Early Christian Life and Thought in Social Context

Understanding the Bible and its World

Early Christian Life and Thought in Social Context

A Reader

Mark Harding

T&T Clark International
A Continuum imprint
The Tower Building, 11 York Road, London SE1 7NX
15 East 26th Street, Suite 1703, New York, NY 10010

First published 2003 by T&T Clark International

www.continuumbooks.com

British Library Cataloguing-in-Publication Data
A catalogue record for this book is available from the British Library

Typeset by ISB Typesetting, Sheffield
Printed and bound in Great Britain by Cromwell Press Ltd, Trowbridge, Wilts

ISBN 0-8264-5603-0 (hardback)
0-8264-5604-9 (paperback)

To
Margaret and Herbert
and
Bon and Les

Remember that it was of your parents you were born;
how can you repay what they have given to you?

(Sirach 7:28)

Contents

Preface

Students of the New Testament and early Judaism have access to several excellent anthologies of sources in the form of C.K. Barrett's *The New Testament Background: Selected Documents* (New York: Harper & Row, 2nd edn, 1987), M. Eugene Boring, Klaus Berger and Carsten Colpe (eds.), *Hellenistic Commentary to the New Testament* (Nashville: Abingdon Press, 1995) and Louis H. Feldman and Meyer Reinhold, *Jewish Life and Thought among Greeks and Romans: Primary Readings* (Minneapolis: Fortress Press, 1996). This book does not seek to replace them, but rather to integrate a coherent account of the historical and social context of the early Christians and Hellenistic, Graeco-Roman with early Jewish and Christian sources.

The book's genesis can be traced to my experience as a teacher of undergraduates in early Judaism and Christian origins. There was no single accessible volume, a textbook, which might combine essential sources and explanatory text that might also serve as a catalyst for further specialist study. *Early Christian Life and Thought in Social Context* is the fruit of the perceived lack of the availability of such a resource. It will serve, I trust, as a self-contained introductory orientation to the contextualized study of Christian origins.

I am greatly indebted to the Department of Ancient History at Macquarie University for according me the status of Associate Fellow. As such I am privileged to have access to the considerable resources of the university's library, access without which the writing of this book could not have been accomplished.

I wish to thank Professor Edwin Judge for permission to use a number of sources from the series *New Documents Illustrating Early Christianity* based at Macquarie. M. Eugene Boring very generously gave permission to use his translation of a marriage contract from Murabba'at. I would like to express my gratitude to the many other publishers for their generous permission to excerpt their material in this book.

I owe a debt of gratitude to Sue, David, Philip and Jami who typed many of the sources and read the manuscript. I would like to thank the Delegates of the Australian College of Theology for timely study leave and my colleagues Helen, Anne and Jennifer for their patience and understanding. Finally, I wish to record my deep appreciation for the unflagging enthusiasm of my wife and our children for this project, and for their willingness to engage with me in the great matter that is the interpretation of the New Testament in our generation.

Mark Harding
12 August 2002

Acknowledgments†

Sources 1, 2, 3, 8, 12, 581, 582 and 583 are reprinted from J.B. Pritchard (ed.), *Ancient Near Eastern Texts Relating to the Old Testament*. Copyright © 1950, 1955 by Princeton University Press. Reprinted with permission of Princeton University Press.

Sources 66, 67, 68, 79 and 515 are reprinted from *Res Gestae Divi Augusti: The Achievements of the Divine Augustus* with an introduction and commentary by P.A. Brunt and J.M. Moore (1967) by permission of Oxford University Press.

Sources 70, 535 and 537 are reprinted by permission of the publishers and the Trustees of the Loeb Classical Library from Appian: *History of Rome*, I (Loeb Classical Library, 2; trans. Harold White; Cambridge, MA: Harvard University Press, 1912).

Sources 28, 31, 34, 38, 50, 51 and 206 are reprinted by permission of the publishers and the Trustees of the Loeb Classical Library from Appian: *History of Rome*, II (Loeb Classical Library, 3; trans. Harold White; Cambridge, MA: Harvard University Press, 1912).

Sources 54, 201, 356 and 476 are reprinted by permission of the publishers and the Trustees of the Loeb Classical Library from Appian: *History of Rome*, III (Loeb Classical Library, 4; trans. Harold White; Cambridge, MA: Harvard University Press, 1913).

Sources 64, 448 and 485 are reprinted by permission of the publishers and the Trustees of the Loeb Classical Library from Appian: *History of Rome*, IV (Loeb Classical Library, 5; trans. Harold White; Cambridge, MA: Harvard University Press, 1913).

Sources 244, 245, 350 and 717 are reprinted by permission of the publishers and the Trustees of the Loeb Classical Library from Apuleius: *The Golden Ass* (trans. W. Adlington; rev. S. Gaselee; Cambridge, MA: Harvard University Press, 1915).

Sources 403, 404, 405, 477 and 560 are reprinted by permission of the publishers and the Trustees of the Loeb Classical Library from Aristotle: *Works*, XXI (Loeb Classical Library, 264; trans. H. Rackham; Cambridge, MA: Harvard University Press, 1944).

Sources 468 and 471 are reprinted by permission of the publishers and the Trustees of the Loeb Classical Library from Aristotle: *Works*, XVI (Loeb Classical Library, 317; trans. H. Rackham; Cambridge, MA: Harvard University Press, 1937).

Sources 464 and 466 are reprinted by permission of the publishers and the Trustees of the Loeb Classical Library from Aristotle: *Works*, XXII (Loeb Classical Library, 193; trans. J.H. Freese; Cambridge, MA: Harvard University Press, 1926).

Source 217 is reprinted by permission of the publishers and the Trustees of the Loeb Classical Library from Aristotle: *Works*, XXIII (Loeb Classical Library, 199; trans. W. Rhys Roberts; Cambridge, MA: Harvard University Press, 1932).

Sources 16, 17 and 18 are reprinted by permission of the publishers and the Trustees of the Loeb Classical Library from Arrian: *Anabasis of Alexander*, I (Loeb Classical Library, 236; trans. P.A. Brunt; Cambridge, MA: Harvard University Press, 1976).

Source 22 is reprinted by permission of the publishers and the Trustees of the Loeb Classical Library from Arrian: *Anabasis of Alexander*, II (Loeb Classical Library, 269; trans. E. Iliff Robson; Cambridge, MA: Harvard University Press, 1933).

Source 343 is reprinted by permission of the publishers and the Trustees of the Loeb

† The Loeb Classical Library ® is a registered trademark of the President and Fellows of Harvard College.

Classical Library from Athenaeus: *Deipnosophistae*, III (Loeb Classical Library, 224; trans. Charles Burton Gulick; Cambridge, MA: Harvard University Press, 1929).

Source 58 is reprinted by permission of the publishers and the Trustees of the Loeb Classical Library from Julius Caesar: *Civil Wars* (Loeb Classical Library, 39; trans. A.G. Peskett; Cambridge, MA: Harvard University Press, 1914).

Sources 502, 503, 504, 505 and 506 are reprinted by permission of the publishers and the Trustees of the Loeb Classical Library from Cato and Varro: *On Agriculture* (Loeb Classical Library, 283; trans. Harrison Boyd Ash and William Davis Hooper; Cambridge, MA: Harvard University Press, 1935).

Sources 225, 226, 227 and 353 are reprinted by permission of the publishers and the Trustees of the Loeb Classical Library from Catullus: *Poems* (Loeb Classical Library, 6; trans. Francis Warre Cornish; Cambridge, MA: Harvard University Press, 1913).

Source 470 is reprinted by permission of the publishers and the Trustees of the Loeb Classical Library from Cicero: *Works*, VII (Loeb Classical Library, 221; trans. L.H.G. Greenwood; Cambridge, MA: Harvard University Press, 1928).

Source 592 is reprinted by permission of the publishers and the Trustees of the Loeb Classical Library from Cicero: *Works*, X (Loeb Classical Library, 324; trans. Louis E. Ford; Cambridge, MA: Harvard University Press, 1937).

Source 493 is reprinted by permission of the publishers and the Trustees of the Loeb Classical Library from Cicero: *Works*, XI (Loeb Classical Library, 158; trans. N.H. Watts; Cambridge, MA: Harvard University Press, 1923).

Source 354 is reprinted by permission of the publishers and the Trustees of the Loeb Classical Library from Cicero: *Works*, XVI (Loeb Classical Library, 213; trans. Clinton Walker Keyes; Cambridge, MA: Harvard University Press, 1928).

Sources 323, 383, 384, 391 and 392 are reprinted by permission of the publishers and the Trustees of the Loeb Classical Library from Cicero: *Works*, XIX (Loeb Classical Library, 268; trans. H. Rackham; Cambridge, MA: Harvard University Press, 1933).

Source 220 is reprinted by permission of the publishers and the Trustees of the Loeb Classical Library from Cicero: *Works*, XXII (Loeb Classical Library, 7; trans. E.O. Winstedt; Cambridge, MA: Harvard University Press, 1912).

Source 221 is reprinted by permission of the publishers and the Trustees of the Loeb Classical Library from Cicero: *Works*, XXIV (Loeb Classical Library, 97; trans. E.O. Winstedt; Cambridge, MA: Harvard University Press, 1918).

Sources 61 and 218 are reprinted by permission of the publishers and the Trustees of the Loeb Classical Library from Cicero: *Works*, XXV (Loeb Classical Library, 205; trans. W. Glynn Williams; Cambridge, MA: Harvard University Press, 1927).

Source 219 is reprinted by permission of the publishers and the Trustees of the Loeb Classical Library from Cicero: *Works*, XXVII (Loeb Classical Library, 230; trans. W. Glynn Williams; Cambridge, MA: Harvard University Press, 1926).

Source 548 is reprinted by permission of the publishers and the Trustees of the Loeb Classical Library from Cicero: *Works*, XXVIII (Loeb Classical Library, 462; trans. W. Glynn Williams, M. Cary and Mary Isobel Henderson; Cambridge, MA: Harvard University Press, 1972).

Sources 19 and 25 are reprinted by permission of the publishers and the Trustees of the Loeb Classical Library from Curtius: *History of Alexander* (Loeb Classical Library, 369; trans. John C. Rolfe; Cambridge, MA: Harvard University Press, 1946).

Source 422 is reprinted by permission of the publishers and the Trustees of the Loeb Classical Library from Demosthenes: *Works*, VI (Loeb Classical Library, 351; trans. A.T. Murray; Cambridge, MA: Harvard University Press, 1939).

Source 531 is reprinted by permission of the publishers and the Trustees of the Loeb Classical Library from Dio Cassius: *Roman History*, I (Loeb Classical Library, 32; trans. Earnest Cary; Cambridge, MA: Harvard University Press, 1914).

Sources 153 and 154 are reprinted by permission of the publishers and the Trustees of the Loeb Classical Library from Dio Cassius: *Roman History*, V (Loeb Classical Library, 82; trans. Earnest Cary; Cambridge, MA: Harvard University Press, 1917).

Sources 69, 76, 77, 338, 409, 497, 514 and 526 are reprinted by permission of the publishers and the Trustees of the Loeb Classical Library from Dio Cassius: *Roman History*, VI (Loeb Classical Library, 83; trans. Earnest Cary; Cambridge, MA: Harvard University Press, 1917).

Sources 86, 87, 344, 345 and 596 are reprinted by permission of the publishers and the Trustees of the Loeb Classical Library from Dio Cassius: *Roman History*, VII (Loeb Classical Library, 175; trans. Earnest Cary; Cambridge, MA: Harvard University Press, 1924).

Sources 101, 103, 104, 184, 200, 204 and 557 are reprinted by permission of the publishers and the Trustees of the Loeb Classical Library from Dio Cassius: *Roman History*, VIII (Loeb Classical Library, 176; trans. Earnest Cary; Cambridge, MA: Harvard University Press, 1925).

Sources 23, 342, 533 and 534 are reprinted by permission of the publishers and the Trustees of the Loeb Classical Library from Diodorus Siculus: *Histories*, VIII (Loeb Classical Library, 422; trans. C. Bradford Welles; Cambridge, MA: Harvard University Press, 1963).

Sources 393, 394, 395, 432 and 438 are reprinted by permission of the publishers and the Trustees of the Loeb Classical Library from Diogenes Laertius: *Lives of Eminent Philosophers*, II (Loeb Classical Library, 185; trans. R.D. Hicks; Cambridge, MA: Harvard University Press, 1925).

Sources 376, 377, 382, 387, 390, 396, 454, 473 and 602 are reprinted by permission of the publishers and the Trustees of the Loeb Classical Library from Epictetus: *Discourses*, I (Loeb Classical Library, 131; trans. W.A. Oldfather; Cambridge, MA: Harvard University Press, 1925).

Sources 348, 388, 389, 397, 450 and 566 are reprinted by permission of the publishers and the Trustees of the Loeb Classical Library from Epictetus: *Discourses*, II (Loeb Classical Library, 218; trans. W.A. Oldfather; Cambridge, MA: Harvard University Press, 1928).

Sources 199, 711 and 713 are reprinted by permission of the publishers and the Trustees of the Loeb Classical Library from Eusebius: *Ecclesiastical History*, I (Loeb Classical Library, 153; trans. Kirsopp Lake; Cambridge, MA: Harvard University Press, 1926).

Sources 385 and 408 are reprinted by permission of the publishers and the Trustees of the Loeb Classical Library from Aulus Gellius: *Attic Nights*, II (Loeb Classical Library, 200; trans. John C. Rolfe; Cambridge, MA: Harvard University Press, 1927).

Source 496 is reprinted by permission of the publishers and the Trustees of the Loeb Classical Library from Aulus Gellius: *Attic Nights*, III (Loeb Classical Library, 212; trans. John C. Rolfe; Cambridge, MA: Harvard University Press, 1927).

Sources 10 and 210 are reprinted by permission of the publishers and the Trustees of the Loeb Classical Library from Herodotus: *Histories*, I (Loeb Classical Library, 117; trans. A.D. Godley; Cambridge, MA: Harvard University Press, 1926).

Source 9 is reprinted by permission of the publishers and the Trustees of the Loeb Classical Library from Herodotus: *Histories*, II (Loeb Classical Library, 118; trans. A.D. Godley; Cambridge, MA: Harvard University Press, 1938).

Sources 63 and 224 are reprinted by permission of the publishers and the Trustees of the Loeb Classical Library from Horace: *Odes and Epodes* (Loeb Classical Library, 33; trans. C.E. Bennett; Cambridge, MA: Harvard University Press, 1927).

Sources 14, 15, 240, 241 and 336 are reprinted by permission of the publishers and the Trustees of the Loeb Classical Library from Isocrates: *Works*, I (Loeb Classical Library, 209; trans. George Norlin; Cambridge, MA: Harvard University Press, 1928).

Source 242 is reprinted by permission of the publishers and the Trustees of the Loeb Classical Library from Isocrates: *Works*, III (Loeb Classical Library, 373; trans. LaRue Van Hook; Cambridge, MA: Harvard University Press, 1945).

Sources 406, 411, 427, 428, 429, 430, 431, 495, 499, 500, 501, 511, 513, 517, 542, 561, 570, 600 and 601 are reprinted by permission of the publishers and the Trustees of the Loeb Classical Library from Juvenal: *Satires* (Loeb Classical Library, 91; trans. G.G. Ramsay; Cambridge, MA: Harvard University Press, 1940).

Sources 39, 214, 319 and 322 are reprinted by permission of the publishers and the Trustees of the Loeb Classical Library from Livy: *History of Rome*, I (Loeb Classical Library, 114; trans. B.O. Foster; Cambridge, MA: Harvard University Press, 1936).

Source 349 is reprinted by permission of the publishers and the Trustees of the Loeb Classical Library from Livy: *History of Rome*, XI (Loeb Classical Library, 313; trans. Evan T. Sage; Cambridge, MA: Harvard University Press, 1936).

Source 509 is reprinted by permission of the publishers and the Trustees of the Loeb Classical Library from Lucian: *Works*, I (Loeb Classical Library, 14; trans. A.M. Harmon; Cambridge, MA: Harvard University Press, 1913).

Source 337 is reprinted by permission of the publishers and the Trustees of the Loeb Classical Library from Lucian: *Works*, III (Loeb Classical Library, 130; trans. A.M. Harmon; Cambridge, MA: Harvard University Press, 1921).

Sources 65, 372 and 373 are reprinted by permission of the publishers and the Trustees of the Loeb Classical Library from Lucretius: *On the Nature of the Universe* (Loeb Classical Library, 181; trans. W.H.D. Rouse; Cambridge, MA: Harvard University Press, 1937).

Sources 97, 100, 352, 398, 519, 520, 521 and 572 are reprinted by permission of the publishers and the Trustees of the Loeb Classical Library from Martial: *Epigrams*, I (Loeb Classical Library, 94; trans. D.R. Shackleton Bailey; Cambridge, MA: Harvard University Press, 1993).

Sources 197, 423, 437, 455, 498 and 512 are reprinted by permission of the publishers and the Trustees of the Loeb Classical Library from Martial: *Epigrams*, II (Loeb Classical Library, 95; trans. D.R. Shackleton Bailey; Cambridge, MA: Harvard University Press, 1993).

Source 508 is reprinted by permission of the publishers and the Trustees of the Loeb Classical Library from Martial: *Epigrams*, II (Loeb Classical Library; trans. Walter C.A. Ker; Cambridge, MA: Harvard University Press, 1920).

Source 237 is reprinted by permission of the publishers and the Trustees of the Loeb Classical Library from Ovid: *Works*, I (Loeb Classical Library, 41; trans. Grant Showerman; Cambridge, MA: Harvard University Press, 1977).

Sources 238, 239, 494 and 611 are reprinted by permission of the publishers and the Trustees of the Loeb Classical Library from Ovid: *Works*, II (Loeb Classical Library, 232; trans. J.H. Mozely; Cambridge, MA: Harvard University Press, 1979).

Sources 346, 347, 487, 510 and 599 are reprinted by permission of the publishers and the Trustees of the Loeb Classical Library from Petronius: *The Satyricon* (Loeb Classical Library, 15; trans. Michael Heseltine and E.H. Warmington; Cambridge, MA: Harvard University Press, 1969).

Sources 579 and 636 are reprinted by permission of the publishers and the Trustees of the Loeb Classical Library from Pliny the Elder: *Natural History*, II (Loeb Classical Library, 352; trans. H. Rackham; Cambridge, MA: Harvard University Press, 1942).

Sources 339, 362, 558 and 559 are reprinted by permission of the publishers and the Trustees of the Loeb Classical Library from Pliny the Elder: *Natural History*, VIII (Loeb Classical Library, 418; trans. W.H.S. Jones; Cambridge, MA: Harvard University Press, 1963).

Source 325 is reprinted by permission of the publishers and the Trustees of the Loeb Classical Library from Pliny the Elder: *Natural History*, IX (Loeb Classical Library, 394; trans. H. Rackham; Cambridge, MA: Harvard University Press, 1952).

Source 556 is reprinted by permission of the publishers and the Trustees of the Loeb Classical Library from Pliny: *Letters and Panegyricus*, I (Loeb Classical Library, 55; trans. Betty Radice; Cambridge, MA: Harvard University Press, 1969).

Sources 222, 525, 526, 714 and 715 are reprinted by permission of the publishers and the Trustees of the Loeb Classical Library from Pliny: *Letters and Panegyricus*, II (Loeb Classical Library, 59; trans. Betty Radice; Cambridge, MA: Harvard University Press, 1969).

Source 447 is reprinted by permission of the publishers and the Trustees of the Loeb Classical Library from Plutarch: *Lives*, II (Loeb Classical Library, 47; trans. Bernadotte Perrin; Cambridge, MA: Harvard University Press, 1914).

Sources 341 and 489 are reprinted by permission of the publishers and the Trustees of the Loeb Classical Library from Plutarch: *Lives*, IV (Loeb Classical Library, 80; trans. Bernadotte Perrin; Cambridge, MA: Harvard University Press, 1916).

Sources 20, 21, 24, 62 and 539 are reprinted by permission of the publishers and the Trustees of the Loeb Classical Library from Plutarch: *Lives*, VII (Loeb Classical Library, 99; trans. Bernadotte Perrin; Cambridge, MA: Harvard University Press, 1919).

Sources 424, 425, 426 and 603 are reprinted by permission of the publishers and the Trustees of the Loeb Classical Library from Plutarch: *Moralia*, II (Loeb Classical Library, 222; trans. F.C. Babbitt; Cambridge, MA: Harvard University Press, 1928).

Sources 40, 41 and 212 are reprinted by permission of the publishers and the Trustees of the Loeb Classical Library from Polybius: *Histories*, I (Loeb Classical Library, 128; trans. W.R. Paton; Cambridge, MA: Harvard University Press, 1922).

Sources 43, 44, 45 and 446 are reprinted by permission of the publishers and the Trustees of the Loeb Classical Library from Polybius: *Histories*, II (Loeb Classical Library, 137; trans. W.R. Paton; Cambridge, MA: Harvard University Press, 1922).

Sources 32, 46, 324, 528, 544 and 545 are reprinted by permission of the publishers and the Trustees of the Loeb Classical Library from Polybius: *Histories*, III (Loeb Classical Library, 159; trans. W.R. Paton; Cambridge, MA: Harvard University Press, 1923).

Sources 30, 47, 48 and 213 are reprinted by permission of the publishers and the Trustees of the Loeb Classical Library from Polybius: *Histories*, IV (Loeb Classical Library, 159; trans. W.R. Paton; Cambridge, MA: Harvard University Press, 1925).

Sources 33 and 35 are reprinted by permission of the publishers and the Trustees of the Loeb Classical Library from Polybius: *Histories*, V (Loeb Classical Library, 160; trans. W.R. Paton; Cambridge, MA: Harvard University Press, 1926).

Sources 36 and 49 are reprinted by permission of the publishers and the Trustees of the Loeb Classical Library from Polybius: *Histories*, VI (Loeb Classical Library, 161; trans. W.R. Paton; Cambridge, MA: Harvard University Press, 1927).

Sources 234, 235 and 236 are reprinted by permission of the publishers and the Trustees of the Loeb Classical Library from Propertius: *Elegies* (Loeb Classical Library, 18; trans. H.E. Butler; Cambridge, MA: Harvard University Press, 1933).

Sources 458, 465 and 467 are reprinted by permission of the publishers and the Trustees of the Loeb Classical Library from Quintilian: *Institutio Oratoria*, I (Loeb Classical Library,

124; trans. H.E. Butler; Cambridge, MA: Harvard University Press, 1920).

Sources 52, 53, 469, 490, 491, 492, 547 and 550 are reprinted by permission of the publishers and the Trustees of the Loeb Classical Library from Sallust: *Works* (Loeb Classical Library, 116; trans. J.C. Rolfe; Cambridge, MA: Harvard University Press, 1931).

Source 453 is reprinted by permission of the publishers and the Trustees of the Loeb Classical Library from *Scriptores Historiae Augustae*, I (Loeb Classical Library, 139; trans. David Magie; Cambridge, MA: Harvard University Press, 1921).

Sources 459 and 460, 461 and 462 are reprinted by permission of the publishers and the Trustees of the Loeb Classical Library from Seneca the Elder: *Controversiae and Suasoriae*, I (Loeb Classical Library, 463; trans. M. Winterbottom; Cambridge, MA: Harvard University Press, 1974).

Sources 461 and 462 are reprinted by permission of the publishers and the Trustees of the Loeb Classical Library from Seneca the Elder: *Controversiae and Suasoriae*, II (Loeb Classical Library, 464; trans. M. Winterbottom; Cambridge, MA: Harvard University Press, 1974).

Source 386 is reprinted by permission of the publishers and the Trustees of the Loeb Classical Library from Seneca: *Works*, I (Loeb Classical Library, 214; trans. J.W. Basore; Cambridge, MA: Harvard University Press, 1928).

Sources 243 and 565 are reprinted by permission of the publishers and the Trustees of the Loeb Classical Library from Seneca: *Works*, II (Loeb Classical Library, 254; trans. J.W. Basore; Cambridge, MA: Harvard University Press, 1932).

Sources 340, 368, 379, 381, 452 and 523 are reprinted by permission of the publishers and the Trustees of the Loeb Classical Library from Seneca: *Works*, IV (Loeb Classical Library, 75; trans. Richard M. Gummere; Cambridge, MA: Harvard University Press, 1917).

Sources 380, 472 and 564 are reprinted by permission of the publishers and the Trustees of the Loeb Classical Library from Seneca: *Works*, V (Loeb Classical Library, 76; trans. Richard M. Gummere; Cambridge, MA: Harvard University Press, 1920).

Sources 543 and 597 are reprinted by permission of the publishers and the Trustees of the Loeb Classical Library from Seneca: *Works*, VI (Loeb Classical Library, 77; trans. Richard M. Gummere; Cambridge, MA: Harvard University Press, 1925).

Source 161 reprinted by permission of the publishers and the Trustees of the Loeb Classical Library from Strabo: *Geography*, VII (Loeb Classical Library, 241; trans. Horace Leonard Jones; Cambridge, MA: Harvard University Press, 1983).

Sources 55, 56, 57, 59, 60, 71, 78, 84, 85, 151 and 529 are reprinted by permission of the publishers and the Trustees of the Loeb Classical Library from Suetonius: *The Twelve Caesars*, I (Loeb Classical Library, 31; trans. John C. Rolfe; Cambridge, MA: Harvard University Press, 1951).

Sources 88, 91, 92, 93, 95, 98, 102, 176, 196, 449, 518, 598 and 710 are reprinted by permission of the publishers and the Trustees of the Loeb Classical Library from Suetonius: *The Twelve Caesars*, II (Loeb Classical Library, 38; trans. John C. Rolfe; Cambridge, MA: Harvard University Press, 1914).

Sources 215 and 216 are reprinted by permission of the publishers and the Trustees of the Loeb Classical Library from Tacitus, *Works*, I (Loeb Classical Library, 35; trans. M. Hutton; Cambridge, MA: Harvard University Press, 1914).

Sources 94, 96, 451 and 538 are reprinted by permission of the publishers and the Trustees of the Loeb Classical Library from Tacitus, *Works*, II (Loeb Classical Library, 111; trans. Clifford H. Moore; Cambridge, MA: Harvard University Press, 1925).

Sources 72, 73, 74, 75, 80, 82, 185, 486, 530, 546 and 580 are reprinted by permission of the publishers and the Trustees of the Loeb Classical Library from Tacitus, *Works*, III

(Loeb Classical Library, 249; trans. Clifford H. Moore and John Jackson; Cambridge, MA: Harvard University Press, 1931).

Sources 83, 436 and 540 are reprinted by permission of the publishers and the Trustees of the Loeb Classical Library from Tacitus, *Works*, IV (Loeb Classical Library, 249; trans. John Jackson; Cambridge, MA: Harvard University Press, 1937).

Sources 81, 555 and 709 are reprinted by permission of the publishers and the Trustees of the Loeb Classical Library from Tacitus, *Works*, V (Loeb Classical Library, 322; trans. John Jackson; Cambridge, MA: Harvard University Press, 1937).

Source 211 is reprinted by permission of the publishers and the Trustees of the Loeb Classical Library from Thucydides: *Peloponnesian War*, I (Loeb Classical Library, 108; trans. Charles Forster Smith; Cambridge, MA: Harvard University Press, 1928).

Sources 549, 551, 552 and 553 are reprinted by permission of the publishers and the Trustees of the Loeb Classical Library from *Remains of Old Latin*, III (Loeb Classical Library, 329; trans. E.H. Warmington; Cambridge, MA: Harvard University Press, 1938).

Source 479 is reprinted by permission of the publishers and the Trustees of the Loeb Classical Library from *Remains of Old Latin*, IV (Loeb Classical Library, 357; trans. E.H. Warmington; Cambridge, MA: Harvard University Press, 1940).

Sources 228, 229, 230, 231, 232, 233 and 507 are reprinted by permission of the publishers and the Trustees of the Loeb Classical Library from Virgil: *Works*, I (Loeb Classical Library, 63; trans. H. Rushton Fairclough; Cambridge, MA: Harvard University Press, 1935).

Source 13 is reprinted by permission of the publishers and the Trustees of the Loeb Classical Library from Xenophon: *Works*, II (Loeb Classical Library, 89; trans. Carleton L. Bownson; Cambridge, MA: Harvard University Press, 1921).

Source 594 is reprinted from M. Stern, *Greek and Latin Authors on Jews and Judaism*, I (Jerusalem: Israel Academy of Sciences and Humanities, 1976).

Source 478 is reprinted from N. Lewis and M. Reinhold, *Roman Civilization: Sourcebook I, The Republic* (New York: Harper and Row, 1966).

Sources 522, 527 and 554 are reprinted from N. Lewis and M. Reinhold, *Roman Civilization: Sourcebook II, The Empire* (New York: Harper and Row, 1966).

Sources 375 and 378 are reprinted from E. Bevan, *Later Greek Religion* (London: Dent, 1927).

Sources 316, 360, 480, 532, 568, 571, 616 and 622 are reprinted from Adolf Deissmann, *Light from the Ancient East* (London: Hodder & Stoughton, 4th edn, 1927).

Sources 26, 191, 249, 250, 251, 252, 254, 255, 256, 257, 258, 259, 268, 270, 433, 695 and 700 are reprinted from James H. Charlesworth, *Old Testament Pseudepigrapha*, I, copyright © 1983 by James H. Charlesworth. Used by permission of Doubleday, a division of Random House, Inc.

Sources 114, 116, 148, 274, 275, 276, 277, 278, 284, 294, 295, 298, 317, 609, 697, 699 and 706 are reprinted from James H. Charlesworth, *Old Testament Pseudepigrapha*, II, copyright © 1985 by James H. Charlesworth. Used by permission of Doubleday, a division of Random House, Inc.

Sources 90, 180, 182, 304, 305, 412, 418, 463, 578, 585, 610, 617 and 620 are reprinted by permission of the publishers and the Trustees of the Loeb Classical Library from Josephus: *Works*, I (Loeb Classical Library, 186; trans. H.St.J. Thackeray; Cambridge, MA: Harvard University Press, 1926).

Sources 99, 149, 150, 155, 156, 159, 160, 164, 165, 169, 174, 175, 177, 178, 179, 181, 306, 626, 631, 633, 658 and 659 are reprinted by permission of the publishers and the Trustees of the Loeb Classical Library from Josephus: *Works*, III (Loeb Classical Library, 203; trans. H.St.J. Thackeray; Cambridge, MA: Harvard University Press, 1927).

Sources 183, 186, 187, 188, 189, 193, 194, 536, 586, 607 and 618 are reprinted by permission of the publishers and the Trustees of the Loeb Classical Library from Josephus: *Works*, III (Loeb Classical Library, 210; trans. H.St.J. Thackeray; Cambridge, MA: Harvard University Press, 1928).

Source 280 is reprinted by permission of the publishers and the Trustees of the Loeb Classical Library from Josephus: *Works*, IV (Loeb Classical Library, 242; trans. H.St.J. Thackeray; Cambridge, MA: Harvard University Press, 1930).

Source 363 is reprinted by permission of the publishers and the Trustees of the Loeb Classical Library from Josephus: *Works*, V (Loeb Classical Library, 281; trans. H.St.J. Thackeray and Ralph Marcus; Cambridge, MA: Harvard University Press, 1934).

Source 7 is reprinted by permission of the publishers and the Trustees of the Loeb Classical Library from Josephus: *Works*, VI (Loeb Classical Library, 326; trans. Ralph Marcus; Cambridge, MA: Harvard University Press, 1937).

Sources 27, 109, 110, 111, 113, 124, 126, 128, 144, 145, 147, 584, 589, 593, 604, 605, 615, 624 and 632 are reprinted by permission of the publishers and the Trustees of the Loeb Classical Library from Josephus: *Works*, VII (Loeb Classical Library, 365; trans. Ralph Marcus; Cambridge, MA: Harvard University Press, 1937).

Sources 157, 488, 524 and 606 are reprinted by permission of the publishers and the Trustees of the Loeb Classical Library from Josephus: *Works*, VIII (Loeb Classical Library, 410; trans. Ralph Marcus and Allen Wikgren; Cambridge, MA: Harvard University Press, 1963).

Sources 163, 166, 170, 171, 172, 595 and 684 are reprinted by permission of the publishers and the Trustees of the Loeb Classical Library from Josephus: *Works*, IX (Loeb Classical Library, 433; trans. L.H. Feldman; Cambridge, MA: Harvard University Press, 1965).

Sources 89 and 686 are reprinted by permission of the publishers and the Trustees of the Loeb Classical Library from Josephus: *Works*, X (Loeb Classical Library, 456; trans. L.H. Feldman; Cambridge, MA: Harvard University Press, 1965).

Sources 399 and 400 are reprinted by permission of the publishers and the Trustees of the Loeb Classical Library from Philo: *Works*, I (Loeb Classical Library, 226; trans. F.H. Colson and G.H. Whitaker; Cambridge, MA: Harvard University Press, 1929).

Source 401 is reprinted by permission of the publishers and the Trustees of the Loeb Classical Library from Philo: *Works*, IV (Loeb Classical Library, 261; trans. F.H. Colson and G.H. Whitaker; Cambridge, MA: Harvard University Press, 1932).

Source 320 is reprinted by permission of the publishers and the Trustees of the Loeb Classical Library from Philo: *Works*, VI (Loeb Classical Library, 289; trans. F.H. Colson and G.H. Whitaker; Cambridge, MA: Harvard University Press, 1935).

Sources 441, 541, 619 and 678 are reprinted by permission of the publishers and the Trustees of the Loeb Classical Library from Philo: *Works*, VII (Loeb Classical Library, 320; trans. F.H. Colson; Cambridge, MA: Harvard University Press, 1935).

Sources 634 and 635 are reprinted by permission of the publishers and the Trustees of the Loeb Classical Library from Philo: *Works*, IX (Loeb Classical Library, 363; trans. F.H. Colson; Cambridge, MA: Harvard University Press, 1941).

Sources 588, 590 and 591 are reprinted by permission of the publishers and the Trustees of the Loeb Classical Library from Philo: *Works*, X (Loeb Classical Library, 379; trans. F.H. Colson; Cambridge, MA: Harvard University Press, 1962).

Sources 292, 300, 301, 333, 444, 563, 667, 672, 674, 682, 683, 712 and 716 are reprinted by permission of the publishers and the Trustees of the Loeb Classical Library from *Apostolic Fathers*, I (Loeb Classical Library, 24; trans. Kirsopp Lake; Cambridge, MA: Harvard University Press, 1912).

Source 326 is reprinted from Herodas, *Mime IV: Dedications and Sacrifices to Asklepios* ll. 1–20, in A.D. Knox (ed.) with notes by A.C. Headlam, *Mimes and Fragments* (Cambridge: Cambridge University Press, 1922).

Source 208 is reprinted from J. Neusner, *The Mishnah: A New Translation* (New Haven: Yale University Press, 1988), p. 315.

Sources 289, 290, 312 and 687 are reprinted from Bentley Layton, *The Gnostic Scriptures* (Garden City, NY: Doubleday, 1987).

Sources 190, 192, 209, 419, 456, 613, 614 and 621 are reprinted from C.G. Montefiore and H. Loewe, *A Rabbinic Anthology,* copyright © 1974 by Schocken Books, a division of Random House, Inc. used by permission of Schocken Books, a division of Random House, Inc.

Source 625 is reprinted from S. Singer (trans.), *The Authorised Daily Prayer Book* (London: Eyre and Spottiswoode, 10th edn, 1916).

Sources 327, 328 and 407 are reprinted from G.H.R. Horsley, *New Documents Illustrating Early Christianity* (Macquarie University: Ancient History Documentary Research Centre, 1981). Used by permission of the Ancient History Documentary Research Centre, Macquarie University.

Sources 359 and 361 are reprinted from G.H.R. Horsley, *New Documents Illustrating Early Christianity*, II (Macquarie University: Ancient History Documentary Research Centre, 1982). Used by permission of the Ancient History Documentary Research Centre, Macquarie University.

Sources 195, 573, 575, 576 and 623 are reprinted from G.H.R. Horsley, *New Documents Illustrating Early Christianity*, III (Macquarie University: Ancient History Documentary Research Centre, 1983). Used by permission of the Ancient History Documentary Research Centre, Macquarie University.

Sources 574 and 577 are reprinted from G.H.R. Horsley, *New Documents Illustrating Early Christianity*, IV (Macquarie University: Ancient History Documentary Research Centre, 1987). Used by permission of the Ancient History Documentary Research Centre, Macquarie University.

Source 663 is reprinted from Stephen R. Llewelyn, *New Documents Illustrating Early Christianity*, VIII (Macquarie University: Ancient History Documentary Research Centre, 1998). Used by permission of the Ancient History Documentary Research Centre, Macquarie University.

Source 445 is reprinted from Viktor A. Tcherikover and Alexander Fuks (eds.), *Corpus Papyrorum Judaicarum*, I (Cambridge, MA: Harvard University Press, 1957 [for Magnes Press]). Used by permission of Magnes Press.

Sources 198, 202, 203, 416, and 608 are reprinted from Viktor A. Tcherikover and Alexander Fuks (eds.), *Corpus Papyrorum Judaicarum*, II (Cambridge, MA: Harvard University Press, 1960 [for Magnes Press]). Used by permission of Magnes Press.

Source 415 is reprinted from M. Eugene Boring, Klaus Berger and Carsten Colpe (eds.), *Hellenistic Commentary to the New Testament* (Nashville: Abingdon Press, 1995). Used by permission of the translator, M. Eugene Boring.

Source 413 is reprinted from Naphtali Lewis (ed.), *Judean Desert Studies: The Documents from the Bar Kokhba Period in the Cave of Letters* (Jerusalem: Israel Exploration Society, 1989).

Source 207 is reprinted from Yigael Yadin, *Bar-Kokhba* (London: Weidenfeld and Nicolson, 1971).

Source 358 is reprinted from A.S. Hunt, *The Oxyrhynchus Papyri, Part VIII* (London: Egypt Exploration Society, 1911).

Source 374 is reprinted from B.P. Grenfell and A.S. Hunt, *Oxyrhynchus Papyri, Part II* (London: Egypt Exploration Fund, 1899).

Source 562 is reprinted from B.P. Grenfell, A.S. Hunt and C.C. Edgar, *Oxyrhynchus Papyri, Part IV* (London: Egypt Exploration Society, 1904).

Source 567 is reprinted from B.P. Grenfell and A.S. Hunt, *The Oxyrhynchus Papyri, Part I* (London: Egypt Exploration Society, 1898).

Source 410 is reprinted from B.P. Grenfell, A.S. Hunt and J.G. Smyly, *Tebtunis Papyri* (London: Egypt Exploration Fund, 1902).

Source 481 is reprinted from A.D. Nock, *Early Gentile Christianity and its Hellenistic Background* (New York: Harper & Row, 1964).

Sources 691 and 693 are reprinted from L.H. Mills (trans.), *The Zend Avesta*, in F. Max Müller (ed.), *The Sacred Books of the East*, XXXI (Oxford: Oxford University Press, 1887), pp. 30, 390-91.

Source 692 is reprinted from E.W. West (trans.), *The Pahlavi Texts*, in F. Max Müller (ed.), *The Sacred Books of the East*, V (Oxford: Oxford University Press, 1880), pp. 121-29.

Sources 205 and 313 are reprinted from Alexander Roberts and James Donaldson (eds.), *Ante-Nicene Fathers*, I (Grand Rapids: Eerdmans, repr. of the 1885–96 edition published by T. & T. Clark, 1987).

Sources 260, 261, 262, 269, 279, 293, 417, 637, 638, 639, 640, 641, 642, 643, 644, 645, 646, 647, 648, 649, 650, 651, 652, 653, 654, 655, 656, 657 and 701 are reprinted from Geza Vermes, *The Complete Dead Sea Scrolls in English* (Harmondsworth: Penguin Books, 1997). Copyright © G. Vermes, 1962, 1965, 1968, 1975, 1995, 1997. Reproduced by permission of Penguin Books Ltd.

Source 281 is reprinted from M. Maher, *Targum Pseudo-Jonathan: Genesis* (Edinburgh: T. & T. Clark, 1992). Reproduced by permission of T. & T. Clark.

Sources 369, 370 and 371 are reprinted from C. Bailey, *Epicurus: The Extant Remains* (Oxford: Oxford University Press, 1926). Reprinted by permission of Oxford University Press.

Sources (Old Testament) 4, 5, 6, 11, 29, 37, 105, 106, 107, 108, 118, 120, 122, 125, 246, 247, 248, 253 and 694 are reprinted from the New Revised Standard Version of the Bible, copyright © 1989 by the Division of Christian Education of the National Council of Churches of Christ in the USA. Used by permission. All rights reserved.

Sources (Apocrypha) 112, 115, 117, 119, 121, 123, 127, 129, 130, 131, 132, 133, 134, 135, 136, 137, 138, 139, 140, 141, 142, 143, 271, 282, 283, 285, 286, 296, 302, 303, 434, 442, 662 and 696 are reprinted from the New Revised Standard Version of the Bible, copyright © 1989 by the Division of Christian Education of the National Council of Churches of Christ in the USA. Used by permission. All rights reserved.

Sources (New Testament) 158, 162, 167, 168, 173, 223, 263, 264, 265, 266, 267, 272, 273, 287, 288, 291, 297, 299, 307, 308, 309, 310, 311, 314, 315, 318, 321, 329, 330, 331, 332, 334, 335, 355, 357, 364, 365, 366, 367, 402, 414, 420, 421, 435, 439, 440, 443, 457, 474, 475, 482, 483, 484, 569, 612, 627, 628, 629, 630, 660, 661, 664, 665, 666, 668, 669, 670, 671, 673, 675, 676, 677, 679, 680, 681, 685, 688, 689, 690, 698, 702, 703, 704, 705, 707 and 708 are reprinted from the New Revised Standard Version of the Bible, copyright © 1989 by the Division of Christian Education of the National Council of Churches of Christ in the USA. Used by permission. All rights reserved.

Abbreviations

ANET	James B. Pritchard (ed.), *Ancient Near Eastern Texts Relating to the Old Testament* (Princeton: Princeton University Press, 1950)
ANF	Alexander Roberts and James Donaldson (eds.), *Anti-Nicene Fathers* (10 vols.; Grand Rapids: Eerdmans; repr. of the 1885–96 edn published by T. & T. Clark, 1987)
ANRW	Hildegard Temporini and Wolfgang Haase (eds.), *Aufstieg und Niedergang der römischen Welt: Geschichte und Kultur Roms im Spiegel der neueren Forschung* (Berlin: W. de Gruyter, 1972–)
BJRL	*Bulletin of the John Rylands Library*
CIJ	*Corpus inscriptionum judaicarum*
CIL	*Corpus inscriptionum latinarum*
CPJ	Viktor A. Tcherikover and A. Fuks (eds.), *Corpus Papyrorum Judaicorum* (vols. 1, 2; Cambridge, MA: Harvard University Press, 1957, 1960)
DJD	Discoveries in the Judaean Desert
DOTT	D. Winton Thomas (ed.), *Documents from Old Testament Times* (New York: Harper & Row, 1961)
ICC	International Critical Commentary
IEJ	*Israel Exploration Journal*
JAC	*Jahrbuch für Antike und Christentum*
JJS	*Journal of Jewish Studies*
JSOT	*Journal for the Study of the Old Testament*
LCL	Loeb Classical Library
Mur	Murabbaʿat
NewDocs	*New Documents Illustrating Early Christianity* (vols. 1, 2, 3, 4: G.H.R. Horsley [1981, 1982, 1983, 1987]; vol. 7: S.R. Llewelyn with R.A. Kearsley [1994]; vol. 8: S.R. Llewelyn [1998]; Macquarie University: Ancient History Documentary Research Centre)
NovT	*Novum Testamentum*
NRSV	New Revised Standard Version
NTS	*New Testament Studies*
OTP	James Charlesworth (ed.), *Old Testament Pseudepigrapha* (2 vols.; Garden City, NY: Doubleday, 1983, 1985)
RB	*Revue biblique*
RevQ	*Revue de Qumran*
SBLDS	SBL Dissertation Series
SBLMS	SBL Monograph Series
SNTSMS	Society for New Testament Studies Monograph Series

Introduction

This book is offered to the tertiary student and the interested reader. It is the author's hope that reading the excerpts from early Christian literature juxtaposed with writings extracted from Greek, Roman and Jewish writers of the Hellenistic and Graeco-Roman eras will promote a fuller understanding of the political and social milieu in which the early churches were founded and the New Testament came to be written. I also trust that readers with a grasp of the New Testament and Christian origins will be moved to undertake a more thorough study of the Hellenistic, Graeco-Roman and Jewish background of early Christianity than this book can provide. In addition, should readers turn from the literary sources excerpted in this book to read the complete works from which they are taken, then its production will have served a laudable purpose indeed.

This is a book pre-eminently about the early Christians and their cultural environment especially within early Judaism, or, rather, the Judaisms, of the Second Temple period. To explain that environment, especially the political realities, which confronted the early Christians, I have chosen to take the story back to the sixth century, to the career of Cyrus the Persian. It was he who brought the power of the Babylonians to an end 50 years after they had captured Jerusalem, destroyed the First Temple and ended Judah's political independence. Cyrus permitted any captive Jews who wanted to return to their land to do so. Several thousand chose to return immediately, taking with them a body of diverse articulations of their Jewish heritage which crystallized into the Hebrew Bible, and which was to be further supplemented in the restored Jewish state. The exile had galvanized the community to consolidate their historical memories, prophetic oracles, and other writings. The ranks of these Jews were later swelled during the Persian era by other Jewish returnees. It is possible that they took with them an appreciation of certain aspects of Zoroastrianism, the religion of their Persian overlords. From this time belief in cosmological dualism and the soul's ascent to heaven after death, and even the resurrection of the body, which had hitherto not been present in Judaism, can be traced in the Jewish literary output. These beliefs had a significant life in both Judaism and in Christianity.

This book takes its initial impetus from the stories of imperial enterprise. Imperialism is not an endeavour we willingly excuse. Nevertheless the stories of imperial aggrandizement are remarkable. Whether it is the Persians, Greeks or Romans who are the imperialists, the stories reveal the determination and drive both to conquer and to sustain power over others. Indeed, aristocratic Romans regarded such activity as a manly virtue. Imperial adventure was the stage on which the quest for fame and glory was played out. In Roman times too there was a steady interest in the imperial and military exploits of the great ones of the past since it was believed that they could furnish models that might propel latter-day men of virtue to emulate the fame of their predecessors. The stories echoed in this book are the stories of great and terrible deeds—magnetic and fascinating, but terrible all the same.

The quest for empire, and the violent effort necessarily expanded to sustain it, is the most insular and self-interested of human social endeavours. Yet, as the historical and cultural record demonstrates, in the midst of one people's attempt to wield and maintain domination over others, the conquerors themselves frequently learn from cultures other than their own and adopt values of the defeated as their own. Radically inward-looking and insular civilizations that turn conqueror are liable to be brought to a position of affirming the worth of the cultural values of those who are the victims of their violence. That the conquered assimilate the cultural values of their conquerors is the other side of the equation. For example, even after the repudiation of the brutal hellenizing programme of Antiochus IV Epiphanes in Judaea in the 160s BCE, the progress of hellenism among the Jews of that land was little checked even if its most outrageous expressions were quashed.

Early Christian Life and Thought in Social Context is essentially a dialogue between a selection of sources and my interpretation of them. There is no lack of excellent New Testament introductions. But whereas conventional presentations of the background of the New Testament usually relegate the sources to passing references in footnotes, I have deliberately cited them in the body of the text and kept my own commentary to a minimum. There can be no history writing without the historian giving his or her shape to an account of the significance of the data, whether that data be literary documents or the *realia* of archaeology. I have sought to allow the sources to be heard without injecting too much of my own sense of their significance for understanding early Christianity.

The majority of the documents excerpted emanate from literate and well-educated Hellenistic and Graeco-Roman circles. The scope of these corpora makes it inevitable that historians will turn first to these witnesses with regard to the historical and social conditions of the early Christians. The work of the Jewish historian Josephus is a particularly fruitful treasury especially with respect to information about and reflection on the tragic events that unfolded in first century CE Palestine. The publication of inscriptions and papyri has meant that scholars have access in many instances to the writing of people of those in the lower socio-economic strata whose voice is only rarely heard in the classics. I trust that readers will find the selection of sources in this book broad enough for them to feel that a diversity of social experiences and viewpoints has been engaged.

The book is divided into eight parts. Each of these is further divided into topics. Each topic has two sections: a brief orientation is followed by a selection of primary sources, sometimes prefaced by explanatory notes. Footnotes throughout the book direct the reader to further ancient sources or to discussion in scholarly journals and monographs.

Parts 1 and 2 deal with the political landscape. They bring together sources tracing and illustrating the political realities in which the New Testament churches were founded. To provide some perspective, Part 1 begins some five and a half centuries before the common era with the Persian empire builders, progressing to Alexander the Great and his successors before whom the Persian hegemony was brushed aside, and then proceeds to chart the irresistible rise of Rome and the consolidation of its empire. In the main, the sources selected represent the point of view of imperial aggrandizers and their apologists. However, rising above the clamour of aggression, the conquered and the victims of violence are also heard. The occasional voices of critique and protest are also to be encountered. Part 2 is concerned with the same imperial realities from a Jewish point of view. The Jews of Judaea found themselves swept up in the designs of the Romans for security on their eastern frontier. This resulted in the loss of political independence for Judaea under a succession of imperial masters and supervising agents. The imposition of direct Roman rule and the incorporation of Judaea into the empire marks the beginning of an unfolding tragedy that scores the Roman presence in Judaea and Galilee at the very time of the mission of Jesus and his earliest followers until the extinction of the vestiges of the Jewish state in 135 CE.

Literary endeavour is an important medium of cultural identity. Accordingly Parts 3 and 4 are devoted to the literature of the Graeco-Roman era. The former is given over selectively to the literature of the Greeks and

Romans, especially their historians, biographers, letter writers, moralists and poets. Part 4 surveys the literature of the early Jews and Christians, their apocalypses, testaments, prayers and hymns. I attempt to account for the New Testament Gospels and their content. In the main, the literature surveyed is that produced by the cultural elites.

Part 5 provides an orientation to Graeco-Roman religion. The emphasis here falls on the Greek and Roman cults and the manner in which those who owed allegiance to the gods approached and worshipped them. The mystery cults are also surveyed, as are occult practices and the cult of the ruler. Part 6 focuses on the sophisticated, reflective pursuit of philosophical speculation. In contrast with the emphasis in religion with cultic decorum and propriety, much of the output of the philosophers of the Graeco-Roman era was concerned with matters of theology. The thought of the major Graeco-Roman philosophical schools—Stoicism, Epicureanism, and the Academy—is outlined, as is the thought of the Alexandrian Jewish thinker Philo.

The final two parts of the book focus on ordered life during the empire. Part 7 surveys Graeco-Roman society in general. Topics engaged include the social hierarchy, the economy of the era, education and rhetoric, the family and the role of women, the violence of the arena, warfare and the atrocities committed in the name of personal fame and empire. There are occasional excursions into Jewish and Christian perspectives. Part 8 is devoted to early Jews and Christians in society. Jewish religious institutions are surveyed, such as the Temple and the synagogue, as are the major groups of Jews, including Pharisees, Sadducees, the Essenes, and the Dead Sea sect. It concludes with an account of the genesis of the Christian movement and its beliefs, and includes sources detailing the encounter of the Romans with early Christians.

1. The Political Landscape: The Persian, Hellenistic and Roman Empires

1.1. The Rise of Persia

In the tenth century BCE there was a brief flowering of a unified, independent kingdom of Israel under David and Solomon. In the absence of other contenders for hegemony, the kings extended their control from the hill country to all of Palestine, from the border of Egypt in the south to the Euphrates in the north (1 Kings 4:21–22). However, Israel's ascendancy was shortlived. During the ninth and eighth centuries the resurgent Assyrians established a presence in Syria and Palestine, eventually absorbing the northern kingdom (Israel) based in Samaria in 722 and almost toppling the southern kingdom (Judah) with its capital in Jerusalem in 701.

Towards the end of the seventh century BCE, the kingdom of Babylon, a vassal of the Assyrians, rebelled, brought Assyrian hegemony over Babylonia to an end, and embarked on a programme of imperial aggrandizement. The Babylonians captured Jerusalem in 586 BCE, destroyed the Temple, and deported the upper echelons of the society. The Medes also threw off Assyrian suzerainty. In 612 their king, Cyaxares, destroyed Nineveh, the capital of Assyria. He also succeeded in bringing the troublesome Scythians to heel and extended his overlordship to the tribes of the Persian plateau. The empire of the Medes, however, was soon eclipsed.

In 559 Cyrus assumed the throne of Anshan, a region of Elam in Persia.[1] The Median king, Astyages, was his suzerain. Cyrus fomented a revolt by Persian tribes against the Medes. In 550 he vanquished Astyages, becoming ruler of both Media and Persia. In 547, Croesus, the king of Lydia (in eastern Asia Minor), crossed the River Halys in the district of Pteria to stop Cyrus's advance westwards. After an inconclusive engagement, Croesus, in charge of a smaller army than that commanded by Cyrus, decided to return to Sardis, his capital, and call for reinforcements from his allies, namely, the Egyptians, Babylonians and Spartans. After a brief siege, Sardis was captured. Cyrus was now undisputed master of the east, north and north-west of Babylon. The capture of Babylon was his next goal.[2]

Under Nabonidus (555–539 BCE), the last king of Babylon, the Babylonian Empire was rocked by the neglect of the city and its traditional religious festivals. Nabonidus, a former military commander from Harran in north-west Mesopotamia, worshipped a pantheon, the chief of which was the moon god Sin. Nabonidus spent much of his time at Sin's sanctuary, Tema, in northwest Arabia. Babylon was left in the charge of his son, Belshazzar (see Daniel 5). The so-called Nabonidus Chronicle laments the neglect of the traditional rituals. The king was absent from the New Year festival for 11 years. As an indispensable player in the mythic drama, his absence jeopardized the order of the cosmos as established by Marduk, the chief god of the Babylonian pantheon, who in the Babylonian creation myth was the creator god and the upholder of the created order in the face of the primeval chaos. The New Year festival ritually enacted the defeat of chaos by Marduk in the person of the king and proclaimed the pre-eminence of Babylon in the created order. In 539 Cyrus's troops besieged and entered Babylon.[3] Cyrus restored the traditional worship of Babylon, re-establishing the gods 'banished' by Nabonidus in their shrines. Cyrus assumed the throne of Babylon as a Babylonian king, acknowledging the gods of Babylon and the religious traditions of other nations. He set about restoring the gods and their images to their rightful, ancestral places of worship—including those brought to Babylon by Nebuchadrezzar II (605–562 BCE).

Sources[4]

The Nabonidus Chronicle recounts Cyrus's rise to power over both Media and Persia. In the following extract King Ishtumegu is the Median king Astyages.

1. [King Ishtumegu] called up his troops and marched against Cyrus, king of Anshan, in order to me[et him in battle]. The army of Ishtumegu revolted against him and in fetters they de[livered him] to Cyrus.
   (From the Nabonidus Chronicle [*ANET* p. 305])

The Cyrus Cylinder reports that Cyrus accepted the crown from Marduk's hand. Marduk had finally found someone to restore religious and, therefore, cosmic order. The priesthood of the god supported Cyrus. Note that the Cylinder graphically depicts Marduk marching along with Cyrus 'like a real friend' (# [Source] 3).

2. [The images of Babyl]on(ia), male and female, he returned to their cellas,
   [The…who] had abandoned their [cha]pels he returned to their mansions,
   [Their wrath] he appeased, their mind he put at rest,
   […those whose power was] at a low he brought back to life
   [Because] their food is served (to them) [regular]ly…

   [To the inhabitants of] Babylon a (joyful) heart is given now
   [They are like prisoners when] the prisons are opened
   [Liberty is restored to] those who were surrounded by oppression
   [All rejoice] to look upon him as king!
   (From Nabonidus and the Clergy of Babylon [*ANET* p. 315])

3. The worship of Marduk, the king of the gods, he (Nabonidus) [chang]ed into abomination, daily he used to do evil against his (i.e. Marduk's) city…

   He (Marduk) scanned and looked (through) all the countries, searching for a righteous ruler willing to lead him (i.e. Marduk) (in the annual procession). (Then) he announced the name of Cyrus, king of Anshan, declared him to be(come) the ruler of all the world…

   (He) ordered him to march against his city Babylon. He made him set out on the road to Babylon going at his side like a real friend… Without any battle, he made him enter his town Babylon, sparing Babylon any calamity. He delivered into his (i.e. Cyrus') hands Nabonidus, the king who did not worship him (i.e. Marduk). All the inhabitants of Babylon as well as of the entire country of Sumer and Akkad, princes and governors (included), bowed to him (Cyrus) and kissed his feet, jubilant that he (had received) the kingship, and with shining faces. Happily they greeted him as a master through whose help they had come (again) to life from death (and) had all been spared damage and disaster, and they worshiped his (very) name.
   (From the Cyrus Cylinder [*ANET* pp. 315–16])

It is possible that there were Jews in exile who also supported Cyrus. In the following two excerpts from the prophecy of Second Isaiah, God is depicted as promoting the cause of Cyrus in the interests of bringing the Babylonian exile of the Jews to an end. Similarities between the following passages and the excerpts from the Cyrus Cylinder cited above on the score of divine initiative are obvious.

4. Who has roused a victor from the east, summoned him to his service?
   He delivers up nations to him, and tramples kings under foot;
   he makes them like dust with his sword, like driven stubble with his bow.
   He pursues them and passes on safely, scarcely touching the path with his feet.
   (Isaiah 41:2–3.
   See also Isaiah 41:25)

5. This says the Lord, your Redeemer, who formed you in the womb:

I am the Lord, who made all things, who alone stretched out the heavens, who by myself spread out the earth;
who frustrates the omens of liars, and makes fools of diviners;
who turns back the wise, and makes their knowledge foolish;
who confirms the word of his servant, and fulfills the prediction of his messengers;
who says of Jerusalem, 'It shall be inhabited,' and of the cities of Judah, 'They shall be rebuilt, and I will raise up their ruins';
who says to the deep, 'Be dry—I will dry up your rivers';
who says of Cyrus, 'He is my shepherd, and he shall carry out all my purpose';
and who says of Jerusalem, 'It shall be rebuilt,' and of the temple, 'Your foundation shall be laid.'
Thus says the Lord to his anointed, to Cyrus, whose right hand I have grasped to subdue nations before him and strip kings of their robes, to open doors before him—and the gates shall not be closed:
I will go before you and level the mountains,
I will break in pieces the doors of bronze and cut through the bars of iron,
I will give you the treasures of darkness and riches hidden in secret places,
so that you may know that it is I, the LORD, the God of Israel, who call you by your name.
For the sake of my servant Jacob, and Israel my chosen,
I call you by your name, I surname you, though you do not know me.
(Isaiah 44:24–45:4.
Cf. Ezra 1:1)

The book of Daniel ascribes the capture of Babylon and the reorganization of the Empire to the otherwise unknown 'Darius the Mede'.[5] The following two extracts from the Bible and Josephus present a distinctive Jewish view of the capture of Babylon.

6. That very night Belshazzar, the Chaldean king, was killed. And Darius the Mede received the kingdom, being about sixty-two years old. It pleased Darius to set over the kingdom one hundred and twenty satraps, stationed throughout the whole kingdom… (Daniel 5:30–6:1. 2 Chronicles 36:22–23 [#105] and Ezra 1:1–4 nominate Cyrus, King of Persia, as the heir to the Babylonian Empire)

7. Now Darius, who with his relative Cyrus put an end to the Babylonian sovereignty, was in his sixty-second year when he took Babylon; he was a son of Astyages but was called another name among the Greeks. (Josephus, *Antiquities* 10.248)

Cyrus restored the traditional religion of Babylon and its former imperial domains. The Cyrus Cylinder declares the unequivocal willingness of the Persians to grant religious 'freedom' to former vassal territories ruled by the Babylonians, and to restore the worship of traditional gods to captured peoples, including the exiled Jews.

8. (As to the region) from…as far as Ashur and Susa, Agade, Eshunna, the towns Zamban, Me-Turnu, Der as well as the region of the Gutians, I returned to (these) sacred cities on the other side of the Tigris, the sanctuaries of which have been ruins for a long time, the images which (used) to live therein and established for them permanent sanctuaries. I (also) gathered all their (former) inhabitants and returned (to them) their habitations. Furthermore, I resettled upon the command of Marduk, the great lord, all the gods of Sumer and Akkad whom Nabonidus has brought into Babylon to the anger of the lord of the gods, unharmed, in their (former) chapels, the places which make them happy. (From the Cyrus Cylinder [*ANET* p. 316]. Cf. 2 Chronicles 36:22–23 [#105]; Ezra 1:1–4)

1.2. The Persian Empire

For the next 200 years the Persians lay claim to a vast tract of land from the Greek city-states of the Ionian coast in the west to the Indus Valley in the east. Persian territory was organized into administrative provinces called satrapies. In Darius I's time there were 20 of these. During his reign tribute was levied on each satrapy. This replaced the rather less formal bestowal of gifts which was the practice under Cyrus and his son and successor Cambyses. The satraps were appointed both from the ranks of the Persian nobility and the royal family. Darius used Aramaic as the administrative *lingua franca* of his empire.

Cambyses captured Egypt, bringing an end to the institution of pharaohs. His successors, Darius I and Xerxes (485–465 BCE), attempted to enfold the Greek city-states of the mainland into the Persian imperial organization. Invasion attempts were frustrated by the destruction of the Persian fleet by storm off the promontory of Mount Athos in 490 and resounding Greek victories over Darius at Marathon (490 BCE) during the first campaign, and over Xerxes at Salamis (480) and Plataea (479) during the second. Persian activity in Greece is attested for the period of the Peloponnesian War (431–421, 415–404). The mid-fourth-century Macedonian kings Philip II and Alexander the Great were prepared to confront decisively the threat and actuality of Persian aggression.

Sources

The fifth-century BCE historian Herodotus preserves a lengthy catalogue of the tribute paid by each Persian satrapy.[6]

9. Having done so in Persia, he [Darius] divided his dominions into twenty governments, called by the Persians satrapies; and doing so and appointing governors, he ordained that each several nation should pay him tribute; to this end he united each nation with its closest neighbours, and, beyond these nearest lands, assigned those that were farther off some to one and some to another nation.
(Herodotus, *Histories* 3.89)[7]

In the following passage Herodotus preserves a record of the wealth of the satrapy of Babylon in his own times.

10. There are many proofs of the wealth of Babylon, but this in especial. All the land ruled by the great King is parceled out for the provisioning of himself and his army, besides that it pays tribute: now the territory of Babylon feeds him for four out of the twelve months in the year, the whole of the rest of Asia providing for the other eight. Thus the wealth of Assyria is one third of the whole wealth of Asia. The governorship, which the Persians call 'satrapy', of this land is by the greatest of all the governorships; seeing that the daily revenue of Tritantaechmes son of Artabazus, governing this province by the king's will, was an artaba full of silver (the artaba is a Persian measure, containing more by three Attic choenixes than an Attic medimnus), and besides war chargers he had in his stables eight hundred stallions, and sixteen thousand brood mares, each stallion serving twenty mares. Moreover he kept so great a number of Indian dogs that four great villages of the plain were appointed to provide food for the dogs and eased from all other burdens. Such were the riches of the governor of Babylon.
(Herodotus, *Histories* 1.192)[8]

The Bible bears witness to the Persian ascendancy and the incorporation of Judah into the Persian Empire (see Ezra 5:3, 6; 6:6, 13; Nehemiah 3:7). In the passage below, Nehemiah contrasts his own mild rule under Persian patronage with that of his rapacious predecessors.

11. Moreover from the time that I was appointed to be their governor in the land of Judah, from the twentieth year to the thirty-second year of King Artaxerxes, twelve years, neither I nor my brothers ate the food allowance of the governor. The former governors who were before me laid heavy burdens on the people, and took food and wine from them, besides forty shekels of silver. Even their servants lorded it over the people. But I did not do so, because of the fear of God. Indeed, I devoted myself to the work of this wall, and acquired no land; and all my servants were gathered there for the work. Moreover there were at my table one hundred fifty people, Jews and officials, beside those who came to us from the nations around us. Now that which was prepared for one day was one ox and six choice sheep; also fowls were prepared for me, and every ten days skins of wine in abundance; yet with all this I did not

demand the food allowance of the governor, because of the heavy burden of labor on the people.
(Nehemiah 5:14–18)

The Behistun inscription testifies to Darius's defeat of rival claimants to the throne. He was directed, so the inscription claims, by Ahuramazda, the god of the Persians. His son Xerxes forbade the worship of gods other than Ahuramazda (see #12). The following text provides important early insights into Zoroastrianism, the religion of the Persians. Note the belief in blessedness after death for the faithful (see also #691–92). This was a view which significantly influenced Judaism and, in turn, Christianity.

12. Ahuramazda is the great god who gave (us) this earth, who gave (us) that sky, who gave (us) mankind, who gave to his worshipers prosperity, who made Xerxes, the king, (rule) the multitudes (as) only king, give alone orders to the other (kings).

I am Xerxes, the great king, the only king (lit.: king of kings), the king of (all) countries (which speak) all kinds of languages, the king of this (entire) big and far(-reaching) earth,—the son of king Darius, the Achaemenian, a Persian, son of a Persian, an Aryan of Aryan descent (lit.: seed).

Thus speaks king Xerxes: These are the countries—in addition to Persia—over which I am king under the 'shadow' of Ahuramazda, over which I hold sway, which are bringing their tribute to me—whatever is commanded them by me, that they do and they abide by my law(s)—: Media, Elam, Arachosia, Urartu, Drangiana, Parthia, (H)aria, Bactria, Sogdia, Chorasmia, Babylonia, Assyria, Sattagydia, Sardis, Egypt, the Ionians who live on the salty sea and (those) who live beyond (lit.: on the other shore of) the salty sea, Maka, Arabia, Gandara, India, Cappadocia, Da'an, the Amyrgian Cimmerians, the Cimmerians (wearing) pointed caps, the Skudra, the Akupish, Libya, Banneshu (Carians) (and) Kush.

Thus speaks king Xerxes: After I became king, there were (some) among these countries (names of which) are written above, which revolted (but) I crushed (lit.: killed) these countries, after Ahuramazda had given me his support, under the 'shadow' of Ahuramazda, and I put them (again) into their (former political) status. Furthermore, there were among these countries (some) which performed (religious) service (lit.: festival) to the 'Evil (God)s,' (but) under the 'shadow' of Ahuramazda I destroyed (lit.: eradicated) these temples of the 'Evil (God)s' and proclaimed (as follows): 'You must not perform (religious) service to the 'Evil (God)s' (any more)!' Whatever formerly (religious) service was performed to the 'Evil (God)s,' I, myself, performed a (religious) service to Ahuramazda and the *arta* (cosmic order) reverently. Furthermore, there were other things which were done in a bad way, and these (too) I made in the correct way.

All these things which I did, I performed under the 'shadow' of Ahuramazda and Ahuramazda gave me his support until I had accomplished everything.

Whosoever you are, in future (days) who thinks (as follows): 'May I be prosperous in this life and blessed after my death!'—do live according to this law which Ahuramazda has promulgated: 'Perform (religious) service (only) for Ahuramazda and the *arta* (cosmic order) reverently.' A man who lives according to this law which Ahuramazda has promulgated, and (who) performs (religious) service (only) to Ahuramazda and the *arta* (cosmic order) reverently, will be prosperous while he is alive—(when) dead—he will become blessed.

Thus speaks king Xerxes: May Ahuramazda protect me, my family and these countries from all evil. This I do ask of Ahuramazda and this Ahuramazda may grant me!
(Foundation Tablet from Persepolis [*ANET* pp. 316–17])

1.3. Philip II of Macedonia

Throughout the classical era, unity among the Greek city-states (*poleis*) was rarely achieved except in the face of external threats during the early fifth century from Persian forces under kings Darius I and Xerxes. These were beaten off in memorable Greek campaigns against the invaders. Yet at times later in the century and early in the fourth century BCE one or more of the city-states actively sought Persian military aid in promoting the cause of hegemony over the others. For example, during the final stages of the Peloponnesian War against the Athenians and her empire (427–405), the Spartans concluded an alliance with the Persians. Indeed, the Peace of Antalcidas (387 BCE) was mediated by the Spartans whose hegemony over the other Greek city-states after the War had turned oppressive. The terms of the treaty required those Greeks not already under Athenian hegemony to submit to the Persians and to the possibility of Persian interference in relations between them.

Hopelessly divided among themselves and almost constantly warring against one another, the city-states were unable to withstand the imperial pretensions and designs of the Macedonian dynasty, which, in the fourth century, produced two able kings, Philip II and Alexander the Great. They sought hegemony over all Greeks. The Macedonians they ruled were regarded as semi-barbarians by the Greeks. Nevertheless, under Philip II (359–336 BCE), father of Alexander, the city-states were steadily incorporated into the Macedonian sphere of influence. A decisive battle at Chaeronea in 338 fought by Philip against troops of a Greek confederacy led by Athens and Thebes put an end to the hopes of the remaining independent *poleis*. Athens, in particular, the only potential rival to Macedonian pretensions, was no longer able to claim hegemony over other Greeks.

Athenian politics of the era reveal responses to the designs of the Macedonians which were both defiant and accommodationist, but yet fervently pan-hellenic and anti-barbarian. Isocrates the rhetorician (436–338 BCE), an older contemporary of the great Athenian orator Demosthenes, articulated a long-cherished hope that the Greek city-states would unite and invade the Persian empire in the name of the defence of the Greek homeland. He expressed these hopes in a great discourse entitled *Panegyricus*, in which he argued that Athens had the right to lead a Greek expedition against the barbarian Persians. The future of civilization, he argued forcibly, was at stake.

Sources

In the following decree Xenophon records the humiliating terms of the Peace of Antalcidas in 387 BCE.

13. 'King Artaxerxes thinks it just that the cities in Asia should belong to him, as well as Clazomenae and Cyprus among the islands, and that the other Greek cities, both small and great, should be left independent, except Lemnos, Imbros, and Scyros; and these should belong, as of old, to the Athenians. But whichever of the two parties does not accept this peace, upon them I will make war, in company with those who desire this arrangement, both by land and sea, with ships and with money'.
(Xenophon, *Hellenica* 5.1.31)

Isocrates had the incessant warfare of the city-states in mind in when he began a campaign to link all Greek city-states in a war against the Persians (see his *Panegyricus* 173, 182). He succinctly underscored the cultural divide between Greeks and Persians in the following extract from his *Panegyricus*. This work was published in 380 BCE, well before the rise of the Macedonians.

14. Most of their [the Persian] population is a mob without discipline or experience of dangers, which has lost all stamina for war and has been trained more effectively for servitude [*douleia*] than are the slaves in our country. Those, on the other hand, who stand highest in repute among them have never governed their lives by dictates of equality or of common interest or of loyalty to the state; on the contrary, their whole existence consists of insolence toward some, and servility towards others—a manner of life than which nothing could be more demoralizing to human nature. Because they are rich, they pamper their bodies; but because they are subject to one man's power, they keep their souls in a state of

abject and cringing fear, parading themselves at the door of the royal palace, prostrating [*proskunountes*] themselves, and in every way schooling themselves to humility of spirit, falling on their knees before a mortal man, addressing him as a divinity, and thinking more lightly of the gods than of men.
(Isocrates, *Panegyricus* 150–51)[9]

In 346 BCE, after the concluding of the Peace of Philocrates which brought about an end to ten years of warfare between the Macedonians and Athens for control of the northern city of Amphipolis, Isocrates wrote his discourse *To Philip*. With a lasting peace now possible, he saw a fresh opportunity for Philip, King of Macedonia, to carry out his longstanding grand vision of a campaign against Persia.[10] He proceeded to lay before Philip the example of his legendary hero ancestor, Heracles, who conducted a successful campaign against barbarian Troy, then the greatest power in Asia.

15. For since you have no need to follow alien examples but have before you one from your own house, have we not then the right to expect that you will be spurred on by this and inspired by the ambition to make yourself like the ancestor of your race? I do not mean that you will be able to imitate Heracles in all his exploits; for even among the gods there are some who could not do that; but in the qualities of the spirit, in devotion to humanity, and in the good will which he cherished toward the Hellenes, you can come close to his purposes… And mark that I am summoning you to an undertaking in which you will make expeditions, not with the barbarians against men who have given you no just cause, but with the Hellenes against those upon whom it is fitting that the descendants of Heracles should wage war.
(Isocrates, *To Philip* 113–15)[11]

Isocrates's vision was thwarted by further fruitless Athenian resistance to the Macedonians. After the battle of Chaeronea, at which Athens was defeated, and just before his death, Isocrates wrote a letter to Philip in which he returned to his grand agenda, urging him to pursue the 'unsurpassable' glory of compelling the Persian king to do whatever he might command. 'For then will naught be left for you', Isocrates argued, 'except to become a god' (*Letter to Philip* II.5)[12]

1.4. Alexander the Great

Philip was assassinated in 336 BCE in circumstances that pointed to the possible involvement of Alexander, his son, and his mother Olympias, who had been displaced by Philip for another queen. Thus Alexander (b. 356) became king.

On ascending the throne of Macedonia, Alexander immediately re-asserted Macedonian control of the Greek city-states before crossing the Hellespont and embarking on the conquest of the Persian empire. The first confrontation occurred in 334, the battle of Granicus (in northwest Asia Minor, near ancient Troy) over Darius III's satraps. The subjugation of Persian forces in Asia Minor quickly followed. In the following year, Alexander prepared to meet Darius and his troops at Issus in northern Syria. Darius's forces outnumbered those Alexander commanded. Although Darius escaped the field of battle, his mother, wife and children were captured.[13] Subsequently all of Syria, Palestine and Egypt fell to Alexander.

Among the many cities Alexander founded on the Greek model throughout his territory was a new city in Egypt called Alexandria.[14] The city had a body of free citizens, and political institutions and an educational system analogous to what might be found operating in a Greek *polis*. Alexandria was destined to become the centre of Greek rule in Egypt for the next three centuries. It became the home of a sizeable Greek-speaking Jewish population, and, with Rome and Antioch, the largest of the cities of the Graeco-Roman world.

Alexander now turned his attention eastwards. He captured Babylon. On entering the city he sacrificed to Marduk, and sought to rebuild the temples allegedly destroyed by Xerxes.[15] The last and final confrontation with Darius occurred in 331 at Gaugamela in northern Mesopotamia. Darius was present at the battle, and fled when it became clear his forces would be defeated. He was later assassinated as the pursuing Alexander was about to overtake him. Alexander's victory left the eastern Persian empire vulnerable to his troops.

After the death of Darius, Alexander began to adopt Persian dress and expected to receive the honour of prostration (*proskunēsis*) (see Arrian, *Anabasis of Alexander* 4.9.9), the custom by which inferiors respectfully approached superiors in Persia. These innovations were not well received among his Macedonian troops. In particular, the expectation of prostration was resented since to Greeks it implied the divine status of one to whom it was offered. The philosopher Callisthenes spoke out against the novelty. His later execution was based on trumped-up charges, according to extant sources. Earlier Alexander had been directly responsible for the murder of Cleitus at a banquet after criticizing Alexander's adoption of Persian ways.[16] At the height of his power Alexander was risking alienating members of his inner circle. Alexander also had 30,000 youths educated in Greek and Greek customs (cf. Daniel 1).

In 327 Alexander reached the Indus valley in modern Pakistan. After winning several military engagements and establishing military fortresses, which he garrisoned with Macedonian (Thracian) veterans, and having concluded military alliances with local Indian kings, Alexander turned back to organize his vast domain. He had hoped valiantly that he might bring unity to his vast territory. That task was to prove too great, at least for one man. In 323 Alexander died in Babylon, only 33 years old.

At Alexander's death the empire he had forged faced no external threats to the east or west. Alexander's son by his Bactrian wife Roxane had not yet been born. Both were later murdered.

Sources

As Darius considered his tactics at Issus, the historian Arrian provides the following assessment of the supernatural forces conspiring to bring about the defeat of the Persians and the ascendancy of Alexander. Darius and his advisers believed that Alexander's delayed arrival on the plains of Mesopotamia was the result of indecision and failure of nerve. Darius, however, clearly underestimated Alexander's ability and resolve.

16. [I]ngratiating courtiers...encouraged him to conclude that Alexander was no longer willing to advance further, but was hesitating on hearing of Darius' own approach. On all sides they egged him on, telling him that he would trample the Macedonian force underfoot with his cavalry. Amyntas, however, persisted that Alexander would come wherever he found Darius to be, and urged him to remain where he was. But the worse counsels prevailed, as they were more agreeable to hear at the time; moreover, some divine power led Darius into the very position where his cavalry did not much help him, nor the number of his men and javelins and arrows, where he could make no display even of the splendour of his army, but delivered the victory easily to Alexander and his force. In fact it was destined that the Persians should forfeit the sovereignty of Asia to Macedonians, just as Medes had lost it to Persians, and Assyrians even earlier to Medes.
(Arrian, *Anabasis of Alexander* 2.6.4–7)

Alexander's speech to his generals and senior officers reveals contempt for the way of life of the 'barbarian' Persians (cf. #14).

17. 'We Macedonians...are to fight Medes and Persians, nations long steeped in luxury, while we have now long been inured to danger by the exertions of campaigning. Above all it will be a fight of free men against slaves. And so far as Greek will meet Greek, they will not be fighting for like causes; those with Darius will be risking their lives for pay, and poor pay too; the Greeks on our side will fight as volunteers

in the cause of Greece. As for our barbarian troops, Thracians, Paeonians, Illyrians, Agrianians, the most robust and warlike races of Europe, will be ranged against the most indolent and softest tribes of Asia. In addition you have Alexander commanding against Darius.'
(Arrian, *Anabasis of Alexander* 2.7.4–5)

Alexander's visit to the Temple of Ammon.

The relationship between Heracles and Philip II is also canvassed in #15. As a result of the visit to the oracle, Alexander began to style himself son of Zeus Ammon.

18. (3) After this a longing seized Alexander to pay a visit to Ammon in Libya, for one reason to consult the god, since the oracle of Ammon was said to be infallible, and to have been consulted by Perseus, when he was sent by Polydectes against the Gorgon, and by Heracles when he was on his way into Lybia to find Antaeus, and into Egypt to find Busiris. Alexander sought to rival Perseus and Heracles, as he was descended from them both; and in addition he himself traced his birth in part to Ammon, just as the legends traced that of Heracles and Perseus to Zeus. In any case he set out for Ammon with this idea, hoping to secure more exact knowledge of his affairs, or at least to say he had secured it…
(4) The district (Siwah) in which the Temple of Ammon lies is desert all around, covered with sand, and without water. But the site in the centre, which is small (for its broadest stretch only comes to about forty stades), is full of garden trees, olives and palms, and of all the surrounding country it alone catches the dew. A spring, too, rises from it, not at all like other springs which rise from the ground. For at midday the water is cold to the taste and even more to the touch, as cold as can be, but when the sun sinks towards evening it is warmer, and from evening on it grows warmer and warmer till midnight, and at midnight it is at its warmest; but after midnight it cools off in turn, and from dawn onwards it is already cold, but coldest at midday. This change occurs regularly every day. Then there are natural salts in this district, to be obtained by digging; some are taken by priests of Ammon to Egypt. Whenever they are going off to Egypt, they pack the salt into baskets woven of palm leaves, to be conveyed as a present to the king or to someone else. The grains of this salt are large, some of them have been known to be more than three fingers' breadth, and clear as crystal. Egyptians and others who are particular about religious observance use this salt in their sacrifices, as being purer than the sea-salts. Now Alexander surveyed the site with wonder, and made his enquiry of the god; he received the answer his heart desired, as he said, and turned back for Egypt, by the same route according to Aristobulus, but according to Ptolemy son of Lagos, by a different way, direct to Memphis.
(Arrian, *Anabasis of Alexander* 3.3.1–2; 4.1–5)

Alexander sought to bring unity to his vast territory. In the following extract from the first-century CE Roman historian Quintus Curtius, Alexander addresses his Persian and Macedonian troops.

19. 'It is for this reason that I myself united in marriage with me Roxanê, daughter of the Persian Oxyartes, not disdaining to rear children from a captive. Then later, when I desired to propagate the stock of my race more extensively, I took to wife a daughter of Darius and set the example to my nearest friends of begetting children from captives, in order that by this sacred alliance I might abolish all distinction between vanquished and victor. Therefore believe that in my eyes you are soldiers of our blood, not brought in from outside. Asia and Europe now belong to one and the same kingdom; I give you the arms of the Macedonians, I have made you old soldiers instead of new and foreign ones; you are both my citizens and my soldiers. All things take on the same colour; it is neither unbecoming for the Persians to simulate the manners of the Macedonians, nor for the Macedonians to copy those of the Persians. Those ought to have the same rights who are to live under the same sovereign.'
(Curtius, *History of Alexander* 10.3.11–14)

Alexander's adoption of Persian ways (#20–21).

20. From thence he marched into Parthia, where, during a respite from fighting, he first put on the barbaric dress, either from desire to adapt himself to the native customs, believing that community of race and custom goes far towards softening the hearts of men; or else this was an attempt to introduce the obeisance [Greek *proskunēsis*] among the Macedonians, by accustoming them little by little to put up with changes and alterations in his mode of life. However, he did not adopt the famous Median fashion of dress, which was altogether barbaric and strange, nor did he assume trousers, or sleeved vest, or tiara, but carefully devised a fashion which was midway between the Persian and the Median, more modest than the one and more stately than the other. At first he wore this only in intercourse with the Barbarians and with his companions at home, then people generally saw him riding forth or giving audience in this attire. The sight was offensive to the Macedonians, but they admired his other high qualities and thought they ought to yield to him in some things which made for his pleasure or his fame.
(Plutarch, *Alexander* 45.1–3)

21. [H]e adapted his own mode of life still more to the customs of the country, and tried to bring these into closer agreement with Macedonian customs, thinking that by a mixture and community of practice which produced good will, rather than by force, his authority would be kept secure while he was far away. For this reason, too, he chose out thirty thousand boys and gave orders that they should learn the Greek language and be trained to use Macedonian weapons, appointing many instructors for this work.
(Plutarch, *Alexander* 47.3. Cf. 71.1).

1.5. Alexander's Achievement

There can be no doubting the esteem in which Alexander was held in antiquity, both by contemporaries and subsequent generations. In his own time and later he was admired, even revered, as a proponent of Greek civilization to the 'barbarian' east. Alexander also believed himself to be divinely guided and divinely inspired.

It is scarcely true to call the loose confederation of Alexander's conquests an empire. Much of the territory he conquered reverted to local, independent rule after his death. At the eastern margins, Alexander's military outposts in the Indus valley were quickly overcome. In Asia Minor, Pontus and Pergamum were also able to regain their independence.[17]

But Alexander did facilitate the spread of the Greek language, together with the accoutrements of Greek civilization, throughout his domain. The founding of cities based on Greek precedents across the breadth of his march undoubtedly served as bastions of Greek cultural values. However, Alexander's attempts to bring Persians into partnership embittered powerful elements of his military machine.

Sources

At the beginning and conclusion of his account of Alexander's career Arrian offers assessments of the king's prodigious and unprecedented accomplishments. The conclusion of his account follows.

22. If, however, Alexander committed any error through haste or in anger, or if he went some distance in the direction of Eastern arrogance, this I do not regard as important; if readers will consider in a spirit of charity Alexander's youth, his unbroken success, and those courtiers who associate with kings to flatter but not to improve them, and who always will so associate with kings to their harm. But I do know that to Alexander alone of the kings of old did repentance for his faults come, by reason of his noble nature; while most people, if they have admitted any error, by defending their misdeed, as if it were a good deed, think that they will conceal their error; and this is a great mistake. For I at least feel that the only cure for sin is a confession of sin and evidence of repentance, since the offended

party will not feel the offences so grievous if the offender agrees that he did not well; and for the man himself this good hope is left behind for the future, that he will not so offend again if he appear grieved at the errors of the past. But that he referred his birth to a god, even this I do not altogether think to be a grave fault, if it was not perhaps a mere device to impress his subjects, and to appear more dignified. In point of fact I hold him no less famous a king than Minos, Aeacus, or Radamanthus; they traced their origin back to Zeus, and yet this was not associated by men of old with any arrogance; nor yet Theseus' descent from Poseidon, nor Ion's from Apollo. Moreover, I feel that the adoption of Persian equipage was a device, both towards the Persians, so that their King might not appear wholly removed from them, and towards the Macedonians, to mark some reversion from Macedonian abruptness and arrogance; for the same reason, I suspect, he drafted into their ranks the Persian troops who carried the 'golden apples,' and the Persian nobles into their cavalry squadrons. And his carousings, as Aristobulus says, were prolonged not for the wine, for Alexander was no wine-bibber, but from a spirit of comradeship.

Whosoever speaks evil of Alexander, let him speak such evil, not merely by producing what deserves evil-speaking, but gathering all that Alexander did into a single whole; let such a one consider first himself, his own personality, his own fortunes, and then on the other hand Alexander, what he became, and the height of human prosperity which he reached, having made himself king, beyond all contradiction, of both continents, and having spread his fame over the widest possible span; let such a one, I say, consider of whom he speaks evil; himself being more puny, and busied about puny things, and not even bringing these to success. For I myself believe that there was at that time no race of mankind, no city, no single individual, whither the name of Alexander had not reached. And so not even I can suppose that a man quite beyond all other men was born without some divine influence. Moreover, oracles are said to have prophesied Alexander's death, and visions coming to different persons, and dreams, dreamed by different persons; there was also the general regard of mankind leading to this same conclusion, and the memory of one more than human; and even now there are other oracles, after this great gap of time, which have been delivered to the Macedonian race, and all tending to the highest estimation of him. True it is that I myself have quarrelled with certain acts in my history of Alexander's deeds, but I am bold to admire Alexander himself; and those acts I blamed, both for the sake of my veracity, and also for the general benefit of mankind; and that is why I myself too took up this history, not without the help of God.
(Arrian, *Anabasis of Alexander* 7.29–30)[18]

After his meteoric career, speculation concerning Alexander's alleged superhuman origins continued to circulate. In the extracts below, Diodorus Siculus and Plutarch report the tradition of his parentage and lineage.

23. On his father's side Alexander was a descendant of Heracles and on his mother's he could claim the blood of the Aeacids, so that from his ancestors on both sides he inherited the physical and moral qualities of greatness.
(Diodorus Siculus, *Histories* 17.1.5)[19]

24. [A] serpent was once seen lying stretched out by the side of Olympias [Alexander's mother] as she slept, and we are told that this, more than anything else, dulled the ardour of Philip's attentions to his wife, so that he no longer came often to sleep by her side, either because he feared that some spells and enchantments might be practised upon him by her, or because he shrank from her embraces in the conviction that she was the partner of a superior being.
(Plutarch, *Alexander* 2.4)[20]

Alexander's founding of cities throughout the Ancient Near East organized on the Greek model had lasting cultural implications.

The founding of Alexandria in the Caucasus.

25. A site for founding a city was chosen at the foot of the mountain and seven thousand

from the subdued nations were permitted to settle in the new city, as well as those soldiers whose services the king had ceased to make use of. This city also its inhabitants called Alexandria.
(Curtius, *History of Alexander* 7.3.23)

Later Jewish memories of the rapacity of Alexander and his armies have been preserved in the early Jewish collection known as the *Sibylline Oracles*. The oracle cited below is of indeterminate date.

26. An oracle on Alexander the Great.

But Macedonia will bring forth a great affliction for Asia
and a very great grief for Europe will spring up
from the race of Cronos, the progeny of bastards and slaves.
She will conquer even the fortified city of Babylon.
Having been called mistress of every land which the sun beholds,
she will perish by evil fate,
leaving a name among her much-wandering posterity.
(*Sibylline Oracles* 3.381–87)[21]

1.6. Alexander's Successors (the *diadochoi*)

Alexander left his mark on a vast area, one that had been administered by the Persians before him. Not surprisingly Alexander's Indian conquests soon reverted to Indian control. Alexander had also founded a number of Greek cities, such as Alexandria in Egypt, in which he settled his veterans, and which also served as military and administrative centres. Later these cities became highly significant as cultural and economic outposts. In the main, the empire was ruled after the Persian model. However, the Macedonian and Greek elites were predominant.

At Alexander's death his generals found themselves as his 'heirs'. Each one sought to establish his control and stamp his authority over his own sphere of influence. They also fought interminably among themselves, each one seeking to establish hegemony over the others. This warfare ceased with the defeat at the battle of Ipsus in 301 of Antigonus I Monophthalmus, satrap of Phrygia, by a coalition of Seleucus I and the surviving *diadochoi*.[22] This ended any attempt to unite Alexander's domains under one ruler.

The most significant areas of the former empire of Alexander were Syria and Egypt. In Syria, Seleucus I, initially satrap of Babylon, established a dynasty. He founded Antioch on the Orontes, his later capital (Appian, *History of Rome* 11.57). His territory initially extended as far east as the Indus. Throughout the third century BCE the Seleucids sought control over Palestine, which was in Egyptian hands until 200 BCE when Antiochus III defeated Ptolemy V Epiphanes at the battle of Panium.[23] These struggles are recorded in Daniel 11 as prophecies *ex eventu*. By 129, the year of the death of Antiochus VII, Seleucid territory had shrunk to a small area in northern Syria.[24]

Antiochus III, nicknamed 'the Great' because of his conquests in the east, provoked Roman intervention against him. In 195, the Carthaginian general Hannibal, who was fleeing the Romans, reached Antiochus. Antiochus found himself in a position to challenge the eastward expansion of Roman power. However, he and his new ally Hannibal were defeated at battles at Thermopylae, Rhodes and Magnesia. By the terms of the Treaty of Apamea (188 BCE), the Romans denied the Seleucids access to their possessions north of the Taurus Mountains. They imposed a heavy indemnity on Antiochus and his successors, contributing to the decline of the dynasty. The terms are cited below (#33). Antiochus also fostered a ruler cult of himself, his predecessors and his queen.

Heavy-handed Syrian intervention in the politics and religious affairs of Jerusalem during the reign of Antiochus IV Epiphanes (175–164 BCE) precipitated the Maccabaean revolt (see topic 2.4 below). As Syria became increasingly embroiled in fighting between rival claimants to the throne, it became steadily apparent that Rome would have to intervene in Syria. Parthian forces beyond the Euphrates threatened to overwhelm the Mediterranean east. In 126 BCE the Parthians captured Babylon. Accordingly, in 64 BCE Pompey annexed Syria for Rome, sweeping away the Seleucid dynasty, and establishing a strong Roman military presence along what was now her eastern frontier.

Ptolemy I's dynasty ruled Egypt until the death of Cleopatra VII in 30 BCE when the Romans annexed Egypt. At the height of Ptolemaic prestige, Polybius records Egyptian control of Coele-Syria, Cyprus, the 'lesser kingdoms' of Asia Minor, and 'the islands'. Supervision was exercised over Thrace and Macedonia (see Polybius, *Histories* 5.34.6–7). The competition between the Ptolemies and the Seleucids resulted in Palestine becoming the battleground between the two powers. The decisive battle of Raphia (217 BCE) saw the defeat of Antiochus III by Ptolemy IV and the confirmation of Egyptian hegemony over Coele-Syria, though the former was able to assert Syrian control after his victory over Ptolemy V at the battle of Panium.

Antiochus IV invaded Egypt, besieged Alexandria and threatened to revive hopes of a single Greek kingdom in the east to rival the eastward imperial pretensions of Rome. Anxious to secure Roman support for his move, Antiochus sent envoys to Rome. Roman anxiety, particularly on the score of the securing of a reliable corn supply from Egypt is well documented throughout the Graeco-Roman era. In Antiochus's day Rome intervened in Egypt in the person of G. Popilius Laenas, who prevented Antiochus from pressing his claim on Egypt (Polybius, *Histories* 29.27).

Sources

From his Palestinian Jewish perspective, Josephus comments as follows on the era of the *diadochoi*.

27. Having overthrown the Persian empire and settled the affairs of Judaea in the manner described above [see *Antiquities* 11.313–47], Alexander, the king of Macedon, died. And his empire fell to the share of many, Antigonus becoming master of Asia, and Seleucus of Babylon and the nations thereabouts, while Lysimachus ruled the Hellespont, Cassander held Macedon, and Ptolemy, the son of Lagus, took Egypt. But, as these quarrelled and fought jealously with one another, each for his own kingdom, the result was that continual and prolonged wars arose, and the cities suffered through their struggles and lost many of their inhabitants, so that all of Syria at the hands of Ptolemy, the son of Lagus, who was then called *Soter* [Saviour], suffered the reverse of that which was indicated by his surname.
(Josephus, *Antiquities* 12.1–3)[25]

The following passages from Appian and the Bible survey the struggles among the *diadochoi*. In the first, the energy and success of Seleucus I in establishing his own kingdom are recorded. Seleucus had already re-asserted his control over Babylon.

28. He [Seleucus] also acquired the kingdom of Media, slaying with his own hand in battle Nicator whom Antigonus had left as satrap of that country. He afterwards waged many wars with Macedonians and barbarians. The two principal ones were with Macedonians, the second with Lysimachus, king of Thrace, the first with Antigonus at Ipsus in Phrygia, where Antigonus commanded in person and fought in person although he was above eighty years of age. Antigonus was killed in the battle, and then all the kings who had been in league with Seleucus against him divided his territory among themselves. At this division all Syria from the Euphrates to the sea, also inland Phrygia, fell to the lot of Seleucus. Always lying in wait for the neighbouring nations, strong in arms and persuasive in diplomacy, he acquired Mesopotamia, Armenia, the so-called Seleucid Cappadocia, the Persians, Parthians, Bactrians, Arabs, Tapyri, Sogdiani, Arachotes, Hyrcanians, and all the other adjacent peoples that had been subdued by Alexander, as far as the river Indus, so that he ruled over a wider empire in Asia than any of his predecessors

except Alexander. For the whole region from Phrygia to the Indus was subject to Seleucus. He crossed the Indus and waged war with Androcottus, king of the Indians, who dwelt on the banks of that stream, until they came to an understanding with each other and contracted a marriage relationship.
(Appian, *History of Rome* 11.55)

29. 'Then the king of the south shall grow strong, but one of his officers shall grow stronger than he and shall rule a realm greater than his own realm. After some years they shall make an alliance, and the daughter of the king of the south shall come to the king of the north to ratify the agreement. But she shall not retain her power, and his offspring shall not endure. She shall be given up, she and her attendants and her child and the one who supported her.

In those times a branch from her roots shall rise up in his place. He shall come against the army and enter the fortress of the king of the north, and he shall take action against them and prevail. Even their gods, with their idols and with their precious vessels of silver and gold, he shall carry off to Egypt as spoils of war. For some years he shall refrain from attacking the king of the north; then the latter shall invade the realm of the king of the south, but will return to his own land'.
(Daniel 11:5–9. See also Josephus, *Antiquities* 12.129–37)[26]

The advancing power of Rome caused the Greek city-states to consider their response. The excerpt from the following speech is heavily dependent on the Greek experience of Philip II, Alexander and their successors.

The speech of Chlaeneas, the Aetolian.

30. 'Men of Lacedaemon [Sparta], I am convinced indeed that no one would venture to deny that the slavery of Greece owes its origin to the kings of Macedon, but the matter may be looked at thus. There was once a group of Greek cities in Thrace founded by the Athenians and Chalcidians, of which Olynthus was the most eminent and powerful. Philip, by selling the inhabitants into slavery and making an example of it, not only obtained possession of the Thracian cities, but intimidated the Thessalians into submission. When, shortly afterwards, he had defeated the Athenians in a battle he made a generous use of his success, not with the object of benefiting the Athenians, far from it, but in order that his kindness to them might induce others to obey his orders without resistance. The prestige of your city still survived then and it seemed as if in time you would be the leading power in Greece. Consequently, alleging as sufficient any pretext that offered itself, he came here with his army and inflicted great damage, cutting the crops and trees and burning the homesteads, and finally partitioning your cities and your territory, he assigned part of it to the Argives, part to the Tegeans and Megalopolitans, and part to the Messenians, wishing to confer ill-merited benefits on all of them if by doing so he could only damage you. He was succeeded by Alexander. That king again, because he thought there was left in Thebes a little spark of the Greece that once was, destroyed that city in the manner that you all, I take it, know.

And as for the successors of Alexander, need I tell you in detail how they treated the Greeks? For no one is so indifferent to facts as not to have heard how Antipater after his victory over the Greeks at Lamia treated the unhappy Athenians as well as the other Greeks in the harshest manner, going so far in his wanton and lawless violence as to appoint and send round to the different cities exile-hunters to catch those who had opposed or in any way offended the royal house of Macedon. Some forcibly driven out of the temples and others dragged from the altars perished by torture, while those who escaped were expelled from the whole of Greece, having no single place of refuge except the territory of the Aetolian League. And who is ignorant of the actions of Cassander, Demetrius, and Antigonus Gonatus, all so recent that the memory of them is quite vivid? Some of them by introducing garrisons to cities and others by planting tyrannies left no city with the right to call itself unenslaved. Leaving them aside, I will now pass to the last Antigonus [Antigonus III Doson], in case any of you, regarding his action without suspicion, con-

sider themselves under a debt of gratitude to the Macedonians. It was not for the purpose of saving the Achaeans that Antigonus undertook the war against you, nor because he disapproved of the tyranny of Cleomenes and desired to save Sparta. If anyone entertains such a notion he must be very simple-minded. But seeing that his own power would not be safe if you acquired the supremacy in the Peloponnesus, that Cleomenes was just the man to effect this and that Fortune was working for you splendidly, he came here actuated both by fear and envy, not to help the Peloponnesians but to cut short your hopes and humiliate your prestige. So instead of affection for the Macedonians because they did not plunder your city when masters of it, you should consider them your enemies and hate them for preventing you more than once when you had the power of attaining supremacy in Greece.'
(Polybius, *Histories* 9.28–29)[27]

Antiochus III was a considerable figure in the Seleucid dynasty, not least because he threatened the expanding power of the Romans.

31. Antiochus (the son of Seleucus and grandson of Antiochus), king of the Syrians, the Babylonians and other nations, was the sixth in succession from that Seleucus who succeeded Alexander in the government of the Asiatic countries around the Euphrates. He invaded Media and Parthia, and other countries that revolted from his ancestors, and performed many exploits, from which he was named Antiochus the Great. Elated by his successes, and by the title which he had derived from them, he invaded Coele-Syria and a portion of Cilicia and took them away from Ptolemy Philopator [the translator suggests instead Ptolemy Epiphanes], king of Egypt, who was still a boy. Filled with unbounded ambition, he marched against the Hellespontines, the Aeolians, and the Ionians as though they belonged to him as the ruler of Asia, because they had been formerly subjects of the Asiatic kings. Then he crossed over to Europe, brought Thrace under his sway, and reduced by force those who would not obey him. He fortified Chersonesus and rebuilt Lysimacheia, which Lysimachus, who ruled Thrace after Alexander, built as a stronghold against the Thracians themselves, but which they destroyed after his death. Antiochus repeopled it, calling back the citizens who had fled, redeeming those who had been sold as slaves, bringing in others, supplying them with cattle, sheep, and iron for agricultural purposes, and omitting nothing that might contribute to its speedy completion as a stronghold; for the place seemed to him to be admirably situated to hold all Thrace in subjection, and a convenient base of supplies for all the other operations that he contemplated.
(Appian, *History of Rome* 11.1)

Despite an inauspicious beginning of the battle of Raphia, Ptolemy IV was eventually victorious. Polybius concludes his narrative with the following observation.

32. Such was the result of the battle of Raphia fought by the kings for the possession of Coele-Syria. After paying the last honours to the dead Antiochus returned to his own kingdom with his army, and Ptolemy took without resistance Raphia and the other towns, each community endeavouring to anticipate its neighbours in going over to him and resuming its allegiance. Possibly all men at such times are more or less disposed to adapt themselves to the needs of the hour, and the natives of these parts are naturally more prone than others to bestow their affections at the bidding of circumstances. But at this juncture it was only to be expected that they should act so, as their affection for the Egyptian kings was of no recent growth; for the peoples of Coele-Syria have always been more attached to that house than to the Seleucidae. So now there was no extravagance of adulation to which they did not proceed, honouring Ptolemy with crowns, sacrifices, altars dedicated to him and every distinction of the kind.
(Polybius, *Histories* 5.86.7–11)

In the aftermath of the battle of Zama, Hannibal escaped eastwards to the court of Antiochus III. This led to a successful Roman campaign against the Seleucids and their

Greek allies. In 188, by the terms of the treaty of Apamea, the Romans imposed a heavy indemnity on Antiochus and his successors, contributing to the decline of the dynasty and, in all probability, to the measures taken by Antiochus IV Epiphanes to secure a foothold in Egypt.

33. The terms in detail were as follows: 'There shall be friendship between Antiochus and the Romans for all time if he fulfils the conditions of the treaty: King Antiochus and his subjects shall not permit the passage through their territory of any enemy marching against the Romans and their allies or furnish such enemy with any supplies: the Romans and their allies engage to act likewise towards Antiochus and his subjects: Antiochus shall not make war on the inhabitants of the islands or of Europe: he shall evacuate all cities, lands, villages, and forts on this side of the Taurus as far as the river Halys and all between the valley of Taurus and the mountain ridges that descend to Lycaonia: from all such places he is to carry away nothing except the arms borne by his soldiers, and if anything has been carried away, it is to be restored to the same city: he shall not receive either soldiers or others from the kingdom of Eumenes: if there be any men in the army of Antiochus coming from the cities which the Romans take over, he shall deliver them up at Apamea: if there be any from the kingdom of Antiochus dwelling with the Romans and their allies, they may remain or depart at their good pleasure: Antiochus and his subjects shall give up the slaves of the Romans and of their allies, both those taken in war and those who deserted, and any prisoners of war they have taken, if there be such: Antiochus shall give up, if it be in his power, Hannibal son of Hamilcar, the Carthaginian, Mnasilochus the Acarnanian, Thoas the Aetolian, Eubulidas and Philo the Chalcidians, and all Aetolians who have held public office: he shall surrender all the elephants now in Apamea and not keep any in future: he shall surrender his long ships with their gear and tackle and in future he shall not possess more than ten decked ships of war, nor shall he have any galley rowed by more than thirty oars, nor a moneres to serve in any war in which he is the aggressor: his ships shall not sail beyond the Calycadnus and the Sarpedonian promontory unless conveying tribute, envoys or hostages: Antiochus shall not have permission to hire mercenaries from the lands under the rule of the Romans, or to receive fugitives: all houses that belonged to the Rhodians and their allies in the dominions of Antiochus shall remain their property as they were before he made war on them; likewise if any money is owing to them they may exact payment, and if anything has been abstracted from them it shall be sought for and returned: merchandise meant for Rhodes shall be free from duties as before the war: if any of the cities which Antiochus has to give up have been given by him to others, he shall withdraw from these also the garrisons and the men in possession of them: and if any cities afterwards wish to desert to him, he shall not receive them: Antiochus shall pay to the Romans twelve thousand talents of the best Attic money in twelve years, paying a thousand talents a year, the talent not to weigh less than eighty Roman pounds, and five hundred and forty thousand modii of corn: he shall pay to King Eumenes three hundred and fifty talents in the next five years, paying seventy talents a year at the same time that is fixed for his payments to the Romans and in lieu of the corn, as Antiochus estimated it—one hundred and twenty-seven talents and twelve hundred and eight drachmas, the sum Eumenes agreed to accept as a satisfactory payment to his treasury: Antiochus shall give twenty hostages, replacing them every three years, not below eighteen years of age and not above forty: if any of the money he pays does not correspond to the above stipulations, he shall make it good in the following year: if any of the cities or peoples against which Antiochus is forbidden by this treaty to make war begin first to make war on him, he may make war on such, provided he does not exercise sovereignty over any of them or receive them into his alliance: all grievances of both parties are to be submitted to a lawful tribunal: if both parties

desire to add any clauses to this treaty or to remove any by common decree, they are at liberty to do so.'
(Polybius, *Histories* 21.42)[28]

Antiochus III was succeeded by his son Seleucus IV, who was soon assassinated and replaced by Antiochus IV, a younger son of Antiochus III.

34. Afterward, on the death of Antiochus the Great, his son Seleucus succeeded him, and gave his son Demetrius as a hostage to the Romans in place of his brother Antiochus [later Antiochus IV]. When the latter arrived at Athens on his way home, Seleucus was assassinated as the result of a conspiracy of a certain Heliodorus [see 2 Maccabees 3:1–40], one of the court officers; but when Heliodorus sought to possess himself of the government he was driven out by Eumenes and Attalus, who installed Antiochus therein in order to secure his good-will; for, by reason of certain bickerings, they also had already grown suspicious of the Romans. Thus Antiochus, the son of Antiochus the Great, ascended the throne of Syria. He was called Epiphanes (the Illustrious) by the Syrians, because when the government was seized by usurpers he showed himself to be a true king. Having cemented his friendship and alliance with Eumenes he governed Syria and the neighbouring nations with a firm hand. He appointed Timarchus a satrap of Babylon and Heraclides as treasurer, two brothers, both of whom had been his favourites. He also made an expedition against Artaxias, king of Armenia, and took him prisoner.
(Appian, *History of Rome* 11.45)

Antiochus IV took the throne in 175 BCE. Fragmentary detail concerning him from Polybius, *Histories* 26, is preserved by Athenagoras. For negative Jewish assessments of this controversial king, see #118–19.

35. Polybius in his 26th Book calls him Epimanes (the Madman) instead of Epiphanes owing to his conduct. For not only did he condescend to converse with common people, but even with the meanest of the foreigners who visited Antioch. And whenever he heard that any of the younger men were at an entertainment, no matter where, he would come in with a fife and other music so that most of the guests got up and ran off in astonishment. He would often, moreover, doff his royal robe and pick up a toga and so make the circuit of the market-place.
(Polybius, *Histories* 26.1a. See also *Histories* 26.1)

In 169 BCE Antiochus embarked on an invasion of Egypt.[29] He was repulsed at Alexandria. He sent envoys to Rome, seeking Roman endorsement of his claims (see Polybius, *Histories* 28.22). His designs were received with considerable unease by the Roman senate. It dispatched Gaius Popilius Laenas to bring the war to an end (see Polybius, *Histories* 29.2.1–3).

36. At the time when Antiochus approached Ptolemy and meant to occupy Pelusium, Caius Popilius Laenas, the Roman commander, on Antiochus greeting him from a distance and then holding out his hand, handed to the king, as he had it by him, the copy of the senatus-consultum, and told him to read it first, not thinking it proper, as it seems to me, to make the conventional sign of friendship before he knew if the intentions of him who was greeting him were friendly or hostile. But when the king, after reading it, said he would like to communicate with his friends about this intelligence, Popilius acted in a manner which was thought to be offensive and exceedingly arrogant. He was carrying a stick cut from a vine, and with this he drew a circle round Antiochus and told him he must remain inside this circle until he gave his decision about the contents of the letter. The king was astonished at this authoritative proceeding, but, after a few moments' hesitation, said he would do all that the Romans demanded. Upon this Popilius and his suite all grasped him by the hand and greeted him warmly. The letter ordered him to put an end at once to the war with Ptolemy [Ptolemy VI Philometor]. So, as a fixed number of days were allowed to him, he led his army back to Syria, deeply hurt

and complaining indeed, but yielding to circumstances for the present. Popilius after arranging matters in Alexandria and exhorting the two kings there to act in common, ordering them also to send Polyaratus to Rome, sailed for Cyprus, wishing to lose no time in expelling the Syrian troops that were in the island. When they arrived, finding that Ptolemy's generals had been defeated and that the affairs of Cyprus were generally in a topsy-turvy state, they soon made the Syrian army retire from the country, and waited until the troops took ship for Syria. In this way the Romans saved the kingdom of Ptolemy, which had almost been crushed out of existence: Fortune having so directed the matter of Perseus and Macedonia that when the position of Alexandria and the whole of Egypt was almost desperate, all was again set right simply owing to the fact that the fate of Perseus had been decided. For had this not been so, and had not Antiochus been certain of it, he would never, I think, have obeyed the Roman behests.
(Polybius, *Histories* 29.27)

The book of Daniel 'predicts' the intervention of the Romans (the 'Kittim'). 'Kittim' is a term used frequently in the Dead Sea Scrolls to designate the Romans. It originally denoted Cyprus (see Isaiah 23:1 [Heb.]; Jeremiah 2:10 [Heb.]). See also Part 2 n. 22.

37. 'At the time appointed he [the "contemptible person" of 11:21; i.e. Antiochus Epiphanes] shall return and come into the south, but this time it shall not be as it was before. For ships of Kittim shall come against him, and he shall lose heart and withdraw.'
(Daniel 11:29–30a)

The decay of the Seleucids c. 150–63 BCE.

38. During this time Syria had many kings, succeeding each other at brief intervals, but all of the royal lineage, and there were many changes and revolts from the dynasty. The Parthians, who had previously revolted from the rule of the Seleucidae, seized Mesopotamia, which had been subject to that house. Tigranes, the son of Tigranes, king of Armenia, who had subdued many of the neighbouring nations which had kings of their own, and from these exploits had acquired the title of King of Kings, attacked the Seleucidae because they would not acknowledge his supremacy. Antiochus Pius was not able to withstand him, and Tigranes conquered all the Syrian peoples this side of the Euphrates as far as Egypt. He took Cilicia at the same time (for this was also subject to the Seleucidae) and put his general, Magadates, in command of all these conquests for fourteen years.

When the Roman general, Lucullus, was pursuing Mithridates, who had taken refuge in the territory of Tigranes, Magadates went with his army to Tigranes' assistance. Thereupon Antiochus, the son of Antiochus Pius, entered Syria clandestinely and assumed the governance with the consent of the people. Nor did Lucullus, who first made war on Tigranes and wrested his newly acquired territory from him, object to Antiochus exercising his ancestral authority. But Pompey, the successor of Lucullus, when he had overthrown Mithridates, allowed Tigranes to reign in Armenia and expelled Antiochus from the government of Syria, although he had done the Romans no wrong. The real reason for this was that it was easy for Pompey, with an army under his command, to annex a large, defenceless empire, but the pretence was that it was unnatural for the Seleucidae, whom Tigranes had dethroned, to govern Syria, rather than the Romans who had conquered Tigranes.

In this way the Romans, without fighting, came into possession of Cilicia, inland Syria and Coele-Syria, Phoenicia, Palestine, and all the other countries bearing the Syrian name from the Euphrates to Egypt and the sea. The Jewish nation alone still resisted, and Pompey conquered them, sent their king, Aristobulus, to Rome, and destroyed their greatest, and to them holiest, city, Jerusalem, as Ptolemy, the first king of Egypt, had formerly done...
(Appian, *History of Rome* 11.48–50. See also 11.70)

1.7. Early Rome

Rome, a city near the mouth of the Tiber, was founded, according to legend in 753 BCE, by the Latin brothers Romulus and Remus. However, the roots of the Latin people reached back to Aeneas, the ancestor of the founders. Aeneas, with his father, Anchises, and son, Ascanius, together with other refugees from Troy, fled the carnage of the Trojan War and arrived at the site of Alba Longa some three centuries before the founding of Rome. The Aeneas story has been famously perpetuated in Virgil's *Aeneid*. The founding of the city represents the confederation and consolidation of small Latin tribes which had moved out of the hill country to occupy the several 'hills' of the later city.

Rome was ruled by a succession of kings until the expulsion of the last of them, Tarquinius Superbus, in 510 BCE. In fact the last two, and possibly last three, kings of Rome were Etruscans. They were a neighbouring tribe that had forged an empire north of Rome in Etruria and Tuscany. They traded with the Greek east and with Carthage in North Africa. The Carthaginians, a sea-faring people, were originally from Phoenicia. In addition the Etruscans influenced the culture of the Romans, not least in terms of the contours of their religious observances and the shape of their political institutions. This influence persisted long after Etruscan dominance had come to an end.

During the monarchy, the Senate, an aristocratic body of the male heads of the leading propertied families, appointed the king, having secured the support of the citizenry (plebs). The people gathered to ratify the appointment of the king, to hear his pronouncements and to play their part in the civic religious rites. After the expulsion of Tarquinius Superbus, Rome became a Republic. The term 'king' (Latin *rex*) was thereafter studiously avoided. Kingly power (*imperium*) was now vested in two annually elected magistrates, called consuls. They were elected by the people in assembly; their choice ratified by the Senate. Each consul could veto the initiatives of the other. In times of crisis they could be granted extraordinary, though temporary, powers as dictators.

During the fourth century and early third century the plebs were able to secure for themselves a number of important concessions protecting their rights. The most significant of these was the right of the Council of the Plebs to elect their own magistrates, called tribunes. The power of the tribunes, termed *potestas*, was invested in protecting plebs from summary punishment by patrician magistrates. The person of tribunes was inviolate. By the time of the Lex Hortensia, enacted by the dictator L. Hortensius in 287 BCE, the plebeians had won the right to contest one of the consulships and to be admitted to the Senate. The Lex Hortensia effectively bestowed pre-eminent legislative power on the Council of the Plebs. However, subsequent events were to return the balance of power decisively in favour of the patricians. From 280 BCE there was a prolonged period of warfare in which patrician families played dominant roles.

In 390 BCE Rome was sacked by the Gauls. Her putative Latin allies failed to come to her aid. This event, effectively demonstrating the vulnerability of Rome, galvanized the city to protect its position in Italy, coercing, if need be, the various tribes to accept Roman hegemony. Ultimately this brought the Romans into conflict with the Greek colonies of southern Italy. In 280 the city of Thurii appealed for Roman help against the city-state of Tarentum. The Tarentines sought the aid of Pyrrhus, king of Epirus on the Adriatic coast. A series of inconclusive battles between the king and the Romans in Italy and Sicily resulted in his withdrawal in 275. This left Rome in effective control of central and southern Italy, including the southern Greek cities. Direct conflict between Rome (and her allies) and Carthage followed. In 273, as a mark of the increasing attention the Romans were attracting from the Hellenistic east, Ptolemy II of Egypt recognized the enhanced role Rome was now playing in the western Mediterranean.

Sources

The apotheosis of Romulus.

Proculus Julius assures the plebeians that Romulus has been assumed into heaven. Romulus's last words, according to Livy, set the tone for Roman history.

39. 'Quirites [citizens of Rome], the Father of this City, Romulus, descended suddenly from the sky at dawn this morning and appeared to me. Covered with confusion, I stood reverently before him, praying that it may be vouchsafed me to look upon his face without sin. "Go," said he, "and declare to the Romans the will of Heaven that my Rome shall be the capital of the world; so let them cherish the art of war, and let them know and teach their children that no human strength can resist Roman arms." So saying,' he concluded, 'Romulus departed on high.'
(Livy, *History of Rome* 1.16.6–7)

Polybius traces the growth of the power of Rome in the opening book of his *Histories*. At the outset, the historian anticipates the subsequent record of Roman imperial aggression.

40. For it was owing to their defeat of the Carthaginians in the Hannibalic War that the Romans, feeling that the chief and most essential step in their scheme of universal aggression had now been taken, were first emboldened to reach out their hands to grasp the rest and to cross with an army to Greece and the continent of Asia.
(Polybius, *Histories* 1.3.6)

The capture of the city, with the exception of the capitol, by the Gauls in 390 BCE had the following consequences, which Polybius narrates.[30]

41. The Romans, after making a truce on conditions satisfactory to the Gauls and being thus contrary to their expectation reinstated in their home and as it were now started on the road of aggrandizement, continued in the following years to wage war on their neighbours. After subduing all the Latins by their valour and the fortune of war, they fought first against the Etruscans, then against the Celts, and next against the Samnites, whose territory was conterminous with that of the Latins on the East and North. After some time the Tarentines, fearing the consequences of their insolence to the Roman envoys, begged for the intervention of Pyrrhus. (This was in the year preceding the expedition of those Gauls who met with the reverse at Delphi and then crossed to Asia.) The Romans had ere this reduced the Etruscans and Samnites and had vanquished the Italian Celts in many battles, and they now for the first time attacked the rest of Italy not as if it were a foreign country, but as if it rightfully belonged to them. Their struggle with the Samnites and Celts had made them veritable masters in the art of war, and after bravely supporting this war with Pyrrhus and finally expelling himself and his army from Italy, they continued to fight with and subdue those who had sided with him. When, with extraordinary good fortune, they had reduced all these peoples and made all the inhabitants of Italy their subjects excepting the Celts, they undertook the siege of Rhegium now held by certain of their compatriots.
(Polybius, *Histories* 1.6.3–8)

The Romans make preparations for the conquest of the world.

42. It appears to me not to be foreign to my general purpose and original plan to call the attention of my readers to the vast scope of operations of the two states Rome and Carthage, and the diligence with which they pursued their purposes. For who can help admiring the way in which, although they had on their hands such a serious war for the possession of Italy, and another no less serious for the possession of Spain, and though they were in each case both of them quite uncertain as to their prospects of success and in an equally perilous position, they were yet by no means content with the undertakings on which they were thus engaged, but disputed likewise the possession of Sardinia and Sicily, not only entertaining hopes of conquest all the world over, but laying in supplies and making preparations for the purpose? It is indeed when we come to look

> into the details that our admiration is fully aroused. The Romans had two complete armies for the defence of Italy under the two consuls and two others in Spain, the land forces there being commanded by Gnaeus Cornelius Scipio and the fleet by Publius Cornelius Scipio; and of course the same was the case with the Carthaginians. But besides this a Roman fleet lay off the coast of Greece to observe the movements of Philip, commanded first by Marcus Valerius and later by Publius Sulpicius, while at the same time Appius with a hundred quinqueremes and Marcus Claudius Marcellus with a land force protected their interests in Sicily, Hamilcar doing the same on the part of the Carthaginians.
> (Polybius, *Histories* 8.1)

1.8. Rome Acquires an Empire

In defending itself against local enemies and maintaining its power, Rome extended its influence first over the sophisticated Etruscans, and later over the other tribes surrounding Rome. This happened by conquest and by the contracting of alliances. Moreover, the Romans, like the other major powers of that era, came to learn from the cultures they encountered. From the eighth century BCE Greeks had been establishing colonies in southern Italy and Sicily. The Etruscans, the Romans and their respective neighbours learned the art of writing from the Greeks. Rome was to find itself especially attracted to the culture of the Greeks, though at times Romans were repulsed by what were considered Greek moral excesses. While these contacts did mean that Rome was drawn culturally into the culture of the eastern Mediterranean, they were also to result in the penetration of Roman military power into the Greek and non-Greek east as well.

By 264 BCE Rome had become the dominant power in central and southern Italy. Unrest fomented by the Gauls in northern Italy just before the Second Punic War drew Roman troops into that region also. By the beginning of the War, Rome was undisputed master of all Italy. This position had been secured by the perceived need to consolidate her own situation. Her hegemony, extended by conquest and confederation, had been hard fought and won with gritty determination and perseverance.

Two long and critical campaigns on land and sea against Carthage in the third century BCE (264–241, 218–202) determined that Rome would not only dominate all of Italy but also acquire an overseas empire. The power of her legions on land was complemented by a navy. The first provinces of the empire were Sardinia and Corsica, followed soon after by Sicily. These were annexed before the Second Punic War. Their incorporation was designed to forestall renewed Carthaginian threats to the Roman sphere of influence. The Romans had well anticipated a second Carthaginian challenge. In the midst of great military crises, Rome and her allies were to uncover depths of resilience and fortitude that were to see the Carthaginians driven out of Italy and the emergence of Rome as the dominant force in the western Mediterranean.

Hannibal, one of the greatest of ancient military commanders, boldly, and with alacrity, invaded Italy after marching through Spain, southern Gaul, and the Alps. Roman troops were defeated in Italy at battles at Trebia (218) and Trasimene (217). However, despite these crushing defeats, Rome's allies in central Italy refused to join or to supply Hannibal, who, as a result, was eventually unable to capture Rome. In 216 there followed an even more disastrous rout of the Romans at Cannae on the southeastern coast of Italy—one of the most devastating defeats the Romans ever endured.

Hannibal withdrew to southern Italy. Some support from the Greek cities of the region was forthcoming. Galvanized by the disaster at Cannae, Rome redoubled the war effort, increasing the number of legions. Hannibal, by contrast, found himself unable to increase his fighting force. Moreover, expected overseas help from the Macedonians did not materialize.[31] The welcome intervention in Italy of Hasdrubal, Hannibal's brother, was cut short when he was defeated and killed at the battle of the Metaurus.

Rome counter-attacked through Spain. Under the able leadership of Scipio Africanus, Carthaginian hold on Spain was broken by 206. Scipio subsequently invaded North Africa. At the battle of Zama (202), the Romans crushed the Carthaginians, adopting the same tactics used against them at Cannae. The war was effectively brought to an end. Once the retreating Carthaginians had abandoned the peninsula, Spain was added to the provinces of the empire. Hannibal, who had urged the Cathaginians to make peace, was entrusted by Rome to ensure that the indemnity Rome had imposed was paid.

In 198 BCE Antiochus III of Syria had broken a century of Egyptian hegemony over Palestine, including Judaea. He now turned his attention westward, to the Greek mainland, seeking to extend his imperial pretensions there. This brought him inevitably into conflict with the Romans. Hannibal, who had fled Carthage in 196 after being accused of plotting against Rome, arrived at the court of Antiochus III in Ephesus in 195. According to Polybius, Antiochus was invited to invade Greece by the Aetolians. In an alliance with Antiochus and the king of Bithynia, Hannibal took part in Antiochus's invasion of Greece in 192. Antiochus's designs were decisively checked by Roman victories at Thermopylae in Greece and at Magnesia in Asia Minor in 190. Hannibal was defeated by the Rhodians in a sea battle in the same year, fleeing by way of Crete to Persias I of Bithynia. Hannibal committed suicide when it was clear that Persias would hand him over to the Roman general T. Quinctius Flaminius. These victories effectively rendered Rome master of the whole Mediterranean basin, west and east.

The Romans imposed a huge 15,000 talent war-indemnity, the greatest it ever demanded, on the defeated Antiochus by the terms of the Treaty of Apamea in 188, the terms of which also precluded the Seleucids from their territories in Asia Minor west of Mount Taurus. Funding the indemnity proved difficult. In the same year Antiochus was assassinated in the act of plundering a temple to pay the Romans. A steady decline of Seleucid fortunes followed. In 168 Rome, under L. Aemilius Paulus, also secured a victory over Perseus II, king of Macedonia, who had foolishly gone to war against the Romans. The Macedonian defeat was the last battle featuring the Macedonian phalanx. In 146 Carthage was razed at the conclusion of the Third Punic War.

Over the next century Rome was drawn increasingly into affairs in Greece, Asia Minor and Syria. In 146 Corinth was destroyed after a serious of attempts on the part of Macedonians and Greeks to resist the encroachment of Roman influence. Achaea was incorporated into the empire after 146. In 88, Mithridates VI, King of Pontus, and Tigranes, King of Armenia, overran Asia Minor, slaughtering thousands of Romans and Italians. In the resultant war, the Roman dictator Sulla defeated the Pontic armies. Mithridates resurfaced ten years later. This time he was defeated by Lucullus, though, once again, not decisively. Mithridates continued to harass the Romans until his death in 63 BCE.

The alarming depredations of pirates throughout the Mediterranean resulted in a special command given to Pompey by the Senate to conduct a sweep of the sea from west to east.[32] His brief gave him the pretext to invade Pontus, Armenia and Syria. Syria, together with Bithynia, Crete and Pontus, was annexed. Thus Rome steadily added provinces, determined to draw into her orbit any sources of potential instability, and to head off any challenges to her hard-won dominance. The threat from the Parthians beyond the Euphrates was becoming too critical to allow an increasingly weak Seleucid dynasty to manage its affairs independently. Rome was very aware of the threat posed to the eastern Mediterranean, and to her own interests, by the Parthians and by tribes living in Armenia. Syria represented a vulnerable point in Rome's imperial defences because of the limitless expanse of territory beyond, inhabited as it was by warlike semi-nomadic tribes that had already severely curtailed Seleucid dominance. Indeed, Roman anxieties were realized in the military disaster that overtook Roman legions under the leadership of Crassus at the hands of the Parthians at the battle of Carrhae in 53 BCE. In 39 the Parthians, led by Pacorus (son of the Parthian king) and the renegade Roman Q. Labienus, swept into Syria and Judaea, killing Decidius Saxa the Roman governor of Syria. Pacorus set up Antigonus, brother of Hyrcanus II, as king of the Jews in Jerusalem.

Mark Antony, anxious to prosecute a Mesopotamian campaign planned by Caesar, was defeated by the Parthians in 36 BCE. Three captured standards were returned to the Romans in 20 BCE. Attempts to come to terms with the Parthians occupied each Roman emperor until the establishment in 62 CE of a secure agreement in which Rome recognized a Parthian puppet in the Kingdom of Armenia and the Parthians agreed not to cross the Euphrates.

Rome's policy of involvement in areas of potential instability also drew her attention to Palestine. Pompey successfully besieged Jerusalem in 63 BCE. As in the case of Armenia, Rome was prepared to allow Judaea to be ruled by the local dynasty under careful scrutiny. For this purpose Rome was to find able custodians of her interests in the form of Antipater and his sons Phasael and Herod.

Meanwhile Roman power was also being extended in Gaul and Germany. Between 55 and 49 BCE, Julius Caesar enlarged Roman control over territory that included modern-day France and Belgium. He also invaded Britain, an area not annexed until the more extensive occupation and campaigns initiated during the reign of the emperor Claudius in 43 CE.

Sources

Once in Italy Hannibal had a succession of resounding and reverberating victories over the Romans. However, despite these early successes no town allied with Rome went over to Hannibal.

43. The Carthaginians...crossed the Apennines and descended into the territory of the Samnites, which was very fertile and had not for long been visited by war, so that they had such abundance of provisions that they could not succeed either in using or in destroying all their booty. They also overran the territory of Beneventum, a Roman colony, and took the city of Telesia, which was unwalled and full of all manner of property. The Romans continued to hang on their rear at a distance of one or two days' march, refusing to approach nearer and engage the enemy. Hannibal, consequently, seeing that Fabius, while obviously wishing to avoid a battle, had no intention of withdrawing altogether from the open country, made a bold dash at Falernum in the plain of Capua, counting with certainty on one of two alternatives: either he would compel the enemy to fight or make it plain to everybody that he was winning and that the Romans were abandoning the country to him. Upon this happening he hoped that the towns would be much impressed and hasten to throw off their allegiance to Rome. For up to now, although the Romans had been beaten in two battles, not a single Italian city had revolted to the Carthaginians, but all remained loyal, although some suffered much. From which one may estimate the awe and respect that the allies felt for the Roman state.
(Polybius, *Histories* 3.90.7–14)

The most stunning of Hannibal's victories came at Cannae in 216 BCE. In the following extract Polybius describes Hannibal's tactics.

44. The advanced guards were the first to come into action, and at first when only the light infantry were engaged neither side had the advantage; but when the Spanish and Celtic horse on the left wing came into collision with the Roman cavalry, the struggle that ensued was truly barbaric; for there were none of the normal wheeling evolutions, but having once met they dismounted and fought man to man. The Carthaginians finally got the upper hand, killed most of the enemy in the mellay, all the Romans fighting with desperate bravery, and began

to drive the rest along the river, cutting them down mercilessly, and it was now that the heavy infantry on each side took the place of the light-armed troops and met. For a time the Spaniards and Celts kept their ranks and struggled bravely with the Romans, but soon, borne down by the weight of the legions, they gave way and fell back, breaking up the crescent. The Roman maniples, pursuing them furiously, easily penetrated the enemy's front, since the Celts were deployed in a thin line while they themselves had crowded up from the wings to the centre where the fighting was going on. For the centres and wings did not come into action simultaneously, but the centres first, as the Celts were drawn up in a crescent and a long way in advance of their wings, the convex face of the crescent being turned towards the enemy. The Romans, however, following up the Celts and pressing on to the centre and that part of the enemy's line which was giving way, progressed so far that they now had the heavy-armed Africans on both of their flanks. Hereupon the Africans on the right wing facing to the left and then beginning from the right charged upon the enemy's flank, while those on the left faced to the right and dressing by the left, did the same, the situation itself indicating to them how to act. The consequence was that, as Hannibal had designed, the Romans, straying too far in pursuit of the Celts, were caught between the two divisions of the enemy, and they now no longer kept their compact formation but turned singly or in companies to deal with the enemy who was falling on their flanks.
(Polybius, *Histories* 3.115)

The response of the Romans to the disaster at Cannae.

45. The result of the battle being as I have described, the general consequences that had been anticipated on both sides followed. The Carthaginians by this action became at once masters of almost all the rest of the coast, Tarentum immediately surrendering, while Argyrippa and some Campanian towns invited Hannibal to come to them, and the eyes of all were now turned to the Carthaginians, who had great hopes of even taking Rome itself at the first assault. The Romans on their part owing to this defeat at once abandoned all hope of retaining their supremacy in Italy, and were in the greatest fear about their own safety and that of Rome, expecting Hannibal every moment to appear. It seemed indeed as if Fortune were taking part against them in their struggle with adversity and meant to fill the cup to overflowing; for but a few days afterwards, while the city was yet panic-stricken, the commander they had sent to Cisalpine Gaul was surprised by the Celts in an ambush and he and his force utterly destroyed. Yet the Senate neglected no means in its power, but exhorted and encouraged the populace, strengthened the defences of the city, and deliberated on the situation with manly coolness. And subsequent events made this manifest. For though the Romans were now incontestably beaten and their military reputation shattered, yet by the peculiar virtues of their constitution and by wise counsel they not only recovered their supremacy in Italy and afterwards defeated the Carthaginians, but in a few years made themselves masters of the whole world.
(Polybius, *Histories* 3.118.1–9. Cf. 6.58.7–13)

Philip V of Macedonia heard news of the defeats suffered by the Romans early in the Second Punic War. Demetrius of Pharos advised him to settle quickly the Aetolian War in which he was engaged in order to be free to prepare for an invasion of Italy.

46. The whole of Greece, he [Demetrius of Pharos] said, was even now and would be in the future subservient to him, the Achaeans being his partisans by inclination and the spirit of the Aetolians being cowed by what had happened during the war. An expedition, however, to Italy was the first step towards the conquest of the world, an enterprise which belonged to none more properly than to himself. And now was the time, after this disaster to the Roman arms. By such words as these he soon aroused Philip's ambition, as I think was to be expected in the case of a king so young, who had achieved so much success, who had such a

reputation for daring, and above all who came of a house which we may say had always been inclined more than any other to covet universal dominion.
(Polybius, *Histories* 5.101.9–102.1)[33]

In 210, during the Second Punic War, Rome succeeded in securing the supply of corn from Egypt. The continued security of this resource was a perennial Roman priority.

47. The Romans sent envoys to Ptolemy wishing to procure a supply of corn, as they were suffering from a great scarcity of it, all the crops in Italy up to the gates of Rome having been destroyed by the armies, and no help from abroad having been forthcoming, since all over the world except in Egypt there were wars in progress and hostile forces in the field. The scarcity at Rome had reached such a pitch that the Sicilian medimnus cost fifteen drachmae. But in spite of this distress the Romans did not neglect their military preparations…
(Polybius, *Histories* 9.11a)

The battle of Zama (202 BCE).

48. As the whole battle was a hand-to-hand affair… the [Carthaginian] mercenaries at first prevailed by their courage and skill, wounding many of the Romans, but the latter still continued to advance, relying on their admirable order and on the superiority of their arms. The rear ranks of the Romans followed close on their comrades, cheering them on, but the Carthaginians behaved like cowards, never coming near their mercenaries nor attempting to back them up, so that finally the barbarians gave way, and thinking that they had evidently been left in the lurch by their own side, fell upon those they encountered in their retreat and began to kill them. This actually compelled many of the Carthaginians to die like men; for as they were being butchered by their own mercenaries they were obliged against their will to fight both against these and against the Romans, and as when at bay they showed frantic and extraordinary courage, they killed a considerable number both of their mercenaries and of the enemy. In this way they even threw the cohorts of the *hastati* into confusion, but the officers of the *principes*, seeing what was happening, brought up their ranks to assist, and now the greater number of the Carthaginians and their mercenaries were cut to pieces where they stood, either by themselves or by the *hastati*. Hannibal did not allow the survivors in their flight to mix with his own men but, ordering the foremost ranks to level their spears against them, prevented them from being received into his force. They were therefore obliged to retreat towards the wings and the open ground beyond. The space which separated the two armies still on the field was now covered with blood, slaughter, and dead bodies, and the Roman general was placed in great difficulty by this obstacle to his completing the rout of the enemy. For he saw that it would be very difficult to pass over the ground without breaking his ranks owing to the quantity of slippery corpses which were still soaked in blood and had fallen in heaps and the number of arms thrown away at haphazard. However, after conveying the wounded to the rear and recalling by bugle those of the *hastati* who were still pursuing the enemy, he stationed the latter in the fore part of the field of battle, opposite the enemy's centre, and making the *principes* and *triarii* close up on both wings ordered them to advance over the dead. When these troops had surmounted the obstacles and found themselves in a line with the *hastati* the two phalanxes closed with the greatest eagerness and ardour. As they were nearly equal in numbers as well as in spirit and bravery, and were equally well armed, the contest was for long doubtful, the men falling where they stood out of determination, until Massanissa and Laelius, returning from the pursuit of the cavalry, arrived providentially at the proper moment. When they fell on Hannibal's army from the rear, most of the men were cut down in their ranks, while of those who took to flight only quite a few escaped, as the cavalry were close on them and the country was level. More than fifteen hundred Romans fell, the Carthaginian loss amounted to twenty thousand killed and nearly the same number of prisoners.
(Polybius, *Histories* 15.13–14)

The destruction of Carthage (146 BCE) at the conclusion of the Third Punic War (149–146 BCE).

49. Scipio [Aemilianus], when he looked upon the city as it was utterly perishing and in the last throes of its complete destruction, is said to have shed tears and wept openly for his enemies. After being wrapped in thought for long, and realizing that all cities, nations, and authorities must, like men, meet their doom; and this happened to Ilium, once a prosperous city, to the empires of Assyria, Media, and Persia, the greatest of their time, and to Macedonia itself, the brilliance of which was so recent, either deliberately or the verses escaping him, he said:

A day will come when sacred Troy shall perish,
And Priam and his people shall be slain [*Iliad* 6.448–49].

And when Polybius [the historian] speaking with freedom to him, for he was his teacher, asked him what he meant by the words, they say that without any attempt at concealment he named his own country, for which he feared when he reflected on the fate of all things human. Polybius actually heard him and recalls it in his history. (Polybius, *Histories* 38.22)[34]

While the Romans were preparing for war against Mithridates, King of Pontus, the king ordered the massacre of Romans and Italians in the province of Asia in 88 BCE. The death toll was 80,000.

50. Mithridates built a large number of ships for an attack on Rhodes, and wrote secretly to his satraps and city governors that on the thirtieth day thereafter they should set upon all Romans and Italians in their towns, and upon their wives and children and their freedmen of Italian birth, kill them and throw their bodies out unburied, and share their goods with King Mithridates. He threatened to punish any who should bury the dead or conceal the living, and proclaimed rewards to informers and to those who should kill persons in hiding. To slaves, who killed or betrayed their masters he offered freedom, to debtors, who did the same to their creditors, the remission of half of their debt. These secret orders Mithridates sent to all the cities at the same time. When the appointed day came disasters of the most varied kinds occurred throughout Asia, among which were the following:

The Ephesians tore way the fugitives, who had taken refuge in the temple of Artemis, and were clasping the images of the goddess, and slew them. The Pergameans shot with arrows those who had fled to the temple of Aesculapius, while they were still clinging to his statues. The people of Adramyttium followed into the sea those who sought to escape by swimming, and killed them and drowned their children. The Caunii, who had been made subject to Rhodes after the war against Antiochus and had been lately liberated by the Romans, pursued the Italians who had taken refuge about the statue of Vesta in the senate-house, tore them from the shrine, first killed the children before their mothers' eyes, and then killed the mothers themselves and their husbands after them. The citizens of Tralles, in order to avoid the appearance of blood-guiltiness, hired a savage monster named Theophilus, of Paphlagonia, to do the work. He conducted the victims to the temple of Concord, and there murdered them, chopping off the hands of some who were embracing the sacred images. Such was the awful fate that befell the Romans and Italians in Asia, men, women, and children, their freedmen and slaves, all who were of Italian blood; by which it was made very plain that it was quite as much hatred of the Romans as fear of Mithridates that impelled the Asiatics to commit these atrocities. But they paid a double penalty for their crime—one at the hands of Mithridates himself, who ill-treated them perfidiously not long afterward, and the other at the hands of Cornelius Sulla. (Appian, *History of Rome* 12.22–23)[35]

Appian describes Pompey's triumph in 62 BCE at the conclusion of his successful eastern campaign that had begun in 67 BCE.

51. His [Pompey's] chariot was followed by the officers who had shared the campaigns with him, some on horseback and others on foot. When he arrived at the Capitol he did not put any of the prisoners to death, as had

been the custom of other triumphs, but sent them all home at the public expense, except the kings. Of these Aristobulus alone was at once put to death and Tigranes somewhat later. Such was the character of Pompey's triumph.
(Appian, *History of Rome* 12.117)[36]

1.9. Late Republican Roman Politics

The creation of an empire and the success of Roman arms abroad was to have a profound impact on domestic politics. The large number of slaves now available by reason of Roman conquests encouraged the creation of huge estates (*latifundia*) in Italy and the provinces, worked by slave labour. Massive numbers of slaves came onto the market—80,000 Sardinians in 176 BCE and 150,000 Epirotes in 167, though not all of these were brought to Italy. Whereas arable land had been the domain of peasant farmers, large parcels of idle or captured land was now frequently leased out by the Senate to wealthy speculators and then farmed at minimal cost by their slaves. Not surprisingly free small-hold farmers were increasingly forced off the land. The landless flocked to Rome creating a large pool of unemployed. The brothers Tiberius and Gaius Gracchus, tribunes in 133 and 122 respectively, attempted land reform. Their proposals were designed to limit the amount of land taken up by speculators for the creation of *latifundia*. The surplus was to be re-allocated to the landless. The proposals of the Gracchi won overwhelming popular support in the Council of the Plebs. Both tribunes bypassed the Senate, which was expected to veto the proposals. Gaius Gracchus gave the Knights the right to collect lucrative Asian taxes. He also gave them seats on the juries, hitherto the preserve of the Senate. Both Gracchi were assassinated, and large numbers of their followers executed. The attempt at agrarian reform was further frustrated by the repeal of Gracchan laws prohibiting the selling of land (see Appian, *Civil Wars* 1.27).

After 100 BCE the unquestioned pre-eminence and prestige of the Senate came increasingly under threat from popular generals who began to recruit troops not from the landed, but from among the unpropertied (*proletarii*). The fact that they were resourceless served to accentuate their vulnerability on discharge; they had no land on which to settle. They demanded land in return for their labour on behalf of Roman interests. Generals, such as Marius and Sulla, were only too happy to promote the demands of their veterans by sponsoring laws designed to grant their veterans access to land.

When two or more such generals happened to be operating at once, conflict between them invariably resulted. Roman politics became more and more an arena in which the competition among the great popular generals for sole power was played out, often accompanied by massacres and proscriptions of opponents. Power was wielded by those who could command the unquestioned loyalty of his troops. Custom, by which Senatorial politics had been guided, was no match for the ambitious general whose troops owed a higher allegiance to him than to the Roman constitution.

The earliest of the popular generals were Marius and Sulla, both of whom were given extraordinary powers by the Senate to deal with military emergencies. Marius took command of operations against Jugurtha in North Africa and against marauding German tribes. Sulla put down the revolt of the Roman allies in Italy in the Social War (91–89 BCE). He was also instrumental in defeating Mithridates in the First Mithridatic War soon after. Civil war between rival generals resulted in the domination of Sulla, who, after defeating all opposition, endeavoured to reinstate the Senate as the prime political institution in Rome. His retirement in 79 led to further political instability as a new generation of generals sought the upper hand. Pompey emerged as the most able of these. In 67 the Senate bestowed on Pompey an extraordinary command with wide-ranging powers designed to rid the Mediterranean of pirates. His speedy success allowed him to devote more time and energy to bringing much of the east, Palestine and Syria included, under Roman influence.[37]

A triumvirate of Pompey, the wealthy Crassus, and Julius Caesar dominated Roman politics during the 50s. Crassus was killed in 53 at the battle of Carrhae while fighting the Parthians. Civil War broke out between Pompey and Caesar. Pompey fled after his defeat at the battle of Pharsalus in 48 BCE, and was assassinated soon after his arrival in Egypt.

This left Caesar in supreme command. However, he progressively alienated influential senators who regarded his growing power with suspicion. In addition to his other honours, the Senate granted him perpetual dictatorship in early 44, an office that could be revoked. A perpetual dictatorship (like a monarchy) would lock out the noble families from power and patronage. Caesar was assassinated in 44. Among those implicated were some of those who had been the beneficiaries of his clemency. The 18-year-old Octavian, Caesar's adopted son, and Mark Antony defeated the conspirators at Philippi. Their victory led to proscriptions of their enemies in Rome.[38] However, Octavian and Antony soon fell out. The conflict was only brought to an end with Octavian's defeat of Antony and Cleopatra, queen of Egypt, at the battle of Actium in 31 BCE, and their subsequent suicide.

Ronald Syme's observations of late Republican-era politics are worth citing as a fitting conclusion to this account of the turbulence of the period:

> The political life of the Roman Republic was stamped and swayed, not by parties and programmes of a modern and parliamentary character, not by the ostensible opposition between Senate and People, Optimates and Populares, nobiles, and novi homines, but by the strife for power, wealth and glory.[39]

He adds: 'The competition was fierce and incessant. Family influence and wealth did not alone suffice. From ambition or from safety, politicians formed compacts. *Amicitia* was a weapon of politics, not a sentiment based on congeniality.'[40]

Sources

Sallust accounts for the spiral of violence that afflicted Rome in the first century BCE.

52. Now the institution of parties and factions, with all their attendant evils, originated at Rome a few years before this as the result of peace and of an abundance of everything that mortals prize most highly. For before the destruction of Carthage [146 BCE] the people and senate of Rome together governed the republic peacefully and with moderation. There was no strife among the citizens either for glory or for power; fear of the enemy preserved the good morals of the state. But when the minds of the people were relieved of that dread, wantonness and arrogance naturally arose, vices which are fostered by prosperity. Thus the peace for which they had longed in time of adversity, after they had gained it proved to be more cruel and bitter than adversity itself. For the nobles began to abuse their position and the people their liberty, and every man for himself robbed, pillaged, and plundered. Thus the community was split into two parties, and between these the state was torn to pieces.

    But the nobles had the more powerful organization, while the strength of the commons [plebs] was less effective because it was incompact and divided among many. Affairs at home and in the field were managed according to the will of a few men, in whose hands were the treasury, the provinces, public offices, glory and triumphs. The people were burdened with military service and poverty. The generals divided the spoils of war with a few friends. Meanwhile the parents or little children of the soldiers, if they had a powerful neighbour, were driven from their homes. Thus, by the side of power, greed arose, unlimited and unrestrained, violated and devastated everything, respected nothing, and held nothing sacred, until it finally brought about its own downfall. For as soon as nobles were found who preferred true glory to unjust power, the state began to be disturbed and civil dissension to arise like an upheaval of the earth.

For example, when Tiberius and Gaius Gracchus, whose forefathers had added greatly to the power of the republic in the Punic and other wars, began to assert the freedom of the commons and expose the crimes of the oligarchs, the nobility, who were guilty, were therefore panic stricken. They accordingly opposed the acts of the Gracchi, now through the allies and the Latin cities and again through the knights, whom the hope of an alliance with the senate had estranged from the commons. And first Tiberius, then a few years later Gaius, who had followed in his brother's footsteps, were slain with the sword, although one was a tribune and the other a commissioner for founding colonies; and with them fell Marcus Fulvius Flaccus. It must be admitted that the Gracchi were so eager for victory that they had not shown a sufficiently moderate spirit; but a good man would prefer to be defeated rather than to triumph over injustice by establishing a bad precedent.

The nobles then abused their victory to gratify their passions; they put many men out of the way by the sword or by banishment, and thus rendered themselves for the future rather dreaded than powerful. It is this spirit which has commonly ruined great nations, when one party desires to triumph over another by any and every means and to avenge itself on the vanquished with excessive cruelty. But if I should attempt to speak of the strife of parties and of the general character of the state in detail or according to the importance of the theme, time would fail me sooner than material.
(Sallust, *War with Jugurtha* 41–42)[41]

Marius was a *novus homo*, a 'new man', i.e. not a member of the elite families. In the following speech he parades his humble origins.

53. 'Compare me now, fellow citizens, a "new man", with those haughty nobles. What they know from hearsay and reading, I have seen either with my own eyes or done with my own hands. What they have learned from books I have learned by service in the field; think now for yourselves whether words or deeds are worth more. They scorn my humble birth, I their worthlessness; I am taunted with my lot in life, they with their infamies. For my part, I believe that all men have one and the same nature, but that the bravest is the best born; and if the fathers of Albinus and Bestia could now be asked whether they would prefer to have me or those men for their descendants, what do you suppose they would reply, if not that they desired to have the best possible children?'
(Sallust, *War with Jugurtha* 85.13–16)

Sulla's proscriptions.

Victorious in a civil war against Marius, Sulla entered Rome and immediately began to change the Roman political landscape. He did this by means of extreme violence.

54. Sulla…called the Roman people together in an assembly and made them a speech, vaunting his own exploits and making other menacing statements in order to inspire terror. He finished by saying that he would bring about a change which would be beneficial to the people if they would obey him, but of his enemies he would spare none, but would visit them with the utmost severity. He would take vengeance by strong measures on the praetors, quaestors, military tribunes, and everybody else who had committed any hostile act after the day when the consul Scipio violated the agreement made with him. After saying this he forthwith proscribed about forty senators and 1600 knights. He seems to have been the first to make a formal list of those whom he punished, to offer prizes to assassins and rewards to informers, and to threaten with punishment those who should conceal the proscribed. Shortly afterward he added the names of other senators to the proscription. Some of these, taken unawares, were killed where they were caught, in their houses, in the streets, or in the temples. Others were hurled through mid-air and thrown at Sulla's feet. Others were dragged through the city and trampled on, none of the spectators daring to utter a word of remonstrance against these horrors. Banishment was inflicted upon some and confiscation upon others. Spies were searching every-

where for those who had fled from the city, and those whom they caught they killed.

There was much massacre, banishment, and confiscation also among those Italians who had obeyed Carbo, or Marius, or Norbanus, or their lieutenants. Severe judgments of the courts were rendered against them throughout all Italy on various charges—for exercising military command, for serving in the army, for controlling money, for rendering other service, or even giving counsel against Sulla...
(Appian, *Civil Wars* 1.95–96)[42]

The First Triumvirate.

55. Of the two other candidates for this office, Lucius Lucceius and Marcus Bibulus, Caesar joined forces with the former, making a bargain with him that since Lucceius had less influence but more funds, he should in their common name promise largess to the electors from his own pocket. When this became known, the aristocracy authorized Bibulus to promise the same amount, being seized with fear that Caesar would stick at nothing when he became chief magistrate, if he had a colleague who was heart and soul with him. Many of them contributed to the fund, and even Cato did not deny that bribery under such circumstances was for the good of the commonwealth.

So Caesar was chosen consul with Bibulus. With the same motives the aristocracy took care that provinces of the smallest importance should be assigned to the newly elected consuls; that is, mere woods and pastures. Thereupon Caesar, especially incensed by this slight, by every possible attention courted the goodwill of Gnaeus Pompeius [Pompey], who was at odds with the senate because of its tardiness in ratifying his acts after his victory over king Mithridates. He also patched up a peace between Pompeius and Marcus Crassus, who had been enemies since their consulship, which had been one of constant wrangling. Then he made a compact with both of them, that no step should be taken in public affairs which did not suit any one of the three.
(Suetonius, *Julius Caesar* 19)[43]

Julius Caesar (#56–62).

Caesar's ancestry.

56. When quaestor, he [Caesar] pronounced the customary orations from the rostra in praise of his aunt Julia and his wife Cornelia, who had both died. And in the eulogy of his aunt he spoke in the following terms of her paternal and maternal ancestry and that of his own father: 'The family of my aunt Julia is descended by her mother from the kings, and on her father's side is akin to the immortal Gods; for the Marcii Reges (her mother's family name) go back to Ancus Marcius, and the Julii, the family of which ours is a branch, to Venus. Our stock therefore has at once the sanctity of kings, whose power is supreme among mortal men, and the claim to reverence which attaches to the Gods, who hold sway over kings themselves'.
(Suetonius, *Julius Caesar* 6.1)

Caesar's campaign in Germany and in Britain.

57. During the nine years of his command this is in substance what he did. All that part of Gaul which is bounded by the Pyrenees, the Alps and the Cévennes, and by the Rhine and Rhone rivers, a circuit of some 3,200 miles, with the exception of some allied states which had rendered him good service, he reduced to the form of a province; and imposed upon it a yearly tribute of 40,000,000 sesterces. He was the first Roman to build a bridge and attack the Germans beyond the Rhine; and he inflicted heavy losses upon them. He invaded the Britons too, a people unknown before, vanquished them, and exacted moneys and hostages. Amid all these successes he met with adverse fortune but three times in all: in Britain, where his fleet narrowly escaped destruction in a violent storm; in Gaul, when one of his legions was routed at Gergovia; and on the borders of Germany, when his lieutenants Titurius and Aurunculeius were ambushed and slain.
(Suetonius, *Julius Caesar* 25)

Ordered by the Senate to disband his legions on the eve of his return to Italy after his long but victorious campaigns in Gaul, Caesar refused. He knew that without an army he was liable to be the target of legal moves against him by the supporters of Pompey.

Caesar reflects on the causes of the civil war between himself and Pompey.

58. All these speakers [those advising negotiation with Caesar] encounter opposition and are confronted with speeches from the consul, from Scipio, and from Cato. Cato is goaded on by his old quarrels with Caesar and vexation at his defeat. Lentulus is moved by the greatness of his debts, by the prospect of a military command and a province, and by the lavish bribes of rulers claiming the title of king, and boasts among his friends that he will prove a second Sulla to whom shall fall the supreme command. Scipio is stimulated by the same hope of a province and of armies, which he thinks that kinship will entitle him to share with Pompeius; also by the dread of the law courts, by the flattery of certain powerful men who had then great influence in public affairs and in the law courts, and by his own and their ostentatious character. Pompeius, urged on by Caesar's enemies and by his desire that no one should be on the same level of authority with himself, had completely withdrawn himself from Caesar's friendship and become reconciled with their common enemies, most of whom he had himself imposed upon Caesar at the time of their connexion by marriage. Stirred, too, by the discredit attaching to his diversion of two legions from their route by Asia and Syria and his appropriation of them for his own power and supremacy, he was eager that the issue should be brought to the arbitrament of war.
(Caesar, *Civil Wars* 1.4)[44]

The clemency of Caesar.

59. Even in avenging wrongs he was by nature most merciful, and when he got hold of the pirates who had captured him, he had them crucified, since he had sworn beforehand that he would do so, but ordered their throats be cut first... The slave Philemon, his amanuensis, who had promised Caesar's enemies that he would poison him, he merely punished by death, without torture...

He certainly showed admirable self-restraint and mercy, both in his conduct of the civil war and in the hour of victory. While Pompey announced that he would treat as enemies those who did not take up arms for the government, Caesar gave out that those who were neutral and of neither party should be numbered among his friends. He freely allowed all those whom he had made centurions on Pompey's recommendation to go over to his rival. When conditions of surrender were under discussion at Ilerda, and friendly intercourse between the two parties was constant, Afranius and Petreius, with a sudden change of purpose, put to death all of Caesar's soldiers whom they found in their camp; but Caesar could not bring himself to retaliate in kind. At the battle of Pharsalus he cried out, 'Spare your fellow citizens', and afterwards allowed each of his men to save any one man he pleased of the opposite party. And it will be found that no Pompeian lost his life except in battle, save only Afranius and Faustus, and the young Lucius Caesar; and it is believed that not even these men were slain by his wish, even though the two former had taken up arms again after being pardoned, while Caesar had not only cruelly put to death the dictator's slaves and freedmen with fire and sword, but had even butchered the wild beasts which he had procured for the entertainment of the people. At last, in his latter years, he went so far as to allow all those whom he had not yet pardoned to return to Italy, and to hold magistracies and the command of armies: and he actually set up the statues of Lucius Sulla and Pompey, which had been broken to pieces by the populace. After this, if any dangerous plots were formed against him, or slanders uttered, he preferred to quash rather than to punish them. Accordingly, he took no further notice of the conspiracies which were detected, and of meetings by night, than to make known by proclamation that he was aware of them; and he thought it enough to give public warning to those who spoke ill of him, not to persist in their conduct, bearing with good nature the attacks on his reputation made by the scurrilous volume of Aulus Caecina and the abusive lampoons of Pitholaus.
(Suetonius, *Julius Caesar* 74–75)[45]

After reviewing the evidence for Caesar's restraint and mercy, Suetonius sets forth the reasons why it was thought that Caesar deserved to be assassinated.

60. Yet after all, his other actions and words so turn the scale, that it is thought that he abused his power and was justly slain…

No less arrogant were his public utterances, which Titus Ampius records: that the state was nothing, a mere name without body or form; that Sulla did not know his A. B. C. when he laid down his dictatorship; that men ought now to be more circumspect in addressing him, and to regard his word as law. So far did he go in his presumption, that when a soothsayer once reported direful inwards without a heart, he said: 'They will be more favourable when I wish it; it should not be regarded as a portent, if a beast has no heart'.

But it was the following action in particular that roused deadly hatred against him. When the Senate approached him in a body with many highly honorary decrees, he received them before the temple of Venus Genetrix without rising. Some think that when he attempted to get up, he was held back by Cornelius Balbus; others, that he made no such move at all, but on the contrary frowned angrily on Gaius Trebatius when he suggested that he should rise. And this action of his seemed the more intolerable, because when he himself in one of his triumphal processions rode past the benches of the tribunes, he was so incensed because a member of the college, Pontius Aquila by name, did not rise, that he cried: 'Come then, Aquila, take back the republic from me, you tribune'; and for several days he would not make a promise to any one without adding, 'That is, if Pontius Aquila will allow me'.

To an insult which so plainly showed his contempt for the Senate he added an act of even greater insolence; for at the Latin Festival, as he was returning to the city, amid the extravagant and unprecedented demonstrations of the populace, someone in the press placed on his statue a laurel wreath with a white fillet tied to it; and when Epidius Marullus and Caesetius Flavus, tribunes of the commons, gave orders that the ribbon be removed from the wreath and the man taken off to prison, Caesar sharply rebuked and deposed them, either offended that the hint at regnal power had been received with so little favour, or, as he asserted, that he had been robbed of the glory of refusing it. But from that time on he could not rid himself of the odium of having aspired to the title of monarch, although he replied to the commons, when they hailed him as king, 'I am Caesar and no king', and at the Lupercalia, when the consul Antony several times attempted to place a crown upon his head as he spoke from the rostra, he put it aside and at last sent it to the Capitol, to be offered to Jupiter Optimus Maximus. Nay, more, the report had spread in various quarters that he intended to move to Ilium or Alexandria, taking with him the resources of the state, draining Italy by levies, and leaving the charge of the city to his friends; also that at the next meeting of the Senate Lucius Cotta would announce as the decision of the Fifteen, that inasmuch as it was written in the books of fate [*Sibylline Oracles*] that the Parthians could be conquered only by a king, Caesar should be given that title.

It was this that led the conspirators to hasten in carrying out their designs, in order to avoid giving their assent to this proposal…

(Suetonius, *Julius Caesar* 76–80)[46]

Marcus Tullius Cicero (106–43 BCE), a *novus homo*, was the greatest orator of the day. He was elected consul in 63 BCE. He was progressively alienated from the powerful generals of the 50s and 40s. A staunch defender of the rapidly eroding conventions of the Republic, his delighted response to news of the assassination of Caesar is apparent in the following letter written to L. Minucius Basilus, who was one of the conspirators.

61. Cicero to Basilus (written 15 [?] March 44 BCE).

I greet you. I am delighted on your account, and rejoice on my own; I love you, and have your interests at heart; I want you to love me too, and should like to know how you are, and what is going on.

(Cicero, *Letters to his Friends* 6.15)

Basilus was later murdered by his slaves (see #448).

Assessment of Caesar's life.

62. At the time of his death Caesar was fully fifty-six years old, but he had survived Pompey not much more than four years, while of the power and dominion which he had sought all his life at so great risks, and barely achieved at last, of this he had reaped no fruit but the name of it only, and a glory which had awakened envy on the part of his fellow citizens. However, the great guardian-genius of the man, whose help he had enjoyed through life, followed upon him even after death as an avenger of his murder, driving and tracking down his slayers over every land and sea until not one of them was left, but even those who in any way soever either put hand to the deed or took part in the plot were punished.
(Plutarch, *Julius Caesar* 69.1–2)

Horace on the battle of Philippi (42 BCE).

63. O friend oft led with me into extremest peril, when Brutus was leader of our hosts, who hath restored thee as a citizen to thy country's gods and to the sky of Italy, O Pompey [Sextus Pompeius, Pompey the Great's son], first of my comrades, with whom I many a time have beguiled the lagging day with wine, first garlanding my locks with Syrian nard? With thee I knew Philippi's day and its headlong rout, leaving my shield ingloriously behind, when Valour's self was beaten down and threatening hosts ignobly bit the dust. But me in my terror Mercury bore swiftly through the foe in a dense cloud; thee the wave drew back again into the abyss of war and bore once more on troubled waters.
(Horace, *Odes* 2.7 ll. 1–16)

Proscriptions in Rome under the Second Triumvirate.

64. As soon as the triumvirs were by themselves they joined in making a list of those who were to be put to death. They put on the list those whom they suspected because of their power, and also their personal enemies, and they exchanged their own relatives and friends with each other for death, both then and later. For they made additions to the catalogue from time to time, in some cases on the ground of enmity, in others for a grudge merely, or because the victims were friends of their enemies or enemies of their friends, or on account of their wealth, for the triumvirs needed a great deal of money to carry on the war, since the revenue from Asia had been paid to Brutus and Cassius, who were still collecting it, and the kings and satraps were contributing. So the triumvirs were short of money because Europe, and especially Italy, was exhausted by wars and exactions; for which reason they levied very heavy contributions from the plebeians and finally even from women, and contemplated taxes on sales and rents. By now, too, some were proscribed because they had handsome villas or city residences. The number of senators who were sentenced to death and confiscation was about 300, and of the knights about 2000. There were brothers and uncles of the triumvirs in the list of the proscribed, and also some of the officers serving under them who had had some difficulty with the leaders, or with their follow-officers.
(Appian, *Civil Wars* 4.5; Cicero was one who perished [see Appian, *Civil Wars* 4.19])

Lucretius's prayer for peace.

65. Cause meanwhile the savage works of war to sleep and be still over every land and sea. For you alone can delight mortals with quiet peace, since Mars mighty in battle rules the savage works of war, who often casts himself upon your lap wholly vanquished by the ever-living wound of love, and thus looking upward, with shapely neck thrown back, feeds his eager eyes with love, gaping upon you, goddess, and, as he lies back, his breath hangs upon your lips. There as he reclines, goddess, upon your sacred body, do you, bending around him from above, pour from your lips sweet coaxings, and for your Romans, illustrious one, crave quiet peace. For in this time of our country's troubles neither can I do my part with untroubled mind, nor can the noble scion of the Memmii at such a season be wanting to the common weal. (I pray to you for peace,) for the very nature of divinity must necessarily

> enjoy immortal life in the deepest peace, far removed and separated from our affairs; for without any pain, without danger, itself mighty by its own resources, needing us not at all, it is neither propitiated with services nor touched by wrath.
> (Lucretius, *On the Nature of the Universe* 1.29–49)[47]

1.10. Augustus

Octavian, in effect, exercised monarchic rule over Rome and the empire until his death in 14 CE. Once the threat posed by Antony and Cleopatra had been extinguished, Octavian was able to 'restore' the Republic, wracked by civil strife and its institutions repeatedly marginalized by a succession of ruthless generals. In a symbolically laden gesture, he handed back the government of Rome and the Empire to the Senate. Octavian then withdrew to private life, choosing the honorific title 'princeps', 'first citizen'. However, he also accepted from the Senate the title 'Augustus', a term usually signifying the immense dignity and gravity of the gods, as well as styling himself 'Caesar'.[48] A cult of Rome and Augustus was initiated in the east. Augustus introduced this cult into Gaul, though he did not countenance worship of himself from Roman citizens.

The overwhelming majority of the legions were personally loyal to him, a loyalty underscored by an oath administered in 32 BCE as he prepared for war with Antony. Real power in the state and empire resided in Augustus. Realizing this the Senate took care to maintain good public relations with him. It voted him the consular and pro-consular powers he required, as well as a huge province comprising the more unsettled areas of the empire, such as Syria, and the economically crucial Egypt. These were governed by his personal representatives. Augustus might have grasped this power and wielded it by force in defiance of the Senate. As it was his pro-consular imperium was extended by the Senate throughout the time of his principate.

Propagandists could speak about the restoration of the Republic, but in reality Augustus was 'king'. He and all his successors adopted the name 'Caesar'. The term 'rex' was never used. There could be no return to the days of the city-state, but it made good political sense to maintain good relations with that class of men who had the expertise to run internal affairs and the affairs of those provinces most secure from destabilizing influences, and who were used to the opportunities to enhance their fame in the service of the state. The emperor saw to it that the legions were loyal, and that his men ruled those provinces that were vulnerable (such as Syria and Germania). Greece (Achaea) could be entrusted to a Senatorial proconsul, but Syria, too recently 'liberated', and too defensively sensitive to allow anything but an imperial nominee, was governed by a legate appointed by Augustus. From 31 BCE Egypt was ruled by another imperial nominee, an equestrian prefect, in control of legionary troops.

By the time of the birth of Jesus, authority in Rome and throughout the empire was being exercised by what amounts to a hereditary monarchy. Power was invested in one man, a man who had his agents overseas and at home, and who were responsible to him and to him alone. Indeed the whole empire owed allegiance to Augustus (see #68 and #72).[49]

Sources

The benefits bestowed on the world by Augustus.

Augustus offers these remarks on his role in the years following the assassination of Julius Caesar.

> 66. At the age of nineteen on my own responsibility and at my own expense I raised an army, with which I successfully championed the liberty of the republic when it was oppressed by the tyranny of a faction. On that account the senate passed decrees in my honour enrolling me in its order in the consulship of Gaius Pansa and Aulus Hirtius, assigning me the right to give my opinion among the consulars and giving me imperium. It ordered me as a propraetor to provide in concert with the consuls that the republic

should come to no harm. In the same year, when both consuls had fallen in battle, the people appointed me consul and triumvir for the organization of the republic.

I drove into exile the murderers of my father, avenging their crime through tribunals established by law; and afterwards, when they made war on the republic, I twice defeated them in battle.
(Augustus, *Res Gestae Divi Augusti* 1)

67. I undertook many civil and foreign wars by land and sea throughout the world, and as victor I spared the lives of all citizens who asked for mercy. When foreign peoples could safely be pardoned I preferred to preserve rather than to exterminate them. The Roman citizens who took the soldier's oath of obedience to me numbered about 500,000. I settled rather more than 300,000 of these in colonies or sent them back to their home towns after their period of service; to all these I assigned lands or gave money as rewards for their military service. I captured six hundred ships, not counting ships smaller than triremes.
(Augustus, *Res Gestae Divi Augusti* 3)

Augustus's assessment of himself as bringer of peace.

68. In my sixth and seventh consulships, after I had extinguished civil wars, and at a time when with universal consent I was in complete control of affairs, I transferred the republic from my power to the dominion of the senate and people of Rome. For this service of mine I was named Augustus by decree of the senate, and the door-posts of my house were publicly wreathed with bay leaves and a civic crown was fixed over my door and a golden shield was set in the Curia Julia, which, as attested by the inscription thereon, was given me by the senate and people of Rome on account of my courage, clemency, justice and piety. After this time I excelled all in influence, although I possessed no more official power than others who were my colleagues in the several magistracies.
(Augustus, *Res Gestae Divi Augusti* 34)

Augustus sought to restore the architectural fabric of Rome and reduced indebtedness to the state.

69. He [Augustus] cancelled all obligations which had been given to the public treasury previous to the battle of Actium, except those secured by buildings, and he burned the old notes of those who were indebted to the state. As for religious matters, he did not allow the Egyptian rites to be celebrated inside the pomerium, but made provision for the temples; those which had been built by private individuals he ordered their sons and descendants, if any survived, to repair, and the rest he restored himself.
(Dio Cassius, *Roman History* 53.2.3–4)

Appian astutely observes that Rome began as a monarchy and ended up as one.

70. Although holding the empire of so many and such great nations the Romans laboured five hundred years with toil and difficulty to establish their power firmly in Italy itself. Half of this time they were under kings, but having expelled them and sworn to have kingly rule no longer, they henceforward adopted aristocracy, and chose their rulers yearly. In about the two hundred years next succeeding the five hundred their dominion increased greatly, they acquired unexampled foreign power, and brought the greater part of the nations under their sway. Gaius (Julius) Caesar having got the upper hand of his rivals possessed himself of the sovereignty, which he strengthened, systematised, and secured, and, while preserving the form and name of the republic, made himself the absolute ruler of all. In this way the government, from that time to this, has been a monarchy; but they do not call their rulers kings, out of respect, as I think, for the ancient oath. They call them imperators (emperors), that being the title also of those who formerly held the chief command of the armies for the time being. Yet they are very kings in fact.
(Appian, *History of Rome* Preface 6.
See also his comment in *Civil Wars* 1.6)

The pax romana.

71. The temple of Janus Quirinus, which had been closed but twice before his [Augustus's] time since the founding of the city, he closed three times in a far shorter period, having won peace on land and sea. He twice

entered the city in an ovation, after the war of Philippi, and again after that in Sicily, and he celebrated three regular triumphs for his victories in Dalmatia, at Actium, and at Alexandria, all on three successive days. (Suetonius, *Augustus* 22)[50]

Tacitus, however, is quite prepared to denigrate Augustus's achievements. The following extract chronicles Augustus's progressive acquisition of the functions of government and the mute acquiescence of the populace.

72. When the killing of Brutus and Cassius had disarmed the Republic; when Pompey [Sextus Pompeius, son of Pompey the Great] had been crushed in Sicily, and, with Lepidus thrown aside and Antony slain, even the Julian party was leaderless but for the Caesar; after laying down his triumviral title and proclaiming himself a simple consul content with tribunician authority to safeguard the commons, he first conciliated the army by gratuities, the populace by cheapened corn, the world by the amenities of peace, then step by step began to make his ascent and to unite in his own person the functions of the senate, the magistracy, and the legislature. Opposition there was none: the boldest spirits had succumbed on stricken fields or by proscription-lists; while the rest of the nobility found a cheerful acceptance of slavery the smoothest road to wealth and office, and, as they had thriven on revolution, stood now for the new order and safety in preference to the old order and adventure. Nor was the state of affairs unpopular in the provinces, where administration by the Senate and People had been discredited by the feuds of the magnates and the greed of the officials, against which there was but frail protection in a legal system for ever deranged by force, by favouritism, or (in the last resort) by gold. (Tacitus, *Annals* 1.2)

Tacitus continues in this vein. In the passage below the historian laments the passing of the Republic and the old Roman values.

73. War at the time was none, except an outstanding campaign against the Germans, waged more to redeem the prestige lost with Quintilius Varus and his army than from any wish to extend the empire or with any prospect of an adequate recompense. At home all was calm. The officials carried the old names; the younger men had been born after the victory of Actium; most even of the elder generation, during the civil wars; few indeed were left who had seen the Republic.

It was thus an altered world, and of the old, unspoilt Roman character not a trace lingered. Equality was an outworn creed, and all eyes looked to the mandate of the sovereign—with no immediate misgivings, so long as Augustus in the full vigour of his prime upheld himself, his house, and peace. But when the wearing effects of bodily sickness added themselves to advancing years, and the end was coming and new hopes dawning, a few voices began idly to discuss the blessings of freedom; more were apprehensive of war; others desired it; the great majority merely exchanged gossip derogatory to their future masters:—'Agrippa, fierce-tempered, and hot from his humiliation, was unfitted by age and experience for so heavy a burden. Tiberius Nero was mature in years and tried in war, but had the old, inbred arrogance of the Claudian family, and hints of cruelty, strive as he would repress them, kept breaking out. He had been reared from the cradle in a regnant house; consulates and triumphs had been heaped on his youthful head: even during the years when he lived at Rhodes in ostensible retirement and actual exile, he had studied nothing save anger, hypocrisy, and secret lasciviousness. Add to the tale of his mother with her feminine caprice: they must be slaves, it appeared, to the distaff, and to a pair of striplings as well, who in the interval would oppress the state and in the upshot rend it asunder!'
(Tacitus, *Annals* 1.3–4.
See also the observation in *Annals* 1.7 that the Roman upper classes were 'rushing into slavery')

The following two passages from Tacitus are extracts from two set speeches articulating opposing views of Augustus's constitutional actions by which he restored the Republic in 27 BCE. In the first the speaker presents a set of arguments majoring on the benefits accorded the state by Augustus's actions.

74. According to some, 'filial duty and the needs of a country, which at the time had no room for law, had driven him to the weapons of civil strife—weapons which could not be either forged or wielded with clean hands. He had overlooked much in Antony, much in Lepidus, for the sake of bringing to book the assassins of his father. When Lepidus grew old and indolent, and Antony succumbed to his vices, the sole remedy for his distracted country was government by one man. Yet he organized the state, not by instituting a monarchy or a dictatorship, but by creating the title of First Citizen [*princeps*]. The empire had been fenced by the ocean or distant rivers. The legions, the provinces, the fleets, the whole administration, had been centralized. There had been law for the Roman citizen, respect for the allied communities; and the capital itself had been embellished with remarkable splendour. Very few situations had been treated by force, and then only in the interests of general tranquility'.
(Tacitus, *Annals* 1.9)

In the second passage, the speaker argues that Augustus was motivated by lust for power and that he was responsible for the violence and bloodshed that accompanied his path to power and the consolidation of sole rule.

75. On the other side it was argued that 'filial duty and the critical position of the state had been used merely as a cloak: come to the facts, and it was from the lust of dominion that he excited the veterans by his bounties, levied an army while yet a stripling and a subject, seduced the legions of a consul [those of Antony], and affected a leaning to the Pompeian side. Then, following his usurpation by senatorial decree of the symbols and powers of the praetorship, had come the deaths of Hirtius and Pansa,—whether they perished by the enemy's sword, or Pansa by poison sprinkled on his wound, and Hirtius by the hands of his own soldiery, with the Caesar to plan the treason. At all events, he had possessed himself of both their armies, wrung a consulate from the unwilling senate, and turned against the commonwealth the arms which he had received for the quelling of Antony. Then proscription of citizens and the assignments of land had been approved not even by those who executed them. Grant that Cassius and the Bruti were sacrificed to inherited enmities—though the moral law required that private hatreds should give way to public utility—yet Pompey was betrayed by the simulacrum of a peace, Lepidus by the shadow of a friendship: then Antony, lured by the Tarentine and Brundisian treaties and a marriage with his sister, had paid with life the penalty of that delusive connexion. After that there had been undoubtedly peace, but peace with bloodshed—the disasters of Lollius and of Varus, the execution at Rome of a Varro, an Egnatius, an Iullus'.
(Tacitus, *Annals* 1.10)

The worship of and divine honours accorded Augustus.

76. And when Caesar had actually carried out his promises, the name Augustus was at length bestowed upon him by the senate and by the people. For when they wished to call him by some distinctive title, and men were proposing one title and another and urging its selection, Caesar was exceedingly desirous of being called Romulus, but when he perceived that this caused him to be suspected of desiring the kingship, he desisted from his efforts to obtain it, and took the title of 'Augustus', signifying that he was more than human; for all the most precious and sacred objects are termed *augusta*. Therefore, they addressed him also in Greek as *Sebastos*, meaning the *august* personage, from the passive of the verb *sebazo*, 'to revere.'
(Dio Cassius, *Roman History* 53.16.6–8)[51]

1.11. The Roman Empire in Early Imperial Times

At the beginning of the Principate, there were 60 legions under arms.[52] Thirty-two of these were demobbed after the battle of Actium. This meant that land had to be found, and either purchased or confiscated from its owners. Many veterans were settled in Spain. The family of the Senecas were thrown off the land.

For most of Augustus's Principate, Rome maintained 28 legions, all but three serving in

Imperial provinces. In 9 CE three legions commanded by Varus were lost in a military disaster in the Teutoberg Forest between the sources of the Rhine and the Danube.[53] Augustus had intended to establish the German border beyond the Rhine to the Elbe. This severe setback effectively rendered the goal unattainable. By the time of the death of Augustus in 14 CE, 25 legions were in arms. Four of these were stationed in Syria, three in Spain, two in Egypt, one in Africa, eight along the Rhine, and seven along the Danube.

If Germany proved a difficult battleground for Roman forces, Rome was more successful north of the Danube. In 106 CE the emperor Trajan (98–117) incorporated Dacia (modern Rumania) into the empire. He also made territorial gains in Mesopotamia, establishing two new provinces of Mesopotamia and Assyria, and annexing Armenia. At its height the empire comprised 43 provinces. The Emperor Hadrian—Trajan's adopted son, heir and successor—abandoned Trajan's eastern acquisitions. The Emperor Valerian (270–75) abandoned Dacia.

The Senate continued to send consuls who had completed their one-year term to govern the provinces Augustus allowed to them, such as Achaea. Imperial provinces were governed by governors appointed by the emperor. These governors were either legates of senatorial rank or equestrian prefects. Augustus and his successors also used procurators who looked after the emperor's financial interests, paid the army and collected the taxes. Censuses were taken on a regular basis to ensure that taxation assessments were levied equitably.

The Romans often annexed provinces after the rule of a local client king under close Roman supervision during whose rule tribute was collected.

Sources

Augustus and the empire.

77. In this way he [Augustus] had his supremacy ratified by the senate and by the people as well. But as he wished even so to be thought democratic, while he accepted all the care and oversight of the public business, on the ground that it required some attention on his part, yet he declared he would not personally govern all the provinces, and that in the case of such provinces as he should govern he would not do so indefinitely; and he did, in fact, restore to the senate the weaker provinces, on the ground that they were peaceful and free from war, while he retained the more powerful, alleging that they were insecure and precarious and either had enemies on their borders or were able on their own account to begin a serious revolt. His professed motive in this was that the senate might fearlessly enjoy the finest portion of the empire, while he himself had the hardships and the dangers; but his real purpose was that by this arrangement the senators should be unarmed and unprepared for battle, while he alone had arms and maintained soldiers. Africa, Numidia, Asia, Greece with Epirus, the Dalmatian and Macedonian districts, Crete and the Cyrenaic portion of Libya, Bithynia with Pontus which adjoined it, Sardinia and Baetica, were held to belong to the people and the senate; while to Caesar belonged the remainder of Spain,—that is, the district of Tarraco and Lusitania,—and all the Gauls,—that is, Gallia Narbonensis, Gallia Lugdunensis, Aquitania, and Belgica, both the natives themselves and the aliens among them. For some of the Celts, whom we call Germans, had occupied all the Belgic territory along the Rhine and caused it to be called Germany, the upper portion extending to the sources of that river, and the lower portion reaching to the British Ocean. These provinces, then, together with Coele-Syria, as it is called, Phoenicia, Cilicia, Cyprus and Egypt, fell at that time to Caesar's share; for afterwards he gave Cyprus and Gallia Narbonensis back to the people, and for himself took Dalmatia instead. This same course was followed subsequently in the case of other provinces also, as the progress of my narrative will show; but I have enumerated these provinces in this way because at the present time each one of them is governed separately, whereas in the beginning and for a long period thereafter they were administered two and three together. The others I

have not mentioned because some of them were acquired later, and the rest, even if they were already subjugated, were not being governed by the Romans, but either had been left autonomous or had been attached to some kingdom or other. All of them which came into the Roman empire after this period were added to the provinces of the one who was emperor at the time.
(Dio Cassius, *Roman History* 53.12)

Augustus and client kingdoms.

78. (48) Except in a few instances he restored the kingdoms of which he gained possession by the right of conquest to those from whom he had taken them or joined them with other foreign nations. He also united the kings with whom he was in alliance by mutual ties, and was very ready to propose or favour intermarriages or friendships among them. He never failed to treat them all with consideration as integral parts of the empire, regularly appointing a guardian for such as were too young to rule or whose minds were affected, until they grew up or recovered; and he brought up the children of many of them and educated them with his own.

(60) His friends and allies among the kings each in his own realm founded a city called Caesarea, and all joined in a plan to contribute the funds for finishing the temple of Jupiter Olympius, which was begun at Athens in ancient days, and to dedicate it to his Genius; and they would often leave their kingdoms and show him the attentions usual in dependents, clad in the toga and without the emblems of royalty, not only at Rome, but even when he was traveling through the provinces.
(Suetonius, *Augustus* 48, 60)

Egypt as a Roman province.

Egypt was governed by equestrians. These legates were imperial nominees in control of legionary troops. The extract below from Tacitus mentions Tiberius Alexander, nephew of the Jewish philosopher Philo, Prefect of Egypt at the time of the year of the four emperors. Tiberius Alexander had been procurator of Judaea in 46–48.[54]

79. I [Augustus] added Egypt to the empire of the Roman people. Greater Armenia I might have made a province after its king, Artaxes had been killed, but I preferred, following the model set by our ancestors, to hand over that kingdom to Tigranes, son of King Artavasdes and grandson of King Tigranes; Tiberius Nero, who was then my stepson, carried this out. When the same people later rebelled and went to war, I subdued them through the agency of my son Gaius and handed them over to be ruled by King Ariobarzanes, son of Artabazus King of the Medes, and after his death to his son Artavasdes. When he was killed, I sent Tigranes, a scion of the royal Armenian house, to that kingdom. I recovered all the provinces beyond the Adriatic sea towards the east, together with Cyrene, the greater part of them being then occupied by kings. I had previously recovered Sicily and Sardinia which had been seized in the slave war.
(Augustus, *Res Gestae Divi Augusti* 27)[55]

Roman anxiety on the score of Egypt is the subject of the following passage from Tacitus.

80. In the consulate of Marcus Silanus and Lucius Norbanus, Germanicus set out for Egypt to view its antiquities, though the reason given was solicitude for the province. He did, in fact, lower the price of corn by opening the state granaries, and adopted many practices popular with the multitude, walking without his guards, his feet sandalled and his dress identical with that of the Greeks: an imitation of Publius Scipio, who is recorded to have done the like in Sicily, although the Carthaginian war was still raging. Tiberius passed a leniently worded criticism on his dress and bearing, but rebuked him with extreme sharpness for overstepping the prescription of Augustus by entering Alexandria without the imperial assent. For Augustus, among the other secrets of absolutism, by prohibiting all senators or Roman knights of the higher rank from entering the country without permission, kept Egypt isolated; in order that Italy might not be subjected to starvation by anyone who contrived, with however slight a garrison against armies however formidable,

to occupy the province and the key-positions by land and sea.
(Tacitus, *Annals* 2.59)[56]

In c. 50 CE some of the soldiers lost in the Teutoberg Forest catastrophe of 9 CE were repatriated.

81. [A] panic was caused in Upper Germany by an incursion of Chattan marauders. Thereupon, the legate Publius Pomponius sent the auxiliary Vangiones and Nemetes, supported by allied cavalry, with instructions to head off the raiders, or, if they scattered, to envelop and surprise them. The general's plan was seconded by the activity of the troops. They separated into two columns; one of which, marching to the left, entrapped a newly-returned detachment of pillagers, who, after employing their booty in a debauch, were sleeping off the effects. The exultation of the men was heightened by the fact that, after forty years, they had redeemed from slavery a few survivors of the Varian disaster.
(Tacitus, *Annals* 12.27)

Roman depredations in Germany led to the revolt of Civilis in 69 CE. The following passage traces the origins of the revolt.

82. So then Civilis, having determined to revolt, concealed for the time his deeper purpose, and being ready to determine his other plans by the event, began to make trouble in the following way. At the orders of Vitellius a levy of the young Batavians was now being made. This burden, which is naturally grievous, was made the heavier by the greed and licence of those in charge of the levy: they hunted out the old and the weak that they might get a price for letting them off; again they dragged away the children to satisfy their lust, choosing the handsomest—and the Batavian children are generally tall beyond their years. These acts aroused resentment, and the leaders in the conspiracy, on which they were now determined, persuaded the people to refuse the levy. Civilis called the leaders of his tribe and the boldest of the common people into a sacred grove under the pretext of giving a banquet, and when he saw that the night and revelry had fired their spirits, he began to speak of the honour and the glory of their tribe, then passed on to count over the wrongs, the extortion practised on them, and all the rest of the misfortunes of slavery.
(Tacitus, *Histories* 4.14)

1.12. Augustus's Successors (14–138 CE)

The sustaining of the great achievement of Augustus in bringing about an end to two generations of civil war was dependent on a smooth succession. To this end, Augustus adopted as heir his stepson Tiberius, son of his wife Livia from a previous marriage. Augustus had no living sons.

Tiberius proved to be an able administrator and political savant, particularly early in his reign. He also maintained a careful watch on the excesses of foreign cults. The Jews were expelled from Rome in 19 CE. In the same year, after a scandal, the priests of Isis were crucified, the temple razed and the statue of the goddess thrown into the Tiber (see Josephus, *Antiquities* 18.65–80). Under the influence of Sejanus, Tiberius's trusted Praetorian Prefect, his suspicions on the score of the loyalty of senators and advisors were aroused and inflamed. At the suggestion of Sejanus, Tiberius retired to Capri in 26. The Emperor's links with Rome and the Senate were secured by agents such as Sejanus. Sejanus, plotting to succeed the aging Tiberius, dealt ruthlessly with perceived rivals, including Tiberius's son Drusus, who was poisoned in 23. However, in 31 Tiberius was prevailed upon by family members to denounce Sejanus for treason. He was put to death soon afterward.[57]

Tiberius was succeeded by Gaius, nicknamed Caligula. He was the son of the able soldier Germanicus, who, it was believed, had been poisoned in 19 CE by Piso, the legate of Syria. Once installed, Gaius soon developed signs of mental instability. His intention to set up a statue of himself in the Jerusalem temple had the potential to plunge the province of Judaea into open revolt (see #170). Increasingly erratic and tyrannical, Gaius was assassinated in 41. His unprepossessing uncle,

Claudius, a brother of Germanicus and something of a scholar, was pressed into taking on the role of emperor.

Claudius rose to the occasion, proving to be an able administrator and a social reformer. Like Tiberius, he took ruthless action against foreign cults, seeking to protect the ancestral dignity of Roman cultic observance from the unseemly excesses of newly arrived cults. After a riot in the city, he had no hesitation in banning the re-established Jews from Rome in 49, a fact attested by Suetonius. He also outlawed Druidism, a factor that led to unrest in southern Britain, and expelled astrologers from Italy. He died in 54, possibly by poison administered by his wife Agrippina. Nero, Agrippina's 17-year-old son by a former marriage, who was adopted by Claudius in 50, succeeded him. Brittanicus, Claudius's natural son, was passed over.

Nero had the good fortune to have the services of two able advisors—the philosopher Seneca the Younger and Burrus.[58] Like Gaius, he too soon began to evidence signs of megalomania. Claudius's young son Brittanicus was poisoned in 55. Agrippina was murdered in 59. The restraint exercised by Nero's advisors was removed in the early 60s. Burrus died in 62.[59] Seneca was forced to retire in the same year, and compelled to commit suicide in 65.[60] The Christians were blamed for the devastating fire that broke out in Rome in 64, and were cruelly punished.

The empire, more or less at peace for two generations, became the theatre of a number of destabilizing challenges to Roman authority late in Nero's reign. The Parthian settlement broke down when the Roman client king of Armenia, Tigranes, found himself threatened by a Parthian army. Roman reinforcements were decimated at Rhandeia in 62 before another accommodation could be reached with the Parthians. Galba and Vindex led revolts against Nero from bases in the provinces. Revolts also broke out in Britain, led by Boudicca, and in Palestine. The latter revolt, which broke out in 66, constituted the most serious threat to Roman power and prestige in the first century. Vespasian was sent with three legions to prosecute the war. In 68 the Senate, no longer able to tolerate Nero's excesses, outlawed him.[61] He committed suicide.[62]

The year 68–69, the year of 'four emperors', saw all the horrors of the instability of the Civil Wars of the previous century revisited upon the Roman state. Tacitus remarks that it became apparent that emperors could be made outside of Rome (*Histories* 1.4). Galba, Vitellius and Vespasian were first hailed by their troops outside of Italy. Finally, Vespasian, the general in command of the Roman troops in Palestine, was proclaimed emperor by his army.

Vespasian fought his way into Rome, establishing himself in 69, but not before the destruction of the Temple of Jupiter Capitolinus by fire.[63] Vespasian was not a member of the Julio-Claudian family. His sons, Titus and Domitian, each succeeded him. The able Titus died after two years in office. Domitian (81–96) repressed political dissenters and the *literati*, including a number of aristocratic Romans accused of 'atheism' and conspiracy. The philosopher Dio Chrysostom was one forced into exile. Domitian is also reported to have insisted that he be addressed as *dominus et deus* (lord and god). He was assassinated in 96. The elderly Nerva, a prominent senator, was pressed into accepting office.

The emperors Trajan (98–117) and Hadrian (117–38) are universally regarded as two of Rome's most astute emperors. Trajan, who had been adopted by Nerva, had been commander of the Roman forces in upper Germany. He extended Rome's northern and eastern imperial boundaries, annexing Dacia, Armenia and Mesopotamia. Attempting to consolidate Rome's eastern boundaries, Hadrian withdrew from the latter two imperial acquisitions, and fixed the eastern limit of the empire at the Euphrates. Both emperors were confronted with serious revolts, both instigated by Rome's eastern Jewish populations. The revolt of Jews in Egypt, Cyrene, Mesopotamia and Cyprus (115–17) and the second Jewish Revolt in Palestine (132–35) were ruthlessly put down.

Roman citizenship was a substantial privilege in the first century, especially in the east where there were fewer citizens. Manumitted slaves were admitted to the citizen ranks, as were auxiliary troops on discharge. In earlier times whole Italian communities had been granted citizenship. Citizens enjoyed the protection of Roman law, including the right to appeal to the emperor (see Acts 25:10), were given the right to make legally binding contracts and the ability to contract legal marriages, and often the right to vote and stand as candidates in elections in Rome.

Sources

Tacitus reports conditions before the 'reign of terror', which scarred the principate of Tiberius, as follows.[64]

83. It will be opportune, I take it, as this year brought the opening stages of deterioration in the principate of Tiberius, to review in addition the other departments of state and the methods by which they were administered up to that period. First, then, public affairs—together with private affairs of exceptional moment—were treated in the senate, and discussion was free to the leading members, their lapses into subserviency being checked by the sovereign himself. In conferring offices, he took into view the nobility of a candidate's ancestry, the distinction of his military service, or the brilliance of his civil attainments, and left it sufficiently clear that no better choice had been available. The consulate had its old prestige; so had the praetorship: the powers even of the minor magistracies were exercised; and the laws, apart from the process in cases of treason, were in proper force. On the other hand, the corn-tribute, the monies from indirect taxation, and other public revenues, were handled by companies of Roman knights. The imperial property was entrusted by the Caesar to men of tested merit, at times to a personal stranger on the strength of his reputation; and his agents, once installed, were retained quite indefinitely, many growing grey in the service originally entered. The populace, it is true, was harassed by exorbitant food-prices, but in that point no blame attached to the emperor: he spared, indeed, neither expense nor pains in order to neutralize the effects of unfruitful soils or boisterous seas. He saw to it that the provinces were not disturbed by fresh impositions and that the incidence of the old was not aggravated by magisterial avarice or cruelty: corporal punishment and the forfeiture of estates were not in vogue. His demesnes in Italy were few, his establishment of slaves unassuming, his household limited to a small number of freedmen; and, in the event of a dispute between himself and a private citizen, the decision rested with a court of justice.

    All this, not gracefully indeed, but in his grim and often dreaded fashion, he nevertheless observed, until by the death of Drusus the whole was overthrown.
    (Tacitus, *Annals* 4.6–7)[65]

The prosecution of foreign cults under Tiberius (19 CE).

84. He abolished foreign cults, especially the Egyptian and the Jewish rites, compelling all who were addicted to such superstitions to burn their religious vestments and all their paraphernalia. Those of the Jews who were of military age he assigned to provinces of less healthy climate, ostensibly to serve in the army; the others of that same race or of similar beliefs he banished from the city, on pain of slavery for life if they did not obey. He banished the astrologers as well, but pardoned such as begged for indulgence and promised to give up their art.
    (Suetonius, *Tiberius* 36)[66]

Caligula's brutality.

85. (11) Yet even at that time [before he became emperor] he could not control his natural cruelty and viciousness, but he was a most eager witness of the tortures and executions of those who suffered punishment, reveling at night in gluttony and adultery, disguised in a wig and a long robe, passionately devoted besides to the theatrical arts of dancing and singing, in which Tiberius very willingly indulged him, in the hope that through these his savage nature might be softened.

(32) His acts and words were equally cruel, even when he was indulging in relaxation and given up to amusement and feasting. While he was lunching or reveling capital examinations by torture were often made in his presence, and a soldier who was an adept at decapitation cut off the heads of those who were brought from prison.
(Suetonius, *Gaius* 11, 32.1)

Claudius took action against the Jews and the clubs (voluntary associations). Roman sensibilities on the potential of the clubs for social dislocation is discussed in part 7 (#525–57).

86. As for the Jews, who had again increased so greatly that by reason of their multitude it would have been hard without raising a tumult to bar them from the city, he did not drive them out, but ordered them, while continuing their traditional mode of life, not to hold meetings. He also disbanded the clubs, which had been reintroduced by Gaius [Caligula].
(Dio Cassius, *Roman History* 60.6.6)

Claudius and the empire.

87. Next he restored Commagene to Antiochus, since Gaius, though he had himself given him the district, had taken it away again; and Mithridates the Iberian, whom Gaius had summoned and imprisoned, was sent home again to resume his throne. To another Mithridates, a lineal descendant of Mithridates the Great, he granted Bosporus, giving to Polemon some land in Cilicia in place of it. He enlarged the domain of Agrippa of Palestine, who, happening to be in Rome, had helped him to become emperor, and bestowed on him the rank of consul; and to his brother Herod he gave the rank of praetor and a principality. And he permitted them to enter the senate and to express their thanks to him in Greek.
(Dio Cassius, *Roman History* 60.8.1–3)

The banishing of the Jews from Rome and the abolition of the religion of the Druids.

88. Since the Jews constantly made disturbances at the instigation of Chrestus [*impulsore Chresto*], he expelled them from Rome... He utterly abolished the cruel and inhuman religion of the Druids among the Gauls, which under Augustus had merely been prohibited to Roman citizens...
(Suetonius, *Claudius* 25.4, 5. See also #598)

According to Josephus, Poppaea, Nero's consort, was sympathetic to Judaism. In the early 60s CE the Jewish king Agrippa II added a storey to his palace overlooking the Temple in Jerusalem in order to observe the priestly round. The eminent men of the city countered by building a high wall blocking out not only Agrippa's view but the view into the Temple precincts of the soldiers in the Antonia. Despite the opposition of Festus, the procurator, and Agrippa II, Nero resolved the dispute in the favour of the Jews.

89. Nero, after a full hearing, not only condoned what they [the Jews] had done, but also consented to leave the building as it was. In this he showed favour to his wife Poppaea, who was a worshipper of God [Greek *theosebēs*] and who pleaded on behalf of the Jews.
(Josephus, *Antiquities* 20.195)[67]

In the late 50s the young Josephus embarked on a mission to Rome on behalf of some priests imprisoned by the procurator Felix. Josephus's ship was wrecked off the Italian coast.

90. About daybreak, through God's good providence, we sighted a ship of Cyrene, and I and certain others, about eighty in all, outstripped the others and were taken on board. Landing safely at Dicaearchia, which the Italians call Puteoli, I formed a friendship with Aliturus, an actor who was a special favourite of Nero and of Jewish origin. Through him I was introduced to Poppaea, Caesar's consort, and took the earliest opportunity of soliciting her aid to secure the liberation of the priests. Having, besides this favour, received large gifts from Poppaea, I returned to my own country.
(Josephus, *Life* 15–16)[68]

91. [Nero] dearly loved Poppaea, whom he married twelve days after his divorce from Octavia, yet he caused her death too by kicking her when she was pregnant and ill, because she scolded him for coming home

late from the races. By her he had a daughter, Claudia Augusta, but lost her when she was still an infant.
(Suetonius, *Nero* 35.3.
See also Tacitus, *Annals* 16.6)

Nero as arsonist.

92. [U]nder cover of displeasure at the ugliness of the old buildings and the narrow, crooked streets, he set fire to the city so openly that several ex-consuls did not venture to lay hands on his chamberlains although they caught them on their estates with tow and firebrands, while some granaries near the Golden House, whose room he particularly desired, were demolished by engines of war and then set on fire, because their walls were of stone. For six days and seven nights destruction raged, while the people were driven for shelter to monuments and tombs. At that time, besides an immense number of dwellings, the houses of leaders of old were burned, still adorned with trophies of victory, and the temples of the gods vowed and dedicated by the kings and later in the Punic and Gallic wars, and whatever else interesting and noteworthy had survived from antiquity.
(Suetonius, *Nero* 38.1–2)[69]

Nero's throne in the east.

93. Astrologers had predicted to Nero that he would one day be repudiated, which was the occasion of that well known saying of his: 'A humble art affords us daily bread', doubtless uttered to justify him in practicing the art of lyre-playing, as an amusement while emperor, but a necessity for a private citizen. Some of them, however, had promised him the rule of the East, when he was cast off, a few expressly naming the sovereignty of Jerusalem, and several the restitution of all his former fortunes.
(Suetonius, *Nero* 40.2.
Cf. #95–96 and *Sibylline Oracles* 5.137–54)

Vespasian was sent with three legions to prosecute the war against the Jews.

94. The war against the Jews was being directed with three legions by Flavius Vespasianus, whom Nero had selected as general. Neither Vespasian's desires nor sentiments were opposed to Galba, for he sent his son, Titus, to pay his respects and to show his allegiance to him, as we shall tell at the proper time. The secrets of Fate, and the signs and oracles which predestined Vespasian and his sons for power, we believed only after his success was secured.
(Tacitus, *Histories* 1.10)

Fears of Nero's return.

95. He met his death in the thirty-second year of his age, on the anniversary of the murder of Octavia, and such was the public rejoicing that the people put on liberty-caps [close-fitting felt caps given to slaves on manumission] and ran about all over the city. Yet there were some who for a long time decorated his tomb with spring and summer flowers, and now produced his statues on the rostra in the fringed toga, and now his edicts, as if he were still alive and would shortly return and deal destruction to his enemies. Nay more, Vologaesus, king of the Parthians, when he had sent envoys to the senate to renew his alliance, earnestly begged this too, that honour be paid to the memory of Nero. In fact, twenty years later, when I was a young man, a person of obscure origin appeared, who gave out that he was Nero, and the name was still in such favour with the Parthians that they supported him vigorously and surrendered him with great reluctance.
(Suetonius, *Nero* 57)[70]

At the outset of his work, the *Histories*, Tacitus surveys the turbulent era from the death of Nero (68 CE) to the death of Domitian (96 CE).

96. The history on which I am entering is that of a period rich in disasters, terrible with battles, torn by civil struggles, horrible even in peace. Four emperors fell by the sword; there were three civil wars, more foreign wars, and often both at the same time. There was success in the East, misfortune in the West. Illyricum was disturbed, the Gallic provinces wavering, Britain subdued and immediately let go. The Sarmatae and Suebi rose against us; the Dacians won fame by defeats inflicted

and suffered; even the Parthians were almost roused to arms through the trickery of a pretended Nero. Moreover, Italy was distressed by disasters unknown before or returning after the lapse of ages. Cities on the rich fertile shores of Campania were swallowed up or overwhelmed; Rome was devastated by conflagrations, in which her most ancient shrines were consumed and the very Capitol fired by citizens' hands. Sacred rites were defiled; there were adulteries in high places. The sea was filled with exiles, its cliffs made foul with the bodies of the dead. In Rome there was more awful cruelty. High birth, wealth, the refusal or acceptance of office—all gave ground for accusations, and virtues caused the surest ruin. The rewards of the informers were no less hateful than their crimes; for some, gaining priesthoods and consulships as spoils, others obtaining positions as imperial agents and secret influence at court, made havoc and turmoil everywhere, inspiring hatred and terror. Slaves were corrupted against their masters, freedmen against their patrons; and those who had no enemy were crushed by their friends.

Yet this age was not so barren of virtue that it did not display noble examples. Mothers accompanied their children in flight; wives followed their husbands into exile; relatives displayed courage, sons-in-law firmness, slaves a fidelity which defied even torture. Eminent men met the last necessity with fortitude, rivalling in their end the glorious deaths of antiquity. Besides the manifold misfortunes that befell mankind, there were prodigies in the sky and on the earth, warnings given by thunderbolts, and prophecies of the future, both joyful and gloomy, uncertain and clear. For never was it more fully proved by awful disasters of the Roman people or by indubitable signs that the gods care not for our safety, but for our punishment.
(Tacitus, *Histories* 1.2–3)

Martial, the epigramist, celebrates the building of the Flavian Amphitheatre, known today as the Colosseum, on the very site of some of Nero's building excesses.

97. Where the starry colossus sees the constellations at close range and lofty scaffolding rises in the middle of the road, once gleamed the odious halls of a cruel monarch, and in all Rome there stood a single house. Where rises before our eyes the august pile of the Amphitheater, was once Nero's lake. Where we admire the warm baths, a speedy gift, a haughty tract of land had robbed the poor of their dwellings. Where the Claudian colonnade unfolds its wide-spread shade, was the outermost part of the palace's end. Rome has now been restored to herself, and under your rule, Caesar, the pleasances that belonged to a master now belong to the people.
(Martial, *On the Spectacles* 2)

Prophecies regarding Vespasian as the ruler from the east destined to rule the world.

98. (4.5–6) There had spread over all the Orient an old and established belief that it was fated at that time for men coming from Judaea to rule the world. This prediction, referring to the emperor of Rome, as afterwards appeared from the event, the people of Judaea took to themselves; accordingly they revolted and after killing their governor, they routed the consular ruler of Syria as well, when he came to the rescue, and took one of his eagles. Since to put down this rebellion required a considerable army with a leader of no little enterprise, yet one to whom so great power could be entrusted without risk, Vespasian was chosen for the task, both as a man of tried energy and as one in no wise to be feared because of the obscurity of his family and name. Therefore there were added to the forces in Judaea two legions with eight divisions of cavalry and ten cohorts. He took his elder son [Titus] as one of his lieutenants, and as soon as he reached his province he attracted the attention of the neighbouring provinces also; for he at once reformed the discipline of the army and fought one or two battles with such daring, that in the storming of a fortress he was wounded in the knee with a stone and received several arrows in his shield…

(5.6) When he consulted the oracle of the god of Carmel in Judaea, the lots were highly encouraging, promising that whatever he planned or wished, however great it might be, would come to pass; and one of his high-born prisoners, Josephus by name,

as he was being put in chains, declared most confidently that he would soon be released by the same man, who would then, however, be emperor [see #99]. Omens were also reported from Rome: Nero in his latter days was admonished in a dream to take the sacred chariot of Jupiter Optimus Maximus from its shrine to the house of Vespasian and from there to the Circus. Not long after this, too, when Galba was on his way to the elections which gave him his second consulship, a statue of the Deified Julius of its own accord turned towards the East; and on the field of Betriacum, before the battle began, two eagles fought in the sight of all, and when one was vanquished, a third came from the direction of the rising sun and drove off the victor.
(Suetonius, *Vespasian* 4.5–6, 5.6)[71]

Josephus predicts that Vespasian will be emperor.

Vespasian learned that Josephus, the commander of Galilee, had been captured at Jotapata. He ordered his life to be spared in order to send him to Nero.

99. On hearing this [that he was to be sent to the Emperor], Josephus expressed a desire for a private interview with him [Vespasian]. Vespasian having ordered all to withdraw except his son Titus and two of his friends, the prisoner thus addressed him: 'You imagine, Vespasian, that in the person of Josephus you have taken a mere captive; but I come to you as a messenger of greater destinies. Had I not been sent on this errand by God, I knew the law of the Jews and how it becomes a general to die. To Nero do you send me? Why then? Think you that (Nero and) those who before your accession succeed him will continue? You will be Caesar, Vespasian, you will be emperor, you and your son here. Bind me then yet more securely in chains and keep me for yourself; for you, Caesar, are master not of me only, but of land and sea and the whole human race. For myself, I ask to be punished by stricter custody, if I have dared to trifle with the words of God'. To this speech Vespasian, at the moment, seemed to attach little credit, supposing it to be a trick of Josephus to save his life. Gradually, however, he was led to believe it, for God was already rousing in him thoughts of empire and by other tokens foreshadowing the throne.
(Josephus, *Jewish War* 3.399–404)

Josephus was protected by the Flavians, who become his patrons (#305).

In the following epigram Martial refers to Domitian taking the name Germanicus in 84 CE. His father, Vespasian, and brother, Titus, celebrated a famous triumph in 70 CE after the end of the Jewish Revolt. The young Domitian had taken part in the Roman expedition.

100. Crete gave a great name, Africa a greater, borne by victorious Scipio and by Metellus. Germany bestowed a nobler when the Rhine was subjugated; you were worthy of this name, Caesar, even as a boy. Your brother won Idumean triumphs along with your father, but the laurel given for the Chatti is all yours.
(Martial, *Epigrams* 2.2)

Domitian banishes the philosophers.

101. Many others also perished as a result of this same charge of philosophizing, and all the philosophers that were left in Rome were banished once more. One Juventius Celsus, however, who had taken a leading part in conspiring with certain others against Domitian and had been accused of this, saved his life in a remarkable way. When he was on the point of being condemned, he begged that he might speak to the emperor in private, and thereupon did obeisance before him and after repeatedly calling him 'master' and 'god' (terms that were already being applied to him by others), he said: 'I have done nothing of this sort, but if I obtain a respite, I will pry into everything and will not only bring information against many persons for you but also secure their conviction.' He was released on this condition, but did not report any one; instead, by advancing different excuses at different times, he lived until the death of Domitian.
(Dio Cassius, *Roman History* 67.13.3–4)

Domitian is reported to have insisted that he be addressed as *dominus et deus*.

102. When he became emperor, he did not hesitate to boast in the senate that he had conferred their power on both his father and his brother, and that they had but returned him his own; nor on taking back his wife after their divorce, that he had 'recalled her to his divine couch'. He delighted to hear the people in the amphitheatre shout on his feast day: 'Good Fortune attend our Lord and Mistress'. Even more, in the Capitoline competition, when all the people begged him with great unanimity to restore Palfurius Sura, who had been banished some time before from the senate, and on that occasion received the prize for oratory, he deigned no reply, but merely had a crier bid them be silent. With no less arrogance he began as follows in issuing a circular letter in the name of his procurators, 'Our Master and our God [*dominus et deus noster*] bids that this be done.' And so the custom arose of henceforth addressing him in no other way even in writing or in conversation. He suffered no statues to be set up in his honour in the Capitol, except of gold and silver of a fixed weight. He erected so many and such huge vaulted passage-ways and arches in the various regions of the city, adorned with chariots and triumphal emblems, that on one of them someone wrote in Greek: 'It is enough' [Latin *arci*; Greek *arkei*].
(Suetonius, *Domitian* 13.1–2.
Cf. Martial, *Epigrams* 5.8; and #101)

Domitian puts Flavius Clemens to death.

103. At this time the road leading from Sinuessa to Puteoli was paved with stone. And the same year Domitian slew, along with many others, Flavius Clemens the consul, although he was a cousin and had to wife Flavia Domitilla, who was also a relative of the emperor's. The charge brought against them both was that of atheism, a charge on which many others who drifted into Jewish ways were condemned. Some of these were put to death, and the rest were at least deprived of their property. Domitilla was merely banished to Pandateria. But Glabrio, who had been Trajan's colleague in the consulship, was put to death, having been accused of the same crimes as most of the others, and, in particular, of fighting as a gladiator with wild beasts. Indeed, his prowess in the arena was the chief cause of the emperor's anger against him, an anger prompted by jealousy. For in Glabrio's consulship Domitian had summoned him to his Alban estate to attend the festival called the Juvenalia and had imposed on him the task of killing a large lion; and Glabrio not only had escaped all injury but had despatched the lion with most accurate aim.

As a consequence of his cruelty the emperor was suspicious of all mankind, and from now on ceased to repose hopes of safety in either the freedmen or yet the prefects, whom he usually caused to be brought to trial during their very term of office. He had first banished and now slew Epaphroditus, Nero's freedman, accusing him of having failed to defend Nero; for he wished by the vengeance that he took on Nero's behalf to terrify his own freedmen long in advance, so that they should venture no similar deed. Yet it availed him naught, for he became the object of a conspiracy in the following year, and perished in the consulship of Gaius Valens (who died after entering upon the consulship in his ninetieth year) and of Gaius Antistius.
(Dio Cassius, *Roman History* 67.14)[72]

Trajan conquers the Dacians.

104. Trajan...conducted the war with safe prudence rather than with haste, and eventually, after a hard struggle, vanquished the Dacians. In the course of the campaign he himself performed many deeds of good generalship and bravery, and his troops ran many risks and displayed great prowess on his behalf. It was here that a certain horseman, after being carried, badly wounded, from the battle in the hope that he could be healed, when he found that he could not recover, rushed from his tent (for his injury had not yet reached his heart) and, taking his place one more in the line, perished after displaying great feats of valour. Decebalus, when his capital and all his territory had been occupied and he was himself in danger of being captured, committed suicide; and his head was brought to Rome. In this way Dacia became subject to the Romans, and Trajan founded cities there. The treasures of

Decebalus were also discovered, though hidden beneath the river Sargetia, which ran past his palace. With the help of some captives Decebalus had diverted the course of the river, made an excavation in its bed, and into the cavity had thrown a large amount of silver and gold and other objects of great value that could stand a certain amount of moisture; then he had heaped stones over them and piled on earth, afterwards bringing the river back into its course. He also had caused the same captives to deposit his robes and other articles of a like nature in caves, and after accomplishing this had made away with them to prevent them from disclosing anything. But Bicilis, a companion of his who knew what had been done, was seized and gave information about these things.
(Dio Cassius, *Roman History* 68.14)

Notes

1. Cyrus, so the legends recounted, had been a 'persecuted baby'. This narrative motif appears in Ancient Near Eastern literature as early as the third millennium BCE. See *ANET* p. 119 and the tradition concerning Sargon of Akkad (fl. 2350 BCE). The motif also appears in the Bible (Moses—Exodus 1:15–2:4; Jesus—Matthew 2:13–22).
2. Cyrus was an exceptionally energetic soldier (see #4). This played no small part in his military successes. Herodotus, *Histories* 1.79. Cf. Julius Caesar in Suetonius, *Julius Caesar* 57; Plutarch, *Julius Caesar* 17.5.
3. While Cyrus's troops besieged and entered Babylon, they were led, not by Cyrus, but by Gobryas, a Median general, who had served Nabonidus as governor of Gutium. See the Nabonidus Chronicle (*ANET* p. 306). Herodotus describes the method used by the Persian troops to enter the well-fortified and provendered city of Babylon. On his way to the city Cyrus's troops spent a summer 'punishing' the river Gyndes by diverting the stream into 360 canals for drowning one of his sacred white horses. When Cyrus arrived at the city gates, he was challenged by a Babylonian army, which he defeated. The Babylonians now retired, confident that they could withstand any siege. The subsequent capture of the city was unprecedented. See Herodotus, *Histories* 1.191; Xenophon, *Cyropaedia* 7.5.15–34.
4. Citations of documents from Ancient Near Eastern texts show the translator's interpretative glosses in parentheses ( ) and textual emendations in square brackets [ ].
5. According to Daniel 9:1, Darius the Mede was a son of Ahasuerus (Xerxes), and a Median by birth. Darius I of Persia is known to Nehemiah and Ezra (Nehemiah 12:22; Ezra 4:5, 24; 5:6; 6:1). The tradition of 'Darius the Mede' may have resulted from the confusion of Cyrus's capture of the city with that of Darius I (522–486 BCE), who captured Babylon when it revolted from Persian control soon after his accession (Herodotus, *Histories* 3.159). Josephus also repeats the biblical tradition about the role of 'Darius the Mede' in his account of the events of 539 (see #7 above). The Nabonidus Chronicle ascribes the appointment of satraps to Gobryas (see *ANET* p. 306).
6. Something of the burden of the imperial system can be observed in Herodotus, *Histories* 3.92 in which the ninth satrapy is recorded as paying an annual tribute of 1000 talents of silver and 500 eunuch boys. Although not part of the Persian Empire and not required to pay an annual tribute, gifts were required of several peoples, including the distant Colchians and their neighbours who donated 100 boys and girls every fourth year (see Herodotus, *Histories* 3.97). Rapid communications and a postal service were features of the Persian empire (see Esther 3:13–15a). Cyrus and his successors appointed officials, termed 'eyes' and 'ears', whose task was to report directly to the king in matters concerning the interests of the king throughout the empire. See Xenophon, *Cyropaedia* 8.2.10; Aeschylus, *Persians* 978–80.
7. The Persians, however, did not pay tribute (see Herodotus, *Histories* 3.97).
8. A medimnus was a liquid measure equal to 11 and a half gallons (c. 50 litres). There were 48 choenixes in one medimnus.
9. The later adoption of Persian customs by Alexander, especially the expectation that he receive prostration (*proskunēsis*), was heavily resented by his Greek troops. See the passage

from Plutarch's *Life of Alexander* cited below (#20).

10. See, e.g., Isocrates, *To Philip* 9 (cf. *Panegyricus* 17).
11. See also *To Philip* 122–23. Isocrates concludes his discourse by urging Philip to undertake the expedition against Persia, confident that he will perceive such an undertaking as his duty as a Greek.
12. The great orator Demosthenes, on the other hand, laments the lost glory of Athens and her steadily eroding hegemony over other Greeks. See, e.g., his *First Philippic*.
13. In response to Darius's letter requesting the safe return of his family after they were captured at Issus, and reproaching Alexander for his unprovoked aggression, Alexander defended his invasion of the Persian Empire in a litany of grievances, some ancient but others more recent, including the meddling of Darius in Greek and Macedonian affairs (see Arrian, *Anabasis of Alexander* 2.14.4–9). On learning that Alexander had accorded respect to his captured family, Darius proclaimed Alexander as deserving lord of Asia (see *Anabasis of Alexander* 4.20.1–3).
14. See Diodorus Siculus, *Histories* 17.52.1–2, 5; Arrian, *Anabasis of Alexander* 3.1.
15. For Alexander's capture of Babylon and his restoration of its temples, see Arrian, *Anabasis of Alexander* 3.16.4; 7.17.1–3; Strabo, *Geography* 16.5. Cf. Herodotus, *Histories* 1.181.
16. See Arrian, *Anabasis of Alexander* 4.8.4–9.
17. Not all ancient commentators were prepared to laud Alexander and his Macedonians. See the speech of Chlaeneas the Aetolian in Polybius, *Histories* 9.28–29 (cited in the next topic [1.6] at #30). The Bible preserves negative images of the violence and depredations occasioned by Alexander in his campaigns. See Daniel 7; 8; 11:3–4 and Zechariah 9:1–8.
18. Cf. Arrian, *Anabasis of Alexander* 1.12.1–5. See also Diodorus Siculus, *Histories* 17.1.3–4; Curtius, *History of Alexander* 10.5.26–37.
19. The Aeacids could claim Achilles as their ancestor, and ultimately the god Zeus, as their progenitor. See Plutarch, *Alexander* 2.1; Arrian, *Anabasis of Alexander* 7.29.3 (see #22 above); and cf. Plutarch, *Alexander* 28.6.
20. Cf. stories regarding Augustus's and Nero's conception in Suetonius, *Augustus* 94 and Tacitus, *Annals* 11.11. The traditions of the birth of Jesus recorded in Matthew 1:18–25 and Luke 1:26–38 should also be consulted. See also #317 and the comment prefacing it.
21. See also the oracle that follows this one concerning the successors of Alexander (3.388–400).
22. For the battle of Ipsus, see Appian, *History of Rome* 11.55 (see #28). See Sidney Smith (ed.), *Babylonian Historical Texts* (Hildesheim: Georg Olms, 1975), pp. 124–49 (a chronicle concerning the *diadochoi*) and pp. 150–59 (account of the reign of Antiochus I). See also M.M. Austin, *The Hellenistic World from Alexander to the Roman Conquest: A Selection of Ancient Sources in Translation* (Cambridge: Cambridge University Press, 1981), pp. 39–92.
23. See Polybius, *Histories* 16.18. Incidentally, the Rosetta Stone celebrates Ptolemy's majority and coronation as pharaoh at Memphis in 197 BCE.
24. For a chronicle of Syria from Alexander to the annexation of the Seleucid empire by the Romans, see Appian, *History of Rome* 11.52–70.
25. The early Jewish author of 1 Maccabees had cause to rue the accomplishment of Alexander and his successors who ruled in the same vein. His concise assessment of Alexander's successors sets the tone for the presentation of the depredations of Antiochus IV Epiphanes and his history of the Maccabaean revolt (see 1 Maccabees 1:1–9).
26. See Polybius, *Histories* 5.80–86 for the battle of Raphia. Most of book 2 deals with the campaigns of Ptolemy IV and Antiochus III.
27. The speech is countered by Lysicus, the Acarnanian. Lysicus mounts a defence of Macedonian policy, pointing out the benefits bestowed by them on the Greeks. See Polybius, *Histories* 9.35.2–4.
28. For the terms of the Treaty of Apamea, see also Livy, *History of Rome* 37.45.3; Appian, *History of Rome* 11.38–39.
29. See also Polybius, *Histories* 28.18–20. 2 Maccabees 5:1 states that Antiochus conducted two invasions of Egypt. See also Daniel 11:25–28, 29–30. My view is that there was one invasion only (see 1 Maccabees 1:16–19; Josephus, *Antiquities* 12.242–45. Note the sources brought together at #124–27.

30. Cf. Sallust, *War with Catiline* 6.3–7.
31. In a potentially ominous development for the Romans, a treaty between Philip V and Hannibal was concluded in 215. The treaty proved ineffectual. For the terms, see Polybius, *Histories* 7.9.
32. For Pompey's campaign against the pirates, see Appian, *History of Rome* 12.92–96; Plutarch, *Pompey* 26–27.
33. See also Polybius, *Histories* 5.104 for the speech of Agelaus of Naupactus delivered in 217 BCE advocating that the warring Aetolians and Achaeans close ranks against the Romans.
34. For the speech Appian puts into the mouth of Cornelius Scipio Aemilianus, the Roman general overseeing the destruction of the city, see his *History of Rome* 8.81.
35. See also Plutarch, *Sulla* 85. There is evidence that the Romans were guilty of extortion in Asia. Having narrated the self-inflicted death of Mithridates, Appian reflects on his achievements and recalls Roman regard for a worthy foe. See Appian, *History of Rome* 12.112–13.
36. According to Josephus, Aristobulus (the Jewish 'king') was not executed at the conclusion of the triumph. Josephus relates his escape from Rome and his return to Judaea to continue the fight against Rome and her Jewish clients (*Jewish War* 1.171–74).
37. Note the observation of Ronald Syme to the effect that the general had to be a politician. 'The necessities of world-empire and the ambition of generals led to the creation of extraordinary commands in the provinces' (*Roman Revolution* [Cambridge: Cambridge University Press, 1939], p. 15). See also Syme's comment on the importance of patronage and clients. The general's legionaries 'were a host of clients, looking to their leader for spoil in war and estates in Italy when their campaigns were over' (*Roman Revolution*, p. 15).
38. For looting and famine in Rome during the civil wars of Octavian and Antony, see Appian, *Civil Wars* 5.18.
39. Syme, *Roman Revolution*, p. 11.
40. Syme, *Roman Revolution*, p. 12. *Amicitia* means 'friendship'.
41. For a study of violence in the era, see A.W. Lintott, *Violence in Republican Rome* (Oxford: Clarendon Press, 1968).
42. See also Plutarch, *Sulla* 31–32 for Sulla's butchery and the proscriptions. See Plutarch, *Marius* 43 for revenge exacted on the supporters of Sulla.
43. See also Cicero, *Letters to Atticus* II.21 for his sense of alienation from the new order.
44. Caesar suggested that both he and Pompey disband their armies (see Caesar, *Civil Wars* 1.9). This offer was refused. Caesar subsequently crossed the Rubicon, the boundary between Cisalpine Gaul and Italy proper, thus precipitating the Civil War.
45. See also Caesar, *Civil Wars* 1.23. For Caesar's clemency after the battle of Pharsalus, see Plutarch, *Julius Caesar* 46. See also Plutarch, *Pompey* 65.2.
46. See also Plutarch, *Julius Caesar* 60.1–3.
47. See also Horace, *Odes* 2.1; Virgil, *Georgics* 1.498–514. Horaces reflects on the safety and security bestowed on the Roman world by Augustus in *Odes* 4.5, 15.
48. Augustus also became *pontifex maximus* in 12 BCE, and *pater patriae* in 2 BCE (see *Res Gestae Divi Augusti* 35).
49. For an assessment of Augustus and his achievement, see Dio Cassius, *Roman History* 56.43.4.
50. The gates of the temple of Janus had been closed in the reign of Numa and after the First Punic War in 235 BCE. The gates stood open whenever Rome was at war. See, e.g., Virgil, *Aeneid* 7.601–615.
51. See also Tacitus, *Annals* 1.10; Suetonius, *Augustus* 100; Ovid, *Metamorphoses* 15.870. Libations to Augustus (while still living) are mentioned in Horace, *Odes* 4.5 ll. 31–36. For the precedent of the dedication of temples to Augustus, see Tacitus, *Annals* 1.78 (in Spain at the colony of Tarraco).
52. Suetonius, *Augustus* 23.
53. Six years after the destruction of Varus and his legions, Germanicus and his troops re-visited the site of the catastrophe. Tacitus movingly depicts the scene (*Annals* 1.61–62). See also #73, #75 and #81.
54. Tiberius Alexander was the first official to acknowledge Vespasian as emperor. See Tacitus, *Histories* 2.79, 81.
55. See also Suetonius, *Augustus* 18.
56. Roman anxiety on the score of Egypt had been crucial in the Roman intervention in 169 BCE when Antiochus Epiphanes invaded that land. See #36 above.

57. For Sejanus's death, see Suetonius, *Tiberius* 55. In *Satires* 10.56–80, 88–113 Juvenal remarks on the passing fame of the great ones, such as Sejanus. See also #540 for the execution of Sejanus's children.
58. When Claudius married Agrippina, she procured the return of Seneca from banishment. He had been banished after being charged with adultery with Germanicus's daughter Julia Livilla. For the public prominence of Seneca in Nero's reign, see Tacitus, *Annals* 12.8. See Tacitus, *Annals* 13.2 for the influence for good of Seneca and Burrus, given Nero's predilection towards vice. In his treatise *On Mercy* 2–4 Seneca flatteringly puts into words the impossibly lofty thoughts of Nero on the subject of his merciful dealings as emperor.
59. Burrus may have been poisoned (Suetonius, *Nero* 35), or he may have succumbed to cancer (Tacitus, *Annals* 14.51).
60. See Tacitus, *Annals* 14.52; 15.60, 63. See *Annals* 15.73 for attacks on Gallio, Seneca's brother (mentioned in Acts 18:12–17). Note also the Gallio inscription at Delphi. For text, see C.K. Barrett, *The New Testament Background: Selected Documents* (San Francisco: Harper and Row, rev. edn, 1989), pp. 51–52.
61. For Nero as charioteer, actor, and poet see Tacitus, *Annals* 14.14–16.
62. There were rumours that Nero had been revived. See Tacitus, *Histories* 2.8; Suetonius, *Nero* 57. This rumour colours the imagery of the Beast's attack on Rome with a Parthian army (the 'ten kings') in Revelation 17:15–18.
63. The destruction of the Temple of Jupiter Capitolinus by fire happened as Vespasian's troops marched on Rome. Vespasian's brother Sabinus, a senator, and his retinue had been besieged in the Capitol by forces loyal to Vitellius (see Tacitus, *Histories* 3.71–72). For the rebuilding and re-dedication of the temple, see *Histories* 4.53.
64. See also Suetonius, *Tiberius* 57, 61; Dio Cassius, *Roman History* 58.11.5.
65. Drusus, Tiberius's only son, died in 23 CE. The 'reign of terror' began with the rise of Sejanus after the death of Drusus.
66. See also #86, #88 and #598 for the expulsion of the Jews by Claudius in 49 CE.
67. A few years later, Poppaea did do the Jews a disservice. In *Antiquities* 20.252, Josephus reports that a friend of Poppaea, Cleopatra, married Gessius Florus, a knight from Glazomenae, and that through Cleopatra's influence with Poppaea she was able to secure for him the post of procurator of Judaea. Florus's mismanagement of his duties inflamed Jewish opposition, and was a major cause of the Revolt which broke out in 66 (see #178).
68. It has been suggested that Poppaea's influence may have been crucial in deflecting any blame for the fire of Rome from the Jews (H.H. Scullard, *From the Gracchi to Nero* [London: Methuen, 1963], p. 320).
69. Nero had hoped to call the rebuilt city Neropolis (see Suetonius, *Nero* 55). For the extent of the fire, see Tacitus, *Annals* 15.40–41.
70. Note Tacitus, *Histories* 1.2 (#96); Suetonius, *Domitian* 6. The myth of the return of Nero from the dead (Nero *redivivus*) is important for understanding the presentation of the Beast in Revelation 13 and 17. On this see #263 and the discussion preceding it.
71. See also Tacitus, *Histories* 1.10; 2.1; 5.13; Dio Cassius, *Roman History* 66.1.
72. See also Suetonius, *Domitian* 15 and Eusebius, *Ecclesiastical History* 3.17–20. The persecution is possibly alluded to in *1 Clement* 1.1.

2. The Jews under Persians, Greeks and Romans: 539 BCE–135 CE

2.1. The Jews under Persian Rule

The historical narrative of the Hebrew Bible ends with Israel nominally restored to the land of Judaea from exile in Babylon. The foundation of the rebuilt Jerusalem Temple was soon laid, though the building was not completed until some 20 years later in the reign of Darius I. From this point in time it is proper to refer to the people who looked to the Temple as the community focus as 'Jews' (*yehudhim*). In effect Jewish territory in Palestine was coterminous with the city and environs of Jerusalem.

The Jews were able to return from exile as a result of the policies instigated by Cyrus, the Persian king who captured the city of Babylon in 539 BCE and decreed that all captured and displaced peoples were free to return home to re-establish the threads of national and religious life. The policy of the Persians, however, did not mean that Judaea was autonomous. Judaea was incorporated into the Empire as a district within a province. At times the Empire included Asia Minor and Egypt and, in the east, stretched as far as the Indian subcontinent.

The Persians termed their provinces 'satrapies'. The satrapy 'Beyond the River', i.e. west of the Euphrates from the Persian perspective, included Palestine (see Ezra 4:17; 5:3).[1] The satrap was stationed in Damascus. A Persian governor was usually stationed in Samaria, a district included in the satrapy, and in which the territory of the Jews fell. Consequently Jewish affairs were frequently mediated through the local Persian governor stationed in Samaria. However, during a time of considerable hardship and vulnerability for the Jews, Nehemiah, a Jewish servant in the royal court of Susa, was appointed by the Persian king Artaxerxes I, to govern the Jews from Jerusalem. Nehemiah's mission brought him into potential conflict with Sanballat, the Persian governor of Samaria, and local officials, anxious lest a rebuilt Jerusalem pose a threat to their own interests in the region.

Information of the period is patchy. However, it is clear that the returning Jews found that they were sharing the land with other ethnic minorities. Jews and non-Jews lived in somewhat uneasy relationships within the borders of what had once been the territory of the earlier Kingdom of Judah. The books of Ezra and Nehemiah, as well 1 Esdras and the writings of Josephus, do provide insights into social and religious matters. It was a time of cultural consolidation for the Jews. Of significance in this regard are the reforms of Ezra, a scribe, who travelled from Babylon during the reign of either Artaxerxes I or II. Ezra's reforms had the effect of mandating a rigorous distinction between Jews and Gentiles, marriage only within the Jewish community, and the enforcement of the Sabbath laws. These laws and impositions, clearly reflected in the Pentateuch, especially the so-called 'holiness code' of Leviticus 17–26, were retrojected to the time of the great lawgiver, Moses. The book of Nehemiah records the reading of the law. In effect the books of Moses, known as the Torah, were now regarded as authoritative and canonical. The attitude in which Moses is held in Ezra and Nehemiah is vital for understanding the Torah-centred ethos of early Judaism.

It is possible that hopes of a restoration of the Davidic monarchy were invested in one of the early leaders of the Jews in the period, namely, Zerubbabel, who had returned to Judaea in 520 BCE. He was descended from the Davidic kings who had ruled Judah down to 586 BCE. These hopes are expressed in the oracles of the prophets Haggai and Zechariah (see, e.g., Haggai 2:23; Zechariah 4:7). Those hopes came to nothing. It is reasonable to surmise that any political protest on the part of the Jews was repressed by the Persians. Nevertheless, the Persian period seems to have been tolerant as far as the religious sensibilities of the Jews were concerned. The fact that large Jewish populations continued to live throughout the Persian empire (e.g. in Babylon) is a testimony to their inoffensive rule.

During the Persian period Judaism become a 'world' religion. Judaea was incorporated into a monetarized economy, which brought economic volatility and risk.[2] Babylon became a great centre of world Jewry, and even more so after 135 CE and the extinction of hopes for political autonomy.

Sources

The Cyrus Cylinder, already cited above (see #3), bears witness to the magnanimity of Cyrus in dealing generously with peoples displaced by the Babylonians.

105. In the first year of King Cyrus of Persia, in fulfillment of the word of the LORD spoken to Jeremiah [see Jeremiah 25:11; 29:10], the LORD stirred up the spirit of King Cyrus of Persia so that he sent a herald throughout all his kingdom and also declared in a written edict: 'Thus says King Cyrus of Persia: The LORD, the God of heaven, has given me all the kingdoms of the earth, and has charged me to build him a house in Jerusalem, which is in Judah. Whoever is among you of all his people, may the LORD his God be with him! Let him go up.'
(2 Chronicles 36:22–23)[3]

Nehemiah, a Jewish servant in the royal court of Susa, was appointed by the Persian king Artaxerxes I, to govern the Jews from Jerusalem (see Nehemiah 2:1–8). Nehemiah 8 records the reading of the book of the law, and its translation into Aramaic, which had by then replaced Hebrew as the *lingua franca*.

106. (1) [A]ll the people gathered together into the square before the Water Gate. They told the scribe Ezra to bring the book of the law of Moses, which the LORD had given to Israel. Accordingly, the priest Ezra brought the law before the assembly, both men and women and all who could hear with understanding... He read from it facing the square before the Water Gate from early morning until midday, in the presence of the men and the women and those who could understand; and the ears of all the people were attentive to the book of the law.

(7) Also Jeshua, Bani, Sherebiah, Jamin, Akkub, Shabbethai, Hodiah, Maaseiah, Kelita, Azariah, Jozabad, Hanan, Pelaiah, the Levites, helped the people understand the law, while the people remained in their places. So they read from the book, from the law of God, with interpretation. They gave the sense, so that the people understood the reading.
(Nehemiah 8:1–3, 7–8)

The reading of the Mosaic Law during the time of Nehemiah.

107. (1) On that day they read from the book of Moses in the hearing of the people; and in it was found written that no Ammonite or Moabite should enter the assembly of God...

(3) When the people heard the law, they separated from Israel all those of foreign descent.

(15) In those days I saw in Judah people treading wine presses on the sabbath, and bringing in heaps of grain and loading them on donkeys; and also wine, grapes, figs, and all kinds of burdens, which they brought into Jerusalem on the sabbath day; and I warned them at that time against selling food.

(23) In those days I saw Jews who had married women of Ashdod, Ammon, and Moab; and half of their children spoke the language of Ashdod, and they could not speak the language of Judah, but spoke the language of various peoples. And I contended with them and cursed them and beat some of them and pulled out their hair; and I made them take an oath in the name of God, saying, 'You shall not give your daughters to their sons, or take their daughters for your sons or for yourselves'.
(Nehemiah 13:1, 3, 15, 23–25)[4]

2.2. Judaea under Greek Rule (336–175 BCE)

The hill country of Palestine remained an economic backwater for much of the period.[5] Historical sources for Alexander's campaign in Palestine are few. After the battle of Issus (fought in October 333 BCE), Alexander pressed southwards along the coast. His general Parmenio captured Damascus while Alexander captured Sidon and began what was to be a long siege of Tyre.[6] After reducing Tyre, he continued his march down through coastal Palestine on his way to extricate Egypt from Persian control. After another costly, though briefer, siege, he destroyed Gaza, which was then resettled with his own veterans.

According to Josephus, who draws on traditions not paralleled in the extant Greek and Roman histories, Alexander had significant dealing with the Jews and Samaritans at this time. These traditions are not credible. Josephus records Alexander's contact with the high priest, Jaddua, in Jerusalem. Alexander had sought his help supplying his troops besieging Tyre and requested him to send the tribute the city customarily sent to Darius. Alexander proceeded to invest Gaza. Josephus, unlike the Graeco-Roman historians, who agree that he now pressed on to Egypt, reports Alexander's respectful visit to Jerusalem, dutifully offering sacrifice in the Temple under the high priest's supervision (*Antiquities* 11.336–37). Jews did serve in Alexander's army.[7]

There are few Jewish sources for the period immediately after Alexander. Josephus himself is largely dependent on one source, the *Letter of Aristeas*, for his sketchy account of Jewish relationships with the Ptolemies and Seleucids in *Antiquities* 12.1–153. The *Letter* culminates with the translation of the law into Greek, a work authorized by Ptolemy II Philadelphus (see #114). One can only surmise that under the Ptolemies, as under the Persians, Judaea was left more or less to its own devices. Tribute would have been paid and an Egyptian garrison would have been stationed in Jerusalem.

Ptolemy I (Soter), Josephus reports, not only captured Jerusalem but also deported numbers of Jews from Judaea and Jerusalem as well as Samaritans to Egypt. Other Jews migrated to Egypt of their own accord. Those deported from Jerusalem were assigned to Ptolemy's garrisons, since their reputation for keeping their oaths was unquestioned, as evidenced by the incident recorded by Josephus in *Antiquities* 11.318–20 (cf. 12.147–53).

3 Maccabees could be termed a novella. It is based on an improbable incident which occurred in the aftermath of the battle of Raphia (217 BCE), at which Ptolemy IV defeated Antiochus III. Ptolemy had sought access to the Most Holy Place in the Jerusalem Temple, only to face the mass protest of the people and the intervention of God himself. He returned to Alexandria resolved to punish the Jewish population of Egypt, a purpose that God also thwarted.

Egyptian hegemony over Syria ended in 200. Antiochus III finally managed to wrest control of Palestine, including Judaea, from the Ptolemies. There had been rivalry between the leading Jerusalem families concerning the matter of allegiance. A continuation of these rivalries was to have disastrous consequences for Judaean Jews once Antiochus IV Epiphanes became king in 175 BCE. Josephus describes the depredations that occasioned Antiochus III's vigorous, though not always successful, prosecution of war against the Ptolemy IV Philopator and his son and successor Ptolemy V Epiphanes.

Josephus portrays Antiochus as grateful for Jewish compliance in the capture of Judaea from the Ptolemies, writing a letter to his governor of Coele-Syria and Phoenicia, indicating his indebtedness to the Jews. He offered to restore Jerusalem and to underwrite repairs to the Temple and its worship, declared his intention to re-populate the city by bringing back Jews who had been dispersed abroad, remitted certain taxes and granted relief from tribute every third year (see *Antiquities* 12.138–44). He also published a decree throughout his entire kingdom underscoring the sanctity of the Temple. The letter of guarantee and the decree are generally regarded as possessing doubtful authenticity. Josephus himself records that many doubted the authenticity of proclamations such as these because they were not known outside Jewish records (see *Antiquities* 14.187). If they did exist, Antiochus IV set them aside.

In *Antiquities* 12.154–236, Josephus includes a more-or-less self-contained narrative of Joseph, the son of Tobias, and his son Hyrcanus. It is often called the Tobiad 'romance'. The narrative shows that the Tobiads were taxation agents for the Ptolemies. Joseph's wealth and influence came as the result of tax farming. Father and son are presented as resourceful self-promoters, quite prepared to exact tribute rapaciously. Tobias also appears in the Zenon papyri (see #445). Josephus's story shows the extent of the hellenization that was occurring in the upper ranks of Jewish society at the time.

Sources

Though difficult to date, Zechariah 9–14 was probably written during the Greek ascendancy in the late fourth or third century BCE.

108. Rejoice greatly, O daughter Zion!
Shout aloud, O daughter Jerusalem!
Lo, your king comes to you; triumphant and victorious is he,
humble and riding on a donkey,
on a colt, the foal of a donkey.
He will cut off the chariot from Ephraim
and the war horse from Jerusalem;
and the battle bow shall be cut off,
and he shall command peace to the nations;
his dominion shall be from sea to sea,
and from the River to the ends of the earth.
As for you also, because of the blood of my covenant with you,
I will set your prisoners free from the waterless pit.
Return to your stronghold, O prisoners of hope;
today I declare that I will restore to you double.
For I have bent Judah as my bow;
I have made Ephraim its arrow.
I will arouse your sons, O Zion,
against your sons, O Greece,
and wield you like a warrior's sword.
(Zechariah 9:9–13)

Josephus reports the capture of Jerusalem by Ptolemy I after the death of Alexander.

109. [Ptolemy] seized Jerusalem by resorting to cunning and deceit. For he entered the city on the Sabbath as if to offer sacrifice, and, as the Jews did not oppose him—for they did not suspect any hostile act—and, because of their lack of suspicion and the nature of day, were enjoying idleness and ease, he became master of the city without difficulty and ruled it harshly.
(Josephus, *Antiquities* 12.4)[8]

Josephus describes the circumstances of the annexation of Judaea by Antiochus III.

110. When Antiochus the Great ruled over Asia it was the lot of the Jews to undergo great hardships through the devastation of their land, as did also the inhabitants of Coele-Syria. For while he was at war with Ptolemy Philopator and with his son Ptolemy, surnamed Epiphanes, they had to suffer, and whether he was victorious or defeated, to experience the same fate; so that they were in no way different from a storm-tossed ship which is beset on either side by heavy seas, finding themselves crushed between the successes of Antiochus and the adverse turn of his fortunes. When, however, Antiochus had defeated Ptolemy [trans.: Josephus seems to mean Ptolemy IV Philopator here although Ptolemy V Epiphanes makes better sense of the historical record], he annexed Judaea. And on the death of Philopator his son sent out a great force with Scopas as general against the people of Coele-Syria, and he took many of their cities and also our nation, which went over to him after being attacked. But not long afterwards Antiochus defeated Scopas in a battle near the sources of the Jordan, and destroyed a great part of his army. And later, when Antiochus took possession of the cities in Coele-Syria which Scopas had held, and Samaria, the Jews of their own will went over to him and admitted him to their city and made abundant

provision for his entire army and his elephants; and they readily joined his forces in besieging the garrison which had been left by Scopas in the citadel of Jerusalem.
(Josephus, *Antiquities* 12.129–33)[9]

The setting and commencement of the Tobiad 'romance'.

111. (154) After this [the annexation of Judaea and Jerusalem] Antiochus made a treaty of friendship with Ptolemy, and gave him his daughter Cleopatra in marriage, making over to him as her dowry Coele-Syria, Samaria, Judaea and Phoenicia. And when the tribute was divided between the two sovereigns, the prominent men purchased the right to farm the taxes in their several provinces and, collecting the sum fixed, paid it to the royal pair.

(175) Now when the day came round on which the rights to farm taxes in the cities were to be sold, bids were made by those eminent in rank in the various provinces. When the sum of taxes from Coele-Syria and from Phoenicia and Judaea with Samaria added up to eight thousand talents, Joseph came forward and accused the bidders of having made an agreement to offer the king a low price for the taxes, whereas he for his part promised to give double that amount and send over to the king the property of those who had been remiss toward his house; for this right was sold along with that of farming the taxes.
(Josephus, *Antiquities* 12.154–55, 175–76)[10]

2 Maccabees testifies to the saintliness of the high priest Onias III (d. c. 170 BCE).

112. While the holy city was inhabited in unbroken peace and the laws were strictly observed because of the piety of the high priest Onias and his hatred of wickedness, it came about that the kings themselves honoured the place and glorified the temple with the finest presents, even to the extent that King Seleucus of Asia defrayed from his own revenues all the expenses connected with the service of the sacrifices.
(2 Maccabees 3:1–3)

International recognition of the Jews.

There is little do ubt that Greek city-states of the Hellenistic era were aware of the existence of the Jews of Judaea. Josephus records the text of an early letter written by the Spartan king Areus, probably Areus I who reigned from 309–264 BCE. Its genuineness is doubtful.

113. 'Areios, king of the Lacedaemonians, to Onias [Onias I], greeting. We have come upon a certain document from which we have learned that the Jews and Lacedaemonians are of one race and are related by descent from Abraham. It is right, therefore, that you as our brothers should send to us to make known whatever you may wish. We also shall do this, and shall consider what is yours as our own, and what is ours we shall also share with you.'
(Josephus, *Antiquities* 12.226–27)[11]

2.3. Judaism and Hellenism in Judaea

The conquests of Alexander the Great, as well as the consolidation of territory controlled by his generals and their successors, created a climate conducive to the wide dissemination of Greek cultural values and institutions. In addition, Alexander and his successors founded cities, such as Alexandria (Egypt) and Antioch (on the Orontes), the two most prominent cities in the Hellenistic east, which were based on Greek models. These, and cities like them, became outposts of Greek cultural values amid the populations of 'barbarians' (i.e. unsophisticated non-Greek speakers).

Hellenism impinged on the Jews of Palestine, not least because this was the culture of their economic and political masters, whether Egyptian Ptolemies or Syrian Seleucids. However, Palestine was not an exclusively Jewish enclave. Many native non-Jews also lived there. They were Greek speakers and shared Greek values. Egyptian Jews were even more exposed to Greek culture. Ptolemy II Philadelphus (285–246 BCE) sponsored the translation of the Pentateuch into Greek. Alexandrian Jews could not read Hebrew.[12]

During the third century BCE it is clear that Judaean Jews were increasingly coming into contact with Greek culture. Greek was used as the language of diplomacy. Palestine was regularly traversed by Greek-speaking troops. There were newly founded Greek cities of Gaza and Samaria, and later Sebaste and Caesarea. Throughout Palestine, Jews and Gentiles lived more or less as neighbours with every possibility that influences flowed both ways. The Tobiad 'romance' reveals a Jewish aristocratic family under quite definite Greek influence. In c. 170 BCE there was established in Jerusalem itself that most culturally Greek of institutions, namely, a gymnasium (with an ephebate) that was much frequented by priests (see #117; 2 Maccabees 4:7–10, 12–15). Greek loan words began appearing in Aramaic texts emanating from Palestine, such as the names of the musical instruments in Daniel 3. The use of Greek philosophical and ethical terms are encountered within Jewish documents such as *4 Maccabees* (c. 50 CE) and Josephus's *Antiquities*. It has also been suggested that schools set up in Palestine to teach the Torah were modelled on Greek schools designed to teach the epics of Homer, the foundational classics of the Greeks. Greek was the language of a number of biblical books, notably 1 Maccabees, and the Additions to Esther and to Daniel. A surprisingly large number of Jerusalem ossuary inscriptions are in Greek, and some are in Greek and Hebrew (or Aramaic). Letters of the era, such as those of Bar Kokhba, are in Greek and Hebrew.[13]

However, the influence of Greek culture was also resisted. It has been argued that the book of Sirach (early second century BCE) issues warnings concerning the dangers posed by Gentile, specifically Greek, ways. The book of *Jubilees* is far more explicit in its repudiation of the influence of Greek culture, especially in its condemnation of nudity, a possible reaction to the gymnasium established in Jerusalem once Antiochus IV Epiphanes came to the Syrian throne (see 1 Maccabees 1:11–15; 2 Maccabees 4:7–17). Whereas 1 Maccabees holds Jewish 'renegades' responsible for this development, the writer of 2 Maccabees is under no misapprehension that it was the high priest Jason who was responsible for the introduction of Greek ways. In 2 Maccabees Jason offers to establish a gymnasium and to 'enroll the people of Jerusalem as citizens of Antioch' (2 Maccabees 4:9). Jerusalem was becoming a Greek city with the expected cultural and civic institutions. The effect on the daily sacrificial round was subversive. It is clear that there was Jewish support for a hellenizing programme designed to redress economic and cultural marginalization (1 Maccabees 1:11).

In response a reactive movement grew up in this period which resisted the inroads of Greek cultural values in Judaism. The movement's adherents were called the Hasidim and was the spiritual ancestor of Pharisaism and possibly Essenism. The comparative peace of the Jews in Palestine after the wars of Antiochus III and Ptolemy IV and V had concluded was soon to be shattered. It is not clear from the sources whether Antiochus IV set out deliberately to provoke the Jews. Power struggles within the priestly families, and Seleucid financial bankruptcy, play their part. In 170 BCE, those tensions contributed to a decisive repudiation of Greek values in Jerusalem itself.

Sources

The translation of the Septuagint by 72 Jewish translators in the time of Ptolemy II.

114. (301) Demetrius [the king's librarian] took the men with him, traversed the mile-long jetty into the sea toward the island, crossed the bridge, and went in the direction of the north. There he assembled them in a house which had been duly furnished near the shore—a magnificent building in a very quiet situation—and invited the men to carry out the work of translation, all that they would require being handsomely provided. They set to completing their several tasks, reaching agreement among themselves on each by comparing versions. The result of their agreement thus was made into a fair copy by Demetrius. The business of their meeting occupied them until the ninth hour, after which they were free for bodily rest and relaxation, everything which they desired being furnished on a lavish scale...

(307)... The outcome was such that in seventy-two days the business of translation was completed, just as if such a result was achieved by some deliberate design. When it was completed, Demetrius assembled the company of the Jews in the place where the task of the translation had been finished, and read it to all, in the presence of the translators, who received a great ovation from the crowded audience for being responsible for great blessings. Likewise also they gave an ovation to Demetrius and asked him, now that he had transcribed the whole Law, to give a copy to their leaders. As the books were read, the priests stood up, with the elders from among the translators and from the representatives of the 'Community,' and with the leaders of the people, and said, 'Since this version has been made rightly and reverently, and in every respect accurately, it is good that this should remain exactly so, and that there should be no revision.' There was general approval of what they said, and they commanded that a curse should be laid, as was their custom, on anyone who should alter the version by any addition or change to any part of the written text, or any deletion either. This was a good step taken, to ensure that the words were preserved completely and permanently in perpetuity.
(*Letter of Aristeas* 301–303, 307–311)

The following two documents reveal something of the reaction to the inroads of Greek culture. In second-century BCE Rome, Marcus Portius Cato conducted a similar campaign against the subversion of traditional Roman virtues and values.

115. Woe to timid hearts and to slack hands, and
 to the sinner who walks a double path!
 Woe to the fainthearted who have no trust!
 Therefore they will have no shelter.
 Woe to you who have lost your nerve! What
 will you do when the Lord's reckoning
 comes?
 (Sirach 2:12–14)

116. But from all the beasts and all the cattle he [God] granted to Adam alone that he might cover his shame. Therefore it is commanded in the heavenly tablets to all who will know the judgment of the Law that they should cover their shame and they should not be uncovered as the gentiles are uncovered.
(*Jubilees* 3:30–31)

The gymnasium and the extent of hellenization in Jerusalem under Jason in the period 175–169 BCE.

117. In those days certain renegades came out from Israel and misled many, saying, 'Let us go and make a covenant with the Gentiles around us, for since we separated from them many disasters have come upon us'. This proposal pleased them, and some of the people eagerly went to the king, who authorized them to observe the ordinances of the Gentiles. So they built a gymnasium in Jerusalem, according to Gentile custom, and removed the marks of circumcision, and abandoned the holy covenant. They joined with the Gentiles and sold themselves to do evil.
(1 Maccabees 1:11–15)[14]

2.4. Antiochus IV Epiphanes and Priestly Politics in Judaea

Antiochus is portrayed in the Jewish sources as an implacable enemy of Jews and Judaism. It has been suggested that the imposition of Greek ways was designed to unify his diverse kingdom particularly in the face of the Roman threat.[15] There could be no room for (religious) autonomy. He took the name 'Epiphanes', a name designed to advertise the perception that he was a god 'manifest' on earth. Some, however, called him 'Epimanes', 'mad'. As a child Antiochus had been taken hostage to Rome after his father's defeat at the battle of Magnesia in 190 BCE.[16] Hanging over the heads of Antiochus III and his successors was the spectre of the war indemnity imposed after the peace of Apamea in 188.

Antiochus's accession in 175 coincided with a power struggle in Jerusalem within the temple establishment that had begun in the reign of his predecessor, Seleucus IV. Jason, the brother of the high priest Onias III, offered the king a bribe to be made high priest. He also promised to establish a gymnasium in Jerusalem, and to enroll the people of the city as citizens of Antioch (see 2 Maccabees 4:19). With the support of many in Jerusalem, Jason inaugurated Greek-style athletic contests in the city. A stadium was built (see 1 Maccabees 1:14; 2 Maccabees 4:9, 12). Greek dress became the 'rage'. The athlete's wide-brimmed hat was worn. The athletes competed naked. Moreover there were reports that the Jewish athletes were removing the marks of their circumcision by surgery (see #117; cf. 1 Corinthians 7:18). The deposing of Onias is presented as prophecy in the book of Daniel which speaks of an 'anointed one [who] shall be cut off and shall have nothing' (see 9:26; #122). According to 2 Maccabees 4:7–10 Jason was responsible for promoting a vigorous and thoroughgoing Hellenizing programme.

Later Jason sent Menelaus, brother of Simon the Captain of the Temple, to carry tribute to Antiochus. Menelaus promised the king a larger sum of money than had Jason for the high priestly office. Jason in his turn found himself deposed. The Jews would not accept Menelaus, a Benjaminite, as high priest. In 169, returning from his military campaign in Egypt where he had been warned by the Romans not to proceed, Antiochus entered the city and supported Menelaus with a show of strength. Antiochus put down the revolt savagely and successfully, looting the Temple treasury as well.

Two years later, his general fought his way into the city on the Sabbath, and established a garrison of Macedonian soldiers and Jewish 'renegades' in a commanding fortress, called the Akra in the city of David (the Ophel).[17] The Temple was then appropriated to the worship of Olympian Zeus (2 Maccabees 6:2). The active proscription of the Jewish religion and culture followed. An altar called the 'abomination which causes desolation' (see Daniel 9:27; 11:31; 12:1) was placed over the existing one for the sacrificing of swine (Josephus, *Antiquities* 12.253). Altars were set up all over the country. Circumcision was banned on pain of death. The famous martyrology of 2 Maccabees 7 details in graphic terms the lengths the Syrians were prepared to go to prosecute those infringing Antiochus's statutes as well as the defiant heroism of those Jews prepared to disobey.

Sources

Antiochus IV in the Jewish sources.

118. [There] shall arise a contemptible person on whom royal majesty had not been conferred; he shall come in without warning and obtain the kingdom [Syria] through intrigue.
(Daniel 11:21)[18]

119. From them [the successors of Alexander] came forth a sinful root, Antiochus Epiphanes, son of King Antiochus; he had been a hostage in Rome. He began to reign in one hundred thirty-seventh year of the kingdom of the Greeks.
(1 Maccabees 1:10)

The book of Daniel presents the rapacity of Antiochus in the following terms.

120. Armies shall be utterly swept away and broken before him [Antiochus], and the prince of the covenant as well [Onias III, the high priest].
(Daniel 11:22)

The deposing of Onias III.

121. When Seleucus died and Antiochus, who was called Epiphanes, succeeded to the kingdom, Jason the brother of Onias obtained the high priesthood by corruption, promising the king at an interview three hundred sixty talents of silver, and from another source of revenue eighty talents. In addition to this he [Jason] promised to pay one hundred fifty more if permission were given to establish by his authority a gymnasium and a body of youth for it, and to enrol the people of Jerusalem as citizens of Antioch. When the king assented and Jason came to office, he at once shifted his compatriots over to the Greek way of life.

He set aside the existing royal concessions to the Jews, secured through John the

father of Eupolemus, who went on the mission to establish friendship and alliance with the Romans; and he destroyed the lawful ways of living and introduced new customs contrary to the law. He took delight in establishing a gymnasium right under the citadel, and he induced the noblest of the young men to wear the Greek hat. There was such an extreme of Hellenization and increase in the adoption of foreign ways because of the surpassing wickedness of Jason, who was ungodly and no true high priest, that the priests were no longer intent upon their service at the altar. Despising the sanctuary and neglecting the sacrifices, they hurried to take part in the unlawful proceedings in the wrestling arena after the signal for the discus-throwing, disdaining the honors prized by their ancestors and putting the highest value upon Greek forms of prestige. For this reason heavy disaster overtook them, and those whose ways of living they admired and wished to imitate completely became their enemies and punished them. It is no light thing to show irreverence to the divine laws—a fact that later events will make clear.
(2 Maccabees 4:7–17)

Daniel 9:24–27 also alludes to the troubled events surrounding the removal of Onias III (see v. 26), the intrigues surrounding the office of the high priest, and the subsequent giving over of the temple to idolatrous worship for a half week of years (i.e. three and a half years).

122. 'Seventy weeks are decreed for your people and your holy city: to finish the transgression, to put an end to sin, and to atone for iniquity, to bring in everlasting righteousness, to seal both vision and prophet, and to anoint a most holy place. Know therefore and understand: from the time that the word went out to restore and rebuild Jerusalem until the time of an anointed prince, there shall be seven weeks; and for sixty-two weeks it shall be built again with streets and moat, but in a troubled time. After the sixty-two weeks, an anointed one shall be cut off and shall have nothing, and the troops of the prince who is to come shall destroy the city and the sanctuary. Its end shall come with a flood, and to the end there shall be war. Desolations are decreed. He shall make a strong covenant with many for one week, and for half of the week he shall make sacrifice and offering cease; and in their place shall be an abomination that desolates, until the decreed end is poured out upon the desolator.'
(Daniel 9:24–27)[19]

Three years later, Jason, who had deposed Onias III, was himself deposed by Menelaus.

123. After a period of three years Jason sent Menelaus, the brother of the previously mentioned Simon, to carry the money to the king and to complete the records of essential business. But he, when presented to the king, extolled him with an air of authority, and secured the high priesthood for himself, outbidding Jason by three hundred talents of silver. After receiving the king's orders he returned, possessing no qualification for the high priesthood, but having the hot temper of a cruel tyrant and the rage of a savage wild beast. So Jason, who after supplanting his own brother was supplanted by another man, was driven as a fugitive into the land of Ammon.
(2 Maccabees 4:23–26)[20]

Antiochus IV's campaign in Egypt (see also #36).

124. But Antiochus, in whose own kingdom things were going well, determined to march against Egypt because he coveted it and also because he held in contempt the sons of Ptolemy, who were still weak and not yet able to govern so great a state. And so he arrived at Pelusium with a great force, and circumventing Ptolemy Philometor by cunning, occupied Egypt; and after he had arrived in the neighbourhood of Memphis and taken possession of this city, he set out for Alexandria with the intention of reducing it by siege and getting into his power the Ptolemy who was reigning there. He was, however, repelled not only from Alexandria, but also from the whole of Egypt, for the Romans instructed him to keep away from the country, as we have already related somewhere in an earlier passage. But I shall give a detailed account of this king, how he became master of Judaea and the temple; for since in my first work I mentioned these

things only in summary fashion, I have thought it necessary now to go back and give a more exact account of them.
(Josephus, *Antiquities* 12.242–45)[21]

The following documents narrate the ravaging of Jerusalem in 169 and 167 BCE by Antiochus's forces, followed by the outlawing of Jewish customs and desecration of the temple by Antiochus.

125. After subduing Egypt, Antiochus returned in the one hundred forty-third year [169 BCE]. He went up against Israel and came to Jerusalem with a strong force. He arrogantly entered the sanctuary and took the golden altar, the lampstand for the light, and all its utensils. He took also the table for the bread of the Presence, the cups for drink offerings, the bowls, the golden censers, the curtain, the crowns, and the gold decoration on the front of the temple; he stripped it all off. He took the silver and the gold, and the costly vessels; he took also the hidden treasures that he found. Taking them all, he went into his own land.
(1 Maccabees 1:20–24.
Cf. Josephus, *Against Apion* 2.83–84)

126. Two years later [in 167 BCE], as it happened, in the hundred and forty-fifth year, on the twenty-fifth day of the month which by us is called Chasleu, and by the Macedonians Apellaios, in the hundred and fifty-third Olympiad, the king went up to Jerusalem, and by pretending to offer peace, overcame the city by treachery. But on this occasion he did not spare even those who admitted him, because of the wealth of the temple, but through greed—for he saw much gold in the temple and an array of very costly dedicatory-offerings of other kinds—, and for the sake of taking this as spoil, he went so far as to violate the treaty which he had made with them. And so he stripped the temple, carrying off the vessels of God, the golden lampstands and the golden altar and table and the other altars, and not even forbearing to take the curtains, which were made of fine linen and scarlet, and he also emptied the temple of its hidden treasures, and left nothing at all behind, thereby throwing the Jews into deep mourning. Moreover he forbade them to offer the daily sacrifices which they used to offer to God in accordance with their law, and after plundering the entire city, he killed some of the people, and some he took captive together with their wives and children, so that he number of those taken alive came to some ten thousand. And he burnt the finest parts of the city, and pulling down the walls, built the *Akra* (citadel) in the Lower City; for it was high enough to overlook the temple, and it was for this reason that he fortified it with high walls and towers, and stationed a Macedonian garrison therein. Nonetheless there remained in the *Akra* those of the people who were impious and of bad character, and at their hands the citizens were destined to suffer many terrible things.
(Josephus, *Antiquities* 12.248–52)

127. 'At the time appointed he shall return and come into the south, but this time it shall not be as it was before. For ships of Kittim [Rome] shall come against him, and he shall lose heart and withdraw. He shall be enraged and take action against the holy covenant. He shall turn back and pay heed to those who forsake the holy covenant. Forces sent by him shall occupy and profane the temple and fortress. They shall abolish the regular burnt offering and set up the abomination that makes desolate. He shall seduce with intrigue those who violate the covenant; but the people who are loyal to their God shall stand firm and take action. The wise among the people shall give understanding to many; for some days, however, they shall fall by sword and flame, and suffer captivity and plunder. When they fall victim, they shall receive a little help, and many shall join them insincerely. Some of the wise shall fall, so that they may be refined, purified, and cleansed, until the time of the end, for there is still an interval until the time appointed'.
(Daniel 11:29–35. Daniel combines events that seem to have taken place in 169 [Antiochus's withdrawal from Egypt] and 167 [action taken against the Temple and its aftermath])[22]

The enforced hellenization of Judaea and the outlawing of Judaism. The events of 167.

128. The king [Antiochus] also built a pagan altar upon the temple-altar, and slaughtered swine thereon, thereby practising a form of

sacrifice neither lawful nor native to the religion of the Jews. And he compelled them to give up the worship of their own God, and to do reverence to the gods in whom he believed; he then commanded them to build sacred places in every city and village, and to set up altars on which to sacrifice swine daily. He also ordered them not to circumcise their children, threatening to punish anyone who might be found acting contrary to these orders. He also appointed overseers who should assist in compelling them to carry out his instructions. And so, many of the Jews, some willingly, others through fear of the punishment which had been prescribed, followed the practices ordained by the king, but the worthiest people and those of noble soul disregarded him, and held their country's customs of greater account than the punishment with which he threatened them if they disobeyed; and being on that account maltreated daily, and enduring bitter torments, they met their death. Indeed, they were whipped, their bodies were mutilated, and while still alive and breathing, they were crucified, while their wives and the sons whom they had circumcised in despite of the king's wishes were strangled, the children being made to hang from the necks of their crucified parents. And wherever a sacred book or copy of the Law was found, it was destroyed; as for those in whose possession it was found, they too, poor wretches, wretchedly perished.
(Josephus, *Antiquities* 12.253–56.
Cf. 1 Maccabees 1:41–53)

The author of 1 Maccabees also describes graphically the measures by which Judaism was effectively outlawed.

129. Now on the fifteenth day of Chislev, in the one hundred forty-fifth year, they erected a desolating sacrilege on the altar of burnt-offering. The also build altars in the surrounding towns of Judah, and offered incense at the doors of the houses and in the streets. The books of the law that they found they tore to pieces and burned with fire. Anyone found possessing the book of the covenant, or anyone who adhered to the law, was condemned to death by decree of the king. They kept using violence against Israel, against those who were found month after month in the towns. On the twenty-fifth day of the month they offered sacrifice on the altar that was on top of the altar of burnt offering. According to the decree, they put to death the women who had their children circumcised, and their families and those who circumcised them; and they hung the infants from their mothers' necks. But many in Israel stood firm and were resolved in their hearts not to eat unclean food. They chose to die rather than to be defiled by food or to profane the holy covenant; and they did die. Very great wrath came upon Israel.
(1 Maccabees 1:54–64)[23]

The author of 2 Maccabees had access to historical sources that present the imposed religion as an explicit Greek innovation. After the revolt of Judas Maccabaeus, the ancestral customs of the Jews were actively proscribed.

130. Not long after this [Judas' escape to the wilderness], the king sent an Athenian senator to compel the Jews to forsake the laws of their ancestors and no longer to live by the laws of God; and to pollute the temple in Jerusalem and to call it the temple of Olympian Zeus, and to call the one in Gerizim [the temple of the Samaritans] the temple of Zeus-the-Friend-of-Strangers, as did the people who lived in that place.
(2 Maccabees 6:1–2)[24]

2.5. The Maccabaean Revolt (167–164 BCE) and its Aftermath

At a sacrifice to Olympian Zeus at a place in Judaea called Modein, a member of a priestly family called Mattathias refused to sacrifice, killed the Jew who came forward to do it, and then killed the Syrian officer overseeing the sacrifice. His grandfather was named Asmoneaus—hence the name 'Hasmonaean' for the family which exercised authority for the next 130 years in Judaea. Judas, the eldest of Mattathias's sons, became known by the nickname, 'Maccabaeus', which means the 'Hammer'. After fierce battles against Antiochus's generals, the Maccabaean guerillas were finally able to re-enter Jerusalem.[25]

Antiochus, busy in the eastern regions of his empire, is portrayed by the author of 1 Maccabees being informed of the success of the Maccabaean guerillas. Quite improbably the king repented of his sacrilege and desecration of the Jerusalem Temple, and died soon after in 164.[26] Josephus takes issue with Polybius and insists that Antiochus was struck down because he dared to commit sacrilege against the Temple in Jerusalem.[27] The Syrians, though defeated, were not driven from Judaea or, indeed, from Jerusalem. The Syrian garrison, still supported by renegade Jews, was still present in the lower city. The Temple had been cleansed, an action celebrated in the Jewish festival Hanukkah—the 'festival of lights'.[28] Nevertheless, Jerusalem was re-fortified. The struggle for independence continued during the succeeding years as the Maccabaean brothers found themselves fighting a succession of Syrian kings and pretenders. Judas and his brothers campaigned against unfriendly neighbours and supported Jews in Galilee (*Antiquities* 12.327–53).

After Antiochus IV's death his son Antiochus Eupator reinforced the hand of those forces still prepared to resist the Hasmonaeans, using the Jerusalem citadel, still under Syrian control, as their base. Although the Temple was now firmly in Hasmonaean hands, there was still a war to be prosecuted.

A new high priest, Alcimus, was appointed by Antiochus Eupator, son of Antiochus IV, after Menelaus had been killed (*Antiquities* 12.388–89). At that point Onias IV went into voluntary exile in Egypt. At first Alcimus was acceptable to the Hasidim, but he later massacred 60 of them. He also opposed Judas Maccabaeus.[29]

The Maccabaean emergency had a number of significance ramifications for early Judaism. The revolt brought the family of the Hasmonaeans to the fore. They were the great heroes of the resistance. The dynasty supplied the high priests for the period 152–137 BCE. In later New Testament times, the family, though eclipsed politically by Herod and the Roman presence in Judaea, achieved great popularity among the Jews in Palestine because they symbolized opposition to Gentile incursions. Indeed the spirit of the revolt lived on in the early Jewish era and reaches into the modern era.

In 161 Judas Maccabaeus took the step of initiating and entering a pact of friendship with Rome. This was an astute move on Judas' part given Rome's increasing interest in the Eastern Mediterranean and in Egypt, already evidenced by their intervention against Antiochus III and now his son Antiochus IV. Both Jews and Romans had a vested interest in keeping Syria weak. The book of 1 Maccabees reports the initial awakening of awareness of the presence and power of the Romans in the region. Given its suspicion of the ambitions of the Seleucids, Rome would not have been averse to a strong Jewish state. 2 Maccabees 4:11 knows of an earlier pact with the Romans.

Judas was slain in battle in 160 BCE.[30] However, his brothers, especially Jonathan and Simon, who were high priests in succession, continued the fight for Jewish independence.

Sources

The author of 1 Maccabees depicts the scene at the sacrifice in Modein.

131. But Mattathias answered and said in a loud voice: 'Even if all the nations that live under the rule of the king obey him, and have chosen to obey his commandments, everyone of them abandoning the religion of their ancestors, I and my sons and my brothers will continue to live by the covenant of our ancestors. Far be it from us to desert the law and the ordinances. We will not obey the king's words by turning aside from our religion to the right hand or to the left.'

When he had finished speaking these words, a Jew came forward in the sight of all to offer sacrifice on the altar in Modein, according to the king's command. When Mattathias saw it, he burned with zeal and his heart was stirred. He gave vent to righteous anger; he ran and killed him on the altar. At the same time he killed the king's officer who was forcing them to sacrifice, and he tore down the altar. Thus he burned for zeal for the law, just as Phinehas did against Zimri son of Salu [Numbers 25:1–15].

Then Mattathias cried out in the town with a loud voice, saying: 'Let every one who is zealous for the law and supports the covenant come out with me!' Then he and his sons fled to the hills and left all that they had in the town.
(1 Maccabees 2:19–28)[31]

At the outbreak of the Maccabaean Revolt, the writer of 1 Maccabees reports the actions of a group of ill-fated Jews.

132. At that time many who were seeking righteousness and justice went down to the wilderness to live there, they, their sons, their wives, and their livestock, because troubles pressed heavily upon them. And it was reported to the king's officers, and to the troops in Jerusalem the city of David, that those who had rejected the king's command had gone down to the hiding places in the wilderness. Many pursued them, and overtook them; they encamped opposite them and prepared for battle against them on the sabbath day. They said to them, 'Enough of this! Come out and do what the king commands, and you will live.' But they said, 'We will not come out, nor will we do what the king commands and so profane the sabbath day.' Then the enemy quickly attacked them. But they did not answer them or hurl a stone at them or block up their hiding places, for they said, 'Let us all die in our innocence; heaven and earth testify for us that you are killing us unjustly.' So they attacked them on the sabbath, and they died, with their wives and children and livestock, to the number of a thousand persons.

When Mattathias and his friends learned of it, they mourned for them deeply. And all said to their neighbors: 'If we all do as our kindred have done and refuse to fight with the Gentiles for our lives and for our ordinances, they will quickly destroy us from the earth.' So they made this decision that day: 'Let us fight against anyone who comes to attack us on the sabbath day; let us not all die as our kindred died in their hiding places.'
(1 Maccabees 2:29–41)[32]

The Hasidim join Mattathias.

133. Then there united with them a company of Hasideans, mighty warriors of Israel, all who offered themselves willingly for the law. And all who became fugitives to escape their troubles joined them and reinforced them. They organized an army, and struck down sinners in their anger and renegades in their wrath; the survivors fled to the Gentiles for safety. And Mattathias and his friends went around and tore down the altars; they forcibly circumcised all the uncircumcised boys that they found within the borders of Israel. They hunted down the arrogant and the work prospered in their hands. They rescued the law out of the hands of the Gentiles and kings, and they never let the sinner gain the upper hand.
(1 Maccabees 2:42–48)

The cleansing of the Temple (#134–35).

134. Then Judas detailed men to fight against those in the citadel until he had cleansed the sanctuary. He chose blameless priests devoted to the law, and they cleansed the sanctuary and removed the defiled stones to an unclean place. They deliberated what to do about the altar of burnt offering, which had been profaned. And they thought it best to tear it down, so that it would not be a lasting shame to them that the Gentiles had defiled it. So they tore down the altar, and stored the stones in a convenient place on the temple hill until a prophet should come to tell what to do with them.
(1 Maccabees 4:41–46)

135. Early in the morning on the twenty-fifth day of the ninth month, which is the month of Chislev, in the one hundred forty-eighth year, they rose and offered sacrifice, as the law directs, on the new altar of burnt offering that they had built. At the very season and on the very day that the Gentiles had profaned it, it was dedicated with songs and harps and lutes and cymbals. All the people fell on their faces and worshiped and blessed Heaven, who had prospered them. So they celebrated the dedication of the altar for

eight days, and joyfully offered burnt offerings; they offered a sacrifice of well-being and a thanksgiving offering. They decorated the front of the temple with golden crowns and small shields; they restored the gates and the chambers for the priests, and fitted them with doors. There was very great joy among the people, and the disgrace brought by the Gentiles was removed. Then Judas and his brothers and all the assembly of Israel determined that every year at that season the days of dedication of the altar should be observed with joy and gladness for eight days, beginning with the twenty-fifth day of the month of Chislev.
(1 Maccabees 4:52–59)

A famous incident during a battle against the forces of Antiochus Eupator (Antiochus IV's son) is cited below. Unfortunately for the Jews, the example of Eleazer's bravery was not followed. The Jewish army fled the field of battle on which this incident took place.

136. Now Eleazer, called Avaran, saw that one of the animals [i.e. the Syrian war elephants] was equipped with royal armour. It was taller than all the others, and he supposed that the king [Antiochus Eupator] was on it. So he gave his life to save his people and to win for himself an everlasting name. He courageously ran into the midst of the phalanx to reach it; he killed men right and left, and they parted before him on both sides. He got under the elephant, stabbed it from beneath, and killed it; but it fell to the ground upon him and he died.
(1 Maccabees 6:43–46)[33]

Judas Maccabaeus' overtures to Rome.

137. (1) Now Judas heard of the fame of the Romans, that they were very strong and were well-disposed toward all who made an alliance with them, that they pledged friendship to those who came to them, and that they were very strong. He had been told of their wars and of the brave deeds that they were doing among the Gauls, how they had defeated them and forced them to pay tribute, and what they had done in the land of Spain to get control of the silver and gold mines there, and how they had gained control of the whole region by their planning and patience, even though the place was far distant from them... (5) They had crushed in battle and conquered Philip, and King Perseus of the Macedonians, and the others who rose up against them. They also had defeated Antiochus the Great, king of Asia, who went to fight against them with one hundred twenty elephants and with cavalry and chariots and a very large army... (12b) They have subdued kings far and near, and as many as have heard of their fame have feared them. Those whom they wish to help and to make kings, they make kings, and those whom they wish they depose; and they have been greatly exalted. Yet for all this not one of them has put on a crown or worn purple as a mark of pride, but they have built for themselves a senate chamber, and every day three hundred twenty senators constantly deliberate concerning the people, to govern them well. They trust one man each year to rule over them and to cotrol all their land; they all heed the one man, and there is no envy or jealousy among them.
(1 Maccabees 8:1–4a, 5–6, 12b–16)[34]

Judas and an embassy travelled to Rome to conclude an alliance. They addressed the Senate as follows.

138. 'Judas, who is also called Maccabeus, and his brothers and the people of the Jews have sent us to you to establish alliance and peace with you, so that we may be enrolled as your allies and friends.'
(1 Maccabees 8:20)

The text of the Romans' reply was inscribed on bronze and sent to Jerusalem. The author of 1 Maccabees cites the text.

139. (23) 'May all go well with the Romans and with the nation of the Jews at sea and on land forever, and may sword and enemy be far from them. If war comes first to Rome or to any of their allies in all their dominion, the nation of the Jews shall act as their allies wholeheartedly, as the occasion may indicate to them. To the enemy that makes war they shall not give or supply grain, arms, money, or ships, just as Rome has decided; and they

> shall keep their obligations without receiving any return. In the same way, if war comes first to the nation of the Jews, the Romans shall willingly act as their allies, as the occasion may indicate to them. And to their enemies there shall not be given grain, arms, money, or ships, just as Rome has decided; and they shall keep these obligations and do so without deceit. Thus on these terms the Romans make a treaty with the Jewish people…
>
> (31) Concerning the wrongs that King Demetrius is doing to them, we have written to him as follows, "Why have you made your yoke heavy on our friends and allies the Jews? If now they appeal again for help against you, we will defend their rights and fight you on sea and on land."'
> (1 Maccabees 8:23–29, 31–33)[35]

In 161 BCE, during the high priesthood of Alcimus, the Hasidim attempted to come to terms with the Syrians led by Bacchides, the Governor of the Province Beyond the River for King Demetrius I Soter (a son of Seleucus IV) and 'renegade' Jews.

140. Then a group of scribes appeared in a body before Alcimus and Bacchides to ask for just terms. The Hasideans were first among the Israelites to seek peace from them. For they said, 'A priest of the line of Aaron has come with the army, and he will not harm us.' Alcimus spoke peaceable words to them and swore this oath to them, 'We will not seek to injure you or your Friends.' So they trusted him; but he seized sixty of them and killed them in one day…
(1 Maccabees 7:12–16a)

2.6. The Hasmonaeans and the Coming of the Romans

By 164 BCE Antiochus was dead. While Syrian forces had been worsted in clashes with Jews under Maccabaean leadership, their power and influence was still potent. The Temple had been re-dedicated and purified in 164, but a Syrian garrison was still present in Jerusalem in the Akra. The struggle for independence from Seleucid control continued in the ensuing years. To some extent Jewish affairs were still managed and controlled by Seleucid power brokers. For their part Jewish leaders still courted the backing of the Seleucids.

After the death of Judas Maccabaeus in 160, the Jews acclaimed Jonathan military leader. In 152 Alexander Balas, son of Antiochus IV, appointed him high priest. For his part Jonathan supported Alexander in his struggle to consolidate the Seleucid throne. In 143 Jonathan was murdered by Syrian agents. He had changed sides on the assurance that his new patron, Demetrius, would guarantee autonomy for Jerusalem. Demetrius had the backing of Rome.

Simon (high priest 143–134), another Maccabaean brother, was appointed by popular acclamation at the time of an emergency sparked by the appearance of a large army commanded by the Syrian general Trypho. Simon was confirmed in the position by Demetrius, his Seleucid patron. Independence for Jerusalem did result, thus bringing to fulfilment the objectives of the instigators of the Maccabaean revolt. The Syrian garrison was withdrawn. Significantly, it was anticipated by the people that Simon's descendants would enjoy the high priestly power 'until a trustworthy prophet should arise' (1 Maccabees 14:41). By this means a dynasty of high priests was created and the Hasmonaean line legitimated. Hasmonaean tenure of the high priesthood was a likely cause of the break between the priestly group that formed the nucleus of the Qumran community, which supported the 'Righteous Teacher' in his struggle with the so-called 'Wicked Priest'.

John Hyrcanus (134–104) is mentioned at the conclusion of 1 Maccabees. The book was probably written in his reign as a defence of the Hasmonaean establishment. Hyrcanus was Simon Maccabeus's third son. A new threat to Roman, not to mention Seleucid, interests arose beyond the Euphrates in the form of the Parthians. Hyrcanus was eager to build on the pact of friendship with Rome. In the absence of significant power in Palestine, he also began enlarging his territory. Hyrcanus took the opportunity of destroying the Samaritan temple (128 BCE) and forcibly judaized the hitherto Gentile areas of Galilee and Idumaea in 104 BCE. He captured Samaria in 109 BCE. He also captured the region known as the Decapolis and the east bank of the Jordan. During Hyrcanus's high priesthood, the sources first mention two of the major Jewish groups, namely, the Sadducees and Pharisees.

Aristobulus I (104–103) took the title of king (Josephus, *Antiquities* 13.301). He imprisoned his brothers (except for the next oldest [Antigonus] whom he loved but later murdered out of envy [13.304]), and imprisoned his mother, starving her to death.[36] He was nicknamed 'Philhellene' (*Antiquities* 13.318).[37]

Alexander Jannaeus (103–76) succeeded Aristobulus. He was married to Salome Alexandra, the wife of Aristobulus I. He had been one of the imprisoned brothers of that high priest (*Antiquities* 13.302, 320). He ruled an extensive kingdom, approximating to Solomon's borders. He also took the title 'king' and achieved renown as a warrior king. Jannaeus pursued a fierce campaign against the Pharisees, though he was reconciled to them near his death. Aristobulus II (67–63) was able to depose his older brother Hyrcanus II when Salome, their mother, died.

Jannaeus had appointed Antipater as governor of Idumaea, a region that had only recently been judaized. Antipater, who was an Idumaean, was regarded as a semi-Jew. He backed the deposed Hyrcanus in the struggle for the high priesthood. With Arab help he attacked Jerusalem on Hyrcanus's behalf.

Meanwhile, Rome was facing a crisis with the restive Parthians. The crumbling of Seleucid hegemony in the region made Roman intervention in Jewish affairs more likely. Pompey, who had been given a wide-ranging command in the east ostensibly to deal with the threat of pirates in the Mediterranean, was drawn into Syrian and Judaean politics. Vitally interested in the security of the whole region, Pompey chose to support the claims of Hyrcanus II against his brother Aristobulus, who refused to comply with this decision. Subsequently Pompey marched on Jerusalem and besieged it, capturing the city in 63 BCE. In the midst of the carnage, the curious Pompey penetrated the Most Holy Place beyond the veil in the Temple. He found nothing there. From the point of view of the Jews, Pompey had committed a great sacrilege. There was no looting of the sanctuary (unlike the looting perpetrated by Antiochus IV Epiphanes a century before). Aristobulus was taken to Rome with thousands of his supporters, who, ultimately, swelled the Jewish population there. Aristobulus eventually found his way back to Palestine.

Hyrcanus was re-established as high priest, and as 'ethnarch' (not 'king') of the Jews. He served as high priest from 63–40. Aristobulus and his sons continued to make trouble in Judaea over the next 25 years. Rome now imposed tribute on Judaea, which was incorporated into the new Roman province of Syria with its administrative base at Antioch (the old Seleucid capital). Pompey redrew the map of Palestine. The Decapolis, ten Greek cities east of the Jordan, was separated from Hasmonaean control and their Greek populations restored. Samaria was also made independent of control from Jerusalem. While one cannot yet speak of direct Roman rule of Israel, the settlement engineered by Pompey constituted the first step. Rome was attempting a political settlement that allowed for protection of its own interests while leaving the task of political management to trusted clients, in this case, Hyrcanus II. In the meantime the gifted Antipater and his sons Phasael and Herod took every opportunity to impress the Romans with their willingness to cooperate with and further Roman interests in Judaea. In this way Judaea was placed under the control of the Roman legate in Antioch.

There had been some contact between the Jews and Rome before the time of Pompey. In 161, after the end of the Maccabaean Revolt, Judas Maccabaeus had concluded a pact of friendship with Rome (see #137–38). The treaty was renewed under Simon (see 1 Maccabees 14:25–49), allegedly based on a precedent going back to the embassy of John the father of Eupolemus (2 Maccabees 4:11), to a time before the Maccabaean revolt. Rome also proclaimed protection of Jewish populations in 20 Greek cities of the Empire.

In 55 BCE Julius Caesar appointed Antipater as 'procurator' of Judaea. Hyrcanus was also able to elicit significant protection for diaspora Jews from Caesar, namely, exemption from serving in the army (since marching on the Sabbath and worship of military standards compromised a Jewish life commitment). Caesar also granted some tax concessions to the Jews. In 44, a month before his assassination, Caesar agreed to allow the rebuilding the walls of Jerusalem. Antipater was poisoned in 43.[38]

Sources

After the death of Jonathan Maccabaeus in 143 BCE, Simon Maccabaeus declared his preparedness to complete the objectives of the Maccabaean Revolt. The people responded by acclaiming him high priest in his brother's stead.

141. 'You yourselves know what great things my brothers and I and the house of my father have done for the laws and the sanctuary; you know also the wars and the difficulties that my brothers and I have seen. By reason of this all my brothers have perished for the sake of Israel, and I alone am left. And now, far be it from me to spare my life in any time of distress, for I am not better than my brothers. But I will avenge my nation and the sanctuary and your wives and children, for all the nations have gathered together out of hatred to destroy us.'

The spirit of the people was rekindled when they heard these words, and they answered in a loud voice, 'You are our leader in place of Judas and your brother Jonathan. Fight our battles, and all that you say to us we will do'. So he [Simon] assembled all the warriors and hurried to complete the walls of Jerusalem, and he fortified it on every side. He sent Jonathan son of Absalom to Joppa, and with him a considerable army; he drove out its inhabitants and remained there.
(1 Maccabees 13:3–11)

Simon presided over the surrender of the citadel into Hasmonaean hands (see 1 Maccabees 13:49–51). The capture marked the beginning of independence for Judaea. The following poem reflects on the return to plenty and peace (cf. Micah 4:4).

142. The land had rest all the days of Simon.
He sought the good of his nation;
his rule was pleasing to them,
as was the honour shown him, all his days.
To crown all his honours he took Joppa for a harbor,
and opened a way to the isles of the sea.
He extended the borders of his nation,
and gained full control of the country.
He gathered a host of captives;
he ruled over Gazara and Beth-zur and the citadel,
and he removed its uncleanness from it;
and there was none to oppose him.
They tilled their land in peace;
the ground gave its increase,
and the trees of the plains their fruit.
Old men sat in the streets;
they all talked together of good things,
and the youths put on splendid military attire.
He supplied the towns with food,
and furnished them with the means of defense,
until his renown spread to the ends of the earth.
He established peace in the land,
and Israel rejoiced with great joy.
All the people sat under their own vines and fig trees,
and there was none to make them afraid.
No one else was left in the land to fight them,
and the kings were crushed in those days.
He gave help to all the humble among his people;
he sought out the law, and did away with all the renegades and outlaws.
He made the sanctuary glorious,
and added to the vessels of the sanctuary.
(1 Maccabees 14:4–15)

The solemn proclamation of Simon's great deeds.

143. 'The Jews and their priests have resolved that Simon should be their leader and high

priest forever, until a trustworthy prophet should arise, and that he should be governor over them and that he should take charge of the sanctuary and appoint officials over its tasks and over the country and the weapons and the strongholds, and that he should take charge of the sanctuary, and that he should be obeyed by all, and that all contracts in the country should be written in his name, and that he should be clothed in purple and wear gold.'
(1 Maccabees 14:41–43)

Hyrcanus and the Pharisees.

During Hyrcanus's high priesthood the sources first mention two of the major Jewish groups, namely, the Sadducees and Pharisees. The latter had earned John's wrath because he came to believe that they agreed with the view of one of them, Eleazar, that he was illegitimate (see further *Antiquities* 13.293–95 and the machinations of Jonathan, a Sadducee).

144. As for Hyrcanus, the envy of the Jews was aroused against him by his own successes and those of this sons; particularly hostile to him were the Pharisees, who are one of the Jewish schools, as we have related above [*Antiquities* 13.171–73]. And so great is their influence with the masses that even when they speak against a king or high priest, they immediately gain credence. Hyrcanus too was a disciple of theirs, and was greatly loved by them. And once he invited them to a feast and entertained them hospitably, and when he saw that they were having a very good time, he began by saying that they knew he wished to be righteous and in everything he tried to please God and them—for the Pharisees profess such beliefs; at the same time he begged them, if they observed him doing anything wrong or straying from the right path, to lead him back to it and correct him. But they testified to his being altogether virtuous, and he was delighted with their praise. However, one of the guests, named Eleazar, who had an evil nature and took pleasure in dissension, said, 'Since you have asked to be told the truth, if you wish to be righteous, give up the high-priesthood and be content with governing the people'. And when Hyrcanus asked him for what reason he should give up the high-priesthood, he replied, 'Because we have heard from our elders that your mother was a captive in the reign of Antiochus Epiphanes.' But the story was false, and Hyrcanus was furious with the man, while all the Pharisees were very indignant.
(Josephus, *Antiquities* 13.288–92)[39]

Alexander Jannaeus ruled an extensive kingdom. He took the title 'king' and achieved renown as a warrior. Jannaeus was at war with the Seleucid Demetrius III Eukairos, and had been worsted in a previous battle. However, Jannaeus emerged victorious in the struggle. He took fearful revenge on those Jews who had supported Demetrius.

145. Alexander thereupon fled to the mountains, where out of pity for him at this reverse six thousand Jews gathered to his side. And at this Demetrius withdrew in alarm. But later on the Jews fought against Alexander and were defeated, many of them dying in battle. The most powerful of them, however, he shut up and besieged in the city of Bethoma, and after taking the city and getting them into his power, he brought them back to Jerusalem; and there he did a thing that was as cruel as could be: while he feasted with his concubines in a conspicuous place, he ordered some eight hundred of the Jews to be crucified, and slaughtered their children and wives before the eyes of the still living wretches. This was the revenge he took for the injuries he has suffered; but the penalty he exacted was inhuman for all that, even though he had, as was natural, gone through very great hardships in the wars he had fought against them, and had finally found himself in danger of losing both his life and his throne…
(Josephus, *Antiquities* 13.379–81)[40]

A perspective on the moral bankruptcy of the Hasmonaean dynasty.

146. Their wealth was extended to the whole earth,
and their glory to the end of the earth.
They exalted themselves to the stars,
they said they would never fall.
They were arrogant in their possessions,
and they did not acknowledge (God).

Their sins were in secret, and even I did not
know.
Their lawless actions surpassed the gentiles
before them;
they completely profaned the sanctuary of
the Lord.
(*Psalms of Solomon* 1:4–8)

Pompey's command in the east, ostensibly bestowed for action against the pirates, extended to bringing the war against Mithridates to a close and to his settling the Armenian and Syrian situations. The dissension between competing parties within Judaea brought decisive action on Pompey's part.

Pompey captures Jerusalem.

147. (69) Now when the siege-engine was brought up, the largest of the towers was shaken and fell, making a breach through which the enemy poured in; first among them was Cornelius Faustus, the son of Sulla, who with his soldiers mounted the wall, and after him the centurion Furius, with those who followed him, on the other side, and between them Fabius, another centurion, with a strong and compact body of men. And there was slaughter everywhere. For some of the Jews were slain by the Romans, and others by their fellows; and there were some who hurled themselves down the precipices, and setting fire to their houses, burned themselves within them, for they could not bear to accept their fate. And so of the Jews there fell some twelve thousand, but of the Romans only very few. One of those taken captive was Absalom, the uncle and at the same time father-in-law of Aristobulus. And not light was the sin committed against the sanctuary, which before that time had never been entered or seen. For Pompey and not a few of his men went into it and saw what it was unlawful for any but the high priests to see. But though the golden table was there and the sacred lampstand and the libation vessels and a great quantity of spices, and beside these, in the treasury, the sacred moneys amounting to two thousand talents, he touched none of these because of piety, and in this respect also he acted in a manner worthy of his virtuous character. And on the morrow he instructed the temple servants to cleanse the temple and to offer the customary sacrifice to God, and he restored the high priesthood to Hyrcanus because in various ways he had been useful to him and particularly because he had prevented the Jews throughout the country from fighting on Aristobulus' side; and those responsible for the war he executed by beheading. He also bestowed on Faustus and the others who had mounted the wall with alacrity fitting rewards for their bravery. And he made Jerusalem tributary to the Romans, and took from its inhabitants the cities of Coele-Syria which they had formerly subdued, and placed them under his own governor; and the entire nation, which before had raised itself so high, he confined within its own borders...

(77) For this misfortune which befell Jerusalem Hyrcanus and Aristobulus were responsible, because of their dissension. For we lost our freedom and became subject to the Romans, and the territory which we had gained by our arms and taken from the Syrians we were compelled to give back to them, and in addition the Romans exacted of us in a short space of time more than ten thousand talents; and the royal power which had formerly been bestowed on those who were high priests by birth became the privilege of commoners... Now Pompey gave over to Scaurus Coele-Syria and the rest of Syria, as far as the Euphrates river and Egypt, and two Roman legions, and then went off to Cilicia, making haste to reach Rome. And with him he took Aristobulus in chains, together with his family; for he had two daughters and as many sons; but one of them, Alexander, got away, while the younger son, Antigonus, was carried off to Rome together with his sisters.
(Josephus, *Antiquities* 14.69–75, 77–79)[41]

The assassination of Pompey was interpreted by the writer of the late first-century BCE *Psalms of Solomon* as evidence of the exercise of God's justice (see 2:22–37). The hand of that justice was also perceived in Pompey's incursion of 63 BCE.

148. Arrogantly the sinner broke down the
strong walls with a battering ram and
you did not interfere.
Gentile foreigners went up to your place of
sacrifice;

they arrogantly trampled (it) with their sandals.
Because the sons of Jerusalem defiled the sanctuary of the Lord,
they were profaning the offerings of God with lawless acts;
Because of these things he said, 'Remove them far from me;
they are not sweet-smelling.'
The beauty of his glory was despised before God;
it was completely disgraced.
The sons and the daughters (were) in harsh captivity,
their neck in a seal, a spectacle among the gentiles.
He did (this) to them according to their sins,
so that he abandoned them to the hands of those who prevailed.
For he turned away his face from their mercy;
(from) young and old and their children once again,
for they sinned once again by not listening.
And the heavens were weighed down,
and the earth despised them,
for no one on (the earth) had done what they did.
And the earth shall know all your righteous judgments, O God.
(*Psalms of Solomon* 2:1–10)

The rise of Antipater.

During Mithridates's campaign in Egypt at the end of the civil war between Pompey and Julius Caesar, Antipater, who had previously been loyal to the now dead Pompey, led troops loyal to Julius Caesar in a decisive victory over the Mithridates.

149. The praise bestowed by Caesar at the time on the hero of the day and the hopes which it excited spurred Antipater to further ventures in his service. Showing himself on all occasions the most daring of fighters, and constantly wounded, he bore the marks of his valour on almost every part of his person. Later, when Caesar had settled affairs in Egypt and returned to Syria, he conferred on Antipater the privilege of Roman citizenship with exemption from taxes, and by other honours and marks of friendship made him an enviable man. It was to please him that Caesar confirmed the appointment of Hyrcanus to the office of high-priest. (Josephus, *Jewish War* 1.193–94)

Caesar and the Jews.

Antigonus, the son of Aristobulus, the high priest deposed by Pompey in 63 BCE, now accused Antipater and Hyrcanus before Caesar. However, Antipater's war service proved crucial in the debate, and resulted in his further promotion.

150. After hearing both speakers [Antigonus and Antipater], Caesar pronounced Hyrcanus to be the more deserving claimant to the high-priesthood, and left Antipater free choice of office. The latter, replying that it rested with him who conferred the honour to fix the measure of the honour, was then appointed viceroy of all Judaea. He was further authorized to rebuild the ruined walls of the metropolis. Orders were sent by Caesar to Rome for these honours to be graven in the Capitol, as a memorial of his own justice and of Antipater's valour. (Josephus, *Jewish War* 1.199–200)[42]

Jews mourn the death of Caesar.

151. At the height of the public grief a throng of foreigners went about lamenting each after the fashion of his country, above all the Jews, who even flocked to the place for several successive nights. (Suetonius, *Julius Caesar* 84.5)

2.7. Herod's Early Career

Herod was born in c. 74 BCE. In 47 Antipater assigned his sons Phasael and Herod the oversight of Judaea and Galilee respectively. Herod proved himself an able, if ruthless, campaigner. He rooted out the bandits infesting areas of the territory (see #152). They had supported the risings of Aristobulus and his sons. Their leader was a certain Hezekiah, whose descendants were to play an important part in the violent resistance to the Roman presence in Palestine in successive generations.

Herod executed Hezekiah and many of his supporters. News of this was greeted with alarm by the Sanhedrin who objected to Herod's pretentious use of summary capital punishment. Herod was increasingly helpful to the cause of furthering Roman interests. In the late 40s, Mark Antony appointed Phasael and Herod tetrarchs of Judaea and Galilee.

The year 40 saw Parthian advances across the Euphrates. Antigonus (son of Aristobulus II) offered them 1000 talents and 500 women to replace Hyrcanus and to eject Phasael and Herod.[43] With Parthian support, Antigonus captured Jerusalem. The brothers found themselves confined to the Baris. Phasael committed suicide rather than fall into enemy hands. Herod managed to escape with his fiancée, Mariamme, and his supporters to Masada. Mariamme was Hyrcanus's granddaughter, and the daughter of Alexander (a son of Aristobulus II's) and Alexandra (Hyrcanus's daughter). Hyrcanus was also captured. Reports say that his ears were cut off (though there is some suggestion that Antigonus bit them off[44]) to disqualify him, as a disfigured person, from holding priestly office. Hyrcanus was taken to Babylon.

By late 40 Herod was in Rome. Antony and Octavian championed and promoted his cause for authority in Palestine. He was decreed 'king' by the Senate. However, he was unable to take control in his kingdom until 37. Rome's probable intention was for Herod to rule Judaea until his death when the province would become fully Roman. However, in 23 Herod was given the considerable privilege of being free to nominate a successor.

Sources

Herod and the bandits.

152. Herod, energetic by nature, at once found material to test his metal. Discovering that Ezekias [Hezekiah], a brigand-chief, at the head of a large horde, was ravaging the district on the Syrian frontier, he caught him and put him and many of the brigands to death [see also *Antiquities* 14.159–60]. This welcome achievement was immensely admired by the Syrians. Up and down the villages and in the towns the praises of Herod were sung, as the restorer of their peace and possessions. This exploit, moreover, brought him to the notice of Sextus Caesar, a kinsman of the great Caesar and governor of Syria. Phasael, on his side, with a generous emulation, vied with his brother's reputation; he increased his popularity with the inhabitants of Jerusalem, and kept the city under control without any tactless abuse of authority. Antipater, in consequence, was courted by the nation as if he were king and universally honoured as lord of the realm. Notwithstanding this, his affection for Hyrcanus and his loyalty to him underwent no charge.
(Josephus, *Jewish War* 1.204–207)

In 40 the Roman Labienus deserted to the Parthians. This event had significant ramifications for Judaea.

153. The manner of Labienus' coming among the Parthians, and what he did in conjunction with Pacorus, was as follows. He was an ally of Brutus and Cassius, having before the battle [of Philippi] been sent to Orodes [King of Parthia] to secure some reinforcements, was detained by him a long time while the king was waiting the turn of events and hesitating to join forces with him, yet fearing to refuse. Later, when the news of the defeat reached him, and it appeared to be the intention of the victors to spare none who had resisted them, Labienus remained among the barbarians, choosing to live with them rather than to perish at home. Now as soon as Labienus was aware of Antony's demoralization, of his passion [for Cleopatra], and of his departure for Egypt, he persuaded the Parthian king to make an attack upon the Romans. For he declared their armies were either destroyed utterly or impaired, while the remainder of the troops were in a state of mutiny and would again be at war; and he accordingly advised the king to subjugate Syria and the adjoining districts, while Caesar was busy in Italy with Sextus and Antony was indulging his passion in Egypt.
(Dio Cassius, *Roman History* 48.24.4–7)[45]

Gaius Sosius was appointed the Governor of Syria in 38 BCE. He set about restoring Roman control over the province. Incidentally, Dio Cassius's remarks in the extract below about the Jews reveal considerable anti-Jewish sentiment.

154. This officer [Gaius Sosius] subdued the Aradii, who had been besieged up to this time and had been reduced to hard straits by famine and disease, and also captured in battle Antigonus, who had put to death the Roman guards that were with him, and reduced him by siege when he took refuge in Jerusalem. The Jews, indeed, had done much injury to the Romans, for the race is very bitter when aroused to anger, but they suffered far more themselves. The first of them to be captured were those who were fighting for the precinct of their god, and then the rest on the day even then called the day of Saturn. And so excessive were they in their devotion to religion that the first set of prisoners, those who had been captured along with the temple, obtained leave from Sosius, when the day of Saturn came around again, and went up into the temple and there performed all the customary rites, together with the rest of the people. These people Antony entrusted to a certain Herod to govern; but Antigonus he bound to a cross and flogged,—a punishment no other king had suffered at the hands of the Romans,—and afterwards slew him.
(Dio Cassius, *Roman History* 49.22.3–6)

The Roman Senate decrees Herod 'king'.

155. Antony was moved with compassion at his reversal of fortune; and influenced by the recollection of Antipater's hospitality, but above all by the heroic qualities of the man in front of him, determined then and there to make him king of the Jews whom he had himself previously appointed tetrarch. Besides admiration for Herod, he had as strong an incentive in the aversion for Antigonus, whom he regarded as a promoter of sedition and an enemy of Rome. Caesar [Octavian] proved a yet more ready champion than Antony, as his memory recalled the part which Antipater had borne with his own father in the Egyptian campaigns, his hospitality and invariable loyalty, while his eyes rested on Herod and read his enterprising character. So he convened the Senate, to which Messala, seconded by Atratinus, presented Herod and dwelt on the services rendered by his father and his own goodwill towards the Roman people; demonstrating at the same time that Antigonus was their enemy, not only from the earlier quarrel which they had had with him, but because he had also just been guilty of contempt of Rome in accepting his crown from Parthian hands. These words stirred the Senate, and when Antony came forward and said that with a view to the war with Parthia it was expedient that Herod should be king, the proposal was carried unanimously. The meeting was dissolved and Antony and Caesar left the senate-house with Herod between them, preceded by the consuls and the other magistrates, as they went to offer sacrifice and to lay up the decree in the Capitol. On this, the first day of his reign, Herod was given a banquet by Antony.
(Josephus, *Jewish War* 1.282–85)

2.8. Palestine under Herod the Great and Archelaus (37 BCE–6 CE)

The Romans prosecuted the war against the Parthians, and were able to help Herod in his struggle with Antigonus. Sosius captured Jerusalem. Fortunately, Herod was able to restrain the Roman troops from looting the temple (see Josephus, *Antiquities* 14.482–86). The troublesome Antigonus was captured and executed. The last male Hasmonaeans were now the aged Hyrcanus, who was brought back from Babylon, and the 16-year-old Aristobulus III (Mariamme's brother and Herod's brother-in-law). The now mutilated Hyrcanus had been rendered unfit for high priestly office. Herod was unwilling to promote the popular Aristobulus III. Herod summoned Hananel, a priest living in Babylon, to be his first high priest. However he was soon replaced by Aristobulus. His mother was a friend of Cleopatra of Egypt. Herod did not dare risk offending her. Cleopatra longed to extend her borders to their Ptolemaic limit. This would mean reducing Herod's territory and asserting control over Judaean affairs. Enthusiasm greeted Aristobulus as he officiated at the Feast of Tabernacles in 36. This was too much for Herod, who took a political risk and had the boy drowned.

The war between Octavian and Antony culminated in the naval battle of Actium in 31 BCE at which Octavian was victorious. However, Herod had supported the vanquished. To forestall the chance of being replaced by Hyrcanus, Herod had him executed on a charge of treason. Octavian was wise enough to perceive in Herod a loyal servant. In 27 BCE Augustus gave Herod a number of Greek cities on the coast of Palestine and in Gaulinitis (Golan Heights) in the interior. This was a sparsely populated area. Herod established new cities there. He also founded Sebaste and Caesarea.

By 37 Herod had married Mariamme. It was a tumultuous match. In 29 BCE Herod had Mariamme executed.[46] He was increasingly unable to manage his household, and became even more cruel and suspicious. The sons of Herod and Mariamme were Alexander and Aristobulus. Both were regarded by the people as Hasmonaeans. Both had been educated in Rome. Herod regarded them as his heirs. Reports of intrigues, both real and imagined, were fed by Herod's eldest son, Antipater. Grimly, Herod ordered both sons strangled in 7 BCE. Antipater himself was executed a few days before Herod died in 4.

In 5 BCE Herod set up a huge gilt eagle over the gate to the Temple. This aroused opposition on the basis of the second commandment, which prohibits the making of images (Exodus 20:4; Deuteronomy 5:8). Spurred on by the news that Herod was dying, some rabbis hacked the eagle down. Herod took fearful revenge. He burnt the chief perpetrators alive. On his death bed Herod ordered the internment of a large number of Jews in the hippodrome at Jericho. He issued orders that on his death they too were to be put to death so that grief, not joy, would greet the news of his own death.

Herod was what one might call a hellenized Jew. He lavished money on gymnasia, theatres, hippodromes, public lavatories, temples, wild beast shows, and athletics. He sponsored the Olympic Games in 9 BCE (see *War* 1.426–27). He bestowed benefactions on Greek cities with sizable Jewish populations. He frequently visited Antioch, and paved the two mile-long main street with marble. But no benefactions were bestowed on Alexandria (*Antiquities* 15.267–76), Cleopatra's capital. He was careful, however, not to antagonize the religious sensibilities of his Jewish subjects.[47]

Herod was a great builder. His greatest monument in this regard was Caesarea, a city complete with statues of Roma (Rome) and Augustus.[48] He also built Sebaste as well as impressive fortresses throughout his territory, namely, Masada, Machaerus and Herodium. He also enhanced the patriarchal sites of Hebron and Mamre. Jerusalem was also beautified by Herod. Chief among his considerable architectural enterprises was the rebuilding of the Temple. The work was begun in 23/22 BCE. Work on the site was only finished as war was breaking out in 66 CE.

On Herod's death in 4 BCE, the kingdom was divided by the emperor Augustus (acting with the Senate), Herod's nominated executor, into four segments called tetrarchies ('fourths'). Archelaus became 'ethnarch', an honorary title meaning 'ruler of a nation', of Judaea. Antipas became tetrarch of Galilee and Perea. Philip became tetrarch of the northern districts of Trachonitus and Ituraea. As ethnarch Archelaus had no jurisdiction over his brothers, but the title he enjoyed anticipated the possibility of his becoming 'king' of the Jews, as Herod had himself envisaged in his will, with precedence over his brothers.

Hopes were expressed that Archelaus would be a milder ruler than his father. However, even before he had left for Rome to have his father's will ratified he had caused the bloodshed of several thousands in Jerusalem during Passover. At the time of the sacrifices, he sent his troops into the Temple to quell demonstrations during the mourning of those killed in the aftermath of the eagle affair in the last days of Herod's rule. This brutal beginning (cf. Matthew 2:22) did not augur well for his chances of securing Roman favour. The incident was used against him in 6 CE when the Romans chose to remove him and to impose direct Roman rule on Judaea.

In 4 BCE some Jews made representations to the Emperor to have the Herods removed in favour of direct Roman rule. When Archelaus left Palestine for Rome to defend the terms of his father's will, Varus, the Roman legate in Syria, was required to put down civil unrest in Judaea and Galilee. Two thousand bandits were crucified, including the son of the bandit chief Hezekiah whom Herod had executed in 46.

By 6 CE it was clear that Judaea could not be governed effectively by Archelaus. In sympathy with Judaean Jews, 8000 Jews gathered in the precincts of Apollo on the Palatine in Rome to demonstrate against Archelaus. He was summoned to Rome and banished to Vienne in Gaul.[49] Judaea (but not Galilee) became a Roman province governed by equestrian prefects under the supervision of the Roman legate in Syria stationed at Antioch with legionary troops.

Sources

Herod's domestic turmoil.

156. Herod had five children by Mariamme, two daughters and three sons. The youngest son died in the course of his training in Rome; to the two elder sons [Alexander and Aristobulus] he gave a princely education, both out of respect for their mother's illustrious parentage, and because they had been born after his accession to the throne. But a still stronger influence in their favour was Herod's passion for Mariamme, the consuming ardour of which increased from day to day, so that he was insensible to the troubles of which his beloved one was the cause; for Mariamme's hatred of him was as great as was his love for her. As the events of the past gave her just reason for aversion, and her husband's love enabled her to speak plainly, she openly upbraided him with the fate of her grandfather Hyrcanus [the former high priest Hyrcanus II] and her brother Jonathan [Aristobulus III]. For Herod had not spared even this poor lad; he had bestowed upon him in his seventeenth year the office of high-priest, and then immediately after conferring this honour had put him to death, because, on the occasion of a festival, when the lad approached the altar, clad in the priestly vestments, the multitude with one accord burst into tears. He was, consequently, sent by night to Jericho, and there, in accordance with instructions, plunged into a swimming-bath by the Gauls and drowned.
(Josephus, *Jewish War* 1.435–37)

Josephus describes Herod's founding of several cities, including Sebaste.

157. When, therefore, the city had been made safe for him by the palace in which he lived, and the temple by the strong fortress called Antonia, which had been built by him, he thought of making a third rampart against the entire nation out of Samaria, which he called Sebaste, for he believed that this place would give him no less security against the country (than the others), since it was only a day's journey from Jerusalem and would be equally useful for controlling affairs in the city and in the country. And he built a fortress for the entire nation in the place formerly called Straton's Tower but by him named Caesarea. And in the Great Plain he founded a site for some of his picked cavalrymen, to whom he gave allotments, (namely) the place called Gaba in Galilee, and in Peraea (he rebuilt) Esebonitis. These several measures for security he kept thinking up from time to time, and he placed garrisons throughout the entire nation so as to minimize the chance of their taking things into their own hands and plunging into disturbances such as they continually made when the slightest incitement was given, and to keep them from starting any trouble without his learning of it through some of his men who were stationed near them at all times and thus could discover and prevent it. And at this time, being eager to fortify

Samaria, he arranged to have settled in it many of those who had fought as his allies in war and many of the neighbouring populations. This he did because of his ambition to erect it as a new (city) by his own action, for hitherto it had not been among the famous cities, and even more because he made his ambitious scheme a source of security to himself. He also changed the city's name, calling it Sebaste, and apportioned the near-by territory, which was the best in the country, among its inhabitants in order that they might find prosperity so soon as they came together to live there. He surrounded the city with a strong wall, using the steep slope of the place as a means of strengthening it. And he enclosed an area that was not of the same size as that of the former city but did not fall short of that of the most renowned cities, for it was twenty stades (in circumference). Within it, at its centre, he consecrated a precinct of one and a half stades (in circumference), which was adorned in a variety of ways, and in it he erected a temple which in size and beauty was among the most renowned. The various parts of the city he also adorned in a variety of ways, and seeing the necessity of security, he made it a first-class fortress by strengthening its outer walls. He also made it splendid in order to leave to posterity a monument of the humanity that arose from his love of beauty.
(Josephus, *Antiquities* 15.292–98)[50]

The New Testament witness to the megalomania of Herod.

158. (1) In the time of King Herod, after Jesus was born in Bethlehem of Judea, wise men from the East came to Jerusalem, asking, 'Where is the child who has been born king of the Jews? For we observed his star at its rising, and have come to pay him homage.' When King Herod heard this, he was frightened, and all Jerusalem with him; and calling together all the chief priests and scribes of the people, he inquired of them where the Messiah was to be born.

(12) And having been warned in a dream not to return to Herod, they left for their own country by another road.

Now after they [the wise men] had left, an angel of the Lord appeared to Joseph in a dream and said, 'Get up, take the child and his mother, and flee to Egypt, and remain there until I tell you; for Herod is about to search for the child, to destroy him.' Then Joseph got up, took the child and his mother by night, and went to Egypt, and remained there until the death of Herod.

(16) When Herod saw that he had been tricked by the wise men, he was infuriated, and sent and killed all the children in and around Bethlehem who were two years old or under, according to the time that he had learned from the wise men.
(Matthew 2:1–4, 12–15a, 16)

Trouble in Judaea in 4 BCE.

Josephus describes the bloodshed at Passover in 4 BCE. He begins by noting the demonstration in the Temple in support of the two rabbis who had been executed by Herod for cutting down the golden eagle erected by him over its great gate.

159. The promoters of the mourning for the doctors stood in a body in the temple, procuring recruits for their faction. This alarmed Archelaus, who, wishing to prevent the contagion from spreading to the whole crowd, sent in a tribune in command of a cohort, with orders to restrain by force the ringleaders of the sedition. Indignant at the appearance of the troops, the whole crowd pelted them with stones; most of the cohort were killed, while their commander was wounded and escaped with difficulty. Then, as if nothing serious had happened, the rioters returned to their sacrifices. Archelaus, however, now felt that it would be impossible to restrain the mob without bloodshed, and let loose upon them his entire army, the infantry advancing in close order through the city, the cavalry by way of the plain. The soldiers falling unexpectedly upon the various parties busy with their sacrifices slew about three thousand of them and dispersed the remainder among the neighbouring hills. The heralds of Archelaus followed and ordered everyone to return home; so they all abandoned the festival and departed.
(Josephus, *Jewish War* 2.10–13)

Archelaus now left for Rome to defend the terms of his father's will.

Varus, the Syrian legate, marched to Jerusalem to restore order. He left one of his legions in the city to quell the disturbances. These troops under Sabinus were besieged in the palace adjacent to the Temple precincts. The situation deteriorated elsewhere.

160. (55) Meanwhile, the country also, in various districts, was a prey to disorder, and the opportunity induced numbers of persons to aspire to sovereignty. In Idumaea, two thousand of Herod's veterans formed up in arms and took the field against the royal troops. They were opposed by Achiab, the king's cousin, who, avoiding an engagement in the plain, fell back on the strongest positions. At Sepphoris in Galilee Judas, son of Ezechias, the brigand-chief who in former days infested the country and was subdued by King Herod, raised a considerable body of followers, broke open the royal arsenals, and, having armed his companions, attacked the other aspirants to power.

In Peraea Simon, one of the royal slaves, proud of his tall and handsome figure, assumed the diadem. Perambulating the country with the brigands whom he had collected, he burnt down the royal palace at Jericho and many other stately mansions, such incendiarism providing him with an easy opportunity for plunder...

(60) Now, too, a mere shepherd had the temerity to aspire to the throne. He was called Athrongaeus, and his sole recommendations, to raise such hopes, were vigour of body, a soul contemptuous of death, and four brothers resembling himself...

(65) [A]t the period of which we are speaking, these men were making the whole of Judaea one scene of guerrilla warfare.
(Josephus, *Jewish War* 2.55–57, 60, 65)[51]

The banishment of Archelaus.

161. [Herod's] sons were not successful, but became involved in accusations; and one of them [Archelaus] spent the rest of his life in exile, having taken up his abode among the Allobrogian Gauls, whereas the others [Antipas and Philip], by much obsequiousness, but with difficulty, found leave to return home, with a tetrarchy assigned to each.
(Strabo, *Geography* 16.46)

2.9 Roman Rule in Judaea (6–37 CE)

The first period of direct Roman rule in Judaea lasted from 6 CE till 41 at which time Agrippa I, the grandson of Herod the Great, was appointed king. The second period of direct Roman rule lasted from 44–66 during which Roman rule was also imposed on Galilee. The transition to direct rule in 6 CE was marked by a census. This prompted the revolt of Judas the Galilaean, whose action was centred on Judaea. Quirinius, Legate of Syria, conducted the census as a preliminary to taxation.

The governors were drawn from the equestrian class, the second class in the Roman class structure, and appointed by the emperor. The term 'prefect' was given to governors of the equestrian class and was applied to the governors of Judaea till 41 CE. Thereafter the term 'procurator' was used.[52] It was not unusual for the Romans to give responsibility for managing difficult and/or sensitive provinces to men of this rank. Egypt was also governed by an equestrian prefect. The governors of Judaea had 'auxiliary' troops at their disposal. They were commanded by a tribune.[53] Auxiliaries were not Roman citizens, and were recruited from the provinces. The historical record shows that the Romans found the Jews difficult to govern. Josephus's narrative of the period abounds with accounts of banditry and brutal Roman responses to protests and peasant revolts ending in the crucifixions of those captured.

Little is known of the first three Prefects, Coponius, Ambivius and Gratus, who governed successively from 6 to 26 CE. The disturbances of 6 CE engineered by Judas the Galilaean (see #629 and #658) at the time of the full integration of Judaea into the Roman imperial administration appear to have been short-lived.

Much more is known about Pontius Pilate's tenure.[54] Both Josephus, and to a lesser extent Philo,[55] have access to information about him. The New Testament adds its own witness.[56] We meet a somewhat chastened and vacillating Pilate in the passion narratives of the Gospels, especially in the account of the trial of Jesus in Luke and John.[57] Because the Jews lost the right of capital punishment, Jesus had to be put to death by the order of Pilate.[58]

Josephus mentions several incidents that occurred during his office. Early in his rule, he brought his troops from Caesarea, the headquarters of the Roman imperial rule in Judaea, into Jerusalem by night. Each unit of soldiers had military standards which were the focus of worship. The portrait of the emperor was depicted on them, though some standards were aniconic. Pilate, using iconic standards, had them veiled. When the Jews discovered this, there was great anger. Many Jews followed Pilate to Caesarea, where there was a peaceful protest. When confronted by Pilate's troops they declared that they preferred to die than to tolerate the standards. Pilate backed down. He was held in suspicion thereafter. He made a second attempt to bring standards into Jerusalem, this time of the aniconic variety bearing inscriptions rather than a portrait.[59] Again the Jews staged a protest, Pilate again succumbing. He also seized some of the Temple treasure to contribute to the building of an aqueduct. He argued that its provision would enhance Temple ablutions. However, there was a great outcry. At the next festival, Pilate had his soldiers mingle with the crowd of pilgrims with concealed clubs. At the first sign of a demonstration, Pilate ordered the soldiers into action.

At the end of his tenure Pilate sent his troops to break up a Samaritan attempt to assert their independence. They had gathered on Gerizim to secure the tabernacle vessels. They appealed to Syrian legate, Vitellius, who sent Pilate to Tiberius early in 37. Vitellius and his successor Petronius show themselves to be sensitive in their dealings with the Jews. Thereafter, the high priestly vestments were given into the hands of the Jews by Tiberius.

Sources

The census.

There is no evidence of an empire-wide registration such as that reported by Luke below.

162. In those days a decree went out from Emperor Augustus that all the world should be registered. This was the first registration and was taken while Quirinius was governor of Syria. All went to their own towns to be registered.
(Luke 2:1–2)[60]

The governorships of the first three prefects—Coponius and Ambivius (both appointed by Augustus), and Gratus (appointed by Tiberius)—are briefly noted by Josephus.

163. (29) During the administration of Judaea by Coponius, who, as I have said, had been dispatched with Quirinius, an event occurred which I shall now describe. When the Festival of Unleavened Bread, which we call Passover, was going on, the priests were accustomed to throw open the gates of the temple after midnight. This time, when the gates were first opened, some Samaritans, who had secretly entered Jerusalem, began to scatter human bones in the porticoes and throughout the temple. As a result, the priests, although they had previously observed no such custom, excluded everyone from the temple, in addition to taking other measures for the greater protection of the temple. Not long afterwards Coponius returned to Rome. His successor in office was Marcus Ambivulus...

(176) He [Tiberius]... took the precaution of not dispatching governors continually to the subject-peoples who had been brought to ruin by so many thieves; for the governors would harry them utterly like flies. Their natural appetite for plunder would be reinforced by their expectation of being speedily deprived of that pleasure. The record of Tiberius' acts will bear out my account of his humour in such matters. For during the twenty-two years that he was emperor he sent altogether two men, Gratus and Pilate, his successor, to govern the Jewish nation.
(Josephus, *Antiquities* 18.29–31, 176–77)

Pilate and the incident of the iconic standards.

164. Pilate, being sent by Tiberius as procurator to Judaea, introduced into Jerusalem by night and under cover the effigies of Caesar which are called standards. This proceeding, when day broke, aroused immense excitement among the Jews; those on the spot were in consternation, considering their laws to have been trampled under foot, as those laws permit no image to be erected in the city; while the indignation of the townspeople stirred the countryfolk, who flocked together in crowds. Hastening after Pilate to Caesarea, the Jews implored him to remove the standards from Jerusalem and to uphold the laws of their ancestors. When Pilate refused, they fell prostrate around his house and for five whole days and nights remained motionless in that position.

On the ensuing day Pilate took his seat on his tribunal in the great stadium and summoning the multitude, with the apparent intention of answering them, gave the arranged signal to his armed soldiers to surround the Jews. Finding themselves in a ring of troops, three deep, the Jews were struck dumb at this unexpected sight. Pilate, after threatening to cut them down, if they refused to admit Caesar's images, signalled to the soldiers to draw their swords. Thereupon the Jews, as by concerted action, flung themselves in a body on the ground, extended their necks, and exclaimed that they were ready rather to die than to transgress the law. Overcome with astonishment at such intense religious zeal, Pilate gave orders for the immediate removal of the standards from Jerusalem.
(Josephus, *Jewish War* 2.169–74)

The aqueduct incident.

165. On a later occasion he [Pilate] provoked a fresh uproar by expending upon the construction of an aqueduct the sacred treasure known as *Corbonus*; the water was brought from a distance of 400 furlongs. Indignant at this proceeding, the populace formed a ring round the tribunal of Pilate, then on a visit to Jerusalem, and besieged him with angry clamour. He, forseeing the tumult, had interspersed among the crowd a troop of his soldiers, armed but disguised in civilian dress, with orders not to use their swords, but to beat any rioters with cudgels. He now from his tribunal gave the agreed signal. Large numbers of the Jews perished, some from the blows which they received, others trodden to death by their companions in the ensuing flight. Cowed by the fate of the victims, the multitude was reduced to silence.
(Josephus, *Jewish War* 2.175–77)

2.10. Herod Antipas

Antipas was tetrarch of Galilee and Peraea from 4 BCE. This is the 'Herod' who executed John the Baptist (see Mark 6:14–29; Matthew 14:1–12). He is mentioned several times in the Gospels. The Lukan Jesus calls him 'that fox'.[61] The wife of his steward followed Jesus and provided for him out of her means (with other women, see Luke 8:3). At Jesus' arraignment, as recorded in Luke 23, Antipas wanted to see Jesus perform a miracle. Antipas was the founder of the town of Tiberias on the western shore of the Sea of Galilee.

Both the New Testament and Josephus recount the difficulties of Antipas with respect to his marriage to Herodias. Antipas had earlier married the daughter of a neighbouring Arabian ruler. Herodias, who was the daughter of Aristobulus (a son of Herod the Great who had been strangled on his father's orders in 7 BCE), had been married to Herod Philip, Antipas's half-brother. Herodias was Antipas's and Herod Philip's niece. Antipas's Arabian wife returned to her father. Antipas found himself facing a potential threat on his eastern frontier, and was confronted by John the Baptist who, according to the Gospels, kept denouncing the marriage of Antipas and Herodias.[62] Herodias was ambitious for Antipas. She urged him to seek the glorious title 'king' (he is called 'king' in Mark 6:14 since that was the popular term). Her ambition had disastrous results.

Sources

Antipas and the death of John the Baptist.

The Baptist is an important enough figure in early Judaism for Josephus to record his death and his beliefs. Subsequently John became more significant in Christianity than in Judaism. Josephus is narrating Herod Antipas's defeat at the hands of his former father-in-law Aretas in 37 CE.

166. But to some of the Jews the destruction of Herod's army seemed to be divine vengeance, and certainly a just vengeance, for his treatment of John, surnamed the Baptist. For Herod had put him to death, though he was a good man and had exhorted the Jews to lead righteous lives, to practise justice towards their fellows and piety towards God, and so doing to join in baptism. In his view this was a necessary preliminary if baptism was to be acceptable to God. They must not employ it to gain pardon for whatever sins they had committed, but as a consecration of the body implying that the soul was already thoroughly cleansed by right behaviour. When others too joined the crowds about him, because they were aroused to the highest degree by his sermons, Herod became alarmed. Eloquence that had so great an effect on mankind might lead to some form of sedition, for it looked as if they would be guided by John in everything that they did. Herod decided therefore that it would be much better to strike first and be rid of him before his work led to an uprising, than to wait for an upheaval, get involved in a difficult situation and see his mistake. Though John, because of Herod's suspicions, was brought in chains to Machaerus, the stronghold that we have previously mentioned, and there put to death, yet the verdict of the Jews was that the destruction visited upon Herod's army was a vindication of John, since God saw fit to inflict such a blow on Herod.
(Josephus, *Antiquities* 18.116–19)[63]

Antipas heard about the miracles Jesus was doing in Galilee. He concluded that John the Baptist had been raised from the dead.

167. For Herod himself had sent men who arrested John, bound him, and put him in prison on account of Herodias, his brother Philip's wife, because Herod had married her. For John had been telling Herod, 'It is not lawful for you to have your brother's wife.' And Herodias had a grudge against him, and wanted to kill him. But she could not, for Herod feared John, knowing that he was a righteous and holy man, and he protected him. When he heard him, he was greatly perplexed; and yet he liked to listen to him. But an opportunity came when Herod on his birthday gave a banquet for his courtiers and officers and for the leaders of Galilee. When his daughter Herodias came in and danced, she pleased Herod and his guests; and the king said to the girl, 'Ask me for whatever you wish, and I will give it.' And he solemnly swore to her, 'Whatever you ask me, I will give you, even half of my kingdom.' She went out and said to her mother, 'What should I ask for?' She replied, 'The head of John the baptizer.' Immediately she rushed back to the king and requested, 'I want you to give me at once the head of John the Baptist on a platter.' The king was deeply grieved; yet out of regard for his oaths and for the guests, he did not want to refuse her. Immediately the king sent a soldier of the guard with orders to bring John's head. He went and beheaded him in the prison, brought his head on a platter, and gave it to the girl. Then the girl gave it to her mother. When his disciples heard about it, they came and took his body, and laid it in a tomb.
(Mark 6:17–29)

Pilate and Antipas.

Jesus has been arrested and brought before Pilate, who is told that Jesus has been active in Galilee as well as Judaea. The following extract is unique to the Gospel of Luke.

168. When Pilate heard this, he asked whether the man was a Galilean. And when he learned that he was under Herod's jurisdiction, he sent him off to Herod, who was himself in Jerusalem at that time. When Herod saw Jesus, he was very glad, for he had been wanting to see him for a long time, because he had heard about him and was hoping to see him perform some sign. He questioned him at some length, but Jesus gave him no answer. The chief priests and the scribes stood by, vehemently accusing him. Even Herod with his soldiers treated him with contempt and mocked him; then

he put an elegant robe on him, and sent him back to Pilate. That same day Herod and Pilate became friends with each other; before this they had been enemies.
(Luke 23:6–12)

The banishment of Antipas (39 CE).

169. Gaius, on being proclaimed emperor, liberated Agrippa [son of Aristobulus, son of Herod the Great, executed in 7 BCE] and gave him, with the title of king, the tetrarchy of Philip [see Luke 3:1], now deceased. Agrippa's arrival to take possession of his kingdom aroused the envy and ambition of Herod the tetrarch. But it was above all his wife Herodias [Agrippa's sister] who instigated the tetrarch to aspire to a throne; she reproached him for his indolence and told him that it was only his reluctance to set sail and wait upon Caesar which kept him out of promotion. 'Now that he has made a king of Agrippa, a mere commoner,' she said, 'surely he could not hesitate to confer the same title on a tetrarch.' Yielding to these solicitations, Herod presented himself to Gaius, who punished him for his cupidity by banishing him to Spain. For an accuser had followed him in the person of Agrippa, to whose kingdom Gaius annexed his rival's tetrarchy. Herod died in Spain, whither his wife had accompanied him into exile.
(Josephus, *Jewish War* 2.181–83. In *Antiquities* 18.252, Josephus reports that Antipas was banished to Lyons in Gaul)

2.11. Agrippa I and II

Agrippa I was the brother of Herodias. He was born in 10 BCE. He grew up and was educated in Rome. He was a close friend of the later Emperor Caligula and a childhood companion of Caligula's successor, Claudius. After a few years of Roman administration, the territory ruled formerly by Philip, namely, Trachonitus and Ituraea, was given by Caligula to Agrippa I in 37 CE. With the land went the eminent title 'king'.

This elevation of the previously penniless and spendthrift Agrippa, prompted Antipas to go to Rome in 39 seeking to be made king also (#169). Herodias accompanied him. However, Caligula bestowed his territory on Agrippa, who was now declared King of Galilee, and banished Antipas. In 41 CE Caligula was succeeded by Claudius. The Senate now declared Agrippa King of Judaea as well. Direct Roman rule was withdrawn. In a bold experiment, the Romans had restored the kingdom ruled by King Herod to his grandson. In one stroke the Emperor had set Jewish Palestine on course towards a potentially peaceful solution to the problems faced by direct Roman administration. Agrippa was popular with the Jews. His grandmother had been the Hasmonaean princess Mariamme I.

He was instrumental in persuading Caligula not to set up a statue of himself in the Jerusalem Temple, at least momentarily. According to Josephus, after the assassination of Caligula Agrippa convinced Claudius to accept the opportunity of becoming emperor (*Antiquities* 19.236). According to Josephus, Agrippa also persuaded Claudius to guarantee Jewish equal citizenship privileges in ethnically-troubled Alexandria (see *Antiquities* 19.279–85)[64] and to uphold Jewish rights throughout the empire. He executed the apostle James the brother of John (Acts 12:2; #685) and imprisoned Peter. But by 44 Agrippa was dead. Both the book of Acts and Josephus relate the events that led to his death.

With his death Galilee came under direct Roman rule for the first time. Judaea reverted to Roman rule. This was a crushing blow to Jewish political hopes. Agrippa's death was greeted with enthusiasm and delight by the Gentile citizens of Caesarea (see Josephus, *Antiquities* 19.357–58), this despite the fact that, like Herod the Great, he had lavished gifts on Gentile cities with Jewish minorities.

Agrippa II was only 17 when his father died. He was considered too young by the Roman administration to assume the territory of his father. He was given the title 'king', but ruled only an insignificant portion of land northwest of Galilee. He appears in Acts 25–26.[65] Agrippa urged Jewish restraint at the outbreak of the War in 66 CE, reminding the

Jews of the might of Rome. On his death in c. 105 CE his territory was subsumed into the Roman province of Syria.

Sources

The Temple statue affair.

170. Meanwhile, there was civil strife in Alexandria between the Jewish inhabitants and the Greeks. Three delegates were chosen by each of the factions and appeared before Gaius. One of the Alexandrian delegates was Apion, who scurrilously reviled the Jews, asserting, among other things, that they neglected to pay the honours due to the emperor. For while all the subject peoples in the Roman empire had dedicated altars and temples to Gaius and had given him the same attentions in all other respects as they did the gods, these people alone scorned to honour him with statues and to swear by his name. And so Apion spoke many angry words by which he hoped that Gaius would be moved, as might be expected. Philo, who stood at the head of the delegation of the Jews, a man held in the highest honour, brother of Alexander the alabarch and no novice in philosophy, was prepared to proceed with the defence against these accusations. But Gaius cut him short, told him to get out of his way, and, being exceedingly angry, made it clear that he would visit some outrage upon them. Philo, having thus been treated with contumely, left the room, saying to the Jews who accompanied him that they should be of good courage, for Gaius' wrath was a matter of words, but in fact he was now enlisting God against himself.

Indignant at being so slighted by the Jews alone, Gaius dispatched Petronius as his legate to Syria to succeed Vitellius in this office. His orders were to lead a large force into Judaea and, if the Jews consented to receive him, to set up an image of Gaius in the temple of God. If, however, they were obstinate, he was to subdue them by force of arms and so set it up. Petronius took over Syria and hastened to carry out the commands of the emperor. Gathering together as many auxiliaries as possible, he marched at the head of two legions of the Roman army to Ptolemaïs, intending to spend the winter there and towards spring to engage in war without fail. He wrote Gaius what he had in mind to do. The latter commended him for his zeal and bade him abate nothing but wage war vigorously against them if they persisted in disobedience.
(Josephus, *Antiquities* 18.257–62)[66]

The Jews vigorously opposed Petronius, who realized that Caligula's demand would only plunge the whole province into war. Petronius therefore resolved to resist the demand knowing that he risked death. Caligula also changed his mind, in deference to a request from Agrippa at a lavish banquet. However when the emperor ascertained from Petronius that the Jews were resisting his demand he resolved to press ahead with his plan. Providentially, news of his assassination reached Petronius before the letter from the emperor demanding his suicide.

Josephus reports Claudius's empire-wide edict upholding Jewish rights. The issue of Jewish rights is also addressed in topic 8.5 (see especially #608).

171. 'Tiberius Claudius Caesar Augustus Germanicus Pontifex Maximus, of tribunician power, elected consul for the second time, speaks: Kings Agrippa and Herod, my dearest friends, having petitioned me to permit the same privileges to be maintained for the Jews throughout the empire under the Romans as those in Alexandria enjoy, I very gladly consented, not merely in order to please those who petitioned me, but also because in my opinion the Jews deserve to obtain their request on account of their loyalty and friendship to the Romans. In particular, I did so because I hold it right that not even Greek cities should be deprived of these privileges, seeing that they were in fact guaranteed for them in the time of the divine Augustus. It is right, therefore, that the Jews throughout the whole world under our sway should also observe the customs of their fathers without let or hindrance. I enjoin upon them also by these presents to avail themselves of this kindness in a more reasonable spirit, and not to set at nought

the beliefs about the gods held by other peoples but to keep their own laws. It is my will that the ruling bodies of the cities and colonies and municipia in Italy and outside Italy, and the kings and other authorities through their own ambassadors, shall cause this edict of mine to be inscribed, and keep it posted for not less than thirty days in a place where it can plainly be read from the ground.'
(Josephus, *Antiquities* 19.287–91)

Both Josephus and Acts report the death of Agrippa I (#172–73).

172. After the completion of the third year of his reign over the whole of Judaea, Agrippa came to the city of Caesarea, which had previously been called Strato's Tower. Here he celebrated spectacles in honour of Caesar, knowing that these had been instituted as a kind of festival on behalf of Caesar's well-being. For this occasion there were gathered a large number of men who held office or had advanced to some rank in the kingdom. On the second day of the spectacles, clad in a garment woven completely of silver so that its texture was indeed wondrous, he entered the theatre at daybreak. There the silver, illumined by the touch of the first rays of the sun, was wondrously radiant and by its glitter inspired fear and awe in those who gazed intently upon it. Straightway his flatterers raised their voices from various directions—though hardly for his good—addressing him as a god. 'May you be propitious to us,' they added, 'and if we have hitherto feared you as a man, yet henceforth we agree that you are more than mortal in your being.' The king did not rebuke them nor did he reject their flattery as impious. But shortly thereafter he looked up and saw an owl perched on a rope over his head. At once, recognizing this as a harbinger of woes, just as it had once been of good tidings [*Antiquities* 18.200], he felt a stab of pain in his heart. He was also gripped in his stomach by an ache that he felt everywhere at once and that was intense from the start. Leaping up he said to his friends: 'I, a god in your eyes, am now bidden to lay down my life, for fate brings immediate refutation of the lying words lately addressed to me. I, who was called immortal by you, am now under sentence of death. But I must accept my lot as God wills it. In fact I have lived in no ordinary fashion but in the grand style that is hailed as true bliss.' Even as he was speaking these words, he was overcome by more intense pain. They hastened, therefore, to convey him to the palace; and the word flashed about to everyone that he was on the very verge of death. Straightway the populace, including the women and children, sat in sackcloth in accordance with their ancestral custom and made entreaty to God on behalf of the king. The sound of wailing and lamentations prevailed everywhere. The king, as he lay in his lofty bedchamber and looked down on the people as they fell prostate, was not dry-eyed himself. Exhausted after five straight days by the pain in his abdomen, he departed this life in the fifty-fourth of his life and the seventh of his reign.
(Josephus, *Antiquities* 19.343–50)

173. Now Herod was angry with the people of Tyre and Sidon. So they came to him in a body; and after winning over Blastus, the king's chamberlain, they asked for a reconciliation, because their country depended on the king's country for food. On an appointed day Herod put on his royal robes, took his seat on the platform, and delivered a public address to them. The people kept shouting, 'The voice of a god, and not of a mortal!' And immediately, because he had not given the glory to God, an angel of the Lord struck him down, and he was eaten by worms and died.
(Acts 12:20–23)

Agrippa II (#174–75).

The following two extracts are from Agrippa's speech in Jerusalem in 66 after the massacre of the cohorts. Having listed the nations which have submitted to the Romans, Agrippa appeals to the Jews in the following terms.

174. 'What are the troops, what is the armour, on which you rely? Where is your fleet to sweep the Roman seas? Where is your treasury to meet the cost of your campaigns? Do you really suppose that you are going to war

with Egyptians or Arabs? Will you shut your eyes to the might of the Roman empire and refuse to take the measure of your own weakness? Have not our forces been constantly defeated even by the neighbouring nations, while theirs have never met with a reverse throughout the whole known world? Nay, even that world has not sufficed for their ambition. For, not content with having for their frontiers on the east the Euphrates, on the north the Ister [the Danube], on the south Libya explored into desert regions, on the west Gades, they have sought a new world beyond the ocean and carried their arms as far as the Britons, previously unknown to history. I ask you, then, are you wealthier than the Gauls, stronger than the Germans, more intelligent than the Greeks, more numerous than all the peoples of the world? What is it which inspires you with confidence to defy the Romans?'
(Josephus, *Jewish War* 2.361–64)

175. 'The only refuge, then, left to you is divine assistance. But even this is ranged on the side of the Romans, for, without God's aid, so vast an empire could never have been built up. Consider, too, the difficulty of preserving your religious rules from contamination, even were you engaging a less formidable foe; and how, if compelled to transgress the very principles on which you chiefly build your hopes of God's assistance, you will alienate Him from you. If you observe your sabbath customs and refuse to take any action on that day, you will undoubtedly be easily defeated, as were your forefathers by Pompey, who pressed the siege most vigorously on the days when the besieged remained inactive; if, on the contrary, you transgress the law of your ancestors, I fail to see what further object you will have for hostilities, since your one aim is to preserve inviolate all the institutions of your fathers. How could you invoke the aid of the Deity, after deliberately omitting to pay Him the service which you owe Him?'
(Josephus, *Jewish War* 2.390–94)

The Jews banished Agrippa from the city.

2.12. Judaea and Galilee (44–66 CE)

E. Mary Smallwood observes that the period 44–66 is 'largely the story of the progressive breakdown of law and order throughout the province'.[67] The period witnessed the slide into anarchy which eventually overwhelmed the province in 66. There was trouble with bandits throughout this time.

During the procuratorship of Fadus (44–46) there was no major upheaval in Galilee and Judaea when direct Roman rule was reimposed. However, a certain Theudas, whom Josephus calls a false prophet, did mount a demonstration—the first of its kind.[68] Josephus tells us that he led some thousands to the Jordan in the expectation that it would divide. The subsequent Roman massacre was unnecessary. According to Josephus, Fadus rid Judaea of bandits. They soon returned. The mid 40s saw difficult economic times; a famine during the middle of the decade (see Acts 11:27–30) would have only fuelled banditry.

The next procurator was Tiberius Alexander, a nephew of the Alexandrian Jewish philosopher and apologist, Philo. He executed the bandit sons of Judas the Galilaean, who had been active in 6 CE. Alexander had a very distinguished later career. He was Prefect of Egypt in 66 CE and later Praetorian prefect.[69] His father had paid for the gilding of the doors of the Temple.

During the procuratorship of Cumanus (48–52) there were two serious confrontations between the Roman authorities and the Jewish population. During Passover, a soldier (a Greek from Judaea) exposed himself to the crowd from the battlements. Stone-throwing greeted this outrage. Many died in the resulting melee.[70] An imperial slave was attacked about 12 miles north of the city by bandits. Cumanus sent in the troops. The villages in the vicinity suspected of harbouring the bandits were put to the sword. A soldier extricated a Torah scroll from a burning synagogue. In full view of the Jews, he tore it in half and threw it on the fire. Cumanus had the offending soldier beheaded.

Finally, Cumanus failed to intervene in a dispute between Samaritans and Galilaeans. The former had killed a number of Galilaeans on their way to a feast. Cumanus had accepted a bribe not to take action. The Jerusalem mob took vengeance. Once again the procurator sent in his troops. Finally the Syrian legate was called in. He deposed Cumanus and found against the Samaritans. Two high priests and some Samaritan prisoners were sent to Rome. Josephus observes that at this time the land was infested with brigands.

Felix (52–59), the next procurator, was a freedman.[71] He appears in the book of Acts.[72] There was a great increase in banditry during his procuratorship. Many were sent in chains to Rome. Moreover, the *sicarii* ('daggermen') made their first appearance in Jerusalem. They assassinated Jonathan (a former high priest) who had urged Claudius to nominate Felix as procurator (see #659). Josephus also charts the appearance of more false prophets, whom he also calls 'charlatans' (*goai*). One of these, at the head of several thousand followers (called 'assassins' in Acts and Josephus), occupied the Mount of Olives awaiting the collapse of the walls of Jerusalem.

Felix's comparatively long period in office saw a dramatic worsening of an already tense situation. Finally, there was an outbreak of violence at Caesarea. The Jews there argued that they had a right to equality with Gentiles as citizens, a privilege from which they had been excluded, thus threatening the power enjoyed by the non-Jewish citizenry. Felix sent two deputations to Rome for Nero to hear the case. Nero rejected the Jewish claim to equal civic rights (*isopoliteia*), deciding in favour of the status quo. In 66 CE bloody riots between Jews and Greeks played a major part in precipitating the Revolt.

The last three procurators—Festus (60–62), Albinus (62–64) and Gessius Florus (64–66)—all failed to overcome the problem of banditry. Festus died in office. He appears in Acts 25. Albinus deposed the high priest (Annas II) who had killed James, the brother of Jesus, during the interregnum (see #686). Josephus and Tacitus agree that Florus's procuratorship was disastrous.[73] Josephus claims that he was in collusion with the bandits and actually provoked the revolt to divert attention from his misrule. Many Jews sought to emigrate to escape the ravages of the bandits.

Sources

Claudius and his freedmen.

176. Of his freedmen he had special regard for the eunuch Posides, whom he even presented with the headless spear at his British triumph, along with those who had served as soldiers. He was equally fond of Felix, giving him the command of cohorts and of troops of horse, as well as of the province of Judaea; and he became the husband of three queens. Also of Harpocras, to whom he granted the privilege of riding through the city in a litter and of giving public entertainments. Still higher was his regard for Polybius, his literary adviser, who often walked between the two consuls. But most of all he was devoted to his secretary Narcissus and his treasurer Pallas, and he gladly allowed them to be honoured in addition by a decree of the senate, not only with immense gifts, but even with the insignia of quaestors and praetors. Besides this he permitted them to amass such wealth by plunder, that when he once complained of the low state of his funds, the witty answer was made that he would have enough and to spare, if he were taken into partnership by his two freedmen.
(Suetonius, *Claudius* 28)

The activities of the false prophets.

177. Besides these [the sicarii] there arose another body of villains, with purer hands but more impious intentions, who no less than the assassins ruined the peace of the city. Deceivers and impostors, under the pretence of divine inspiration fostering revolutionary changes, they persuaded the multitude to act like madmen, and led them out into the

desert under the belief that God would there give them tokens of deliverance. Against them Felix, regarding this as but the preliminary to insurrection, sent a body of cavalry and heavy-armed infantry, and put a large number to the sword.

A still worse blow was dealt at the Jews by the Egyptian false prophet. A charlatan, who had gained for himself the reputation of a prophet, this man appeared in the country, collected a following of about thirty thousand dupes, and led them by a circuitous route from the desert to the mount called the mount of Olives. From there he proposed to force an entrance into Jerusalem and, after overpowering the Roman garrison, to set himself up as tyrant of the people, employing those who poured in with him as his bodyguard. His attack was anticipated by Felix, who went to meet him with the Roman heavy infantry, the whole population joining him in the defence. The outcome of the ensuing engagement was that the Egyptian escaped with a few of his followers; most of his force were killed or taken prisoners; the remainder dispersed and stealthily escaped to their several homes.

No sooner were these disorders reduced than the inflammation, as in a sick man's body, broke out again in another quarter. The impostors and brigands, banding together, incited numbers to revolt, exhorting them to assert their independence, and threatening to kill any who submitted to Roman domination and forcibly to suppress those who voluntarily accepted servitude. Distributing themselves in companies throughout the country, they looted the houses of the wealthy, murdered their owners, and set the villages on fire. The effects of their frenzy were thus felt throughout all Judaea, and every day saw this war being fanned into fiercer flame.

(Josephus, *Jewish War* 2.258–65)[74]

Gessius Florus.

In 66 Florus took 17 talents from the Temple treasury to help pay his staff. Mocked by outraged citizens of the city, he demanded the Jewish leaders hand over the culprits. The leaders, comprising (as Josephus says) the most eminent people, refused.

178. This speech [from the Jewish leaders] merely increased the exasperation of Florus, who now shouted to the soldiers to sack the agora known as the 'upper market,' and to kill any whom they encountered. The troops, whose lust for booty was thus backed by their general's order, not only plundered the quarter which they were sent to attack, but plunged into every house and slaughtered the inmates. There ensued a stampede through the narrow alleys, massacre of all who were caught, every variety of pillage; many of the peaceable citizens were arrested and brought before Florus, who had them first scourged and then crucified. The total number of that day's victims, including women and children, for even infancy received no quarter, amounted to about three thousand six hundred. The calamity was aggravated by the unprecedented character of the Romans' cruelty. For Florus ventured that day to do what none had ever done before, namely, to scourge before his tribunal and nail to the cross men of equestrian rank, men who, if Jews by birth, were at least invested with that Roman dignity.

(Josephus, *Jewish War* 2.305–308. Cf. Philo, *Flaccus* 72.83–85 for this crucifixion of Jews in Alexandria in the late 30s CE)

2.13. The First Jewish Revolt

Josephus writes that the Jewish War was 'the greatest of wars' (see *Jewish War* 1.1). This is an exaggeration, of course, but the war was a major conflict in the historical context. It took four years to break the back of Jewish resistance, and another four to capture the remaining fortresses, all in the control of the Sicarii, culminating in 73/74 with the famous capture of Masada (see #193 below).

The war was also fought at a critical time for Rome. After the suicide of Nero in 68, there were four emperors (Galba, Otho, Vitellius and Vespasian) during the following 12 months. Vespasian had been the general prosecuting the war against the Jews. Subsequently, his son Titus took charge of the war until the fall of Jerusalem. It was he who burned the Temple, and in whose honour the arch of Titus was erected with its relief sculptures depicting the booty from the Temple carried in the triumph.

The war broke out in 66. Sacrifices for the Roman emperor ceased in late summer. This move was instigated by the hawkish Eleazar, the Captain of the Temple. One of the cohorts of Roman troops was massacred in the Antonia palace by Eleazar and his men. The other cohort was cut to pieces on its way out of the city under promise of safe conduct. Josephus describes a massacre of Jews in Caesarea which he times to coincide with the massacre of the second cohort in Jerusalem. For him it is clear evidence of divine retribution on the Jews.[75] This was the signal for massacres of Jews and Gentiles all over Palestine.[76] Yet the moderates were still a force to be reckoned with in Jerusalem politics, and Josephus counted himself one of their number.[77]

In the midst of this, Menahem the leader of the sicarii arrived in Jerusalem. He was a grandson of the bandit leader Ezekias, whom Herod had killed in his campaign against the bandits in 47 BCE, and son of Judas the Galilaean (6 CE). He entered the city like a king (*Jewish War* 2.444). However, after assassinating a former high priest, Menahem was himself murdered. His men withdrew to Masada, which they had captured from the Romans and held till 74 when it was re-taken.

The Syrian legate, Gallus, overran Galilee as he hastened to restore order in Jerusalem. He camped outside the city during the Feast of Tabernacles in 66. However, he was attacked by surprise and suffered heavy casualties. Nevertheless, Gallus began the siege. Yet he was forced to withdraw just when a breach was about to be made. It was now November. There could be no fighting in the cold and wet of winter. However, his withdrawal to Caesarea proved to be a disaster. His troops were harried all the way.

The high priests, led by Annas II (the high priest who had been responsible for the murder of James the Lord's brother), organized the city for the war to come in the offensive of 67. The aristocratic conservatives were still in control.[78] Palestine was divided into military districts. Josephus was sent as military governor to Galilee, which he fortified. He had a rival by the name of John of Gischala, a bandit leader. He was critical of Josephus's perceived lack of urgency, and won extremist support. However, by the 67 offensive, Josephus was in full control of the war effort in Galilee.

In 67 Vespasian was appointed by Nero to take charge of the Roman forces. He came with 60,000 troops (twice the number under the command of Gallus), including three legions.[79] In Galilee the Jewish armies melted away (*Jewish War* 3.59–64). Josephus defended Jotapata. However, the Romans successfully besieged the city. Josephus survived a suicide pact (*Jewish War* 3.387–91) and was captured when the city fell. Taken before Vespasian he prophesied that he, Vespasian, was the one from Judaea who was destined to be ruler of the world (#98–99). The prophecy was well known in Jewish circles and not unknown to the Romans.[80] By 68 Jerusalem was isolated. Bandits streamed into the city, ousting the moderates and plunging the city into anarchy.[81] Many Jews fled to Jamnia. However, Nero's death brought a halt in the war. Vespasians's orders lapsed. Not until 69 was there a further Roman advance.

In Jerusalem there was a bitter power struggle between John of Gischala and his bandits and the high priestly leadership led by Eleazar and his party whom Josephus calls Zealots.[82] They controlled the inner courts of the Temple. John and his partisans controlled the outer courts. They eventually overwhelmed the Zealots, and Eleazar was killed.[83] Another bandit group led by Simon bar Gioras also entered the city.

In 69 Titus appeared before Jerusalem. There were mutilations and crucifixions of those who endeavoured to escape. As the Romans were taking the Antonia, the daily sacrifices stopped. There were no more victims left to be sacrificed. Josephus testifies to the appalling conditions which the defenders endured.[84]

The city was finally taken in the late summer of 70. According to Josephus the Temple was destroyed on 10 Ab, on the same date that Nebuchadnezzar had captured Jerusalem (see

Jeremiah 52:12–13), an anniversary that is still commemorated.[85] The Temple was burned, but not before the looting of the treasure, some of which was included in Titus's triumph. The soldiers sacrificed to their standards within the temple precincts.[86] Josephus sought to absolve Titus of responsibility for the fire. However, the fact that the Temple was used for military purposes would have been sufficient cause for Titus to order its destruction.

Many Jewish captives were put to death in the beast shows in Syria (see *Jewish War* 7.37–39). The fittest were taken to Rome for the triumph. John of Gischala was captured and sentenced to life imprisonment (*Jewish War* 6.433–34). Simon bar Gioras was executed at the conclusion of the triumph (see *Jewish War* 7.154–57). However, Titus did not revoke Jewish rights in Antioch as he was urged to do (see #607).

Josephus writes that more than one million lost their lives in the war. Tacitus puts the figure at 600,000.[87] Although the city was effectively destroyed, some impressive parts were left standing as an example to future generations (see #187).

Sources

The massacre of the cohorts in Jerusalem in 66 and its aftermath in Judaea and further afield.

179. For, to add to its heinousness, the massacre took place on the sabbath, a day on which from religious scruples Jews abstain even from the most innocent acts.

The same day and at the same hour, as it were by the hand of Providence, the inhabitants of Caesarea massacred the Jews who resided in their city; within one hour more than twenty thousand were slaughtered, and Caesarea was completely emptied of Jews, for the fugitives were arrested by orders of Florus and conducted, in chains, to the dockyards. The news of the disaster at Caesarea infuriated the whole nation; and parties of Jews sacked the Syrian villages and the neighbouring cities, Philadelphia, Heshbon and its district, Gerasa, Pella and Scythopolis.
(Josephus, *Jewish War* 2.456–58.
See also *Jewish War* 2.477–80, 559–61)

180. There was much looting, contrary to our intention; for we, after our conference with Capella and the leading men of Tiberias, had left Bethmaus for Upper Galilee. Jesus [son of Sapphias] and his followers then massacred all the Greek residents in Tiberias and any others who, before the outbreak of hostilities, had been their enemies.
(Josephus, *Life* 67)

Josephus garrisons Galilee.

181. The Jews who had pursued Cestius, on their return to Jerusalem, partly by force, partly by persuasion, brought over to their side such pro-Romans as still remained; and, assembling in the Temple, appointed additional generals to conduct the war. Joseph, son of Gorion, and Ananus the high priest were elected to the supreme control of affairs in the city, with a special charge to raise the height of the walls. As for Eleazar, son of Simon, notwithstanding that he had in his hands the Roman spoils, the money taken from Cestius, and a great part of the public treasure, they did not entrust him with office, because they observed his despotic nature, and that his subservient admirers conducted themselves like his bodyguard. Gradually, however, financial needs and the intrigues of Eleazar had such influence with the people that they ended by yielding the supreme command to him.

Other generals were selected for Idumaea, namely, Jesus son of Sapphas, one of the chief priests, and Eleazar, son of the high-priest Neus; and the existing governor of Idumaea, Niger, called the Peraean because he was a native of Peraea beyond Jordan, received instructions to act under the orders of these officers. Nor were the other districts neglected; Joseph, son of Simon, was sent to take command at Jericho, Manasseh to Peraea, John the Essene to the province of Thamna, with Lydda, Joppa and Emmaus also under his charge. John, son of Ananias, was appointed commanding officer of the provinces of Gophna and Acrabetta; Josephus, son of Matthias was given the two Galilees, with the addition of Gamala, the strongest city in that region.

Each of these generals executed his commission to the best of his zeal or ability. As for Josephus, on his arrival in Galilee, he made it his first care to win the affection of the inhabitants, knowing that this would be of the greatest advantage to him, however he might otherwise fail. He realized that he would conciliate the leaders by associating them with him in his authority, and the people at large, if his orders were in the main given through the medium of their local acquaintances. He, therefore, selected from the nation seventy persons of mature years and the greatest discretion and appointed them magistrates of the whole of Galilee, and seven individuals in each city to adjudicate upon petty disputes, with instructions to refer more important matters and capital cases to himself and the seventy. (Josephus, *Jewish War* 2.562–71)

As a member of the entourage of Titus, Josephus observes the horrors of the siege of Jerusalem (#182–83).

182. Again, when at last Jerusalem was on the point of being carried by assault, Titus Caesar repeatedly urged me to take whatever I would from the wreck of my country, stating that I had his permission. And I, now that my native place had fallen, having nothing more precious to take and preserve as a solace for my personal misfortunes, made request to Titus for the freedom of some of my countrymen; I also received by his gracious favour a gift of sacred books. Not long after I made petition for my brother and fifty friends, and my request was granted. Again, by permission of Titus, I entered the Temple, where a great multitude of captive women and children had been imprisoned, and liberated all the friends and acquaintances whom I recognized, in number about a hundred and ninety; I took no ransom for their release and restored them to their former fortune. Once more, when I was sent by Titus Caesar with Cerealius and a thousand horse to a village called Tekoa, to prospect whether it was a suitable place for an entrenched camp, and on my return saw many prisoners who had been crucified, and recognized three of my acquaintances among them, I was cut to the heart and came and told Titus with tears what I had seen. He gave orders immediately that they should be taken down and receive the most careful treatment. Two of them died in the physician's hands; the third survived. (Josephus, *Life* 417–21)

183. The total number of prisoners taken throughout the entire war amounted to ninety-seven thousand, and of those who perished during the siege, from first to last, to one million one hundred thousand. Of these the greater number were of Jewish blood, but not natives of the place; for, having assembled from every part of the country for the feast of unleavened bread, they found themselves suddenly enveloped in the war, with the result that this overcrowding produced first pestilence, and later the added and more rapid scourge of famine. (Josephus, *Jewish War* 6.420–21)

Roman reporting of the siege and capture of Jerusalem (#184–85).

184. Titus, who had been assigned to the war against the Jews, undertook to win them over by certain representations and promises; but, as they would not yield, he now proceeded to wage war upon them. The first battles he fought were indecisive; then he got the upper hand and proceeded to besiege Jerusalem. This city had three walls, including the one that surrounded the temple. The Romans, accordingly, heaped up mounds against the outer wall, brought up their engines, joined battle with all who sallied forth to fight and repulsed them, and with their slings and arrows kept back all the defenders of the wall; for they had many slingers and bowmen that had been sent by some of the barbarian kings. The Jews also were assisted by many of their countrymen from the region round about and by many who professed the same religion, not only from the Roman empire but also from beyond the Euphrates; and these, also, kept hurling missiles and stones with no little force on account of their higher position, some being flung by the hand and some hurled by means of engines. They also made sallies both night and day, whenever occasion offered, set fire to the siege engines, slew many of their assailants, and undermined the Romans' mounds by removing the earth through tunnels driven under the wall. As for the battering-rams, sometimes they

threw ropes around them and broke them off, sometimes they pulled them up with hooks, and again they used thick planks fastened together and strengthened with iron, which they let down in front of the wall and thus fended off the blows of still others. But the Romans suffered most hardship from the lack of water; for their supply was of poor quality and had to be brought from a distance. The Jews found in their underground passages a source of strength; for they had these tunnels dug from inside the city and extending out under the walls to distant points in the country, and going out through them, they would attack the Romans' water-carriers and harass any scattered detachments. But Titus stopped up all these passages.

In the course of these operations many on both sides were wounded and killed. Titus himself was struck on the left shoulder by a stone, and as a result of this accident that arm was always weaker. In time, however, the Romans scaled the outside wall, and then, pitching their camp between this and the second circuit, proceeded to assault the latter. But here they found the conditions of fighting different; for now that all the besieged had retired behind the second wall, its defence proved an easier matter because its circuit was shorter. Titus therefore once more made a proclamation offering them immunity. But even then they held out, and those of them that were taken captive or deserted kept secretly destroying the Romans' water supply and slaying any troops that they could isolate and cut off from the rest; hence Titus would no longer receive any Jewish deserters. Meanwhile some of the Romans, too, becoming disheartened, as often happens in a protracted siege, and suspecting, furthermore, that the city was really impregnable, as was commonly reported, went over to the other side. The Jews, even though they were short of food, treated these recruits kindly, in order to be able to show that there were deserters to their side also.

Though a breach was made in the wall by means of engines, nevertheless, the capture of the place did not immediately follow even then. On the contrary, the defenders killed great numbers that tried to crowd through the opening, and they also set fire to some of the buildings near by, hoping thus to check the further progress of the Romans, even though they should gain possession of the wall. In this way they not only damaged the wall but at the same time unintentionally burned down the barrier around the sacred precinct, so that the entrance to the temple was now laid open to the Romans. Nevertheless, the soldiers because of their superstition did not immediately rush in; but at last, under compulsion from Titus, they made their way inside. Then the Jews defended themselves much more vigorously than before, as if they had discovered a piece of rare good fortune in being able to fight near the temple and fall in its defence. The populace was stationed below in the court, the senators [the members of the Sanhedrin] on the steps, and the priests in the sanctuary itself. And though they were but a handful fighting against a far superior force, they were not conquered until a part of the temple was set on fire. Then they met death willingly, some throwing themselves on the swords of the Romans, some slaying one another, others taking their own lives, and still others leaping into the flames. And it seemed to everybody, and especially to them, that so far from being destruction, it was victory and salvation and happiness to them that they perished along with the temple. Yet even under these conditions many captives were taken, among them Bargiora [Simon bar Gioras], their leader; and he was the only one to be executed in connexion with the triumphal celebration.

Thus was Jerusalem destroyed on the very day of Saturn, the day which even now the Jews reverence most. From that time forth it was ordered that the Jews who continued to observe their ancestral customs should pay an annual tribute of two denarii to Jupiter Capitolinus. In consequence of this success both generals received the title of *imperator*, but neither got that of Judaïcus, although all the other honours that were fitting on the occasion of so magnificent a victory, including triumphal arches, were voted to them.
(Dio Cassius, *Roman History* 65.4.1–7.2)[88]

185. It is said that Titus first called a council and deliberated whether he should destroy such a mighty temple. For some thought that a consecrated shrine, which was famous beyond all other works of men, ought not to be razed, arguing that its preservation would bear witness to the moderation of Rome, while its destruction would for ever brand her cruelty. Yet others, including Titus himself, opposed, holding the destruction of this temple to be a prime necessity in order to wipe out more completely the religion of the Jews and the Christians; for they urged that these religions, although hostile to each other, nevertheless sprang from the same sources; the Christians had grown out of the Jews: if the root were destroyed, the stock would easily perish.
(Tacitus, *Histories* Fragment 2)

Josephus blamed the Jewish extremists and absolved the Romans for the burning of the Temple.

186. Titus then withdrew to Antonia, determined on the following day, at dawn, to attack with his whole force, and invest the temple. That building, however, God, indeed long since, had sentenced to the flames; but now in the revolution of the years had arrived the fated day, the tenth of the month Lous, the day on which of old it had been burnt by the king of Babylon. The flames, however, owed their origin and cause to God's own people. For, on the withdrawal of Titus, the insurgents, after a brief respite, again attacked the Romans, and an engagement ensued between the guards of the sanctuary and the troops who were endeavouring to extinguish the fire in the inner court; the latter routing the Jews and pursuing them right up to the sanctuary. At this moment, one of the soldiers, awaiting no orders and with no horror of so dread a deed, but moved by some supernatural impulse, snatched a brand from the burning timber and, hoisted up by one of his comrades, flung the fiery missile through a low golden door, which gave access on the north side to the chambers surrounding the sanctuary. As the flame shot up, a cry, as poignant as the tragedy, arose from the Jews, who flocked to the rescue, lost to all thought of self-preservation, all husbanding of strength, now that the object of all their past vigilance was vanishing.
(Josephus, *Jewish War* 6.249–53)

In the following two extracts Josephus describes the action taken by the Roman troops once the capture of the city was complete.

187. The army now having no victims either for slaughter or plunder, through lack of all objects on which to vent their rage—for they would assuredly never have desisted through a desire to spare anything so long as there was work to be done—Caesar ordered the whole city and the temple to be razed to the ground, leaving only the loftiest of the towers, Phasael, Hippicus, and Mariamme, and the portion of the wall enclosing the city on the west: the latter as an encampment for the garrison that was to remain, and the towers to indicate to prosperity the nature of the city and of the strong defences which had yet yielded to Roman prowess. All the rest of the wall encompassing the city was so completely levelled to the ground as to leave future visitors to the spot no ground for believing that it had ever been inhabited. Such was the end to which the frenzy of revolutionaries brought Jerusalem, that splendid city of worldwide renown.
(Josephus, *Jewish War* 7.1–4)[89]

188. Titus, removing his troops from Caesarea-on-sea, now passed to Caesarea Philippi so called, where he remained for a considerable time, exhibiting all kinds of spectacles. Here many of the prisoners perished, some being thrown to wild beasts, others compelled in opposing masses to engage one another in combat.
(Josephus, *Jewish War* 7.23–24)

The spoils from the Jerusalem Temple.

189. The spoils in general were borne in promiscuous heaps; but conspicuous above all stood out those captured in the temple at Jerusalem. These consisted of a golden table, many talents in weight, and a lampstand, likewise made of gold, but constructed on a different pattern from those which we use in ordinary life. Affixed to a pedestal was a cen-

tral shaft, from which there extended slender branches, arranged trident-fashion, a wrought lamp being attached to the extremity of each branch; of these there were seven, indicating the honour paid to that number among the Jews. After these, and last of all the spoils, was carried a copy of the Jewish Law.
(Josephus, *Jewish War* 7.148–50)[90]

The following two extracts record Jewish reflection on the destruction of the Temple.

190. Simeon the Just said: 'Upon three things the world is based: upon the Torah, upon the Temple Service, and upon the doing of loving deeds.' As regards the third, it is said, 'I desire love, and not sacrifice.' The world at the beginning was created only by love, as it is said, 'The world is built by love [Psalm 89:2].' It happened that R. Johanan b. Zakkai went out from Jerusalem, and R. Joshua followed him, and he saw the burnt ruins of the Temple, and he said, 'Woe is it that the place, where the sins of Israel find atonement, is laid waste.' Then said R. Johanan, 'Grieve not, we have an atonement equal to the Temple, the doing of loving deeds,' as it is said, 'I desire love, and not sacrifice.'
(*Aboth de Rabbi Nathan* IV, 11a)

191. And I, Baruch, went to the holy place and sat on the ruins and wept and said:
'O that my eyes were springs,
and my eyelids, that they were a fountain of tears.
For how shall I be sad over Zion,
and lament over Jerusalem?
For at the place where now I am prostrate,
the high priests used to offer sacrifices,
and placed thereon incense of fragrant spices.
Now, however, that of which we are proud has become dust,
and that which our soul desired is ashes.'
(*2 Baruch* 35)[91]

2.14. Palestine 70–135 CE

Legionary troops with auxiliaries were now stationed in Jerusalem. Caesarea continued to be the capital of the province. The size of the military was two to three times larger than under the earlier procurators and prefects. A military colony was established by Vespasian at Emmaus. In the short term the strong presence of seasoned Roman troops was sufficient to dissuade the Jews to revolt again. In Samaria, Flavia Neapolis (the modern Nablus) was founded by Vespasian. It was largely a Gentile city, and subsequently proved one of the most significant towns of Palestine.

In the diaspora of North Africa there were some disturbances immediately related to the end of the War. In Alexandria and Cyrenaica, sicarii who had escaped from Palestine, stirred up strife in the early 70s. Vespasian ordered the burning down of the temple at Leontopolis, which had been built by Onias IV (see #586). In Cyrenaica there was a large Jewish population. Both there and at Alexandria there was considerable popular support for the sicarii. Their leader promised signs in the desert to those who would follow him (about 2000 poorer Jews). They were cut down by the Roman soldiers in a repeat of earlier violent responses to protests in Judaea in the 40s and 50s.

The Temple site was now a defiled place. It was the home of the iconic standards of the military occupants. Yet there was no effort to proscribe Judaism. The diaspora remained largely quiet, at least until Trajan's reign, and the disturbances of 115–17 in Cyprus, Cyrene, and Alexandria. Jews were not forbidden access to Jerusalem, though it is clear that the Temple cult had been extinguished as a practical expression of Jewish piety towards God.[92]

The Temple tax was diverted to the coffers in Rome, ostensibly to pay for the rebuilding of the Temple of Jupiter Capitolinus after the fire of 69 that destroyed it at the time of Vespasian's siege of the city.[93] The *fiscus Judaicus* was paid by all Jews, male and female, from the ages of 3 to 62.[94] Before 70 only males aged 20–50 were required to pay the tax to support the Jerusalem cultus.

A rabbi, Jonathan ben Zakkai, escaped Jerusalem during the siege. He requested permission from the Romans to set up a school in Jamnia.[95] Under Roman auspices, the rabbis under ben Zakkai presided over a re-grouping of Jewish *intelligentsia*, now that there was no temple and no priestly aristocracy.[96] The legal decisions (*halakoth*) promulgated at Jamnia became normative. In all probability the extent of the Hebrew canon was settled at this time. A compendium of rabbinic oral tradition, much of it emanating from the period after 70, was published in the Mishnah of c. 200 CE. The Jewish synagogue liturgy, including the 'Eighteen Benedictions', also reached definitive forms during this period. *2 Baruch* and *4 Ezra* provide an eloquent witness to the sombre religious mood of Palestinian Jews.[97] Scholars surmise that there was a growing messianic movement during the period. Eusebius preserves a number of reports from the Christian author Hegesippus (first half of the second century CE) in which Vespasian, Domitian and Trajan cracked down on potential messianic threats. Christians were caught up in this exercise.[98]

Sources

Rabbi Johanan ben Zakkai set up a rabbinic school after being smuggled out of Jerusalem in a coffin by his friends, and brought before Vespasian.

192. Then they opened the coffin, and he stood before Vespasian. He said, 'Are you R. Johanan b. Zakkai? What shall I give you?' He replied, 'All I ask of you is that I may go to Jabneh and teach my disciples there, and fix a place of prayer there, and carry out all the commandments.' He answered, 'Go, and all that it pleases you to do there, do.' (*Aboth de Rabbi Nathan* IV, 11b–12a)

The capture of Masada (#193–94).

Masada was the last of the citadels in rebel hands to fall. A fortress had been first built there by Jonathan Maccabaeus (Josephus, *Jewish War* 7.285). Herod built an impressive palace. The Jewish defenders were well provendered. Masada's well-nigh impregnable position brought out the best in Roman tenacity and perseverance. The Romans, under Silva, first constructed a wall around the rock.

193. The Roman general, having now completed his wall surrounding the whole exterior of the place...and taken the strictest precautions that none should escape, applied himself to the siege. He had discovered only one spot capable of supporting earthworks. For in rear of the tower which barred the road leading from the west to the palace and the ridge, was a projection of rock, of considerable breadth and jutting far out, but still three hundred cubits below the elevation of Masada; it was called Leuce. Silva, having accordingly ascended and occupied this eminence, ordered his troops to throw up an embankment. Working with a will and a multitude of hands, they raised a solid bank to the height of two hundred cubits. This, however, being still considered of insufficient stability and extent as an emplacement for the engines, on top of it was constructed a platform of great stones fitted closely together, fifty cubits broad and as many high. The engines in general were similarly constructed to those first devised by Vespasian and afterwards by Titus for their siege operations; in addition a sixty-cubit tower was constructed entirely cased in iron, from which the Romans by volleys of missiles from numerous quick-firers and *ballistae* quickly beat off the defenders on the ramparts and prevented them from showing themselves. Simultaneously, Silva, having further provided himself with a great battering-ram, ordered it to be directed without intermission against the wall, and having, though with difficulty, succeeded in effecting a breach, brought it down in ruins. The Sicarii, however, had already hastily built up another wall inside, which was not likely to meet with a similar fate from the engines; for it was pliable and calculated to break the force of the impact, having been constructed as follows. Great beams were laid lengthwise and contiguous and joined at the extremities; of these there were two parallel rows a wall's breadth apart, and the intermediate space was filled with earth. Further, to prevent the soil from dispersing as the mound rose, they clamped, by other transverse beams, those laid longitudinally. The work thus presented to the enemy the appearance of masonry, but the blows of the engines were weakened, battering upon a yielding material which, as it settled down

> under the concussion, they merely served to solidify. Observing this, Silva, thinking it easier to destroy this wall by fire, ordered his soldiers to hurl at it showers of burning torches. Being mainly made of wood, it quickly caught fire, and, from its hollow nature becoming ignited right through blazed up in a volume of flame. At the first outbreak of the fire, a north wind which blew in the faces of the Romans caused them an alarm; for, diverting the flame from above, it drove it against them, and the fear that all their engines would be burnt up had almost reduced them to despair. Then suddenly the wind veering, as if by divine providence, to the south and blowing with full force in the opposite direction, wafted and flung the flames against the wall, which now through and through was all ablaze. The Romans, thus blessed by God's aid, returned rejoicing to their camp, with the determination of attacking the enemy on the morrow; and throughout that night they kept stricter watch lest any of them should secretly escape. (Josephus, *Jewish War* 7.304–319)

It is clear that the situation was now hopeless. The leader of the Sicarii, Eleazar, delivers a set speech, an extract from which follows. It expresses as eloquently as anything else in the *Jewish War* Josephus's theology of the causes and outcome of the revolt. Eleazar proposes that the defenders, together with their wives and children, commit suicide rather than fall into the hands of the Romans. He is presented as a descendant of Judas the Galilaean who had induced the Jews to revolt at the time of the census of Quirinius in 6 CE (see *Jewish War* 7.253).

194. 'Long since, my brave men, we determined neither to serve the Romans nor any other save God, for He alone is man's true and righteous Lord [see *Jewish War* 2.118]; and now the time is come which bids us verify that resolution by our actions. At this crisis let us not disgrace ourselves; we who in the past refused to submit even to a slavery involving no peril, let us not now, along with slavery, deliberately accept the irreparable penalties awaiting us if we are to fall alive into Roman hands. For as we were the first of all to revolt, so are we the last in arms against them. Moreover, I believe that it is God who has granted us this favour, that we have it in our power to die nobly and in freedom—a privilege denied to others who have met with unexpected defeat. Our fate at break of day is certain capture, but there is still the free choice of a noble death with those we hold most dear. For our enemies, fervently though they pray to take us alive, can no more prevent this than we can now hope to defeat them in battle. Maybe, indeed, we ought from the very first—when, having chosen to assert our liberty, we invariably experienced such hard treatment from one another, and still harder from our foes—we ought, I say, to have read God's purpose and to have recognized that the Jewish race, once beloved of Him, had been doomed to perdition. For had he continued to be gracious, or but lightly incensed, he would never have overlooked such wholesale destruction or have abandoned His most holy city to be burnt and razed to the ground by our enemies. But did we forsooth hope that we alone of all the Jewish nation would survive and preserve our freedom, as persons guiltless towards God and without a hand in crime—we who had even been the instructors of the rest? Mark, now, how He exposes the vanity of our expectations, by visiting us with such dire distress as exceeds all that we could anticipate. For not even the impregnable nature of this fortress has availed to save us; nay, though ample provisions are ours, piles of arms, and a superabundance of every other requisite, yet we have been deprived, manifestly by God Himself, of all hope of deliverance. For it was not of their own accord that those flames which were driving against the enemy turned back upon the wall constructed by us; no, all this betokens wrath at the many wrongs which we madly dared to inflict upon our countrymen. The penalty for those crimes let us pay not to our bitterest foes, the Romans, but to God through the act of our own hands. It will be more tolerable than the other. Let our wives thus die undishonoured, our children unacquainted with slavery; and, when they are gone, let us render a generous service to each other, preserving our liberty as a noble winding-sheet. But first let us destroy our chattels and the

fortress by fire; for the Romans, well I know, will be grieved to lose at once our persons and the lucre. Our provisions only let us spare; for they will testify, when we are dead, that it was not want which subdued us, but that, in keeping with our initial resolve, we preferred death to slavery.'
(Josephus, *Jewish War* 7.323–36)[99]

A governor of Judaea under Vespasian.

The following text is a translation of a Latin inscription discovered near the site of the Temple.

195. Imperator Caesar Vespasian Augustus, Imperator Titus Caesar Vespasian son of the Augustus; legion X Fretensis (set this up) when Lucius Antonius Saturninus was legate of Augustus as pro-praetor.
(*New Docs* III, p. 122)

The 'Jewish' tax (#196–98).

Suetonius is describing the financial straits in which Domitian found himself by virtue of his building programmes.

196. Besides other taxes, that on the Jews was levied with the utmost rigour, and those were prosecuted who without publicly acknowledging that faith yet lived as Jews, as well as those who concealed their origin and did not pay the tribute levied upon their people. I recall being present in my youth when the person of a man ninety years old was examined before the procurator and a very crowded court, to see whether he was circumcised.
(Suetonius, *Domitian* 12.2)

197. Chrestus, if you return no man's presents, then don't give any to me or send any in return for mine; I shall think you sufficiently generous. But if you make return to Apicius and Lupus and Gallus and Titius and Caesius, you will lick a cock—not mine, which is well-behaved and diminutive, but one that comes from burned-out Jerusalem, one lately doomed to pay taxes.
(Martial, *Epigrams* 7.55)

Ostracon from Apollinopolis Magna in the Nile Delta (75 CE).

The *aparchai* ('firstfruits') was a tax levied in addition to the 'Jewish tax'.

198. Paid by Marous daughter of Akietos, in respect of the two-denar tax on the Jews for the 7th year of Vespasian, 8 drachmai 2 obols; in respect of the *aparchai*, 1 drachme. Akyntas Kaikillias, freedman of Sarra, 8 drachmai 2 obols; in respect of the *aparchai*, 1 drachme.
(*CPJ* no. 171)

2.15. The Revolts of 115–17 CE

Trajan was busy in Mesopotamia dealing with the troublesome Parthians when a revolt of Egyptian Jews broke out. The Prefect was defeated by a Jewish army. A violent pogrom resulted in the decimation of the Jewish population of Alexandria. In neighbouring Cyrenaica, another violent revolt broke out. Temples were damaged. Milestones near Cyrene point to roads destroyed by Jewish rebels. The revolt was put down savagely. Three thousand veterans were stationed in Cyrene to assist in the repopulation. In Cyprus, Salamis was devastated by the Jews. All Jews were banned from the island. Even those Jews sheltering or shipwrecked were to be put to death. Dio Cassius reports a death toll of 220,000 in Cyrene and 240,000 in Egypt. The historian, writing in c. 220 CE, speaks of the exclusion of Jews from Cyprus as still in force. Until at least 200 CE there was an annual festival at Oxyrhynchus commemorating the defeat of the Jews.[100]

The Jews of Mesopotamia also revolted while Trajan was involved with the Parthians. The general, Quietus, who put down the revolt, was rewarded with the governorship of Palestine. However, there were no massacres on the scale of North Africa. Babylonian Jews assumed leadership of Jews elsewhere.

Sources

Eusebius reports the revolts of 115–17.

199. While the teaching of our Saviour and the church were flourishing daily and moving on to further progress the tragedy of the Jews was reaching the climax of successive woes [the revolts of 115–17 and the second Jewish

revolt of 132–35]. In the course of the eighteenth year of the reign of the Emperor a rebellion of the Jews again broke out and destroyed a great multitude of them. For both in Alexandria and in the rest of Egypt and especially in Cyrene, as though they had been seized by some terrible spirit of rebellion, they rushed into sedition against their Greek fellow citizens, and increasing the scope of the rebellion in the following year started a great war while Lupus was governor of all Egypt. In the first engagement they happened to overcome the Greeks, who fled to Alexandria and captured and killed the Jews in the city, but though thus losing the help of the townsmen, the Jews of Cyrene continued to plunder the country of Egypt and to ravage the districts in it under their leader Lucuas. The Emperor sent against them Marcius Turbo with land and sea forces including cavalry. He waged war vigorously against them in many battles for a considerable time and killed many thousands of Jews, not only those of Cyrene but also those of Egypt who had rallied to Lucuas, their king. The Emperor suspected that the Jews in Mesopotamia would also attack the inhabitants and ordered Lucius Quietus to clean them out of the province. He organized a force and murdered a great multitude of the Jews there, and for this reform was appointed governor of Judaea by the Emperor.
(Eusebius, *Ecclesiastical History* 4.2)

The revolt in Cyrene.

200. Meanwhile the Jews in the region of Cyrene had put a certain Andreas at their head, and were destroying both the Romans and the Greeks. They would eat the flesh of their victims, make belts for themselves of their entrails, anoint themselves with their blood and wear their skins for clothing; many they sawed in two, from the head downwards; others they gave to wild beasts, and still others they forced to fight as gladiators. In all two hundred and twenty thousand persons perished. In Egypt, too, they perpetrated many similar outrages, and in Cyprus, under the leadership of a certain Artemion. There, also, two hundred and forty thousand perished, and for this reason no Jew may set foot on that island, but even if one of them is driven upon its shores by a storm he is put to death. Among others who subdued the Jews was Lusius, who was sent by Trajan.
(Dio Cassius, *Roman History* 68.32.1–3)[101]

Appian, who was pursued by the Jews in the Nile Delta,[102] mentions the Jews and the revolt in Egypt in his *Civil Wars*. He is narrating the tour of Egypt by Caesar in the wake of his victory over Pompey at Pharsalus, after which Pompey was assassinated in Egypt.

201. Caesar could not bear to look at the head of Pompey when it was brought to him, but ordered that it be buried, and set apart for it a small plot of ground near the city [Alexandria] which was dedicated to Nemesis, but in my time, while the Roman emperor Trajan was exterminating the Jewish race in Egypt, it was devastated by them in the exigencies of the war.
(Appian, *Civil Wars* 2.90)

Jewish victories in the Hermopoulite District (June 116–January 117 CE).

202. The one hope and expectation that was left was the push of the massed villagers from our district against the impious Jews; but now the opposite has happened. For on the 20th (?) our forces fought and were beaten and many of them were killed... now, however, we have received the news from men coming from... that another legion of Rutilius arrived at Memphis on the 22nd and is expected.
(*CPJ* no. 438)

Confiscation of Jewish property in Egypt (117/118 [?] CE).

203. Aquillius Pollio, strategos of the Herakleopolite nome, to his dearest Apollonios, strategos of the Oxyrhynchite nome, greeting.

Be good enough to receive two letters which I have written, one to you, and one to Sabinus, strategos of the Kynopolite nome, about the schedule of the property formerly held by the Jews, and the schedule itself. Retain your own copy, and transmit the other to the Lykopolite nome...
(*CPJ* no. 445)

2.16. The Second Jewish Revolt 132–35 CE

Hadrian built a new city called Aelia Capitolina on the site of Jerusalem and built a temple to Jupiter on the site of the former temple. He also intensified the Roman ban on castration decreed by emperors Titus and Domitian.[103] This practice was placed on a par with circumcision. These initiatives were sufficient provocation for the second revolt of 132–35.

This revolt, unlike the first, was messianic. In rabbinic literature the leader of the Jewish armies is called Bar Koziba, which means 'son of the lie' or 'liar'. This name was concocted by his opponents. However, recent discoveries of coins and texts call him Simon bar Kosiba, prince of Israel. Prominence was also given to a certain Eleazar the Priest. There has been speculation that the Jewish revolutionaries were intending to restore the cult. The Jewish leadership is reminiscent of the Aaronic and Davidic messiahs expected in some of the Qumran texts.

Rabbi Akiba affirmed the messianic status of bar Kosiba and called him 'bar Kokhba', which means 'son of a star', a reference to the description of a coming ruler anticipated in Numbers 24:17. The revolt was undertaken for political independence. This objective is advertised on bar Kokhba's coins, some of which bear the legend 'for the freedom of Jerusalem'.

The rebels had to be rooted out cave by cave. Julius Severus, governor of Britain, took charge of the war effort. The final battle of the campaign took place at Bether, 10 kilometres southwest of Jerusalem. The town was captured on 9 Ab, the anniversary of the two previous destructions of the Jerusalem Temple! Ten rabbis, including Akiba, were particularly revered as martyrs of the cause. Bar Kokhba was killed.[104] It was said that there were so many slaves on offer that each fetched as much as a horse. All Jews were banned from Jerusalem. Thereafter the city was home to a Gentile population. Under Constantine, Jews were allowed into the city on the anniversary of its capture to weep at what is now called the 'wailing wall'. Dio Cassius puts the number of those who died in battle at 580,000. Those who died by disease and plague, he writes, are 'past finding out'.

The circumcision ban remained; amounting to a ban on Judaism. The Romans also desecrated the Samaritan holy place. Hadrian was execrated by the Jews, more so than Titus. The Romans were increasingly regarded as enemies of the Jews in the midrashic literature.

Important documentary finds in Hebrew, Aramaic, and Greek dating from the period after 70 CE up to and including the second revolt have been discovered at Murabba'at and Naḥal Ḥever in the Judaean desert.

Sources

Dio Cassius reports the second Jewish revolt.

204. At Jerusalem he founded a city in place of the one which had been razed to the ground, naming it Aelia Capitolina, and on the site of the temple of the god he raised a new temple to Jupiter. This brought on a war of no slight importance nor of brief duration, for the Jews deemed it intolerable that foreign races should be settled in their city and foreign religious rites planted there. So long, indeed, as Hadrian was close by in Egypt and again in Syria, they remained quiet, save in so far as they purposely made of poor quality such weapons as they were called upon to furnish, in order that the Romans might reject them and they themselves might thus have the use of them; but when he went farther away, they openly revolted. To be sure, they did not dare try conclusions with the Romans in the open field, but they occupied the advantageous positions in the country and strengthened them with mines and walls, in order that they might have places of refuge whenever they should be hard pressed, and might meet together unobserved under ground; and they pierced these subterranean passages from above at intervals to let in air and light.

At first the Romans took no account of them. Soon, however, all Judaea had been stirred up, and the Jews everywhere were showing signs of disturbance, were gathering together, and giving evidence of great hostility to the Romans, partly by secret and partly by overt acts; many outside nations, too, were joining them through eagerness for gain, and the whole earth, one might almost say, was being stirred up over the matter. Then, indeed, Hadrian sent against them his best generals. First of these was Julius Severus, who was dispatched from Britain, where he was governor, against the Jews. Severus did not venture to attack his opponents in the open at any one point, in view of their numbers and their desperation, but by intercepting small groups, thanks to the number of his soldiers and his under-officers, and by depriving them of food and shutting them up, he was able, rather slowly, to be sure, but with comparatively little danger, to crush, exhaust and exterminate them. Very few of them in fact survived. Fifty of their most important outposts and nine hundred and eighty-five of their most famous villages were razed to the ground. Five hundred and eighty thousand men were slain in the various raids and battles, and the number of those that perished by famine, disease and fire was past finding out. Thus nearly the whole of Judaea was made desolate, a result of which the people had had forewarning before the war. For the tomb of Solomon, which the Jews regard as an object of veneration, fell to pieces of itself and collapsed, and many wolves and hyenas rushed howling into their cities. Many Romans, moreover, perished in this war. Therefore Hadrian in writing to the senate did not employ the opening phrase commonly affected by the emperors, 'If you and your children are in health, it is well; I and the legions are in health.'
(Dio Cassius, *Roman History* 69.12.1–14.3. Cf. Eusebius, *Ecclesiastical History* 4.6)

Christians were persecuted by bar Kokhba and made to blaspheme Jesus Christ.

205. For in the Jewish war which lately raged, Barchochebas, the leader of the revolt of the Jews, gave orders that Christians alone should be led to cruel punishments, unless they would deny Jesus Christ and utter blasphemy.
(Justin, *Apology* 1.31)[105]

Appian recounts the decay and overthrow of the Seleucid empire by Pompey and his annexation of the much of the eastern Mediterranean. He notes Pompey's capture of Jerusalem, proceeding to make the following remarks about Vespasian's and Hadrian's destructions of 70 and 135 respectively.

206. It [Jerusalem] was afterward rebuilt and Vespasian destroyed it again, and Hadrian did the same in our time. On account of these rebellions the poll-tax imposed upon all Jews is heavier than that imposed upon the surrounding peoples…
(Appian, *History of Rome* 11.50)[106]

A letter of Bar Kokhba.

A number of letters from the rebel leader have been discovered in caves in the Judaean desert.

207. From Shimeon bar Kosiba to the men of En-gedi.

To Masabala and to Yehonathan bar Be'ayan, peace. In comfort you sit, eat and drink from the property of the House of Israel, and care nothing for your brothers.
(Yadin, *Bar-Kokhba*, p. 133)

Jewish reflection on the second Jewish revolt (#208–209).

208. On the ninth of Ab the decree was made against our forefathers that they should not enter the land, the first Temple and the second (Temple) were destroyed, Betar was taken, and the city was ploughed up (after the war of Hadrian).

When Ab comes, rejoicing diminishes.
(*m. Taanit* 4.6)

209. Rabbi [b. Judah] could preach four and twenty sermons on 'The Lord has swallowed up and not pitied' (Lamentations 2:2), but R. Johanan (b. Nappaha) could preach sixty on the same verse. What! R. Johanan could

preach more than R. Judah! Yes, but R. Judah (135–200 CE) lived nearer the time of the Destruction than R. Johanan (died 279 CE), and when R. Judah used to preach, there were present old men who remembered the Destruction, and when he preached about it (and mentioned things that happened) they would weep, and were so afflicted that they would depart: therefore R. Judah shortened his addresses (and did not say all that he might, so as not to trouble them). R. Judah (b. Ilai) said that R. Judah the Prince used to expound 'The voice is the voice of Jacob, but the hands are the hands of Esau' (Genesis 27:22) thus: Hark! the voice of Jacob, crying out for what Esau's hands have wrought in Bethar. R. Simeon b. Yohai said, 'My teacher Akiba used to expound Num. 24:17 ("A star has gone forth from Jacob") as "A liar has gone forth from Jacob".' Nevertheless, when R. Akiba (first) saw Bar Koziba (= liar, i.e. Bar Kokba), he said, 'This is King Messiah.' Johanan b. Torta said to him, 'Akiba, grass will sprout through your cheeks ere the son of David comes.' R. Johanan said: Hark! the voice of Hadrian Caesar slaying eighty thousand myriads in Bethar! R. Johanan said: Eighty thousand pairs of trumpeters surrounded Bethar, each one of whom was set over countless hosts…

Bethar was captured and Bar Koziba slain. They brought his head to Hadrian who asked, 'Who slew this man?' A Samaritan said, 'It was I.' Hadrian said, 'Show me his body.' He showed it to him, and there was a snake entwined round it. Hadrian said, 'Had not God slain him, no man could have done so.'…

The Romans continued the slaughter till horses were plunged in blood to their nostrils, and the blood-stream whirled weights of forty seahs, till it reached the sea, forty miles distant. They say that on one stone they found the brains of three hundred infants. They found also three piles of capsules of phylacteries, each pile weighing nine seahs…

(*Jerusalem Talmud, Ta'anit* IV, section 8, f. 68d, l. 43).

Notes

1. In his list of the 20 Persian satrapies and the tribute they paid, Herodotus (*Histories* 3.91) describes the geographical boundaries of this satrapy, the fifth in his list. Note the preference given to Babylon.
2. See Choon-Leong Seow, 'The Socioeconomic Context of "The Preacher's Hermeneutic" ', *Princeton Seminary Bulletin* 17 (1996), pp. 168–95. Economic difficulties are readily apparent in Nehemiah 5:3–5. Note also the evidence of vigorous trade in Nehemiah 13:15–22. The book of Ecclesiastes, Seow argues, was composed against the backdrop of economic volatility.
3. Cf. Ezra 1:1–4; 1 Esdras 2:1–15; Josephus, *Antiquities* 11.1–18. The practice of Jews sending money home to Jerusalem antagonized local rulers (see #592).
4. A comparison between the mandates of this code and those of the 'Holiness Code' of Leviticus 17–26 is warranted.
5. The so-called Samaria papyri written in c. 375–335 BCE bear witness to life in the period. For texts, see D.M. Gropp *et al.*, *Wadi Daliyeh II and Qumran Cave 4* (DJD, 28; Oxford: Clarendon Press, 2001).
6. Josephus (*Antiquities* 11.317) reports that Alexander captured Damascus.
7. Josephus cites the report of Hecataeus of Abdera that Jews serving in Alexander's army refused to rebuild the ruined temple of Bel in Babylon, and were exempted by Alexander from the task only after enduring punishments and fines (see *Against Apion* 1.192). Josephus notes Hecataeus's observation that Jews served both Alexander and his successors, and relates Hecataeus's eye-witness account of the Jewish archer, Meshullam, who served in a detachment of Jewish cavalry in Alexander's army (*Against Apion* 1.201–204).
8. Josephus proceeds to cite Agatharchides of Cnidus, the Greek historian of the *diadochoi*, as the corroborator of this fact (*Antiquities* 12.7). Note the comment of Plutarch (see #603).
9. See also Polybius, *Histories* 5.70, Daniel 11:11–19.
10. Joseph's father was Tobias (see #445), who held the office of kleruch under the Ptolemies.
11. Cf. 1 Maccabees 12:19–23; 2 Maccabees 5:9.

According to Josephus, the Pergamenes also claimed friendship with the Jews dating to the time of Abraham (*Antiquities* 14.255).

12. This version, which became part of what is now called the Septuagint, provided an important medium for the dissemination of Jewish religious values. The *Letter of Aristeas* recounts the work of translation.
13. See J.A. Fitzmyer, 'The Languages of Palestine in the First Century A.D.', in *idem*, *A Wandering Aramean: Collected Aramaic Essays* (SBLMS, 25; Chico, CA: Scholars Press, 1979), pp. 29–56.
14. See also 2 Maccabees 4:7–17, 18–20; Josephus, *Antiquities* 12.240–41.
15. Josephus claims Antiochus had long planned an invasion of Judaea (*Jewish War* 1.32). See also Tacitus, *Histories* 5.8 on the purpose of Antiochus with respect to Judaea.
16. See 1 Maccabees 1:10; Appian, *History of Rome* 11.39.
17. See Herbert G. May (ed.), *The Oxford Bible Atlas* (London: Oxford University Press, 2nd edn, 1974), p. 80. The *Akra* is not to be confused with Nehemiah's Baris, later the site of Herod the Great's Antonia fortress (see Ralph Marcus's notes in his translation of Josephus, *Antiquities* 12–14 [LCL; Cambridge, MA: Harvard University Press, 1933], pp. 128–29, 382–83).
18. There is a reference in this document to the possible usurpation of Seleucus IV's throne by Antiochus IV.
19. See also Josephus, *Jewish War* 1.32. 2 Maccabees eulogizes Onias III. His death in Daphne and Antiochus's response are narrated in 2 Maccabees 4:30–38.
20. In 2 Maccabees 4:23–29 Menelaus was a brother of Simon, the Captain of the Temple (see 2 Maccabees 3:4), and a Benjaminite. As such he had no rightful claim to priestly, let along high priestly, office. Menelaus had Onias murdered at Daphne near Antioch (2 Maccabees 4:30–34). Jason had been the last Zadokite high priest. Now there was a high priest from the tribe of Benjamin, who held the office with Syrian patronage.
21. Both 2 Maccabees 5:1 and Daniel 11:25, 29 (cf. the Qumran fragment 4Q248) speak of two Egyptian campaigns. See discussion in Part 1 (at n. 29).
22. The 'little help' mentioned here may be a reference to the Maccabaean insurgents. The 'wise among the people' may refer to the Hasidim (or Hasidaeans) (see also 1 Maccabees 2:42). The Hasidim may have been the forerunners of the Jewish groups later known as the Pharisees and the Essenes, as well as of the Qumran sectarians. 'Kittim', the Hebrew term for Cyprus, has become a term for the Romans here. Like Cyprus, Rome was a land across the sea. 'Kittim' could be conveniently used to denote the Romans. 'Kittim' is used frequently of Rome in the Qumran *pesharim* (see, e.g., #642).
23. For martyrdoms see 1 Maccabees 1:44; 2 Maccabees 6:18–31; 2 Maccabees 7 (#696); Josephus, *Antiquities* 12.255–56.
24. Cf. Josephus, *Jewish War* 1.34–35.
25. Josephus, *Antiquities* 12.316–26; 1 Maccabees 4:36–61.
26. 1 Maccabees 6:1–17. See also 2 Maccabees 1:11–17 for another account, and note Polybius, *Histories* 31.9.
27. Josephus, *Jewish War* 1.39; *Antiquities* 12.354–59.
28. See John 10:22 ('Renewal'), Josephus, *Antiquities* 12.235.
29. See 1 Maccabees 7:25. For Alcimus, see also 1 Maccabees 9:54, 55–56; 2 Maccabees 14:7; Josephus, *Antiquities* 12.20.
30. Josephus, *Jewish War* 1.47; cf. 1 Maccabees 9:5–18. Judas' burial is narrated in 1 Maccabees 9:19–21.
31. See also the parallel account in Josephus, *Antiquities* 12.265–72.
32. See also Josephus, *Antiquities* 12.274, 276–77.
33. Cf. Josephus, *Jewish War* 1.41–46. For the circumstances surrounding Antiochus Eupator's accession in 163 BCE, see 1 Maccabees 6:17
34. See also Josephus, *Jewish War* 1.38.
35. Cf. Josephus, *Antiquities* 12.414–17.
36. See Josephus, *Antiquities* 13.302; *Jewish War* 1.71.
37. The first mention of the Essenes, a separatist sect opting out of the Temple establishment, dates from this time. Josephus documents a prophecy of John the Essene regarding Antigonus (*Antiquities* 13.311–13).
38. See Josephus, *Antiquities* 14.277–84; *Jewish War* 1.229–35. Note E. Mary Smallwood's assessment of Antipater: 'So died the states-

man who had grasped the fact that, once Rome had the east under her heel, voluntary cooperation was the only practical course for the Jews' (*The Jews under Roman Rule* [Leiden: E.J. Brill, 1981], p. 47).

39. Eleazar is referring to the regulation in Leviticus 21:14.
40. See also Josephus, *Jewish War* 1.96–98. Note also the Qumran text 4QpNahum 1 which speaks of the 'furious young lion' who executes revenge on the 'seekers after smooth things' (i.e. the Pharisees) who had been in league with Demetrius.
41. See also Diodorus Siculus, *Histories* 40.4; Appian, *History of Rome* 12.106; Cicero, *Pro Flacco* 67; Dio Cassius, *Roman History* 27.16.4; Plutarch, *Pompey* 39.2; Florus, *Epitome of Roman History* 1.40.30. See also Josephus's mention of other historians, namely, Strabo, Nicolas and Livy, who recorded the siege of the city in the accounts of the career of Pompey in *Antiquities* 14.68. Note also Josephus's reflections on the capture of the city in *Antiquities* 14.77–79.
42. Suetonius reports that many Jews were present at Caesar's funeral in 44 BCE (see his *Julius Caesar* 84, #151).
43. See Josephus, *Antiquities* 14.331.
44. Josephus, *Jewish War* 1.270.
45. Labienus proceeded to invade the coastal plain with Pacorus, Orodes's son. After capturing Antioch, Labienus pursued and captured Saxa the governor of Syria, whom he put to death. Pacorus made himself ruler of Syria. Some of the fear engendered by the 'hordes' beyond the Euphrates can be glimpsed in the New Testament book of Revelation (see 9:13–19; 16:12). It was also believed that Nero would return from the dead at the head of a Parthian army (see Suetonius, *Nero* 57). This is also reflected in the progress of the Beast at the head of an infernal army towards Rome (Revelation 17:16–18).
46. See *Antiquities* 15.232–37; 15.247–52. In the *Jewish War*, Josephus blames Mariamme for the chaos in his household. In the more moralistic *Antiquities*, Josephus regards Herod as a monster.
47. According to the fourth-century CE writer Macrobius, Augustus, when he learned that Herod had ordered the killing of young boys in Syria under two years old, including his son, is supposed to have quipped that he would rather be Herod's pig (Greek *hus*) than his son (Greek *huios*) (*Saturnalia* 2.4.11).
48. For other Caesareas established at the time see Suetonius, *Augustus* 60.
49. Dio Cassius, *Roman History* 55.27.6.
50. Herod built a temple to Augustus in Sebaste.
51. Varus returned to Judaea and Galilee and put down the various rebellions. In 9 CE Varus lost his life, and three legions, in a military disaster in the Teutoberg Forest.
52. No difference in status was implied as the post continued to be filled by equestrians. The term 'procurator' was used by Claudius in his administration (41–54 CE) and afterwards. See the Pontius Pilate inscription in H.G. May (ed.), *Oxford Bible Atlas*, p. 116 and Barrett, *New Testament Background*, 155–56. Note also A.N. Sherwin-White, *Roman Society and Roman Law in the New Testament* (Oxford: Oxford University Press, 1963), pp. 6–8.
53. The tribune Claudias Lysias is encountered in Acts 23:26.
54. According to Tacitus, *Annals* 1.80, Tiberius prolonged the terms of military commanders.
55. Philo describes Pilate in *On the Embassy to Gaius* (the *Legatio*) as 'naturally inflexible, a blend of self-will and relentlessness, stubborn' (300–301), adding that his rule was characterized by 'briberies, insults, robberies, outrages, wanton injuries, executions without trial, the ceaseless and supremely vicious cruelty—vindictive, furious temper…' (302–303) (see #588).
56. Luke 13:1 refers to an otherwise unknown incident in which Pilate is said to have mingled the blood of some Galilaeans with their sacrifices. This may have happened while they were in the act of sacrificing. It is more likely, however, that the incident happened while they were making their way to Jerusalem on pilgrimage. Herod Antipas and Pilate, so Luke 23:6–12 relates, were at enmity. The New Testament also knows of an 'insurrection' in which Barabbas had committed murder (Mark 15:7).
57. Luke has Pilate declare Jesus innocent on three occasions. Luke also portrays the Jews as the crucifiers of Jesus. See Mark Harding, 'On the Historicity of Acts: Comparing Acts 9:23–5 with 2 Cor 11:32–3', *NTS* 39 (1993), pp. 518–38. Pilate shows some concern for Jewish religious scruples in John 18:29.

58. See Josephus, *Jewish War* 2.117. There is some question whether the Sanhedrin might have had the power of capital punishment since both Stephen and James were put to death. Perhaps this was allowed when the sanctity of the Temple was at stake (see Acts 6:13; 21:29).
59. For the aniconic standards incident, see Philo, *On the Embassy to Gaius* 298–305 (#588).
60. Quirinius, Legate of Syria, conducted the census as a preliminary to taxation. He had been consul in 12 BCE. Quirinius crucified 2000 Jews in Jerusalem. Crucifixions were an integral part of Roman policy. Josephus observes (*Jewish War* 5.450) that they were 'spectacles designed to induce capitulation'. Quirinius's character is assessed in Tacitus, *Annals* 3.48; Suetonius, *Tiberius* 49. Luke has made an error in synchronizing the birth of Jesus at the end of Herod's reign with the census conducted in 6 CE. Acts 5:37 also attests the revolt fomented by Judas the Galilaean that took place at the time of the census.
61. See Luke 13:32. Luke may have Ezekiel 13:4 in mind. The 'fox' undermines the rule of God over his people.
62. See Mark 6:18; Matthew 14:4.
63. By contrast with Josephus, the Gospels are clear that John's baptism was a baptism of repentance with a view to the forgiveness of sins (see Mark 1:4).
64. The Jews did not actually possess citizenship rights in Alexandria. See the Letter of Claudius cited at #608.
65. Paul had an audience with him at which he exclaimed, 'You almost persuade me to become a Christian' (Acts 26:28).
66. Josephus wrote his *Against Apion* to counter the baneful influence of Apion's anti-Judaism. The statue and the threat of Jewish insurrection is also noted in Tacitus, *Histories* 5.9 (and the emended text of *Annals* 12.54).
67. Smallwood, *The Jews under Roman Rule*, p. 257.
68. See also Acts 5:36. This is probably the same Theudas mentioned by Josephus but whose activity is placed at the time of the census in 6 CE.
69. He had also been among the first to support the campaign of Vespasian for emperor. See Suetonius, *Vespasian* 6.
70. This incident clearly resulted in a considerable loss of life. Josephus records in the *Antiquities* that 20,000 died; in his *Jewish War* the figure is 30,000.
71. Tacitus, a patrician, writes: 'Claudius made Judaea a province [i.e. 44 CE] and entrusted it to Roman knights or to freedmen; one of the latter, Antonius Felix, practised every kind of cruelty and lust, wielding the power of king with all the instincts of a slave' (*Histories* 5.9). In the *Annals* 12.54, Tacitus reports that Cumanus and Felix exercised joint control over Samaria and Galilee respectively. Cumanus was made the scapegoat for the outrages of Felix. Incidentally, Felix was the brother of Pallas, the financial secretary of the emperor Claudius (see *Annals* 12.54).
72. See Acts 24. Felix was 'rather well informed about the Way' (v. 22). Note his response to Paul's preaching in v. 25.
73. See Josephus, *Jewish War* 2.277–78. Tacitus, *Histories* 5.10, writes: 'The Jew's patience lasted till Gessius Florus became procurator'. Tacitus recognized that the Jews were being poorly (even criminally) governed.
74. Acts records 4000 followers (Acts 21:38). However, Josephus records a less likely 30,000. Paul was mistaken for him when arrested in the temple precincts.
75. Josephus puts the figure at 20,000 killed (see *Jewish War* 2.457).
76. See Lee I. Levine, 'The Jewish–Greek Conflict in First Century Caesarea', *JJS* 25 (1974), pp. 281–97; U. Rappaport, 'Jewish-Pagan Relations and the Revolt against Rome in 66–70 C.E.', in Lee I. Levine, *The Jerusalem Cathedra: Studies in the History, Archaeology, Geography and Ethnography of the Land of Israel* (Jerusalem: Wayne State University Press, 1981), pp. 81–95.
77. At this point, according to Eusebius (*Ecclesiastical History* 3.5.3), the Christians took the opportunity to escape from Jerusalem to Pella (just east of the Jordan near the Sea of Galilee). See also Matthew 24:15; Mark 13:14; Luke 21:21.
78. By 66 CE each section of the populace, even the high priests and the aristocracy, was inciting revolt and contributing to the war effort. Indeed the aristocrats are the leading figures in the initial stages, and there are large numbers of well-born Jews in Jerusalem up till the last assault (including Josephus's own brother and his 50 friends, as well as his mother, who

were in prison [*Jewish War* 5.544]). Martin Goodman (*The Ruling Classes of Judaea: The Origins of the Jewish Revolt Against Rome A.D. 66–70* [Cambridge: Cambridge University Press, 1987]) argues that the aristocracy could not maintain their privilege and prestige presiding over Judaean social affairs on Rome's behalf unless they too rebelled against the Romans. Upper-class leadership of the revolt was critical in ensuring its initial success. Banditry alone could not have carried a war against the Romans. One suspects that Josephus has overstated the role of the 'rabble' in precipitating the war.

79. These were the 5th, 10th and 15th. See Josephus, *Jewish War* 3.65, 66–69.
80. See Numbers 24:17; Josephus, *Jewish War* 3:62–63, 350–54, 399–402; cf. Tacitus, *Histories* 2.1; 5.13; Suetonius, *Vespasian* 4–5 (#98).
81. According to Martin Goodman ('The First Jewish Revolt: Social Conflict and the Problem of Debt', *JJS* 33 [1982], pp. 417–27), the problem of indebtedness contributed to the bandit problem. Wealth from the diaspora flowed into Jerusalem for the support of the cult, but there was little benefit bestowed on the populace. There is evidence of conspicuous consumption in Jerusalem. In addition, the wealthy were not 'evergetes', i.e. they did not bestow benefactions on the general populace, unlike Herod. Instead they lent their money to small landowners who, in the difficult times that troubled Judaea and Galilee, defaulted on their loans and found themselves dispossessed. Early in the war the refugee mob from the countryside burned the debt-archives in Jerusalem as their first action on reaching the city (see Josephus, *Jewish War* 2.427).
82. The 'Zealots' were neither a party nor a grouping in the period before the War. Rather there were individuals 'zealous' for the honour of God. The Old Testament priest Phineas (see Numbers 25) was the role model, the 'zealot' par excellence. In Mark 3:18 Jesus is recorded choosing a disciple called Simon the 'Zealot' (or Simon the 'Cananaean', a title derived from the Hebrew word used in Numbers 25 to denote the disposition of Phinehas).
83. With the help of Idumaeans smuggled into the city, John of Gischala also managed to kill the former High Priests Annas (Ananus) and Jesus. See Josephus, *Jewish War* 4.305, 310–11, 312–25.
84. In *Jewish War* 6.201–219, at the height of the siege, Josephus records an incident of cannibalism—a mother eating her baby. For Josephus, the incident compounds the injustice of the rebel cause. See further discussion in S. Mason, *Josephus and the New Testament* (Peabody, MA: Hendrikson, 1992), pp. 11–14.
85. Jews still commemorate the anniversary of the destructions on the 9th Ab (see #208).
86. See Josephus, *Jewish War* 6.316; and cf. 1QpHab 6 (see #642).
87. See Tacitus, *Histories* Fragment 3. In his *Histories* 5.13, the number of the besieged is put at 600,000.
88. See also Tacitus, *Histories* Fragment 1. For text see Tacitus, *Works*, II (LCL, 111; trans. Clifford H. Moore; Cambridge, MA: Harvard University Press, 1925), p. 221.
89. Titus left the 10th legion to garrison the site with some cavalry and infantry (Josephus, *Jewish War* 7.5). It was now too late to travel to Rome. He took the 5th and 15th with him as he made his way northwards. He re-visited the now-ruined Jerusalem on his way from Antioch to Egypt. See Josephus, *Jewish War* 7.112–15.
90. The triumph culminated in the execution of Simon bar Gioras (*Jewish War* 7.132–57).
91. Cf. Josephus, *Jewish War* 6.267–70; *Odes of Solomon* 4; *4 Ezra* 10:21–23; *2 Baruch* 10:6–11:3.
92. Julian (emperor 361–63 CE) wanted to rebuild the temple to undermine the Christians' arguments that their movement was the legitimate heir of Judaism.
93. See Suetonius, *Domitian* 12.
94. See *CPJ* II, p. 114; Smallwood, *The Jews under Roman Rule*, pp. 371–76. The tax was levied, at least during Domitian's reign not only on Jews but also on those living as Jews (#196–97).
95. See *Aboth de Rabbi Nathan* IV, 11b–12a (Montefiore and Loewe, *Rabbinic Anthology*, p. 266) (#192).
96. Note Schürer's observation that the Pharisees and the rabbis 'entered the heritage of the Sadducees and the priests'. See his *The History of the Jewish People in the Age of Jesus*

Christ (175 B.C.–A.D. 135), I (rev. and ed. Geza Vermes and Fergus Millar; Edinburgh: T. & T. Clark, 1973), p. 524.

97. Was the catastrophe a punishment from God? *2 Baruch* 6–8 portrays the angels of God actually permitting the Romans to enter the city after the removal of the sacred furniture and the vestments. *4 Ezra* is much less certain about the reason for the disaster.

98. A number of descendants of Jesus were interrogated according to Eusebius, *Ecclesiastical History* 3.12; 19–20. In 3.32 Eusebius reports the execution (during Trajan's reign) of Bishop Simeon of Jerusalem, reputedly a cousin of Jesus. Domitian also purged high status pro-Jewish sentiment (see Suetonius, *Vespasian* 15). In 95 he executed his cousin (the father of his appointed heirs) Flavius Clemens on a charge of atheism and drifting into Jewish ways, and exiled Clemens's wife Flavia Domitilla. See also Suetonius, *Domitian* 12.2 (#196) and Dio Cassius, *Roman History* 67.14.1–3 (#103).

99. According to Josephus, there were seven survivors of the suicide pact (see *Jewish War* 7.399).

100. See comment on no. 450 in *CPJ* II, p. 258 (= P.Oxy 705). Two papyri in *CPJ* II (nos. 447, 449) record damage to property caused by the Jews in Oxyrhynchus and elsewhere in the Fayyum during the revolt.

101. The *sicarii* were active in Cyrene in the aftermath of the first revolt (see Josephus, *Jewish War* 7.437–41).

102. Fragment 19 of Appian's *History* is translated and discussed by Alain M. Gowing, *The Triumphal Narratives of Appian and Cassius Dio* (Ann Arbor: University of Michigan Press, 1992), pp. 13–16.

103. According to Dio Cassius, *Roman History* 67.2.3, Titus, Domitian's brother and predecessor, had had a favourite who was a eunuch. Domitian banned castration because he wanted to insult Titus's memory. Circumcision was not a peculiarly Jewish custom. It was practised by the Colchians, Ethiopians and Egyptians.

104. According to the *Midrash on Lamentations* II, 2, section 4, his head was shown to Hadrian, who remarked: 'If his God had not slain him who could have overcome him?' Text in H. Freedman and Maurice Simon (eds.), *Midrash Rabbah, Lamentations* (London/New York: Soncino, 1983), p. 159. See also #209.

105. See also Eusebius, *Ecclesiastical History* 4.8.4.

106. The previous sections of Appian are cited at #38.

3. Graeco-Roman Literature

3.1. History

The writing of 'history' (*historia*) can be traced to the fifth-century BCE Greek writer Herodotus. He was born in c. 490 BCE at Halicarnassus in southwest Asia Minor. He is often called the 'father of history', though he himself did not invent the genre. Herodotus's methodology is transparent. He used eye-witnesses (see *Histories* 2.99, 147; 4.81) and written sources (*Histories* 2.24; 5.3), and attempted to verify what he had been told.[1]

What distinguishes history from other genres of prose is the attempt to craft a narrative of past events regarded as significant for the present. Some historians sought to account for the causes of events—in Herodotus's case, the cause of the Persian Wars fought by the Greeks against the invaders during two famous campaigns in 490 and 480–479 BCE. But history also had a didactic and moral purpose in common with moral philosophy, and which was also closely allied to the purpose of rhetoric, the art of persuasion. Behind the great historians of Greece and Rome lies the sense that history has a public purpose to affirm and inculcate the ethical values of society.[2]

Other Greeks, and later, Romans, proceeded to emulate Herodotus's achievement. Thucydides (c. 460–395 BCE) turned his investigative powers to the events of the Peloponnesian War fought by Athens and her allies against a league headed by Sparta (431–21, 415–404), in which he, an Athenian general exiled before the outbreak of the war, was a participant on the Peloponnesian side.

Thucydides's methodology regarding speeches should be noted (#211). Historians did not think that it was either edifying or entertaining to report verbatim what was said on such occasions even if such reports were available. Rather they sought to provide the sense of what had been said, rendering the speech in accordance with rhetorical conventions. In this way historians were able to make their speeches more effective as vehicles of persuasion for their discerning audience. Mirroring the debates of citizen assemblies, historians frequently presented speeches in pairs, encapsulating contrasting points of view of the speakers as proponents of different courses of action. Speeches were also presented in elaborate style, once again demonstrating the pervasive influence of rhetoric.[3]

The later Polybius (c. 201–120 BCE) was a Greek from Megalopolis in Arcadia who, with other scions of the Achaean League, had been taken as a hostage to Rome at the end of the Macedonian Wars in 149 BCE. Enjoying the patronage of the powerful family of the Scipios, he turned his attention to the great theme of tracing the rise of the power and universal influence of the Romans. Polybius was acutely aware of the chronic inability of Greeks to unite against a common enemy, and the ubiquitous, divisive self-interest of Greek city-states. For all his military genius and stupendous achievement, even Alexander had been unable to establish a lasting, unified Greek hegemony over those areas he had conquered in the name of Greek civilization. Rome, by contrast, had achieved in Polybius's own day what no Greek power had been able to achieve. He saw his task as one of describing as accurately as possible the manner in which Rome had come to exercise world-wide dominion and to account for the unprecedented phenomenon of Roman success.

In Flavius Josephus (c. 36–100 CE) early Judaism produced a historian of considerable ability (see Part 4, topic 4.6). He wrote in Greek. He owed much to Polybius insofar as he too was highly impressed by the overwhelming military resources and force the Romans were able to bring to bear on those who endeavoured to resist them. Indeed,

Josephus insisted that the Romans were being guided and given success by God himself. Like many of his contemporaries, the young, urbane Josephus had the opportunity to visit Rome (#90). Like Polybius he too came to enjoy the patronage of a dominant Roman family. When captured during the Jewish War he came to the attention of Vespasian and his sons, spending the rest of the war and the remainder of his life under their protection. His warnings to the Jews of Jerusalem took on the force of personal experience of the superabounding might of the Romans, their cause promoted by God.

Generally, the Romans adapted Greek literary models. Latin history writing of the first century BCE and CE is no exception. Livy and Tacitus, the greatest of the Roman historians, belong to the great tradition of history writing.

Sources

Herodotus describes his purpose in writing the *Histories* in its opening section.

210. What Herodotus the Halicarnassian has learnt by inquiry [*historia*] is here set forth: in order that so the memory of the past may not be blotted out from among men by time, and that great and marvellous deeds done by Greek and foreigners [*barbaroi*] and especially the reason why they warred against each other may not lack renown.
(Herodotus, *Histories* 1.1)

Thucydides considers the methodology he used, especially with respect to the speeches, at the outset of his *Peloponnesian War*.

211. As to the speeches that were made by different men, either when they were about to begin the war or when they were already engaged therein, it has been difficult to recall with strict accuracy the words actually spoken, both for me as regards that which I myself heard, and for those who from various other sources have brought me reports. Therefore the speeches are given in the language in which, as it seemed to me, the several speakers would express, on the subjects under consideration, the sentiments most befitting the occasion, though at the same time I have adhered as closely as possible to the general sense of what was actually said. But as to the facts of the occurrences of the war, I have thought it my duty to give them, not as ascertained from any chance informant nor as seemed to me probable, but only after investigating with the greatest possible accuracy each detail, in the case both of the events in which I myself participated and of those regarding which I got my information from others. And the endeavour to ascertain these facts was a laborious task, because those who were eye-witnesses of the several events did not give the same reports about the same things, but reports varying according to their championship of one side or the other, or according to their recollection. And it may well be that the absence of the fabulous from my narrative will seem less pleasing to the ear; but whoever shall wish to have a clear view both of the events which have happened and of those which will some day, in all human probability, happen again in the same or a similar way—for these to adjudge my history profitable will be enough for me. And, indeed, it has been composed, not as a prize-essay to be heard for the moment, but as a possession for all time.
(Thucydides, *Peloponnesian War* 1.22)

Polybius discusses the purpose of history and the methodology the historian should employ (#213). After criticizing contemporaries who indulge in emotive writing to evoke pity, he offers the following observation.

212. A historical author should not try to thrill his readers by such exaggerated pictures, nor should he, like a tragic poet, try to imagine the probable utterances of his characters or reckon up all the consequences probably incidental to the occurrences with which he deals, but simply record what really happened and what really was said, however commonplace. For the object of tragedy is not the same as that of history but quite the opposite. The tragic poet should thrill and charm his audience for the moment by the verisimilitude of the words he puts into his characters' mouths, but it is the task of the historian to instruct and convince for all time serious students by the

truth of the facts and the speeches he narrates, since in the one case it is the probable that takes precedence, even if it be untrue, the purpose being to create illusion in spectators, in the other it is the truth, the purpose being to confer benefit on learners. (Polybius, *Histories* 2.56.10–12)[4]

213. The peculiar function of history is to discover, in the first place, the words actually spoken, whatever they were, and next to ascertain the reason why what was done or spoken led to failure or success. For the mere statement of a fact may interest us but is of no benefit to us: but when we add the cause of it, study of history becomes fruitful. For it is the mental transference of similar circumstances to our own times that gives us the means of forming presentiments of what is about to happen, and enables us at certain times to take precautions and at others by reproducing former conditions to face with more confidence the difficulties that menace us. But a writer who passes over in silence the speeches made and the causes of events and in their place introduces false rhetorical exercises and discursive speeches, destroys the peculiar virtue of history. (Polybius, *Histories* 12.25b)

Livy comments on the scope of his history of Rome. Note the moralizing intent.

214. Whether I am likely to accomplish anything worthy of the labour, if I record the achievements of the Roman people from the foundation of the city, I do not really know, nor if I knew would I dare to avouch it; perceiving as I do that the theme is not only old but hackneyed, through the constant succession of new historians, who believe either that in their facts they can produce more authentic information, or that in their style they will prove better than the rude attempts of the ancients. Yet, however, this shall be, it will be a satisfaction to have done myself as much as lies in me to commemorate the deeds to the foremost people of the world; and if in so vast a company of writers my own reputation should be obscure, my consolation would be the fame and greatness of those whose renown will throw mine into the shade. Moreover, my subject involves infinite labour, seeing that it must be traced back above seven hundred years, and that proceeding from slender beginnings it has so increased as now to be burdened by its own magnitude; and at the same time I doubt not that to most readers the earliest origins and the period immediately succeeding them will give little pleasure, for they will be in haste to reach these modern times, in which the might of a people which has long been very powerful is working its own undoing. I myself, on the contrary, shall seek in this an additional reward for my toil, that I may avert my gaze from the troubles which our age has been witnessing for so many years, so long at least as I am absorbed in the recollection of the brave days of old, free from every care which, even if it could not divert the historian's mind from the truth, might nevertheless cause it anxiety.

Such traditions as belong to the time before the city was founded, or rather was presently to be founded, and are rather adorned with poetic legends than based upon trustworthy historical proofs, I purpose neither to affirm nor to refute. It is the privilege of antiquity to mingle divine things with human, and so to add dignity to the beginnings of cities; and if any people ought to be allowed to consecrate their origins and refer them to a divine source, so great is the military glory of the Roman People that when they profess that their Father and the Father of their Founder was none other than Mars, the nations of the earth may well submit to this also with as good a grace as they submit to Rome's dominion. But to such legends as these, however they shall be regarded and judged, I shall, for my own part, attach no great importance. Here are the questions to which I would have every reader give his close attention—what life and morals were like; through what men and by what policies, in peace and in war, empire was established and enlarged; then let him note how, with the gradual relaxation of discipline, morals first gave way, as it were, then sank lower and lower, and finally began the downward plunge which has brought us to the present time, when we can endure neither our vices nor their cure.

What chiefly makes the study of history wholesome and profitable is this, that you

> behold the lessons of every kind of experience set forth as on a conspicuous monument; from these you may choose for yourself and for your own state what to imitate, from these mark for avoidance what is shameful in the conception and shameful in the result. For the rest, either love of the task I have set myself deceives me, or no state was ever greater, none more righteous or richer in good examples, none ever was where avarice and luxury came into the social order so late, or where humble means and thrift where so highly esteemed and so long held in honour. For true it is that the less men's wealth was, the less was their greed. Of late, riches have brought in avarice, and excessive pleasures the longing to carry wantonness and licence to the point of ruin for oneself and of universal destruction.
> (Livy, *History of Rome* Preface 1–12)[5]

3.2. Biography

Biography and history are related in so far as the character and life of particular great ones who are the proponents of historical cause and effect are set within a wider historical context.[6] On occasion Greek and Roman historians present developed biographies of certain characters within the scope of their work, though subservient to their wider purpose in writing.[7]

In Graeco-Roman times the genre is represented, *inter alia*, by Plutarch's many Greek and Roman *Lives*, Tacitus's *Agricola*, Lucian's *Life of Demonax*, and Philostratus's *Life of Apollonius*. Unlike their modern counterparts, Graeco-Roman biography did not seek to give an exhaustive, definitive account of someone's life. Rather, biography had a more defined and restricted scope, namely, a didactic and ethical purpose closely linked with individuals who are the subjects of the genre. The influence of rhetoric is also detectible. Indeed, the influence of the encomium, a speech highlighting the achievements and moral excellence of the character of a particular person, can be traced in Graeco-Roman biographies. Tacitus's *Agricola* (the historian's father-in-law) is a fine example of an encomiastic biography.

Biographers were intentionally selective in their choice of material since the biographer hoped to present to the audience something of the character of his subject, believing that this was able to modify the character of the audience. Graeco-Roman biography, therefore, reads something like a moral sermon, or a moral treatise in which negative and positive examples and paradigms or models are presented to the audience for their instruction in the moral life.[8] There is a sense in biography of the subject's persona and significance continuing to influence later generations, long after the death of the subject.[9]

Biography, therefore, grew out of the rhetoric of praise in which the deeds of the subject were advertised and acclaimed. The classical and Graeco-Roman world was an oral culture. Strictly speaking Graeco-Roman biography is not historical in the sense we use that term today. Presentation of facts through rigorous use and analysis of sources was not the purpose of biography, nor, for that matter, history. Moral exhortation had priority. Nevertheless the biographer was required to present his work in a plausible fashion. There was no excuse for invention and untruth that produced an implausible and therefore unpersuasive account.

People today have different standards for assessing the worth and integrity of literary works. We would find it highly improbable and implausible that a biography of a great statesman leader might begin with an account of the omens that attended his birth, or the suggestion that the wise of the day foresaw great things for the infant, or that his mother had somehow been impregnated by a god. But that is exactly how many biographies and the New Testament Gospels Matthew and Luke begin.

Sources

Tacitus's life of his father-in-law Agricola (#215–26).

Gnaeus Julius Agricola was a distinguished senator and politician, who had enjoyed a successful governorship of Britain.

215. To hand down to posterity the works and ways of famous men was a custom of the past: our age has not yet abandoned it even now, indifferent though it be to its own affairs, whenever, at least, some great and notable virtue has overcome and surmounted the vice common alike to small states and great—ignorance of what is right and jealousy.

But in our fathers' times, just as it was easy, and there was more scope, to do deeds worth recording, so also there was inducement then to the most distinguished men of ability to publish such records of virtue. Partisanship or self-seeking was not the motive: a good conscience was its own reward; indeed, many men even counted it not presumption, but self-respect, to narrate their own lives. A Rutilius, a Scaurus, could do so without being disbelieved or provoking a sneer; so true is it that virtues are best appreciated in those ages which most readily give them birth; but in these times, even though I was about to write the life of a man who was already dead, I had to seek permission which I should not have needed, had invective been my purpose; so harsh was the spirit of age, so cynical towards virtue.
(Tacitus, *Agricola* 1)

216. If there be any habitation for the spirits of the just; if, as wise men will have it, the soul that is great perish not with the body, may you rest in peace, and summon us, your household, from weak repinings and womanish tears to the contemplation of those virtues which it were impiety to lament or mourn. Let reverence rather, let thankfulness, let imitation even, if our strength permit, be our tribute to your memory: this is true respect, this is kinship's duty. This would I say to wife and daughter, so to venerate the memory of husband and of father as to ponder each word and deed within their hearts, and to cling to the lineaments and features of the soul rather than the body.

Not that I think that the image wrought of bronze or marble should be forbidden, but vain alike and passing is the face of man and its likeness: only the form of the soul remains, to be known and shown not through the materials and artistry of another but only in your own character.

Whatever we have loved in Agricola, whatever we have admired, abides, and will abide, in the hearts of men, in the procession of the ages, by the records of history. Many of the ancients will forgetfulness engulf as though neither fame nor name were theirs. Agricola, whose story here is told, will outlive death, to be our children's heritage.
(Tacitus, *Agricola* 46)

3.3. Letters

A vast deposit of letters survives from the Graeco-Roman era, much of it in papyrus form. All classes of society wrote letters—from kings, aristocrats and philosophers down to semi-literate peasants—in varying degrees of literateness and facility. Artemon, the collector and publisher of Aristotle's corpus of letters, is reported to have defined a letter as 'half a conversation'. As is the case today, ancient letters were extensions of and substitutes for the medium of conversation.

Modern scholars have identified three characteristics of Graeco-Roman letters. These are 'philophronesis', 'parousia' and 'homilia'. Letters are the expression of a friendly relationship between the writer and the person addressed (*philophronēsis*), the letter writer addresses the recipient as though physically present (*parousia*), and the writer continues the dialogue begun while the two parties were present (*homilia*). The use of established epistolary formulas, often noted by scholars, served to reconnect the writer and the recipient.

There remain a number of letter writing manuals from the Graeco-Roman era. Scholars have observed that letter writing was incorporated into the secondary school curriculum. Letter-writing exercises were set to elicit the young students' facility in character impersonation.

The earliest extant theoretical discussion of letter writing occurs as a digression in the treatise *On Style*, a work attributed to Demetrius of Phalerum (c. 300 BCE). Towards the end of the classical era the art of letter writing was incorporated into the rhetorical handbooks. Letters, as Demetrius observed, quite properly used an unornamented 'plain' style, avoiding the stylized, well-crafted and highly inventive rhetorical techniques of oratory. Nevertheless, as the author of *On Style* observes, letter writers need to be attentive to the occasional need to write with attention to rhetorical effect, especially for the purpose of moral exhortation.

In the Graeco-Roman world there was a hortatory tradition in which a letter writer appealed to the addressee to continue to live in a certain way, the writer commending perseverance in the ways of conventional morality and traditional wisdom already adopted by the addressee. This appeal on the part of the writer was reinforced not just by reminder but also by positive and negative examples, as well as by reminder to the addressee to of what he already knows of the ethical lifestyle. This mode of address, frequently encountered in letters and treatises, is called paraenesis. Isocrates, the fourth-century BCE Athenian rhetorician, wrote a number of treatises which are the earliest extant literary articulations of paraenetic address.

Another major mode of address, termed protrepsis, urged the addressee to change his or her life-orientation. Often the writer exhorts the addressee to take up the life of philosophical contemplation as the sure path to virtue and to cultivate a life of philosophical detachment from the world and its ephemeral pleasures. The literary model for this mode of exhortation was Aristotle's lost *Protrepticus*, a treatise addressed to Themison, king of Cyprus. Both *Epistle* 7 attributed to Plato and Isocrates's *Busiris* are good examples of the protreptic mode of discourse.

It has been observed that much of the extant hortatory epistolary literature was written by or attributed to philosophers, both Greek and Latin, keeping in touch with their students, clients or family members. These letters articulate a tradition of 'psychagogy', i.e. pastoral care or guidance.

Sources

The nature and style of a letter.

217. (223) We will next treat of epistolary style, since it too should be plain. Artemon, the editor of Aristotle's *Letters*, says that a letter ought to be written in the same manner as a dialogue, a letter being regarded by him as one of the two sides of a dialogue.

There is perhaps some truth in what he says, but not the whole truth. The letter should be a little more studied than the dialogue, since the latter reproduces an extemporary utterance, while the former is committed to writing and is (in a way) sent as a gift.

Who (one may ask) would, in conversation with a friend, so express himself as does Aristotle when writing to Antipater on the subject of the aged exile? 'If he is doomed to wander to the uttermost parts of the earth, an exile hopeless of recall, it is clear that we cannot blame men (like him) who wish to return home—to Hades.' A man who conversed in that fashion would seem not be talking but to be making an oratorical display.

(227) The letter, like the dialogue, should abound in glimpses of character. It may be said that everybody reveals his own soul in letters. In every other form of composition it is possible to discern the writer's character, but in none so clearly as in the epistolary.

The length of a letter, no less than its style, must be kept within due bounds. Those that are too long, and further are rather stilted in expression, are not in sober truth letters but treatises with the heading 'My dear So-and-So.' This is true of many of Plato's, and of that of Thucydides.

(231) If anyone should write of logical subtleties or questions of natural history in a letter, he writes indeed, but not a letter. A letter is designed to be the heart's good wishes in brief; it is the exposition of a simple subject in simple terms.

Ornament, however, it may have in the shape of friendly bits of kindly advice, mixed with a good few proverbs. This last is the only philosophy admissible in it—the proverb being the wisdom of a people, the

wisdom of the world. But the man who utters sententious maxims and exhortations seems to be no longer talking familiarly in a letter but to be speaking *ex cathedra.*
(Demetrius, *On Style* 223–25, 227–28, 231–32)[10]

Different kinds of letters.[11]

Cicero to C. Scribonius Curio.

218. That there are many kinds of letters you are well aware; there is one kind, however, about which there can be no mistake,—for indeed letter-writing was invented just in order that we might inform those at a distance if there were anything which it was important for them or for ourselves that they should know. A letter of this kind you will of course not expect from me; for as regards your own affairs you have correspondents and messengers at home, while as regards mine there is absolutely no news to tell you. There remain two kinds of letters which have a great charm for me, the one intimate and humorous, the other austere and serious. Which of the two it least beseems me to employ, I do not quite see. Am I to jest with you by letter? On my oath, I don't think there is a citizen in existence who can laugh in these days. Or am I to write something more serious? What is there that can possibly be written by Cicero to Curio, in the serious style, except on public affairs? Ah! but in this regard my case is just this, that I dare not write what I feel, and I am not inclined to write what I don't feel.
(Cicero, *Letters to his Friends* 2.4.1 [53 BCE])

Quintus Cicero (Cicero's brother) to Marcus Cicero.

219. In the matter of Tiro, my dear Marcus, as surely as I hope to see you, and my son Cicero, and my darling Tullia, and your son, you have done what gave me extreme pleasure, when you preferred that he whose position was so unworthy of him should be our friend rather than a slave. Believe me, when I had perused your letter, and his, I jumped for joy, and I not only thank, but I congratulate you too.

For if Statius's faithful service is so constant a pleasure to me, how inestimable should such good qualities be in your man, when we think too of his literary and conversational powers, and his refinement—merits which outweigh even those qualities which minister to our personal comfort. I have every reason, and each the strongest possible, to love you, and I have this reason also, I mean that you sent me the news in precisely the proper way. All of you was revealed to me in your letter. I have promised Sabinus's serving-men to do all they asked, and I shall do so.
(Cicero, *Letters to his Friends* 16.16 [54/53 BCE])[12]

Cicero clearly sees the letter as a substitute for conversation in person. Note the following excerpt from one of his letters to Atticus. It reveals not only the keenness with which absence of friends is felt but also something of the daily life of the wealthy patron.

220. Believe me, there is nothing I want so much at the present time as a person with whom I can share anything that causes me the least anxiety, a man of affection and common sense, to whom I can speak without affectation, reserve, or concealment. My brother, who is the most unaffected of persons and most affectionate, is away. Metellus is not a human being, but 'sea-shore and airy void and desert waste.' And you whose conversation and advice have so often lightened my load of care and anxiety, who have aided me in my political life, been my confidant in my family affairs, and shared my conversation and projects—where are you? So utterly am I deserted, that the only moments of repose I have are those which are spent with my wife, my little daughter, and darling boy. For my grand and showy friendships bring some public *éclat*, but of private satisfaction they have none. And so, when my house has been crowded with the morning *levée* and I have gone down to the forum amid a throng of friends, I cannot find in the whole company a single man with whom I can jest freely or whisper familiarly. So I look forward with longing to your coming and in fact urge you to hurry: for I have many cares and anxieties, which I

fancy would be banished by a single walk and talk in your sympathetic hearing.
(Cicero, *Letters to Atticus* 1.18 [60 BCE])[13]

Cicero's letters contain vignettes of life in the late Republic. The following is contained in a letter to Atticus.

221. I detest Cleopatra; and the voucher for her promises, Ammonius, knows I have good reason to do so. Her promises were all things that had to do with learning and not derogatory to my dignity, so I could have mentioned them even in a public speech. Sara, besides being a knave, I have noticed is also impertinent to me. Once, and only once, have I seen him in my house; and then, when I asked politely what he wanted, he said he wanted Atticus. But the insolence of the queen herself, when she was in her villa across the river, I cannot mention without great indignation. So no dealings with them. They don't credit me with any spirit or even any feelings at all.
(Cicero, *Letters to Atticus* 15.15 [44 BCE])

A letter of advice.

222. Pliny to Valerius (?) Maximus.

I know you need no telling, but my love for you prompts me to remind you to keep in mind and put into practice what you know already, or else it would be better for you to remain ignorant. Remember that you have been sent to the province of Achaia, to the pure and genuine Greece, where civilization and literature, and agriculture, too, are believed to have originated; and you have been sent to set in order the constitution of free cities, and are going to free men who are both men and free in the fullest sense, for they have maintained their natural rights by their courage, merits, and friendly relationships, and finally by treaty and sanction of religion. Respect the gods their founders and the names they bear, respect their ancient glory and their very age, which in man commands our veneration, in cities our reverence. Pay regard to their antiquity, their heroic deeds, and the legends of their past. Do not detract from anyone's dignity, independence, or even pride, but always bear in mind that this is the land which provided us with justice and gave us laws, not after conquering us but at our request; that it is Athens you go to and Sparta you rule, and to rob them of the name and shadow of freedom, which is all that now remains to them, would be an act of cruelty, ignorance and barbarism. (Illness is the same in a slave as in a free man, but you will have observed how a doctor will treat the free man with more kindness and consideration.) Remember what each city was once, but without looking down on it for being so no longer; do not allow yourself to be hard or domineering, and have no fear that you will be despised for this. No one who bears the insignia of supreme authority is despised unless his own meanness and ignobility show that he must be the first to despise himself. It is a poor thing if authority can only test its powers by insults to others, and if homage is to be won by terror; affection is far more effective than fear in gaining you your ends. Fear disappears at your departure, affection remains, and, whereas fear engenders hatred, affection develops into genuine regard. Never, never forget (I must repeat this) the official title you bear, and keep clearly in mind what it means to establish order in the constitution of free cities, for nothing can serve a city like ordered rule and nothing is so precious as freedom; nor can anything equal the disgrace should order be overthrown and freedom give place to servitude. You are moreover your own rival; you bring with you the excellent reputation you won during your quaestorship in Bithynia, you bring the Emperor's recognition and your experience as tribune, praetor, and holder of your present office, given you as a reward for your services. You must then make every effort not to let it appear that you were a better, kinder, and more experienced administrator in a remote province than in one nearer Rome, and when dealing with servile rather than free men, when you were elected by lot instead of being the Emperor's choice, and at a time when you were raw and unknown before being tested and proved by experience. And, besides, as you have often heard and read, it is far more shameful to lose a reputation than not to win one.

Please believe, as I said at the start, that this letter was intended not to tell, but to

remind you of your duties—though I know I am telling you as well, as I am not afraid of letting my affection carry me too far; there is no danger of excess where there ought to be no limits.
(Pliny the Younger, *Letters* 8.24)[14]

Philosophers kept in touch with their pupils by letters, reminding them of the teaching of the master, and exhorting them to maintain their commitment to it. Examples can be found in the writings of Epicurus (see his letters to Herodotus and Menoeceus, cited at #369 and #371) and Seneca (*Moral Epistles*). In the New Testament 1 Thessalonians should be seen as such a letter. Although Paul would have rejected the epithet 'philosopher' in favour of 'apostle', he does keep in touch with the communities he founded through letters, anxious to maintain his guidance of each. 1 Thessalonians is probably the first of the extant Pauline corpus. Note the image of motherly succour (2:1–12) and the stress on maintaining the integrity of the community (4:9–12) in the extract below.

223. (2:1) You yourselves know, brothers and sisters, that our coming to you was not in vain, but though we had already suffered and been shamefully mistreated at Philippi, as you know, we had courage in our God to declare to you the gospel of God in spite of great opposition. For our appeal does not spring from deceit or impure motives or trickery, but just as we have been approved by God to be entrusted with the message of the gospel, even so we speak, not to please mortals, but to please God who tests our hearts. As you know and as God is our witness, we never came with words of flattery or with a pretext for greed; nor did we seek praise from mortals, whether from you or from others, though we might have made demands as apostles of Christ. But we were gentle among you, like a nurse tenderly caring for her own children. So deeply do we care for you that we are determined to share with you not only the gospel of God but also our own selves, because you have become very dear to us.

You remember our labor and toil, brothers and sisters; we worked night and day, so that we might not burden any of you while we proclaimed to you the gospel of God. You are witnesses, and God also, how pure, upright, and blameless our conduct was toward you believers. As you know, we dealt with each one of you like a father with his children, urging and encouraging you and pleading that you lead a life worthy of God, who calls you into his own kingdom and glory…

(4:9) Now concerning love of the brothers and sisters, you do not need to have anyone write to you, for you yourselves have been taught by God to love one another; and indeed you do love all the brothers and sisters throughout Macedonia. But we urge you, beloved, to do so more and more, to aspire to live quietly, to mind your own affairs, and to work with your own hands, as we directed you, so that you may behave properly toward outsiders and be dependent on no one.
(1 Thessalonians 2:1–12; 4:9–12)

3.4. Poetry

Rome produced a number of poets of distinction, many of whom were active during the principate of Augustus. Lucretius (c. 94–55 BCE), a devotee of Epicurus, wrote passionate poetry intended to persuade and instruct.[15] Horace eulogized Augustus and his achievement. Catullus wrote some fine love poems. Propertius wrote intensely wrought poems that betray a tortured individual. Ovid is remembered as a writer of erotic love poetry. Virgil is the best known of all. His fourth *Eclogue* contains a prophecy of a 'messianic' figure. He was regarded as a pre-Christian prophet by later church Fathers. The *Georgics* idealize farming as a noble vocation (see #507). The third *Georgic* is a eulogy of Augustus. His *Aeneid* portrays Aeneas as the great exemplar of the Stoic.[16]

Sources

Horace (65–68 BCE) served under Brutus and Cassius at Philippi (42 BCE). Pardoned, he was able to concentrate on writing under the patronage of Augustus. Suetonius's biography of him survives.

The benefits bestowed on the world by Augustus.

224. Sprung from the blessed gods, best guardian of the race of Romulus, too long already art thou absent. Come back, for thou didst pledge a swift return to the sacred council of the Fathers. To thy country give again, blest leader, the light of thy presence! For when, like spring, thy face has beamed upon the folk, more pleasant runs the day, and brighter shines the sun. As with vows, with omens, and with prayers a mother calls the son whom the South wind with his envious gales keeps lingering far from his sweet home across the stretch of the Carpathian Sea for longer than a year, and from the curving shore turns not her face; so, moved by loyal love, his country yearns for Caesar. For when he is here, the ox in safety roams the pastures; Ceres and benign Prosperity makes rich the crops; safe are the seas o'er which our sailors course; Faith shrinks from blame; polluted by no stain, the home is pure; custom and law have stamped out the taint of sin; mothers win praise because of children like unto their sires; while Vengeance follows close on guilt.

Who would fear the Parthian, who the icy Scythian, who the hordes rough Germany doth breed, while Caesar lives unharmed? Who would mind the war in wild Iberia? On his own hillside each man spends the day, and weds his vines to waiting trees; thence gladly repairs to the feast, and at the second course invokes thee as a god. Thee with many a prayer, thee with pure wine poured from bowls, he worships; and mingles thy majesty with his household gods, like Greece mindful of Castor and great Hercules.

'Long holidays, blest leader, vouchsafe unto Hesperia!' So do we pray, dry-lipped, when day begins: so pray we, flushed with wine, when the sun sinks beneath the Ocean. (Horace, *Odes* 4.5)[17]

Catullus (c. 84–54 BCE) wrote love poetry dedicated to Lesbia, as well as epigrammatical pieces. He also wrote a number of longer poems.

225. Let us live, my Lesbia, and love, and value at one farthing all the talk of crabbed old men.

Suns may set and rise again. For us, when the short light has once set, remains to be slept the sleep of one unbroken night.

Give me a thousand kisses, then a hundred, then another thousand, then a second hundred, then yet another thousand, then a hundred. Then, when we have made up many thousands, we will confuse our counting, that we may not know the reckoning, nor any malicious person blight them with evil eye, when he knows that our kisses are so many.
(Catullus, *Poems* 5)

226. You shall have a good dinner at my house, Fabullus, in a few days, please the gods, if you bring with you a good dinner and plenty of it, not forgetting a pretty girl and wine and wit and all kinds of laughter. If, I say, you bring all this, my charming friend, you shall have a good dinner; for the purse of your Catullus is full of cobwebs. But on the other hand you shall have from me love's very essence, or what is sweeter or more delicious than love, if sweeter there be; for I will give you some perfume which the Venuses and Loves gave to my lady; and when you snuff its fragrance, you will pray the gods to make you, Fabullus, nothing but nose.
(Catullus, *Poems* 13)

227. Sirmio, bright eye of peninsulas and islands, all that in liquid lakes or vast ocean either Neptune bears: how willingly and with what joy I revisit you, scarcely trusting myself that I have left Thynia and the Bithynian plains, and that I see you in safety. Ah, what is more blessed than to put cares away, when the mind lays by its burden, and tired with labour of far travel we have come to our own home and rest on the couch we longed for? This it is which alone is worth all these toils. Welcome, lovely Sirmio, and rejoice in your master, and rejoice ye too, waters of the Lydian lake, and laugh out aloud all the laughter you have in your home.
(Catullus, *Poems* 31)

Virgil (70–19 BCE) was a towering figure in Roman literature whose work exerted a powerful influence on subsequent Roman and Christian literature. His major work, the *Aeneid*, is a masterpiece of myth-making. In the first selection, Virgil contemplates the dislocation of the era of civil war. His farm was confiscated by Octavian eager to provide land for his veterans.

228. But we must go hence—some to the thirsty Africans, some to reach Scythia and Crete's swift Oaxes, and the Britons, wholly sundered from all the world. Ah, shall I ever, long years hence, look again on my country's bounds, on my humble cottage with its turf-clad roof—shall I, long years hence, look amazed on a few ears of corn, once my kingdom? Is a godless soldier to hold these well-tilled fallows? a barbarian these crops? See to what strife has brought our unhappy citizens! For these have we sown our fields! Now, Meliboeus, graft your pears, plant your vines in rows! Away, my goats! Away, once happy flock! No more, stretched in some mossy grot, shall I watch you in the distance hanging from a bushy crag; no more songs shall I sing; no more, my goats, under my tending, shall you crop flowering lucerne and bitter willows!
(Virgil, *Eclogue* 1.64–78)

The following poem, the fourth *Eclogue*, has commanded close attention from Christian writers and theologians for understandable reasons. It holds out the promise of a son born to a contemporary figure who will usher in an era of peace and plenty. Its thought is uncannily similar in tone to Isaiah 7:14, a passage that Christians have always associated with the birth of Christ (see Matthew 1:23).

229. Sicilian Muses, let us sing a somewhat loftier strain. Not all do the orchards please and the lowly tamarisks. If our song is of the woodland, let the woodland be worthy of a consul.

Now is come the last age of the song of Cumae; the great line of the centuries begins anew. Now the Virgin returns, the reign of Saturn returns; now a new generation descends from heaven on high. Only do thou, pure Lucina, smile on the birth of the child, under whom the iron brood shall first cease, and a golden race spring up throughout the world! Thine own Apollo now is king!

And in thy consulship, Pollio, yea in thine, shall this glorious age begin, and the mighty months commence their march; under thy sway, any lingering traces of our guilt shall become void, and release the earth from its continual dread. He shall have the gift of divine life, shall see heroes mingled with gods, and shall himself be seen of them, and shall sway a world to which his father's virtues have brought peace.

But for thee, child, shall the earth untilled pour forth, as her first pretty gifts, straggling ivy with foxglove everywhere, and the Egyptian bean blended with the smiling acanthus. Uncalled, the goats shall bring home their udders swollen with milk, and the herds shall fear not huge lions; unasked, thy cradle shall pour forth flowers for thy delight. The serpent, too, shall perish, and the false poison-plant shall perish; Assyrian spice shall spring up on every soil.

But soon as thou canst read of the glories of heroes and thy father's deeds, and canst know what valour is, slowly shall the plain yellow with the waving corn, on wild brambles shall hang the purple grape, and the stubborn oak shall distil dewy honey. Yet shall some few traces of olden sin lurk behind, to call men to essay the sea in ships, to gird towns with walls, and to cleave the earth with furrows. A second Tiphys shall then arise, and a second Argo to carry chosen heroes; a second warfare, too, shall there be, and again shall a great Achilles be sent to Troy.

Next, when now the strength of years has made thee man, even the trader shall quit the sea, nor shall the ship of pine exchange wares; every land shall bear all fruits. The earth shall not feel the harrow, nor the vine the pruning-hook; the sturdy ploughman, too, shall now loose his oxen from the yoke. Wool shall no more learn to counterfeit varied hues, but of himself the ram in the meadows shall change his fleece, now to sweetly blushing purple, now to a saffron yellow; of its own will shall scarlet clothe the grazing lambs.

'Ages such as these, glide on!' cried to their spindles the Fates, voicing in unison the fixed will of Destiny!

Enter on thy high honours—the hour will soon be here—O thou dear offspring of the gods, mighty seed of a Jupiter to be!

Behold the world bowing with its massive dome—earth and expanse of sea and heaven's depth! Behold, how all things exult in the age that is at hand! O that then the last days of a long life may still linger for me, with inspiration enough to tell of thy deeds! Not Thracian Orpheus, not Linus shall vanquish me in song, though his mother be helpful to the one, and his father to the other, Calliope to Orpheus, and fair Apollo to Linus. Even Pan, were he to contend with me and Arcady be judge, even Pan, with Arcady for judge, would own himself defeated.

Begin, baby boy, to know thy mother with a smile—to thy mother ten months have brought the weariness of travail. Begin, baby boy! Him on whom his parents have not smiled, no god honours with his table, no goddess with her bed!
(Virgil, *Eclogue* 4)

Virgil's Aeneid *(#230–33).*

Virgil's epic ranks with Homer's *Odyssey* and *Iliad* as the greatest poetic works to survive the classical and Graeco-Roman eras.

The selection below is from Book 1. Aeneas, his ships, and demoralized fellow travellers are heading towards Latium having escaped the destruction of Troy. Jupiter assures Venus, Aeneas's mother and heavenly champion, that once settled in Italy the descendants of Aeneas will become a mighty nation, *Troy redivivus* (see also *Aeneid* 1.198–207). Jupiter offers a review of the history of Rome.

230. 'Spare thy fear, Lady of Cythera; thy children's fates abide unmoved. Thou shalt see Lavinium's city and its promised walls; and thou shalt raise on high to the starry heaven great-souled Aeneas. No thought has turned me. This thy son—for, since this care gnaws at thy heart, I will speak and, further unrolling the scroll of fate, will disclose its secrets—shall wage a great war in Italy, shall crush proud nations, and for his people shall set up laws and city walls; till the third summer has seen him reigning in Latium and three winters have passed in camp since the Rutulians were laid low. But the lad Ascanius, now surnamed Iulus—Ilus he was, while the Ilian state stood firm in sovereignty—shall fulfil in empire thirty great circles of rolling months, shall shift his throne from Lavinium's seat, and, great in power, shall build the walls of Alba Longa. Here then for thrice a hundred years unbroken shall the kingdom endure under Hector's race, until Ilia, a royal priestess, shall bear to Mars her twin offspring. Then Romulus, proud in the tawny hide of the she-wolf, his nurse, shall take up the line, and found the walls of Mars and call the people Romans after his own name. For these I set neither bounds nor periods of empire; dominion without end have I bestowed. Nay, harsh Juno, who now in her fear troubles sea and earth and sky, shall change to better counsels and with me cherish the Romans, lords of the world, and the nation of the gown. Thus is it decreed. There shall come a day, as the sacred seasons glide past, when the house of Assaracus shall bring into bondage Phthia, and famed Mycenae, and hold lordship over vanquished Argos. From this noble line shall be born the Trojan Caesar, who shall limit his empire with ocean, his glory with the stars, a Julius, name descended from great Iulus! Him, in days to come, shalt thou, anxious no more, welcome to heaven, laden with Eastern spoils; he, too, shall be invoked in vows. Then shall wars cease and the rough ages soften; hoary Faith and Vesta, Quirinus with his brother Remus, shall give laws. The gates of war, grim with iron and close-fitting bars, shall be closed; within, impious Rage, sitting on savage arms, his hands fast bound behind with a hundred brazen knots, shall roar in the ghastliness of blood-stained lips.'
(Virgil, *Aeneid* 1.257–96)

Book 6 of the *Aeneid* is a mirror of Book 12 of the *Iliad*. Aeneas's father Anchises has died on the way to Latium. Aeneas is granted the opportunity of visiting his father in the underworld. Having crossed over he meets heroes from the past, and sees the still unforgiving Dido of Carthage (ll. 450–76) whom he had abandoned. In the following Aeneas hears the torments of those in hell.

231. Suddenly Aeneas looks back, and under a cliff on the left sees a broad castle, girt with

triple wall and encircled with a rushing flood of torrent flames—Tartarean Phlegethon, that rolls along thundering rocks. In front stands the huge gate, and pillars of soil adamant, that no might of man, nay, not even the sons of heaven, may uproot in war; there stands the iron tower, soaring high, and Tisiphone, sitting girt with bloody pall, keeps sleepless watch o'er the portal night and day. Therefrom are heard groans and the sound of the savage lash; withal, the clank of iron and dragging of chains. Aeneas stopped, rooted to the spot in terror of the din. 'What forms of crime are these? Say, O maiden! With what penalties are they scourged? What cry so loud uprises?' Then the seer thus began to speak: 'Famed chieftain of the Teucrians, no pure soul may tread the accursed threshold; but when Hecate set me over the groves of Avernus, she taught me the god's penalties and guided me through all. Gnosian Rhadamanthus holds here his iron sway; he chastises, and hears the tale of guilt, exacting confession of crimes, whenever in the world above any man, rejoicing in vain deceit, has put off atonement until death's late hour. Straightway avenging Tisiphone, girt with the lash, leaps on the guilty to scourge them, and with left hand brandishing her grim snakes, calls on her savage sister band. Then at last, grating on harsh, jarring hinge, the infernal gates open. Seest thou what sentry sits in the doorway? what shape guards the threshold? The monstrous Hydra, still fiercer, with her fifty black gaping throats, dwells within. Then Tartarus itself yawns sheer down, stretching into the gloom twice as far as is yon sky's upward view to heavenly Olympus. Here the ancient sons of Earth, the Titan's brood, hurled down by the thunderbolt, writhe in the lowest abyss. Here, too, I saw the twin sons of Aloeus, giant in stature, whose hands essayed to tear down high Heaven and thrust down Jove from his realm above. Salmoneus, too, I saw, who paid a cruel penalty while aping Jove's fires and the thunders of Olympus. He, borne by four horses and brandishing a torch, rode triumphant through the Greek peoples and his city in the heart of Elis, claiming as his own the homage of deity. Madman! to mimic the storm-clouds and inimitable thunder with brass and the tramp of horn-footed horses! But the Father Almighty amid thick clouds launched his bolt—no firebrands he, nor pitch-pines' smoky glare—and drave him headlong with furious whirlwind. Likewise one might see Tityos, nursling of Earth, the universal mother. Over nine full acres his body is stretched, and a monstrous vulture with crooked beak gnaws at his deathless liver and vitals fruitful for anguish; deep within the breast he lodges and gropes for his feast; nor is any respite given to the filaments that grow anew. Why tell of the Lapithae, Ixion and Pirithoüs, over whom hangs a black crag that now, yea now, would seem to slip and fall? High festal couches gleam with frames of gold, and before their eyes is spread a banquet in royal splendour. Yet, reclining hard by, the eldest Fury stays their hands from touch of the table, springing forth with uplifted torch and thunderous cries.

'Here were they who in lifetime hated their brethren, or smote a sire, and entangled a client in wrong; or who brooded in solitude over wealth they had won, nor set aside a portion for their kin—the largest number this; who were slain for adultery; or who followed unholy warfare, and feared not to break faith with their lords—all these, immured, await their doom. Seek not to learn that doom, or what form of crime, or fate, o'erwhelmed them! Some roll a huge stone, or hang outstretched on spokes of wheels; hapless Theseus sits and evermore shall sit, and Phlegyas, most unblest, gives warning to all and with loud voice bears witness amid the gloom: *Be warned; learn ye to be just and not to slight the gods!* This one sold his country for gold, and fastened on her a tyrant lord; he made and unmade laws for a bribe. This forced his daughter's bed and a marriage forbidden. All dared a monstrous sin, and what they dared attained. Nay, had I a hundred tongues, a hundred mouths, and voice of iron, I could not sum up all the forms of crime, or rehearse all the tale of torments.'

(Virgil, *Aeneid* 6.548–627)

Aeneas is granted a sight of the Blissful Groves, a haven for worthy heroes.

232. This at length performed and the task of the goddess fulfilled, they came to a land of joy, the green pleasaunces and happy seats of the Blissful Groves. Here an ampler ether clothes the meads with roseate light, and they know their own sun, and stars of their own. Some disport their limbs on the grassy wrestling-ground, vie in sports, and grapple on the yellow sand; some trip it in the dance and chant songs. There, too, the long-robed Thracian priest matches their measures with the seven clear notes, striking them now with his fingers, now with his ivory quill. Here is Teucer's olden line, family most fair, high-souled heroes born in happier years—Ilus and Assaracus and Dardanus, Troy's founder. From afar he marvels at their phantom arms and chariots. Their lances stand fixed in the ground, and their steeds, unyoked, browse freely over the plain. The selfsame pride in chariot and arms that was theirs in life, the selfsame care in keeping sleek steeds, attends them when hidden beneath the earth. Lo! others he sees, to right and left, feasting on the sward, and chanting in chorus a joyous paean within a fragrant laurel grove, whence, in the world above, the full flood of the Eridanus rolls amid the forest.

Here is the band of those who suffered wounds, fighting for fatherland; those who in lifetime were priests and pure, good bards, whose songs were meet for Phoebus; or they who ennobled life by truths discovered and they who by service have won remembrance among men—the brows of all bound with snowy fillet. These, as they streamed round, the Sibyl thus addressed, Musaeus before all; for he is centre of the vast throng that gazes up to him, as with shoulders high he towers aloft: 'Say, happy souls, and thou best of bards, what land, what place holds Anchises? For his sake are we come, and have sailed across the great rivers of Erebus.'
(Virgil, *Aeneid* 6.637–71)

Anchises offers the following account of the journey of the soul. While a select few souls remain forever in Elysium, the majority return in time to animate new earthly bodies.

233. 'First, the heaven and earth, and the watery plains, the shining orb of the moon and Titan's star, a spirit within sustains, and mind, pervading its members, sways the whole mass and mingles with its mighty frame. Thence the race of man and beast, the life of winged things, and the strange shapes ocean bears beneath his glassy floor. Fiery is the vigour and divine the source of those life-seeds, so far as harmful bodies clog them not, nor earthly limbs and mortal frames dull them. Hence their fears and desires, their griefs and joys; nor discern they the light, pent up in the gloom of their dark dungeon. Nay, when at their last day life is fled, still not all the evil, alas! not all the plagues of the body quit them utterly; and it must needs be that many a taint, long linked in growth, should in wondrous wise become deeply ingrained. Therefore are they schooled with penalties, and for olden sins pay punishment: some are hung stretched out to the empty winds; from some the stain of guilt is washed away under swirling floods or burned out in fire. Each of us suffers his own spirit; then through wide Elysium are we sent, a few of us to abide in the joyous fields; till lapse of days, when time's cycle is complete, takes out the inbred taint and leaves unsoiled the ethereal sense and pure flame of spirit. All these, when they have rolled time's wheel through a thousand years, the god summons in vast throng to the river of Lethe, in sooth that, reft of memory, they may revisit the vault above and conceive desire to return again to the body.'
(Virgil, *Aeneid* 6.724–51)

Like Virgil, the land of Propertius (c. 50–52 BCE) and his family was confiscated at the end of the 40s. A critic of the political establishment, he eschewed the normal political and military career path for a life devoted to love as a vocation.

234. Wherefore, Cynthia, when at last death shall seal my eyes, hear thou the order of my funeral. For me let no procession walk with long array of masks, let no trumpet make vain wailing for my end. Let no last bed on posts of ivory be strewn for me, let not my dead body lie on a couch of cloth-of-gold; no line of attendants with sweet-scented platters for me, only the humble obsequies that mark a poor man's death.

Costly enough shall be my funeral train if three little books go with me to the grave, that I may bear them to Persephone as my most precious offering. And thou shalt follow, thy breast all bare and torn, nor shalt thou weary of calling upon my name, but shalt imprint the last kiss upon my clay-cold lips, when the casket of onyx with its gift of Syrian nard is bestowed upon me. Then when the fire beneath hath burned me to an ash, let a tiny earthen urn receive my ghost, and over my little tomb let a laurel be planted to o'ershade the spot, where the fire of death hath ceased to burn; and thereon be these two verses: HE THAT NOW LIES NAUGHT BUT UNLOVELY DUST, ONCE SERVED ONE LOVE AND ONE LOVE ONLY.
(Propertius, *Elegies* 2.13A ll. 1–36)

235. Yet do ye mortals inquire after the uncertain hour of death, and of the path by which your doom shall draw a nigh, and in the unclouded heaven ye seek by the art the Phoenicians found of old what star is good, what star is ill for man. Whether on foot we follow the flying Parthian or with our fleet attack the Briton, blind are the perils both by land and sea. And again thou weepest that thy life is threatened by the storm of war, when Mars on this side and on that mingles the wavering ranks; thou dreadest also fire for thy house and ruin, and tremblest lest thou put cups of dark poison to thy lips. The lover only knows when and by what death he shall perish, and fears nor weapons nor blasts of the North Wind. Yea, even though he sit at the oar among the reeds of Styx and gaze on the dismal sails of the boat of hell, if the faint whisper of his mistress' voice cry out and call him back from the dead, he will return over that road that the eternal ordinance hath sealed.
(Propertius, *Elegies* 2.27)

236. Caesar [Augustus] our god plans war against rich Ind and would cleave with his fleet the waters of the pearl-bearing sea. Great is the prize, men of Rome: furthest earth prepares triumphs for thee, Tiber, and Euphrates shall flow beneath thy sway. Late shall that province come beneath Ausonia's rods, yet it shall surely come; Parthia's trophies shall become familiar with Latin Jupiter. Go now, ye prows well skilled in war, unfurl your sails; ye war-horses, ply the task ye know so well! I sing you prospering omens. Avenge Crassus and his slaughter! Go forth and make fair the pages of Rome's story!

O father Mars and ye fires of fate, that burn for holy Vesta, I implore you, may that day come ere I die, on which I shall see Caesar's chariots laden with spoils and his steeds oft halting at sound of the people's cheers; then as I lie reclined on the bosom of my beloved I will read the names of captured cities, and will turn mine eyes to gaze at the shafts that were hurled by flying horsemen, at the bows of trousered warriors and the captive chiefs that sit beneath the arms that once they bore.

Venus, keep safe thine offspring; may that life, that before thine eyes still preserves Aeneas' line, live through all ages! Be the spoil theirs whose toil has won it! Enough for me to be able to cheer them on the Sacred Way.
(Propertius, *Elegies* 3.4)

Ovid (43 BCE –17 CE) was a member with Horace and Propertius of the *litterati* gathered around Augustus. Banished by the emperor in 8 CE, he spent the rest of his life at Tomis on the Black Sea.

Ovid's *Amores* is a collection of frequently erotic and passionate love poems.

237. 'Twas sultry, and the day had passed its mid hour; I laid my members to rest them on the middle of my couch. One shutter of my window was open, the other shutter was closed; the light was such as oft in woodland, or as the faint glow of the twilight when Phoebus just is taking leave, or when night has gone and still the day is not sprung. It was such a light as shrinking maids should have whose timid modesty hopes to hide away—when lo! Corinna comes, draped in tunic girded round, with divided hair falling over fair, white neck—such as 'tis said was famed Semiramis when passing to her bridal chamber, and Lais loved of many men.

I tore away the tunic—and yet 'twas fine, and scarcely marred her charms; but still she struggled to have the tunic shelter her. Even while thus she struggled, as one who would not overcome, was she overcome—and 'twas not hard—by her own betrayal. As she stood before my eyes with drapery laid all aside, nowhere on all her body was sign of fault. What shoulders, what arms did I see—and touch! How suited for caress the form of her breasts! How smooth her body beneath the faultless bosom! What a long and beautiful side! How youthful fair her thigh!

Why recount each charm? Naught did I see not worthy of praise, and I clasped her undraped form to mine.

The rest, who does not know? Outwearied, we both lay quiet in repose.

May my lot bring many a midday like to this!
(Ovid, *Amores* 1.5)

Ovid's *Art of Love* was written for men and women. It purports to be a manual of courtship leading to sexual intimacy. Like the *Amores* the *Art of Love* is replete with erotic content. Ovid includes a catalogue of fashionable poets, which includes himself, in 3.329–48.

238. Such openings will the Circus afford to a new courtship, and the melancholy sand scattered on the busy Forum. Often has Venus' Boy fought upon that sand, and he who watched the wounds has himself been wounded. While he is speaking and touching her hand and asking for the book, and inquiring which is winning as he lays his stake, he feels the winged barb and groans with the wound, and is himself part of the show which he is watching.

What when Caesar of late brought on Persian and Athenian vessels under the fashion of a naval fight? Why, youths and maidens came from either sea: the mighty world was in our city. Who found not in that crowd some object for his passion? alas! how many did a foreign love o'erthrow!
(Ovid, *Art of Love* 1.163–76)

239. First let assurance come to your minds, that all women can be caught; spread but your nets and you will catch them. Sooner would birds be silent in spring, or grasshoppers in summer, or the hound of Maenalus flee before the hare than a woman persuasively wooed resist a lover: nay, even she, whom you will think cruel, will be kind. And as stolen love is pleasant to a man, so is it also to a woman; the man dissembles badly: she conceals desire better. Did it suit us males not to ask any woman first, the woman, already won, would play the asker.
(Ovid, *Art of Love* 1.269–78)

3.5. Moral Treatises

The Hellenistic and Graeco-Roman eras produced essays or treatises designed to inculcate the good life. Often written by philosophers, these works exhort the reader to pursue a life orientated to high moral standards. There were two basic modes of exhortation. In the first, termed paraenesis, the writer exhorted the reader to continue pursuing a set of moral precepts to which the reader is already orientated. In the second, protrepsis, the writer urged the reader to turn from a less worthy life orientation to embrace a life of moral seriousness.

Sources

Paraenesis.

The following extracts are from the collection of moral treatises by (or associated with) the fourth-century BCE Athenian rhetorician Isocrates. They well illustrate the tendency in this mode of exhortation to recall what the addressee already knows. Note the appeal to conventional morality in #241.

240. Nay, if you will but recall also your father's principles, you will have from your own house a noble illustration of what I am telling you. For he did not belittle virtue nor pass his life in indolence; on the contrary, he trained his body by toil, and by his spirit he withstood dangers. Nor did he love wealth inordinately; but, although he enjoyed the good things at his hand as became a mortal, yet he cared for his possessions as if he had been immortal. Neither did he order his existence sordidly, but was a lover of beauty, munificent in his manner of life, and gener-

ous to his friends; and he prized more those who were devoted to him than those who were his kin by blood; for he considered that in the matter of companionship nature is a much better guide than convention, character than kinship, and freedom of choice than compulsion.
(Isocrates, *To Demonicus* 9–10)

241. First of all, then, show devotion to the gods, not merely by doing sacrifice, but also by keeping your vows; for the former is but evidence of a material prosperity, whereas the latter is proof of a noble character. Do honour to the divine power at all times, but especially on occasions of public worship; for thus you will have the reputation both of sacrificing to the gods and of abiding by the laws.

Conduct yourself toward your parents as you would have your children conduct themselves toward you.

Train your body, not by the exercises which conduce to strength, but by those which conduce to health. In this you will succeed if you cease your exertions while you still have energy to exert yourself.

Be not fond of violent mirth, nor harbour presumption of speech; for the one is folly, the other madness.

Whatever is shameful to do you must not consider it honourable even to mention. Accustom yourself to be, not of a stern, but of a thoughtful, mien; for through the former you will be thought self-willed, through the latter, intelligent. Consider that no adornment so becomes you as modesty, justice, and self-control; for these are the virtues by which, as all men are agreed, the character of the young is held in restraint.

Never hope to conceal any shameful thing which you have done; for even if you do conceal it from others, your own heart will know.

Fear the gods, honour your parents, respect your friends, obey the laws.

Pursue the enjoyments which are of good repute; for pleasure attended by honour is the best thing in the world, but pleasure without honour is the worst.

Guard yourself against accusations, even if they are false; for the multitude are ignorant of the truth and look only to reputation. In all things resolve to act as though the whole world would see what you do; for even if you conceal your deeds for the moment, later you will be found out. But most of all will you have the respect of men, if you are seen to avoid doing things which you would blame others for doing.
(Isocrates, *To Demonicus* 13–17)

Protrepsis.

242. I have learned of your fairmindedness, Polycrates, and of the reversal in your life, through information from others; and having myself read certain of the discourses which you have written, I should have been greatly pleased to discuss frankly with you and fully the education with which you have been obliged to occupy yourself. For I believe that when men through no fault of their own are unfortunate and so seek in philosophy a source of gain, it is the duty of all who have had a wider experience in that occupation, and have become more thoroughly versed in it, to make this contribution voluntarily for their benefit. But since we have not yet met one another, we shall be able, if we ever do come together, to discuss the other topics at greater length; concerning those suggestions, however, by which at the present time I might be of service to you, I have thought I should advise you by letter, though concealing my views, to the best of my ability, from everyone else. I am well aware, however, that it is instinctive with most persons when admonished, not to look to the benefits they receive but, on the contrary, to listen to what is said with the greater displeasure in proportion to the rigour with which their critic passes their faults in review. Nevertheless, those who are well disposed toward any persons must not shrink from incurring such resentment, but must try to effect a change in the opinion of those who feel this way toward those who offer them counsel.
(Isocrates, *Busiris* 1–3)

Consolation.

A number of treatises offering consolation to the grieving are extant from the Graeco-Roman era. The following extract is from

Seneca's *To Marcia*. They articulate a stoic view of death and grief.

243. Reflect that there are no ills to be suffered after death, that the reports that make the Lower World terrible to us are mere tales, that no darkness is in store for the dead, no prison, no blazing streams of fire, no river of Lethe, that no judgement-seats are there, nor culprits, nor in that freedom so unfettered are there a second time any tyrants. All these things are the fancies of the poets, who have harrowed us with groundless terrors. Death is a release from all suffering, a boundary beyond which our ills cannot pass—it restores us to that peaceful state in which we lay before we were born. If anyone pities the dead, he must also pity those who have not been born. Death is neither a good nor an evil; for that only which is something is able to be a good or an evil. But that which is itself nothing and reduces all things to nothingness consigns us to neither sphere of fortune; for evils and goods must operate upon something material.
(Seneca, *To Marcia, On Consolation* 19.4–5)

3.6. The Novel

The only complete novel from the Graeco-Roman era is the justly famous *Golden Ass* of Apuleius. Written in c. 130 CE the work tells the adventures of the well-born Lucius. He visits Milo, spending some time as his guest. He is turned into an ass following a dalliance with the slave-girl Fotis. She panders to his overweening curiosity in the magic arts of her mistress, Milo's wife. After many adventures, at the conclusion of the novel, Lucius seeks the aid of the goddess Isis and is finally released from his asinine form and initiated into the mysteries of the goddess (#350). In the extract below Lucius is addressed by a priest.

Sources

244. 'O my friend Lucius, after the endurance of so many labours and the escape of so many tempests of fortune, thou art now at length come to the port and haven of rest and mercy. Neither did thy noble lineage, thy dignity, neither thy excellent doctrine anything avail thee; but because thou didst turn to servile pleasures, by a little folly of thy youthfulness, thou hast had a sinister reward of thy unprosperous curiosity. But howsoever the blindness of fortune tormented thee in divers dangers, so it is that now by her unthoughtful malice thou art come to this present felicity of religion. Let fortune go and fume with fury in another place; let her find some other matter to execute her cruelty; for fortune hath no puissance against them which have devoted their lives to serve and honour the majesty of our goddess. For what availed the thieves? The beasts savage? Thy great servitude? The ill, toilsome, and dangerous ways? The fear of death every day? What availed all those, I say, to cruel fortune? Know thou that now thou art safe, and under the protection of that fortune that is not blind but can see, who by her clear light doth lighten the other gods: wherefore rejoice, and take a convenable countenance to thy white habit, and follow with joyful steps the pomp of this devout and honourable procession; let such, which be not devout to the goddess, see and acknowledge their error: "Behold, here is Lucius that is delivered from his former so great miseries by the providence of the goddess Isis, and rejoiceth therefore and triumpheth of victory over his fortune." And to the end thou mayest live more safe and sure, make thyself one of this holy order, to which thou wast but a short time since pledged by oath, dedicate thy mind to the obeying of our religion, and take upon thee a voluntary yoke of ministry: for when thou beginnest to serve and honour the goddess, then shalt thou feel the more the fruit of liberty.'
(Apuleius, *Golden Ass* 11.15)

Lucius's hymn in praise of Isis.

245. 'O holy and blessed dame, the perpetual comfort of human kind, who by Thy bounty and grace nourishest all the world, and bearest a great affection to the adversities of the miserable as a loving mother, Thou takest no rest night or day, neither art Thou idle at any time in giving benefits and succouring all men as well on land and sea; Thou art she that puttest away all storms

and dangers from men's life by stretching forth Thy right hand, whereby likewise Thou dost unweave even the inextricable and entangled web of fate, and appeasest the great tempests of fortune, and keepest back the harmful course of the stars. The gods supernal do honour Thee; the gods infernal have Thee in reverence; Thou dost make all the earth to turn, Thou givest light to the sun, Thou governest the world, Thou treadest down the power of hell. By Thy mean the stars give answer, the seasons return, the gods rejoice, the elements serve: at Thy commandment the winds do blow, the clouds nourish the earth, the seeds prosper, and the fruits do grow. The birds of the air, the beasts of the hill, the serpents of the den, and the fishes of the sea do tremble at Thy majesty: but my spirit is not able to give Thee sufficient praise, my patrimony is unable to satisfy Thy sacrifices; my voice hath no power to utter that which I think of Thy majesty, no, not if I had a thousand mouths and so many tongues and were able to continue for ever. Howbeit as a good religious person, and according to my poor estate, I will do what I may: I will always keep Thy divine appearance in remembrance, and close the imagination of Thy most holy godhead within my breast.'
(Apuleius, *Golden Ass* 11.25)[18]

Notes

1. See Herodotus, *Histories* 2.19, 44, 75, 113, 118; 6.19. Note also Tacitus, *Annals* 3.16 for the testimony of eye-witnesses and the reporting of both sides of an issue, and *Annals* 15.53 on recording statements of differing points of view. Cf. Suetonius, *Claudius* 1.
2. The difference between 'annals' and 'history', as discussed by Aulus Gellius, is instructive. 'The books of annals merely made known what happened and in what year it happened, which is like writing a diary, which the Greeks call ἐφημερίς [*ephēmeris*]. For my part, I realize that it is not enough to make known what has been done, but that one should show with what purpose and for what reason things were done' (*Attic Nights* 5.18.8).
3. Note also Cicero, *Laws* 1.5: 'History is a branch of study which is predominantly the concern of the orator'.
4. Elsewhere Polybius writes that 'past events make us pay particular attention to the future, that is to say if we really make thorough inquiry in each case into the past' (*Histories* 12.25e.6).
5. Note the moralizing impulse in Tacitus, *Annals* 3.65; and in *Histories* 1.7, 72; 2.30 (on the moral decadence of Otto and Vitellius), 2.62, 64 (on the revealing of character). See also the digression in *Histories* 2.38 on the character of Rome itself; and *Histories* 2.73 on Vitellius's and Roman immorality and excess.
6. See Polybius, *Histories* 10.21.5–8 for the different scope of biography and history.
7. See, e.g., Polybius's biographical sketch of Scipio Aemilianus in *Histories* 18.35.9.
8. See Plutarch, *Marius* 2.3; *Sulla* 30.5; *Caesar* 58.4–10 on character as revealed in the subject's life and moral choices.
9. Lucian concludes his *Life* of the Athenian philosopher Demonax by writing: 'These are a very few things out of the many which I might have mentioned, but they will suffice to give my readers a notion of the sort of man he was' (cf. John 20:30–31). Lucian intends his audience to learn moral lessons from the simple and peace-loving example of the philosopher.
10. See also Ovid (*Art of Love* 1.455–68) on the advisability of sending one's beloved a letter; particularly if written in the unadorned style.
11. Cicero distinguished between letters for private consumption and those written for the wider public (*Pro Flacco* 16; 37), and noted the fact that there are different kinds of letters (see *Letters to his Friends* 2.4.1 cited below at #218). Pseudo-Demetrius (second century BCE –third century CE) provides a catalogue and examples of 21 different kinds of letters; Pseudo-Libanius (fourth–sixth centuries CE) extends the list to 41. For texts see Abraham J. Malherbe, *Ancient Epistolary Theorists* (Atlanta: Scholars Press, 1988).
12. Tiro was one of Cicero's slaves who had recently been manumitted.
13. The absence of friends is also taken up, e.g., in *Letters to Atticus* 2.1. See also *Letters to his Friends* 16.16 (#218) and Seneca, *Epistles* 40.1 for the reassuring communication of the writer's personality in letters.

14. This letter should be compared with the three Pastoral Epistles of the New Testament in which the writer advises his protégés who are about to enter significant leadership roles in the Pauline churches. Such letters have been characterized as belonging to a letter type—called *mandata principis* (precepts of the ruler)—in which a social superior sets out the responsibilities he wishes to enjoin on a junior. See also P.Tebt 703, 'Instructions of a Dioecetes to a Subordinate' (late third century BCE).
15. Examples of Lucretius's poetry are cited at #372 and #373. The connection between oratory and the power of poetry to persuade and move was not lost on the Romans. Quintilian argued that secondary schools should concentrate on the reading and teaching of poetry (Michael Grant, *Roman Literature* [Harmondsworth: Penguin Books, 1958], p. 126). Cicero affirmed the connection between poetry and oratory (*De Oratore* 1.70).
16. So Grant, *Roman Literature*, p. 184.
17. See also *Odes* 4.15 for gratitude to Augustus and the return during his principate of the Eagles lost at Carrhae with the army of Crassus.
18. See also the aretalogy cited at #351.

4. Early Jewish and Christian Literature

Introduction

The period between c. 200 BCE and 200 CE bears witness to a diverse array of Jewish writings. The best known to readers of the New Testament are likely to be the books comprising what is usually known as the Old Testament Apocrypha. This collection achieved deutero-canonical status in Orthodox and Roman Catholic churches, and was accepted as scriptural by the majority of the early church Fathers. In addition there is the vast Jewish literary enterprise comprising the midrashim, the targums, and the halakhic literature associated with the rabbis of the first few centuries of the Common Era.

Much of the Jewish literature of the era between c. 200 BCE and 200 CE that is not found in the Hebrew Bible or Greek New Testament, the Apocrypha, or the rabbinic writings has been in gathered up into an artificial collection known as the 'Old Testament Pseudepigrapha', a term that means 'writings falsely ascribed' (i.e. they were written under assumed names). Strictly speaking, however, only the apocalypses of this collection are pseudepigrapha. The collection represents literary works emanating from both Palestine and the diaspora (chiefly Syrian and Alexandrian Judaism).

The books of the Pseudepigrapha, like the works of Josephus, were preserved in the Christian churches, and are often extant only in the languages of those churches—Latin, Greek, Syriac, Slavonic, Georgian, Armenian and Ethiopic. Originally many of the books were composed in Hebrew and Aramaic. Some Hebrew and Aramaic fragments of the books of Tobit, *1 Enoch* and *Jubilees* have been discovered among the Dead Sea Scrolls. Hebrew fragments of the books of Sirach and *Jubilees* have been found among the texts from Masada. There is evidence of occasional Christian interpolation and addition.[1]

Apocalypses are well represented in the Pseudepigrapha. Sections of these apocalypses may be dated as early as the third century BCE. The earliest sections of *1 Enoch* (chapters 1–36) may be the earliest Jewish apocalyptic material of all. Christians, themselves persecuted, identified with the tortured existence that finds expression in many of these works. The eschatological worldview of much of the New Testament is clearly indebted to them. The testament genre is also frequently encountered in the Pseudepigrapha. In the New Testament 2 Peter and 2 Timothy, though formally letters, owe much to the testament. In the Pseudepigrapha, the *Testament of Moses* (*TMos*) and the *Testaments of the Twelve Patriarchs* (*T12P*) are two well-known examples of the genre. Both incorporate apocalyptic scenarios. Prayers and hymns are found both independently and incorporated into other genres. Considerable literary energy was invested in the enterprise of applying and actualizing the narrative traditions of the Hebrew Bible through interpretation and expansion. By this means Jewish communities rooted in the Bible were equipped to meet new challenges and crises. This predilection for expanding the biblical text may have given rise to the way in which the early traditions about Jesus reached their final form. In early Jewish wisdom literature, the law is equated with wisdom (see Wisdom of Solomon; Sirach 24). Temperance and asceticism are prominent among the ethical ideals espoused in Jewish exhortatory literature generally. Hymns and prayers are found across the genres.

The literature of early Christianity is imbued with the conviction that the person and work of Jesus represents a fresh revelation of God among humankind. That conviction is pre-eminently articulated in a new literary genre, the gospel.

4.1. Apocalypses

The term 'apocalypse' derives from a Greek word meaning an unveiling or revelation. In works of the genre the secrets of this world or the world to come are revealed to the seer through angelic mediation. Apocalypses are written pseudonymously. The seer writes in the name of a venerable figure from the past, thus enhancing the authority of the writing. The earliest examples of the genre emanate from third-century BCE Palestine.

Some scholars argue that apocalyptic thinking arose as a protest against the conventional wisdom and expectations entertained by the oppressive establishment exercised either by apostate Jews (from the perspective of the seers) or Gentiles (in the case of Antiochus Epiphanes or the Romans).[2] Apocalyptic writing is characterized by otherworldly journeys, extravagant animal imagery, number symbolism, and visions. Angelic mediation is a constant motif encountered in apocalypses. A consistent theme of eschatological apocalypses is the confident expectation that God will intervene decisively in human affairs marked as they are by injustice. God will bring the rule of the oppressors to a catastrophic end (often by the means of a designated agent), vindicate the beleaguered and persevering, consign the evil to eternal destruction, and usher in a new era of plenty and peace. These characteristics can be found among the latest written sections of the Hebrew Bible, chiefly Isaiah 24–27, 56–66, and Joel 2. Daniel 7–12, written during the Maccabaean Revolt, and the earlier Zechariah 9–14 constitute some of the earliest dateable examples of apocalyptic writing.

In the New Testament the non-pseudonymous book of Revelation is the sole example of the genre. However, there are examples of apocalyptic eschatological speculation in the Gospels (see Matthew 24; Mark 13; Luke 21). Moreover, the undisputed letters of Paul bear the imprint of an apocalyptic worldview. Like the apocalyptic seers, Paul believes in the imminent triumph of God, and, like some of them, believes that God's triumph will be marked by the interposing of a divinely appointed agent, the resurrection of the dead, and the revealing of a new creation.

Sources

Apocalyptic imagery (#246–48).

Occasionally in the Hebrew Bible there are passages in which the language and symbolism of creation myths are used in poetic contexts celebrating the redemptive work of God. These passages afford a glimpse of the imagery which later surfaces in the apocalypses. In the three passages below the writers are alluding to the Israelites' crossing of the Sea (see Exodus 14–15) as evidence of the saving might of God. Readers should compare the imagery of the Enuma Elish (Babylonian Creation Epic) (*ANET* pp. 60–72) and the Ugaritic Baal myths (*DOTT* pp. 129–31).

246. On that day the LORD with his cruel and great and strong sword will punish Leviathan the fleeing serpent, Leviathan the twisting serpent, and he will kill the dragon that is in the sea.
(Isaiah 27:1)

247. Awake, awake, put on strength,
O arm of the LORD!
Awake, as in days of old,
the generations of long ago!
Was it not you who cut Rahab in pieces,
who pierced the dragon?
Was it not you who dried up the sea,
the waters of the great deep;
who made the depths of the sea a way
for the redeemed to cross over?
(Isaiah 51:9–10)

248. Yet God my King is from of old,
working salvation in the earth.
You divided the sea by your might;
you broke the heads of the dragons in the waters.
You crushed the heads of Leviathan;

you gave him as food for the creatures of
the wilderness.
(Psalms 74:12–13)

1 Enoch *(#249–52).*

1 Enoch is a composite work extant as a whole in Ethiopic. There is manuscript evidence of four of the five sections among the Dead Sea corpus, but no manuscript of the second section (chapters 37–71) has been found in the caves. The book exercised considerable influence on early Judaism and Christianity, and was vital in the consolidation of opinion with respect to the work of the eschatological agent (Messiah), demonology, the afterlife and other aspects of the eschaton (see also Jude 6; 14–15). Chapters 1–36 and 72–82 constitute the oldest extant Jewish extra-biblical literature extant. In these two sections the reader is transported to third-century BCE Palestine. The former speculates on the origin and nature of evil, and is dependent on the story of the descent of the 'sons of God' to earth narrated in Genesis 6:1–4 (see also #231, *Aeneid* Book 6). The latter section (chapters 72–82) considers the secrets of the universe as revealed to the seer by the angel Uriel.

The fall of the angels.

249. (7) And they took wives unto themselves, and everyone (respectively) chose one woman for himself, and they began to go unto them. And they taught them magical medicine, incantations, the cutting of roots, and taught them (about) plants. And the women became pregnant and gave birth to great giants whose heights were three hundred cubits. These (giants) consumed the produce of all the people until the people detested feeding them. So the giants turned against (the people) in order to eat them. And they began to sin against birds, wild beasts, reptiles, and fish. And their flesh was devoured the one by the other, and they drank blood. And then the earth brought an accusation against the oppressors.

(10) And then spoke the Most High, the Great and Holy One! And he sent Asuryal to the son of Lamech [Noah], (saying), 'Tell him in my name, "Hide yourself!" and reveal to him the end of what is coming; for the earth and everything will be destroyed. And the Deluge is about to come upon all the earth; and all that is in it will be destroyed. And now instruct him in order that he may flee, and his seed will be preserved for all generations.' And secondly the Lord said to Raphael, 'Bind Azaz'el hand and foot (and) throw him into the darkness!' And he made a hole in the desert which was in Duda'el and cast him there; he threw on top of him rugged and sharp rocks. And he covered his face in order that he may not see light; and in order that he may be sent into the fire on the great day of judgment. And give life to the earth which the angels have corrupted. And he will proclaim life for the earth: that he is giving life to her. And all the children of the people will not perish through all the secrets (of the angels), which they taught to their sons. And the whole earth has been corrupted by Azaz'el's teaching of his (own) actions; and write upon him all sin. And to Gabriel the Lord said, 'Proceed against the bastards and the reprobates and against the children of adultery; and destroy the children of adultery and expel the children of the Watchers from among the people. And send them against one another (so that) they may be destroyed in the fight, for length of days have they not. They will beg you everything—for their fathers on behalf of themselves—because they hope to live an eternal life. (They hope) that each one of them will live a period of five hundred years.' And to Michael God said, 'Make known to Semyaza and the others who are with him, who fornicated with the women, that they will die together with them in all their defilement. And when they and all their children have battled with each other, and when they have seen the destruction of their beloved ones, bind them for seventy generations underneath the rocks of the ground until the day of their judgment and of their consummation, until the eternal judgment is concluded. In those days they will lead them into the bottom of the fire—and in torment—in the prison (where) they will be locked up forever. And at the time when they will burn and die, those who collaborated with them will

be bound together with them from henceforth unto the end of (all) generations. And destroy all the souls of pleasure and the children of the Watchers, for they have done injustice to man. Destroy injustice from the face of the earth. And every iniquitous deed will end, and the plant of righteousness and truth will appear forever and he will plant joy. And then all the righteous ones will escape; and become the living ones until they multiply and become tens of hundreds; and all the days of their youth and the years of their retirement they will complete in peace. And in those days the whole earth will be worked in righteousness, all of her planted with trees, and will find blessing. And they shall plant pleasant trees upon her—vines. And he who plants a vine upon her will produce wine for plenitude. And every seed that is sown on her, one measure will yield a thousand (measures) and one measure of olives will yield ten measures of presses of oil. And you cleanse the earth from all injustice, and from all defilement, and from all oppression, and from all sin, and from all iniquity which is being done on earth; remove them from the earth. And all the children of the people will become righteous, and all nations shall worship and bless me; and they will all prostrate themselves to me. And the earth shall be cleansed from all pollution, and from all sin, and from all plague, and from all suffering; and it shall not happen again that I shall send (these) upon the earth from generation to generation and forever.'
(*1 Enoch* 7, 10)

Enoch makes a second journey where he sees the preliminary and final place of punishment of fallen 'stars'.

250. And I came to an empty place. And I saw (there) neither a heaven above nor an earth below, but a chaotic and terrible place. And there I saw seven stars of heaven bound together in it, like great mountains, and burning with fire. At that moment I said, 'For which sin are they bound, and for what reason were they cast in here.' Then one of the holy angels, Uriel, who was with me, guiding me, spoke to me and said to me, 'Enoch, for what reason are you asking and for what reason do you question and exhibit eagerness? These are among the stars of heaven which have transgressed the commandments of the Lord and are bound in this place until the completion of ten million years, (according) to the number of their sins.' I then proceeded from that area to another place which is even more terrible and saw a terrible thing: a great fire that was burning and flaming; the place had a cleavage (that extended) to the last sea, pouring out great pillars of fire; neither its extent nor its magnitude could I see nor was I able to estimate. At that moment, what a terrible opening is this place and a pain to look at! Then Ura'el, (one) of the holy angels who was with me, responded and said to me, 'Enoch, why are you afraid like this?' (I answered and said), 'I am frightened because of this terrible place and the spectacle of this painful thing.' And he said unto me, 'This place is the prison house of the angels; they are detained here forever.'
(*1 Enoch* 21)

1 Enoch 72–82 is entitled the Book of the Heavenly Luminaries. The section has parallels in other apocalyptic literature of the Enoch tradition. It is a compendium of astronomical lore.

251. (Book) Three: The Book of the Itinerary of the Luminaries of Heaven: the position of each and every one, in respect to their ranks, in respect to their authorities, and in respect to their seasons; each one according to their names and their places of origin and according to their months, which Uriel, the holy angel who was with me, and who (also) is their guide, showed me—just as he showed me all their treatises and the nature of the years of the world unto eternity, till the new creation which abides forever is created.

This is the first commandment of the luminaries: The sun is a luminary whose egress is an opening of heaven, which is (located) in the direction of the east, and whose ingress is (another) opening of heaven, (located) in the west. I saw six openings through which the sun rises and six openings through which it sets. The moon also rises and sets through the same openings, and they are guided by the stars; together with

those whom they lead, they are six in the east and six in the west heaven. All of them (are arranged) one after another in a constant order. There are many windows (both) to the left and the right of these openings. First there goes out the great light whose name is the sun; its roundness is like the roundness of the sky; and it is totally filled with light and heat. The chariot on which it ascends is (driven by) the blowing wind. The sun sets in the sky (in the west) and returns by the northeast in order to go to the east; it is guided so that it shall reach the eastern gate and shine in the face of the sky.
(*1 Enoch* 72:1–5)

A historical review of Israel from just before, up to and including the Maccabaean Revolt as perceived by the seer of 1 Enoch *83–90.*

The sheep represent Israel; those blinded are apostate Jews. The shepherds are the angelic leaders of the people of God. Israel is set upon by wild beasts, Gentile marauders. The ram stands for Judas Maccabaeus.

252. Then, behold lambs were born from those snow-white sheep; and they began to open their eyes and see, and cried aloud to the sheep. But as for the sheep, they (the lambs) cried aloud to them, yet they (the sheep) did not listen to what they (the lambs) were telling them, but became exceedingly deafened, and their eyes became exceedingly dim-sighted. Then I saw in a vision ravens flying above those lambs, and they seized one of those lambs; and then smashing the sheep, they ate them. I kept seeing till those lambs grew horns; but the ravens crushed their horns. Then I kept seeing till one great horn sprouted on one of those sheep, and he opened their eyes; and they had vision in them and their eyes were opened. He cried aloud to the sheep, and all the rams saw him and ran unto him. In spite of this, all those eagles, vultures, ravens, and kites until now continue to rip the sheep, swooping down upon them and eating them. As for the sheep, they remain silent; but the rams are lamenting and crying aloud. Those ravens gather and battle with him (the horned ram) and seek to remove his horn, but without success.

I saw thereafter the shepherds coming; and those vultures and kites cried aloud to the ravens so that they should smash the horn of that ram. But he battled with them, and they fought each other; and he cried aloud, while battling with them, so that (God's) help should come. I kept seeing till that man, who writes down the names of the shepherds and elevates them before the Lord of the sheep, came; it is he who helped him and revealed (to him) everything; thus help came down for that ram. And I kept seeing till the Lord of the sheep came upon them in wrath, and all who saw him fled and fell all into darkness, from before his face. All the eagles, vultures, ravens, and kites gathered, with all the sheep of the field lining up with them; and having thus come together in unity, all of them cooperated in order to smash the horn of the ram. I saw that man who was writing a book by the command of the Lord, for he opened that book (of) destruction which those twelve last shepherds caused; and he revealed before the Lord of the sheep that they had much greater destruction than their predecessors. I kept seeing till the Lord of the sheep came unto them and took in his hand the rod of his wrath and smote the earth; and all the beasts and all the birds of the heaven fell down from the midst of those sheep and were swallowed up in the earth, and it was covered upon them. Then I saw that a great sword was given to the sheep; and the sheep proceeded against all the beasts of the field in order to kill them; and all the beasts and birds of heaven fled from before their face.

Then I kept seeing till a throne was erected in a pleasant land; and he sat upon it for the Lord of the sheep; and he took all the sealed books and opened those very books in the presence of the Lord of the sheep. Then the Lord called those people, the seven first snow-white ones, and ordered them to bring before him (some) from among the star(s) that arose, and from among those stars whose sexual organs were like those of the horses, as well as (that) first star which had fallen down earlier. And they brought them before him. He spoke to the man who was writing in his presence—that (man) being

one of those seven snow-white ones—saying, 'Take those seven shepherds to whom I had handed over the sheep, but who decided to kill many more than they were ordered.' Behold, I saw all of them bound; and they all stood before him. Then his judgment took place. First among the stars, they received their judgment and were found guilty, and they went to the place of condemnation; and they were thrown into an abyss, full of fire and flame and full of the pillar of fire. Then those seventy shepherds were judged and found guilty; and they were cast into that fiery abyss. In the meantime I saw how another abyss like it, full of fire, was opened wide in the middle of the ground; and they brought those blinded sheep, all of which were judged, found guilty, and cast into this fiery abyss, and they were burned—the abyss is to the right of that house; thus I saw those sheep while they were burning—their bones also were burning.
(*1 Enoch* 90:6–27)[3]

The following passage is from Daniel 7. Like *1 Enoch* 90 (see #252 above) it features a review of history culminating in the arrival of a fearsome beast (Alexander and his successors) and a 'little horn', a cipher for Antiochus IV Epiphanes. Yet the seer is confident in God's ability to deliver his people and to place them under his everlasting rule.

253. In the first year of King Belshazzar of Babylon, Daniel had a dream and visions of his head as he lay in bed. Then he wrote down the dream: I, Daniel, saw in my vision by night the four winds of heaven stirring up the great sea, and four great beasts came up out of the sea, different from one another. The first was like a lion and had eagles' wings. Then, as I watched, its wings were plucked off, and it was lifted up from the ground and made to stand on two feet like a human being; and a human mind was given to it. Another beast appeared, a second one, that looked like a bear. It was raised up on one side, had three tusks in its mouth among its teeth and was told, 'Arise, devour many bodies!' After this, as I watched, another appeared, like a leopard. The beast had four wings of a bird on its back and four heads; and dominion was given to it. After this I saw in the visions by night a fourth beast, terrifying and dreadful and exceedingly strong. It had great iron teeth and was devouring, breaking in pieces, and stamping what was left with its feet. It was different from all the beasts that preceded it, and it had ten horns. I was considering the horns, when another horn appeared, a little one coming up among them; to make room for it, three of the earlier horns were plucked up by the roots. There were eyes like human eyes in this horn, and a mouth speaking arrogantly.

As I watched,
thrones were set in place,
and an Ancient One took his throne,
his clothing was white as snow,
and the hair of his head like pure wool;
his throne was fiery flames,
and its wheels were burning fire.
A stream of fire issued
and flowed out from his presence.
A thousand thousands served him,
and ten thousand times ten thousand stood
attending him.
The court sat in judgment,
and the books were opened.

I watched then because of the noise of the arrogant words that the horn was speaking. And as I watched, the beast was put to death, and its body destroyed and given over to be burned with fire. As for the rest of the beasts, their dominion was taken away, but their lives were prolonged for a season and a time.

As I watched in the night visions,
I saw one like a human being
coming with the clouds of heaven.
And he came to the Ancient One
and was presented before him.
To him was given dominion
and glory and kingship,
that all peoples, nations, and languages
should serve him.
His dominion is an everlasting dominion
that shall not pass away,
and his kingship is one
that shall never be destroyed.

As for me, Daniel, my spirit was troubled within me, and the visions of my head terrified me. I approached one of the atten-

> dants to ask him the truth concerning all this. So he said that he would disclose to me the interpretation of the matter: 'As for these four great beasts, four kings shall arise out of the earth. But the holy ones of the Most High shall receive the kingdom and possess the kingdom forever—forever and ever.' (Daniel 7:1–18)[4]

4 Ezra.

4 Ezra was originally composed in Palestine. It was widely known in the early church in its Greek form.[5] Chapters 3–14 comprise seven visions granted Ezra. They were written in the wake of the destruction of Jerusalem in 70 CE.[6] 3:1 purports to set the writing in the 30th year after the destruction of 'our city' (i.e. Jerusalem in 586 BCE). Chapters 3–14 were written probably not much after 120 CE at the latest. The Bar Kokhba revolt (132–35 CE) decisively alienated synagogue from church. It is unlikely, therefore, that *4 Ezra* would have found its way into Christian circles after the revolt.

A major theme of the book is encapsulated in the recurring question: Why has God permitted his people to be delivered into the hands of their enemies? The seer persistently challenges the basic concepts of the Jewish worldview such as that espoused in the Baruch tradition (see n. 8 below). The author is not satisfied that Israel was punished because of her sins. Israel is a nation of sinners, but the sins of her enemies are worse than Israel's (see 3:28–36).

The fourth vision is the turning point of the work (see #254 below). Ezra meets a grieving woman whose son had dropped dead as he entered the wedding chamber. He finds her grief suggestive of Zion, the mother of us all, who is in mourning (10:7). The inhabitants of Zion are in mourning, not just for one son, but for 'our mother' (10:8). He comforts her by reminding her that she will receive her son again at the resurrection (cf. John 11:23–24). Now the grieving woman is transformed into the renewed eschatological Jerusalem (see 10:25–27). This is an overpowering experience for Ezra. The tension between the promises of God and the harsh reality of the destruction of Jerusalem expressed in the first three visions is resolved in terms of the eschatological promise of the renewed city (cf. Revelation 21:1–4). While no answer is given concerning the existence of evil, there is an underscoring of divine promises.

In the fifth vision, the eschatological era is inaugurated by the messiah, who establishes his kingdom on earth. The emphasis here is largely political. The power of Rome (the 'eagle') is waning; its days are numbered. The three Flavian emperors (Vespasian, Titus, Domitian) are overthrown by the messiah (12:22–24). The messiah is depicted as a ravenous, avenging lion (see 12:31–34). The language of the passage 12:31–33 would likely have provided some impetus towards the second revolt of 132–35 CE. After God's judgment of the Romans, he will deliver the remnant of the people of God (12:34). The sixth vision speaks of one like a son of man who, at the head of an angelic army, annihilates his enemies with the breath of his mouth (see 13:8–13; 37–38). He then re-gathers the 10 lost tribes to himself (cf. *Apocalypse of Abraham* 31:1). The seventh vision finds Ezra, portrayed as a second Moses, restoring the 24 books of the Hebrew Bible for public consumption, and the 70 books reserved for the wise alone.[7] By means of his work Ezra prepares the people for patient and godly living while they await the overthrow of the Romans and the vindication of the people of God.

*The eagle vision (*4 Ezra *11).*

254. On the second night I had a dream, and behold, there came up from the sea an eagle that had twelve feathered wings and three heads. And I looked, and behold, he spread his wings over all the earth, and all the winds of heaven blew upon him, and the clouds were gathered about him. And I looked, and out of his wings there grew opposing wings; but they became little, puny wings. But his heads were at rest; the middle head was larger than the other heads, but it also was at rest with them. And I looked, and behold, the eagle flew with his wings, to reign over the earth and

over those who dwell in it. And I saw how all things under heaven were subjected to him, and no one spoke against him, not even one creature that was on the earth. And I looked, and behold, the eagle rose upon his talons, and uttered a cry to his wings, saying, 'Do not all watch at the same time; let each sleep in his own place, and watch in his turn; but let the heads be reserved for the last.'

And I looked, and behold, the voice did not come from his heads, but from the midst of his body. And I counted his opposing wings, and behold, there were eight of them. And I looked, and behold, on the right side one wing arose, and it reigned over all the earth. And while it was reigning it came to its end and disappeared, so that its place was not seen. Then the next wing arose and reigned, and it continued to reign a long time. And while it was reigning its end came also, so that it disappeared like the first. And behold, a voice sounded, saying to it, 'Hear me, you who have ruled the earth all this time; I announce this to you before you disappear. After you no one shall rule as long as you, or even half as long.'

Then the third wing raised itself up, and held the rule like the former ones, and it also disappeared. And so it went with all the wings; they wielded power one after another and then were never seen again. And I looked, and behold, in due course the wings that followed also rose up on the right side in order to rule. There were some of them that ruled, yet disappeared suddenly; and others of them rose up, but did not hold the rule.

After this I looked and behold, the twelve wings and the two little wings disappeared; and nothing remained on the eagle's body except the three heads that were at rest and six little wings. And I looked, and behold, two little wings separated from the six and remained under the head that was on the right side; but four remained in their place. And I looked, and behold, these little wings planned to set themselves up and hold the rule. And I looked, and behold, one was set up, but suddenly disappeared; a second also, and this disappeared more quickly than the first. And I looked, and behold, the two that remained were planning between themselves to reign together; and while they were planning, behold, one of the heads that were at rest (the one which was in the middle) awoke; for it was greater than the other two heads. And I saw how it allied the two heads with itself, and behold, the head turned with those that were with it, and it devoured the two little wings which were planning to reign. Moreover this head gained control of the whole earth, and with much oppression dominated its inhabitants; and it had greater power over the world than all the wings that had gone before.

After this I looked, and behold, the middle head also suddenly disappeared, just as the wings had done. But the two heads remained, which also ruled over the earth and its inhabitants. And I looked, and behold, the head on the right side devoured the one on the left.

Then I heard a voice saying to me, 'Look before you and consider what you see.' And I looked, and behold, a creature like a lion was aroused out of the forest, roaring; and I heard how he uttered a man's voice to the eagle, and spoke, saying, 'Listen and I will speak to you. The Most High says to you, "Are you not the one that remains of the four beasts which I had made to reign in my world, so that the end of my times might come through them? You, the fourth that has come, have conquered all the beasts that have gone before; and you have held sway over the world with much terror, and over all the earth with grievous oppression; and for so long you have dwelt on the earth with deceit. And you have judged the earth, but not with truth; for you have afflicted the meek and injured the peaceable; you have hated those who tell the truth, and have loved liars; you have destroyed the dwellings of those who brought forth fruit, and have laid low the walls of those who did you no harm. And so your insolence has come up before the Most High, and your pride to the Mighty One. And the Most High has looked upon his times, and behold, they are ended, and his ages are completed! Therefore you will surely disappear, you eagle, and your terrifying wings, and your most evil little wings, and your malicious heads, and your most evil talons, and your whole worthless body, so that the whole earth, freed from your violence, may be refreshed and relieved, and may hope for the judgment and mercy of him who made it."'

While the lion was saying these words to the eagle, I looked, and behold, the remaining head disappeared. And the two wings that had gone over to it arose and set themselves up to reign, and their reign was brief and full of tumult. And I looked, and behold, they also disappeared, and the whole body of the eagle was burned, and the earth was exceedingly terrified.
(*4 Ezra* 11:1–12:3)

2 Baruch *(#255–57).*

2 Baruch was also written in Palestine in the wake of the destruction of the Temple in 70 CE. In common with the seers of the other late apocalypses, the writer of *2 Baruch* is seeking to come to terms with the destruction. The work expresses the point of view of the Baruch tradition in which the people of God are exhorted to accept responsibility for their sinfulness.[8] The Romans did not destroy Jerusalem; God's angels allowed this to happen (see chapters 7 and 80); they did so because the people were rebellious. The destruction was therefore the fault of Israel itself.

The destruction of the Temple means that even worse eschatological woes are about to come upon the earth. The anointed one will appear only after great tribulation.[9] However, when he appears the earth will blossom like paradise (see 29:3–30:1).[10] He will reign until the corruption of the present world has ended. In the messianic era, there will be no death and no hatred, and no enmity between people and animals (see chapter 73). The way forward, if the reader wants to participate in this eventuality, is to keep the law (32:1–2; cf. chapters 78–87). The nations, however, will be overthrown (see chapters 39–40; 72–73). The righteous can expect acquittal on that day because they possess a treasure of good works (14:12; 24:1).[11] The righteous dead will be raised incorruptible, as angels.[12] The appearance of a heavenly temple is foreshadowed in 4:2–7.[13]

The angels of God permit the destruction of Jerusalem.

255. Now it happened on the following day that, behold, an army of the Chaldeans surrounded the city. And in the evening I, Baruch, left the people, went outside, and set myself by an oak. And I was grieving over Zion and sighed because of the captivity which had come upon the people. And behold, suddenly a strong spirit lifted me and carried me above the wall of Jerusalem. And I saw, and behold, there were standing four angels at the four corners of the city, each of them with a burning torch in his hands. And another angel came down from heaven and said to them, 'Hold your torches and do not light them before I say it to you. Because I was sent first to speak a word to the earth and then to deposit in it what the Lord, the Most High, has commanded me.' And I saw that he descended in the Holy of Holies and that he took from there the veil, the holy ephod, the mercy seat, the two tables, the holy raiment of the priests, the altar of incense, the forty-eight precious stones with which the priests were clothed, and all the holy vessels of the tabernacle. And he said to the earth with a loud voice:

Earth, earth, earth, hear the word of the mighty God,
and receive the things which I commit to you,
and guard them until the last times,
so that you may restore them when you are ordered,
so that strangers may not get possession of them.
For the time has arrived when Jerusalem will also be delivered up for a time,
until the moment that it will be said that it will be restored forever.
And the earth opened its mouth and swallowed them up.

And after these things I heard this angel saying to the angels who held the torches: Now destroy the walls and overthrow them to their foundations so that the enemies do not boast and say, 'We have overthrown the wall of Zion and we have burnt down the place of the mighty God.' And they restored me to the place where I once stood.

The enemies enter the city

Now the angels did as he had commanded them; and when they had broken up the corners of the wall, a voice was heard from the midst of the temple after the wall had fallen, saying: Enter, enemies, and come, adversaries, because he who guarded the house has left it. And I, Baruch, went away. And it happened after these things that the army of the Chaldeans entered and seized the house and all that is around it. And they carried away the people into captivity and killed some of them. And they put King Zedekiah in irons and sent him to the king of Babylon.
(*2 Baruch* 6–8)

The timing of the End.

256. And he [the angel] answered and said to me: You also will be preserved until that time, namely until that sign which the Most High will bring about before the inhabitants of the earth at the end of days. This then will be the sign: When horror seizes the inhabitants of earth, and they fall into many tribulations and further, they fall into great torments. And it will happen that they will say in their thoughts because of their great tribulations, 'The Mighty One does not anymore remember the earth'; It will happen when they lose hope, that the time will awake.
(*2 Baruch* 25)

257. The apocalypse of the twelve calamities and the coming of the Messiah.

And I answered and said: That tribulation which will be will it last a long time; and that distress, will it embrace many years?

And he [the Lord] answered and said to me: That time will be divided into twelve parts, and each part has been preserved for that for which it was appointed. In the first part: the beginning of commotions. In the second part: the slaughtering of the great. In the third part: the fall of many into death. In the fourth part: the drawing of the sword. In the fifth part: famine and the withholding of rain. In the sixth part: earthquakes and terrors. In the eighth part: a multitude of ghosts and the appearances of demons. In the ninth part: the fall of fire. In the tenth part: rape and much violence. In the eleventh part: injustice and unchastity. In the twelfth part: disorder and a mixture of all that has been before. These parts of that time will be preserved and will be mixed, one with another, and they will minister to each other. For some of these parts will withhold a part of themselves and take from others and will accomplish that which belongs to them and to others; hence, those who live on earth in those days will not understand that it is the end of times.

But everyone who will understand will be wise at that time. For the measure and the calculation of that time will be two parts: weeks of seven weeks.

And I answered and said: It is good that man should come so far and see, but it is better that he should not come so far lest he fall. But I shall also say this: Will he who is incorruptible despise those who are corruptible, and will he despise what happens with those who are corruptible so that he might only look to those who are not corruptible? But when, O Lord, these things will surely come of which you spoke to me before, let me also know this, if I have found grace in your eyes: Is it in one place or in one part of the earth that these things will come or will they be noticed by the whole earth?

And he answered and said to me: That which will happen at that time bears upon the whole earth. Therefore, all who live will notice it. For at that time I shall only protect those found in this land at that time. And it will happen that when all that which should come to pass in these parts has been accomplished, the Anointed One will begin to be revealed. And Behemoth will reveal itself from its place, and Leviathan will come from the sea, the two great monsters which I created on the fifth day of creation and which I shall have kept until that time. And they will be nourishment for all who are left. The earth will also yield fruits ten thousandfold. And on one vine will be a thousand branches, and one branch will produce a thousand clusters, and one cluster will produce a thousand grapes, and one grape will produce a cor of wine. And those who

are hungry will enjoy themselves and they will, moreover, see marvels every day. For winds will go out in front of me every morning to bring the fragrance of aromatic fruits and clouds at the end of the day to distill the dew of health. And it will happen at that time that the treasury of manna will come down again from on high, and they will eat of it in those years because these are they who will have arrived at the consummation of time.
(*2 Baruch* 26–29)

Sibylline Oracles *(#258–59).*

The collection of Jewish and Christian *Sibylline Oracles*, which dates from the early second to the seventh centuries CE, take their inspiration from the oracles ascribed to the Sibyl, and housed in Rome in the Temple of Jupiter, but destroyed in a fire in 83 BCE. There were similar collections in the ancient world. Writers of the collection under review were drawn to the genre because it was a mode of expression commonly known among their non-Jewish and non-Christian contemporaries. The collection is a testimony to the hopes and fears of those living under Roman authority. The following are drawn from the Jewish Oracles 3 and 5 (about 100 CE).

258. The universal rule of Rome will be followed by cataclysmic destruction.

But when Rome will also rule over Egypt
guiding it toward a single goal, then indeed the most great kingdom
of the immortal king will become manifest over men.
For a holy prince will come to gain sway over the scepters of the earth
forever, as time presses on.
Then also implacable wrath will fall upon Latin men.
Three will destroy Rome with piteous fate.
All men will perish in their own dwellings
when the fiery cataract flows from heaven.
Alas, wretched one, when will that day come,
and the judgment of the great king immortal God?
Yet, just for the present, be founded, cities, and all
be embellished with temples and stadia, markets and golden
silver and stone statues so that you may come to the bitter day.
For it will come, when the smell of brimstone spreads
among all men. But I will tell all in turn,
in how many cities mortals will endure evil.
(*Sibylline Oracles* 3.46–62)

259. Oracle against Rome.

You will be among evil mortals, suffering evils,
but you will remain utterly desolate for all ages yet,
(it will exist, but it will remain utterly desolate forever),
despising your soil, because you desired sorcery.
With you are found adulteries and illicit intercourse with boys.
Effeminate and unjust, evil city, ill-fated above all.
Alas, city of the Latin land, unclean in all things,
maenad, rejoicing in vipers, as a widow you will sit
by the banks, and the river Tiber will weep for you, its consort.
You have a murderous heart and impious spirit.
Did you not know what God can do, what he devises?
But you said, 'I alone am, and no one will ravage me.'
But now God, who is forever, will destroy you and all your people,
and there will no longer be any sign of you in that land,
as there was formerly, when the great God found your honors.
Remain alone, lawless one. Mingled with burning fire,
inhabit the lawless nether region of Hades.
(*Sibylline Oracles* 5.162–78)

Eschatological apocalypticism in the Dead Sea Scrolls (#260–62).

The idea of 'New Jerusalem' figures in a number of apocalypses, as well as in the Dead Sea Scrolls. The influence of Ezekiel 40–48 is quite apparent. In the two extracts below and in #269, the translator (Vermes) places textual emendations in square brackets [ ] and interpretative glosses in parentheses ( ). The term *vacat* means there is a break in the original text.

260. [And they] c[al]l [the name of] this (one) [Gate] of Naphtali. And from this gate he measured to the [eastern] gate 25 [s]tadia. And they call this gate Gate of Asher. And he measu[red from] this [ga]te to the eastern corner 25 stadia. *vacat* And he led me into the city, and he measured each block of houses for its length and width, fifty-one reeds by fifty-one, in a square a[ll]...
(4Q554 fragment 1, column 2.8–13)

261. [He] then [showed me the di]mensions of [all] the blo[cks of houses. Between each block there is a street], six reeds = 42 cubits, wide. And the width of the avenues running from east to west: two of them are ten reeds = 70 cubits, wide. And the third, that to the [lef]t (i.e. north) of the Temple, measures eighteen reeds = 126 cubits in width. And the wid[th of the streets] running from south [to north: t]wo of [them] have nine reeds and four cubits = 67 cubits, each street.

[And the] mid[dle street passing through the mid]dle of the city, its [width measures] thirt[een] ree[ds] and one cubit = 92 cubits. And all [the streets of the city] are paved with white stone...marble and jasper.
(5Q15 fragment 1, column 1.1–7.
Cf. Revelation 21:10–21)

262. The son of God he will be proclaimed (or: proclaim himself) and the son of the Most High they will call him. Like the sparks of the vision, so will be their kingdom. They will reign for years on the earth and they will trample all. People will trample people (cf. Daniel 7:23) and one province another province *vacat* until the people of God will arise and all will rest from the sword. Their (the people of God's) kingdom will be an eternal kingdom (cf. Daniel 7:27) and all their path will be in truth. They will jud[ge] the earth in truth and all will make peace. The sword will cease from the earth, and all the provinces will pay homage to them. The Great God (cf. Daniel 2:45) is their helper. He will wage war for them. He will give peoples into their hands and all of them (the peoples) He will cast before them (the people of God). Their dominion will be an eternal dominion (Daniel 7:14) and all the boundaries of...
(4Q246 column 2.1–8 [Aramaic Apocalypse])[14]

The book of Revelation (#263–66).

The New Testament apocalypse bears similarities with its early Jewish counterparts. It utilizes a similar array of symbols to portray those who harass the people of God. It is indebted to the myth of Nero *redivivus*; the idea that the dead Nero would return from the dead with demonic powers at the head of a Parthian army to wreak vengeance on Rome and the worldwide community of believers (see Revelation 17:1–14 [cf. #95; see also #264 below]; 19:19–21).[15] The Messiah appears as the Lamb who was slain (see Revelation 5:6). Final victory belongs to the Lamb who will destroy Beast (Nero *redivivus*) and False Prophet (the imperial priesthood enforcing emperor worship[16]). The Lamb will inaugurate a millennium, to be followed by the Day of Judgment and the creation of a new heaven and a new earth. The book was written to prepare the Christian communities of Asia Minor for the persecution John perceived must shortly overwhelm all believers.

In the following extract the beast (Nero, who had committed suicide) and the false prophet arise out of the sea to seize control of the empire and to confront the people of God.

263. And I saw a beast rising out of the sea, having ten horns and seven heads; and on its horns were ten diadems, and on its heads were blasphemous names. And the beast that I saw was like a leopard, its feet were like a bear's, and its mouth was like a lion's mouth. And the dragon gave it his power and his throne and great authority. One of its heads seemed to have received a death-blow, but its mortal wound had been healed. In amazement the whole earth followed the beast. They worshiped the dragon, for he had given his authority to the beast, and they worshiped the beast, saying, 'Who is like the beast, and who can fight against it?'

The beast was given a mouth uttering haughty and blasphemous words, and it was allowed to exercise authority for forty-two months. It opened its mouth to utter blasphemies against God, blaspheming his name and his dwelling, that is, those who dwell in heaven. Also it was allowed to make war on the saints and to conquer them. It was given authority over every tribe and people and language and nation, and all the inhabitants of the earth will worship it, everyone whose name has not been written from the foundation of the world in the book of life of the Lamb that was slaughtered.

Let anyone who has an ear listen:
If you are to be taken captive,
into captivity you go;
if you kill with the sword,
with the sword you must be killed.
Here is a call for the endurance and faith of the saints.

Then I saw another beast that rose out of the earth; it had two horns like a lamb and it spoke like a dragon. It exercises all the authority of the first beast on its behalf, and it makes the earth and its inhabitants worship the first beast, whose mortal wound had been healed. It performs great signs, even making fire come down from heaven to earth in the sight of all; and by the signs that it is allowed to perform on behalf of the beast, it deceives the inhabitants of earth, telling them to make an image for the beast that had been wounded by the sword and yet lived; and it was allowed to give breath to the image of the beast so that the image of the beast could even speak and cause those who would not worship the image of the beast to be killed. Also it causes all, both small and great, both rich and poor, both free and slave, to be marked on the right hand or the forehead, so that no one can buy or sell who does not have the mark, that is, the name of the beast or the number of its name. This calls for wisdom: let anyone with understanding calculate the number of the beast, for it is the number of a person. Its number is six hundred sixty-six.
(Revelation 13:1–18)[17]

The destruction of Rome.

264. Then one of the seven angels who had the seven bowls came and said to me, 'Come, I will show you the judgment of the great whore who is seated on many waters, with whom the kings of the earth have committed fornication, and with the wine of whose fornication the inhabitants of the earth have become drunk.' So he carried me away in the spirit into a wilderness, and I saw a woman sitting on a scarlet beast that was full of blasphemous names, and it had seven heads and ten horns. The woman was clothed in purple and scarlet, and adorned with gold and jewels and pearls, holding in her hand a golden cup full of abominations and the impurities of her fornication; and on her forehead was written a name, a mystery: 'Babylon the great, mother of whores and of earth's abominations.' And I saw that the woman was drunk with the blood of the saints and the blood of the witnesses to Jesus.
(Revelation 17:1–6)[18]

The millennium, the final judgment, and the end of the beast and dragon.

265. Then I saw an angel coming down from heaven, holding in his hand the key to the bottomless pit and a great chain. He seized the dragon, that ancient serpent, who is the Devil and Satan, and bound him for a thousand years, and threw him into the pit, and locked and sealed it over him, so that he would deceive the nations no more, until the thousand years were ended. After that he must be let out for a little while.

Then I saw thrones, and those seated on them were given authority to judge. I also saw the souls of those who had been beheaded for their testimony to Jesus and for the word of God. They had not worshiped the beast or its image and had not received its mark on their foreheads or their hands. They came to life and reigned with Christ a thousand years. (The rest of the dead did not come to life until the thousand years were ended.) This is the first resurrection. Blessed and holy are those who share in the first resurrection. Over these the second death has no power, but they will be priests of God and of Christ, and they will reign with him a thousand years.
(Revelation 20:1–6)

The new heavens and new earth.

266. Then I saw a new heaven and a new earth; for the first heaven and the first earth had passed away, and the sea was no more. And I saw the holy city, the new Jerusalem, coming down out of heaven from God, prepared as a bride adorned for her husband. And I heard a loud voice from the throne saying,

'See, the home of God is among mortals.
He will dwell with them as their God;
they will be his peoples,
and God himself will be with them;
he will wipe every tear from their eyes.
Death will be no more;
mourning and crying and pain will be no more,
for the first things have passed away.'
(Revelation 21:1–4)

The following passage from the Gospel of Mark has been called the 'Little Apocalypse'. Some scholars have suggested that it was originally an independent apocalypse. It demonstrates a number of the themes of eschatologically orientated apocalyptic writing, such as the nearness of the end, the catastrophic overthrow of the prevailing establishment, and exhortation to the faithful to stand firm in the face of the impending coming of the Son of Man.

267. As he [Jesus] came out of the temple, one of his disciples said to him, 'Look, Teacher, what large stones and what large buildings!' Then Jesus asked him, 'Do you see these great buildings? Not one stone will be left here upon another; all will be thrown down.'

When he was sitting on the Mount of Olives opposite the temple, Peter, James, John, and Andrew asked him privately, 'Tell us, when will this be, and what will be the sign that all these things are about to be accomplished?' Then Jesus began to say to them, 'Beware that no one leads you astray. Many will come in my name and say, "I am he!" and they will lead many astray. When you hear of wars and rumors of wars, do not be alarmed; this must take place, but the end is still to come. For nation will rise against nation, and kingdom against kingdom; there will be earthquakes in various places; there will be famines. This is but the beginning of the birthpangs.

'As for yourselves, beware; for they will hand you over to councils; and you will be beaten in synagogues; and you will stand before governors and kings because of me, as a testimony to them. And the good news must first be proclaimed to all nations. When they bring you to trial and hand you over, do not worry beforehand about what you are to say; but say whatever is given you at that time, for it is not you who speak, but the Holy Spirit. Brother will betray brother to death, and a father his child, and children will rise against parents and have them put to death; and you will be hated by all because of my name. But the one who endures to the end will be saved.

'But when you see the desolating sacrilege set up where it ought not be (let the reader understand), then those in Judea must flee to the mountains; the one on the housetop must not go down or enter the house to take anything away; the one in the field must not turn back to get a coat. Woe to those who are pregnant and to those who are nursing infants in those days! Pray that it may not be in winter. For in those days there will be suffering, such as has not been from the beginning of the creation that God created until now, no, and never will be. And if the Lord had not cut short those days, no one would be saved; but for the sake of the elect, whom he chose, he has cut short those days. And if anyone says to you at that time, "Look! Here is the Messiah!" or "Look! There he is!"—do not believe it. False messiahs and false prophets will appear and produce signs and omens, to lead astray, if possible, the elect. But be alert; I have already told you everything.

'But in those days, after that suffering,
the sun will be darkened,
and the moon will not give its light,
and the stars will be falling from heaven,
and the powers in the heavens will be shaken.

'Then they will see "the Son of Man coming in the clouds" [Daniel 7:13] with great power and glory. Then he will send out the angels, and gather his elect from the four winds, from the ends of the earth to the ends of heaven.

'From the fig tree learn its lesson: as soon as its branch becomes tender and puts forth its leaves, you know that summer is near. So also, when you see these things taking place, you know that he is near, at the very gates. Truly I tell you, this generation will not pass away until all these things have taken place. Heaven and earth will pass away, but my words will not pass away.

'But about that day or hour no one knows, neither the angels in heaven, nor the Son, but only the Father. Beware, keep alert; for you do not know when the time will come. It is like a man going on a journey, when he leaves home and puts his slaves in charge, each with his work, and commands the doorkeeper to be on the watch. Therefore, keep awake—for you do not know when the master of the house will come, in the evening, or at midnight, or at cockcrow, or at dawn, or else he may find you asleep when he comes suddenly. And what I say to you I say to all: Keep awake.' (Mark 13:1–37)[19]

4.2. Testaments

The testament is the genre of the farewell discourse. It is a potent vehicle of moral exhortation, and is frequently encountered in early Jewish literature. In the Hebrew Bible, Genesis 49 and Deuteronomy (see especially chapters 31–34) already purport to be the farewell discourses of Jacob and Moses respectively. Early Jewish testaments generally possess three distinctive characteristics: (1) historical retrospective reviewing the testator's life; (2) ethical exhortation; and (3) prediction of the future.

Sources

Testaments of the Twelve Patriarchs (T12P).

The *Testaments of the Twelve Patriarchs* was originally written in Greek, imitating Hebrew and Aramaic models, and based especially on Genesis 49. The work was written perhaps as early as 200 BCE.[20] Each patriarch urges his descendants to give the descendants of Levi (as eschatological priest) and Judah (as eschatological king) special honour, with the former enjoying priority over the latter.[21] The dual messianic expectation of some Qumran scrolls is paralleled here.[22] The major themes of the *T12P* are devotion to the law (though it is rarely cited), avoidance of sexual sins and the snares of women, anthropological dualism (see especially *Testament of Judah* 20), avoidance of idolatry, and the eventual re-gathering of the people of God after scattering as a result of divine judgment (see *Testament of Levi* 15–16). The law is equated with wisdom (cf. Wisdom of Solomon; Sirach 24).

The *Testament of Levi* is one of the more substantial of the collection. It features a lengthy discourse on the heavens and the storage place of the judgment that is bound to befall the wicked, the future exile of the people of God for their iniquity, as well as considerable material on the terminal defilement of the sanctuary by Levi's priestly descendants.

268. (13) 'And now, my children, I command you:
Fear the Lord your God and with your whole heart,
and walk according to his Law in integrity.
Teach your children letters also,
so that they might have understanding throughout all their lives
as they ceaselessly read the Law of God.
For everyone who knows the Law of God shall be honored
wherever he goes, he shall not be a stranger.
He shall acquire many more friends than his parents,
and many men will want to serve him and to hear the Law from his mouth.
Therefore, my sons, do righteousness on earth
in order that you might find it in heaven.
Sow good things in your souls
and you will find them in your lives.
If you sow evil,
you will reap every trouble and tribulation.
Acquire wisdom in fear of the Lord
because if a captivity occurs,

if cities and territories are laid waste,
if silver and gold and every possession are lost,
nothing can take away the wisdom of the wise man
except the blindness of impiety and the obtuseness of sin.
For if anyone preserves himself from these evil deeds,
his wisdom shall be glorious, even among his opponents;
it will be found to be a homeland in a foreign territory,
and a friend in the midst of his enemies.
Whoever teaches good things and practices them
shall be enthroned with kings,
as was Joseph my brother.'
(18) 'When vengeance will have come upon them [i.e. the members of the future priestly establishment], the priesthood will lapse.
And the Lord will raise up a new priest
to whom all the words of the Lord will be revealed.
He shall effect the judgment of truth over the earth for many days.
And his star shall rise in heaven like a king;
kindling the light of knowledge as day is illumined by the sun.
And he shall be extolled by the whole inhabited world.
This one will shine forth like the sun in the earth;
he shall take away all darkness from under heaven,
and there shall be peace in all the earth.
The heavens shall greatly rejoice in his days
and the earth shall be glad;
the clouds will be filled with joy
and the knowledge of the Lord will be poured out on the earth like the water of the seas.
And the angels of glory of the Lord's presence will be made glad by him.'

(19) 'And now, my children, you have heard everything. Choose for yourselves light or darkness, the Law of the Lord or the works of Beliar.' And his sons replied, 'Before the Lord we will live according to his Law.' And their father said to them, 'The Lord is my witness and his angels are witnesses, and you are witnesses, and I am witness concerning the word from your mouth.' And his sons said, '(We are) witnesses.' Then Levi finished giving instructions to his sons. He stretched out his feet on his bed and was gathered to his fathers, having lived a hundred and thirty-seven years. And they put him in a coffin and later buried him in Hebron with Abraham, Isaac, and Jacob.
(*Testament of Levi* 13; 18:1–5; 19)

A testament from Qumran.

269. I an[nou]nce (this) to you [and al]so I will indeed inform y[ou... For all the Sons of Light] will shine, [and all the Sons] of Darkness will be dark. [For all the Sons of Light]...and by all their knowledge they will...and the Sons of Darkness will be burnt... For all folly and wicked[ness are dar]k, and all [pea]ce and truth are brigh[t. For all the Sons of Light g]o towards the light, towards [eternal] jo[y and rej]oicin[g], and all the Sons of Dar[kness go towards death] and perdition... The people shall have brightness...and they will cause them to live...

And now to you, Amram my son, [I] enjo[in]...and [to] your [son]s, and to their sons I enjoin..., and they gave them to Levi my father, and Levi my father [gave them] to me...and my books in testimony that they might be warned by them...
(4Q548 from the Testament of Amram [4Q543–48])

The Testament of Moses.

The *Testament of Moses* (*TMos*) is a farewell discourse delivered by Moses to Joshua.[23] The Testament appears to have been issued in two editions: one dating from Maccabaean times (see the allusions to Antiochus Epiphanes's persecution of the Jews in chapter 8), the other to the early decades of the first century CE (see chapter 6 which presupposes the death of Herod and the reign of his sons). Its clear expectation of divine irruption into the present age shows that the work is apocalyptic in tone. Chapter 10 rules out an earthly messianic agent in the establishment of the rule of God. God alone will carry the fight to his enemies. The work has also been called the *Assumption of Moses*. Jude 9 may be an allusion to an incident recounted in the lost ending of the work. Both the *T12P* and the *TMos* incorporate apocalyptic scenarios.

In the following extract Moses foretells the era of the Hasmonaean priest-kings followed in chapter 6 by the reign of Herod the Great. His death will be followed by the arrival of the Romans.

270. 'And when the times of exposure come near and punishment arises through kings who (though) sharing their crimes yet punish them, then they themselves will be divided as to the truth. Consequently the word was fulfilled that they will avoid justice and approach iniquity; and they will pollute the house of their worship with the customs of the nations; and they will play the harlot after foreign gods. For they will not follow the truth of God, but certain of them will pollute the high altar by...the offerings which they place before the Lord. They are not (truly) priests (at all), but slaves, yea sons of slaves. For those who are the leaders, their teachers, in those times will become admirers of avaricious persons, accepting (polluted) offerings, and they will sell justice by accepting bribes. Therefore, their city and the full extent of their dwelling places will be filled with crimes and iniquities. For they will have in their midst judges who will act with impiety towards the Lord and will judge just as they please.

'Then powerful kings will rise over them, and they will be called priests of the Most High God. They will perform great impiety in the Holy of Holies. And a wanton king, who will not be of a priestly family, will follow them. He will be a man rash and perverse, and he will judge them as they deserve. He will shatter their leaders with the sword, and he will (exterminate them) in secret places so that no one will know where their bodies are. He will kill both old and young, showing mercy to none.

'Then fear of him will be heaped upon them in their land, and for thirty-four years he will impose judgments upon them as did the Egyptians, and he will punish them. And he will beget heirs who will reign after him for shorter periods of time. After his death there will come into their land a powerful king of the West who will subdue them; and he will take away captives, and a part of their temple he will burn with fire. He will crucify some of them around their city.'
(*Testament of Moses* 5–6)[24]

Testaments are sometimes incorporated into works of other genres. This is the case with Tobit 13 (#271), 1 Maccabees 2:49–70, *Jubilees* 36, as well as *Pseudo-Philo* 19, 23–24, 33 and *2 Baruch* 43–47.

The testament of Tobit.

271. Then Tobit said:
'Blessed be God who lives forever,
because his kingdom lasts throughout all ages.
For he afflicts, and he shows mercy;
he leads down to Hades in the lowest regions in the earth,
and he brings up from the great abyss,
and there is nothing that can escape his hand.
Acknowledge him before the nations, O children of Israel;
for he has scattered you among them.
He has shown you his greatness even there.
Exalt him in the presence of every living being,
because he is our Lord and he is our God;
he is our Father and he is God forever.
He will afflict you for your iniquities,
but will again show mercy on all of you.
He will gather you from all the nations
among whom you have been scattered.
If you turn to him with all your heart and with all your soul,
to do what is true before him,
then he will turn to you
and will no longer hide his face from you.
So now see what he has done for you;
acknowledge him at the top of your voice.
Bless the Lord of righteousness,
and exalt the King of the ages.
In the land of my exile I acknowledge him,
and show his power and majesty to a nation of sinners:
"Turn back, you sinners, and do what is right before him;
perhaps he may look with favor upon you and show you mercy."
As for me, I exalt my God,
and my soul rejoices in the King of heaven.

Let all the people speak of his majesty,
and acknowledge him in Jerusalem.
O Jerusalem, the holy city,
he afflicted you for the deeds of your hands,
but will again have mercy on the children of the righteous.
Acknowledge the Lord, for he is good,
and bless the King of the ages,
so that his tent may be rebuilt in you in joy.
May he cheer all those within you who are captives,
and love all those within you who are distressed,
to all generations forever.
A bright light will shine to all the ends of the earth;
many nations will come to you from far away,
the inhabitants of the remotest parts of the earth to your holy name,
bearing gifts in their hands for the King of heaven.
Generation after generation will give joyful praise in you;
the name of the chosen city will endure forever.
Cursed are all who speak a harsh word against you;
cursed are all who conquer you
and pull down your walls,
all who overthrow your towers
and set your homes on fire.
But blessed forever will be all who revere you.
Go, then, and rejoice over the children of the righteous,
for they will be gathered together
and will praise the Lord of the ages.
Happy are those who love you,
and happy are those who rejoice in your prosperity,
Happy also are all people who grieve with you
because of your afflictions;
for they will rejoice with you
and witness all your glory forever.
My soul blesses the Lord, the great King!
For Jerusalem will be built as his house for all ages.
How happy I will be if a remnant of my descendants should survive
to see your glory and acknowledge the King of heaven.
The gates of Jerusalem will be built with sapphire and emerald,
and all your walls with precious stones.
The towers of Jerusalem will be built with gold,
and their battlements with pure gold.
The streets of Jerusalem will be paved
with ruby and with stones of Ophir.
The gates of Jerusalem will sing hymns of joy,
and all her houses will cry, "Hallelujah!
Blessed be the God of Israel!"
and the blessed will bless the holy name forever and ever.'
(Tobit 13)[25]

The distinctive features of the testament are encountered in the New Testament within other literary genres. John 14–17 is a testament within the Gospel genre; Acts 20:17–38 is a testament within the *Acta* genre. Though epistolary in form, 2 Peter and 2 Timothy are both testamentary in content.

The following two extracts are from the New Testament letter 2 Timothy. The letter purports to be Paul the Apostle's final words to Timothy. Although written primarily to an individual, the community is also addressed (see the closing greeting at #273).

272. You must understand this, that in the last days distressing times will come. For people will be lovers of themselves, lovers of money, boasters, arrogant, abusive, disobedient to their parents, ungrateful, unholy, inhuman, implacable, slanderers, profligates, brutes, haters of good, treacherous, reckless, swollen with conceit, lovers of pleasure rather than lovers of God, holding to the outward form of godliness but denying its power. Avoid them! For among them are those who make their way into households and captivate silly women, overwhelmed by their sins and swayed by all kinds of desires, who are always being instructed and can never arrive at a knowledge of the truth. As Jannes and Jambres opposed Moses, so these people, of corrupt mind and counterfeit faith, also oppose the truth. But they will not make

much progress, because, as in the case of those two men, their folly will become plain to everyone.
(2 Timothy 3:1–9)

273. In the presence of God and of Christ Jesus, who is to judge the living and the dead, and in view of his appearing and his kingdom, I solemnly urge you: proclaim the message; be persistent whether the time is favorable or unfavorable; convince, rebuke, and encourage, with the utmost patience in teaching. For the time is coming when people will not put up with sound doctrine, but having itching ears, they will accumulate for themselves teachers to suit their own desires, and will turn away from listening to the truth and wander away to myths. As for you, always be sober, endure suffering, do the work of an evangelist, carry out your ministry fully.

As for me, I am already being poured out as a libation, and the time of my departure has come. I have fought the good fight, I have finished the race, I have kept the faith. From now on there is reserved for me the crown of righteousness, which the Lord, the righteous judge, will give me on that day, and not only to me but also to all who have longed for his appearing.

Do your best to come to me soon, for Demas, in love with this present world, has deserted me and gone to Thessalonica; Crescens has gone to Galatia, Titus to Dalmatia. Only Luke is with me. Get Mark and bring him with you, for he is useful in my ministry. I have sent Tychicus to Ephesus. When you come, bring the cloak that I left with Carpus at Troas, also the books, and above all the parchments. Alexander the coppersmith did me great harm; the Lord will pay him back for his deeds. You also must beware of him, for he strongly opposed our message.

At my first defense no one came to my support, but all deserted me. May it not be counted against them! But the Lord stood by me and gave me strength, so that through me the message might be fully proclaimed and all the Gentiles might hear it. So I was rescued from the lion's mouth. The Lord will rescue me from every evil attack and save me for his heavenly kingdom. To him be the glory forever and ever. Amen.

Greet Prisca and Aquila, and the household of Onesiphorus. Erastus remained in Corinth; Trophimus I left ill in Miletus. Do your best to come before winter. Eubulus sends greetings to you, as do Pudens and Linus and Claudia and all the brothers and sisters.

The Lord be with your [pl.] spirit. Grace be with you [pl.].
(2 Timothy 4:1–22.
Cf. Acts 20:25–35)

4.3. Expanded and Rewritten Bible

The biblical narratives exercised a formative hold on early Jews and Christians. The predilection of Jews for applying and expanding the traditions of the Hebrew Bible testifies to an adaptability and flexibility in early Judaism which is the hallmark of a living religion. This activity can be traced in the Gospels. The Gospel of Mark was rewritten by Matthew and Luke in much the same way as the writers of the Jewish targums and midrashim expanded and rewrote the books of the Hebrew Bible in the interests of interpretation, bringing to light what was hidden.[26] It has also been argued that the New Testament evangelists communicated their insights about the significance of Jesus by taking the traditions about the character and redemptive work of God in the Hebrew Bible and re-working them into their stories of the Christ event.[27]

Sources

Jubilees.

The second-century BCE book of *Jubilees* is a retelling of the Genesis and Moses narratives, the writer adding non-biblical traditions.[28] It contains the report of the angelic revelation received by Moses on Mount Sinai in the form of a re-presentation jubilee by jubilee of the story of Israel as narrated in Genesis and the early chapters of Exodus.[29] The narrative is prefaced by a predictive prophecy to the effect that the people of God will fall away but will be restored in the last days.

The author seems to be aligned with Hasidic or Essene thought. Zeal for the law of Moses is the pre-eminent theme. Warfare on the Sabbath is forbidden.[30] A critique of the Hasmonaean priesthood is quite explicit in 23:20–21. Nevertheless, the note of considerable political and religious crisis that marks Daniel is missing from *Jubilees*. There is no allusion to any break with the priestly establishment that is apparent in some of the Dead Sea Scrolls. This suggests the book might have been written early in the Hasmonaean era, soon after the Maccabaean wars (alluded to in 23:18–20). The Maccabaean Revolt is counted a failure (see 23:20). Jerusalem 'will be holy' in the eschaton (1:28) and Zion is the 'navel' (*omphalos*) of the whole earth (8:19). The author probably belonged to a priestly family, as indicated by his interest in ritual, the synchronism of ritual times on earth and in heaven, and the fact that Levi is given priority over the sons of Jacob.[31] Like the Qumran community, the book champions a (solar) 364-day year (see 6:32–38). There will be a renewal of the temple cult in the eternal age.[32]

A reworking of the creation account of Genesis 1.

274. And the angel of the presence spoke to Moses by the word of the Lord, saying, 'Write the whole account of creation, that in six days the Lord God completed all his work and all that he created. And he observed a sabbath the seventh day, and he sanctified it for all ages. And he set it (as) a sign for all his works.'

For on the first day he created the heavens, which are above, and the earth, and the waters and all of the spirits which minister before him:
the angels of the presence,
and the angels of sanctification,
and the angels of the spirit of fire,
and the angels of the spirit of the winds,
and the angels of the spirit of the clouds and darkness and snow and hail and frost,
and the angels of resoundings and thunder and lightning,
and the angels of the spirits of cold and heat and winter and springtime and harvest and summer,
and all of the spirits of his creatures which are in heaven and on earth.
And (he created) the abysses and darkness—both evening and night—and light—both dawn and daylight—which he prepared in the knowledge of his heart. Then we saw his works and we blessed him and offered praise before him on account of all his works because he made seven great works on the first day.
(*Jubilees* 2:1–3)

The blessings of the eschatological age.

275. And in this generation children will reproach their parents and their elders on account of sin, and on account of injustice, and on account of the words of their mouth, and on account of great evil which they will do, and on account of their forsaking the covenant which the Lord made between them and himself so that they might be careful and observe all of his commandments and his ordinances and all of his law without turning aside to the right or left. For they all did evil and every mouth speaks of sin and all of their deeds (are) polluted and abominable.

Behold, the land will be corrupted on account of all their deeds, and there will be no seed of the vine, and there will be no oil because their works are entirely faithless. And all of them will be destroyed together: beast, cattle, birds, and all of the fish of the sea on account of the sons of man. Some of these will strive with others, youths and old men and old men with youths, the poor with the rich, the lowly with the great, and the beggar with the judge concerning the Law and the Covenant because they have forgotten the commandments and covenant and festivals and months and sabbaths and jubilees and all of the judgments. And they will stand up with bow and swords and war in order to return them to 'the way,' but they will not be returned until much blood is shed upon the earth by each (group). And those who escape will not be turned back from their evils to the way of righteousness because they will lift themselves up for deceit and wealth so that one shall take everything of his neighbor; and they will pronounce the great name but not in truth or righteousness. And they will pollute the holy of holies with their pollution and with the corruption of their contamination.

And there will be a great plague upon the deeds of that generation from the LORD and he will give them to the sword and to judgment and to captivity and pillage and destruction. And he will rouse up against them the sinners of the nations who have no mercy or grace for them and who have no regard for any persons old or young or anyone. For (they will be) cruel and powerful so that they will act more evilly than any of the sons of men.

And they will cause turmoil in Israel and sin against Jacob;
and much blood will be shed upon the earth;
and there will be no one who will gather and no one who will bury.
In those days, they will cry out and call and pray
to be saved from the hand of the sinners, the gentiles,
but there will be none who will be saved,
and the heads of children will be white with gray hairs,
and an infant three weeks old will look aged
like one whose years (are) one hundred,
and their stature will be destroyed by affliction and torment.
And in those days, children will begin to search the law,
and to search the commandments
and to return to the way of righteousness.
And the days will begin to increase and grow longer
among those sons of men, generation by generation,
and year by year, until
their days approach a thousand years,
and to a greater number of years than days.
And there (will be) no old men and none who is full of days.
Because all of them will be infants and children.
And all of their days they will be complete
and live in peace and rejoicing
and there will be no Satan and no evil (one) who will destroy,
because all of their days will be days of blessing and healing.
And then the Lord will heal his servants,
and they will rise up and see great peace.
And they will drive out their enemies,
and the righteous ones will see and give praise,
and rejoice forever and ever with joy;
and they will see all of their judgments and all of their curses among their enemies.
And their bones will rest in the earth,
and their spirits will increase joy,
and they will know that the Lord is an executor of judgment;
but he will show mercy to hundreds and thousands,
to all who love him.

And you, Moses, write these words because thus it is written and set upon the heavenly tablets as a testimony for eternal generations.
(*Jubilees* 23:16–32)

An excellent example of expansion is the novel-like *Joseph and Aseneth*.[33] This work emanates from Egypt, most probably before the Jewish revolt of 115–17 CE. This work arises out of speculation concerning the marriage of Joseph to Aseneth (recorded in Genesis 41:45), describing them as attractive and charismatic figures. Some scholars have allied the work with the Hellenistic genre of the 'romance', though one cannot rule out biblical models (Esther, Ruth, Tobit and Judith). The book should be associated with the Alexandrian Jewish community.

The work reads as a sapiential novel. It has a moral purpose. On the surface it is a fully-fledged romance narrating the betrothal of Aseneth to Joseph after her conversion to Judaism and the threat posed to the couple by Pharaoh's son in league with Dan and Gad, both of whom are at enmity with Joseph. However, the work also demonstrates the utter hopelessness of Gentile religion. Even one as beautiful and personally attractive as Aseneth, for whom the world exists to serve, must renounce her 'faith' and devote herself to the God of Joseph. Joseph, for his part, is rigorously resolved not to allow himself to be defiled by this paragon of non-Jewish piety. His rebuff of and prayer for Aseneth (chapters 7–8) sound the death knell of her prejudice against him and her religion. The converted Aseneth is given a large share of the book's polemic against idols.

The message of the work is simple and straightforward: those who convert to Judaism will find life and blessing. On the other hand, maintaining one's devotion to the gods will result in death and eternal destruction—a point made in chapter 8 and Aseneth's soliloquies in chapters 11–13. Jews must maintain their distinctiveness over against their non-Jewish neighbours. On the other hand, Gentiles are indirectly exhorted to follow Aseneth into the true faith. Joseph's rebuff is a model for Jews everywhere in their dealings with the claims of Gentile worship. His fear of Aseneth's potential to embroil him in sexual sins is an allegory of the need for Jews everywhere to be wary of the seduction of Gentile religious values.

Aseneth, though a virgin, and beautiful, is unacceptable to Joseph because she worships idols. Joseph sets out the stark choices facing early Jewish men and women.

276. And Aseneth's mother went up to the upper floor and brought her and stood her before Joseph. And Pentephres said to his daughter Aseneth, 'Greet your brother, because he, too, is a virgin like you today and hates every strange woman, as you, too, every strange man.' And Aseneth said to Joseph, 'Be of good cheer, my lord, blessed by the Most High Lord.' And Joseph said to Aseneth, 'May the Lord God who gives life to all (things) bless you.' And Pentephres said to his daughter Aseneth, 'Go up and kiss your brother.' And as Aseneth went up to kiss Joseph, Joseph stretched out his right hand and put it on her chest between her two breasts, and her breasts were already standing upright like handsome apples. And Joseph said, 'It is not fitting for a man who worships God, who will bless with his mouth the living God and eat blessed bread of life and drink a blessed cup of immortality and anoint himself with blessed ointment of incorruptibility to kiss a strange woman who will bless with her mouth dead and dumb idols and eat from their table bread of strangulation and drink from their libation a cup of insidiousness and anoint herself with ointment of destruction. But a man who worships God will kiss his mother and the sister (who is born) of his mother and the sister (who is born) of his clan and family and the wife who shares his bed, (all of) who(m) bless with their mouths the living God. Likewise, for a woman who worships God it is not fitting to kiss a strange man, because this is an abomination before the Lord God.' (*Joseph and Aseneth* 8:1–7)

The Life of Adam and Eve *(#277–78).*

This work dates from the first century CE. It exists in many ancient versions. The book expands the concise narratives provided in the Hebrew Bible. The story of the Fall provides the framework from which this new work takes its shape. In the work humankind is formed out of divine breath and possesses the image of God without the image being obliterated at the Fall. There are two paradises: heavenly and earthly. The former is located in the 'third heaven' (*Life of Adam and Eve* 25; cf. 2 Corinthians 12:2). Adam has a vision of this paradise. Adam and Eve are eventually buried in the earthly paradise that they had tended before Eve's sin caused them both to be ejected from it. The concept of the resurrection of the dead is affirmed (see, e.g., chapter 51). In the first extract below Eve advises Adam to separate himself from her since he is the innocent party. In the second Solomon builds the Temple on the very site where Adam used to pray to God.

277. And Eve said to Adam, 'You live on, my lord. Life is granted to you, since you have done neither the first nor the second error, but I have been cheated and deceived, for I have not kept the command of God. And now separate me from the light of such life, and I will go to the sunset and stay there until I die.' And she began to walk toward the West and to mourn and to weep bitterly with loud sighing. And she made there a shelter while she was three months pregnant. (*Life of Adam and Eve* 18)[34]

278. Then Seth made tablets of stone and clay, and wrote in them the life of his father Adam and his mother Eve, what he had heard from them and his eyes had seen, and he put the tablets in the middle of the house of his father in the oratory where he used to pray to the LORD. And after the

Flood, those written tablets were seen by many persons but were read by no one. The wise Solomon, however, saw the writings and was entreating the LORD, and an angel of the LORD appeared to him, saying, 'I am he who held the hand of Seth, so that he wrote with his finger onto stone, and you shall be wise in writing so that you might know and understand all that is contained on the stones, and where the place of prayer was where Adam and Eve used to worship the LORD God. And it is fitting for you to build the temple of the LORD, the house of prayer, at that place.' Then Solomon completed the temple of the LORD God and called forth those Achillean documents (that is to say, written without the knowledge of words by the finger of Seth, his hand being held by the angel of the LORD). And on the stones themselves was found what Enoch, the seventh from Adam, prophesied before the Flood, speaking of the coming of Christ, 'Behold, the LORD will come in his holiness to pronounce judgment on all and to convict the impious of all their works which they spoke to him, sinners and impious, murmurers and irreligious, who walked according to their lust and whose mouth has spoken pride.'
(*Life of Adam and Eve*, Appendix 51:3–9)[35]

Rewritten Bible at Qumran.

The Genesis Apocryphon, written in Aramaic, was found in cave 1. The work is more free in its use of the biblical material than the targums. In the extract below, Lamech expresses doubts about the paternity of the child (Noah) his wife is carrying.

279. Behold, I thought then within my heart that conception was (due) to the Watchers and the Holy Ones...and to the Giants...and my heart was troubled within me because of this child. Then I, Lamech, approached Bathenosh [my] wife in haste and said to her, '...by the Most High, the Great Lord, the King of all the worlds and Ruler of the Sons of Heaven, until you tell me all things truthfully, if...Tell me [this truthfully] and not falsely...by the King of all the worlds until you tell me truthfully and not falsely.'

Then Bathenosh my wife spoke to me with much heat [and]...said, 'O my brother, O my lord, remember my pleasure...the lying together and my soul within its body. [And I tell you] all things truthfully.'

My heart was then greatly troubled within me, and when Bathenosh my wife saw that my countenance had changed... Then she mastered her anger and spoke to me saying, 'O my lord, O my [brother, remember] my pleasure! I swear to you by the Holy Great One, the King of [the heavens]...that this seed is yours and that [this] conception is from you. This fruit was planted by you... and by no stranger or Watcher or Son of Heaven... [Why] is your countenance thus changed and dismayed, and why is your spirit thus distressed...I speak to you truthfully.'

Then I, Lamech, ran to Methuselah my father, and [I told] him all these things. [And I asked him to go to Enoch] his father for he would surely learn all things from him. For he was beloved, and he shared the lot [of the angels], who taught him all things. And when Methuselah heard [my words...he went to] Enoch his father to learn all things truthfully from him...his will.
(1QapGen 2.1–23)

The life and work of the Jewish historian Josephus will be introduced more fully below (see topic 4.6). Our interest in him here is restricted to his use of Jewish scripture. His *Antiquities* is a presentation in 20 books of the historical traditions of the Jews from creation to the outbreak of the first Jewish Revolt in 66 CE. The retelling of the biblical account (see *Antiquities* 1–11) reveals an apologetic purpose. Josephus demonstrates how venerable Jewish traditions are, and how reasonable the Jewish faith is. This is particularly clear in the passage selected, namely, Josephus's presentation of Abraham as a great inventor, sage and religious reformer.[36]

Josephus retells the story of Abraham.

280. (154)...He [Abraham] was a man of ready intelligence on all matters, persuasive with his hearers, and not mistaken in his inferences. Hence he began to have more lofty conceptions of virtue than the rest of mankind, and determined to reform and change the ideas universally current concerning God. He was thus the first boldly to

declare that God, the creator of the universe, is one, and that, if any other being contributed aught to man's welfare, each did so by His command and not in virtue of its own inherent power. This he inferred from the changes to which land and sea are subject, from the course of sun and moon, and from all the celestial phenomena; for, he argued, were these bodies endowed with power, they would have provided for their own regularity, but, since they lacked this last, it was manifest that even these services in which they cooperate for our greater benefit they render not in virtue of their own authority, but through the might of their commanding sovereign, to whom alone it is right to render our homage and thanksgiving. It was in fact owing to these opinions that the Chaldaeans and the peoples of Mesopotamia rose against him, and he, thinking fit to emigrate, at the will and with the aid of God, settled in the land of Canaan. Established there, he built an altar and offered a sacrifice to God.

(166) For, seeing that the Egyptians were addicted to a variety of different customs and disparaged one another's practices and were consequently at enmity with one another, Abraham conferred with each party and, exposing the arguments which they adduced in favour of their particular views, demonstrated that they were idle and contained nothing true. Thus gaining their admiration at these meetings as a man of extreme sagacity, gifted not only with high intelligence but with power to convince his hearers on any subject which he undertook to teach, he introduced them to arithmetic and transmitted to them the laws of astronomy. For before the coming of Abraham the Egyptians were ignorant of these sciences, which thus travelled from the Chaldaeans into Egypt, whence they passed to the Greeks.

(Josephus, *Antiquities* 1.154–57, 166–68)

Targums.

Targums are Aramaic translations of the biblical text often with interpretive embellishments. The practice was required because Hebrew ceased to be the vernacular of the Jews (see Nehemiah 8:8). There are targums among the corpus of Qumran texts.[37] The most extensive extant targums date from the second century CE. It is argued that the interpretive traditions represented in the targums date from the New Testament period and before.

There is a fine distinction between the targums and works such as the early Jewish *Jubilees* (see #274–75), the Genesis Apocryphon (see #279), the pesharim from Qumran (see #642–44) and the later Midrashim (the term 'midrash' means commentary). *Genesis Rabbah*, one of the earliest of the Midrashim, frequently cites rabbinic authorities of the third century CE. These are more extensive commentaries on and amplifications of the biblical texts, drawing out the meaning of the text for its readers.

The extract below comes from *Targum Pseudo-Jonathan*, the final form of which dates from the eighth century CE, but many of whose interpretative traditions emanate from much earlier. Words and phrases in italics correspond to the interpretive commentary provided by the targumist.

Targum Pseudo-Jonathan *of Genesis 3:1–20.*

In the extract below the term *Memra* is encountered. It is an Aramaic word meaning 'word'. It is used frequently in the targums as a reverential circumlocution for God.

281. 1. Now the serpent was more skilled *in evil* than all the beasts of the field which *the Lord* God had made. And he said to the woman, '*Is it true* that the Lord God said, "You shall not eat of any tree of the garden"?' 2. And the woman said to the serpent, 'We *are allowed* to eat of the fruit of the *other* trees of the garden; 3. but of the fruit of the tree in the middle of the garden *the Lord* said, "You shall not eat of it and you shall not touch it, lest you die."' 4. *At that moment* the serpent *spoke slander against his creator, and* said to the woman, 'You shall not die. *But every craftsman hates his fellow craftsman.* 5. For *it is manifest before the Lord* that on the day on which you eat of it you shall be like the *great angels*, who *are able to* distinguish good *from* evil.' 6. And the woman saw *Sammael the angel of death and she was afraid. She knew* that the tree was good to eat, that *it was a cure* for *the light* of

the eyes, and that the tree was desirable as a source of wisdom. And she took of its fruit and ate; and she also gave to her husband (who was) with her, and he ate. 7. Then the eyes of both of them were *enlightened* and they knew that they were naked *because they were stripped of the clothing of fingernails in which they had been created, and they saw their shame*; and they sewed fig leaves *for themselves*, and they made girdles for themselves. 8. They heard the voice *of the Memra of* the Lord God strolling in the garden at the *decline* of the day; and *Adam* and his wife hid themselves from before the Lord God in the midst of *the trees* in the garden. 9. The Lord God called to *Adam* and said to him, '*Is not the whole world which I created manifest before me, the darkness as well as the light? How then do you imagine in your heart that you can hide yourself from before me? Do I not see the place where you are hiding? And* where *are the commandments that I commanded you?*' 10. He said, 'I heard the voice *of your Memra* in the garden and I was afraid, for I was naked, *because I neglected the commandment you gave me,* and I hid myself f*or shame*.' 11. He said, 'Who told you that you were naked? *Perhaps* you have eaten of *the fruit of* the tree from which I commanded you not to eat?' 12. And *Adam* said, 'The woman you put beside me, she gave me of *the fruit of* the tree, and I ate.' 13. The Lord God said to the woman, 'What is this you have done?' And the woman said, 'The serpent lured me *with his cleverness and led me astray in his wickedness*, and I ate.' 14. Then the Lord God *brought the three of them to judgment, and* he said to the serpent, 'Because you have done this, cursed are you above all cattle, and above all beasts of the field. Upon your belly you shall go about, *and your feet shall be cut off, and you will cast off your skin once every seven years, and the poison of death will be in your mouth*, and you shall eat dust all the days of your life. 15. And I will put enmity between you and the woman, between the offspring *of your children* and the offspring *of her children. And when the children of the woman keep the commandments of the Law, they will take aim and strike you on your head. But when they forsake the commandments of the Law you will take aim* and wound them on *their* heels. *For them, however, there will be a remedy; but for you there will be no remedy; and they are to make peace in the end, in the days of the King Messiah*.' 16. To the woman (he said), 'I will greatly multiply your affliction *in the blood of virginity* and (in) your pregnancies; in pain you shall bear children, yet your desire shall be for your husband; he shall rule over you *both for righteousness and for sin*.' 17. And to Adam he said, 'Because you listened to *the word of* your wife, and ate of *the fruit of* the tree concerning which I commanded you saying, "You shall not eat of it," cursed be the earth because *it did not show you your guilt*; by toil you shall eat of it all the days of your life. 18. Thorns and thistles it shall sprout *and produce* because of you; and you shall eat the plants that are upon the surface of the field.' *Adam answered and said, 'I beseech by thy mercy before you, O Lord, Let me not be reckoned before you as cattle, that I should eat the grass of the surface of the field. I will arise and labor with the labor of my hands, and I will eat of the food of the earth; and thus let there be a distinction before you between the children of men and the offspring of cattle*.' 19. 'By the *labor of your hand* you shall eat *food* until you return to the *dust* from which you were *created*, because dust you are, and to dust you will return; *but from the dust you are destined to arise to render an account and a reckoning of all you have done, on the day of great judgment*.' 20. Adam named his wife Eve, because she was the mother of all *human beings*.
(*Targum Pseudo-Jonathan*, Genesis 3:1–20)

4.4. Wisdom Literature

The wisdom literature of early Judaism and Christianity owes much to the wisdom tradition of the Ancient Near East and more particularly to the Hebrew Bible. This continuity is exemplified in the well-known books of Sirach and Wisdom of Solomon, but also in the literature of Qumran. Ethical exhortation, of course, had a long literary history within the Greek and Roman worlds. In the New Testament the letter of James is heavily indebted to the Hellenistic wisdom tradition. The synoptic Gospels should not be overlooked either. Jesus' sayings are redolent of Jewish wisdom.

Sources

Sirach.

Sirach, also known as Ecclesiasticus, is one of the better known books of the early Jewish era. Translated from the original Hebrew into Greek by the grandson of the author at the end of the first century BCE, it is deeply indebted to the wisdom tradition exemplified especially in the book of Proverbs.

282. Wisdom praises herself,
and tells of her glory in the midst of her people.
In the assembly of the Most High she opens her mouth,
and in the presence of his hosts she tells of her glory:
'I came forth from the mouth of the Most High,
and covered the earth like a mist.
I dwelt in the highest heavens,
and my throne was in a pillar of cloud.
Alone I compassed the vault of heaven
and traversed the depths of the abyss.
Over waves of the sea, over all the earth,
and over every people and nation I have held sway.
Among all these I sought a resting place;
in whose territory should I abide?
'Then the Creator of all things gave me a command,
and my Creator chose the place for my tent.
He said, "Make your dwelling in Jacob,
and in Israel receive your inheritance."
Before the ages, in the beginning, he created me,
and for all the ages I shall not cease to be.
In the holy tent I ministered before him,
and so I was established in Zion.
Thus in the beloved city he gave me a resting place,
and in Jerusalem was my domain.
I took root in an honored people,
in the portion of the Lord, his heritage.
'I grew tall like a cedar in Lebanon,
and like a cypress on the heights of Hermon.
I grew tall like a palm tree in En-gedi,
and like rosebushes in Jericho;
like a fair olive tree in the field,
and like a plane tree beside water I grew tall.
Like cassia and camel's thorn I gave forth perfume,
and like choice myrrh I spread my fragrance,
like galbanum, onycha, and stacte,
and like the odor of incense in the tent.
Like a terebinth I spread out my branches,
and my branches are glorious and graceful.
Like the vine I bud forth delights,
and my blossoms become glorious and abundant fruit.
'Come to me, you who desire me,
and eat your fill of my fruits.
For the memory of me is sweeter than honey,
and the possession of me sweeter than the honeycomb.
Those who eat of me will hunger for more,
and those who drink of me will thirst for more.
Whoever obeys me will not be put to shame,
and those who work with me will not sin.'
All this is the book of the covenant of the Most High God,
the law that Moses commanded us
as an inheritance for the congregations of Jacob.
It overflows, like the Pishon, with wisdom,
and like the Tigris at the time of the first fruits.
It runs over, like the Euphrates, with understanding,
and like the Jordan at harvest time.
It pours forth instruction like the Nile,
like the Gihon at the time of vintage.
The first man did not know wisdom fully,
nor will the last one fathom her.
For her thoughts are more abundant than the sea,
and her counsel deeper than the great abyss.
As for me, I was like a canal from a river,
like a water channel into a garden.
I said, 'I will water my garden
and drench my flower-beds.'
And lo, my canal became a river,
and my river a sea.
I will again make instruction shine forth like the dawn,
and I will make it clear from far away.
I will again pour out teaching like prophecy,
and leave it to all future generations.
Observe that I have not labored for myself alone,
but for all who seek wisdom.
(Sirach 24)

The Wisdom of Solomon.

This book was written in the first century BCE. The author mounts a sustained polemic against the worship of idols.

283. For all people who were ignorant of God
were foolish by nature;
and they were unable from the good things
that are seen to know the one who exists,
nor did they recognize the artisan while paying heed to his works;
but they supposed that either fire or wind or swift air,
or the circle of the stars, or turbulent water,
or the luminaries of heaven were the gods that rule the world.
If through delight in the beauty of these things people assumed them to be gods,
let them know how much better than these is their Lord,
for the author of beauty created them.
And if people were amazed at their power and working,
let them perceive from them
how much more powerful is the one who formed them.
For from the greatness and beauty of created things
comes a corresponding perception of their Creator.
Yet these people are little to be blamed,
for perhaps they go astray
while seeking God and desiring to find him.
For while they live among his works, they keep searching,
and they trust in what they see, because the things that are seen are beautiful.
Yet again, not even they are to be excused;
for if they had the power to know so much
that they could investigate the world,
how did they fail to find sooner the Lord of these things?
But miserable, with their hopes set on dead things, are those
who give the name 'gods' to the works of human hands,
gold and silver fashioned with skill,
and likenesses of animals,
or a useless stone, the work of an ancient hand.
A skilled woodcutter may saw down a tree easy to handle
and skillfully strip off all its bark,
and then with pleasing workmanship
make a useful vessel that serves life's needs,
and burn the cast-off pieces of his work
to prepare his food, and eat his fill.
But a cast-off piece from among them, useful for nothing,
a stick crooked and full of knots,
he takes and carves with care in his leisure,
and shapes it with skill gained in idleness;
he forms it in the likeness of a human being,
or makes it like some worthless animal,
giving it a coat of red paint and coloring its surface red
and covering every blemish in it with paint;
then he makes a suitable niche for it,
and sets it in the wall, and fastens it there with iron.
He takes thought for it, so that it may not fall,
because he knows that it cannot help itself,
for it is only an image and has need of help.
When he prays about possessions and his marriage and children,
he is not ashamed to address a lifeless thing.
For health he appeals to a thing that is weak;
for life he prays to a thing that is dead;
for aid he entreats a thing that is utterly inexperienced;
for a prosperous journey, a thing that cannot take a step;
for money-making and work and success with his hands
he asks strength of a thing whose hands have no strength.
Again, one preparing to sail and about to voyage over raging waves
calls upon a piece of wood more fragile than the ship that carries him.
For it was desire for gain that planned that vessel,
and wisdom was the artisan who built it;
but it is your providence, O Father, that steers its course,
because you have given it a path in the sea,
and a safe way through the waves,
showing that you can save from every danger,
so that even a person who lacks skill may put to sea.
It is your will that works of your wisdom should not be without effect;
therefore people trust their lives even to the smallest piece of wood,
and passing through the billows on a raft they come safely to land.

For even in the beginning, when arrogant giants were perishing,
the hope of the world took refuge on a raft,
and guided by your hand left to the world the seed of a new generation.
For blessed is the wood by which righteousness comes.
But the idol made with hands is accursed, and so is the one who made it—
he for having made it, and the perishable thing because it was named a god.
For equally hateful to God are the ungodly and their ungodliness;
for what was done will be punished together with the one who did it.
Therefore there will be a visitation also upon the heathen idols,
because, though part of what God created, they became an abomination,
snares for human souls
and a trap for the feet of the foolish.
For the idea of making idols was the beginning of fornication,
and the invention of them was the corruption of life;
for they did not exist from the beginning,
nor will they last forever.
For through human vanity they entered the world,
and therefore their speedy end has been planned.
(Wisdom of Solomon 13:1–14:14)

Sentences of Pseudo-Phocylides.

This early Jewish work was written between about 100 BCE and 100 CE.

284. (3) Neither commit adultery nor rouse homosexual passion.
Neither devise treachery nor stain your hands with blood.
Do not become rich unjustly, but live from honorable means.
Be content with what you have and abstain from what is another's.
Do not tell lies, but always speak the truth.
Honor God foremost, and afterward your parents.

(59) Let (your) emotions be moderate, neither great nor overwhelming.
Excess, even of greed, is never a boon to mortals;
and a great luxuriousness draws one to immoderate desires.
Great wealth is conceited and grows to insolence.
Anger that steals over one causes destructive madness.
Rage is a desire, but wrath surpasses (it).
Zeal for good things is noble, but (zeal for) bad things (is) excessive.
Daring in bad deeds is ruinous, but greatly helps a man who works at good deeds.
Love of virtue is worthy, but love of passion increases shame.
A man who is too naïve is called foolish among the citizens.
Eat in moderation, and drink and tell stories in moderation.
Moderation is the best of all, excesses are grievous.

(175) Do not remain unmarried, lest you die nameless.
Give nature her due, you also, beget in your turn as you were begotten.

(213) Guard the youthful prime of life of a comely boy,
because many rage for intercourse with a man.
Guard a virgin in firmly locked rooms,
and do not let her be seen before the house until her wedding day.
(*Sentences of Pseudo-Phocylides* ll. 3–8, 59–69b, 175–76, 213–16)

4 Maccabees *(#285–86).*

4 Maccabees is set during the Maccabaean Revolt. It has been argued that the work represents the essence and style of a synagogue sermon. It dates to the about the middle of the first century CE. Its theme is to argue that the prized virtue of self-control, eagerly sought after in the Graeco-Roman literature of moral exhortation, is best achieved in obedience to the Jewish law.

285. (1) The subject that I am about to discuss is most philosophical, that is, whether devout reason is sovereign over the emotions. So it is right for me to advise you to pay earnest attention to philosophy. For the subject is essential to everyone who is seeking knowledge, and in addition it includes the praise

of the highest virtue—I mean, of course, rational judgment. If, then, it is evident that reason rules over those emotions that hinder self-control, namely, gluttony and lust, it is also clear that it masters the emotions that hinder one from justice, such as malice, and those that stand in the way of courage, namely anger, fear, and pain.

(30b) Observe now, first of all, that rational judgment is sovereign over the emotions by virtue of the restraining power of self-control. Self-control, then, is dominance over the desires. Some desires are mental, others are physical, and reason obviously rules over both. Otherwise, how is it that when we are attracted to forbidden foods we abstain from the pleasure to be had from them? Is it not because reason is able to rule over appetites? I for one think so. Therefore when we crave seafood and fowl and animals and all sorts of foods that are forbidden to us by the law, we abstain because of domination by reason. For the emotions of the appetites are restrained, checked by the temperate mind, and all the impulses of the body are bridled by reason.
(*4 Maccabees* 1:1–4, 30b–35)

In the following extract, seven brothers are brought forward for torture (cf. 2 Maccabees 7). They have already witnessed the excruciatingly painful martyrdom of the elderly Eleazar who, in obedience to the Mosaic law, refused to eat unclean food. The seven brothers face the same fate. A series of arguments is presented by the writer that might have induced the seven to eat unclean food and so escape the tortures and death that await them.

286. But the youths, though about to be tortured, neither said any of these things nor even seriously considered them. For they were contemptuous of the emotions and sovereign over agonies, so that as soon as the tyrant had ceased counseling them to eat defiling food, all with one voice together, as from one mind, said:

'Why do you delay, O tyrant? For we are ready to die rather than transgress our ancestral commandments; we are obviously putting our forebears to shame unless we should practice ready obedience to the law and to Moses our counselor. Tyrant and counselor of lawlessness, in your hatred for us do not pity us more than we pity ourselves. For we consider this pity of yours, which insures our safety through transgression of the law, to be more grievous than death itself. You are trying to terrify us by threatening us with death by torture, as though a short time ago you learned nothing from Eleazar. And if the aged men of the Hebrews because of their religion lived piously while enduring torture, it would be even more fitting that we young men should die despising your coercive tortures, which our aged instructor [Eleazar] also overcame. Therefore, tyrant, put us to the test; and if you take our lives because of our religion, do not suppose that you can injure us by torturing us. For we, through this severe suffering and endurance, shall have the prize of virtue and shall be with God, on whose account we suffer; but you, because of your bloodthirstiness toward us, will deservedly undergo from the divine justice eternal torment by fire.'
(*4 Maccabees* 8:27–9:9)[38]

Jesus and wisdom (#287–90).

Recently scholars have argued that Jesus is best seen as a type of itinerant cynic philosopher. Philosophers in this tradition practised asceticism, exhorted their hearers to adopt a radical self-sufficiency based on a rejection of materialism, and were critical of the establishment.[39] The following extracts from the deposit of the teaching of Jesus show him as a teacher of subversive wisdom.

287. Now when Jesus saw great crowds around him, he gave orders to go over to the other side. A scribe then approached and said, 'Teacher, I will follow you wherever you go.' And Jesus said to him, 'Foxes have holes, and birds of the air have nests; but the Son of Man has nowhere to lay his head.' Another of his disciples said to him, 'Lord, first let me go and bury my father.' But Jesus said to him, 'Follow me, and let the dead bury their own dead.'
(Matthew 8:18–22)

288. 'No one can serve two masters; for a slave will either hate the one and love the other, or be devoted to the one and despise the other. You cannot serve God and wealth.

'Therefore, I tell you, do not worry about your life, what you will eat or what you will drink, or about your body, what you will wear. Is not life more than food, and the body more than clothing? Look at the birds of the air; they neither sow nor reap nor gather into barns, and yet your heavenly Father feeds them. Are you not of more value than they? And can any of you by worrying add a single hour to your span of life? And why do you worry about clothing? Consider the lilies of the field, how they grow; they neither toil nor spin, yet I tell you, even Solomon in all his glory was not clothed like one of these. But if God so clothes the grass of the field, which is alive today and tomorrow is thrown into the oven, will he not much more clothe you—you of little faith? Therefore do not worry, saying, "What will we eat?" or "What will we drink?" or "What will we wear?" For it is the Gentiles who strive for all these things; and indeed your heavenly Father knows that you need all these things. But strive first for the kingdom of God and his righteousness, and all these things will be given to you as well.

'So do not worry about tomorrow, for tomorrow will bring worries of its own. Today's trouble is enough for today.'
(Matthew 6:24–34)

289. Mary said to Jesus, 'What do your disciples resemble?' He said, 'What they resemble is children living in a plot of land that is not theirs. When the owners of the land come they will say, "Surrender our land to us." They, for their part, strip naked in their presence in order to give it back to them, and they give them their land.'
(*Coptic Gospel of Thomas* 21)

290. Jesus said, 'Grapes are not harvested from thorn trees, nor are figs gathered from thorn bushes, for these do not bear fruit. Good people produce good from their store. Evil people produce wicked things from their evil store within their hearts, and say wicked things. For out of the heart's abundance they produce wicked things.'
(*Coptic Gospel of Thomas* 45)[40]

The Letter of James.

This New Testament letter is much indebted to the themes of Hellenistic wisdom.

291. Not many of you should become teachers, my brothers and sisters, for you know that we who teach will be judged with greater strictness. For all of us make many mistakes. Anyone who makes no mistakes in speaking is perfect, able to keep the whole body in check with a bridle. If we put bits into the mouths of horses to make them obey us, we guide their whole bodies. Or look at ships: though they are so large that it takes strong winds to drive them, yet they are guided by a very small rudder wherever the will of the pilot directs. So also the tongue is a small member, yet it boasts of great exploits.

How great a forest is set ablaze by a small fire! And the tongue is a fire. The tongue is placed among our members as a world of iniquity; it stains the whole body, sets on fire the cycle of nature, and is itself set on fire by hell. For every species of beast and bird, of reptile and sea creature, can be tamed and has been tamed by the human species, but no one can tame the tongue—a restless evil, full of deadly poison. With it we bless the Lord and Father, and with it we curse those who are made in the likeness of God. From the same mouth come blessing and cursing. My brothers and sisters, this ought not to be so. Does a spring pour forth from the same opening both fresh and brackish water? Can a fig tree, my brothers and sisters, yield olives, or a grapevine figs? No more can salt water yield fresh.

Who is wise and understanding among you? Show by your good life that your works are done with gentleness born of wisdom. But if you have bitter envy and selfish ambition in your hearts, do not be boastful and false to the truth. Such wisdom does not come down from above, but is earthly, unspiritual, devilish. For where there is envy and selfish ambition, there will also be disorder and wickedness of every kind. But the wisdom from above is first pure, then peaceable, gentle, willing to yield, full of mercy and good fruits, without a trace of partiality or hypocrisy. And a harvest of righteousness is sown in peace for those who make peace.
(James 3:1–18)

The two ways.

This is a common motif in early Jewish and Christian wisdom literature.

292. There are two Ways, one of Life and one of Death, and there is a great difference between the two Ways.

The Way of Life is this: 'First, thou shalt love the God who made thee, secondly, thy neighbour as thyself; and whatsoever thou wouldst not have done to thyself, do not thou to another.'

Now, the teaching of these words is this: 'Bless those that curse you, and pray for your enemies, and fast for those that persecute you. For what credit is it to you if you love those that love you? Do not even the heathen do the same?' But, for your part, 'love those that hate you,' and you will have no enemy. 'Abstain from carnal' and bodily 'lusts.' 'If any man smite thee on the right cheek, turn to him the other cheek also,' and thou wilt be perfect. 'If any man impress thee to go with him one mile, go with him two. If any man take thy coat, give him thy shirt also. If any man will take from thee what is thine, refuse it not'—not even if thou canst. Give to everyone that asks of thee, and do not refuse, for the Father's will is that we give to all from the gifts we have received. Blessed is he that gives according to the mandate; for he is innocent. Woe to him who receives; for if any man receive alms under pressure of need he is innocent; but he who receives it without need shall be tried as to why he took and for what, and being in prison he shall be examined as to his deeds, and 'he shall not come out thence until he pay the last farthing.' But concerning this it was also said, 'Let thine alms sweat into thine hands until thou knowest to whom thou art giving.'

(*Didache* 1)[41]

4.5. Hymns and Prayers

The early Jewish era abounds with examples of religious poetry in the form of prayers and hymns. In the case of the Qumran Hodayot (1QH), the *Psalms of Solomon* and the *Odes of Solomon* we are in possession of the three major Jewish hymn collections outside the Hebrew Psalter. The Psalter furnishes the models for the hymns of subsequent collections. With the exception of the *Psalms of Solomon*, which is present in the fifth century CE Codex Alexandrinus, the Hodayot and the *Odes* were only brought to light in the modern era in the twentieth century.

Sources

Qumran hymns and prayers.

The following hymn comes from the Qumran Hodayot.[42] It is one of a number of hymns in the collection which is written from the point of view of the beleaguered community leader.

293. I thank Thee, O Lord,
for Thou hast placed my soul
in the bundle of the living,
and hast hedged me about
against all the snares of the Pit.
Violent men have sought after my life
because I have clung to Thy Covenant.
For they, an assembly of deceit,
and a horde of Belial,
know not that my stand
is maintained by Thee,
and that in Thy mercy Thou wilt save my soul
since my steps proceed from Thee.
From Thee it is
that they assail my life,
that Thou mayest be glorified
by the judgement of the wicked,
and manifest Thy might through me
in the presence of the sons of men;
for it is by Thy mercy that I stand.
And I said, Mighty men
have pitched their camps against me,
and have encompassed me
with all their weapons of war.
They have let fly arrows
against which there is no cure,
and the flame of (their) javelins
is like a consuming fire among trees.
The clamour of their shouting
is like the bellowing of many waters,
like a storm of destruction
devouring a multitude of men;
as their waves rear up,
Naught and Vanity spout upward to the stars.
But although my heart melted like water,
my soul held fast to Thy Covenant,
and the net which they spread for me

has taken their own foot;
they have themselves fallen
into the snares which they laid for my life.
But my foot remains upon level ground;
apart from their assembly I will bless Thy Name.
(1QH 10.20–30)

The Psalms of Solomon.

The *Psalms of Solomon* were written in response to the successful siege of Jerusalem by Pompey in 63 BCE and before the destruction of the Temple in 70 CE. The collection is critical of the priestly establishment.[43] The *Psalms* give expression to the challenge to the theology of Israel now that alien invaders have encroached on her land. The psalmist(s) has to face the fact that the Gentiles might destroy the people of God. Theodicy is a theme to which the author refers repeatedly (see, e.g., 2:1, 15–18; 3:3–5). Nevertheless, the psalmist has not abandoned the idea that God will do what is right for the just in this life. The humiliating end of Pompey is an eloquent testimony to that fact (see 2:26–35). The *Psalms* also express a sweeping indictment of the nation after the manner of the Baruch tradition as exemplified especially in Baruch (see #148 and n. 8 above). Josephus is also highly indebted to this way of responding to the disasters that have befallen the people of God. He regularly tests his people to prove their faithfulness. God alerts them to their sins. That there are invaders in the land is meant to discipline the people (see 14:1). Eternal life can be hoped for (see 2:31; 3:12).

The following psalm is the last of the collection in the *Psalms of Solomon*. It is particularly significant for its emphatic articulation of a royal messianic hope.

294. O Lord, your mercy is upon the works of your hands forever.
(You show) your goodness to Israel
with a rich gift.
Your eyes (are) watching over them and none of them will be in need.
Your ears listen to the hopeful prayer of the poor,
Your compassionate judgments (are) over the whole world,
and your love is for the descendants of Abraham, an Israelite.
Your discipline for us (is) as (for) a firstborn son, an only child,
to divert the perceptive person from unintentional sins.
May God cleanse Israel for the day of mercy in blessing,
for the appointed day when his Messiah will reign.
Blessed are those born in those days,
to see the good things of the Lord
which he will do for the coming generation;
(which will be) under the rod of discipline of the Lord Messiah,
in the fear of his God,
in wisdom of spirit,
and of righteousness and of strength,
to direct people in righteous acts, in the fear of God,
to set them all in the fear of the Lord
A good generation (living) in the fear of God,
in the days of mercy.
Pause.
Our God is great and glorious
living in the highest (heavens),
who arranges the stars into orbits
(to mark) time of the hours from day to day.
And they have not deviated from their course,
which he appointed them.
Their course each day is in the fear of God,
from the day God created them forever.
And they have not wandered
from the day he created them, from ancient generations.
They have not veered off their course
except when God directed them
by the command of his servants.
(*Psalms of Solomon* 18)

The Odes of Solomon.

The collection entitled the *Odes of Solomon* was only discovered in the early twentieth century. They were known previously only by notations in lists of apocryphal books, excerpts in the Coptic *Pistis Sophia*, and a Latin quote in the late third-/early fourth-century Latin writer Lactantius.[44] The collection is an early attempt to articulate the significance of the coming of the Messiah for Christians who were once Jews. The *Odes* are rather negative towards Gentiles.[45] The Messiah is portrayed in 36:4 as the 'greatest among the great ones'. The *Odes* were originally composed in c. 100 CE. The parallels with 1QH, the Fourth Gospel and the Letters of Ignatius suggest this early date. It is quite possible that Antioch was the place where they were composed.

295. The dove fluttered over the head of our Lord Messiah,
because he was her Head.
And she sang over him,
and her voice was heard.
Then the inhabitants were afraid,
and the foreigners were disturbed.
The bird began to fly,
and every creeping thing died in its hole.
And the chasms were opened and closed;
and they were seeking the Lord as those who are about to give birth.
But he was not given to them for nourishment,
because he did not belong to them.
But the chasms were submerged in the submersion of the Lord,
and they perished in that thought with which they had remained from the beginning.
For they labored from the beginning;
and the end of their labor was life.
And all of them who were lacking perished,
because they were not able to express the word so that they might remain.
And the Lord destroyed the thoughts,
of all those who had not the truth with them.
For they were lacking in wisdom,
they who exalted themselves in their mind.
So they were rejected,
because the truth was not with them.
For the Lord declared his way,
and spread out his grace.
And those who recognized it
knew his holiness.
Hallelujah.
(*Odes of Solomon* 24)

The *Prayer of Manasseh* was written in the first century BCE. It expands on the presentation of Manasseh's reign (687–642 BCE) in 2 Kings 21:1–18 and 2 Chronicles 33:1–20. Manasseh is portrayed as the worst of Judah's kings, instituting a vigorous programme of idolatry. There is a note in 2 Chronicles 33:12, 19 to the effect that Manasseh was taken into captivity to Babylon. While there he repented of his sins. The *Prayer* purports to be the prayer in which he expressed that repentance.

296. O Lord Almighty,
God of our ancestors,
of Abraham and Isaac and Jacob
and of their righteous offspring;
you who made heaven and earth
with all their order;
who shackled the sea by your word of command,
who confined the deep
and sealed it with your terrible and glorious name;
at whom all things shudder,
and tremble before your power,
for your glorious splendor cannot be borne,
and the wrath of your threat to sinners is unendurable;
yet immeasurable and unsearchable
is your promised mercy,
for you are the Lord Most High,
of great compassion, long-suffering, and very merciful,
and you relent at human suffering.
O Lord, according to your great goodness
you have promised repentance and forgiveness
to those who have sinned against you,
and in the multitude of your mercies
you have appointed repentance for sinners,
so that they may be saved.
Therefore you, O Lord, God of the righteous,
have not appointed repentance for the righteous,
for Abraham and Isaac and Jacob, who did not sin against you,
but you have appointed repentance for me,
who am a sinner.
(*Prayer of Manasseh* 1–8)

The New Testament contains a number of what might reasonably be termed liturgical hymns. Colossians 1:15–20 and Philippians 2:5–11 are well-known examples. The Gospel of Luke contains two superb hymns, which are called the Magnificat and Benedictus in ecclesiastical circles. It has been suggested that they have been adapted from originals written during the Maccabaean Revolt.[46] Both hymns celebrate the saving intervention of God, and the vindication of his chosen ones.

The Song of Mary.

297. And Mary said,
'My soul magnifies the Lord,
and my spirit rejoices in God my Savior,
for he has looked with favor on the lowliness of his servant.
Surely, from now on all generations will call me blessed;
for the Mighty One has done great things for me,
and holy is his name.
His mercy is for those who fear him
from generation to generation.
He has shown strength with his arm;
he has scattered the proud in the thoughts of their hearts.
He has brought down the powerful from their thrones,
and lifted up the lowly;
he has filled the hungry with good things,
and sent the rich away empty.
He has helped his servant Israel,
in remembrance of his mercy,
according to the promise he made to our ancestors,
to Abraham and to his descendants forever.'
(Luke 1:46–55.
Cf. Luke 1:68–79)

The following prayer derives from the work *Joseph and Aseneth*.[47] Aseneth, daughter of the priest of On, has fallen in love with Joseph. His rejection of her as an idolater brings about her conversion to Judaism. This is the first prayer she prays on her spiritual journey.

298. Lord God of my father Israel,
the Most High, the Powerful One of Jacob,
who gave life to all (things)
and called (them) from the darkness to the light,
and from the error to the truth,
and from the death to the life;
you, Lord, bless this virgin,
and renew her by your spirit,
and form her anew by your hidden hand,
and make her alive again by your life,
and let her eat your bread of life,
and drink your cup of blessing,
and number her among your people
that you have chosen before all (things) came into being,
and let her enter your rest
which you have prepared for your chosen ones,
and live in your eternal life for ever (and) ever.
(*Joseph and Aseneth* 8:10–11)

The 'Lord's Prayer'.

299. 'When you are praying, do not heap up empty phrases as the Gentiles do; for they think that they will be heard because of their many words. Do not be like them, for your Father knows what you need before you ask him.

Pray then in this way:

Our Father in heaven,
hallowed be your name.
Your kingdom come.
Your will be done,
on earth as it is in heaven.
Give us this day our daily bread.
And forgive us our debts,
as we also have forgiven our debtors.
And do not bring us to the time of trial,
but rescue us from the evil one.'

(Matthew 6:7–13.[48]
See also Luke 11:2–4)

A prayer from *1 Clement*, an early Christian work (c. 95 CE).

300. Grant us to hope on thy name, the source of all creation, open the eyes of our heart to know thee, that thou alone art the highest in the highest and remainest holy among the holy. Thou dost humble the pride of the haughty, thou dost destroy the imaginings of nations, thou dost raise up the humble and abase the lofty, thou makest rich and makest poor, thou dost slay and make alive, thou alone art the finder of spirits and art God of all flesh, thou dost look on the abysses, thou seest into the works of man, thou art the helper of those in danger, the saviour of those in despair, the creator and watcher over every spirit; thou dost multiply nations upon earth and hast chosen out from them all those that love thee through Jesus Christ thy beloved child, and through him hast thou taught us, made us holy, and brought us to honour.

We beseech thee, Master, to be our 'help and succour.' Save those of us who are in affliction, have mercy on the lowly, raise the fallen, show thyself to those in need, heal the sick, turn again the wanderers of thy people, feed the hungry, ransom our prisoners, raise up the weak, comfort the faint-hearted; let all 'nations know thee, that thou art God alone,' and that Jesus Christ is thy child, and that 'we are thy people and the sheep of thy pasture.'

For thou through thy operations didst make manifest the eternal fabric of the world; thou, Lord, didst create the earth. Thou that art faithful in all generations, righteous in judgment, wonderful in strength and majesty, wise in thy creation, and prudent in establishing thy works, good in the things which are seen, and gracious among those that trust in thee, O 'merciful and compassionate,' forgive us our iniquities and unrighteousness, and transgressions, and short-comings. Reckon not every sin of thy servants and handmaids, but cleanse us with the cleansing of thy truth, and 'guide our steps to walk in holiness of heart, to do the things which are good and pleasing before thee' and before our rulers. Yea, Lord, 'make thy face to shine upon us' in peace 'for our good' that we may be sheltered by thy mighty hand, and delivered from all sin by 'thy uplifted arm,' and deliver us from them that hate us wrongfully. Give concord and peace to us and to all that dwell on the earth, as thou didst give to our fathers who called on thee in holiness with faith and truth, and grant that we may be obedient to thy almighty and glorious name, and to our rulers and governors upon the earth.

Thou, Master, hast given the power of sovereignty to them through thy excellent and inexpressible might, that we may know the glory and honour given to them by thee, and be subject to them, in nothing resisting thy will. And to them, Lord, grant health, peace, concord, firmness that they may administer the government which thou hast given them without offence. For thou, heavenly Master, king of eternity, hast given to the sons of men glory and honour and power over the things which are on the earth; do thou, O Lord, direct their counsels according to that which is 'good and pleasing' before thee, that they may administer with piety in peace and gentleness the power given to them by thee, and may find mercy in thine eyes. O thou who alone art able to do these things and far better things for us, we praise thee through Jesus Christ, the high priest and guardian of our souls, through whom be glory and majesty to thee, both now and for all generations and for ever and ever. Amen.
(*1 Clement* 59:3–61:3)

The following prayer was prayed at an early eucharist.

301. But after you are satisfied with food, thus give thanks: 'We give thanks to thee, O Holy Father, for thy Holy Name which thou didst make to tabernacle in our hearts, and for the knowledge and faith and immortality which thou didst make known to us through Jesus thy Child. To thee be glory for ever. Thou, Lord Almighty, didst create all things for thy Name's sake, and didst give food and drink to men for their enjoyment, that they might give thanks to thee, but us hast thou blessed with spiritual food and drink and eternal light through thy Child. Above all we give thanks to thee for that thou art mighty. To thee be glory forever. Remember, Lord, thy Church, to deliver it from all evil and to make it perfect in thy love, and gather it together in its holiness from the four winds to thy kingdom which thou hast prepared for it. For thine is the power and the glory for ever. Let grace come and let this world pass away. Hosannah to the God of David. If any man be holy, let him come! if any man be not, let him repent: Maran atha, Amen.'

But suffer the prophets to hold Eucharist as they will.
(*Didache* 10)[49]

4.6. Jewish Historiography

1 Maccabees.

1 Maccabees was originally written in Hebrew. It opens with an account of the struggles of the priestly Hasmonaean family against the Syrian

king Antiochus IV Epiphanes. Mattathias, the head of the family, initiated what is known as the Maccabaean Revolt. Together with his five sons he and his followers began a guerilla war against the Syrians and their Jewish collaborators. With the death of Mattathias, leadership of the revolt passed to his eldest son Judas, nicknamed the Hammer (Maccabaeus). In 164 the rebels recaptured Jerusalem and re-instituted the worship of God in a cleansed Temple. The book narrates the concluding of a treaty with Rome and the death of Judas in 160. An account of the high priesthoods of Judas's younger brothers Jonathan and Simon takes the account down to 143 BCE. The book closes with a summary of the reign of John Hyrcanus I (134–104 BCE). The book seeks to legitimate the Hasmonaean dynasty, and portrays the family as the saviour of the nation.

Sources

Judas succeeds his father Mattathias.

302. Then his son Judas, who was called Maccabeus, took command in his place. All his brothers and all who had joined his father helped him; they gladly fought for Israel.
He extended the glory of his people.
Like a giant he put on his breastplate;
he bound on his armor of war and waged battles,
protecting the camp by his sword.
He was like a lion in his deeds,
like a lion's cub roaring for prey.
He searched out and pursued those who broke the law;
he burned those who troubled his people.
Law-breakers shrank back for fear of him;
all the evildoers were confounded;
and deliverance prospered by his hand.
He embittered many kings,
but he made Jacob glad by his deeds,
and his memory is blessed forever.
He went through the cities of Judah;
he destroyed the ungodly out of the land;
thus he turned away wrath from Israel.
He was renowned to the ends of the earth;
he gathered in those who were perishing.
(1 Maccabees 3:1–9)

2 Maccabees.

The work known as 2 Maccabees is an engaging epitome (summary) of a five-volume work (now lost) written by Jason of Cyrene (see 2:19–32). It was created before the capture of Jersualem in 63 BCE (see 15:37). The scope of the work is the background of the Maccabaean revolt, the piety of the high priest Onias III, and the career of Judas Maccabaeus. It commences with two letters written to Jews in Egypt exhorting them to observe the new feast of Hanukkah, which commemorates the cleansing of the Temple at the end of the revolt. The piety of the deposed high priest Onias III is eulogized.[50] The career of Judas is closely linked with Onias, a victim of treachery, and who appears to Judas on the eve of his victory over the Syrian general Nicanor. Nevertheless Jonathan and Simon, the later high priests, are disparaged by the epitomist as though he contested the legitimacy of the Hasmonaean high priestly line.

Judas Maccabaeus exhorts his soldiers who are about to engage Nicanor in battle. Onias and Jeremiah appear to Judas in a dream.

303. He [Judas] armed each of them not so much with confidence in shields and spears as with the inspiration of brave words, and he cheered them all by relating a dream, a sort of vision, which was worthy of belief.

What he saw was this: Onias, who had been high priest, a noble and good man, of modest bearing and gentle manner, one who spoke fittingly and had been trained from childhood in all that belongs to excellence, was praying with outstretched hands for the whole body of the Jews. Then in the same fashion another appeared, distinguished by his gray hair and dignity, and of marvelous majesty and authority. And Onias spoke, saying, 'This is a man who loves the family of Israel and prays much for the people and the holy city—Jeremiah, the prophet of God.' Jeremiah stretched out his right hand and gave to Judas a golden sword, and as he gave it he addressed him thus: 'Take this holy sword, a gift from God, with which you will strike down your adversaries.'
(2 Maccabees 15:11–16)

Flavius Josephus.

Josephus was born in Palestine into an aristocratic priestly family in c. 36 CE. He died in c. 100 CE in Rome having enjoyed the patronage of the three Flavian emperors, including the granting of Roman citizenship. He wrote four works: *The Jewish War*, *The Jewish Antiquities*, an autobiography (the *Life*), and *Against Apion*—written in that order. In the *Life*, Josephus presents himself as a precocious and gifted child. As a teenager he made a thorough examination of the three major groups within Judaism, learning as much as he could about the Pharisees, the Sadducees, and the Essenes. He spent three years as the 'zealot' (follower) of Bannus, a hermit. After this time he entered political life representing the interests of the most influential group, the Pharisees.

At the outbreak of the first Jewish War in 66, Josephus was appointed by the aristocratic leadership as the general in charge of organizing resistance to the Romans in Galilee (see #181). However, in the campaign of 67, Vespasian quickly captured the fortified cities of the region and besieged Josephus in Jotapata. Josephus survived a suicide pact, claiming that God had revealed to him the fact that the Jewish cause was lost and that the Roman emperors were destined to rule the world. When taken to Vespasian, he was prompted by the Spirit to pronounce the Roman general and his son, Titus, as future emperors. By 69 Vespasian was indeed emperor. Josephus, who had impressed the Romans, spent the remainder of the War as a guest of and an adviser to the Romans. He was the target of malicious attacks immediately after the War (see *Jewish War* 7.499–50; *Life* 424–25), but was steadfastly protected by his Flavian patrons.

Josephus made use of the work of his contemporary, Nicolas of Damascus, as well as the work of many Graeco-Roman writers such as Strabo and Hecataeus of Abdera.

Josephus's early life.

304. While still a mere boy, about fourteen years old, I won universal applause for my love of letters; insomuch that the chief priests and the leading men of the city used constantly to come to me for precise information on some particular in our ordinances. At about the age of sixteen I determined to gain personal experience of the several sects into which our nation is divided. These, as I have frequently mentioned, are three in number—the first that of the Pharisees, the second that of the Sadducees, and the third that of the Essenes. I thought that, after a thorough investigation, I should be in a position to select the best. So I submitted myself to hard training and laborious exercises and passed through the three courses. Not content, however, with the experience thus gained, on hearing of one named Bannus, who dwelt in the wilderness, wearing only such clothing as trees provided, feeding on such things as grew of themselves, and using frequent ablutions of cold water, by day and night, for purity's sake, I became his devoted disciple. With him I lived for three years and, having accomplished my purpose, returned to the city. Being now in my nineteenth year I began to govern my life by the rules of the Pharisees, a sect having points of resemblance to that which the Greeks call the Stoic school. (Josephus, *Life* 9–12)[51]

Josephus's enjoyment of Flavian patronage.

305. (422) When Titus had quelled the disturbances in Judaea, conjecturing that the lands which I held at Jerusalem would be unprofitable for me, because a Roman garrison was to be quartered there, he gave me another parcel of ground in the plain. On his departure for Rome, he took me with him on board, treating me with every mark of respect. On our arrival in Rome I met with great consideration from Vespasian. He gave me a lodging in the house which he had occupied before he became Emperor; he honoured me with the privilege of Roman citizenship; and he assigned me a pension. He continued to honour me up to the time of his departure from this life, without any abatement in his kindness towards me.

(428) The treatment which I received from the Emperors continued unaltered. On Vespasian's decease Titus, who succeeded to

> the empire, showed the same esteem for me as did his father, and never credited the accusations to which I was constantly subjected. Domitian succeeded Titus and added to my honours. He punished my Jewish accusers, and for a similar offence gave orders for the chastisement of a slave, a eunuch and my son's tutor. He also exempted my property in Judaea from taxation—a mark of the highest honour to the privileged individual. Moreover, Domitia, Caesar's wife, never ceased conferring favours upon me.
> (Josephus, *Life* 422–23, 428–29)

Josephus's preface to the Jewish War.

306. The war of the Jews against the Romans—the greatest not only of the wars of our own time, but, so far as accounts have reached us, well nigh of all that ever broke out between cities or nations—has not lacked historians. Of these, however, some, having taken no part in the action, have collected from hearsay casual and contradictory stories which they have then edited in a rhetorical style; while others, who witnessed the events, have, either from flattery of the Romans or from hatred of the Jews, misrepresented the facts, their writings exhibiting alternatively invective and encomium, but nowhere historical accuracy. In these circumstances, I—Josephus, son of Matthias, a Hebrew by race, a native of Jerusalem and a priest, who at the opening of the war myself fought against the Romans and in the sequel was perforce an onlooker—propose to provide the subjects of the Roman Empire with a narrative of the facts, by translating into Greek the account which I previously composed in my vernacular tongue and sent to the barbarians in the interior.
(Josephus, *Jewish War* 1.1–3)[52]

4.7. Gospels

The four New Testament Gospels present a life of Jesus, selective to be sure, but an ordered chronological account with the story moving towards a climax and its denouement. Consequently, the link with Graeco-Roman biography has often been noted. Matthew and Luke underscore this link by providing accounts of Jesus' birth and his genealogy. Luke especially is concerned to evoke the conventions of Graeco-Roman historiography and to improve stylistically on his predecessors (see Luke 1:1–4). In common with the biographers, all four evangelists provide the reader with an account of Jesus' public career; and there is a prominent exemplary aspect to each Gospel, each presenting the character of Jesus.

By aligning the four Gospels with Graeco-Roman biography, one could not pretend to have explained their *function* satisfactorily. Before all else the Gospels are affirmations in literary form of the claims of the early Christian preaching that Jesus is the Messiah of Jewish expectation. The form of Mark's Gospel follows the outline of the sermons in Acts.[53] The Gospels of Matthew and Luke follow Mark's pattern. The conventions of biography do not, therefore, adequately explain the Gospel genre or the Gospel content, or what I take to be their purpose in the communities for whom they were written. Ultimately it was the content and shape of the early Christian message about Jesus which was the source of the written Gospels and gave them shape.

We should not expect historical accuracy for every deed and saying of Jesus. Analysis of the conventions of Graeco-Roman biography (or Classical, Hellenistic or Roman historiography for that matter) shows that we must not expect the evangelists to have been possessed of a modern methodology which stresses dispassionate, careful evaluating of sources, the weighing of evidence, and consistent cross-questioning of witnesses. The evangelists were not historians and biographers in the modern sense.

Mark's Gospel, the earliest of the canonical Gospels, is a written 'proclamation' (*kerygma*). It encapsulates in written form the essence of the message about Jesus along the lines of the early preaching. Matthew and Luke follow suit. All the Gospels incorporate kerygmatically shaped pieces of tradition. In other words, the Gospels contain in themselves many re-statements of the gospel—the 'good news' of God's intervention in the affairs of people in the person of Jesus. Therefore, reading a Gospel puts one in touch with the gospel of Christ. To read a Gospel is to engage with the significance of all that Jesus did and said for the community for whom that Gospel was written.[54] The Gospels are designed to affirm and strengthen faith, as well as evoke it, in the community of faith. As one scholar has aptly remarked, Gospels reinforced the 'social implications of belief in Jesus as Messiah and Son of God'.[55]

While there are important parallels between the Gospels and Graeco-Roman biography, their content and form suggest that, in the first-century context, they are distinctive and unique literary creations. Outside the New Testament, there is a large corpus of early Christian literature which also falls into the Gospel genre. Some of these are Infancy Gospels, that is, they concentrate on the infancy and childhood of Jesus. Some are rather Gnostic in their thrust. These stress that eternal life is defined as the possession of those who have the knowledge and insight Jesus imparts to his followers. Some of these extra-canonical Gospels, like the *Coptic Gospel of Thomas*, are collections of parables and aphorisms with very little narrative and little or no eschatological focus.

The New Testament Gospels were all written by c. 100 CE. Mark is commonly regarded as the earliest of the four and the Fourth Gospel the last written. Mark might have reached the form in which we now have it during or soon after the Jewish War (66–70). The date of the sources used by the evangelists obviously ante-dates the final form of each of the Gospels. It is highly likely that Luke and Matthew both used Mark and a collection of sayings of Jesus called Q, the initial letter of the German word *Quelle* (source). Special material unique to Matthew (M) and unique to Luke (L), as well as the Gospel of John, complete the picture of Gospel sources. It is possible that there were editions of the three Gospels—Matthew, Mark and Luke—predating the final form of each.

Certain literary features of the Gospels strongly suggest the incorporation by the evangelists of settled literary or oral traditions. The four passion narratives seem to have been the first material about Jesus committed to writing. There is considerable agreement in the order of events in the four accounts. The same might be said for the material designated as belonging to the putative sayings source Q.

Furthermore, the Gospels exhibit certain Jewish traits, the chief of which is the homily based on a passage(s) from the Bible. Jesus frequently cites scripture and proceeds to illuminate the meaning for his readers. There is a similar use of scripture in the early Christian teaching in Acts by Peter and Paul. Fulfilment is the chief note of much early Christian use of scripture, especially in Matthew and Luke–Acts.

Affinities between Graeco-Roman biography and the Gospel genre do begin to break down on closer analysis. The conventions do not adequately explain the Gospel genre or the Gospel content. I believe that the Gospels are quite unprecedented. Ultimately it was the content and shape of the early Christian message about Jesus which lie behind the genre.

Sources

The preface to the Gospel of Luke.

307. Since many have undertaken to set down an orderly account of the events that have been fulfilled among us, just as they were handed on to us by those who from the beginning were eye-witnesses and servants of the word, I too decided, after investigating everything carefully from the very first, to write an orderly account for you, most excellent Theophilus, so that you may know the truth concerning the things about which you have been instructed.
(Luke 1:1–4)

A summary of early Christian preaching.

308. 'You know the message he sent to the people of Israel, preaching peace by Jesus Christ—he is Lord of all. That message spread throughout Judea, beginning in Galilee after the baptism that John announced: how God anointed Jesus of Nazareth with the Holy Spirit and with power; how he went about doing good and healing all who were

oppressed by the devil, for God was with him. We are witnesses to all that he did both in Judea and in Jerusalem. They put him to death by hanging him on a tree; but God raised him on the third day and allowed him to appear, not to all the people but to us who were chosen by God as witnesses, and who ate and drank with him after he rose from the dead. He commanded us to preach to the people and to testify that he is the one ordained by God as judge of the living and the dead. All the prophets testify about him that everyone who believes in him receives forgiveness of sins through his name.'
(Acts 10:36–43)[56]

In the following two passages from the Gospel of Matthew, the evangelist cites scripture to underscore its fulfilment in the advent and ministry of Jesus.

309. He [Jesus] left Nazareth and made his home in Capernaum by the sea, in the territory of Zebulun and Naphtali, so that what had been spoken through the prophet Isaiah might be fulfilled:
'Land of Zebulun, land of Naphtali,
on the road by the sea, across the Jordan,
Galilee of the Gentiles—
the people who sat in darkness
have seen a great light,
and for those who sat in the region and shadow of death
light has dawned' [Isaiah 9:1–2].
(Matthew 4:13–17)

310. When Jesus became aware of this, he departed. Many crowds followed him, and he cured all of them, and he ordered them not to make him known. This was to fulfill what had been spoken through the prophet Isaiah:
'Here is my servant, whom I have chosen,
my beloved, with whom my soul is well-pleased.
I will put my Spirit upon him,
and he will proclaim justice to the Gentiles.
He will not wrangle or cry aloud,
nor will anyone hear his voice in the streets.
He will not break a bruised reed
or quench a smoldering wick
until he brings justice to victory.
And in his name the Gentiles will hope'
[Isaiah 42:1–4].
(Matthew 12:15–21)[57]

Jesus' preferred mode of instruction was the parable. The point of a parable is to draw a comparison or an analogy. Jesus' parables are about the Kingdom of God. In the first selection Jesus teaches about the supreme value of the Kingdom and the necessary sacrifices that must be made to possess it (vv. 44–46) and about the judgment that will bring a decisive end to the present indiscriminate mixture of righteous and evil in the Kingdom. The second comes from the *Coptic Gospel of Thomas*, and bears a relationship to the third of the parables cited at #311.

The parable of the buried treasure.

311. 'The kingdom of heaven is like treasure hidden in a field, which someone found and hid; then in his joy he goes and sells all that he has and buys that field.

'Again, the kingdom of heaven is like a merchant in search of fine pearls; on finding one pearl of great value, he went and sold all that he had and bought it.

'Again, the kingdom of heaven is like a net that was thrown into the sea and caught fish of every kind; when it was full, they drew it ashore, sat down, and put the good into baskets but threw out the bad. So it will be at the end of the age. The angels will come out and separate the evil from the righteous and throw them into the furnace of fire, where there will be weeping and gnashing of teeth.'
(Matthew 13:44–50)

The parable of the intelligent fisherman.

312. And he [Jesus] said, 'What human beings resemble is an intelligent fisherman who, having cast his net into the sea, pulled the net up out of the sea full of little fish. The intelligent fisherman, upon finding among them a fine large fish, threw all the little fish back into the sea, choosing without any effort the big fish. Whoever has ears to hear should listen!'
(*Coptic Gospel of Thomas* 8)

4.8. The Content of the Gospels in their Literary Setting

On closer analysis much of the extraordinary content of much of the Gospels is not unique. The mid second-century apologist Justin Martyr argues that the singling out of Christians for persecution is unwarranted because what Christians say about Jesus is no different from what their unbelieving contemporaries say about their gods and heroes (see #313).

But the miraculous was not just confined to the scope of mythology. According to their biographers miracles also attended the lives of famous men, especially at conception, birth and death. Readers of the Hebrew Bible will be familiar with the presence of miracles in its narratives. Most proximate of all to the Gospels is the *Life of Apollonius of Tyana* written by Philostratus, an early third-century Pythagorean philosopher. Apollonius, who lived in the late first century, was venerated after his death. Like the Gospels the *Life* is a collection of discourses and miracle stories. Like Jesus, Apollonius was willing to die for his beliefs. Entering a temple he vanished from earth only to reappear after his death to convince a doubting disciple.[58]

However there is a significant matter in the Gospel tradition that needs to be addressed. The Gospels are unanimous in using the language of resurrection to describe what happened to Jesus after his death. As far as I am aware the claims of the New Testament in regard to Jesus' resurrection are unique.

Sources

Justin Martyr on the miraculous element in the Christian preaching.

313. And when we say also that the Word, who is the first-birth of God, was produced without sexual union, and that He, Jesus Christ, our Teacher, was crucified and died, and rose again, and ascended into heaven, we propound nothing different from what you believe regarding those whom you esteem sons of Jupiter. For you know how many sons your esteemed writers ascribed to Jupiter: Mercury, the interpreting word and teacher of all; Aesculapius, who, though he was a great physician, was struck by a thunderbolt, and so ascended to heaven; and Bacchus too, after he had been torn limb from limb; and Hercules, when he had committed himself to the flames to escape his toils; and the sons of Leda, and Dioscuri; and Perseus, son of Danae; and Bellerophon, who, though sprung from mortals, rose to heaven on the horse Pegasus. For what shall I say of Ariadne, and those who, like her, have been declared to be set among the stars? And what of the emperors who die among yourselves, whom you deem worthy of deification, and in whose behalf you produce some one who swears he has seen the burning Caesar rise to heaven from the funeral pyre? And what kind of deeds are recorded of each of these reputed sons of Jupiter, it is needless to tell to those who already know. This only shall be said, that they are written for the advantage and encouragement of youthful scholars; for all reckon it an honourable thing to imitate the gods. But far be such a thought concerning the gods from every well-conditioned soul, as to believe that Jupiter himself, the governor and creator of all things, was both a parricide and the son of a parricide, and that being overcome by the love of base and shameful pleasures, he came in to Ganymede and those many women whom he had violated and that his sons did like actions. But, as we said above, wicked devils perpetrated these things. And we have learned that those only are deified who have lived near to God in holiness and virtue; and we believe that those who live wickedly and do not repent are punished in everlasting fire.

Moreover, the Son of God called Jesus, even if only a man by ordinary generation, yet, on account of His wisdom, is worthy to be called the Son of God; for all writers call God the Father of men and gods. And if we assert that the Word of God was born of God in a peculiar manner, different from ordinary generation, let this, as said above, be no extraordinary thing to you, who say that Mercury is the angelic word of God. But if any one objects that He was crucified, in this also He is on a par with those reput-

ed sons of Jupiter of yours, who suffered as we have now enumerated. For their sufferings at death are recorded to have been not all alike, but diverse; so that not even by the peculiarity of His sufferings does He seem to be inferior to them; but, on the contrary, as we promised in the preceding part of this discourse, we will now prove Him superior—or rather have already proved Him to be so—for the superior is revealed by His actions. And if we even affirm that He was born of a virgin, accept this in common with what you accept of Perseus. And in that we say that He made whole the lame, the paralytic, and those born blind, we seem to say what is very similar to the deeds said to have been done by Aesculapius.
(Justin, *Apology* 1.21–22)

Miracles (#314–16).

Miracles are found in each of the four Gospels and the Acts of the Apostles, though for special reasons John restricts his account of them to seven. Miracles are clearly part of the earliest literary strands of the Gospels.[59] But miracles and divine cures are also attested or claimed elsewhere in Graeco-Roman literature.[60]

Jesus performs miracles.

314. That evening, at sundown, they brought to him all who were sick or possessed with demons. And the whole city was gathered around the door. And he cured many who were sick with various diseases, and cast out many demons; and he would not permit the demons to speak, because they knew him.
(Mark 1:32–34)

God effects miracles through Paul.

315. God did extraordinary miracles through Paul, so that when the handkerchiefs or aprons that had touched his skin were brought to the sick, their diseases left them, and the evil spirits came out of them.
(Acts 19:11–12)

Marble tablet of 138 CE, probably from the Temple of Asclepius in Rome.

316. To Valerius Aper, a blind soldier, the god revealed that he should go and take blood of a white cock, together with honey, and rub them into eyesalve and anoint his eyes three days. And he received his sight, and came and gave thanks publicly to the god.
(Deissmann, *Light from the Ancient East* p. 135.
Cf. John 9:7, 11)

The Virgin birth.

While Mark and John have no nativity narrative, Matthew and Luke agree that Jesus was born of a 'virgin' (Matthew 1:18–25; Luke 1:30–35). Matthew appeals to the passage in Isaiah 7:14: 'the young woman will conceive and bear a son'. In the Greek translation of this passage, the Hebrew word *bethulah* ('young woman') is translated by the word *parthenos* ('virgin'). Once again, there are parallels with contemporary literature. Plato, Alexander the Great, Augustus, Pythagoras and Heracles were all conceived of a divine father.[61]

The *Odes of Solomon* articulate the tradition of the virgin birth of Jesus in the following way.

317. The Holy Spirit opened her bosom,
and mixed the milk of the two breasts of the Father.
Then she gave the mixture to the generation without their knowing,
and those who have received (it) are in the perfection of the right hand.
The womb of the Virgin took (it),
and she received conception and gave birth.
So the Virgin became a mother with great mercies.
And she labored and bore the Son but without pain,
because it did not occur without purpose.
(*Odes of Solomon* 19:4–8)[62]

Martyrdom.

Jesus died a victim of unscrupulous opportunists and of Roman weakness in the face of manipulation by Jewish leaders and the mob. In Luke and Acts in particular, Jesus is presented very much as a martyr of a just and righteous cause (see, e.g., Acts 10:38–39). The accounts of the martyrs Eleazar and the seven brothers in 2 Maccabees 6–7 and *4 Maccabees* provide comparable material.[63]

Resurrection.

The accounts of the post-resurrection appearances of Jesus in Matthew, Luke and John are resolutely consistent in affirming the physicality of the body of Jesus raised from the dead.

The disciples return hastily from Emmaus to Jerusalem, telling their story of how Jesus appeared to them on the road, and how he was made known to them in the breaking of the bread.

318. While they were talking about this, Jesus himself stood among them and said to them, 'Peace be with you.' They were startled and terrified, and thought that they were seeing a ghost. He said to them, 'Why are you frightened, and why do doubts arise in your hearts? Look at my hands and my feet; see that it is I myself. Touch me and see; for a ghost does not have flesh and bones as you see that I have.' And when he had said this, he showed them his hands and his feet. While in their joy they were disbelieving and still wondering, he said to them, 'Have you anything here to eat?' They gave him a piece of broiled fish, and he took it and ate in their presence.
(Luke 24:36–43)

Ascension into heaven (apotheosis) (#319–21).

Apotheosis was rather commonly proclaimed in Graeco-Roman literature, and is encountered in the Hebrew Bible (Genesis 5:24; 2 Kings 2:11) and early Jewish literature (Sirach 44:16; 1 Maccabees 2:58). The hero dies and his body disappears. This is followed by evidence that the deceased has been received into heaven.[64]

The apotheosis of Romulus.

319. When these deathless deeds had been done, as the king was holding a muster in the Campus Martius, near the swamp of Capra, for the purpose of reviewing the army, suddenly a storm came up, with loud claps of thunder, and enveloped him in a cloud so thick as to hide him from the sight of the assembly; and from that moment Romulus was no more on earth.
(Livy, *History of Rome* 1.16.1)

The apotheosis of Moses.

320. [F]or when he was already being exalted and stood at the very barrier, ready at the signal to direct his upward flight to heaven, the divine spirit fell upon him and he prophesied with discernment while still alive the story of his own death...
(Philo, *Moses* 2.291.
Cf. Deuteronomy 34)

Jesus ascends to heaven in the presence of his disciples.

321. Then he [Jesus] led them out as far as Bethany, and, lifting up his hands, he blessed them. While he was blessing them, he withdrew from them and was carried up into heaven. And they worshiped him, and returned to Jerusalem with great joy; and they were continually in the temple blessing God.
(Luke 24:50–53.
Cf. Acts 1:6–11)

Notes

1. There are interpolations in the *Testaments of the Twelve Patriarchs* (*T12P*) and *Sibylline Oracles* 1, 2 and 8. There are Christian additions to the *Martyrdom and Ascension of Isaiah* (3:13–4:22; 6–11), *Sibylline Oracles* (Oracles 6 and 7), and *4 Ezra* (chapters 1–2 [note 2:42–48], 15–16). All texts of the Pseudepigrapha used in this book emanate from the two-volume collection entitled *Old Testament Pseudepigrapha* (*OTP*).
2. See Paul D. Hanson, *The Dawn of Apocalyptic* (Philadelphia: Fortress Press, 1979).
3. Florentino García Martínez argues that the Seer was an Essene, and that he is describing the origin of his community and their ministry to Israel under the symbol of the 'lambs' in the third century BCE (certainly in pre-Maccabaean times). See his 'The Origins of the Essene Movement and of the Qumran Sect', in Florentino García Martínez and Julio Trebolle Barrera, *The People of the Dead Sea Scrolls: Their Writings, Beliefs and Practices* (Leiden: E.J. Brill, 1995), pp. 77–96 (especially pp. 86–91).
4. Note the presentation of the Beast in Revelation 13:1–4 (see #263). It is a composite of the four beasts of Daniel 7.

5. In the Christian Apocrypha, 2 Esdras corresponds to *4 Ezra* (4 Esdras in the Vulgate).
6. See the allusions to the destruction of the city in 3:2; 6:19; 10:48.
7. The 24 books of the Hebrew Bible correspond to the 39 books in the Christian Old Testament. The twelve minor prophets are combined into one book. The two books each of Samuel, Kings, Chronicles and Ezra–Nehemiah are also combined into one each.
8. Baruch, a book of the Apocrypha, is an earlier exemplar of this theology. Josephus's accounting for the destruction of Jerusalem owes much to the Baruch tradition. *4 Ezra*, on the other hand, rejects this approach. Instead the book advances the solution to the problem of evil and the apparent failure of divine promises in terms of God's renewal of the destroyed city and the triumph of the messiah over the Romans. The Baruch tradition is dependent on earlier theology espoused in the book of Deuteronomy, which links continued blessing in the land with covenant faithfulness, and predicts expulsion from the land as punishment for rebellion against God and his law (see especially chapters 28–30).
9. Scholars argue that there are possible affinities between the rabbinic concepts of the messiah and *2 Baruch*. The book plays down the idea of the messianic age as imminent, and encourages obedient living with respect to the Torah as the prerequisite for the blessings of the age to come. Nevertheless there is a vivid expectation in *2 Baruch* of the destruction of Gentile oppressors. See also the mishnaic tractate *Sotah* 9.15.
10. See also *4 Ezra* 13:46–50; *Apocalypse of Abraham* 29:17; Revelation 20:4.
11. Cf. *4 Ezra* 7:77; 8:33; Tobit 4:9.
12. Cf. Mark 12:25; 1 Corinthians 15:52.
13. Cf. *2 Baruch* 59; *4 Ezra* 10; *Apocalypse of Abraham* 25:3; Ezekiel 40–48; *1 Enoch* 90:28–29; 1Q32; 4Q554–55.
14. See also the citation of the first line of column 2 and the comment regarding the title son of God/Most High in #655.
15. One prominent theory is that the Seer of Revelation was aware that Domitian was fostering a cult of himself as Lord and God (see #102) and that Roman aristocrats, such as Flavius Clemens, Domitian's own cousin, were being targeted for their Christian sympathies (see #103). Under such circumstances, John perceived that the faithful must be prepared to face martyrdom at the hands of the Beast who would soon come.
16. See R.H. Charles, *Revelation* (ICC; 2 vols.; Edinburgh: T. & T. Clark, 1920), I, p. 357.
17. The number '666' is usually explained as gematria—number values were assigned to the letters of the Greek alphabet and then added. Six hundred and sixty-six is actually the sum of the numbers assigned to the letters of the Greek, *Nerōn Kaisar* (emperor Nero), when transliterated into their Hebrew equivalent (see Charles, *Revelation*, I, p. 367).
18. Babylon is used several times in early Jewish and Christian literature as a symbol of Rome. See 1 Peter 5:13; *Sibylline Oracles* 5.143.
19. Cf. Matthew 24:1–44; Luke 21:5–38. Though note Luke's greater emphasis on the military destruction of Jerusalem (rather than the end of history).
20. There are some Christian interpolations (e.g. *Testament of Levi* 4:4; 14:2), but no more than 12 in the entire collection. They interrupt the flow of the argument and show evidence Christian credal content.
21. See, e.g., *Testament of Reuben* 6; *Testament of Simeon* 7; *Testament of Judah* 21.
22. Note #700. *Testament of Dan* 5.10, however, anticipates a single agent 'from the tribe of Judah and Levi'.
23. The work was originally written in Hebrew, but is now only extant in one Latin ms., the end of which is lost.
24. Cf. Josephus, *Antiquities* 17.261.
25. Cf. *Jubilees* 36:1–11; 1 Maccabees 2:49–70.
26. See M.D. Goulder, *Midrash and Lection in Matthew* (London: SPCK, 1974).
27. See John Shelby Spong, *Liberating the Gospels: Reading the Gospels with Jewish Eyes* (San Francisco: HarperSanFrancisco, 1996). Spong writes that the reality of God encountered in the ministry of Jesus 'was like the reality of God known in the past' (p. 37). He calls the process by which the evangelists shaped their accounts of the life and work of Jesus a 'midrashic principle'.
28. The book is mentioned in the corpus of the Dead Sea Scrolls (Damascus Document 16.3–4) and is cited in 4Q228. Several manuscripts of the book have also been found among the finds of five Qumran caves and at Masada. The most complete of all the ancient versions is the Ethiopic.

29. A jubilee is a 50-year period. See Leviticus 25.
30. See *Jubilees* 50:12; cf. 1 Maccabees 2:29–42.
31. See 30:18–20; cf. the Qumran Messianic Rule (1QSa).
32. See *Jubilees* 1:17, 29; cf. 11QT 29.
33. This lengthy story is extant in 16 Greek manuscripts. Greek was the probable original language.
34. Eve is repeatedly identified as the source of Adam's sin (18:1; 26:2; 35:2; 44:2). Cf. *2 Enoch* 30:18; Sirach 25:24. Note the contrast with Romans 5:17; *4 Ezra* 3:21 and 7:118 which hold Adam accountable. In the following early Jewish and Christian works, Eve's sin is characterized as being of a sexual nature: 2 Corinthians 11:3; 1 Timothy 2:14 (#435); *Apocalypse of Abraham* 23:1–5; *4 Maccabees* 18:6–8 (#434); *Protevangelium of James* 13:1.
35. The citation at the conclusion of this extract is from *1 Enoch* 1:9, which is also cited in Jude 14–15.
36. Cf. Josephus, *Antiquities* 8.111–18, Solomon's prayer at the dedication of the Temple.
37. Targum of Job (11Q10, 4Q157); Targum of Leviticus (4Q156). There are also what appear to be Greek targums. See Geza Vermes, *The Complete Dead Sea Scrolls in English* (Harmondsworth: Penguin Books, 1998), pp. 440–41.
38. The letter to the Hebrews also bears marked affinities with homiletic style. Note the frequent use of exhortation (usually in the first person plural), and the interspersing of exhortation with didactic passages.
39. See, e.g., F. Gerald Downing, *Christ and the Cynics: Jesus and Other Radical Preachers in First-Century Tradition* (JSOT Manuals, 4; Sheffield: Sheffield Academic Press, 1988); John Dominic Crossan, *The Historical Jesus: The Life of a Mediterranean Jewish Peasant* (San Francisco: HarperCollins, 1991). Note also the extracts at #393–98.
40. Note the parallels with sayings of Jesus recorded in Matthew 7:16; Luke 6:44; Matthew 12:34; Luke 6:45.
41. Note the parallels in Matthew 7:23–24, the Dead Sea Scrolls (#646), and *Epistle of Barnabas* 19.
42. The Qumran Hodayot (1QH) are more fully described in Part 8 (topic 8.12).
43. See, e.g., 1:4–8 cited at #146.
44. No manuscript contains all the *Odes of Solomon*. *Ode* 2 is still lost, as is the beginning of *Ode* 3, and perhaps portions of *Ode* 1. Manuscripts exist in Syriac (tenth and fifteenth century CE, the latter comprising *Odes* 3–42), and the more fragmentary Greek (third century CE), and Coptic (fourth century CE). The original language was Syriac or Aramaic.
45. See *Odes of Solomon* 10:5; 29:8; cf. Matthew 10:5–8; Mark 7:24–30.
46. See P. Winter, 'Magnificat and Benedictus—Maccabaean Psalms?', *BJRL* 37 (1954–55), pp. 328–47. Note also D. Flusser, 'The Magnificat, the Benedictus and the War Scroll', in *idem*, *Judaism and the Origins of Christianity* (Jerusalem: Magnes Press, 1988), pp. 126–49.
47. See #276 and the comments prefacing that extract.
48. For essays on the Lord's Prayer and other prayers of the era, see James H. Charlesworth (ed.), *The Lord's Prayer and Other Prayer Texts from the Greco-Roman Era* (Valley Forge, PA: Trinity Press International, 1994).
49. The phrase 'Maran atha' is Aramaic, meaning 'our Lord, come'. It preserves the liturgical language of the earliest Palestinian and Syrian churches. Yet it has also been transposed into the firmly Greek setting of Paul's first letter to the Corinthians (16:22) without translation. See also Revelation 22:20.
50. Interestingly Onias III does not appear in 1 Maccabees, a book that is concerned to provide a defence of the Hasmonaean establishment.
51. Steve Mason argues that Joesphus did not actually become a Pharisee as stated in the translation by Thackeray above. Mason translates the verb that Thackeray translated as 'govern my life' (*politeuesthai*) as 'entered public affairs'. On this reading Josephus entered politics 'following the school of the Pharisees', i.e. with deference to the Pharisees as the most influential force in Judaean life and politics. See his *Flavius Josephus on the Pharisees: A Composition-critical Study* (Leiden: E.J. Brill, 1991), pp. 325–56.
52. Josephus's vernacular was Aramaic. On the inadequacy of the existing accounts, compare Luke 1:1–4. See *Jewish War* 1.2, 6 for earlier histories of the war. Justus of Tiberias also wrote a history of the war (see Josephus, *Life* 336–60).

53. See, e.g., Acts 10:36–43 and the comment in n. 54 below.
54. The Gospels were written on two levels. At one level they present the life and ministry of Jesus in the early 30s CE, and are proclamations of the message that was at the heart of the foundation of the communities. On another level, they can be read as documents contingent upon the life of the communities for which they were written, and mirror their struggles and joys, their questions and problems. Jesus thus speaks not to his own contemporaries but continues to address successive generations of believers. Thus Mark's Gospel addresses believers facing trauma and the threat of martyrdom; as well as the inroads of false prophets and Messiahs who claim that the dreadful events of the Jewish War are harbingers of an imminent parousia. Like much of John's Gospel, John 9 addresses the problem of dual membership of synagogue and church. The Jews will not accept Christian claims about the status and significance of Jesus. They excommunicate believers. Luke appears to mount a case for the legitimacy of the early Christian movement in the face of potential (or actual) Roman suspicion and Jewish claims that the Jews alone represent the faith that rests on the scriptural deposit found in the Bible. Matthew was written to anchor the community's commitment to the Jewish Law and to Jesus' reinterpretation of it.
55. See David E. Aune, *The New Testament in its Literary Environment* (Philadelphia: Westminster Press, 1986), p. 60.
56. Note the brief chronological outline of Jesus' life, the sense that God is working in and through him to bring 'the good news of peace', stress on Jesus' links with the Baptist, Galilaean ministry—exorcisms, miracles, doing good—death ('they killed him') and resurrection (seen by witnesses). The link between the gospel genre and early Christian preaching was first noted by C.H. Dodd, *The Apostolic Preaching and its Developments* (London: Hodder & Stoughton, 1936).
57. Jesus has just healed a man with a withered hand on the Sabbath in a synagogue (Matthew 12:9–14). He learns that, as a result, the Pharisees 'went out and conspired against him, how to destroy him' (v. 14).
58. The appearance occurred in a dream. See Philostratus, *The Life of Apollonius of Tyana* 8.31.
59. Miracles appear in the earliest sources of the synoptic Gospels, namely, Mark and Q (see Matthew 11:2–6//Luke 7:18–23).
60. See the documents brought together in David R. Cartlidge and David L. Dungan (eds.), *Documents for the Study of the Gospels* (Minneapolis: Fortress Press, 1994), pp. 151–64. Among these are the Epidauros Inscriptions testifying to healings effected by Asklepius (pp. 151–52); an account of the miracles said to be have been performed by Pythagoras (pp. 153–54); miracles performed by Vespasian (according to Tacitus, *Histories* 4.81; cf. Suetonius, *Vespasian* 7) (p. 155); the work of the unnamed Syrian exorcist (recorded in Lucian, *The Lover of Lies* 16; cf. Mark 1:23–26) (p. 156); and the healings effected by the mid first-century CE Jewish rabbi Hanina ben Dosa recorded in the Babylonian Talmud (pp. 157–58). Note also the discussion of Jewish miracle workers in Geza Vermes, *Jesus the Jew* (London: Collins, 1973), pp. 58–82. See also the reports of the exorcisms effected by the Pharisees (Matthew 12:27; Luke 11:19) and the miracles performed by Jesus' disciples (Matthew 10:8; Luke 10:9, 17).
61. See texts excerpted in Cartlidge and Dungan (eds.), *Documents for the Study of the Gospels*, pp. 129–36.
62. Cf. Ignatius, *Letter to the Ephesians* 18:2; 19:1 (#667); *Letter to the Smyrnaeans* 1:1; *Letter to the Trallians* 9:1.
63. See texts excerpted in Cartlidge and Dungan (eds.), *Documents for the Study of the Gospels*, p. 179 (Zeno), pp. 180–81 (Eleazar [*4 Maccabees* 5–6]), pp. 182–83 (Rabbi Akiba). Note also Plato's *Apology*—an account of the death of Socrates.
64. See texts excerpted in Cartlidge and Dungan (eds.), *Documents for the Study of the Gospels*, pp. 185–200.

5. Graeco-Roman Religion

5.1. The Religion of the Greeks and the Romans

No aspect of ancient Greek or Roman life and culture was independent of the pull of the world of the gods. Worship of the gods was an indelible aspect of public life throughout the Hellenistic and Graeco-Roman eras, unifying communities by affirming common traditions and celebrating the significant events of the agrarian calendar. The cyclical round of the civic cult produced occasions for public spectacle in the form of processions, athletic and poetry contests, feasting and celebration. The gods, writes Sean Freyne, were really the 'patrons of human and social institutions and virtues that are required from the good citizen'.[1] There was an ineluctable bond between citizenship and religious practice.

The traditional religious beliefs and practices of the Greeks and Romans of the Hellenistic and Graeco-Roman eras can be traced to pre-classical times. Greek and Roman gods were embodiments of tangible natural phenomena and, especially in the case of the Roman gods, numinous forces present in the natural world. In the case of Roman religiosity of the New Testament era, emperor worship and the cult of the deified *Roma* were powerful symbols of Rome's pre-eminence.[2]

Greek beliefs were given incomparable and enduring mythological expression in the epics of Homer and in the slightly later poetic cosmology of Hesiod. The myths and epics formed the basis of Greek and, by extension, Roman theatre, literature, education and art. The Romans ascribed the pattern and content of their religious practices and beliefs to Romulus (auspices) and King Numa (ritual).[3] The Roman religious ideal, as enunciated, for example, in philosophical writings, stressed the need for level-headed observance. This was termed *religio*. By contrast, *superstitio* denoted observance which was lacking in self-control and marked by fear.[4] While respect was often shown ancient religious rites, no respect could be afforded the Egyptian god Apis or other Egyptian animal deities or the Jewish rites.[5]

The three principal religious acts in ancient Greece and Rome were the offering of sacrifice and prayer and the setting up of dedications (votive offerings). Sacrifice could be offered in praise or thanksgiving or in supplication. Sacrifice was ubiquitous in the ancient world. Sacrifice at the holy place, sanctified by association with the divinity whose shrine it was and whose image the shrine housed, was the central act of the obligation of paying religious homage. In both Greek and Roman communities animal sacrifice was followed by a feast in honour of the god, held either at home or in the temple precincts. The worshippers feasted on that part of the victim that had not been immolated on the altar or given to the temple functionaries. The priests had the right to sell the meat in the market place. This practice issued in moral objections on the part of some early Christians, and is clearly a live issue in 1 Corinthians.[6] Jews were not as troubled since the eating of sacrificial meat was already taboo.

Sacrifices were also accompanied by prayers. The close connection of sacrifice and prayer helped determine that prayer took the form of a contract between the worshipper and the divinity invoked. Prayer was essentially the striking of a bargain with the divinity.[7] In Roman worship reciting the exact, often archaic, invocatory formulae and wording of the formal prayers was obligatory. The time-honoured order of the ritual was required to be kept lest the whole ceremony be rendered ineffective. Carrying out one's religious obligations was perceived as an essential feature of Roman religion, and was characterized by the term *pietas*.

Vows entailed promises of gifts, often in the form of a sacrifice, to be made to a god in expectation of a request being granted. Once the request was granted the sacrifice was made or the gift installed in the shrine. Vows were often made in the context of requests for healing. If the worshipper was healed the votive offering might be rendered in the shape of the healed member. The cult of the healing god Asclepius is very much in the ascendancy in the Graeco-Roman period. Archaeological finds from the Asclepeion at Corinth reveal a large number of effigies of human limbs and body parts, votives offered by healed worshippers.[8]

Neither in Roman nor Greek religion was moral attainment seen as an essential prerequisite of worship. Ethics and the performance of religious duty were not connected.[9] Religious duty, however, did require ritual purity.[10] Philosophers, however, did insist that it was the attitude of the worshipper that counted more than the quality or quantity of the offerings.

Material offerings of grain and wine were also made to the gods. This is particularly evident in the case of the etiquette at Greek and Roman private meals. A portion of the meal was offered on the hearth at the beginning of the Greek meal. At the conclusion a libation was poured to the *agathos daimōn*, the protective spirit of the household. In Roman households small offerings of food and wine were made before the *lararium*, the shrine that held images of the *lares*, the protective deities of the household.[11]

Neither among the Greeks nor the Romans was there a professional priestly caste, although at Rome there was the institution of the *flamen dialis*, the priest of Jupiter, who constituted the only full-time sacerdotal function in Rome. Heads of households functioned as priests with respect to the religious obligations demanded of the household cult. Any citizen might be elected to function in the performance of the civic cult. At Rome the official cult was regulated by *collegia* which comprised elected or appointed public guardians of the religious traditions who served as priests (*pontifices*). The members of the *collegia* regulated and planned civic religious occasions. The *pontifices* ensured that due procedure was followed lest the security and well-being of the Roman state be compromised and subverted by ritual laxity. Only authorized cults could be celebrated within the boundaries (*pomerium*) of Rome. This factor in Roman religious life had the potential for religious confrontations to surface between the guardians of traditional Roman religion and the devotees of innovative cults. However, once their practices had been Romanized and approved by the *collegia*, new cults were allowed entry to Rome.

The critique of conventional religious beliefs by Greek sophists of the fifth century BCE undermined any naive confidence in the gods as traditionally conceived and pictured in the Homeric epics. Socrates made reason the measure of all things, and encouraged enquiry into the meaning of life. From the fourth century, other philosophers contributed to a growing lack of confidence in traditional opinion about the gods by questioning the theology of the Homeric epics and the received myths, and expressing indignation at the immorality of the gods as depicted in the mythic and epic traditions.[12] Philosophers chose to speak of the gods in abstractions or allegorized the myths.[13] The traditional gods, whose existence was rarely denied nevertheless, tended to become marginalized beings in philosophical circles in the face of theological and ethical critique. Traditional civic religious practice was not supported by any meaningful theological assent to the gods as traditionally conceived on the part of sophisticated and philosophically literate worshippers. Such individuals found other avenues for satisfying religious needs no longer wholly answered in the public and civic cults. However, the age-old patterns of the cultic worship of the gods remained an integral, if formal, part of the social fabric of Greeks and Romans. Such worship was traditional, venerable and time-honoured. Apart from affording occasions for public spectacle and celebration, civic worship conducted in the ancient ways enhanced and underscored otherwise tenuous links with ancestral times and communal origins. Atheism was rare.

From the Hellenistic era on, traditional religious observances as practised in homes and the cities of the Mediterranean world was supplemented by a plurality of newer religious expressions. The attraction of these may have had something to do with the objections of the philosophers and the acknowledgment of the moral inadequacies of the gods. Greeks and, later, Romans came increasingly into contact with innovative religious practices and cults, particularly those emanating from the east. New cults and observances found a home in many cities, and were eagerly taken up alongside the traditional observances. The growing popularity of mystery religions which nourished religious sensibilities and individual needs that the traditional cults were not designed to satisfy can be traced in the Hellenistic and Graeco-Roman eras. In Rome, however, the progress of some of these religious imports was severely curtailed since they were perceived as actually or potentially subverting conventional social mores, especially the institution of the family, and, by implication, the whole fabric of Roman society.

There were other causes for the widespread appeal of new cults and mysteries. In the new political climate after Alexander, the Greek city-states found themselves increasingly required to come to terms with unprecedented political realities. From c. 300 BCE Greek civic life was perpetually overshadowed by the concerns of relating to successive and competing leagues, dynasts and empires. A sense of uncertainty pervades the Hellenistic and Graeco-Roman religious landscape as surely as the new empires eclipsed civic independence. Loss of political control in the face of military forces impinging on hitherto proudly independent city-states, forces that had once been relatively manageable (except in very exceptional circumstances and emergencies such as the threat to all Greek city-states posed by the Persian invasions of the early fifth century), expressed itself in attachment on the part of many to new cults and religions. In participating in these non-traditional expressions of religion, individuals might discover a sense of belonging and receive assurances of personal well-being. Not surprisingly in these uncertain times when reversals of fortune could be unexpectedly spectacular, the theistic abstraction Fortune or Luck (*Tyche*) was widely worshipped and her favour sought.[14] Tyche was the patron deity of Antioch.

Sources

Livy reports the systematization of Roman religious practice by King Numa.

322. He then turned his attention to the appointment of priests, although he performed very many priestly duties, especially those which belong to the Flamen Dialis. But inasmuch as he thought that in a warlike nation there would be more kings like Romulus than like Numa, and that they would take the field in person, he did not wish the sacrificial duties of the kingly office to be neglected, and so appointed a flamen for Jupiter, as his perpetual priest, and provided him with a conspicuous dress and the royal curule chair. To him he added two other flamens, one for Mars, the other for Quirinus. In like manner he designated virgins for Vesta's service—a priesthood, this, that derived from Alba and so was not unsuited to the founder's stock. That they might be perpetual priestesses of the temple, he assigned them a stipend from the public treasury, and by the rule of virginity and other observances invested them with awe and sanctity. He likewise chose twelve Salii for Mars Gradivus, and granted them the distinction of wearing the embroidered tunic and over it a bronze breastplate, and bearing the divine shields which men call *ancilia*, while they proceeded through the City, chanting their hymns to the triple beat of their solemn dance. He next choose as pontifex Numa Marcius, son of Marcus, one of the senators, and to him he intrusted written directions, full and accurate, for performing the rites of worship; with what victims, on what days, in what temple, sacrifices should

be offered, and from what sources money was to be disbursed to pay their costs. All other public and private sacrifices he likewise made subject to the decrees of the pontifex, that there might be someone to whom the commons could come for advice, lest any confusion should arise in the religious law through the neglect of ancestral rites and the adoption of strange ones. And not merely ceremonies relating to the gods above, but also proper funeral observances and the propitiation of the spirits of the dead were to be taught by the pontifex as well, and also what prodigies manifested by lightning or other visible sign were to be taken in hand and averted. With the purpose of eliciting this knowledge from the minds of the gods, Numa dedicated an altar on the Aventine to Jupiter Elicius, and consulted the god by augury, that he might learn what portents were to be regarded.
(Livy, *History of Rome* 1.20)

A summary of Roman religion.

Cicero puts the following words into the mouth of Cotta, the Academic.

323. The religion of the Roman people comprises ritual, auspices, and the third additional division consisting of all such prophetic warnings as the interpreters of the Sybil or the soothsayers have derived from portents and prodigies. Well, I have always thought that none of these departments of religion was to be despised, and I have held the conviction that Romulus by his auspices and Numa by his establishment of our ritual laid the foundations of our state, which assuredly could never have been as great as it is had not the fullest measure of divine favour been obtained for it.
(Cicero, *On the Nature of the Gods* 3.5)

Roman religion according to Polybius.

324. [T]he quality in which the Roman commonwealth is most distinctly superior is in my opinion the nature of their religious convictions. I believe that it is the very thing which among other peoples is an object of reproach, I mean superstition [*deisidaimonia*], which maintains the cohesion of the Roman State. These matters are clothed in such pomp and introduced to such an extent into their public and private life that nothing could exceed it, a fact which will surprise many. My own opinion at least is that they have adopted this course for the sake of common people. It is a course which perhaps would not have been necessary had it been possible to form a state composed of wise men, but as every multitude is fickle, full of lawless desires, unreasoned passion, and violent anger, the multitude must be held in by invisible terrors and suchlike pageantry. For this reason I think, not that the ancients acted rashly and at haphazard in introducing among the people notions concerning the gods and beliefs in the terrors of hell, but that the moderns are most rash and foolish in banishing such beliefs.
(Polybius, *Histories* 6.56.6–12)

The ancestors.

The extract below provides an important insight into the Roman desire to emulate one's ancestors and to enhance the fame of the family.

325. In the halls of our ancestors it was otherwise; portraits were the objects displayed to be looked at, not statues by foreign artists, nor bronzes nor marbles, but wax models of faces were set out each on a separate sideboard, to furnish likenesses to be carried in procession at a funeral in the clan, and always when some member of it passed away the entire company of his house that had ever existed was present. The pedigrees too were traced in a spread of lines running near the several painted portraits. The archive-rooms were kept filled with books of records and with written memorials of official careers. Outside the houses and round the doorways there were other presentations of those mighty spirits, with spoils taken from the enemy fastened to them, which even one who bought the house was not permitted to unfasten, and the mansions eternally celebrated a triumph even though they changed their masters.
(Pliny the Elder, *Natural History* 35.6–7)

Sacrifice.

The following extract from a mime by the Greek writer Herodas expresses the sense of contract between the worshippers and the divine world. Herodas flourished in the third century BCE.

326. Hail to thee, Lord Paieon, ruler of Tricca, who hast got as thine habitation sweet Kos and Epidauros, hail to Koronis thy mother withal and Apollo; hail to her whom thou touchest with thy right hand, Hygieia, and those to whom belong these honoured shrines, Panake and Epio and Ieso; hail ye twain which did sack the house and walls of Laomedon healers of savage sicknesses, Podaleirios and Machaon, and what gods and goddesses soever dwell by thine hearth, Father Paieon; come hither with your blessings and accept the aftercourse of this cock whom I sacrifice, herald of the walls of my house. For we draw no bounteous nor ready spring; else might we, perchance, with an ox or stuffed pig of much fatness and no humble cock, be paying the price of cure from diseases that thou didst wipe away, Lord, by laying on us thy gentle hands.
(Herodas, *Mime IV: Dedications and Sacrifices to Asklepios* ll. 1–20)

Invitations to temple banquets (second–third centuries CE) (#327–28).

327. Herais asks you to dine in the (dining-) room of the Sarapeion at a banquet of the Lord Sarapis tomorrow, namely the 11th, from the 9th hour.
(*New Docs* I, p. 5)

328. The god calls you to a banquet being held in the Thoereion tomorrow from the 9th hour.
(*New Docs* I, p. 5)

Early Christian perspectives on food offered to idols (#329–35).

Cultic priests had the right to sell the meat given them (see 1 Corinthians 10:25). Paul has no objection to believers eating such meat, though freedom to partake might be suspended if a believer with a weak conscience on this matter draws attention to the presence of such meat at the table (1 Corinthians 10:25, 27–28). However, there was no doubt in Paul's mind that eating at a temple banquet was to be studiously avoided.

329. [I]f others see you, who possess knowledge, eating in the temple of an idol, might they not, since their conscience is weak, be encouraged to the point of eating food sacrificed to idols?
(1 Corinthians 8:10)

330. Do you not know that those who are employed in the temple service get their food from the temple, and those who serve at the altar share in what is sacrificed on the altar?
(1 Corinthians 9:13)

331. [W]hat pagans [here the Greek has *they*] sacrifice, they sacrifice to demons and not to God. I do not want you to be partners with demons. You cannot drink the cup of the Lord and the cup of demons. You cannot partake of the table of the Lord and the table of demons.
(1 Corinthians 10:20–21)

332. Eat whatever is sold in the meat market without raising any question on the ground of conscience.
(1 Corinthians 10:25)

The issue of whether or not believers should eat meat that had been sacrificed was resolved in the negative among some Christian communities.

333. And concerning food…keep strictly from that which is offered to idols, for it is the worship of dead gods.
(*Didache* 6:3)

334. (Letter to Thyatira)

I have this against you: you tolerate that woman Jezebel, who calls herself a prophet and is teaching and beguiling my servants to practice fornication and to eat food sacrificed to idols.
(Revelation 2:20.
Cf. 2:14)

335. For it has seemed good to the Holy Spirit and to us to impose on you no further burden than these essentials: that you abstain from what has been sacrificed to idols and from blood and from what is strangled and from fornication.…
(Acts 15:28–29)

Sacrifice as homage to the gods.

336. And do not be surprised if throughout my speech I am trying to incline you to a policy of kindness to the Hellenes and of gentleness and humanity. For harshness is, I observe, grievous both to those who exercise it and to those upon whom it falls, while gentleness, whether in man or in the other animals, bears a good name; nay, in the case of the gods also we invoke as the 'Heavenly Ones' those who bless us with good things, while to those who are agents of calamities and punishments we apply more hateful epithets; in honour of the former, both private persons and states erect temples and altars, whereas we honour the latter neither in our prayers nor in our sacrifices, but practise rites to drive away their evil presence.
(Isocrates, *To Philip* 116–17)

Lucian on sacrifice.

Lucian was a second-century CE writer of often scathing satirical pieces.

337. (9) If anybody sacrifices, they [the gods] all have a feast, opening their mouths for the smoke and drinking the blood that is spilt at the altars, just like flies…

(12) When they [humankind] have established altars and formulae and lustral rites, they present their sacrifices, the farmer an ox from the plough, the shepherd a lamb, the goatherd a goat, someone else incense or a cake; the poor man, however, propitiates the god by just kissing his own hand. But those who offer victims (to come back to them) deck the animal with garlands, after finding out far in advance whether it is perfect or not, in order that they may not kill something that is of no use to them; then they bring it to the altar and slaughter it under the god's eyes, while it bellows plaintively—making, we must suppose, auspicious sounds, and fluting low music to accompany the sacrifice! Who would not suppose that the gods like to see all this? And although the notice says that no one is allowed within the holy-water who has not clean hands, the priest himself stands there all bloody, just like the Cyclops of old, cutting up the victim, removing the entrails, plucking out the heart, pouring the blood about the altar, and doing everything possible in the way of piety. To crown it all, he lights a fire and puts upon it the goat, skin and all, and the sheep, wool and all; and the smoke, divine and holy, mounts upward and gradually dissipates into Heaven itself.
(Lucian, *On Sacrifices* 9, 12–13)

Roman suspicion of the religious temperament of non-Romans.

In the following excerpt from Dio Cassius, Maecenas is advising Octavian to be rigorous in excluding religious rites which are not compatible with ancestral Roman practices.

338. Therefore, if you desire to become in very truth immortal, act as I advise; and, furthermore, do you not only yourself worship the Divine Power everywhere and in every way in accordance with the traditions of our fathers, but compel all others to honour it. Those who attempt to distort our religion with strange rites you should abhor and punish, not merely for the sake of the gods (since if a man despises these he will not pay honour to any other being), but because such men, by bringing in new divinities in place of the old, persuade many to adopt foreign practices, from which spring up conspiracies, factions, and cabals, which are far from profitable to a monarchy. Do not, therefore, permit anybody to be an atheist or a sorcerer. Soothsaying, to be sure, is a necessary art, and you should by all means appoint some men to be diviners and augurs, to whom those will resort who wish to consult them on any matter; but there ought to be no workers in magic at all. For such men, by speaking the truth sometimes, but generally falsehood, often encourage a great many to attempt revolutions.
(Dio Cassius, *Roman History* 52.36.1–3)[15]

Prayer at sacrifices.

339. Of the remedies derived from man, the first raises a most important question, and one never settled: have words and formulated incantations any effect? If they have, it would be right and proper to give the credit to mankind. As individuals, however, all our wisest men reject belief in them, although as

a body the public at all times believes in them unconsciously. In fact the sacrifice of victims without a prayer is supposed to be of no effect; without it too the gods are not thought to be properly consulted. Moreover, there is one form of words for getting favourable omens, another for averting evil, and yet another for a commendation. We see also that our chief magistrates have adopted fixed formulas for their prayers; that to prevent a word's being omitted or out of place a reader dictates beforehand the prayer from a script; that another attendant is appointed as a guard to keep watch, and yet another is put in charge to maintain a strict silence; that a piper plays so that nothing but the prayer is heard. Remarkable instances of both kinds of interference are on record: cases when the noise of actual ill omens has ruined the prayer, or when a mistake has been made in the prayer itself...
(Pliny the Elder, *Natural History* 28.10–11)

Fate.

340. Perhaps someone will say: 'How can philosophy help me, if Fate exists? Of what avail is philosophy if God rules the universe? Of what avail is it, if Chance governs everything? For not only is it impossible to change things that are determined, but it is also impossible to plan beforehand against what is undetermined; either God has forestalled my plans, and decided what I am to do, or else Fortune gives no free play to my plans'. Whether the truth, Lucilius, lies in one or in all of these views, we must be philosophers; whether Fate binds us down by an inexorable law, or whether God as arbiter of the universe has arranged everything, or whether Chance drives and tosses human affairs without method, philosophy ought to be our defence. She will encourage us to obey God cheerfully, but Fortune defiantly: she will teach us to follow God and endure Chance. But it is not my purpose now to be led into a discussion as to what is within our own control,—if foreknowledge is supreme, or if a chain of fated events drags us along in its clutches, or if the sudden and the unexpected play the tyrant over us; I return now to my warning and my exhortation, that you should not allow the impulse of your spirit to weaken and grow cold. Hold fast to it and establish it firmly, in order that what is now impulse may become a habit of the mind.
(Seneca, *Epistles* 16.4–6)

5.2. Ruler Cults

The new Hellenistic monarchs began to propagate cults of their predecessors and of members of their families. It had been perceived that Alexander was attempting to foster a cult of himself, arousing considerable opposition among his Macedonian compatriots. Yet there had been Greek rulers before Alexander who had on occasions been offered divine honours as homage for benefactions received and services rendered.

Alexander's right to be ruler of Egypt by virtue of his conquest had been recognized there. As such he was acknowledged as a pharaoh.[16] His famous expedition to the oracle of Ammon at Siwah might also have confirmed the perception of his divine origins. Towards the end of his life, according to Aelian and Hypereides, Alexander instructed the Greek cities to honour him as a god.[17] He was also visited by Greek envoys in Babylon who approached him in a manner that demonstrated that they considered him divine.[18]

From the late fourth century Greek cities were increasingly willing to bestow cultic honours on their overlords and benefactors, often graced with the epithet 'saviour' (*sōtēr*).[19] Directions as to the manner in which such a cult was to be offered were given to the Rhodian enquirers by the oracle of Ammon at Siwah. Demetrius Poliorcetes, king of Macedonia, fostered a cult of himself. After delivering the city in 307, the Athenians honoured him in terms that spoke dramatically of the absence of other gods.

In Ptolemaic Egypt an institutionalized ruler cult emerged from the beginning of the third century. Ptolemy I had established a cult of Alexander as founder of Alexandria by 290 BCE. Ptolemy II, son and successor of Ptolemy I, instituted a cult of his father and his widow. Successive kings deified themselves and their consorts. A similar pattern emerges among the Seleucids, though a ruler cult took longer to be established. Antiochus I (281–261 BCE) deified his father Seleucus I. In the early second century, Antiochus III deified his father and his wife after their death and instituted a cult of his ancestors.[20]

From the time the Romans made their incursions into the eastern Mediterranean, victorious Roman generals were greeted in the east by the bestowal of cultic honours and by a cult of Rome, as the tangible embodiments of incontestable force. The paying of personal cultic honours was not encouraged by the Romans. However, after the assassination of Julius Caesar, Augustus declared his adoptive father a god. Thereafter Augustus titled himself the son of a god (*divis filius*). The fact that Augustus brought about an end to the seemingly endless conflict between competing generals naturally attracted the perception that he was a saviour.

In Rome and Italy Augustus, who perceived well enough the value of the paying of cult to him since he himself introduced it from the east into Gaul, nevertheless sought to deflect the honours paid, not to himself but to his *genius*, his ancestral protecting spirit. The official cult of the emperor was organized in the cities by colleges (*collegia*) of freedmen, called *augustales*. The forms in which the official cult could be rendered to the living emperor were several.

In the early second century Pliny, Governor of Bithynia, tested the loyalty of a number of Christians by demanding they offer a pinch of incense to the image of the emperor Trajan. The difficulties provoked by the ruler cult for Christians, should they be required to pay homage, is well documented. Megalomanic emperors, such as Caligula and Domitian, presumed to be honoured directly with a cult in Rome and Italy.

Sources

The first of the ruler cults was that offered to Lysander of Sparta at the end of the fifth century.

341. For he was the first Greek, as Duris writes, to whom the cities erected altars and made sacrifices as to a god, the first also to whom songs of triumph were sung. One of these is handed down, and begins as follows:—

'The general of sacred Hellas
who came from wide-spaced Sparta
will we sing, O! io! Paean.'
(Plutarch, *Lysander* 18.3)

According to Diodorus Siculus (and him alone of extant writers), Alexander the Great's father, Philip II, instigated a cult of himself.

342. Such was the end of Philip, who had made himself the greatest of the kings in Europe in his time, and because of the extent of his kingdom had made himself a throned companion of the twelve gods.
(Diodorus Siculus, *Histories* 16.95.1)

A hymn to Demetrius Poliorcetes, King of Macedonia, as recorded by Athenaeus (second–third century CE).

343. O son of the most mighty god Poseidon and of Aphrodite, hail! For other gods are either far away, or have not ears, or are not, or heed us not at all; but thee we can see in very presence, not in wood and not in stone, but in truth.
(Athenaeus, *Deipnosophistae* 6.253e)

After the assassination of Julius Caesar, Augustus declared his adoptive father a god. Thereafter Augustus titled himself the son of a god (*divi filius*) (i.e. son of the deified Julius Caesar). This is recorded in Plutarch, *Caesar* 67.8; Suetonius, *Caesar* 85; *Augustus* 52; and *Claudius* 2. Nero rejected worship of himself (Tacitus, *Annals* 15.74), although Nero's daughter by Poppeia was deified after her early death (Tacitus, *Annals* 16.6). Vespasian joked on his deathbed about becoming a god (Suetonius, *Vespasian* 23).

The deification of Augustus.

344. Now these rumours began to be current at a later date. At the time they declared Augustus immortal, assigned to him priests and sacred rites, and made Livia, who was already called Julia and Augusta, his priestess; they also permitted her to employ a lic-

tor when she exercised her sacred office. On her part, she bestowed a million sesterces upon a certain Numerius Atticus, a senator and ex-praetor, because he swore that he had seen Augustus ascending to heaven after the manner of which tradition tells concerning Proculus and Romulus.
(Dio Cassius, *Roman History* 56.46.1–2)

Caligula fosters a cult of himself.

345. Furthermore, though he at first forbade any one to set up images of him, he even went on to manufacture statues himself; and though he once requested the annulment of a decree ordering sacrifices to be offered to his Fortune, and even caused this action of his to be inscribed on a tablet, he afterwards ordered temples to be erected and sacrifices to be offered to himself as to a god.
(Dio Cassius, *Roman History* 59.4.4)

Seneca wrote a satirical piece called the *Apocolocyntosis divi Claudii (The Pumpkinification of Claudius)*. In it he pours scorn on the recently dead Claudius, declared a god by the Senate after his death.

346. Word comes to Jupiter that a stranger had arrived, a man well set up, pretty grey; he seemed to be threatening something for he wagged his head ceaselessly; he dragged the right foot. They asked him what nation he was of; he answered something in a confused mumbling voice: his language they did not understand. He was no Greek and no Roman, nor of any known race. On this Jupiter bids Hercules go and find out what country he comes from; you see Hercules had traveled over the whole world, and might be expected to know all the nations in it. Then Hercules, the first glimpse he got, was really much taken aback, being aware that he hadn't yet even by then seen all the monsters in the world that he might be afraid of; when he saw this new kind of object, with its extraordinary gait, and the voice of no terrestrial beast, but such as you might hear in the leviathans of the deep, hoarse and inarticulate, he thought his thirteenth labour had come upon him. When he looked closer, the thing seemed to be a kind of man.
(Seneca, *Apocolocyntosis divi Claudii* 5)

A debate ensues in the senate of heaven on the merits of admitting Claudius as a fellow god. Augustus speaks in the debate.

347. This man you see, who for so many years has been masquerading under my name, has done me the favour of murdering two Julias, great-granddaughters of mine, one by cold steel and one by starvation; and one great-great-grandson, L. Silanus—see, Jupiter, whether he had a case against him (at least it is your own if you will be fair). Come tell me, blessed Claudius, why of all those you killed, both men and women, without a hearing, why did you not hear their side of the case first, before putting them to death? Where do you find this custom? It is not done in heaven…

Is this he you want now to make a god? Look at his body, born under the wrath of heaven! In fine, let him say the three words quickly, and he may have me for a slave. God! Who will worship this god, who will believe in him? While you make gods of such as he, no one will believe you to be gods.
(Seneca, *Apocolocyntosis divi Claudii* 10, 11)

5.3. Mystery Religions and Eastern Cults

The Hellenistic and Graeco-Roman eras witnessed an interest in participation in mystery cults from all over the Greek and Roman world. Participation in the mysteries endowed worshippers with a sense of the protection of the god and assured them of certain individually appropriated benefits. Mysteries were agrarian in origin. The most famous of all were the Mysteries of Demeter and Persephone at Eleusis, just outside Athens. The cults demanded initiation and, prior to participation in the cult, the attainment of a certain moral and ritual purity. Initiation at Eleusis required both moral and ritual purity and fasting, which was broken at the shrine by a sacred meal. Initiates were sworn to secrecy. Modern understanding of the significance of the rites depends, unfortunately, on unreliable testimony, much of it emanating from early

Christian writers who were hostile to the cults.

Initiation into the Eleusinian Mysteries was eagerly sought regardless of social status or rank. Initiates were sworn to secrecy as to the form the culmination of the ritual took, an oath that was perhaps surprisingly observed since modern interpreters are unsure of the precise shape and meaning of what was actually revealed. We do know this much: the Mysteries commemorated the rape of Persephone by Pluto, and the search conducted by Demeter, her mother and the grain-goddess, in the realm of the underworld (see the *Homeric Hymn to Demeter*). As such the Mysteries evoked the revivifying cycle of the seasons, the burial of seed grain in the earth and its rebirth in the spring to new and nourishing life. After a solemn night procession from Athens to the shrine, worshippers were drawn into the very heart and crisis of the drama, empathically participating in Demeter's search for her daughter and rejoicing in her release from the underworld. The ritual culminated, it has been surmised, in the ineffable revelation of an ear of wheat, symbolizing the release of Persephone and encapsulating the promise of new birth and the return of fertility to the earth. There were several stages through which the worshipper might progress (note Suetonius, *Nero* 34).

The worship associated with Dionysus was also widespread. Dionysiac mysteries celebrated the life-giving fluid in plants, animals and humans, the god of which was Dionysus (Bacchus). Understandably, wine was extolled as a prominent gift of the god. The worship of Dionysus was of Phrygian origin. It had had a somewhat chequered history as a cult import in earlier Greek times, as evidenced in the classical era in Euripides's play, the *Bacchae*. From the early second century the cult found a receptive home in Italy where it was especially popular among freedmen. Despite the evidence of considerable decorum required of worshippers, the Romans, acting on rumours of sexual excesses associated with the Bacchanalia, shut the worship down in 186 BCE. It was only allowed to function again once it had been purged of problematic elements and the number of cultic occasions curtailed. In time the cult attracted the well-born, though aspects of the public celebrations associated with Dionysus might still attract disapproval.[21]

The worship of the female deity Isis, sister and consort of Osiris (Sarapis), was of Egyptian provenance. Her worship spread rapidly throughout the Greek and Roman world, finding ready acceptance especially among women. A shrine was built on Delos by the end of the third century BCE by one Apollonius, a descendent of Egyptian priests, though the cult statue had been present in Apollonius's family for two generations.[22] Her temples were often attended by Egyptian priests. Isis was celebrated as the mother of all that is beneficial in society. Her gifts to humankind, the subject of a number of extant aretalogies, include marriage, childbirth, learning and language—in short all the benefits of civilization. Devotees of the goddess tended to see her as the chief manifestation of the gods. She was also perceived as promoting the equality of men and women, another significant element in the extant hymns. Grand public processions were an attractive hallmark of her worship. There were mystery elements as well for initiates, and a hierarchy of grades through which initiates might progress. The second-century CE writer Apuleius wrote a picaresque novel, the *Golden Ass* (also known as the *Metamorphoses*), which culminates in his initiation into the mysteries of Isis (see #350).

Isis was regularly worshipped in company with Sarapis. Sarapis was in effect a new god created by Ptolemy I as a new cult for Greeks in Egypt, especially in Alexandria. It had been intended that Sarapis be that city's divine patron. The cult found considerable acceptance not only among the Greeks of Egypt and in Ptolemaic domains such as Rhodes but throughout Greece and later Rome. The cult derived from Memphis where the sacred bull, Apis, was identified with Osiris (god of the underworld) after death and became known as Osor-Hapi, graecized as Sarapis. The new god was associated, not surprisingly, with the underworld but also had powers of healing. A feature of the monthly celebrations of the mysteries of Isis and Sarapis was a sacred banquet in the Serapeum, invitations to which have been recovered among the papyri (#327–28). Sarapis was identified with Zeus, Father of All. There were intimations of death and immortality in the cult.

The widespread worship of the Phrygian fertility goddess Cybele, who was honoured as the Great Mother (*magna mater*) of the gods, was the first foreign cult to be admitted to Rome. This happened in 205 BCE during the Second Punic War. The cult gained a certain notoriety because its Phrygian priests had undergone castration as the prerequisite to serving her. Her consort Attis also attracted a cult. He had castrated himself, been turned into a tree, but had come back to life.

The Roman festival, the Megalensia, was held during each April to commemorate the introduction of the cult of Cybele. During Claudius's reign the Megalensia became one of the 16 great Roman festivals. Worshippers joined colleges associated with the temples of the goddess for the organization of cultic celebrations and dinners.[23]

The cult of the Syrian goddess Atargatis also attracted the attention of Romans and Greeks. Processions in honour of this goddess featured the self-flagellation of the priests. The processions were also marked by the frenzied castration of the Galli, the goddess's itinerant priests.[24]

The Mysteries bear witness to the democritization of intimate religious experience. Scholars are divided over the issue of whether or not participation in the Mysteries and the other cults briefly surveyed above offered the hope of a personal salvation and life beyond the grave.[25] It is likely that participation did create a sense of well-being, of assurance that through the drama re-enacted in the cult that all was well in the world. Worshippers were caught up in the numinous made dramatically present and immediate.[26]

Sources

The Eleusinian Mysteries.

Epictetus is commenting on the need for adequate preparations before one embarks on a vocation such as being a philosopher.

348. 'But So-and-so lectures; why shouldn't I too?' Slave, these things are not done recklessly, nor at random, but one ought to be of a certain age, and lead a certain kind of life, and have God as his guide. You say: No. But no man sails out of a harbour without first sacrificing to the gods and invoking their aid, nor do men sow hit-or-miss, but only after first calling upon Demeter; and yet will a man, if he has laid his hand to so great a task as this without the help of the gods, be secure in so doing, and will those who come to him be fortunate in so coming? What else are you doing, man, but vulgarizing the Mysteries, and saying, 'There is a chapel at Eleusis; see there is one here too. There is a hierophant there; I too will make a hierophant. There is a herald there; I too will appoint a herald. There is a torch-bearer there; I too will have a torch-bearer. There are torches there; and here too. The words said are the same; and what is the difference between what is done here and what is done there?'? Most impious man, is there no difference? Are the same acts helpful, if they are performed at the wrong place and at the wrong time? Nay, but a man ought to come also with a sacrifice, and with prayers, and after a preliminary purification, and with his mind predisposed to the idea that he will be approaching holy rites, and holy rites of great antiquity. Only thus do the Mysteries become helpful, only thus do we arrive at the impression that all these things were established by men of old time for the purpose of education and for the amendment of our life. But you are publishing the Mysteries abroad and vulgarizing them, out of time, out of place, without sacrifices, without purification; you do not have the dress which the hierophant ought to wear, you do not have the proper head of hair, nor headband, nor voice, nor age; you have not kept yourself pure as he has, but you have picked up only the words which he utters, and recite them. Have the words a sacred force all by themselves?

(Epictetus, *Discourses* 3.21.10–16)

The suppression of the Bacchanalia in Rome and throughout Italy in 186 BCE.

349. The following year diverted the consuls Spurius Postumius Albinus and Quintus Marcius Philippus from the army and the administration of wars and provinces to the suppression of an internal conspiracy... A nameless Greek came first to Etruria, possessed of none of those many arts which the Greek people, supreme as it is in learning, brought to us in numbers for the cultivation of mind and body, but a dabbler in sacrifices and a fortune-teller; nor was he one who, by frankly disclosing his creed and publicly proclaiming both his profession and his system, filled minds with error, but a priest of secret rites performed by night. There were initiatory rites which at first were imparted to a few, then began to be generally known among men and women. To the religious element in them were added the delights of wine and feasts, that the minds of a larger number might be attracted. When wine had inflamed their minds, and night and the mingling of males with females, youth with age, had destroyed every sentiment of modesty, all varieties of corruption first began to be practised, since each one had at hand the pleasure answering to that to which his nature was more inclined. There was not one form of vice alone, the promiscuous matings of free men and women, but perjured witnesses, forged seals and wills and evidence, all issued from this same workshop: likewise poisonings and secret murders, so that at times not even the bodies were found for burial. Much was ventured by craft, more by violence. This violence was concealed because amid the howlings and the crash of drums and cymbals no cry of the sufferers could be heard as the debauchery and murders proceeded.
(Livy, *History of Rome* 39.8.[27]
Note the testimony of Hispala [39.13.8–14] and the speech of the consul [39.16.6–13])

Apuleius provides some tantalizing insights into the rites associated with Isis and their meaning, stopping short, of course, of revealing the actual content of the revelation.[28] Roman suspicion of the cult was confirmed by the unprincipled behaviour of some of her priests at Rome during the reign of Tiberius as reported by Josephus (*Antiquities* 18.65–80).

Lucius describes his initiation into the Mysteries of Isis in Corinth.

350. Then behold the day approached when as the sacrifice of dedication should be done; and when the sun declined and evening came, there arrived on every coast a great multitude of priests, who according to their ancient order offered me many presents and gifts. Then was all the laity and profane people commanded to depart, and when they had put on my back a new linen robe, the priest took my hand and brought me to the most secret and sacred place of the temple. Thou wouldest peradventure demand, thou studious reader, what was said and done there: verily I would tell thee if it were lawful for me to tell, thou wouldest know if it were convenient for thee to hear; but both thy ears and my tongue should incur the like pain of rash curiosity. Howbeit I will not long torment thy mind, which peradventure is somewhat religious and given to some devotion; listen therefore, and believe it to be true. Thou shalt understand that I approached near unto hell, even to the gates of Proserpine, and after that I was ravished throughout all the elements, I returned to my proper place: about midnight I saw the sun brightly shine, I saw likewise the gods celestial and the gods infernal, before whom I presented myself and worshipped them. Behold now have I told thee, which although thou hast heard, yet it is necessary that thou conceal it; wherefore this only will I tell, which may be declared without offence for the understanding of the profane.
(Apuleius, *Golden Ass* 11.23).

A feature of the monthly celebrations of the mysteries of Isis and Sarapis was a sacred banquet in the Serapeum, invitations to which have been recovered among the papyri (see #327–8 above).

An extract from a personalized aretalogy of Isis.

This is the earliest of the extant aretalogies of Isis. It dates from the second half of the second/first half of the first century BCE. The inscription was located in Maroneia in Macedonia.

351. [F]irst I shall come to your family, making as the beginning of my praises the earliest beginnings of your family. They say that Ge was the mother of all: you were born a daughter to her first. You took Sarapis to live with you, and when you had made your marriage together the world, provided with eyes, was lit up by means of your faces, Helios and Selene. So you are two but have many designations among men. For you are the only ones whom (everyday) life knows as gods. Therefore, how would the account of your praises not be unmanageable when one must praise many gods at the outset? She with Hermes discovered writing; and of this writing some was sacred for initiates, some was publicly available for all. She instituted justice, that each of us might know how to live on equal terms, just as, because of our nature, death makes us equal. She instituted the non-Greek language for some, Greek language for others, in order that the race might be differentiated not only as between men and women, but also between all peoples. You gave laws, but they were called *thesmoi* originally. Accordingly, cities enjoyed tranquillity, having discovered not violence legalised, but law without violence. You made parents honoured by their children, in that you cared for them not only as fathers, but also as gods.
(*New Docs* I, p. 11)

Martial offers this biting epigram, alluding to the practice of emasculation by the devotees of Cybele.

352. Although you are more emasculate than a flabby eunuch, more womanish than the catamite of Celaenae [Attis], whose name the gilded priest of the mad Mother [Cybele] howls, you talk of theaters and rows and edicts and purple stripes and Ides and clasps and property qualifications, and point at poor men with your manicured hand. Whether you have the right to sit on the knights' benches I shall consider, Didymus: you have none to sit on the husbands'!
(Martial, *Epigrams* 5.41)[29]

In the 63rd of Catullus's poems the worshipper of Cybele speaks of himself in the feminine now that he has emasculated himself. He laments his lost manhood.

353. 'O my country that gavest me life! O my country that barest me! leaving whom, ah wretch! as runaway servants leave their masters, I have borne my foot to the forests of Ida, to live among snows and frozen lairs of wild beasts, and visit in my frenzy all their lurking-dens,—where then or in what region do I think thy place to be, O my country? Mine eye-balls unbidden long to turn their gaze to thee, while for a short space my mind is free from wild frenzy. I, shall I from my own home be borne far away into these forests? From my country, my possessions, my friends, my parents, shall I be absent? absent from the market, the wrestling-place, the racecourse, the playground? unhappy, ah unhappy heart, again, again must thou complain. For what form of human figure is there which I had not? I, to be a woman—I who was a stripling, I a youth, I a boy, I was the flower of the playground, I was once the glory of the palaestra: mine were the crowded doorways, mine the warm thresholds, mine the flowery garlands to deck my house when I was to leave my chamber at sunrise. I, shall I now be called—what? a handmaid of the gods, a minister of Cybele? I a Maenad, I part of myself, a barren man shall I be? I, shall I dwell in icy snow-clad regions of verdant Ida, I pass my life under the high summits of Phrygia, with the hind that haunts the woodland, with the boar that ranges the forest? now, now I rue my deed, now, now I would it were undone.'
(Catullus, *Poems* 63.50–73)

Hope in the Mystery religions.

354. For among the many excellent and indeed divine institutions which your Athens has brought forth and contributed to human life, none, in my opinion, is better than those mysteries. For by their means we have been brought out of our barbarous and savage mode of life and educated and refined to a state of civilization; and as the rites are called 'initiations,' so in very truth we have learned from them the beginnings of life,

and have gained the power not only to live happily, but also to die with a better hope. (Cicero, *Laws* 2.14.36)

In the New Testament the terminology of the Mysteries is evoked in contexts which show that the 'mystery' has been publicly revealed in events in recent history and is the subject of the church's preaching.

355. Without any doubt, the mystery of our religion is great:

He was revealed in flesh,
vindicated in spirit,
seen by angels,
proclaimed among Gentiles,
believed in throughout the world,
taken up in glory.

(1 Timothy 3:16.[30]
Cf. 1 Timothy 3:9)

5.4. Oracles, Astrology, Magic and the Occult

Most people's lives were dominated by anxiety and by the overwhelming sense that fate was a power futile to resist. Opportunities to escape were offered in the form of oracular pronouncement as well as astrology and the occult. Dreams were also invested with special authority as a medium of revelation, if correctly interpreted.[31]

During the Hellenistic and Graeco-Roman eras recourse to oracles was a constant aspect of popular religion. Throughout the eastern Mediterranean there were much-frequented oracles of venerable repute. The most famous of these were the Delphic oracle in Greece, and the oracles of Didyma, Claros and Daphne. They offered pilgrims and inquirers insight into the will of the gods, and were frequently invoked by rulers in advance of initiating a war.

The attraction of astrology persisted throughout the era. It was based on the idea that the stars were themselves gods, and that their movements had profound, irresistible effects on earthly events.[32] There is astrological interest among Jews.[33] The Dead Sea Scroll corpus, for instance, contains astrological physiognomies.[34] The astrological symbols featured in the sixth-century CE Beth Alpha mosaics are also significant in this regard. The emperor Tiberius was oblivious to all other religious duties so enthralled was he by astrology.[35]

Attempts to manipulate the darker powers were never far from the surface in Hellenistic and Graeco-Roman religion. The drive to know the future, to secure power and influence over someone, or to ward off sickness, bad fortune or the attack of evil spirits are strongly attested in the sources, including the papyri. Incantations, maledictions and charms are frequently found. The use of magic in the hands of the neophyte might lead to dangerous consequences, as Apuleius's hero, Lucius, discovered. The Acts of the Apostles contains a story set in Ephesus about itinerant Jewish exorcists attempting to cast out demons in the name of the Lord Jesus with alarming consequences for the itinerants (see Acts 19:13–16). In Graeco-Roman times Ephesus was a famous centre of occult learning. In the hands of the practitioner, the power that was believed to be potentially available was considerable.

At times emperors, such as Augustus, attempted to outlaw dealings with the occult out of fear for their own security and that of the empire, testifying to the power that was considered available by unscrupulous means for evil purposes.[36] Incantations in which, among other names of gods, the name of the God of the Jews, and at a later date the name of Jesus, is invoked are surprisingly frequent.[37] Jewish astrologers and exorcists are attested in non-Jewish and Jewish sources.

The literature of early Judaism and the New Testament presupposes the existence of the spirit world. Both Jesus and Paul (see, e.g., Acts 16:18) are portrayed as powerful exorcists.[38] Matthew 12:27 and Luke 11:19 report that among Jesus' contemporaries were those who could cast out demons. The Prayer of Nabonidus from Qumran (4Q242) speaks of a Jewish exorcist who forgives Nabonidus's sins and heals him of his ulcer. Note also Mark 2:1–12 for the relationship between forgiveness and healing. Such stories are not confined to the New Testament and Jewish tradition. The Hellenistic and Graeco-Roman world was fully aware of the powers of the divine man (*theios anēr*).

Sources

Portents and oracles (#356–59).

The civil war between Sulla and his opponents was nearing a crucial juncture. As the opposing forces are being deployed, Appian relates the following.

356. It seems, too, that divine providence foretold to them the results of this war. Mysterious terrors came upon many, both in public and in private, throughout all Italy. Ancient, awe-inspiring oracles were remembered. Many monstrous things happened. A mule foaled, a woman gave birth to a viper instead of a child. There was a severe earthquake divinely sent and some of the temples in Rome were thrown down (the Romans being in any case very seriously disposed towards such things). The Capitol, that had been built by the kings 400 years before, was burned down, and nobody could discover the cause of the fire. All things seemed to point to the multitude of coming slaughters, to the conquest of Italy and of the Romans themselves, to the capture of the city, and to constitutional change.
(Appian, *Civil Wars* 1.83)[39]

The New Testament is not unfamiliar with portents. Matthew reports the following portents at the death and resurrection of Jesus.

357. From noon on, darkness came over the whole land until three in the afternoon. And about three o'clock Jesus cried with a loud voice, 'Eli, Eli, lema sabachthani?' that is, 'My God, my God, why have you forsaken me?' When some of the bystanders heard it, they said, 'This man is calling for Elijah.' At once one of them ran and got a sponge, filled it with sour wine, put it on a stick, and gave it to him to drink. But the others said, 'Wait, let us see whether Elijah will come to save him.' Then Jesus cried again with a loud voice and breathed his last. At that moment the curtain of the temple was torn in two, from top to bottom. The earth shook, and the rocks were split. The tombs also were opened, and many bodies of the saints who had fallen asleep were raised. After his resurrection they came out of the tombs and entered the holy city and appeared to many.
(Matthew 27:45–53)[40]

The oracle cited below emanates from the first century CE.

358. 'O Lord Serapis Helios, beneficent one, is it better for my son Phanias and his wife not to agree now with his father, but to oppose him and make no contract? Tell me this truly. Goodbye.'
(P.Oxy 1148)

Answer from an oracle.

The extract below comes from a Greek papyrus of the end of the first century CE. Its provenance is unknown.

359. Concerning the things about which you asked. You are well. What you desire night and day will be yours. As for what you want the gods will guide you and your livelihood will be for the better and your life will be distinguished.
(*New Docs* II, p. 37)

Magic (#360–65).

360. For those possessed by daemons, an approved charm by Pibechis.

Take oil made from unripe olives, together with the plant mastigia and lotus pith, and boil it with marjoram (very colourless), saying: 'Joel, Ossarthiomi, Emori, Theochipsoith, Sithemeoch, Sothe, Joe, Mimipsothiooph, Phersothi AEEIOYO Joe, Eochariphtha: come out of such an one (and the other usual formulae).'

But write this phylactery upon a little sheet of tin: 'Jaeo, Abraothioch, Phtha, Mesenpsiniao, Pheoch, Jaeo, Charsoc,' and hang it round the sufferer: it is of every daemon a thing to be trembled at, which he fears. Standing opposite, adjure him. The adjuration is this: 'I adjure thee by the god of the Hebrews Jesu, Jaba, Jae, Abraoth, Aia,

Thoth, Ele, Elo, Aeo, Eu, Jiibaech, Abarmas, Jabarau, Abelbel, Lona, Abra, Maroia, Bracion, thou that appearest in fire, thou that art in the midst of earth and snow and vapour, Tannetis: let thy angel descend, the implacable one, and let him draw into captivity the daemon as he flieth around this creature which God formed in his holy paradise.'
(*Paris Magical Papyrus*, ll. 3007–3027 [Deissmann, *Light from the Ancient East*, pp. 259–60])

The Greek text cited below is a love charm. Scholars are unable to provide a date or a provenance. It is in the form of a lead tablet. The name of the god invoked is rendered in parentheses by a succession of vowels.

361. I ask for and request your power and your authority (*nomina barbara*). Bring Termoutis whom Sophia bore, to Zoel whom Droser bore, with crazed and unceasing, everlasting love, now quickly!
(*New Docs* II, p. 45)

Jewish magic.

362. There is yet another branch of magic, derived from Moses, Jannes [cf. 2 Timothy 3:8], Lotapes [the translator later explains that Lotapes is a corruption for 'Yahweh'], and the Jews, but living many thousand years after Zoroaster.[41]
(Pliny the Elder, *Natural History* 30.11)

Eleazar, a Jewish exorcist.

363. And God granted him [King Solomon] knowledge of the art used against demons for the benefit and healing of men. He also composed incantations by which illnesses are relieved, and left behind forms of exorcisms with which those possessed by demons drive them out, never to return. And this kind of cure is of very great power among us to this day, for I have seen a certain Eleazar, a countryman of mine, in the presence of Vespasian, his sons, tribunes and a number of other soldiers, free men possessed by demons, and this was the manner of the cure: he put to the nose of the possessed man a ring which had under its seal one of the roots prescribed by Solomon, and then, as the man smelled it, drew out the demon through his nostrils, and, when the man at once fell down, adjured the demon never to come back into him, speaking Solomon's name and reciting the incantations which he had composed. Then, wishing to convince the bystanders and prove to them that he had this power, Eleazar placed a cup or footbasin full of water a little way off and commanded the demon, as it went out of the man, to overturn it and make known to the spectators that he had left the man.
(Josephus, *Antiquities* 8.45–48)

Bar Jesus, a Jewish magician, encounters Paul and Barnabas.

364. So, being sent out by the Holy Spirit, they [Paul and Barnabas] went down to Seleucia; and from there they sailed to Cyprus. When they arrived at Salamis, they proclaimed the word of God in the synagogues of the Jews. And they had John also to assist them. When they had gone through the whole island as far as Paphos, they met a certain magician, a Jewish false prophet, named Bar-Jesus. He was with the proconsul, Sergius Paulus, an intelligent man, who summoned Barnabas and Saul and wanted to hear the word of God. But the magician Elymas (for that is the translation of his name) opposed them and tried to turn the proconsul away from the faith. But Saul, also known as Paul, filled with the Holy Spirit, looked intently at him and said, 'You son of the devil, you enemy of all righteousness, full of all deceit and villainy, will you not stop making crooked the straight paths of the Lord? And now listen—the hand of the Lord is against you, and you will be blind for a while, unable to see the sun.' Immediately mist and darkness came over him, and he went about groping for someone to lead him by the hand. When the proconsul saw what happened, he believed, for he was astonished at the teaching about the Lord
(Acts 13:4–12)

Jewish exorcists in Ephesus.[42]

365. [S]ome itinerant Jewish exorcists tried to use the name of the Lord Jesus over those who had evil spirits, saying, 'I adjure you by

the Jesus whom Paul proclaims.' Seven sons of a Jewish high priest named Sceva were doing this. But the evil spirit said to them in reply, 'Jesus I know, and Paul I know; but who are you?' Then the man with the evil spirit leaped on them, mastered them all, and so overpowered them that they fled out of the house naked and wounded. When this became known to all residents of Ephesus, both Jews and Greeks, everyone was awestruck; and the name of the Lord Jesus was praised. Also many of those who became believers confessed and disclosed their practices. A number of those who practiced magic collected their books and burned them publicly; when the value of these books was calculated, it was found to come to fifty thousand silver coins. So the word of God grew mightily and prevailed. (Acts 19:13–20)

Paul proclaims freedom from slavery in the religious sphere. There was considerable attraction in the Christian message which promised that one could be free from the domination of malevolent and capricious supernatural forces.[43] In the second of the extracts (#367), Paul regards every religious impulse, except that informed by the freedom proclaimed in Christ, as beggarly, elemental and enslaving.

366. For I am convinced that neither death, nor life, nor angels, nor rulers, nor things present, nor things to come, nor powers, nor height, nor depth, nor anything else in all creation, will be able to separate us from the love of God in Christ Jesus our Lord. (Romans 8:38–39)

367. Formerly, when you did not know God, you were enslaved to beings that by nature are not gods. Now, however, that you have come to know God, or rather to be known by God, how can you turn back again to the weak and beggarly elemental spirits? How can you want to be enslaved to them again? You are observing special days, and months, and seasons, and years. I am afraid that my work for you may have been wasted. (Galatians 4:8–11)

Notes

1. Sean Freyne, *The World of the New Testament* (Wilmington, DE: Michael Glazier, 1980), p. 23.
2. The cult of the emperor and of Roma, write John E. Stambaugh and David L. Balch, 'served a religious purpose in its veneration of palpable uncontested power, a political purpose in focusing allegiance to the empire and its ruler, and a social purpose in the way it involved wealthy freedmen in the responsibilities of the cult administration' (*The New Testament in its Social Environment* [Philadelphia: Westminster Press, 1986], p. 130).
3. See Cicero, *On the Nature of the Gods* 2.12; 3.2.5 for affirmation of his belief in the traditional cult and auspices as instituted by Numa and Romulus respectively.
4. See Stambaugh and Balch, *The New Testament in its Social Environment*, p. 135.
5. Pomponia Graecina was indicted for devotion to 'foreign superstition' (Judaism?), but was acquitted by her husband (see Tacitus, *Annals* 13.32). On the suspicion with which foreign cults were held in general, see Suetonius, *Augustus* 93; Cicero, *On the Nature of the Gods* 2.72. For the outlawing of the Druids, see Suetonius, *Claudius* 25.
6. See 1 Corinthians 8 and 10:14–30, and the sources gathered at #329–35. Paul's guarded permission to eat such meat at home is not shared by the seer of Revelation. See Revelation 2:14, 20.
7. See Stambaugh and Balch, *The New Testament in its Social Environment*, p. 129.
8. See Everett Ferguson, *Backgrounds of Early Christianity* (Grand Rapids: Eerdmans, 1987), p. 176.
9. However, see Ferguson, *Backgrounds of Early Christianity*, p. 144, for a brief discussion of the moral catechism that was rehearsed at each monthly sacrifice of the private religious association at Lydian Philadelphia. Such requirements were very much the exception.
10. Ferguson, *Backgrounds of Early Christianity*, pp. 143–44.
11. For worship of the lares, see Petronius, *Satyricon* 60.
12. See Cicero, *On the Nature of the Gods* 1.16. Protagoras of Abdera, a sophist, was an

agnostic. He was exiled, and his books burned (*On the Nature of the Gods* 1.63).

13. For theistic abstractions see Cicero, *On the Nature of the Gods* 2.61 (Honour, Wealth). Reason, Faith and Virtue appear in 3.88. Concord and other abstractions are mentioned in 2.79.
14. The popularity of *Tyche*, Sean Freyne observes, was 'based on the observation that everybody's life is subject to forces and events outside and beyond their control and comprehension'. See his *World of the New Testament*, p. 23. For 'Luck', see Petronius, *Satyricon* 55.
15. See also Plutarch, *Superstition* 166B (cited at #603). Cf. Juvenal on Egyptian religion, *Satires* 15.1–13. Foreign cults were held in suspicion. The cult of Magna Mater (Livy, *History of Rome* 29.10–14), the Bacchanalia, and the cult of Isis, not to mention Judaism and Christianity, were all the subject of Roman opposition. See #349 on the Bacchanalia.
16. See F.W. Wallbank, *The Hellenistic World* (Glasgow: Fontana, 1981), p. 42.
17. See Wallbank, *The Hellenistic World*, p. 41.
18. Arrian, *Anabasis of Alexander* 7.23.2.
19. See Pausanias, *Description of Greece* 1.8.6 for the title bestowed by the Rhodians upon Ptolemy I.
20. Wallbank, *The Hellenistic World* 216.
21. See Seneca, *Natural Questions* 7.32.3.
22. Stambaugh and Balch, *The New Testament in its Environment*, pp. 41–43. For the origins of the cult see Tacitus, *Histories* 4.83–84.
23. At a later date it also featured the taurobolium in which a member of the college descended into a pit, over which a bull was sacrificed. The blood gushed down over the worshipper, who thus considered himself renewed, even reborn.
24. Apuleius describes a procession in honour of the Syrian goddess Atargatis in his *Golden Ass* 8.27–28.
25. See Stambaugh and Balch, *The New Testament in its Environment*, p. 132. The Mysteries, they write, 'promised a special intimacy with the divinity and a carefree immortality beyond the grave'. This assurance was delivered through participation in the ritual, the shared meal and the revelations. See also #354.
26. See also Freyne, *World of the New Testament*, p. 40.
27. In 186 BCE, after the scandal, the consuls Quintus Marcius and Spurius Posthumius wrote a letter to the people of Ager Teuranus in which they inform the town of the Senate's decisions regarding the regulation of the worship of Bacchus. See E.H. Warmington, *Remains of Old Latin*, IV (Cambridge, MA: Harvard University Press, 1940), pp. 254–59 (= *CIL* 1.2.581).
28. See also Ovid, *Art of Love* 1.77–78; Juvenal, *Satires* 6.486–89, 526–41; 9.22–26.
29. See the description of a procession in honour of Cybele in Lucretius, *On the Nature of the Universe* 2.608–643.
30. See also Romans 16:25; 1 Corinthians 15:51; Ephesians 1:9; 3:4; Colossians 1:26.
31. For dreams, see, e.g., Suetonius, *Augustus* 91, 92, 95; *Tiberius* 69; *Galba* 4. Note also the importance of visions in dreams in the New Testament (see, e.g., Matthew 1:20; 2:19, 22; Acts 16:9).
32. See Petronius, *Satyricon* 39; Suetonius, *Tiberius* 69; Tacitus, *Histories* 2.78.
33. Amulets are worn by Jewish soldiers in 2 Maccabees 12:40 (contrast Deuteronomy 7:25–26). On astrology in early Judaism, see James H. Charlesworth, 'Jewish Interest in Astrology during the Hellenistic and Roman Period', *ANRW* 2.20.2 (1987), pp. 926–50.
34. See 4Q186, 534, 561. For texts see Vermes, *Complete Dead Sea Scrolls in English*, pp. 357–59.
35. Claudius banned astrologers (see Tacitus, *Annals* 12.52).
36. See Suetonius, *Tiberius* 63. It was feared that spells and incantations had been used against Germanicus, resulting in his death (see Tacitus, *Annals* 2.69).
37. For texts see H.D. Betz, *Greek Magical Papyri in Translation* (Chicago: Chicago University Press, 2nd edn, 1992). See the use of the name of Jesus in Mark 9:38–40; Acts 19:13. Jesus is portrayed as a magician by Celsus (see Origen, *Against Celsus* 1.6 [ANF 4.398–99]).
38. In Mark 3:22–32 Jesus is accused of being a sorcerer. Jesus responds by arguing that his work is to overthrow the work of the devil, and to release his captives.
39. For further accounts of prodigies in Rome and elsewhere see Appian, *Civil Wars* 2.36, 68; 4.4; for bad omens just before Caesar was assassinated, see 2.116. See also Plutarch,

Sulla 7 for portents as signs of the changing of the ages.

40. An earthquake occurs in Matthew 28:2 when Jesus is raised (cf. 27:51). Note the connection between earthquake and theophany in Exodus 19:18. Note also the guiding star of Matthew 2:1–2. The birth of great men is often attended by portents in the heavens.
41. According to the elder Pliny (*Natural History* 30.3) magic arose in Persia with Zoroaster. He lived, so Pliny informs his audience, 6000 years before the death of Plato.
42. Ephesus was a noted centre of occult practice. See Ferguson, *Backgrounds of Early Christianity*, p. 180. See also Ignatius's comments on the implications of the Christ-event in #667, an extract drawn from his *Letter to the Ephesians*.
43. See further Acts 8:9–24; Matthew 12:22–30; Mark 3:22–32; 9:38–40.

6. Philosophy

Introduction

Philosophy approached the great issues of the purpose of life and the nature of the universe without recourse to mythology. By the first century CE philosophy had a long history of seeking to establish the parameters of a rational discourse, and had deconstructed naively held religious convictions about the gods articulated in myth. Nevertheless, perceptions about the existence of the divine world were affirmed in the philosophical schools, Stoicism especially.

Philosophers concerned themselves not just with abstract thought about the nature of the universe but strove to formulate the principles of the good life. In the Graeco-Roman era ethics was the foundation of philosophical schools and of philosophical reflection. The aim of philosophy was to investigate and to inculcate right living; to formulate a consistent and coherent life-commitment based on rationally determined principles. Religion, by contrast, was not concerned with ethics but with ritual rectitude and decorum (Latin *pietas*) in the religious sphere. Philosophical discourse, however, debated how one ought to live.

The value of philosophy lay in its discipline of self-criticism. In the face of the temptation to surrender to one's passions, the philosophical enterprise of the Graeco-Roman era generally strove to identify the kind of life that was lived in harmony with nature. Seneca, like many of his contemporaries, counselled rising above passionate, unbridled life options. The goal of philosophy, he argued, was self-control, self-possession. In the extract that follows, Seneca articulates an attractive vision of the philosopher as a person of moderation. Slaves, artisans and labourers were not the intended audience of such exhortation.

Sources

368. The first thing which philosophy undertakes to give is fellow-feeling with all men; in other words, sympathy and sociability. We part company with our promise if we are unlike other men. We must see to it that the means by which we wish to draw admiration be not absurd and odious. Our motto, as you know, is 'Live according to Nature'; but it is quite contrary to nature to torture the body, to hate unlaboured elegance, to be dirty on purpose, to eat food that is not only plain, but disgusting and forbidding. Just as it is a sign of luxury to seek out dainties, so it is madness to avoid that which is customary and can be purchased at no great price. Philosophy calls for plain living, but not for penance; and we may perfectly well be plain and neat at the same time. This is the mean of which I approve; our life should observe a happy medium between the ways of a sage and the ways of the world at large; all men should admire it, but they should understand it also. (Seneca, *Epistles* 5.4–5)

6.1. Epicureanism

According to Lucretius, Epicurus (341–270 BCE) was the philosopher *par excellence* who was prepared to critique accepted ideas about the gods. Epicurus based his philosophy on the relentlessly materialistic cosmology of the fifth-century BCE philosopher Democritus, which taught that all things were made of atoms and had come into being by chance. In Epicurus's teaching the gods did exist, but they did so in perfect bliss, ignorant of humankind, and were uninvolved in the world. Epicurus called this state of existence *ataraxia*. This freedom from disturbance enjoyed by the gods was precisely the goal of human life. The goal could be achieved if humankind pursued truly pleasurable activities. Epicurus sought these goals in a withdrawn community with his disciples in which men and women enjoyed equal status.[1] It was commonly believed, erroneously, that Epicurus tolerated moral licence.[2] Such living challenged commonly held beliefs and values about gender roles, and the perception that public life necessarily required being engaged in the competitive quest for fame and honour.[3] He also wrote letters to scattered followers (see #369 and #371 below).

Sources

Epicurus to Herodotus.

369. And besides all these matters in general we must grasp this point, that the principal disturbance in the minds of men arises because they think that these celestial bodies are blessed and immortal, and yet have wills and actions and motives inconsistent with these attributes; and because they are always expecting or imagining some everlasting misery, such as is depicted in legends, or even fear the loss of feeling in death as though it would concern them themselves; and, again, because they are brought to this pass not by reasoned opinion, but rather by some irrational presentiment, and therefore, as they do not know the limits of pain, they suffer a disturbance equally great or even more extensive than if they had reached this belief by opinion.

But peace of mind is being delivered from all this, and having a constant memory of the general and most essential principles.

Wherefore we must pay attention to internal feelings and to external sensations in general and in particular, according as the subject is general or particular, and to every immediate intuition in accordance with each of the standards of judgement. For if we pay attention to these, we shall rightly trace the causes whence arose our mental disturbance and fear, and, by learning the true causes of celestial phenomena and all other occurrences that come to pass from time to time, we shall free ourselves from all which produces the utmost fear in other men.
(Epicurus, *To Herodotus* 81–82)

Extracts from Epicurus's Principal Doctrines.

370. (12) A man cannot dispel his fear about the most important matters if he does not know what is the nature of the universe but suspects the truth of some mythical story. So that without natural science it is not possible to attain our pleasures unalloyed.

(21) He who has learned the limits of life knows that that which removes the pain due to want and makes the whole of life complete is easy to obtain; so that there is no need of actions which involve competition.

(28) The same conviction which has given us confidence that there is nothing terrible that lasts for ever or even for long, has also seen the protection of friendship most fully completed in the limited evils of this life.

(40) As many as possess the power to procure complete immunity from their neighbours, these also live most pleasantly with one another, since they have the most certain pledge of security, and after they have enjoyed the fullest intimacy, they do not lament the previous departure of a dead friend, as though he were to be pitied.
(Epicurus, *Principal Doctrines* 12, 21, 28, 40)

Epicurus to Menoeceus.

371. The things which I used unceasingly to commend to you, these do and practice, considering them to be the first principles of the good life. First of all believe that god is a being immortal and blessed, even as the common idea of a god is engraved on men's minds, and do not assign to him anything alien to his immortality or ill-suited to his blessedness: but believe about him everything that can uphold his blessedness and immortality. For gods there are, since the knowledge of them is by clear vision. But they are not such as the many believe them to be: for indeed they do not consistently represent them as they believe them to be. And the impious man is not he who denies the gods of the many, but he who attaches to the gods the beliefs of the many. For the statements of the many about the gods are not conceptions derived from sensation, but false suppositions, according to which the greatest misfortunes befall the wicked and the greatest blessings (the good) by the gift of the gods. For men being accustomed always to their own virtues welcome those

like themselves, but regard all that is not of their nature as alien.

Become accustomed to the belief that death is nothing to us. For all good and evil consists in sensation, but death is deprivation of sensation. And therefore a right understanding that death is nothing to us makes the mortality of life enjoyable, not because it adds to it an infinite span of time, but because it takes away the craving for immortality. For there is nothing terrible in life for the man who has truly comprehended that there is nothing terrible in not living. So that the man speaks but idly who says that he fears death not because it will be painful when it comes, but because it is painful in anticipation. For that which gives no trouble when it comes, is but an empty pain in anticipation. So death, the most terrifying of ills, is nothing to us, since so long as we exist, death is not with us; but when death comes, then we do not exist. It does not then concern either the living or the dead, since for the former it is not, and the latter are no more...

We must consider that of desires some are natural, others vain, and of the natural some are necessary and others merely natural; and of the necessary some are necessary for happiness, others for the repose of the body, and others for very life. The right understanding of these facts enables us to refer all choice and avoidance to the health of the body and (the soul's) freedom from disturbance [*ataraxia*], since this is the aim of the life of blessedness. For it is to obtain this end that we always act, namely, to avoid pain and fear. And when this is once secured for us, all the tempest of the soul is dispersed, since the living creature has not to wander as though in search of something that is missing, and to look for some other thing by which he can fulfil the good of the soul and the good of the body. For it is then that we have need of pleasure, when we feel pain owing to the absence of pleasure; (but when we do not feel pain), we no longer need pleasure. And for this cause we call pleasure the beginning and the end of the blessed life. For we recognize pleasure as the first good innate in us, and from pleasure we begin every act of choice and avoidance, and to pleasure we return again, using the feeling as the standard by which we judge every good.

And since pleasure is the first good and natural to us, for this very reason we do not choose every pleasure, but sometimes we pass over many pleasures, when greater discomfort accrues to us as the result of them: and similarly we think many pains better than pleasures, since a greater pleasure comes to us when we have endured pains for a long time. Every pleasure then because of its natural kinship to us is good, yet not every pleasure is to be chosen: even as every pain also is an evil, yet not all are always of a nature to be avoided. Yet by scale of comparison and by the consideration of advantages and disadvantages we must form our judgement on all these matters. For the good on certain occasions we treat as bad, and conversely the bad as good.

And again independence of desire [*autarkeia*] we think a great good—not that we may at all times enjoy but a few things, but that, if we do not possess many, we may enjoy the few in the genuine persuasion that those have the sweetest pleasure in luxury who least need it, and that all that is natural is easy to be obtained, but that which is superfluous is hard. And so plain savours bring us a pleasure equal to a luxurious diet, when all the pain due to want is removed; and bread and water produce the highest pleasure, when one who needs them puts them to his lips. To grow accustomed therefore to simple and not luxurious diet gives us health to the full, and makes a man alert for the needful employments of life, and when after long intervals we approach luxuries disposes us better towards them, and fits us to be fearless of fortune.

When, therefore, we maintain that pleasure is the end, we do not mean the pleasures of profligates and those that consist in sensuality, as is supposed by some who are either ignorant or disagree with us or do not understand, but freedom from pain in the body and from trouble in the mind. For it is not continuous drinkings and revellings, nor the satisfaction of lusts, nor the enjoyment of fish and other luxuries of the wealthy table, which produce a pleasant life, but

sober reasoning, searching out the motives for all choice and avoidance, and banishing mere opinions, to which are due the greatest disturbance of the spirit.
(Epicurus, *To Menoeceus* 123–32)

In Lucretius Rome produced a philosopher/poet of passion for the Epicurean cause. In his *On the Nature of the Universe*, Lucretius integrated Epicurean doctrine with poetry of great artistry. Lucretius was especially motivated to mediate Epicurus's dispelling of any grounds his audience may have had for fearing death. Since humans are comprised of atoms, which on death are dispersed, and since the gods are not concerned with us or with the world, but live a life of blissful ease (see, e.g., *On the Nature of the Universe* 6.70–90), there can be no rational grounds for thinking that there is life after death and no possibility that the gods might deal with us malevolently. To think otherwise is to be guilty of superstition and impiety with respect to the gods.

Lucretius on the evils of religion and superstition.

372. Therefore, since treasures profit nothing for our body, nor noble birth nor the glory of royalty, we must further think that for the mind also they are unprofitable; unless by chance, when you behold your legions seething over the spacious Plain as they evoke war in mimicry, established firm with mighty supports and a mass of cavalry, marshalled all in arms cap-à-pie and all full of one spirit, then these things scare your superstitious fears and drive them in panic flight from your mind, and death's terrors then leave your heart unpossessed and free from care. But if we see these things to be ridiculous and a mere mockery, if in truth men's fears and haunting cares fear neither the clang of arms nor wild weapons, if they boldly mingle with kings and sovereigns of the world, if they respect not the sheen of gold nor the glowing light of crimson raiment, why doubt you that this power wholly belongs to reason, especially since life is one long struggle in the dark? For just as children tremble and fear all things in blind darkness, so we in the light fear, at times, things that are no more to be feared than what children shiver at in the dark and imagine to be at hand. This terror of the mind, therefore, and this gloom must be dispelled, not by the sun's rays nor the bright shafts of day, but by the aspect and law of nature.
(Lucretius, *On the Nature of the Universe* 2.37–61)

In the following extract Lucretius expounds on the irrationality of the fear of death. Note also his critique of the culture of the pursuit of fame.

373. Moreover, avarice and the blind lust of distinction, which drive wretched men to transgress the bounds of law, and sometimes by sharing and scheming crime to strive night and day with exceeding toil to climb the pinnacle of power, these sores of life in no small degree are fed by the fear of death. For in general degrading scorn and bitter need are seen to be far removed from sweetness and stability of life, and a lingering as it were before the gates of death; from which men desiring to escape afar and to remove themselves far away, driven by false terror, amass wealth by civil bloodshed and greedily multiply riches, piling murder upon murder; cruelly they rejoice at the mournful death of a brother, they hate and they fear a kinsman's hospitality. In like manner and through the same fear, they are often consumed with envy that before their very eyes he is clothed in power, he is the sight of the town, who parades in shining pomp, while they complain that they themselves are wallowing in darkness and mire. Some wear out their lives for the sake of a statue and a name. And often it goes so far, that for fear of death men are seized by hatred of life and of seeing the light, so that with sorrowing heart they devise their own death, forgetting that this fear is the fountain of their cares: it induces one man to violate honour, another to break the bonds of friendship, and in a word to overthrow all natural feeling; for often before now men have betrayed fatherland or beloved parents in seeking to avoid the regions of Acheron. For as children tremble and fear everything in the blind darkness, so we in the light sometimes fear what is no more to be feared than the things that children in the dark hold in terror and imagine

will come true. This terror, therefore, and darkness of the mind must be dispersed, not by rays of the sun nor the bright shafts of daylight, but by the aspect and law of nature. (Lucretius, *On the Nature of the Universe* 3.59–93. For fear of avenging furies see Philo, *Flaccus* 175)

Extracts from an Augustan-era (?) papyrus fragment of Epicurean philosophy.

374. 'Nor indeed, even when this further statement is made by the ordinary man. "I fear all the gods and worship them, and to them I wish to make every sacrifice and offering." It may perhaps imply more taste on his part than the average, nevertheless by this formula he has not yet reached the trustworthy principle of religion. But do you, sir, consider that the most blessed state lies in the formation of a just conception concerning the best thing that even we can possibly imagine to exist; and reverence and worship this idea.

'But let there be no question of fear in this, nor any assumption that your action will buy the favour of the gods. For why, "by Zeus," to use the vulgar phrase, do you fear them? Is it because you think that you do them an injury? Is it not plain in that case that you are making them inferior? Are you not then regarding the divine power as something mean, if it is inferior to you?' (P.Oxy 215)

6.2. Stoicism

Whereas Epicurus and his successors taught that the gods were uninvolved and uncaring with respect to the universe and humankind, stoicism repeatedly stressed the reality of divine providence. As a philosophical school Stoicism originated with Zeno of Citium (c. 333–262 BCE), who taught in Athens in the *Stoa Poikilē* (the Painted Colonnade), from which the school took its name. Stoics argued that there existed in the universe a unifying principle (*logos*), a law of nature, in which all humankind participated. In the context of the later extent of the Roman empire, such a view took on a new significance in the Graeco-Roman era. It was right for people to live in harmony with universal law according to the particle of divine reason each has received. Not surprisingly Stoicism was the dominant school of philosophy during the first century CE because it functioned as a philosophical analogue of the political reality of the empire. Early Judaism perceived the Torah in a similar way to the Stoic conception of a universal principle (see Sirach 24:5–8, 22). The Jewish philosopher Philo was the foremost Jewish representative of engagement with Stoic ideas (see topic 6.5 below).

By Imperial times Stoicism was largely concerned with ethics. Seneca and Epictetus taught that one ought to live in accord with nature, that nature taught the fundamental equality of all humankind, and that, regardless of status, all were bound under the obligation to live in accordance with that universal law. Not surprisingly Stoic philosophers were among the few who raised their voices against slavery and the horrors of the arena.

Sources

Cleanthes was Zeno's successor in the Stoic school. The following extract from his works has achieved considerable fame.

375. Thou, O Zeus, art praised above all gods: many are Thy names and Thine is all power for ever.
The beginning of the world was from Thee: and with law Thou rulest over all things.
Unto Thee may all flesh speak: for we are Thy offspring.
Therefore will I raise a hymn unto Thee: and will ever sing of Thy power.
The whole order of the heavens obeyeth Thy word; as it moveth around the earth.
With little and great lights mixed together: how great art Thou, King above all for ever!
Nor is anything done upon earth apart from Thee: nor in the firmament, nor in the seas:
Save that which the wicked do: by their own folly.
But Thine is the skill to set even the crooked straight: what is without fashion is fashioned and the alien akin before Thee.

Thus hast Thou fitted together all things in one: the good with the evil:
That Thy word should be one in all things: abiding for ever.
Let folly be dispersed from our souls: that we may repay Thee the honour, wherewith Thou has honoured us:
Singing praise of Thy works for ever: as becometh the sons of men.
(Cleanthes, 'Hymn to Zeus')[4]

Human beings are 'fragments of God' (#376–77).

376. Will you not, therefore, seek the true nature of the good in that quality the lack of which in all creatures other than man prevents you from using the term 'good' of any of these? 'But what then? Are not those creatures also works of God?' They are, but they are not of primary importance, nor portions of Divinity. But you are a being of primary importance; you are a fragment of God; you have within you a part of Him. Why, then, are you ignorant of your own kinship? Why do you not know the source from which you have sprung? Will you not bear in mind, whenever you eat, who you are that eat, and whom you are nourishing? Whenever you indulge in [sexual] intercourse with women, who you are that do this? Whenever you mix in society, whenever you take physical exercise, whenever you converse, do you not know that you are nourishing God, exercising God? You are bearing God about with you, you poor wretch, and know it not! Do you suppose I am speaking of some external God, made of silver or gold? It is within yourself that you bear Him, and do not perceive that you are defiling Him with impure thoughts and filthy actions. Yet in the presence of even an image of God you would not dare to do anything of the things you are now doing. But when God Himself is present within you, seeing and hearing everything, are you not ashamed to be thinking and doing such things as these, O insensible of your own nature, and object of God's wrath!
(Epictetus, *Discourses* 2.8.9–14)

377. If what is said by the philosophers regarding the kinship of God and men be true, what other course remains for men but that which Socrates took when asked to what country he belonged, never to say 'I am an Athenian,' or 'I am a Corinthian,' but 'I am a citizen of the universe'? For why do you say that you are an Athenian, instead of mentioning merely that corner into which your paltry body was cast at birth? Or is it clear you take the place which has a higher degree of authority and comprehends not merely that corner of yours, but also your family and, in a word, the source from which your race has come, your ancestors down to yourself, and from such entity call yourself 'Athenian,' or 'Corinthian'? Well, then, anyone who has attentively studied the administration of the universe and has learned that 'the greatest and most authoritative and most comprehensive of all governments is this one, which is composed of men and God, and that from Him have descended the seeds of being, not merely to my father or to my grandfather, but to all things that are begotten now and that grow upon earth, and chiefly to rational beings, seeing that by nature it is theirs alone to have communion in the society of God, being intertwined with him through the reason,'—why should not such a man call himself a citizen of the universe? Why should he not call himself a son of God? And why shall he fear anything that happens among men? What! Shall kinship with Caesar or any other of them that have great power at Rome be sufficient to enable men to live securely, proof against contempt, and in fear of nothing whatsoever, but to have God as our maker, and father, and guardian,—shall this not suffice to deliver us from griefs and fears?—And wherewithal shall I be fed, asks one, if I have nothing?—And how of slaves, how of runaways, on what do they rely when they leave their masters? On their lands, their slaves, or their vessels of silver? No, on nothing but themselves; and nevertheless food does not fail them. And shall it be necessary for our philosopher, forsooth, when he goes abroad, to depend upon others for his assurance and his refreshment, instead of taking care of himself, and to be more vile and craven than the irrational animals, every one of which is sufficient to himself, and lacks neither its own proper

food nor that way of life which is appropriate to it and in harmony with nature?
(Epictetus, *Discourses* 1.9.1–9)

Musonius Rufus was a Stoic philosopher of the mid first century CE. In the following fragment of his work, he proposes that humankind is made in the image of God.

378. Man alone of terrestrial beings is made after the likeness of God, such that his virtues resemble the Divine ones; for not even in gods can we conceive anything higher than wisdom and righteousness, nay, one may add, than courage and temperance. Just as God then by the presence of these virtues cannot be overcome by pleasure, or overcome by covetousness, just as He rises superior to inordinate desire, to envy and jealousy, and is generous, beneficent, a lover of men—for we think of God as like that—such should we consider His image, Man, to be, when a man is in the condition which accords with his true nature, and, being such, to be what we would crave to be, and being what we would crave to be, to be happy. For the people we call happy are the people who are what we would crave to be. Further, it is nothing impossible for a man to become what we have described. For we could have no conception at all of these virtues, unless we drew it from the nature of Man, having met with men who are really like this, and whom, because they are like this, I might call divine, similitudes of God.
(Musonius Rufus, Fragment)

All humans are citizens of a world polis.

379. The person you are matters more than the place to which you go; for that reason we should not make the mind a bondsman to any one place. Live in this belief: 'I am not born for any one corner of the universe; this whole world is my country'.
(Seneca, *Epistles* 28.4)

Seneca on wisdom and reason (#380–81).

380. Would you know what wisdom has brought forth to light, what she has accomplished? It is not the graceful poses of the body, or the varied notes produced by horn and flute, whereby the breath is received and, as it passes out or through, is transformed into voice. It is not wisdom that contrives arms, or walls, or instruments useful in war; nay, her voice is for peace, and she summons all mankind to concord. It is not she, I maintain, who is the artisan of our indispensable implements of daily use. Why do you assign to her such petty things? You see in her the skilled artisan of life. The other arts, it is true, wisdom has under her control; for he whom life serves is also served by the things which equip life. But wisdom's course is toward the state of happiness; thither she guides us, thither she opens the way for us. She shows us what things are evil and what things are seemingly evil: she strips our minds of vain illusion. She bestows upon us a greatness which is substantial, but she represses the greatness which is inflated, and showy but filled with emptiness; and she does not permit us to be ignorant of the difference between what is great and what is but swollen; nay, she delivers to us the knowledge of the whole of nature and of her own nature. She discloses to us what the gods are and of what sort they are; what are the nether gods, the household deities, and the protecting spirits; what are the souls which have been endowed with lasting life and have been admitted to the second class of divinities, where is their abode and what their activities, powers, and will.

Such are wisdom's rites of initiation, by means of which is unlocked, not a village shrine, but the vast temple of all the gods—the universe itself, whose true apparitions and true aspects she offers to the gaze of our minds. For the vision of our eyes is too dull for sights so great. Then she goes back to the beginnings of things, to the eternal Reason which was imparted to the whole, and to the force which inheres in all the seeds of things, giving them the power to fashion each thing according to its kind.
(Seneca, *Epistles* 90.26–29)

381. For man is a reasoning animal. Therefore, man's highest good is attained, if he has fulfilled the good for which nature designed him at birth. And what is it which this reason demands of him? The easiest thing in the world,—to live in accordance with his own nature. But this is turned into a hard

task by the general madness of mankind; we push one another into vice. And how can a man be recalled to salvation, when he has none to restrain him, and all mankind to urge him on?
(Seneca, *Epistles* 41.8–9)[5]

For Epictetus, living in accordance with nature was the same as living in accordance with reason.

382. As some one was reading the hypothetical arguments, Epictetus said, This also is a law governing hypotheses—that we must accept what the hypothesis or premiss demands. But much more important is the following law of life—that we must do what nature demands.
(Epictetus, *Discourses* 1.26.1)

Philosophy as theology (#383–90).

In Cicero's treatise *On the Nature of the Gods*, the Stoic, Lucilius, argues that divine beings exist.

383. [W]hen we gaze upward to the sky and contemplate the heavenly bodies, what can be so obvious and so manifest as that there must exist some power possessing transcendent intelligence by whom these things are ruled? Were it not so, how comes it that the words of Ennius carry conviction to all readers—

Behold this dazzling vault of heaven, which all mankind as Jove invoke,

ay, and not only as Jove but as sovereign of the world, ruling all things with his nod, and as Ennius likewise says—

father of gods and men,

a deity omnipresent and omnipotent? If a man doubts this, I really cannot see why he should not also be capable of doubting the existence of the sun; how is the latter fact more evident than the former? Nothing but the presence in our minds of a firmly grasped concept of the deity could account for the stability and permanence of our belief in him, a belief which is only strengthened by the passage of the ages and grows more deeply rooted with each successive generation of mankind. In every other case we see that fictitious and unfounded opinions have dwindled away with lapse of time. Who believes that the Hippocentaur or the Chimaera ever existed? Where can you find an old wife senseless enough to be afraid of the monsters of the lower world that were once believed in? The years obliterate the inventions of the imagination, but confirm the judgements of nature.
(Cicero, *On the Nature of the Gods* 2.4–5)[6]

In Cicero's dialogue, *On the Nature of the Gods*, Balbus is the spokesperson for Stoic ideas. Here he presents the Stoic view of the cyclical regeneration of the universe out of fire.

384. In the aether the stars revolve in their courses; these maintain their spherical form by their own internal gravitation, and also sustain their motions by virtue of their very shape and conformation; for they are round, and this is the shape, as I believe I remarked before, that is least capable of receiving injury. But the stars are of a fiery substance, and for this reason they are nourished by the vapours of the earth, the sea and the waters, which are raised up by the sun out of the fields which it warms and out of the waters; and when nourished and renewed by these vapours the stars and the whole aether shed them back again, and then once more draw them up from the same source, with the loss of none of their matter, or only of an extremely small part which is consumed by the fire of the stars and the flame of the aether. As a consequence of this, so our school believe, though it used to be said that Panaetius questioned the doctrine, there will ultimately occur a conflagration of the whole world, because when the moisture has been used up neither can the earth be nourished nor will the air continue to flow, being unable to rise upward after it has drunk up all the water; thus nothing will remain but fire, by which, as a living being and a god, once again a new world may be created and the ordered universe be restored as before.
(Cicero, *On the Nature of the Gods* 2.117–18)[7]

Providence.

In contrast to the Epicureans who taught that the gods took no interest in the world of humankind, the Stoics believed in providence—God's active and beneficent superintending of the cosmos.

385. Those who do not believe that the world was created for God and mankind, or that human affairs are ruled by Providence, think that they are using a strong argument when they say: 'If there were a Providence, there would be no evils.' For they declare that nothing is less consistent with Providence than the existence of such a quantity of troubles and evils in a world which He is said to have made for the sake of man. Chrysippus, arguing against such views in the fourth book of his treatise *On Providence*, says: 'There is absolutely nothing more foolish than those men who think that good could exist, if there were at the same time no evil. For since good is the opposite of evil, it necessarily follows that both must exist in opposition to each other, supported as it were by mutual adverse forces; since as a matter of fact no opposite is conceivable without something to oppose it. For how could there be an idea of justice if there were no acts of injustice? Or what else is justice than the absence of injustice? How too can courage be understood except by contrast with cowardice? Or temperance except by contrast with intemperance? How also could there be wisdom, if folly did not exist as its opposite? Therefore,' said he, 'why do not the fools also wish that there may be truth, but no falsehood? For it is in the same way that good and evil exist, happiness and unhappiness, pain and pleasure. For, as Plato says, they are bound one to the other by their opposing extremes; if you take away one, you will have removed both.'
(Aulus Gellius, *Attic Nights* 7.1.1–6)

386. You ask, 'Why do many adversities come to good men?' No evil can befall a good man; opposites do not mingle. Just as the countless rivers, the vast fall of rain from the sky, and the huge volume of mineral springs do not change the taste of the sea, do not even modify it, so the assaults of adversity do not weaken the spirit of a brave man. It always maintains its poise, and it gives its own colour to everything that happens; for it is mightier than all external things. And yet I do not mean to say that the brave man is insensible to these, but that he overcomes them, and being in all else unmoved and calm rises to meet whatever assails him. All his adversities he counts mere training. Who, moreover, if he is a man and intent upon the right, is not eager for reasonable toil and ready for duties accompanied by danger? To what energetic man is not idleness a punishment? Wrestlers, who make strength of body their chief concern, we see pitting themselves against none but the strongest, and they require of those who are preparing them for the arena that they use against them all their strength; they submit to blows and hurts, and if they do not find their match in single opponents, they engage with several at a time. Without an adversary, prowess shrivels. We see how great and how efficient it really is, only when it shows by endurance what it is capable of. Be assured that good men ought to act likewise; they should not shrink from hardships and difficulties, nor complain against fate; they should take in good part whatever happens, and should turn it to good. Not what you endure, but how you endure, is important.
(Seneca, *On Providence* 2.1–4)

Epictetus's hymn to Providence.

387. [I]f we had sense, ought we to be doing anything else, publicly and privately, than hymning and praising the Deity, and rehearsing His benefits? Ought we not, as we dig and plough and eat, to sing the hymn of praise to God? 'Great is God, that He hath furnished us these instruments wherewith we shall till the earth. Great is God, that He hath given us hands, and power to swallow, and a belly, and power to grow unconsciously, and to breathe while asleep.' This is what we ought to sing on every occasion, and above all to sing the greatest and divinest hymn, that God has given us the faculty to comprehend these things and to follow the path of reason. What then? Since most of you have become blind, ought there not to be someone to fulfil this office for you, and in behalf of all sing the hymn of praise to God? Why, what else can I, a lame old man, do but sing hymns to God? If, indeed, I were a nightingale, I should be

singing as a nightingale; if a swan, as a swan. But as it is, I am a rational being, therefore I must be singing hymns of praise to God. This is my task; I do it, and will not desert this post, as long as it may be given me to fill it; and I exhort you to join me in this same song.
(Epictetus, *Discourses* 1.16.15–21)

388. Does God so neglect His own creatures, His servants, His witnesses, whom alone He uses as examples to the uninstructed, to prove that He both is, and governs the universe well, and does not neglect the affairs of men, and that no evil befalls a good man either in life or in death?—Yes, but what if He does not provide food?—Why, what else but that as a good general He has sounded the recall? I obey, I follow, lauding my commander, and singing hymns of praise about His deeds. For I came into the world when it so pleased Him, and I leave it again at His pleasure, and while I live this was my function—to sing hymns of praise unto God, to myself and to others, be it to one or to many.
(Epictetus, *Discourses* 3.26.28–30)

Epictetus on the nature of true piety (eusebeia).

389. (1) In piety towards the gods, I would have you know, the chief element is this, to have right opinions about them—as existing and as administering the universe well and justly—and to have set yourself to obey them and to submit to everything that happens, and to follow it voluntarily, in the belief that it is being fulfilled by the highest intelligence. For if you act in this way, you will never blame the gods, nor find fault with them for neglecting you.

(5) But it is always appropriate to make libations, and sacrifices, and to give of the firstfruits after the manner of our fathers, and to do all this with purity, and not in a slovenly or careless fashion, nor, indeed, in a niggardly way, nor yet beyond our means.
(Epictetus, *Encheiridion* 31.1, 5)

Imitating God.

390. Now the philosophers say that the first thing we must learn is this: That there is a God, and that He provides for the universe, and that it is impossible for a man to conceal from Him, not merely his actions, but even his purposes and his thoughts. Next we must learn what the gods are like; for whatever their character is discovered to be, the man who is going to please and obey them must endeavour as best he can to resemble them. If the deity is faithful, he also must be faithful; if free, he also must be free; if beneficent, he also must be beneficent; if high-minded, he also must be high-minded, and so forth; therefore, in everything he says and does, he must act as imitator of God.
(Epictetus, *Discourses* 2.14.11–13)

6.3. The Academy

The Roman lawyer and statesman Cicero was a member of the Academy, a school of thought that had its roots in the academy of Plato (c. 429–347 BCE).[8] Under the influence of Arcesilas (c. 316–242 BCE), the School adopted scepticism, an approach to philosophy associated with Pyrrhon (c. 365–275 BCE). This period of the Academy is often termed the 'Middle Academy'. The methodology of the School under sceptic influence was the 'withholding consent from beliefs that are uncertain' (see #392 below). The Middle Academy thus maintained an approach to philosophy that was essentially Socratic in spirit.[9] During the late Republican and Imperial period, the Academy reverted to its Platonic heritage.

Sources

Cicero describes the philosophical method employed in Academic circles of his time.

391. To those again who are surprised at my choice of a system to which to give my allegiance, I think that a sufficient answer has been given in the four books of my *Academica*. Nor is it the case that I have come forward as the champion of a lost cause and of a position now abandoned. When men die, their doctrines do not perish with them, though perhaps they suffer from the loss of their authoritative exponent. Take for example the philosophical method referred to, that of a purely negative

dialectic which refrains from pronouncing any positive judgement. This, after being originated by Socrates, revived by Arcesilas, and reinforced by Carneades, has flourished right down to our own period; though I understand that in Greece itself it is now almost bereft of adherents. But this I ascribe not to the fault of the Academy but to the dullness of mankind. If it is a considerable matter to understand any one of the systems of philosophy singly, how much harder is it to master them all! Yet this is the task that confronts those whose principle is to discover the truth by the method of arguing both for and against all the schools.
(Cicero, *On the Nature of the Gods* 1.11)

392. [P]hilosophy has its origin and starting-point in ignorance, and that the Academic School were well-advised in 'withholding assent' from beliefs that are uncertain: for what is more unbecoming than ill-considered haste? and what is so ill-conceived or so unworthy of the dignity and seriousness proper to a philosopher as to hold an opinion that is not true, or to maintain with unhesitating certainty a proposition not based on adequate examination, comprehension and knowledge?
(Cicero, *On the Nature of the Gods* 1.1)[10]

6.4. Philosophical Itinerants

From the fifth century onwards there were travelling sophists; teachers who made a living not only teaching virtue but also techniques of arguing. Diogenes of Sinope (c. 400–325 BCE) was the first to combine itinerancy with extreme asceticism. The philosophical movement called Cynicism originated with him. For him the good life was attainable for those who satisfied their needs in the most natural and direct way. For this he was called 'dog' (*kuōn*). Cynics are encountered in first-century CE sources. They were caustic public critics of luxury and convention.[11]

Sources

Diogenes learns to adapt himself to all circumstances.

393. He was the first, say some, to fold his cloak because he was obliged to sleep in it as well, and he carried a wallet to hold his victuals, and he used any place for any purpose, for breakfasting, sleeping, or conversing. And then he would say, pointing to the portico of Zeus and the Hall of Processions, that the Athenians had provided him with places to live in. He did not lean upon a staff until he grew infirm; but afterwards he would carry it everywhere, not indeed in the city, but when walking along the road with it and with his wallet...
(Diogenes Laertius, *Lives of Eminent Philosophers* 6.22–23)

The following two extracts provide some insight into the unconventional Cynic spirit.

394. When he [Diogenes] was sunning himself in the Craneum, Alexander came and stood over him and said, 'Ask of me any boon you like.' To which he replied, 'Stand out of my light.'
(Diogenes Laertius, *Lives of Eminent Philosophers* 6.38)

395. Alexander once came and stood opposite him and said, 'I am Alexander the great king.' 'And I,' said he, 'am Diogenes the Cynic.' Being asked what he had done to be called a hound, he said, 'I fawn on those who give me anything, I yelp at those who refuse, and I set my teeth in rascals.'
(Diogenes Laertius, *Lives of Eminent Philosophers* 6.60)

Epictetus on Diogenes (#396–97).

In the following two extracts Epictetus invokes the idea of the philosopher as 'scout', i.e. one who observes accurately and brings a report. Cowards do not make good 'scouts' because they, unlike Diogenes, are too fearful.

396. Diogenes, who before you was sent forth as a scout, has brought us back a different report. He says, 'Death is not an evil, since it is not dishonourable'; he says, 'Ill repute is a noise made by madmen.' And what a report this scout has made us about toil and about pleasure and about poverty! He says, 'To be naked is better than any scarlet robe; and to sleep on the bare ground,' he says, 'is the softest couch.' And he offers as a proof of each statement his own courage, his tran-

quillity, his freedom, and finally his body, radiant with health and hardened. 'There is no enemy near,' says he; 'all is full of peace.' How so, Diogenes? 'Why, look!' says he, 'I have not been struck with any missile, have I, or received any wound? I have not fled from anyone have I?' This is what it means to be a proper scout, but you return and tell us one thing after another. Will you not go away again and observe more accurately, without this cowardice?
(Epictetus, *Discourses* 1.24.6–10)[12]

397. And how is it possible for a man who has nothing, who is naked, without home or hearth, in squalor, without a slave, without a city, to live serenely? Behold, God has sent you the man who will show in practice that it is possible. 'Look at me,' he says, 'I am without a home, without a city, without property, without a slave; I sleep on the ground; I have neither wife nor children, no miserable governor's mansion, but only earth, and sky, and one rough cloak. Yet what do I lack? Am I not free from pain and fear, am I not free? When has anyone among you seen me failing to get what I desire, or falling into what I would avoid? When have I ever found fault with either God or man? When have I ever blamed anyone? Has anyone among you seen me with a gloomy face? And how do I face those persons before whom you stand in fear and awe? Do I not face them as slaves? Who, when he lays eyes upon me, does not feel that he is seeing his king and his master?'
(Epictetus, *Discourses* 3.22.45–49)

A Cynic philosopher, as described by Martial.

398. You often see him, Cosmus, in the recess of our Pallas and by the threshold of the New Temple, an old man with staff and wallet. His bristling hair is white and powdery, his unkempt beard falls on his chest, a threadbare cloak, spouse to his bare pallet, covers him, and the crowd that comes his way gives him the food he barks for. Deceived by fake appearance you take him for a Cynic. He is no Cynic, Cosmus. What then? A dog.
(Martial, *Epigrams* 4.53)

6.5. Philo

Philo (30 BCE–45 CE) was a well-educated Alexandrian Jewish philosopher, who was open to the current trends in Graeco-Roman philosophical thought. His work was preserved in Christian circles. His allegorical method of interpreting scripture was influential in the early church. His genius lay in forging a synthesis of Platonic, Stoic and Jewish thought.[13]

His work might be divided into the following broad categories—midrash (or contemporizing commentary on scripture), allegorical interpretation of scripture, treatises on various topics, and works with an apologetic thrust. In his allegorical interpretations of scripture he emphasized the superiority of the Mosaic law and the surpassing excellence of Israelite heroes, such as Abraham and Moses, who were able to guide the faithful into an ever-deepening relationship with God. In his apologetic works he emerges as a bold defender of Jewish rights against the depredations of anti-Jewish elements in Alexandria, writing *Flaccus* and *On the Embassy to Gaius* to further the Jewish cause.[14]

Philo's nephew, Tiberius Alexander, was procurator of Judaea in 46–48 and Prefect of Egypt at the time of the outbreak of the Jewish revolt in 66. He was an early supporter of Vespasian's quest for the principate. Tiberius Alexander is the only Roman governor of Judaea who, subsequent to holding that position, had a substantial career of which we know.

Sources

The following extract from his work *On the Creation* is a philosophical re-working of the biblical account of the Fall. The work was written as a preface to his exposition of the Mosaic law. He argues that the law of God is in harmony with the law of nature. There is evidence of Platonic influence in Philo. In this extract, for instance, Philo argues that God first created the pattern of the material world in his mind.

399. To speak of or conceive that world which consists of ideas as being in some place is illegitimate; how it consists (of them) we shall know if we carefully attend to some image supplied by the things of this world. When a city is being founded to satisfy the soaring ambition of some king or governor, who lays claim to despotic power and being magnificent in his ideas would fain add a fresh lustre to his good fortune, there comes forward now and again some trained architect who, observing the favourable climate and convenient position of the site, first sketches in his own mind wellnigh all the parts of the city that is to be wrought out, temples, gymnasia, town-halls, market-places, harbours, docks, streets, walls to be built, dwelling-houses as well as public buildings to be set up. Thus after having received in his own soul, as it were in wax, the figures of these objects severally, he carries about the image of a city which is the creation of his mind. Then by his innate power of memory, he recalls the images of the various parts of this city, and imprints their types yet more distinctly in it: and like a good craftsman he begins to build the city of stones and timber, keeping his eye upon his pattern and making the visible and tangible objects correspond in each case to the incorporeal ideas.

Just such must be our thoughts about God. We must suppose that, when He was minded to found the one great city, He conceived beforehand the models of its parts, and that out of these He constituted and brought to completion a world discernible only by the mind, and then, with that for a pattern, the world which our senses can perceive. As, then, the city which was fashioned beforehand within the mind of the architect held no place in the outer world, but had been engraved in the soul of the artificer as by a seal; even so the universe that consisted of ideas would have no other location than the Divine Reason, which was the Author of this ordered frame.
(Philo, *On the Creation* 17–20)[15]

In the following excerpt from the same work Philo characterizes man as 'mind' and woman as 'pleasure'.

400. Pleasure does not venture to bring her wiles and deceptions to bear on the man, but on the woman, and by her means on him. This is a telling and well-made point: for in us mind corresponds to man, the sense to woman; and pleasure encounters and holds parley with the senses first, and through them cheats with her quackeries the sovereign mind itself: for when each sense has been subjugated to her sorceries, delighting in what she proffers, the sense of sight in variegated colours and shapes, that of hearing in harmonious sounds, that of taste in delicate savours, and that of scent in the fragrance of perfumes which it inhales, then all of them receive the gifts and offer them like handmaids to the Reason as to a master, bringing with them Persuasion to plead that it reject nothing whatever. Reason is forthwith ensnared and becomes a subject instead of a ruler, a slave instead of a master, an alien instead of a citizen, and a mortal instead of an immortal. In a word we must never lose sight of the fact that Pleasure, being a courtesan and a wanton, eagerly desires to meet with a lover, and searches for panders, by whose means she shall get one on her hook. It is the senses that act as panders for her and procure the lover. When she has ensnared these she easily brings the Mind under her control. To it, dwelling within us, the senses convey the things seen without, reporting them fully and making them manifest, impressing on it the forms of the several objects, and producing in it the corresponding affection. For it resembles wax, and receives the images that reach it through the senses, by which it apprehends material substances, being incapable, as I have said before, of doing this by itself.
(Philo, *On the Creation* 165–66)

Philo and the logos.

In Greek philosophy *logos* referred to the inherent rationality and order of the universe. For Philo, the *logos* was the principle that enabled humankind to relate to God. He spoke of the *logos* as an intermediary between God and humankind.

401. To His Word [*logos*], His chief messenger, highest in age and honour, the Father of all

has given the special prerogative, to stand on the border and separate the creature from the Creator. This same Word both pleads with the immortal as suppliant for afflicted mortality and acts as ambassador of the ruler to the subject. He glories in this prerogative and proudly describes it in these words 'and I stood between the Lord and you' [Deuteronomy 5:5], that is neither uncreated as God, nor created as you, but midway between the two extremes, a surety to both sides; to the parent, pledging the creature that it should never altogether rebel against the rein and choose disorder rather than order; to the child, warranting his hopes that the merciful God will never forget His own work. For I am the harbinger of peace to creation from that God whose will is to bring wars to an end, who is ever the guardian of peace.
(Philo, *Who is the Heir?* 205–206)

The Gospel of John predicates the existence of another *logos*; also an intermediary, but one that became a human being.

402. (1) In the beginning was the Word [*logos*], and the Word was with God, and the Word was God. He was in the beginning with God. All things came into being through him, and without him not one thing came into being. What has come into being in him was life, and the life was the light of all people. The light shines in the darkness, and the darkness did not overcome it.

(14) And the Word became flesh and lived among us, and we have seen his glory, the glory as of a father's only son, full of grace and truth.
(John 1:1–5, 14)

Notes

1. By contrast Seneca saw the task of philosophers to be engaged with the world. See, e.g., *Epistles* 90.35. Note also Epictetus, *Discourses* 2.20. For the Epicureans and their communities, see Cicero, *About the Ends of Goods and Evils* 1.65.
2. See, e.g., Cicero, *On the Nature of the Gods* 1.93.
3. See Epicurus in section 21 of #370 and Lucretius in #373. The Essenes and the early Christians in Jerusalem also had a community focus in which the quest for acquiring material goods was renounced in favour of the sharing of resources (see #633–34, #681, #687). The early Christians also preached the dangers of the love of wealth (see 1 Timothy 6:10; Hebrews 13:5).
4. Note the similar ideas expressed in Paul's Areopagus speech in which he quotes the third-century BCE Stoic poet Aratus: 'In him we live and move and have our being' (Acts 17:28).
5. See also Marcus Aurelius, *Meditations* 7.30.
6. See also Seneca, *Epistles* 41.3–5.
7. Cf. 2 Peter 3:10.
8. Plato had taught that the changeable world of sense impressions was but a material representation of immaterial, unchangeable 'ideas'. These were perceived by the intellect alone. The highest of the ideas were the virtues such as truth, goodness and beauty. The mind, or reason, must continually assert its rule over the senses (and over pleasure).
9. Socrates (469–399 BCE) spent his time finding out what the pretentious knew, reducing their propositions and definitions to incoherence under his questioning.
10. For Epictetus's criticisms of the Academics, see his *Discourses* 1.5; 2.20.
11. In 1 Thessalonians 2:9 Paul deliberately contrasts the methods he adopted with those of the Cynics. He was not a bitter and harsh critic of his 'disciples'. Rather, he had been like a nurse among them. See Abraham J. Malherbe, '"Gentle as a Nurse": The Cynic Background to 1 Thessalonians 2', *NovT* 12 (1970), pp. 203–217.
12. See also *Discourses* 3.22.23–25.
13. An earlier (possibly second-century BCE) Jewish philosopher, Aristobulus, had also attempted this. Five fragments of his writings, all from Eusebius, can be accessed in *OTP* II, pp. 837–42.
14. See #588 for the citation of *On the Embassy to Gaius* 298–305.
15. Cf. Hebrews 8:1–2, 5; 9:23–24 in which it is argued that the tabernacle and its furnishings are but earthly copies of the realities in heaven. A Platonic influence has long been identified in Hebrews.

7. Graeco-Roman Society

Introduction

First-century CE Graeco-Roman society was organized on an emphatically hierarchical principle. At the pinnacle of the social ranking was the emperor, whose office had emerged out of the competition among the great generals of the preceding century. Next in the hierarchy was the senatorial class drawn from the landed aristocracy of Rome. To qualify as a senator one had to be wealthy, owning 100,000,000 sesterces in property. There were 600 senators. Mirroring the social hierarchy of Rome during the first century, there were local aristocracies, and, sometimes, regional monarchies, each with their own sets of allegiances and social compacts, but all bound to the emperor as supreme.

Originally the equites (or knights or equestrians) were landowners who could afford to go to battle on their own horses. By the time of the principate they were those members of the society who had not come to prominence in politics and the army but were wealthy businessmen, small landowners, craftsmen, shopkeepers, or served in the middle and lower ranks of the army. Many of the Christians mentioned in the New Testament appear to come from this social grouping.

The poor made up the lower ranks of society. They did not possess property, and worked when and where work was available. In Rome they were supported by the monthly grain dole. They could become clients to someone powerful. Freedmen were clients of their former masters.

Slaves possessed no status at all. There had always been those who, for economic reasons, had sold themselves into slavery. During Republican times their ranks had been swelled through capture in warfare. Yet many slaves took on important household and management tasks on behalf of their masters.

7.1. The Household

The household was the basic unit of society, and was a microcosm of the hierarchies operating in the wider society. The household included the immediate family and dependents of the householder, including, of course, his slaves. The householder assumed far-reaching powers and authority over the members of his household, and over his clients as their patron. There were persecutions of minority religions in Rome because the aristocratic guardians of Roman virtue and Roman identity feared the potential undermining of the hierarchy of the household, which, in turn, would spell the end of society as it was known.

Household management was the subject of philosophical discourse, and was the subject of much of Aristotle's treatise called the *Politics*. Extracts from book 1 of this work are included below. Social theory and household management are inseparable in this work. There was a universal acknowledgment that men were by nature fitted for dominance and rule in the household as husbands, fathers and masters. By contrast the members of the household over whom they exercised rule—wives, children and slaves—were regarded as inferior in nature, and duty bound to be submissive to the rule of their superior. Household codes survive which deal with the responsibilities of each of the partners in each of the three pairings of relationships in the household.

In Imperial times the emperor presided over a bureaucracy which was called the household of Caesar.[1] In addition aristocrats owed allegiance to the emperor, and oaths of allegiance were conducted bringing all members of society into a patron–client relationship with the emperor. In effect the whole empire was a macrocosm of the household. At every level of society the dominance of the male over the female, over children and over slaves was underscored.

Sources

The following extracts (#403–405) deal with Aristotle's views on the household. Note his acceptance of slavery as well as his conviction that free men are by nature fitted for rule over their dependents. His picture of the household remained the ideal, if not the reality, throughout the Hellenistic and Graeco-Roman eras.

403. And now that it is clear what are the component parts of the state, we have first of all to discuss household management; for every state is composed of households. Household management falls into departments corresponding to the parts of which the household in its turn is composed; and the household in its perfect form consists of slaves and freemen. The investigation of everything should begin with its smallest parts, and the primary and smallest parts of the household are master and slave, husband and wife, father and children; we ought therefore to examine the proper constitution and character of each of these three relationships, I mean that of mastership, that of marriage (there is no exact term denoting the relation uniting wife and husband), and thirdly the progenitive relationship (this too has not been designated by a special name). Let us then accept these three relationships that we have mentioned. There is also a department which some people consider the same as household management and others the most important part of it, and the true position of which we shall have to consider: I mean what is called the art of getting wealth.

Let us begin by discussing the relation of master and slave, in order to observe the facts that have a bearing on practical utility, and also in the hope that we may be able to obtain something better than the notions at present entertained, with a view to a theoretic knowledge of the subject. For some thinkers hold the function of the master to be a definite science, and moreover think that household management, mastership, statesmanship and monarchy are the same thing, as we said at the beginning of the treatise; others however maintain that for one man to be another man's master is contrary to nature, because it is only convention that makes the one a slave and the other a freeman and there is no difference between them by nature, and that therefore it is unjust for it is based on force. (Aristotle, *Politics* 1.2.1–3)

404. But to resume—it is in a living creature, as we say, that it is first possible to discern the rule both of master and of statesman: the soul rules the body with the sway of a master, the intelligence the appetites with constitutional or royal rule; and in these examples it is manifest that it is natural and expedient for the body to be governed by the soul and for the emotional part to be governed by the intellect, the part possessing reason, whereas for the two parties to be on an equal footing or in the contrary positions is harmful in all cases. Again, the same holds good between man and the other animals: tame animals are superior in their nature to wild animals, yet for all the former it is advantageous to be ruled by man, since this gives them security. Also, as between the sexes, the male is by nature superior and the female inferior, the male ruler and the female subject. And the same must also necessarily apply in the case of mankind generally; therefore all men that differ as widely as the soul does from the body and the human being from the lower animal (and this is the condition of those whose function is the use of the body and from whom this is the best that is forthcoming)—these are by nature slaves, for whom to be governed by this kind of authority is advantageous, inasmuch as it is advantageous to the subject things already mentioned. For he is by nature a slave who is capable of belonging to another (and that is why he does so belong), and who participates in reason so far as to apprehend it but not to possess it; for the animals other than man are subservient not to reason, by apprehending it, but to feelings. And also the usefulness of slaves diverges little from that of animals; bodily service for the necessities of life is forthcoming from both, from slaves and from domestic animals alike. The intention of nature therefore is to make the bodies also of freemen and of slaves different—the latter strong for necessary service, the former erect

and unserviceable for such occupations, but serviceable for a life of citizenship (and that again divides into the employments of war and those of peace); though as a matter of fact often the very opposite comes about—slaves have the bodies of freemen and freemen the souls only; since this is certainly clear, that if freemen were born as distinguished in body as are the statues of the gods, everyone would say that those who were inferior deserved to be these men's slaves; and if this is true in the case of the body, there is far juster reason for this rule being laid down in the case of the soul, but beauty of soul is not so easy to see as beauty of body. It is manifest therefore that there are cases of people of whom some are freemen and the others slaves by nature, and for these slavery is an institution both expedient and just.
(Aristotle, *Politics* 1.2.11–15)

405. Hence there are by nature various classes of rulers and ruled. For the free rules the slave, the male the female, and the man the child in a different way. And all possess the various parts of the soul, but possess them in different ways; for the slave has not got the deliberative part at all, and the female has it, but without full authority, while the child has it, but in an undeveloped form.
(Aristotle, *Politics* 1.5.6)

For the household in the New Testament, see #676.

Clients and patrons (#406–407).

Each householder had his clients for whom he was patron. Many clients were former slaves in the household. Clients were expected to offer service to their patron, perhaps in the form of military service, or voting for the patron, or representing his interests in other ways. The patron, for his part, was expected to further the career of his client. Juvenal makes it clear that, in his eyes, clients were treated more like slaves than partners with mutual obligations and responsibilities.

How clients are 'entertained'—Juvenal on the humiliation endured by clients.

Compare the anticipation of a return favour that is implied by the patron's beneficence with the words of Jesus recorded in Luke 14:12–14.

406. First of all be sure of this—that when bidden to dinner, you receive payment in full for all your past services. A meal is the return which your grand friendship yields you; the great man scores it against you, and though it comes but seldom, he scores it against you all the same. So if after a couple of months it is his pleasure to invite his forgotten client, lest the third place on the lowest couch should be unoccupied, and he says to you, 'Come and dine with me', you are in the seventh heaven! what more can you desire? Now at last has Trebius got the reward for which he must needs cut short his sleep, and hurry with shoe-strings untied, fearing that the whole crowd of callers may have gone their rounds at an hour when the stars are fading or when the chilly wain or Bootes is wheeling slowly round.

And what a dinner after all! You are given wine that fresh-clipped wool would refuse to suck up, and which soon converts your revellers into Corybants....

The great man himself drinks wine bottled in the days when Consuls wore long hair; the juice which he holds in his hand was squeezed during the Social Wars, but never a glass of it will he send to a friend suffering from dyspepsia!

The cup in Virro's hands is richly crusted with amber and rough with beryl: to you no gold is entrusted; or if it is, a watcher is posted over it to count the gems and keep an eye on your sharp finger-nails...

If my lord's stomach is fevered with food and wine, a decoction colder than Thracian hoar-frosts will be brought to him. Did I complain just now that you were given a different wine? Why, the water which you clients drink is not the same. Cups will be handed to you by a Gaetulian groom, or by the bony hand of a blackamoor whom you would rather not meet at midnight when driving past the monuments on the hilly Latin Way. Before mine host stands the very pink of Asia...
(Juvenal, *Satires* 5.12–56)

Deferential greetings to a patron in a papyrus letter (first/second century CE*) (provenance unknown).*

407. Herm…[to Sarapion]…greetings, and that you may always remain in good health in your whole person for long years to come, since your good genius allowed us to greet you with respect and salute you. For as you also make mention of us on each occasion by letter so I here make an act of worship for you in the presence of the lords Dioskouroi and in the presence of the lord Sarapis, and I pray for your safe-keeping during your entire life and for the health of your children and of all your household. Farewell in everything, I beg, my patron and fosterer. Greet all your folk, men and women. All the gods here, male and female, greet you. Farewell. Thoth 16th. (verso) To Sarapion, the lord. (*New Docs* I, p. 57)

7.2. Marriage

The Roman ideal was the once-married person, the *univira*. Even after being widowed it was common for widows to remain unmarried. 1 Timothy 3:2 mandates the requirement that potential presbyters should be husbands of one wife, thus reflecting the prevailing social ideal. Alarmed by falling birth rates, Augustus encouraged marriage as a stimulus to population increase.[2] According to the lex Papia Poppaea (note #409) every woman between the ages of 20 and 50 was required to be married. Claudius proposed to the Senate that free women were to be penalized if they married slaves (Tacitus, *Annals* 12.53). Legislation was passed prohibiting a woman taking a slave as a lover (Suetonius, *Vespasian* 11).

Marriage was seen as the only possible relationship in which legitimate children could be raised. The close guarding of women of marriageable age, especially in Greece, sought to protect the honour of her family. Subsequently, most woman were married at a very young age, soon after puberty. Consequently death rates among women in childbirth are extraordinarily high in Greek and Roman times.[3] Protection of the marriage on the part of husbands occurred as a matter of course lest the marriage and, therefore, family honour be compromized by adultery.[4]

Wives could inherit a maximum of 10% of her husband's estate. However, some women could become wealthy because they inherited their father's estate.

Sources

Old Roman feminine virtues.

408. Those who have written about the life and civilization of the Roman people say that the women of Rome and Latium 'lived an abstemious life'; that is, that they abstained altogether from wine, which in the early language was called *temetum*; that it was an established custom for them to kiss their kinsfolk for the purpose of detection, so that, if they had been drinking, the odour might betray them. But they say that the women were accustomed to drink the second brewing, raisin wine, spiced wine and other sweet-tasting drinks of that kind. And these things are indeed made known in those books which I have mentioned, but Marcus Cato declares that women were not only censured but also punished by a judge no less severely if they had drunk wine than if they had disgraced themselves by adultery.

I have copied Marcus Cato's words from the oration entitled *On the Dowry*, in which it is also stated that husbands had the right to kill wives taken in adultery: 'When a husband puts away his wife,' says he, 'he judges the woman as a censor would, and has full powers if she has been guilty of any wrong or shameful act; she is severely punished if she has drunk wine; if she has done wrong with another man, she is condemned to death.' Further, as to the right to put her to death it was thus written: 'If you should take your wife in adultery, you may with impunity put her to death without trial; but if you should commit adultery or indecency, she must not presume to lay a finger on you, nor does the law allow it.'
(Aulus Gellius, *Attic Nights* 10.23.
See also Tacitus's lament over the corrosion of old Roman virtues, which he saw as a legacy of the principate, at #73)

Augustus encouraged marriage as a stimulus to population increase. Dio Cassius comments on Augustus's decrees regarding marriage and social decorum.

409. Among the laws that Augustus enacted was one which provided that those who had bribed anyone in order to gain office should be debarred from office for five years. He laid heavier assessments upon the unmarried men and upon the women without husbands, and on the other hand offered prizes for marriage and the begetting of children. And since among the nobility there were far more males then females, he allowed all who wished, except the senators, to marry freedwomen, and ordered that their offspring should be held legitimate.

Meanwhile a clamor arose in the senate over the disorderly conduct of the women and of the young men, this being alleged as a reason for their reluctance to enter into the marriage relation; and when they urged him to remedy this abuse also, with ironical allusions to his own intimacy with many women, he at first replied that the most necessary restrictions had been laid down and that anything further could not possibly be regulated by decree in similar fashion. Then, when he was driven into a corner, he said: 'You yourselves ought to admonish and command your wives as you wish; that is what I do.' When they heard that, they plied him with questions all the more, wishing to learn what the admonitions were which he professed to give Livia. He accordingly, though with reluctance, made a few remarks about women's dress and their other adornment, about their going out and their modest behaviour, not in the least concerned that his actions did not lend credence to his words. Another instance of such inconsistency had occurred while he was censor. Some one brought before him a young man who had taken as his wife a married woman with whom he [the young man] had previously committed adultery, and made ever so many accusations against the man, and Augustus was at a loss what to do, not daring to overlook the affair nor yet to administer any rebuke. At length, though with difficulty, he recovered himself and said: 'Our fractious quarrels have borne many terrible fruits; let us, then, forget them and give our attention to the future, that nothing of the sort may occur again.' Inasmuch, too, as certain men were betrothing themselves to infant girls and thus enjoying the privileges granted to married men, but without rendering the service expected of them, he ordered that no betrothal should be valid if the man did not marry within two years of such betrothal,—that is, that the girl must in every case be at least ten years old at her betrothal if the man was to derive any advantages from it, since, as I have stated, girls are held to have reached the marriageable age on the completion of twelve full years.
(Dio Cassius, *Roman History* 54.16)[5]

A marriage contract from Egypt.

410. In the 22nd year of the reign of Ptolemy also called Alexander, the god Philometor, in the priesthood of the priest of Alexander and the rest as written in Alexandria, the 11th of the month Xandicus which is the 11th of Mecheir, at Kerkeosiris in the division of Polemon of the Arsinoite nome. Philiscus son of Apollonius, Persian of the Epigone, acknowledges to Apollonia, also called Kellauthis, daughter of Heraclides, Persian, with her guardian her brother Apollonius, that he has received from her in copper money 2 talents 4000 drachmae, the dowry for Apollonia agreed upon with him. Apollonia shall remain with Philiscus, obeying him as a wife should her husband, owning their property in common with him. Philiscus shall supply to Apollonia all necessaries and clothing and whatever is proper for a wedded wife, whether he is at home or abroad, so far as their property shall admit. It shall not be lawful for Philiscus to bring in any other wife but Apollonia, nor to keep a concubine or lover [*paidikos*: boy], nor to beget children by another woman in Apollonia's lifetime, nor to live in another house over which Apollonia is not mistress, nor to eject or insult or ill-treat her, nor to alienate any of their property to Apollonia's disadvantage. If he is shown to be doing any of these things or does not supply her with necessaries and clothing and the rest as has been said, Philiscus shall forfeit forthwith to

Apollonia the dowry of 2 talents 4000 drachmae of copper. In the same way it shall not be lawful for Apollonia to spend the night or day away from the house of Philiscus without Philiscus' consent or to have intercourse with another man or to ruin the common household or to bring shame upon Philiscus in anything that causes a husband shame. If Apollonia wishes of her own will to separate from Philiscus, Philiscus shall repay her the bare dowry within ten days from the day it is demanded back. If he does not repay it as has been stated he shall forthwith forfeit the dowry he has received increased by one half.
(P.Tebt 104 [92 BCE])

Divorce was common in Graeco-Roman times. It was possible, though not often attested, for a woman to divorce her husband.

Juvenal on divorce.

411. 'Why does Sertorius burn with love for Bibula?' If you shake out the truth, it is the face that he loves, not the wife. Let three wrinkles make their appearance; let her skin become dry and flabby; let her teeth turn black, and her eyes lose their lustre: then will his freedman give her the order, 'Pack up your traps and be off! you've become a nuisance; you are for ever blowing your nose; be off, and quick about it! There's another wife coming who will not sniffle'. But till that day comes, the lady rules the roast, asking her husband for shepherds and Canusian sheep, and elms for her Falernian vines. But that's a mere nothing: she asks for all his slave-boys, all his prison-gangs; everything that her neighbour possesses, and that she does not possess, must be bought. Then in the winter time, when the merchant Jason is shut out from view, and his armed sailors are blocked out by the white booths, she will carry off huge crystal vases, vases bigger still of agate, and finally a diamond of great renown, made precious by the finger of Berenice [sister of the Jewish ruler Agrippa II; see Acts 25:23]. It was given as a present long ago by the barbarian Agrippa to his incestuous sister, in that country where kings celebrate festal Sabbaths with bare feet [see Josephus, *Jewish War* 2.313–14], and where a long-established clemency suffers pigs to attain old age.
(Juvenal, *Satires* 6.142–60)[6]

Marriage and divorce in Judaism and Christianity (#412–21).

Josephus on Jewish marriage customs.

412. What are our marriage laws? The Law recognizes no sexual connexions, except the natural union of man and wife, and that only for the procreation of children. Sodomy it abhors, and punishes any guilty of such assault with death. It commands us, in taking a wife, not to be influenced by dowry, not to carry off a woman by force, nor yet to win her by guile and deceit, but to sue from him who is authorized to give her away the hand of one who is not ineligible on account of nearness of kin. The woman, says the Law, is in all things inferior to the man. Let her accordingly be submissive, not for her humiliation, but that she may be directed; for the authority has been given by God to the man. The husband must have union with his wife alone; it is impious to assault the wife of another. For any guilty of this crime the penalty of death is inexorable, whether he violates a virgin betrothed to another or seduces a married woman. The Law orders all the offspring to be brought up, and forbids women either to cause abortion or to make away with the foetus; a woman convicted of this is regarded as an infanticide, because she destroys a soul and diminishes the race. For the same reason none who has intercourse with a woman who is with child can be considered pure. Even after the legitimate relations of husband and wife ablutions are required. For the Law regards this act as involving a partition of the soul (part of it going) into another place; for it suffers both when being implanted in bodies, and again when severed from them by death. That is why the Law has enjoined purifications in all such cases.
(Josephus, *Against Apion* 2.199–203)

A Jewish marriage contract.

The following document belongs to the Babatha archive found in the Cave of the

Letters near Nahal Hever, a little inland from the western shore of the Dead Sea near Engedi. The cave was excavated in 1961 by Yigael Yadin. The contract is written in Greek, and dates from 5 April 128 CE. The contract was concluded between Shelamzion (Babatha's youthful step-daughter) and Judah Cimber. The bride was given into Cimber's hand by her father.[7]

413. In the consulship of Publius Metilius Nepos for the 2nd time and Marcus Annius Libo on the nones of April, and by the compute of the new province of Arabia year twenty-third on the fifteenth of month Xandikos, in Maoza, Zoara district, Judah son of Eleazar also known as Khthusion, gave over Shelamzion, his very own daughter, a virgin, to Judah surnamed Cimber son of Ananias son of Somalas, both of the village of Engedi in Judaea residing here, for Shelamzion to be a wedded wife to Judah Cimber for the partnership of marriage according to the laws, she bringing to him on account of bridal gift feminine adornment in silver and gold and clothing appraised by mutual agreement, as they both say, to be worth two hundred denarii of silver, which appraised value the bridegroom Judah called Cimber acknowledged that he has received from her by hand forthwith from Judah her father and that he owes to the said Shelamzion his wife together with another three hundred denarii which he promised to give to her in addition to the sum of the aforesaid bridal gift, all accounted toward her dowry, pursuant to his undertaking of feeding and clothing both her and the children to come in accordance with Greek custom upon the said Judah Cimber's good faith and peril and (the security of) all his possessions, both of those which he now possesses in his said home village and here and all those which he may in addition validly acquire everywhere, in whatever manner his wife Shelamzion may choose, or whoever acts through her or for her may choose, to carry out the execution. Judah called Cimber shall redeem this contract for his wife Shelamzion, whenever she may demand it of him, in silver secured in good form, at his own expense interposing no objection. If not, he shall pay to her all the aforestated denarii twofold, she having the right of execution, both from Judah Cimber her husband and upon the possessions validly his, in whatever manner Shelamzion or whoever acts through her or for her may choose to carry out the execution. In good faith the formal question was asked and it was acknowledged in reply that this is thus rightly done.
(Lewis [ed.], *Judean Desert Studies*, no. 18)

Paul on marriage.

Paul's views on marriage in 1 Corinthians 7 are significantly influenced by his conviction that the parousia (the re-appearance of Christ) is imminent. Nevertheless, as in the extract below, there is a far greater acknowledgment in Paul (especially in the letters indisputably by him) of the essential equality and mutual obligations and responsibilities of husband and wife.

414. Now concerning the matters about which you wrote: 'It is well for a man not to touch a woman.' But because of cases of sexual immorality, each man should have his own wife and each woman her own husband. The husband should give to his wife her conjugal rights, and likewise the wife to her husband. For the wife does not have authority over her own body, but the husband does; likewise the husband does not have authority over his own body, but the wife does.
(1 Corinthians 7:1–4. Cf. Jesus' high estimate of celibacy in Matthew 19:10–12)

A Jewish bill of divorce.

The following document emanates from Murabba'at, and dates to c. 111 CE.

415. On the first day [of the month] Marcheshvan, the sixth year, in Masada. By own decision I, Jehoseph bar Niqsan of [ ]h, resident of Masada, today release and dismiss you, Miriam, daughter of Jehonathan of Hanablata, resident of Masada, you who were formerly my wife, so that you have permission to go of your own free will and to

be married to any other Jewish man whom you wish to marry. For my part, I hereby present to you the certificate of dismissal. In addition, I give you the morning gift, and you are to be reimbursed for all your (goods) that have been damaged or destroyed, as is lawful, and I pay fourfold for them. And if you request, I will replace the written document, as long as I am still alive.
(Mur 19)

The following papyrus attests a reciprocal divorce, and is probably Jewish. The document dates from 10 March, 13 BCE. Sambathion, a variant of Sabbathaios (born on the Sabbath), is a common Jewish name in Egypt.

416. To Protarchos, from Apollonia daughter of Sambathion with her guardian, her mother's brother, Herakleides son of Herakleides, and from Hermogenes an Archistrateian. Apollonia and Hermogenes agree that they have dissolved their marriage by an agreement made through the same court in the 13th year of Caesar (Augustus) in the month Pharmouthi. Apollonia agrees that she has duly received back from Hermogenes the dowry of 60 drachmai which he had on her account from her parents Sambathion and Eirene according to the marriage-agreement. They agree therefore that the marriage-agreement is void, and that neither Apollonia nor anyone proceeding on her behalf will proceed against Hermogenes to recover the dowry, and that neither of them will proceed against the other on any matter arising from the marriage or from any other matter arising up to the present day, and that from this day it shall be lawful for Apollonia to marry another man and Hermogenes to marry another woman without penalty, and that whosoever transgresses this agreement shall be liable to the appointed penalty. The 17th year of Caesar (Augustus), Phamenoth 14.
(*CPJ* no. 144)

The writer of this document appeals to creation for the prohibition on divorce. Compare the teaching of Jesus in Mark 10:2–12 cited below (#420).

417. The 'builders of the wall' (Ezekiel 13:10) who have followed after 'Precept'...shall be caught in fornication twice by taking a second wife while the first is alive, whereas the principle of creation is, *Male and female created He them* (Genesis 1:27).
(Damascus Document 4.19–21)

Josephus divorces his wife.

418. At this period I divorced my wife, being displeased at her behaviour.
(Josephus, *Life* 426.
Cf. Deuteronomy 24:1)

Rabbinic comment on divorce.

419. R. Elazar said: If a man divorces his first wife, even the very altar sheds tears because of him.
(*Babylonian Talmud, Giṭṭin* 90b)

The New Testament on divorce.

420. Some Pharisees came, and to test him [Jesus] they asked, 'Is it lawful for a man to divorce his wife?' He answered them, 'What did Moses command you?' They said, 'Moses allowed a man to write a certificate of dismissal and to divorce her.' But Jesus said to them, 'Because of your hardness of heart he wrote this commandment for you. But from the beginning of creation, "God made them male and female" [Genesis 1:27]. "For this reason a man shall leave his father and mother and be joined to his wife, and the two shall become one flesh" [Genesis 2:24]. So they are no longer two, but one flesh. Therefore what God has joined together, let no one separate.'

Then in the house the disciples asked him again about this matter. He said to them, 'Whoever divorces his wife and marries another commits adultery against her; and if she divorces her husband and marries another, she commits adultery.'
(Mark 10:2–12.
Note Matthew 5:31–32; 19:3–9, in which Jesus allows for divorce in the case of 'unchastity' [cf. Deuteronomy 24:1–4])[8]

421. (10) To the married I give this command—not I but the Lord—that the wife should not separate from her husband (but if she does separate, let her remain unmarried or else be reconciled to her husband), and that the husband should not divorce his wife.

> To the rest I say—I and not the Lord—that if any believer has a wife who is an unbeliever, and she consents to live with him, he should not divorce her. And if any woman has a husband who is an unbeliever, and he consents to live with her, she should not divorce him... (15) But if the unbelieving partner separates, let it be so; in such a case the brother or sister is not bound. It is to peace that God has called you.
> (1 Corinthians 7:10–13, 15)

7.3. Attitudes to Women

While sexual intercourse within marriage was chiefly for the bearing of legitimate children, it was common for men to seek sexual release outside of marriage, thus perpetuating a double standard. There existed a class of women called *hetairai*, often of culture and sophistication, who also offered companionship (see #422 below).

The following extracts are illustrative of the regard in which male Graeco-Roman society held women. In her book *Goddesses, Whores, Wives, and Slaves*, Sarah Pomeroy has drawn attention to the fear of women and even misogyny that pervades the sources. The inferiority of women is assumed in Graeco-Roman society, and in Jewish and Christian sources as well. Marriage provided a framework for a husband to foster the potential of his wife to exist in a submissive and decorous context fully expressing the best side of her (inferior) nature. However, failure to rein in the passionate, promiscuous longings of women would dishonour the family and the marriage. Men believed that, given the chance, women would give full rein to the expression of their sexual powers. There is no shortage of indication in the sources that men held a morbid fear of the sexual potency of women and believed that they were capable of exercising a humiliating dominance over any man unable to exercise manly self-control.[9]

Sources

The following extract epigrammatically underscores the role of the wife, as well as the place for women as sharers with men in sexual intimacy and dalliance.

422. For this is what living with a woman as one's wife means—to have children by her and to introduce the sons to the members of the clan and of the deme, and to betroth the daughters to husbands as one's own. Mistresses [*hetairai*] we keep for the sake of pleasure, concubines for the daily care of our persons, but wives to bear us legitimate children and to be faithful guardians of our households.
(Demosthenes, *Against Neaera* 122)

Martial on the elusive equality of marriage partners.

423. You will ask why I don't want to marry a rich wife? I don't want to be my wife's wife. The matron, Priscus, should be below her husband. That's the only way man and woman can be equal.
(Martial, *Epigrams* 8.12)

Plutarch on wifely decorum (#424–26).

424. The lawful wives of the Persian kings sit beside them at dinner, and eat with them. But when the kings wish to be merry and get drunk, they send their wives away, and send for their music-girls and concubines. In so far they are right in what they do, because they do not concede any share in their licentiousness and debauchery to their wedded wives. If therefore a man in private life, who is incontinent and dissolute in regard to his pleasures, commit some peccadillo with a paramour or a maidservant, his wedded wife ought not to be indignant or angry, but she should reason that it is respect for her which leads him to share his debauchery, licentiousness, and wantonness with another woman.
(Plutarch, *Advice to Bride and Groom* 16)

425. Pheidias made the Aphrodite of the Eleans with one foot on a tortoise, to typify for womankind keeping at home and keeping silence. For a woman ought to do her talking either to her husband or through her husband, and she should not feel aggrieved if, like the flute-player, she makes a more impressive sound through a tongue not her own.
(Plutarch, *Advice to Bride and Groom* 32. Cf. 1 Corinthians 14:35–36; 1 Timothy 2:11)

426. [I]f they [women] subordinate themselves to their husbands, they are commended, but if they want to have control, they cut a sorrier figure than the subjects of their control. And control ought to be exercised by the man over the woman, not as the owner has control of a piece of property, but, as the soul controls the body, by entering into her feelings and being knit to her through goodwill. As, therefore, it is possible to exercise care over the body without being a slave to its pleasures and desires, so it is possible to govern a wife, and at the same time to delight and gratify her.
(Plutarch, *Advice to Bride and Groom* 33)

Juvenal's sixth satire is a bitter tirade against women—their power over men, their sexual rapacity, and their shrewishness (#427–31).

427. Why tell of love potions and incantations, of poisons brewed and administered to a stepson, or of the grosser crimes to which women are driven by the imperious power of sex? Their sins of lust are the least of all their sins.
(Juvenal, *Satires* 6.133–35)[10]

428. No sooner has that fellow departed than a palsied Jewess, leaving her basket and her truss of hay, comes begging to her secret ear; she is an interpreter of the laws of Jerusalem, a high priestess of the tree,* a trusty go-between of highest heaven. She, too, fills her palm, but more sparingly, for a Jew will tell you dreams of any kind you please for the minutest of coins.
(Juvenal, *Satires* 6.542–47.
* Note *Satires* 3.10–14 [#600])

429. And what think you of his searching for a wife of the good old virtuous sort? O doctors, lance his over-blooded veins. A pretty fellow you! Why, if you should have the good luck to find a modest spouse, you should prostrate yourself before the Tarpeian threshold, and sacrifice a heifer with gilded horns to Juno; so few are the wives worthy to handle the fillets of Ceres, or from whose kisses their own father would not shrink!
(Juvenal, *Satires* 6.45–51)

430. If you are not to love the woman betrothed and united to you in due form, what reason have you for marrying? Why waste the supper, and the wedding cakes to be given to the well-filled guests when the company is slipping away—to say nothing of the first night's gift of a salver rich with glittering gold inscribed with Dacian or Germanic victories? If you are honestly uxorious, and devoted to one woman, then bow your head and submit your neck ready to bear the yoke. Never will you find a woman who spares the man who loves her; for though she be herself aflame, she delights to torment and plunder him. So the better the man, the more desirable he be as a husband, the less good by far will he get out of his wife. No present will you ever make if your wife forbids; nothing will you ever sell if she objects; nothing will you buy without her consent. She will arrange your friendships for you; she will turn your now-aged friend from the door which saw the beginning of his beard. Panders and trainers can make their wills as they please, as also can the gentlemen of the arena; but you will have to write down among your heirs more than one rival of your own.

'Crucify that slave!' says the wife. 'But what crime worthy of death has he committed?' asks the husband; 'where are the witnesses? who informed against him? Give him a hearing at least; no delay can be too long when a man's life is at stake!' 'What, you numskull? You call a slave a man, do you? He has done no wrong, you say? Be it so; but this is my will and my command: let my will be the voucher for the deed'. Thus does she lord it over her husband. But before long she vacates her kingdom; she flits from one home to another, wearing out her bridal veil; then back she flies again and returns to her own imprints in the bed that she has abandoned, leaving behind her the newly decorated door, the festal hangings on the walls, and the branches green still over the threshold. Thus does the tale of her husbands grow; there will be eight of them in the course of five autumns—a fact worthy of commemoration on her tomb.
(Juvenal, *Satires* 6.200–30)

431. Give up all hope of peace so long as your mother-in-law is alive. It is she that teaches her daughter to revel in stripping and

despoiling her husband; it is she that teaches her to reply to a seducer's love-letters in no unskilled and innocent fashion; she eludes or bribes your guards; it is she that calls in Archigenes [trans. a fashionable doctor of the day] when your daughter has nothing the matter with her, and tosses about the heavy blankets; the lover meanwhile is in secret and silent hiding, trembling with impatience and expectation. Do you really expect the mother to teach her daughter honest ways—ways different from her own? Nay, the vile old woman finds a profit in bringing up her daughter to be vile.
(Juvenal, *Satires* 6.231–41)

Diogenes the Cynic is reported to have said the following:

432. Seeing some women hanged from an olive-tree, he said, 'Would that every tree bore similar fruit.'
(Diogenes Laertius, *Lives of Eminent Philosophers* 6.52)[11]

Early Jewish and Christian views of the promiscuity of women (#433–35).

433. 'For women are evil, my children, and by reason of their lacking authority or power over man, they scheme treacherously how they might entice him to themselves by mean of their looks. And whomever they cannot enchant by their appearance they conquer by a stratagem. Indeed, the angel of the Lord told me and instructed me that women are more easily overcome by the spirit of promiscuity than are men. They contrive in their hearts against men, then by decking themselves out they lead men's minds astray, by a look they implant their poison, and finally in the act itself they take them captive. For a woman is not able to coerce a man overtly, but by a harlot's manner she accomplishes her villainy. Accordingly, my children, flee from sexual promiscuity, and order your wives and your daughters not to adorn their heads and their appearances so as to deceive men's sound minds. For every woman who schemes in these ways is destined for eternal punishment. For it was thus that they charmed the Watchers, who were before the Flood. As they continued looking at the women, they were filled with desire for them and perpetrated the act in their minds. Then they were transformed into human males, and while the women were cohabiting with their husbands they appeared to them. Since the women's minds were filled with lust for these apparitions, they gave birth to giants. For the Watchers were disclosed to them as being as high as the heavens.'
(*Testament of Reuben* 5)

Genesis 3 records the temptation of Eve by the serpent to set aside the command of God with respect to not eating of the tree of the knowledge of good and evil. During the early Jewish era, there arose the view that Eve had been sexually seduced by the serpent.

434. The mother of the seven sons expressed also these principles to her children: 'I was a pure virgin and did not go outside my father's house; but I guarded the rib from which woman was made. No seducer corrupted me on a desert plain, nor did the destroyer, the deceitful serpent, defile the purity of my virginity.'
(*4 Maccabees* 18:6–8)

435. I desire, then, that in every place the men should pray, lifting up holy hands without anger or argument; also that the women should dress themselves modestly and decently in suitable clothing, not with their hair braided, or with gold, pearls, or expensive clothes, but with good works, as is proper for women who profess reverence for God. Let a woman learn in silence with full submission. I permit no woman to teach or to have authority over a man; she is to keep silent. For Adam was formed first, then Eve; and Adam was not deceived, but the woman was deceived and became a transgressor. Yet she will be saved through childbearing, provided they continue in faith and love and holiness, with modesty.
(1 Timothy 2:8–15)[12]

7.4. Sexuality

The moral assessment of sexual desire and activity in the Graeco-Roman world was perceived in terms quite different in the main from modern western society. Sexual activity was a mirror of power relationships in the wider society. The role of males as the natural penetrators of women, who were the penetrated inferiors in intercourse, reflected power relationships with women in the wider society.

Commonly in Greece, and less so in Rome, men indulged in sexual intimacy with younger men and boys. Such activity, as long as it occurred within certain well-defined parameters, was rarely condemned outside Jewish and Christian communities. It was justified, if ever justification was required, as an expression of a deep friendship. Ideally such activity was non-penetrative. By contrast, it was considered shameful for men to be sexually penetrated and for men to act the role of the woman in sexual contact. For a male to be sexually penetrated was to exchange one's manhood for femalehood, and, therefore, to be subject to disgrace and dishonour.

Sources

The pederasty of Tiberius.

Both Tacitus and Suetonius, who is the more explicit, narrate the aging Tiberius's predatory sexual perversions and the sexual violence perpetrated against children.

436. After landing frequently at neighbouring points and visiting the Gardens by the Tiber, he resorted once more to his rocks and the solicitude of the sea, in shame at the sins and lusts whose uncontrollable fires had so inflamed him that, in the kingly style, he polluted with his lecheries the children of free-born parents. Nor were beauty and physical charm his only incitements to lasciviousness, but sometimes a boyish modesty and sometimes a noble lineage. And now were coined the names, hitherto unknown, of *sellarii* and *spintriae*, one drawn from the obscenity of a place, one from the versatility of the pathic; while slaves, commissioned to seek and fetch, plied the willing with gratuities, the reluctant with threats, and, if a kinsman or parent refused compliance, resorted to force, abduction, and the slaking of their own desires as if in a captured city.
(Tacitus, *Annals* 6.1.[13]
See also Suetonius, *Tiberius* 43–44)

The activity of Philaenis is triply shameful. She, who, in Graeco-Roman sexual terms, should be the one penetrated, is in fact the active partner in penetrating boys. Moreover, she assumes the role of a man in penetrating girls.

437. Lesbian Philaenis sodomizes boys and, more cruel than a husband's lust, penetrates eleven girls per diem…
(Martial, *Epigrams* 7.67)

Diogenes the Cynic on effeminacy.

438. Seeing a young man behaving effeminately, 'Are you not ashamed,' he said, 'that your own intention about yourself should be worse than nature's: for nature made you a man, but you are forcing yourself to play the woman.'
(Diogenes Laertius, *Lives of Eminent Philosophers* 6.65)

The New Testament on sexual immorality (#439–40).

Unlike the majority of their Graeco-Roman neighbours, early Jews and Christians subscribed to a higher sexual ethic in which men, not just women, were expected to refrain from pre-marital sexual activity and to remain exclusively monogamous.

439. For you know what instructions we gave you through the Lord Jesus. For this is the will of God, your sanctification: that you abstain from fornication; that each one of you know how to control your own body in holiness and honor, not with lustful passion, like the Gentiles who do not know God; that no one wrong or exploit a brother or sister in this matter, because the Lord is an avenger in all these things, just as we have already told you beforehand and solemnly warned you. For God did not call us to impurity but in holiness.
(1 Thessalonians 4:2–7)

440. Shun fornication! Every sin that a person

commits is outside the body; but the fornicator sins against the body itself.
(1 Corinthians 6:18.
Cf. Hebrews 13:4)

Jewish and Christian attitudes to homosexuality (#441–44).

Jewish and Christian writers regarded homosexuality as a perversion of natural custom. This was affirmed in the Hebrew and Greek Bible (see Leviticus 18:22; 20:13).

441. Much graver than the above [i.e. indulging in sexual intercourse without the intention to procreate] is another evil, which has ramped its way into the cities, namely pederasty. In former days the very mention of it was a great disgrace, but now it is a matter of boasting not only to the active but to the passive partners who habituate themselves to endure the disease of effemination, let both body and soul run to waste, and leave no ember of their male sex-nature to smoulder.
(Philo, *Special Laws* 3.37)

442. [I]t was not enough for them to err about the knowledge of God,
but though living in great strife due to ignorance,
they call such great evils peace.
For whether they kill children in their initiations, or celebrate secret mysteries,
or hold frenzied revels with strange customs,
they no longer keep either their lives or their marriages pure,
but they either treacherously kill one another, or grieve one another by adultery,
and all is a raging riot of blood and murder, theft and deceit, corruption, faithlessness, tumult, perjury,
confusion over what is good, forgetfulness of favors,
defiling of souls, sexual perversion,
disorder in marriages, adultery, and debauchery.
For the worship of idols not to be named
is the beginning and cause and end of every evil.
(Wisdom of Solomon 14:22–27)

443. Therefore God gave them up in the lusts of their hearts to impurity, to the degrading of their bodies among themselves, because they exchanged the truth about God for a lie and worshiped and served the creature rather than the Creator, who is blessed forever! Amen.

For this reason God gave them up to degrading passions. Their women exchanged natural intercourse for unnatural, and in the same way also the men, giving up natural intercourse with women, were consumed with passion for one another. Men committed shameless acts with men and received in their own persons the due penalty for their error.
(Romans 1:24–27)[14]

An aspect of the Way of Light according to the Epistle of Barnabas.

444. Thou shalt not commit fornication, thou shalt not commit adultery, thou shalt not commit sodomy.
(*Epistle of Barnabas* 19:4)

7.5. Slavery

Slavery was ubiquitous in the ancient world. Slaves worked in their thousands on construction, mining, roads and farms. Some wealthy landowners had 2000 slaves. One could become a slave through ruinous financial dealings (see, e.g., Matthew 18:23–35), capture by slave traders, capture in war, or being found guilty in criminal proceedings. Manumission by a Roman citizen brought citizenship to the former slave; their former masters now serving as their patrons.[15] But freedmen were still regarded as socially inferior.[16] In Graeco-Roman times the centre of the slave trade was Delos. Ten thousand slaves could be processed in a day.

Slaves lacked recourse to the usual rights enjoyed by the free population. For instance, slaves were routinely tortured when their masters were accused of crimes. When Germanicus died suddenly, it was widely reported that he had been poisoned. Piso, charged with a range of offences, was suspected. As was routine in judicial investigations, the slaves of the accused man were tortured (Tacitus, *Annals* 3.14).

A venerable tradition affirmed in the philosophical tradition considered slaves as 'less than human', pieces of property.[17] Plato and Aristotle argued that only the independent person was able to devote himself to acquiring virtue.[18] Without self-sufficiency, they claimed, one is dependent on others, that is, on their patronage. The free man, and he alone, was in a position to live the virtuous life.

Close and valued friendships could grow between master and slave (see the epitaph at #573 below). Cicero is surprised by his grief for a slave, his reader Sositheus, who had recently died (*Letters to Atticus* 1.12). However, according to Philo, the Essenes denounced owners of slaves 'for annulling the statutes of man' (see #634). Seneca was also offended by slavery. There are no extant calls from Christians for the freeing of slaves, though Paul certainly hoped that Philemon would not punish his runaway slave Onesimus, but rather receive him as the brother in Christ he now was (see Philemon 15–21). Indeed, Paul counselled slaves not to seek their freedom in the light of the imminence of the parousia (1 Corinthians 7:21–24).

Sources

Sale of a slave-girl (259 BCE).[19]

445. In the 27th year of the reign of Ptolemy, son of Ptolemy, and of his son Ptolemy, the priest of Alexander and of the gods Adelphoi and the kanephorus of Arsinoe Philadelphos being those in office in Alexandria, in the month Xandikos, at Birta of the Ammanitis. Nikanor son of Xenokles, Knidian, in the service of Toubias, sold to Zenon son of Agreophon, Kaunian, in the service of Apollonios the dioiketes, a Sidonian girl named Sphragis, about seven years of age, for fifty drachmai. Guarantor...son of Ananias, Persian, of the troop of Toubias, kleruch...
(*CPJ* no. 1)

Hannibal's enslavement of the population of Saguntum.

446. At length after eight months of hardship and anxiety he took the city by storm. A great booty of money, slaves, and property fell into his hands. The money, as he had determined, he set aside for his own purposes, the slaves he distributed among his men according to rank, and the miscellaneous property he sent off at once to Carthage.
(Polybius, *Histories* 3.17.9–10)[20]

Cato the Elder's treatment of slaves.

447. (1) I regard his treatment of his slaves like beasts of burden, using them to the uttermost, and then, when they were old, driving them off and selling them, as the mark of a very mean nature, which recognizes no tie between man and man but that of necessity. And yet we know that kindness has a wider scope than justice. Law and justice we naturally apply to men alone; but when it comes to beneficence and charity, these often flow in streams from the gentle heart, like water from a copious spring, even down to dumb beasts. A kindly man will take good care of his horses even when they are worn out with age, and of his dogs, too, not only in their puppyhood, but when their old age needs nursing.

(5) We should not treat living creatures like shoes or pots and pans, casting them aside when they are bruised and worn out with service, but, if for no other reason, for the sake of practice in kindness to our fellow men, we should accustom ourselves to mildness and gentleness in our dealings with other creatures. I certainly would not sell even an ox that had worked for me, just because he was old, much less an elderly man, removing him from his habitual place and customary life, as it were from his native land, for a paltry price, useless as he is to those who sell him and as he will be to those who buy him.
(Plutarch, *Marcus Cato* 5.1–2, 5)

Appian relates the death of some of those who had assassinated Caesar.

448. About the same time Minucius Basilus, another of Caesar's murderers, was killed by his slaves, some of whom he was mutilating by way of punishment.
(Appian, *Civil Wars* 3.98)[21]

Claudius frees abandoned slaves.

449. When certain men were exposing their sick and worn out slaves on the Island of Aesculapius [in the Tiber] because of the trouble of treating them, Claudius decreed that all such slaves were free, and that if they recovered, they should not return to the control of their master; but if anyone preferred to kill such a slave rather than to abandon him, he was liable to the charge of murder.
(Suetonius, *Claudius* 25.2)

Freedom brings vulnerability.

450. 'If I am set free,' he [the slave] says, 'immediately it is all happiness, I shall pay no attention to anybody, I talk to everybody as an equal and as one in the same situation in life, I go where I please, I come whence I please, and where I please.' Then he is emancipated, and forthwith, having no place to which to go and eat, he looks for someone to flatter, for someone at whose house to dine. Next he either earns a living by prostitution, and so endures the most dreadful things, and if he gets a manger at which to eat he has fallen into a slavery much more severe than the first; or even if he grows rich, being a vulgarian he has fallen in love with a chit of a girl, and is miserable, and laments, and yearns for his slavery again. 'Why, what was wrong with me? Someone else kept me in clothes, and shoes, and supplied me with food, and nursed me when I was sick; I served him in only a few matters. But now, miserable man that I am, what suffering is mine, who am a slave to several instead of one!'
(Epictetus, *Discourses* 4.1.34–37)

Crucifixion of a runaway slave.

451. A deception, which had a lively success at first, prevailed for only a few days. A man appeared who gave himself out as Scribonianus Camerinus, alleging that he had remained concealed in Istria during Nero's reign, for there the ancient Crassi still possessed clients, lands, and popularity. He accordingly associated with himself, to develop this comedy, a company made up of the dregs of mankind; the credulous common people and some of the soldiers, either deceived by the falsehood or led on by a desire for trouble, were rapidly rallying about him, when he was dragged before Vitellius and questioned as to his identity. No faith was put in his answers; and after he had been recognized by his master as a runaway slave, Geta by name, he suffered the punishment usually inflicted upon slaves.
(Tacitus, *Histories* 2.72.
See also 4.3, 11)

Seneca's view of slaves.

452. (1) I am glad to learn, through those who come from you, that you live on friendly terms with your slaves. This befits a sensible and well-educated man like yourself. 'They are slaves,' people declare. Nay, rather they are men. 'Slaves!' No, comrades. 'Slaves!' No, they are unpretentious friends. 'Slaves!' No, they are our fellow-slaves, if one reflects that Fortune has equal rights over slaves and free men alike...

(5) [W]e maltreat them, not as if they were men, but as if they were beasts of burden. When we recline at a banquet, one slave mops up the disgorged food, another crouches beneath the table and gathers up the left-overs of the tipsy guests. Another carves the priceless game birds; with unerring strokes and skilled hand he cuts choice morsels along the breast or the rump. Hapless fellow, to live only for the purpose of cutting fat capons correctly,—unless, indeed, the other man is still more unhappy than he, who teaches this art for pleasure's sake, rather than he who learns it because he must. Another, who serves the wine, must dress like a woman and wrestle with his advancing years; he cannot get away from his boyhood; he is dragged back to it; and though he has already acquired a soldier's figure, he is kept beardless by having his hair smoothed away or plucked out by the roots, and he must remain awake throughout the night, dividing his time between his master's drunkenness and his lust; in the chamber he must be a man, at the feast a boy. Another, whose duty it is to put a valuation on the guests, must stick to his task, poor fellow, and watch to see whose flattery and whose

immodesty, whether of appetite or of language, is to get them an invitation for to-morrow. Think also of the poor purveyors of food, who note their masters' tastes with delicate skill, who know what special flavours will sharpen their appetite, what will please their eyes, what new combinations will rouse their cloyed stomachs, what food will excite their loathing through sheer satiety, and what will stir them to hunger on that particular day. With slaves like these the master cannot bear to dine; he would think it beneath his dignity to associate with his slave at the same table! Heaven forfend!

(10) Kindly remember that he whom you call your slave sprang from the same stock, is smiled upon by the same skies, and on equal terms with yourself breathes, lives, and dies. It is just as possible for you to see in him a free-born man as for him to see in you a slave. As a result of the massacres in Marius's day, many a man of distinguished birth, who was taking the first steps toward senatorial rank by service in the army, was humbled by fortune, one becoming a shepherd, another a caretaker of a country cottage. Despise, then, if you dare, those to whose estate you may at any time descend, even when you are despising them.

I do not wish to involve myself in too large a question, and to discuss the treatment of slaves, towards whom we Romans are excessively haughty, cruel, and insulting. But this is the kernel of my advice: Treat your inferiors as you would be treated by your betters. And as often as you reflect how much power you have over a slave, remember that your master has just as much power over you. 'But I have no master,' you say. You are still young; perhaps you will have one. Do you not know at what age Hecuba entered captivity, or Croesus, or the mother of Darius, or Plato, or Diogenes?

Associate with your slave on kindly, even on affable, terms; let him talk with you, plan with you, live with you. I know that at this point all the exquisites will cry out against me in a body; they will say: 'There is nothing more debasing, more disgraceful, than this.' But these are the very persons whom I sometimes surprise kissing the hands of other men's slaves. Do you not see even this,—how our ancestors removed from masters everything invidious, and from slaves everything insulting? They called the master 'father of the household,' and the slaves 'members of the household,' a custom which still holds in the mime. They established a holiday on which masters and slaves should eat together,—not as the only day for this custom, but as obligatory on that day in any case. They allowed the slaves to attain honours in the household and to pronounce judgement; they held that a household was a miniature commonwealth.
(Seneca, *Epistles* 47.1, 5–8, 10–14)

The legislation of Hadrian.

453. [Hadrian] forbade masters to kill their slaves, and ordered that any who deserved it should be sentenced by the courts. He forbade anyone to sell a slave or a maid-servant to a procurer or trainer of gladiators without giving a reason therefor… Houses of hard labour for slaves and free he abolished… He issued an order that, if a slave-owner were murdered in his house, no slaves should be examined save those who were near enough to have had knowledge of the murder.
(*Scriptores Historiae Augustae, Life of Hadrian* 18.7–11)

Epictetus was a former slave. Here is his view on the treatment of slaves; a view imbued with the Stoic sensibility regarding the kinship of slave and free.

454. Now when someone asked him [Epictetus] how it was possible to eat acceptably to the gods, he said, If it is done justly and graciously and fairly and restrainedly and decently, is it not also done acceptably to the gods? And when you have asked for warm water and the slave does not heed you; or if he does heed you but brings in tepid water; or if he is not even to be found in the house, then to refrain from anger and not to explode, is not this acceptable to the gods?—How, then, can a man bear with such persons?—Slave, will you not bear with your own brother, who has Zeus as his progenitor and is, as it were, a son born of the same seed as yourself and of the same

sowing from above; but if you have been stationed in a like position above others, will you forthwith set yourself up as a tyrant? Do you not remember what you are, and over whom you rule—that they are kinsmen, that they are brothers by nature, that they are the offspring of Zeus?—But I have a deed of sale for them, and they have none for me.—Do you see whither you bend your gaze, that it is to the earth, that it is to the pit, that it is to these wretched laws of ours, the laws of the dead, and that it is not to the laws of the gods that you look?
(Epictetus, *Discourses* 1.13)

Martial on slavery.

455. You sold a slave yesterday for twelve hundred sesterces, Calliodorus, in order to dine well just once. But well you did not dine. The chief item of the dinner, the pièce de resistance, was a four-pound mullet you had bought. One feels like crying aloud: 'This is no fish, greedy, no, it's a man: Calliodorus, you are a cannibal.'
(Martial, *Epigrams* 10.31)

God and slaves.

456. R. Judah b. Shalom said: If a poor man comes, and pleads before another, that other does not listen to him; if a rich man comes, he listens to, and receives, him at once: God does not act thus: all are equal before Him, women, slaves, rich and poor.
(*Exodus Rabbah*, Beshallaḥ 21.4)[22]

A Christian view on slavery.

457. Let all who are under the yoke of slavery regard their masters as worthy of all honor, so that the name of God and the teaching may not be blasphemed. Those who have believing masters must not be disrespectful to them on the ground that they are members of the church; rather they must serve them all the more, since those who benefit by their service are believers and beloved.
(1 Timothy 6:1–2.
Cf. 1 Corinthians 7:21–24 [in which the nearness of the parousia is the crucial element for Paul]; Ephesians 6:5–9 [see #677])

7.6. Education and Rhetoric

Hellenistic and Graeco-Roman societies were essentially cultures of the spoken word. If one aspired to a role in public life, what mattered was being able to speak effectively, i.e. persuasively, in public. Rhetoric was the means by which all momentous political and judicial decisions were reached.[23] Thus speakers in the assemblies and law courts of the Greek and Roman world were able to determine events of immense weight and significance. The rhetorical theorist Quintilian offered this succinct definition of rhetoric: '[I]f rhetoric is the science of speaking well, its end and highest aim is to speak well'.[24]

Attainment in the craft of rhetoric was considered the highest educational achievement. Training by a rhetor occupied a position at the apex of the Graeco-Roman educational curriculum. Such training could only be afforded by the elite. Moreover, the influence of rhetoric over the earlier stages in the educational process was pervasive. Being able to write well, especially in Roman times, was a laudable aim of youth but being able to speak well was even more highly prized.[25]

Rhetoric as a consciously developed craft first came to the attention of the Greeks in the fifth century with the activity of the Sophists. Their talk was largely dismissed by the philosophers, Socrates and Plato, on the grounds that sophistic oratory was primarily concerned not with truth but with wit and persuasion. Isocrates, however, believed that rhetoric was a craft by which virtuous men could powerfully influence society for the better. Aristotle wrote a highly influential handbook on oratory. It was followed by others, several of which are extant. The techniques and conventions of oratory changed little over the Greek and Roman eras. We can rightly speak of a single rhetorical tradition spanning the late Classical, Hellenistic, Graeco-Roman and late Roman eras.

The literary output of the Greeks and Romans was heavily influenced by rhetoric. Most genres bear the evidence of the craft. History and biography, for example, both have explicit didactic purposes, not least of these being the affirmation by logical argument and appeal to role models of conventional ethical standards. Indeed, Graeco-Roman biography seeks to engender respect for and imitation of the accepted virtues by relating the deeds and achievements of the worthy—be they generals, founders of constitutions or respected philosophers. Rhetoric thus served as a force for the preservation of all that was valued among the Greeks and among the Romans and their subordinated allies.

In the primary stage of education Greek and Roman children learnt their letters. Schools used anthologies of Classical and Hellenistic writings, thus promoting a sense of a shared culture throughout the Graeco-Roman world. In the secondary stage, schools emphasized physical activity, letter writing, simple declamation, and the art of writing character pieces (*prosopopeia*). At the tertiary level the elite were taught by a rhetor.

Public lectures by teachers of rhetoric gave the general population a sense of the standards by which to assess oratorical performance.[26] Paul was aware that he was the subject of invidious comparisons with those more rhetorically effective (2 Corinthians 10:12). He himself could use the conventions of rhetoric (2 Corinthians 11–12), though he claims that he is a 'layman' as far as rhetoric is concerned (see 2 Corinthians 11:6).

Sources

The paedagogus.

458. As regards the boys in whose company our budding orator is to be brought up, I would repeat what I have said about nurses. As regards his paedagogi, I would urge that they should have had a thorough education, or if they have not, that they should be aware of the fact. There are none worse than those, who as soon as they have progressed beyond a knowledge of the alphabet delude themselves into the belief that they are the possessors of real knowledge. For they disdain to stoop to the drudgery of teaching, and conceiving that they have acquired a certain title to authority—a frequent source of vanity in such persons—become imperious or even brutal in instilling a thorough dose of their own folly. Their conduct is not less prejudicial to morals. We are, for instance, told by Diogenes of Babylon, that Leonides, Alexander's paedagogus, infected his pupil with certain faults, which as a result of his education as a boy clung to him even in his maturer years when he had become the greatest of kings.
(Quintilian, *Institutio Oratoria* 1.1.8–9)[27]

In Quintilian's presentation, the youth, having learnt to read and write, moved on to the second stage of education under a teacher of literature (*grammateus*). The third stage in his education was at the hands of the rhetor in whose care the student learned to declaim and to compose speeches. The young man was thus prepared for a career as a public speaker and ideally equipped to function as a statesman (*Institutio Oratoria* 12.1.26). Part of the education curriculum at this level were declamatory exercises, which were termed *controversiae* (in the case of the context of the law court) and *suasoriae* (in the case of the context of the assembly). Some examples from the Elder Seneca follow. In each a situation for ensuing debate is presented.

Controversiae

459. A man with a beautiful wife went off abroad. A foreign trader moved into the woman's neighbourhood. He three times made her propositions of a sexual nature, offering sums of money. She said no. The trader died, leaving her all his wealth in his will, to which he added the clause: 'I found her chaste.' She took the bequest. Then husband returned and accuses her of adultery on suspicion.
(Seneca the Elder, *Controversiae* 2.7)

460. (1.3) An unchaste woman shall be thrown from the rock.

A woman condemned for unchastity appealed to Vesta before being thrown from the rock. She was thrown down and survived. She is sought to pay the penalty again.

[Note the following epigrammatic insertions on this *controversia* both emanating from the rhetorician Fulvius Sparsus].

(1.3.3) (Against the woman)
Thrown down by the gods above, rejected by the gods below: for *her* penalty one would have to construct a special rock.

(1.3.7) (For the woman)
Condemned, she was cast down; acquitted, she descended.
(Seneca the Elder, *Controversiae* 1.3)

Suasoriae

461. The three hundred Spartans sent against Xerxes deliberate whether they too should retreat following the fight of the contingents of three hundred sent from all over Greece.
(Seneca the Elder, *Suasoriae* 2.1)

462. Antony promises to spare Cicero's life if he burns his writings: Cicero deliberates whether to do so.
(Seneca the Elder, *Suasoriae* 7.1)

Josephus on Jewish education.

463. Again the Law does not allow the birth of our children to be made occasions for festivity and an excuse for drinking to excess. It enjoins sobriety in their upbringing from the very first. It orders that they shall be taught to read, and shall learn both the laws and the deeds of their forefathers, in order that they may imitate the latter, and, being grounded in the former, may neither transgress nor have any excuse for being ignorant of them.
(Josephus, *Against Apion* 2.204)

Aristotle on rhetoric.

464. Rhetoric then may be defined as the faculty of discovering the possible means of persuasion in reference to any subject whatever. This is the function of no other of the arts, each of which is able to instruct and persuade in its own special subject; thus, medicine deals with health and sickness, geometry with the properties of magnitudes, arithmetic with number, and similarly with all the other arts and sciences. But Rhetoric, so to say, appears to be able to discover the means of persuasion in reference to any given subject. That is why we say that as an art its rules are not applied to any particular definite class of things.

As for proofs, some are inartificial, others artificial. By the former I understand all those which have not been furnished by ourselves but were already in existence, such as witnesses, tortures, contracts, and the like; by the latter, all that can be constructed by system and by our own efforts. Thus we have only to make use of the former, whereas we must invent the latter.

Now the proofs furnished by the speech are of three kinds. The first depends upon the moral character of the speaker, the second upon putting the hearer into a certain frame of mind, the third upon the speech itself, in so far as it proves or seems to prove.

The orator persuades by moral character when his speech is delivered in such a manner as to render him worthy of confidence; for we feel confidence in a greater degree and more readily in persons of worth in regard to everything in general, but where there is no certainty and there is room for doubt, our confidence is absolute. But this confidence must be due to the speech itself, not to any preconceived idea of the speaker's character; for it is not the case, as some writers of rhetorical treatises lay down in their 'Art,' that the worth of the orator in no way contributes to his powers of persuasion; on the contrary, moral character, so to say, constitutes the most effective means of proof. The orator persuades by means of his hearers, when they are roused to emotion by his speech; for the judgements we deliver are not the same when we are influenced by joy or sorrow, love or hate; and it is to this alone that, as we have said, the present-day writers of treatises endeavour to devote their attention... Lastly, persuasion is produced by the speech itself, when we establish the true or apparently true from the means of persuasion applicable to each individual subject.
(Aristotle, *Art of Rhetoric* 1.2.1–6)

Training in oratory was the pinnacle of a man's preparation for life in civilized society.

465. (9) My aim, then, is the education of the perfect orator. The first essential for such an

one is that he should be a good man, and consequently we demand of him not merely the possession of exceptional gifts of speech, but of all the excellences of character as well. For I will not admit that the principles of upright and honourable living should, as some have held, be regarded as the peculiar concern of philosophy. The man who can really play his part as a citizen and is capable of meeting the demands both of public and private business, the man who can guide a state by his counsels, give it a firm basis by his legislation and purge its vices by his decisions as a judge, is assuredly no other than the orator of our quest. Wherefore, although I admit I shall make use of certain of the principles laid down in philosophical textbooks, I would insist that such principles have a just claim to form part of the subject-matter of this work and do actually belong to the art of oratory. I shall frequently be compelled to speak of such virtues as courage, justice, self-control; in fact scarcely a case comes up in which some one of these virtues is not involved; every one of them requires illustration and consequently makes a demand on the imagination and eloquence of the pleader. I ask you [the dedicatee: Marcellus Victorius] then, can there be any doubt that, wherever imaginative power and amplitude of diction are required, the orator has a specially important part to play? These two branches of knowledge were, as Cicero has clearly shown, so closely united, not merely in theory but in practice, that the same men were regarded as uniting the qualifications of orator and philosopher. Subsequently this single branch of study split into its component parts, and thanks to the indolence of its professors was regarded as consisting of several distinct subjects. As soon as speaking became a means of livelihood and the practice of making an evil use of the blessings of eloquence came into vogue, those who had a reputation for eloquence ceased to study moral philosophy, and ethics, thus abandoned by the orators, became the prey of weaker intellects.

(18) Let our ideal orator then be such as to have a genuine title to the name of philosopher: it is not sufficient that he should be blameless in point of character (for I cannot agree with those who hold this opinion): he must also be a thorough master of the science and the art of speaking, to an extent that perhaps no orator has yet attained. Still we must none the less follow the ideal, as was done by not a few of the ancients, who, though they refused to admit that the perfect sage had yet been found, none the less handed down precepts of wisdom for the use of posterity. Perfect eloquence is assuredly a reality, which is not beyond the reach of human intellect. Even if we fail to reach it, those whose aspirations are highest, will attain to greater heights than those who abandon themselves to premature despair of ever reaching the goal and halt at the very foot of the ascent.

(Quintilian, *Institutio Oratoria* Preface 9–14, 18–20)

The kinds, or 'species', of rhetoric.

466. The kinds of rhetoric are three in number, corresponding to the three kinds of hearers. For every speech is composed of three parts: the speaker, the subject of which he treats, and the person to whom it is addressed, I mean the hearer, to whom the end or object of the speech refers. Now the hearer must necessarily be either a mere spectator or a judge, and a judge either of things past or of things to come. For instance, a member of the general assembly is a judge of things to come; the dicast, of things past; the mere spectator, of the ability of the speaker. Therefore there are necessarily three kinds of rhetorical speeches, deliberative, forensic, and epideictic.

The deliberative kind is either hortatory or dissuasive; for both those who give advice in private and those who speak in the assembly invariably either exhort or dissuade. The forensic kind is either accusatory or defensive; for litigants must necessarily either accuse or defend. The epideictic kind has for its subject praise or blame.

Further, to each of these a special time is appropriate: to the deliberative the future, for the speaker, whether he exhorts or dissuades, always advises about things to come; to the forensic the past, for it is always in reference to things done that one party accuses and the other defends; to the epideictic most appropriately the present, for it is the existing condition of things that all those who praise or blame have in view. It is not uncommon, however, for epideictic speakers to avail themselves of other times, of the past by way of recalling it, or of the future by way of anticipating it.

Each of the three kinds has a different special end, and as there are three kinds of Rhetoric, so there are three special ends. The end of the deliberative speaker is the expedient or harmful; for he who exhorts recommends a course of action as better, and he who dissuades advises against it as worse; all other considerations, such as justice and injustice, honour and disgrace, are included as accessory in reference to this. The end of the forensic speaker is the just or the unjust; in this case also all other considerations are included as accessory. The end of those who praise or blame is the honourable and disgraceful; and they also refer all other considerations to these.

(Aristotle, *Art of Rhetoric* 1.3.1–5)

The characteristics of panegyric or epideictic oratory.

467. This form of oratory is directed in the main to the praise of gods and men, but may occasionally be applied to the praise of animals or even of inanimate objects. In praising the gods our first step will be to express our veneration of the majesty of their nature in general terms: next we shall proceed to praise the special power of the individual god and the discoveries whereby he has benefited the human race. For example, in the case of Jupiter, we shall extol his power as manifested in the governance of all things, with Mars we shall praise his power in war, with Neptune his power over the sea; as regards inventions we shall celebrate Minerva's discovery of the arts, Mercury's discovery of letters, Apollo's of medicine, Ceres' of the fruits of the earth, Bacchus' of wine. Next we must record their exploits as handed down from antiquity. Even gods may derive honour from their descent, as for instance is the case with the sons of Jupiter, or from their antiquity, as in the case of the children of Chaos, or from their offspring, as in the case of Latona, the mother of Apollo and Diana. Some again may be praised because they were born immortal, others because they won immortality by their valour, a theme which the piety of our sovereign has made the glory even of these present times.

There is greater variety required in the praise of men. In the first place there is a distinction to be made as regards time between the period in which the objects of our praise lived and the time preceding their birth; and further, in the case of the dead, we must also distinguish the period following their death. With regard to things preceding a man's birth, there are his country, his parents and his ancestors, a theme which may be handled in two ways. For either it will be creditable to the objects of our praise not to have fallen short of the fair fame of their country and their sires or to have ennobled a humble origin by the glory of their achievements. Other topics to be drawn from the period preceding their birth will have reference to omens or prophecies foretelling their future greatness, such as the oracle which is said to have foretold that the son of Thetis [Achilles] would be greater than his father. The praise of the individual himself will be based on his character, his physical endowments and external circumstances.

(Quintilian, *Institutio Oratoria* 3.7.6–12)

The author of the so-called *Rhetoric to Alexander*, a work associated with Aristotle (but clearly not by him), takes a less-principled view of what the orator was required to do on behalf of his client.

468. The eulogistic [epideictic] species of oratory consists, to put it briefly, in the amplification of creditable purposes and actions and speeches and the attribution of qualities that do not exist, while the vituperative species is the opposite, the minimization of creditable qualities and the amplification of discreditable ones.

(*Rhetoric to Alexander* 1425b36–40. Cf. #471)

Marius's speech to the plebs on being elected to the consulship provides an excellent example of pathos.

469. I am of course well aware that if they ['haughty nobles'] should deign to reply to me, their language would be abundantly eloquent and elaborate. But since after the great honour which you have done me they take every opportunity to rend us both with their invectives, I thought it best not to be silent, for fear that someone might interpret my reticence as due to a guilty conscience. In point of fact, I am confident that I can be injured by no speech; for if they tell the truth, they cannot but speak well of me, and falsehood my life and character refutes. But since it is your judgment in giving me your highest office [that of consul] and a most important commission [command of the war against Jugurtha] which they criticize, consider again and yet again whether you ought to regret those acts. I cannot, to justify your confidence, display family portraits or the triumphs and consulships of my forefathers; but if occasion requires, I can show spears, a banner, trappings and other military prizes, as well as scars on my breast. These are my portraits, these my patent of nobility, not left me by inheritance as theirs were, but won by my own innumerable efforts and perils.

My words are not well chosen; I care little for that. Merit shows well enough in itself. It is they who have need of art, to gloss over their shameful acts with specious words. Nor have I studied Grecian letters. I did not greatly care to become acquainted with them, since they had not taught their teachers virtue. But I have learned by far the most important lesson for my country's good—to strike down the foe, to keep watch and ward, to fear nothing save ill repute, to endure heat and cold alike, to sleep on the ground, to bear privation and fatigue at the same time. It is with these lessons that I shall encourage my soldiers; I shall not treat them stingily and myself lavishly, nor win my own glory at the price of their toil. Such leadership is helpful, such leadership is democratic; for to live in luxury oneself but control one's army by punishments is to be a master of slaves, not a commander. It was by conduct like this that your forefathers made themselves and their country famous; but the nobles, relying upon such ancestors though themselves of very different character, despise us who emulate the men of old, and claim from you all honours, not from desert, but as a debt.
(Sallust, *War with Jugurtha* 85.26–37)

Cicero was the greatest exponent of the craft of oratory of the era.[28] Here is an example of his style from an early (70 BCE) forensic speech against Gaius Verres, who was accused of rapacity as proconsul of Sicily (73–71 BCE). Cicero won the case. Verres chose to go into exile. He was proscribed by Antony at the same time as Cicero in 43 BCE.

470. But nowhere did he [Verres] multiply and magnify the memorials and the proofs of all his evil qualities so thoroughly as in his governorship of Sicily; which island for the space of three years he devastated and ruined so effectually that nothing can restore it to its former condition, and it hardly seems possible that a long lapse of years and a succession of upright governors can in time bring it a partial revival of prosperity. So long as Verres was governing it, its people were protected neither by their own laws, nor by the decrees of the Roman Senate, nor by the rights that belong to all nations alike. None of them has anything left to-day, except what either escaped the notice of this avaricious and intemperate ruffian, or remained over when his greed was glutted. For the space of three years, the law awarded nothing to anybody unless Verres chose to agree; and nothing was so undoubtedly inherited from a man's father or grandfather that the courts would not cancel his right to it, if Verres bade them do so. Countless sums of money, under a new and unprincipled regulation, were wrung from the purses of the farmers; our most loyal allies were treated as if they were national enemies; Roman citizens were tortured and executed like slaves; the guiltiest criminals bought their legal acquittal, while the most honourable and honest men would be prosecuted in absence, and condemned and banished unheard; strongly fortified harbours, mighty and well-defended cities, were left open to the assaults of pirates and buccaneers; Sicilian soldiers and sailors, our allies and our friends, were starved to death; fine fleets, splendidly equipped, were to the great disgrace of our nation destroyed and lost to us.

Famous and ancient works of art, some of them the gifts of wealthy kings, who intended them to adorn the cities where they stood, others the gifts of Roman generals, who gave or restored them to the communities of Sicily in the hour of victory—this same governor stripped and despoiled every one of them. Nor was it only the civic statues and works of art that he treated thus; he also pillaged the holiest and most venerated sanctuaries; in fact, he has not left the people of Sicily a single god whose workmanship he thought at all above the average of antiquity or artistic merit. As to his adulteries and the like vile offences, a sense of decency makes me afraid to repeat the tale of his acts of wanton wickedness: and besides, I would not wish, by repeating it, to add to the calamities of those who have not been suffered to save their children and their wives from outrage at the hands of this lecherous scoundrel. Is it alleged that he did these things so secretly that they were not known everywhere? I do not believe that one human being lives, who has heard the name of Verres spoken, and cannot also repeat the tale of his evil doings. I have therefore more reason to fear criticism for passing over charges of which he is guilty, than for inventing against him charges of which he is innocent. And indeed the purpose of the great audience that has gathered to attend this trial is not, I conceive, to learn the facts of the case from me, but to join me in reviewing the facts that it knows already.
(Cicero, *Against Verres* 1.12–15)

The proper way to use a subject's genealogy in epideictic rhetoric.

471. The proper way to employ genealogy is this. If the ancestors are men of merit, you must enumerate them all from the beginning down to the person you are eulogizing, and at each of the ancestors summarily mention something to his credit. If the first ones are men of merit but the rest do not happen to have done anything remarkable, you must go through the first ones in the same way but omit the inferior ones, explaining that because of the number of ancestors you do not wish to make a long story by mentioning them all, and moreover that it is patent to everybody that the scions of a worthy stock naturally resemble their ancestors. If his early ancestors happen to be undistinguished but those near to his own time are famous, you must mention his descent from the latter and say it would be tedious to dwell on the former, but that you will show that the immediate predecessors of those you are praising were good men, and that it is quite clear that *their* forefathers must have been men of merit, because it is manifestly unlikely that those born from base ancestors could be of that quality. If he has no ancestral distinction in his favour, say that he himself is a fine fellow, suggesting that all men by nature well-endowed with virtue are 'well-born.'
(*Rhetoric to Alexander* 1440b29–1441a8)

In the following extract Seneca discusses the value of a liberal education. Vocational training, by contrast, is not a fitting education for the free-born gentleman.

472. You have been wishing to know my views with respect to liberal studies [*liberalia*]. My answer is this: I respect no study, and deem no study good, which results in money-making. Such studies are profit-bringing occupations, useful only in so far as they give the mind a preparation and do not engage it permanently. One should linger upon them only so long as the mind can occupy itself with nothing greater; they are our apprenticeship, not our real work. Hence you see why 'liberal studies' are so called. It is because they are studies worthy of a free-born gentleman. But there is only one really liberal study,—that which gives a man his liberty. It is the study of wisdom, and that is lofty, brave, and great-souled. All the other studies are puny and puerile. You surely do not believe that there is good in any of the subjects whose teachers are, as you see, men of the most ignoble and base stamp? We ought not to be learning such things; we should have done with learning them.
(Seneca, *Epistles* 88.1–2)[29]

Epictetus on the practice of rhetoric.

473. For why is it that the orator, although he knows that he has composed a good speech,

has memorized what he has written and is bringing a pleasing voice to his task, is still anxious despite all that? Because he is not satisfied with the mere practice of oratory. What, then, does he want? He wants to be praised by his audience. Now he has trained himself with a view to being able to practise oratory, but he has not trained himself with reference to praise and blame. For when did he ever hear any one say what praise is, what blame is, and what is the nature of each? What kinds of praise are to be sought, and what kinds of blame are to be avoided? And when did he ever go through this course of training in accordance with these principles? Why, then, are you any longer surprised because he surpasses all others in the field in which he has studied, but in that in which he has not practised he is no better than the multitude?
(Epicetus, *Discourses* 2.16.5–8)

Rhetorical conventions were, of course, well known, and were occasionally satirized. See, for example, Herodas, *Mimes* 2 (*The Pandar*) and Lucian, *The Fly*. The following passage is from Paul's second letter to the Corinthians. Paul clearly mistrusts the power of rhetoric. He himself claims to be a 'layman' as far as rhetoric is concerned (*idiōtēs tōi logōi*, see 2 Corinthians 11:6).[30]

474. But whatever anyone dares to boast of—I am speaking as a fool—I also dare to boast of that. Are they Hebrews? So am I. Are they Israelites? So am I. Are they descendants of Abraham? So am I. Are they ministers of Christ? I am talking like a madman—I am a better one: with far greater labours, far more imprisonments, with countless floggings, and often near death. Five times I have received from the Jews the forty lashes minus one. Three times I was beaten with rods. Once I received a stoning. Three times I was shipwrecked; for a night and a day I was adrift at sea; on frequent journeys, in danger of rivers, danger from bandits, danger from my own people, danger from Gentiles, danger in the city, danger in the wilderness, danger at sea, danger from false brothers and sisters; in toil and hardship, through many a sleepless night, hungry and thirsty, often without food, cold and naked. And, besides other things, I am under daily pressure because of my anxiety for all the churches. Who is weak, and I am not weak? Who is made to stumble, and I am not indignant?

If I must boast, I will boast of the things that show my weakness. The God and Father of the Lord Jesus Christ (blessed be he forever!) knows that I do not lie. In Damascus, the governor under King Aretas guarded the city of Damascus in order to seize me, but I was let down in a basket through a window in the wall, and escaped from his hands.
(2 Corinthians 11:21b–33)[31]

In 1 Corinthians 2:1–5 Paul reminds his readers that he avoided the use of rhetoric in bringing the message of the Christ event to them.

475. When I came to you, brothers and sisters, I did not come proclaiming the mystery of God to you in lofty words or wisdom. For I decided to know nothing among you except Jesus Christ, and him crucified. And I came to you in weakness and in fear and in much trembling. My speech and my proclamation were not with plausible words of wisdom, but with a demonstration of the Spirit and of power, so that your faith might rest not on human wisdom but on the power of God.
(1 Corinthians 2:1–5)

7.7. The Graeco-Roman Economy

Wealth was primarily invested in land and was concentrated in the hands of the few. Pliny the Younger, for example, possessed extensive estates. The wealthy, such as Crassus the triumvir, were often conspicuous in their activity as politicians, lawyers and generals. Their tombstones herald their services to the state. However, at times individuals did become wealthy against the odds. The extravagantly wealthy freedman Trimalchio (of Petronius's *Satyricon*) is an indication of what might happen when people took a risky financial undertaking which paid off.

Wealth was used to win public office and fame and glory. The wealthy bestowed benefactions which were always given in the expectation that rewards would be reciprocated in the form of honours, inscriptions and the attainment of public office. Benefactions might take the form of public works, donations of food (grain) or the underwriting of a great event.[32] New Testament writers struggled to counter this culture, preaching instead the ideal of service without expecting reward and the virtue of sharing with those who had little. Thus, in 1 Timothy and Titus the requirements of bishops and deacons stress the primacy of moral standing rather than wealth.[33] The celebration of the eucharist at Corinth became an occasion for conspicuous consumption for some, while the poor had nothing and were shamed in the presence of the wealthy (1 Corinthians 11:20–22). Nevertheless, Paul is highly dependent on the support of well-to-do householders who, in Edwin Judge's apt phrase, 'sponsored Christianity to their dependants'.[34] Poverty was not seen as 'virtuous' in Graeco-Roman culture. In Judaism, though the poverty of an honest person is regarded as better than ill-gotten wealth (Proverbs 28:6), poverty was regarded as wretched or as evidence of moral failure. However, in the Gospels the poor are pronounced blessed (see, e.g., Luke 6:20) and the followers of Jesus are exhorted to sell what they possess (see, e.g., Matthew 19:21). Here there is evidence of a disjunction between the ideals of certain communities of early Christians and those prevailing in Jewish and Graeco-Roman society.[35]

Direct taxes were not levied on Roman citizens in the first century CE, though they were liable to pay a range of indirect taxes, e.g. on the manumission of slaves. In Republican times Roman businessmen, who were called *publicani*, paid the taxes (i.e. tribute in the form of poll and land taxes) on conquered territory to the Senate, and reimbursed themselves through farming out the contracts to provincial tax gatherers as their agents. From the beginning of the principate, however, taxes were gathered by officials appointed by the emperor directly. Because taxation was levied on all evenly the burden fell on the poor. The sources of the era frequently testify to the rapacity of the tax gatherers (note Luke 18:11; 19:8), though extortion practised by proconsuls is more frequently attested.

Sources

The historian Appian offers a number of perceptive analyses of economic conditions under the Romans, including the creation of *latifundia*.

476. The Romans, as they subdued the Italian peoples successively in war, used to seize a part of their lands and build towns there, or enrol colonists of their own to occupy those already existing, and their idea was to use these as outposts; but of the land acquired by war they assigned the cultivated part forthwith to the colonists, or sold or leased it. Since they had no leisure as yet to allot the part which then lay desolated by war (this was generally the greater part), they made proclamation that in the meantime those who were willing to work it might do so for a toll of the yearly crops, a tenth of the grain and a fifth of the fruit. From those who kept flocks was required a toll of the animals, both oxen and small cattle. They did these things in order to multiply the Italian race, which they considered the most laborious of peoples, so that they might have plenty of allies at home. But the very opposite thing happened; for the rich, getting possession of the greater part of the undistributed lands, and being emboldened by the lapse of time to believe that they would never be dispossessed, absorbing any adjacent strips and their poor neighbours' allotments, partly by purchase under persuasion and partly by force, came to cultivate vast tracts instead of single estates, using slaves as labourers and herdsmen, lest free labourers should be drawn from agriculture into the army. At the same time the ownership of slaves brought them great gain from the multitude of their progeny,

who increased because they were exempt from military service. Thus certain powerful men became extremely rich and the race of slaves multiplied throughout the country, while the Italian people dwindled in numbers and strength, being oppressed by penury, taxes, and military service. If they had any respite from these evils they passed their time in idleness, because the land was held by the rich, who employed slaves instead of freemen as cultivators.
(Appian, *Civil Wars* 1.7)[36]

The offence of lending money.

477. But, as we said, this art is twofold, one branch being of the nature of trade while the other belongs to the household art; and the latter branch is necessary and in good esteem, but the branch connected with exchange is justly discredited (for it is not in accordance with nature, but involves men's taking things from one another). As this is so, usury is most reasonably hated, because its gain comes from money itself and not from that for the sake of which money was invented. For money was brought into existence for the purpose of exchange, but interest increases the amount of money itself (and this is the actual origin of the Greek word: offspring resembles parent, and interest in money is born of money); consequently this form of the business of getting wealth is of all forms the most contrary to nature.
(Aristotle, *Politics* 1.3.23)[37]

The culture of benefaction *(#478–81).*

An inscription from Aletrium (135–90 BCE).

478. Lucius Betilienus Varus son of Lucius, in accordance with a vote of the [municipal] senate superintended the construction of the works which are recorded below: all the street paths in the town, the colonnade along which people walk to the citadel, a playing field, a sundial, a meat market, the stuccoing of the townhall, seats, a bathing pool; he constructed a reservoir by the gate, an aqueduct about 340 feet long leading into the city and to the hill of the citadel, also the arches and good sound water pipes. As reward for these works the senate made him censor twice and ordered that his son be exempt from military service; and the people bestowed the gift of a statue on him over the title of Censorinus.
(*CIL* volume 1, no. 1529 [Lewis and Reinhold, *Roman Civilization: Sourcebook I, The Republic*, pp. 428–29])

Inscription in a bathing room at Interamna (no date).

479. Quintus Poppaeus and Gaius Poppaeus, sons of Quintus protector [*patron*] of the borough and settlement, give out of their own money a permanent bathing-room for their townsmen, settlers, other residents, strangers, and visitors.
(*CIL* volume 1 part 2, 1903 [Warmington, *The Remains of Old Latin*, IV, p. 149])

The following record of civic honours bestowed on a benefactor is from a marble pedestal in the gymnasium at Pergamum (Roman period).[38]

480. The people honoured Apollodorus, the son of Pyrrhus, with a golden crown and a brazen image by reason of his virtue and goodwill towards them, and because of his good and glorious behaviour when he was Gymnasiarch.
(Deissmann, *Light from the Ancient East*, p. 312)

This famous inscription in honour of Augustus is notable for its use of terms encountered in early Christian writings (see #484). The term 'good tidings' (*euangelion*) is that used for the Christian message, the gospel (see, e.g., Mark 1:1).

481. Since the Providence which has ordered all things and is deeply interested in our life has set it in most perfect order by giving to us Augustus, whom she filled with virtue, that he might benefit mankind, sending him as a savior [*Sōtēr*], both for us and for our descendants, that he might end war and arrange all things, and since he, Caesar, by his appearance [*epiphaneia*] (excelling even our anticipations), surpassing all previous benefactors [*Euergetai*], and not even leaving to posterity any hope of surpassing what he has done, and since the birthday of the god Augustus was the beginning for the world of the good tidings [*euangelion*] that came by reason of him.
(The Priene Inscription [9 BCE])

Early Jews and Christians challenged the benefaction culture. Josephus is cited below on this matter (#488). For Christians, service *without* expecting reward was the ideal—the grace of God having been freely bestowed in Christ (note Luke 14:12–14). Indeed, in the Jerusalem church the sharing of wealth was practised in a manner similar to the Qumran community (see Acts 2:44–47; #681).

482. A dispute also arose among them [Jesus' disciples] as to which one of them was to be regarded as the greatest. But he [Jesus] said to them, 'The kings of the Gentiles lord it over them; and those in authority over them are called benefactors [*euergetai*]. But not so with you; rather the greatest among you must become like the youngest, and the leader like one who serves. For who is greater, the one who is at the table or the one who serves? Is it not the one at the table? But I am among you as one who serves.'
(Luke 22:24–27)

483. '[W]henever you give alms, do not sound a trumpet before you, as the hypocrites do in the synagogues and in the streets, so that they may be praised by others. Truly I tell you, they have received their reward. But when you give alms, do not let your left hand know what your right hand is doing, so that your alms may be done in secret; and your Father who sees in secret will reward you.'
(Matthew 6:2–4)

484. For the grace [*charis*] of God has appeared, bringing salvation [*sōtēria*] to all, training us to renounce impiety and worldly passions, and in the present age to live lives that are self-controlled, upright, and godly, while we wait for the blessed hope and the manifestation [*epiphaneia*] of the glory of our great God and Savior [*sōtēr*], Jesus Christ.
(Titus 2:11–13)

The taxes of Asia.

After the defeat of Cassius and Brutus at Philippi (42 BCE), Antony recalls Julius Caesar's benefits to Rome's provincial clients in Asia, lately supporters of the defeated cause.

485. Octavian then proceeded toward the Adriatic; but when Antony arrived at Ephesus he offered a splendid sacrifice to the city's goddess and pardoned those who, after the disaster to Brutus and Cassius, had fled to the temple as suppliants, except Petronius, who had been privy to the murder of Caesar, and Quintus, who had betrayed Dolabella to Cassius at Laodicea. Having assembled the Greeks and other peoples who inhabited the Asiatic country around Pergamos, and who were present on a peace embassy, and others who had been summoned thither, Antony addressed them as follows; 'Your King Attalus, O Greeks, left you to us in his will, and straightway we proved better to you than Attalus had been, for we released you from the taxes that you had been paying to him, until the action of popular agitators also among us made these taxes necessary. But when they became necessary we did not impose them upon you according to a fixed valuation so that we could collect an absolutely certain sum, but we required you to contribute a portion of your yearly harvest in order that we might share with you the vicissitudes of the seasons. When the publicans, who farmed these collections by the authority of the Senate, wronged you by demanding more than was due, Gaius Caesar remitted to you one-third of what you had paid to them and put an end to their outrages: for he turned over to you the collection of the taxes from the cultivators of the soil. And this was the kind of man that our honourable citizens called a tyrant, and you contributed vast sums of money to the murderers of your benefactor and against us, who were seeking to avenge him.'
(Appian, *Civil Wars* 5.4)[39]

The tax burden in Syria and Judaea early in Tiberius's principate.

Cappadocia became a Roman province when King Archelaus was summoned to Rome and later impeached for treason by Tiberius. Reductions in taxation were decreed at this time for Syria and Judaea.

486. His [Archelaus's] kingdom was converted into a province; and the emperor, announcing that its revenue made feasible a reduction of the one per cent. sale-tax [see *Annals*

1.78—a tax on auctioned goods], fixed it for the future at one half of this amount.—About the same time, the death of the two kings, Antiochus of Commagene and Philopator of Cilicia, disturbed the peace of their countries, where the majority of men desired a Roman governor, and the minority a monarch. The provinces, too, of Syria and Judaea, exhausted by their burdens, were pressing for a diminution of the tribute.
(Tacitus, *Annals* 2.42)

Trimalchio, the freedman, informs his dinner guests how he made his money. After 14 years as a trusted slave, Trimalchio inherited money from his master.

487. [M]y master made me joint residuary legatee with Caesar, and came into an estate fit for a senator. But no one is satisfied with nothing. I conceived a passion for business. I will not keep you a moment—I built five ships, got a cargo of wine—which was worth its weight in gold at the time—and sent them to Rome. You may think it was a put-up job; every one was wrecked, truth and no fairy-tales. Neptune gulped down thirty million in one day. Do you think I lost heart? Lord! no, I no more tasted my loss than if nothing had happened. I built some more, bigger, better and also luckier, so that no one could say I was not a brave man. You know, a huge ship has great gallantry about her. I got another cargo of wine, bacon, beans, perfumes, and slaves. Fortunata [Trimalchio's wife] did a noble thing at that time; she sold all her jewellery and all her clothes, and put a hundred gold pieces into my hand. They were the leaven of my fortune. What God wishes soon happens. I made a clear ten million on one voyage. I at once bought up all the estates which had belonged to my patron. I built a house, and bought slaves and cattle; whatever I touched grew like a honey-comb.
(Petronius, *Satyricon* 76)

A Jewish perspective on the culture of benefaction.

King Herod was a notable benefactor among his Jewish contemporaries. Josephus, commenting on Herod's passion for the honours benefactions were meant to elicit, articulates a distinctively Jewish point of view to the effect that Jews admire righteousness not glory. Josephus shrewdly draws a connection between Herod's benefactions outside of Judaea and his rapacity within his territory, arguing that his passion for honour and fame required harshness towards his subjects by which he financed his benefactions.

488. (153) For Herod loved honours and, being powerfully dominated by this passion, he was led to display generosity whenever there was reason to hope for future remembrance or present reputation, but since he was involved in expenses greater than his means, he was compelled to be harsh toward his subjects...

(156) ... These excesses he committed because of his wish to be uniquely honoured. As evidence that this was the greatest of his passions I can cite what was done by him in honour of Caesar and Agrippa and his other friends. For the very same attentions which he showed to his superiors he expected to have shown to himself by his subjects, and what he believed to be the most excellent gift that he could give another he showed a desire to obtain similarly for himself. But, as it happens, the Jewish nation is by law opposed to all such things and is accustomed to admire righteousness [*to dikaion*] rather than glory [*doxa*]. It was therefore not in his good graces, because it found it impossible to flatter the king's ambition with statues or temples or such tokens. And this seems to me to have been the reason for Herod's bad treatment of his own people and his counsellors, and of his beneficence [*euergesia*] toward foreigners and those who were unattached to him.
(Josephus, *Antiquities* 16.153–54, 156–59)

7.8. Glory and Fame

Greek, Roman and Jewish societies exemplify the values of a shame/honour culture. Honour is defined by Bruce Malina as the 'value of a person in his or her own eyes (that is, one's claim to worth) *plus* that person's value in the eyes of his or her social group'.[40] Men with financial means and drive aspired to the glory that accompanied fame wherever it could be pursued. In Rome especially it was a quest that was carried on in a spirit of competitiveness. Fame was equated with moral goodness, or virtue. Indeed, Tacitus wrote: 'Contempt for fame means contempt for goodness' (*Annals* 4.38). Cicero speaks of the relentless quest of the most honourable men in Rome for fame and glory—for high endeavour that endures beyond death because such enterprise was recognized and perpetuated in tangible forms (see #493 below).

The extracts below illustrate the ruthlessness with which men pursued glory in contrast, so it was perceived, with their forebears who were motivated by more honourable motives in the service of the Roman people. Sallust was an astute observer of the careers of the generals of the first half of the first century BCE. He noted that the Roman state was not well served by this competition among men who were driven by naked ambition and love of money, and who used extreme violence to pursue their ends, even against fellow Romans. The last two generations of the Republic were indeed marked by civil war and catastrophic civil strife as a succession of generals competed against one another for glory. Judaism and Christianity, on the other hand, urged a different quest, one for moral uprightness as defined by the revealed will of God, and for the honour that he might bestow (see #488). The New Testament Gospels take this a step further, commending those who abase themselves (Luke 14:7, 11) and who benefit those who cannot reciprocate (Luke 14:12–14). Following Christ, who had been crucified in shame and weakness, was perceived as a shameful life choice, though one the Christians were sure would result in divine vindication and participation after death in the honour God had bestowed on the risen Christ.[41]

Just as the quest for glory was undertaken in the desire to emulate the achievements of one's ancestors, so failure in the quest inevitably impacted the standing and repute of one's family. If fame and glory was the goal, failing to gain this end was a source of dishonour and shame, not just for the man worsted in the struggle for the limited number of prizes on offer, but also for his family. Shame was the inevitable result of any independent and unauthorized activity by any woman. Men could shame their family by a lack of self-control, or by failure to control one's dependents, or by effeminacy. Shame diminished the standing of the family and brought it into disrepute.

Sources

Marius's lust for fame.

489. At the time of which I speak, deeming the consulship a slight matter in comparison with things to come, his thoughts soared to the Mithridatic war. But here he found a rival in Marius, who was possessed by ambition and a mad desire for fame, those never ageing passions.
(Plutarch, *Sulla* 7.1)

Sulla and glory.

490. Sulla...was a noble of patrician descent, of a family almost reduced to obscurity through the degeneracy of his ancestors. He was well versed alike in Grecian and Roman letters, of remarkable mental power, devoted to pleasure but more devoted to glory [*sed gloriae cupidior*]. In his leisure hours he lived extravagantly, yet pleasure never interfered with his duties, except that his conduct as a husband might have been more honourable. He was eloquent, clever, and quick to make friends. He had a mind deep beyond belief in its power of disguising his purposes, and was generous with many things, especially with money. Before his victory in the civil war he was the most fortunate of all men, but his fortune was never greater than his deserts, and many have hesitated to say whether his bravery or his good luck was the greater. As to what he did later, I know not if one should speak of it rather with shame or with sorrow.
(Sallust, *War with Jugurtha* 95.3–4)

Sallust's extant historical works, *The War with Catiline* and *The War with Jugurtha*, both commence with an analysis of the origin of the pursuit of glory by means of violence that was to become endemic in Roman politics during the first century BCE.

491. (10) But when our country had grown great through toil and the practice of justice, when great kings had been vanquished in war, savage tribes and mighty peoples subdued by force of arms, when Carthage, the rival of Rome's sway, had perished root and branch, and all seas and lands were open, then Fortune began to grow cruel and to bring confusion into all our affairs. Those who had found it easy to bear hardship and dangers, anxiety and adversity, found leisure and wealth, desirable under other circumstances, a burden and a curse. Hence the lust for money first, then for power, grew upon them; these were, I may say, the root of all evils. For avarice destroyed honour, integrity, and all other noble qualities; taught in their place insolence, cruelty, to neglect the gods, to set a price on everything. Ambition [*ambitio*] drove many men to become false; to have one thought locked in the breast, another ready on the tongue; to value friendships and enmities not on their merits but by the standard of self-interest, and to show a good front rather than a good heart. At first these vices grew slowly, from time to time they were punished; finally, when the disease had spread like a deadly plague, the state was changed and a government second to none in equity and excellence became cruel and intolerable.

(11) But at first men's souls were actuated less by avarice than by ambition—a fault, it is true, but not so far removed from virtue; for the noble and the base alike long for glory, honour, and power, but the former mount by the true path, whereas the latter, being destitute of noble qualities, rely upon craft and deception. Avarice implies a desire for money, which no wise man covets; steeped as it were with noxious poisons, it renders the most manly body and soul effeminate; it is ever unbounded and insatiable, nor can either plenty or want make it less. But after Lucius Sulla, having gained control of the state by arms, brought everything to a bad end from a good beginning, all men began to rob and pillage. One coveted a house, another lands; the victors showed neither moderation nor restraint, but shamefully and cruelly wronged their fellow citizens. Besides all this, Lucius Sulla, in order to secure the loyalty of the army which he led into Asia, had allowed it a luxury and license foreign to the manners of our forefathers; and in the intervals of leisure those charming and voluptuous lands had easily demoralized the warlike spirit of his soldiers. There it was that an army of the Roman people first learned to indulge in women and drink; to admire statues, paintings, and chased vases, to steal them from private houses and public places, to pillage shrines, and to desecrate everything, both sacred and profane. These soldiers, therefore, after they had won the victory, left nothing to the vanquished. In truth, prosperity tries the souls even of the wise; how then should men of depraved character like these make a moderate use of victory?

(12) As soon as riches came to be held in honour, when glory, dominion, and power followed in their train, virtue began to lose its lustre, poverty to be considered a disgrace, blamelessness to be termed malevolence. Therefore as the result of riches, luxury and greed, united with insolence, took possession of our young manhood. They pillaged, squandered; set little value on their own, coveted the goods of others; they disregarded modesty, chastity, everything human and divine; in short, they were utterly thoughtless and reckless.

It is worth your while, when you look upon houses and villas reared to the size of cities, to pay a visit to the temples of the gods built by our forefathers, most reverent of men. But they adorned the shrines of the gods with piety, their own homes with glory, while from the vanquished they took naught save the power of doing harm. The men of to-day, on the contrary, basest of creatures, with supreme wickedness are robbing our allies of all that those heroes in the hour of victory had left them; they act as though the one and only way to rule were to wrong.

(14) In a city so great and so corrupt Catiline found it a very easy matter to surround himself, as by a bodyguard, with troops of criminals and reprobates of every kind.
(Sallust, *War with Catiline* 10–12, 14)[42]

Sallust, as we have seen, was particularly aware of the dangers of the pursuit of glory and fame of those without virtue. In the following extract he draws a contrast between the sheer ambition of his contemporaries with the pursuit of fame and glory which motivated men of earlier generations.

492. I have often heard that Quintus Maximus, Publius Scipio, and other eminent men of our country, were in the habit of declaring that their hearts were set mightily aflame for the pursuit of virtue whenever they gazed upon the masks of their ancestors. Of course they did not mean to imply that the wax or the effigy had any such power over them, but rather that it is the memory of great deeds that kindles in the breasts of noble men this flame that cannot be quelled until they by their own prowess have equalled the fame and glory [*fama atque gloria*] of their forefathers.
(Sallust, *War with Jugurtha* 4.5–6)[43]

Cicero has much to say about fame and glory. In the following extract Cicero is appealing to the jury to acquit Archias. In this extract he also refers to his crucial role in putting down the Catiline conspiracy.

493. And the more to incline you so to do, gentlemen of the jury, I will now proceed to open to you my heart, and confess to you my own passion, if I may so describe it, for fame, a passion over-keen perhaps, but assuredly honourable. The measures which I, jointly with you, undertook in my consulship for the safety of the empire, the lives of our citizens, and the common weal of the state, have been taken by my client as the subject of a poem which he has begun; he read this to me, and the work struck me as at once so forcible and so interesting, that I encouraged him to complete it. For magnanimity [*virtus*] looks for no other recognition of its toils and dangers save praise and glory [*laudis et gloriae*]; once rob it of that, gentlemen, and in this brief and transitory pilgrimage of life what further incentive have we to high endeavour? If the soul were haunted by no presage of futurity, if the scope of her imaginings were bounded by the limits set to human existence, surely never then would she break herself by bitter toil, rack herself by sleepless solicitude, or struggle so often for very life itself. But deep in every noble heart dwells a power [*virtus*] which plies night and day the goad of glory, and bids us see to it that the remembrance of our names should not pass away with life, but should endure coeval with all the ages of the future.
(Cicero, *Pro Archia Poeta* 11.28–29)

7.9. Life in the Cities

At the centre of Greek civic life there was a range of institutions including the gymnasium. It provided training for war, education, and gave opportunities for exercise. Gymnasia were maintained by the city and by benefactions (see #480). The business of the gymnasium was conducted in an open courtyard (*palaestra*) surrounded by a colonnade. There were classes for boys and girls at the lower educational levels. By virtue of the curriculum at the secondary level, there was a sense of participating in a common culture and a common heritage underscoring Greek identity, especially in cities like Alexandria with a strong Roman and Jewish presence. Access to citizenship in Greek cities during the Roman era was inextricably linked to membership of the free born, legitimate youth of the city in the gymnasium as ephebes.[44] Cities based on the Greek model can be found all over the empire, including Judaea. Sepphoris, a few miles from Nazareth, was one such city in Galilee. Herod the Great's foundations at Caesarea, Sebaste and elsewhere were cities after the Greek model.

Alexandria, Antioch and Rome were the largest cities of the Graeco-Roman world. As the centre of an empire Rome was a city of magnificent public buildings and a great consumer of the produce of the Mediterranean basin. As in the Greek cities, access to citizenship was closely guarded during the New Testament period. In the extract below (#495) Juvenal protests the barbaric cosmopolitanism of the city, much of this due to the presence of large numbers of slaves. Rome was also a magnet for the enterprising and aspiring from all over the empire.[45] A sizable Jewish minority was resident there.[46]

Life in the cities for the majority of people meant a crowded, noisy existence. While the Romans were attentive to the need to supply fresh water and basic sanitation, there is no doubt that the quality of life for all but the most wealthy was compromised.[47] Juvenal paints a harrowing picture of the dangers of city life and the ever-present threat of fire and building collapses in Rome. Grinding poverty was inescapable. The pressure to provide food for one's dependents was an ever-present reality given the potential for famine and the tenuousness of the corn supply. In such circumstances the lot of slaves might have been envied by free day-workers.

Sources

The splendour of Rome.

494. There was rude simplicity of old, but now golden Rome possesses the vast wealth of the conquered world. See what the Capitol is now, and what it was: you would say they belonged to different Jupiters. The senate-house, which now is most worthy of so august a gathering, was, when Tatius held sway, made of wattles. The Palatine whereon now Phoebus and our chieftains are set in splendour, what was it save the pasture of oxen destined to the plough? Let ancient times delight other folk: I congratulate myself that I was not born till now; this age fits my nature well. Not because now stubborn gold is drawn from out the earth, and shells come gathered from divers shores, nor because mountains diminish as the marble is dug from them, nor because masonry puts to flight the dark-blue waters; but because culture is with us, and rusticity, which survived until our grandsires, has not lasted to our days.
(Ovid, *Art of Love* 3.113–28)

Juvenal offers this assessment of the growing cosmopolitanism of Rome.

495. And now let me speak at once of the race which is most dear to our rich men, and which I avoid above all others; no shyness shall stand in my way. I cannot abide, Quirites, a Rome of Greeks; and yet what fraction of our dregs comes from Greece? The Syrian Orontes has long since poured into the Tiber, bringing with it its lingo and its manners, its flutes and its slanting harp-strings; bringing too the timbrels of the breed, and the trulls who are bidden ply their trade at the Circus.
(Juvenal, *Satires* 3.58–65)

The difference in citizenship between those who live in municipia *and those who live in* colonia.

496. *Municipes*, then, are Roman citizens from free towns, using their own laws and enjoying their own rights, merely sharing with the Roman people an honorary *munus*, or 'privilege' (from the enjoyment of which privilege they appear to derive their name), and bound by no other compulsion and no other law of the Roman people, except such as their own citizens have officially ratified. We learn besides that the people of Caere were the first *municipes* without the right of suffrage, and that it was allowed them to assume the honour of Roman citizenship, but yet to be free from service and burdens, in return for receiving and guarding sacred objects during the war with the Gauls. Hence by contraries those tablets were called *Caerites* on which the censors ordered those to be enrolled whom they deprived of their votes by way of disgrace.

But the relationship of the 'colonies' is a different one; for they do not come into citizenship from without, nor grow from the roots of their own, but they are as it were transplanted from the State and have all the laws and institutions of the Roman people, not those of their own choice. This condition, although it is more exposed to control and less free, is nevertheless thought preferable and superior because of the greatness and majesty of the Roman people, of which those colonies seem to be miniatures, as it were, and in a way copies; and at the same time because the rights of the municipal towns become obscure and invalid, and from ignorance of their existence the townsmen are no longer able to make use of them. (Aulus Gellius, *Attic Nights* 16.13.6–9)[48]

The corn dole in Rome.

497. Augustus limited the number of people to be supplied with grain, a number not previously fixed, to two hundred thousand; and, as some say, he distributed a largess of sixty denarii to each man.
(Dio Cassius, *Roman History* 55.10.1)

Shops in Rome.

498. The audacious retailers had appropriated the entire city; no threshold kept within its bounds. You bade the narrow streets expand, Germanicus [Domitian], and what had lately been a track became a road. No column is girt with chained flagons, and the praetor is not forced to walk through the mud. The razor is not drawn blindly in a dense crowd, not does the grimy cook shop monopolize the whole street. The barber, the taverner, the cook, the butcher keep to their own thresholds. Now it is Rome, it used to be a big shop.
(Martial, *Epigrams* 7.61)

The following two extracts dwell on the danger from fire and building collapse in the city of Rome.

499. Though put out by the departure of my old friend, I commend his purpose to fix his home at Cumae, and to present one citizen to the Sibyl. That is the gate of Baiae, a sweet retreat upon a pleasant shore; I myself would prefer even Prochyta to the Subura! For where has one ever seen a place so dismal and so lonely that one would not deem it worse to live in perpetual dread of fires and falling houses, and the thousand perils of this terrible city, and poets spouting in the month of August!
(Juvenal, *Satires* 3.1–9)

500. Who at cool Praeneste, or at Volsinii amid its leafy hills, was ever afraid of his house tumbling down? Who in modest Gabii, or on the sloping heights of Tivoli? But here we inhabit a city supported for the most part by slender props: for this is how the bailiff holds up the tottering house, patches up gaping cracks in the old wall, bidding the inmates sleep at ease under a roof ready to tumble about their ears. No, no, I must live where there are no fires, no nightly alarms. Ucalegon below is already shouting for water and shifting his chattels; smoke is pouring out of your third-floor attic, but you know nothing of it; for if the alarm begins in the ground-floor, the last man to burn will be he who has nothing to shelter him from the rain but the tiles, where the gentle doves lay their eggs.
(Juvenal, *Satires* 3.190–202)

Noise and danger in the streets of Rome.

501. Most sick people here in Rome perish for want of sleep, the illness itself having been produced by food lying undigested on a fevered stomach. For what sleep is possible in a lodging? Who but the wealthy get sleep in Rome? There lies the root of the disorder. The crossing of wagons in the narrow winding streets, the slanging of drovers when brought to a stand, would make sleep impossible for a Drusus [possibly the Emperor Claudius]—or a sea-calf. When the rich man has a call of social duty, the mob makes way for him as he is borne swiftly over their heads in a huge Liburnian car. He writes or reads or sleeps inside as he goes along, for the closed window of the litter induces slumber. Yet he will arrive before us; hurry as we may, we are blocked by a surging crowd in front, and by a dense mass of people pressing in on us from behind: one man digs an elbow into me, another a hard sedan-pole; one bangs a beam, another a wine-cask, against my head. My legs are beplastered with mud; soon huge feet trample on me from every side, and a soldier plants his hobnails firmly on my toe.

See now the smoke rising from that crowd which hurries as if to a dole: there are a hundred guests, each followed by a kitchener of his own. Corbulo himself could scarce bear the weight of all the big vessels and other gear which that poor little slave is carrying with head erect, fanning the flame as he runs along. Newly-patched tunics are torn in two; up comes a huge fir-log swaying on a wagon, and then a second dray carrying a whole pine-tree; they tower aloft and threaten the people. For if that axle with its load of Ligurian marble breaks down, and pours an overturned mountain on to the crowd, what is left of their bodies? Who can identify the limbs, who the bones? The poor man's crushed corpse wholly disappears, just like his soul. At home meanwhile the folk, unwitting, are washing the dishes, blowing up the fire with distended cheek, clattering over the greasy flesh-scrapers, filling the oil-flasks and laying out the towels. And while each of them is busy over his own task, their master is already sitting, a new arrival, upon the bank, and shuddering at the grim ferryman: he has no copper in his mouth to tender for his fare, and no hope of a passage over the murky flood, poor wretch.

And now regard the different and diverse perils of the night. See what a height it is to that towering roof from which a potsherd comes crack upon my head every time that some broken or leaky vessel is pitched out of the window! See with what a smash it strikes and dints the pavement! There's death in every open window as you pass along at night; you may well be deemed a fool, improvident of sudden accident, if you go out to dinner without having made your will. You can but hope, and put up a piteous prayer in your heart, that they may be content to pour down on you the contents of their slop-basins!

(Juvenal, *Satires* 3.232–77)

7.10. Life in the Countryside

The Graeco-Roman economy was predominately based on agriculture. In Latin literature, poetry especially, a romantic articulation of the farming ideal is frequently expressed. Marcus Portius Cato, the great exemplar of traditional Roman virtues, wrote a treatise on agriculture, as did the polymath Varro. Wealthy Romans and provincials retired to their country estates. Slaves were required to work these, especially the extensive *latifundia* which came into existence in the second century BCE with the increased availability of the manpower required to work the land. Life in the country appealed to those Romans who eagerly sought connection to the more simple virtues of life in the face of the vulgarity of city life.

In Palestine, bandits operating in the countryside seem to have been an endemic problem throughout the 100-year period from the time of the early career of Herod the Great to the outbreak of the Jewish Revolt. Josephus links banditry with religious mania. However, it is likely that the causes of banditry had more to do with economic conditions. There is evidence for the squeezing out of small landholders and the creation of large estates owned by wealthy citizens of Jerusalem.[49] Famine, such as the one which struck the region in the mid 40s CE only exacerbated the problem.

Sources

Farming life.

The growth of large estates was a feature of the era after the Second Punic War. In the following selection Marcus Portius Cato (234–148 BCE), the great exemplar of traditional Roman virtues, enunciates the duties of the overseer of such estates. The availability of slaves made these estates possible. The overseer was a slave who had considerable responsibilities.

502. The following are the duties of the overseer:—

He must show good management. The feast days must be observed. He must withhold his hands from another's goods and diligently preserve his own. He must settle disputes among the slaves; and if anyone commits an offence he must punish him properly in proportion to the fault. He must see that the servants are well provided for, and that they do not suffer from cold or hunger. Let him keep them busy with their work—he will more easily keep them from wrongdoing and meddling. If the overseer sets his face against wrongdoing, they will not do it; if he allows it, the master must not let him go unpunished. He must express his appreciation of good work, so that others may take pleasure in well-doing. The overseer must not be a gadabout, he must always

be sober, and must not go out to dine. He must keep the servants busy, and see that the master's orders are carried out. He must assume that he knows more than the master. He must consider the master's friends his own friends. He must pay heed to anyone to whom he has been bidden to listen. He must perform no religious rites, except on the occasion of the Compitalia at the cross roads, or before the hearth. He must extend credit to no one without orders from the master, and must collect the loans made by the master. He must lend to no one seed-grain, fodder, spelt, wine, or oil. He must have two or three households, no more, from whom he borrows and to whom he lends. He must make up accounts with the master often. He must not hire the same day-labourer or servant or caretaker for longer than a day. He must not want to make any purchases without the knowledge of the master, nor want to keep anything hidden from the master. He must have no hanger-on. He must not consult a fortune-teller, or prophet, or diviner, or astrologer. He must not stint the seed for sowing, for that brings bad fortune. He must see to it that he knows how to perform all the operations of the farm, and actually does perform them often, but not to the extent of becoming exhausted; by so doing he will learn what is in his servant's minds, and they will perform their work more contentedly. Also, he will be less disposed to gad about, will be in better health, and will enjoy his sleep more. He must be the first out of bed, the last to go to bed. Before then he must see that the farmstead is closed, that each one is asleep in his proper place, and that the stock have fodder.
(Cato, *On Agriculture* 5.1–5)

503. See that the housekeeper performs all her duties. If the master has given her to you as wife, keep yourself only to her. Make her stand in awe of you. Restrain her from extravagance. She must visit the neighbouring and other women very seldom, and not have them either in the house or in her part of it. She must not go out to meals, or be a gad-about. She must not engage in religious worship herself or get others to engage in it for her without the orders of the master of the mistress; let her remember that the master attends to the devotions for the whole household. She must be neat herself, and keep the farmstead neat and clean. She must clean and tidy the hearth every night and before she goes to bed.
(Cato, *On Agriculture* 143.1–2)

504. To prevent chafing: When you set out on a journey, keep a small branch of Pontic wormwood under the anus.
(Cato, *On Agriculture* 159)

Marcus Varro (116–27 BCE) stood in the same tradition of reflection on the agricultural enterprise.

505. With regard to the number of slaves required, Cato has in view two bases of calculation: the size of the place, and the nature of the crop grown. Writing of oliveyards and vineyards, he gives two formulas. The first is one in which he shows how an oliveyard of 240 iugera should be equipped; on a place of this size he says that the following thirteen slaves should be kept: an overseer, a housekeeper, five labourers, three teamsters, one muleteer, one swineherd, one shepherd. The second he gives for a vineyard of 100 iugera, on which he says should be kept the following fifteen slaves: an overseer, a housekeeper, ten labourers, a teamster, a muleteer, a swineherd.
(Marcus Terentius Varro, *On Agriculture* 1.18.1.
See Cato, *On Agriculture* 10, 11)[50]

506. Furthermore, it is especially important that the foremen be men who are experienced in farm operations; for the foremen must not only give orders but also take part in the work, so that his subordinates may follow his example, and also understand that there is good reason for his being over them—the fact that he is superior to them in knowledge. They are not to be allowed to control their men with whips rather than with words, if only you can achieve the same result. Avoid having too many slaves of the same nation, for this is a fertile source of domestic quarrels.
(Marcus Terentius Varro, *On Agriculture* 1.17.4–5)

Virgil was a landowner with a profound feeling for the simplicity and integrity of the farming life, combined with a deep sense of belonging to the land of Italy. Here he turns his poetic gifts to describing typical scenes from life on the land.

507. But neither Media's groves, land of wondrous wealth, nor beauteous Ganges, nor Hermus, thick with gold, may vie with Italy's glories—not Bactra, nor India, nor all Panchaea, rich in incense-bearing sand. This land no bulls, with nostrils breathing flame, ever ploughed for the sowing of the monstrous dragon's teeth; no human crop ever bristled with helms and serried lances; but teeming fruits have filled her and the Vine-god's Massic juice; she is the home of olives and of joyous herds. Hence comes the war-horse, stepping proudly o'er the plain; hence thy snowy flocks, Clitumnus, and the bull, that noblest victim, which, oft steeped in thy sacred stream, have led to the shrines of the gods the triumphs of Rome. Here is eternal spring, and summer in months not her own; twice the cattle breed, twice the tree serves us with fruits. But ravening tigers are far away, and the savage seed of lions; no aconite deludes hapless gatherers, nor does the scaly serpent dart his huge rings over the ground, or with his vast train wind himself into a coil. Think, too, of all those noble cities, the achievement of man's toil, all the towns his handiwork has piled high on steepy crags, and the streams that glide beneath those ancient walls. Shall I tell of the seas, washing the land above and below? Or of our mighty lakes? Of thee, Larius, our greatest; and thee, Benacus, with the roaring, surging swell of the sea? Shall I tell of our havens, and the barrier thrown across the Lucrine, and how Ocean roars aloud in wrath, where the Julian waters echo afar as the sea is flung back, and the Tyrrhenian tide pours into the channels of Avernus? Yea, and this land has shown silver-streams and copper-mines in her veins, and has flowed rich with gold. She has mothered a vigorous breed of men, Marsians and the Sabine stock, the Ligurian, inured to hardship, and the Volscian spearmen; yea, the Decii, the Marii, the great Camilli, the Scipios, hardy warriors, and thee, greatest of all, O Caesar, who, already victorious in Asia's farthest bounds, now drivest the craven Indian from our hills of Rome. Hail, land of Saturn, great mother of earth's fruits, great mother of men! 'Tis for thee I essay the theme of olden praise and art; for thee I dare to unseal the sacred founts, and through Roman towns to sing the song of Ascra. (Virgil, *Georgics* 2.136–76)

The following vignette of country life is ascribed to the epigrammist Martial.

508. As you ask what I do while staying in the country I reply shortly. At daybreak I pray to the gods; I visit my servants and afterwards my fields, and to my staff I assign their proper tasks. Then I read and call on Phoebus, and challenge the Muses. After this I rub my body with oil, and with mild gymnastics gladly brace myself, happy in my mind and free from moneylenders. I lunch, drink, sing, play, bathe, dine, go to bed. Provided my small lamp consumes but little oil, such lucubrations as these night furnishes to the nocturnal Muses. (Epigram 1 ascribed to Martial).

7.11. Entertainment

This topic surveys a select number of aspects of Graeco-Roman entertainment, namely, bathing, banqueting, the arena, and social clubs.

The Roman institution of the bath house had spread to all parts of the empire by the New Testament period. It was one feature of daily life that all members of society could enjoy in common. The bath gave ample opportunity for social interaction and were frequently the object of benefactions (see #479). Men and women often bathed together. Members of the Jewish aristocracy also built heated baths after the Roman fashion in their villas.[51] The building of expansive, magnificently appointed baths was by no means infrequent, as the remains of baths in Rome testifies. The imaginative extract from Lucian provides an indication of the expense and elaborate fittings some baths presented to those who patronized them.

Among the Roman upper classes banqueting was part of the social round. Banquets were often excuses for extravagant and wasteful consumption, drunkenness and sexual titilation. Banquets also reinforced social and class distinctions (see #406).

In addition to chariot races, the dubious entertainment provided by the Roman arena is frequently attested in the sources and in archaeological remains. By the first century CE arenas were dotted all over the empire.[52] Unlike the Greeks, who enjoyed athletics and the artistic contests that often accompanied them, the Romans became inured to the spectacles of butchery that characterized the entertainment of the arena during the late Republican and Imperial periods.[53] Indeed, the savagery and cruelty was excused on the basis that it was somehow therapeutic to be a spectator of such events at which men fought each other and against wild animals to the death for the sake of glory. The struggle and enterprise of life, as perceived by such apologists, seemed to be summed up in such contests. The Roman character—warlike, striving, thrusting, competitive, persistently questing for glory—was ideally suited to appreciating the horrors of the arena. By contrast, Greek games seemed 'soft' and unmanly, and suited to a weak and degenerative national temperament. Pliny was one Roman who was offended by what he considered to be the effete, demoralizing spectacle offered by Greek-style games.[54] Wild beast spectacles undermined the ability of animals to maintain their numbers in the wild.[55] Voices raised in protest against the slaughter were few.

The social club provided a social network and a sense of belonging in at least three contexts: (1) societies for professional business men; (2) *collegia sodalicia* for the worship of specific gods; and (3) *collegia tenuiorum*, or burial societies, for the poor.[56] Such clubs provided tangible benefits for their members. The Roman authorities were suspicious of clubs as potential breeding grounds for subversive activity, and closely regulated them (see, e.g., Philo, *Flaccus* 4). This is evident in the correspondence of Pliny to Trajan (see #525–26 below). The New Testament household churches might be seen to be analogous to the clubs insofar as they too promised a sense of belonging.[57]

Sources

Hippias designs a bath house.

509. (5) The entrance is high, with a flight of broad steps of which the tread is greater than the pitch, to make them easy to ascend. On entering, one is received into a public hall of good size, with ample accommodations for servants and attendants. On the left are the lounging-rooms, also of just the right sort for a bath, attractive, brightly lighted retreats. Then, beside them, a hall, larger than need be for the purposes of a bath, but necessary for the reception of the rich. Next, capacious locker-rooms to undress in, on each side, with a very high and brilliantly lighted hall between them, in which are three swimming-pools of cold water; it is finished in Laconian marble, and has two statues of white marble in the ancient technique, one of Hygeia [goddess of health], the other of Aesculapius [god of healing, and father of Hygeia].

(6) On leaving this hall, you come into another which is slightly warmed instead of meeting you at once with fierce heat; it is oblong, and has an apse at each side. Next to it, on the right, is a very bright hall, nicely fitted up for massage, which has on each side an entrance decorated with Phrygian marble, and receives those who come in from the exercising-floor. Then near this is another hall, the most beautiful in the world, in which one can sit or stand with comfort, linger without danger and stroll about with profit. It also is refulgent with Phrygian marble clear to the roof. Next comes the hot corridor, faced with Numidian marble. The hall beyond it is very beautiful, full of abundant light and aglow with colour like that of purple hangings. It contains three hot tubs.

(7) When you have bathed, you need not go back through the same rooms, but can go directly to the cold room through a slightly warmed apartment. Everywhere there is copious illumination and full indoor day-

light. Furthermore, the height of each room is just, and the breadth proportionate to the length; and everywhere great beauty and loveliness prevail, for in the words of noble Pindar, 'Your work should have a glorious countenance.' This is probably due in the main to the light, the brightness and the windows. Hippias, being truly wise, built the room for cold baths to northward, though it does not lack a southern exposure; whereas he faced south, east, and west the rooms that require abundant heat...

(8) ... It has all the good points of a bath—usefulness, convenience, light, good proportions, fitness to its site, and the fact that it can be used without risk. Moreover, it is beautified with all other marks of thoughtfulness—with two toilets, many exits, and two devices for telling time, a water-clock that bellows like a bull, and a sundial. (Lucian, *Hippias* 5–8)

Banquets (#510–13).

Trimalchio's banquet is the most famous section of the extant portion of Petronius's *Satyricon*. In the following extract Petronius describes the serving of the *hors d'oeuvres*.

510. At last we sat down, and boys from Alexandria poured water cooled with snow over our hands. Others followed and knelt at our feet, and proceeded with great skill to pare our hangnails. Even this unpleasant duty did not silence them, but they kept singing at their work. I wanted to find out whether the whole household could sing, so I asked for a drink. A ready slave repeated my order in a chant not less shrill. They all did the same if they were asked to hand anything. It was more like an actor's dance than a gentleman's dining-room. But some rich and tasty whets for the appetite were brought on; for every one had now sat down except Trimalchio, who had the first place kept for him in the new style. A donkey in Corinthian bronze stood on the side-board, with panniers holding olives, white in one side, black in the other. Two dishes hid the donkey; Trimalchio's name and their weight in silver were engraved on their edges. There were also dormice rolled in honey and poppy-seed, and supported on little bridges soldered to the plate. Then there were hot sausages laid on a silver grill, and under the grill damsons and seeds of pomegranate. (Petronius, *Satyricon* 31)

Gluttony.

511. If Atticus dines sumptuously, he is thought a fine gentleman; if Rutilus does the same, people say he has lost his senses: for at what does the public laugh so loudly as at an Apicius reduced to poverty? Every dinner table, all the baths, lounging-places and theatres have their fling at Rutilus; for while still young, active, and warm-blooded, and fit to wear a helmet, he plunges on till he will have to enrol himself—not compelled indeed, but not forbidden by the Tribune—under the rules and royal mandates of a trainer of gladiators. You may see many of these gentry being waited for by an oft-eluded creditor at the entrance to the meat-market—men whose sole reason for living lies in their palate. The greater their straits—though the house is ready to fall, and the daylight begins to show between the cracks—the more luxuriously and daintily do they dine. Meanwhile they ransack all the elements for new relishes; no cost ever stands in the way of their desires; if you look closely into it, the greater the price, the greater the pleasure. So when they want to raise money to go after the rest, they think nothing of pawning their plate, or breaking up the image of their mother; and having thus seasoned their gluttonous delf at a cost of four hundred sesterces, they come down at last to the hotch-potch of the gladiatorial school. It matters much therefore who provides the feast; what is extravagant in Rutilus, gets a fine name in Ventidius, and takes its character from his means. (Juvenal, *Satires* 11.1–23)

Martial proposes a banquet.

512. Her votaries announce the eighth hour to the Pharian heifer [Isis] and the pike-carrying cohort [of the Praetorian Guard] returns to camp as another comes on duty. This hour cools the warm baths, the one preceding pants out immoderate heat, the sixth glows with Nero's excess. Stella, Nepos, Canius, Cerialis, Flaccus, are you coming?

The sigma [a type of banqueting couch] takes seven, we are six; add Lupus. The bailiff's wife has brought me mallows to relieve the stomach and the garden's various wealth. There is sessile lettuce and clipped leeks, belching mint is not to seek, nor the salacious herb. Slices of egg will top mackerel flavoured with rue and there will be a sow's udder wet from tunny's brine. So much for the hors d'oeuvres. The little dinner will be served in one course. A kid, snatched from the jaws of a savage wolf, morsels requiring no carver's knife, workmen's beans and early greens. To these will accrue a chicken and a ham that has already survived three dinners. When my guests are satisfied, I shall offer ripe fruit and leesless wine from a Nomentan flagon twice three years old in Frontinus' consulship. To boot there will be merriment free of malice, frank speech that gives no anxiety the morning after, nothing you would wish you hadn't said. Let my guest talk of Scorpus [a charioteer] and the Green [one of the four racing teams]; let my cups get no man put on trial. (Martial, *Epigrams* 10.48)

Juvenal's banquet will not feature immodest dancing.

513. You may look perhaps for a troop of Spanish maidens to win applause by immodest dance and song, sinking down with quivering buttocks to the floor—such sights as brides behold seated beside their husbands, though it were a shame to speak of such things in their presence... My humble home has no place for follies such as these. The clatter of castanets, words too foul for the strumpet that stands naked in a reeking archway, with all the arts and language of lust, may be left to him who spits upon floors of Lacedaemonian marble; such men we pardon because of their high station. In men of moderate position gaming and adultery are shameful; but when those others do these same things, they are called gay fellows and fine gentlemen. My feast to-day will provide other performances than these. The bard of the *Iliad* will be sung, and the lays of the lofty-toned Maro that contest the palm with his. What matters it with what voice strains like these are read? (Juvenal, *Satires* 11.162–82)

The arena (#514–24).

After Octavian's triumph at the consecration of the shrine to Julius Caesar, there was a series of special events, including the following gladiatorial and beast shows.

514. At the consecration of the shrine to Julius there were all kinds of contests, and the boys of the patricians performed the equestrian exercise called 'Troy,' and men of the same rank contended with chargers, with pairs, and with four-horse teams; furthermore, one Quintus Vitellius, a senator, fought as a gladiator. Wild beasts and tame animals were slain in vast numbers, among them a rhinoceros and a hippopotamus, beasts then seen for the first time in Rome. As regards the nature of the hippopotamus, it has been described by many and far more have seen it. The rhinoceros, on the other hand, is in general somewhat like an elephant, but it has also a horn on its very nose and has got its name because of this. These beasts, accordingly, were brought in, and moreover Dacians and Suebi fought in crowds with one another. (Dio Cassius, *Roman History* 51.22.4–6)

Augustus reviews his contributions to the people of Rome.

515. I gave three gladiatorial games in my own name and five in that of my sons or grandsons; at these games some 10,000 men took part in combat. Twice in my own name and a third time in that of my grandson I presented to the people displays by athletes summoned from all parts. I produced shows in my own name four times and in place of other magistrates twenty-three times. On behalf of the college of *quindecimviri*, as its president, with Marcus Agrippa as colleague, I produced the Secular Games in the consulship of Gaius Furnius and Gaius Silanus. In my thirteenth consulship I was the first to produce the games of Mars, which thereafter in each succeeding year have been produced by the consuls in accordance with a decree of the senate and by statute. I gave beast-hunts of African beasts in my own name or in that of my sons and grandsons in the circus or forum or amphitheatre on twenty-six occasions, on which about 3,500 beasts were destroyed.

I produced a naval show as a show for the people at the place across the Tiber now occupied by the grove of the Caesars, where a site 1,800 feet long and 1,200 broad was excavated. There thirty beaked triremes or biremes and still more smaller vessels were joined in battle. About 3,000 men, besides the rowers, fought in these fleets.
(Augustus, *Res Gestae Divi Augusti* 22–23)[58]

The celebrations of 2 BCE.

516. These matters settled, Augustus dedicated this temple of Mars, although he had granted to Gaius and Lucius once for all the right to consecrate all such buildings by virtue of a kind of consular authority that exercised in the time-honoured manner. And they did, in fact, have the management of the Circensian games on this occasion, while their brother Agrippa took part along with the boys of the first families in the equestrian exercise called 'Troy.' Two hundred and sixty lions were slaughtered in the Circus. There was a gladiatorial combat in the Saepta, and a naval battle between the 'Persians' and the 'Athenians' was given on the spot where even to-day some relics of it are still pointed out. These, it will be understood, were the names given to the contestants; and the 'Athenians' prevailed as of old. Afterwards water was let into the Circus Flaminius and thirty-six crocodiles were there slaughtered. Augustus, however, did not serve as consul during all these days, but after holding office for a short time, gave the title of the consulship to another.
(Dio Cassius, *Roman History* 55.10.6–8)

Commentating on the arrest and execution of Sejanus in 31 CE, Juvenal made the following remark about the fickleness of the Roman mob and its propensity for 'bread and circuses'.

517. And what does the mob of Remus say? It follows fortune, as it always does, and rails against the condemned. That same rabble, if Nortia had smiled upon the Etruscan, if the aged Emperor had been struck down unawares, would in that very hour have conferred upon Sejanus the title of Augustus. Now that no one buys our votes, the public has long since cast off its cares; the people that once bestowed commands, consulships, legions and all else, now meddles no more and longs eagerly for just two things—Bread and Games [*panem et circenses*]!
(Juvenal, *Satires* 10.72–81)

Claudius at the arena.

518. At any gladiatorial show, either his own or another's, he gave orders that even those who fell accidentally should be slain, in particularly the net-fighters, so that he could watch their faces as they died. When a pair of gladiators had fallen by mutually inflicted wounds, he at once had some little knives made from both their swords for his use. He took such pleasure in the combats with wild beasts and of those that fought at noonday, that he would go down to the arena at daybreak and after dismissing the people for luncheon at midday, he would keep his seat and in addition to the appointed combatants, he would for trivial and hasty reasons match others, even of the carpenters, the assistants, and men of that class, if any automatic device, or pageant, or anything else of the kind, had not worked well. He even forced one of his pages to enter the arena just as he was, in his toga.
(Suetonius, *Claudius* 34)[59]

In 80 CE Martial published his *Liber de Spectaculis* (*Book on Shows*), which is his response to the spectacles offered by the Emperor Titus in the newly completed Colosseum.[60] The following extract reminds us that the execution of condemned criminals was a prominent feature of the entertainment.

519. As Prometheus, bound on Scythian crag, fed the tireless bird with his too abundant breast, so did Laureolus, hanging on no sham cross, give his naked flesh to a Caledonian boar. His lacerated limbs lived on, dripping gore, and in all his body, body there was none. Finally he met with the punishment he deserved; the guilty wretch had plunged a sword into his father's throat or his master's, or in his madness had robbed a temple of its secret gold, or laid a cruel torch to Rome. The criminal had outdone the misdeeds of ancient story; in him, what had been a play became an execution.
(Martial, *On the Spectacles* 9)[61]

Martial was moved by the slaughter of animals in the Colosseum to write a number of epigrams on the subject. Two of these follow.

520. Amid the cruel perils of Caesar's hunt a light spear had pierced a pregnant sow. One of her litter lept out of the hapless mother's wound. Savage Lucina, was *this* a delivery? She would have wished to die wounded by further weapons, so that the sad path might open for all her brood. Who denies that Bacchus sprang from his mother's death? Believe that a deity was so given birth: so born was a beast.
(Martial, *On the Spectacles* 14)

521. A tigress, wont to lick the hand of the fearless trainer, rare glory from the Hyrcanian mountains, fiercely tore a wild lion with rabid tooth; a novelty, unknown in any times. She dared do no such thing while she lived in the high forests, but since she has been among us she has gained ferocity.
(Martial, *On the Spectacles* 21)

Inscription from Pompeii.

522. Twenty pairs of gladiators of Decimus Lucretius Satrius Valens, lifetime flamen of Nero son of Caesar Augustus, and ten pairs of gladiators of Decimus Lucretius Valens, his son, will fight at Pompeii on April 8, 9, 10, 11, 12. There will be a full card of wild beast combats, and awnings [for the spectators]. Aemilius Celer [painted this sign], all alone in the moonlight.
(*CIL* volume 4, no. 3,884 [Lewis and Reinhold, *Roman Civilization: Sourcebook II, The Empire*, p. 359])

Seneca protests the barbarities of the arena.

523. But nothing is so damaging to good character as the habit of lounging at the games; for then it is that vice steals subtly upon one through the avenue of pleasure. What do you think I mean? I mean that I come home more greedy, more ambitious, more voluptuous, and even more cruel and inhuman,—because I have been among human beings. By chance I attended a mid-day exhibition, expecting some fun, wit, and relaxation,—an exhibition at which men's eyes have respite from the slaughter of their fellow-men. But it was quite the reverse. The previous combats were the essence of compassion; but now all the trifling is put aside and it is pure murder. The men have no defensive armour. They are exposed to blows at all points, and no one ever strikes in vain. Many persons prefer this programme to the usual pairs and to the bouts 'by request.' Of course they do; there is no helmet or shield to deflect the weapon. What is the need of defensive armour, or of skill? All these mean delaying death. In the morning they throw men to the lions and the bears; at noon, they throw them to the spectators. The spectators demand that the slayer shall face the man who is to slay him in his turn; and they always reserve the latest conqueror for another butchering. The outcome of every fight is death, and the means are fire and sword. This sort of thing goes on while the arena is empty. You may retort: 'But he was a highway robber; he killed a man!' And what of it? Granted that, as a murderer, he deserved this punishment, what crime have you committed, poor fellow, that you should deserve to sit and see this show? In the morning they cried 'Kill him! Lash him! Burn him! Why does he meet the sword in so cowardly a way? Why does he strike so feebly? Why doesn't he die game? Whip him to meet his wounds! Let them receive blow for blow, with chests bare and exposed to the stroke!' And when the games stop for the intermission, they announce: 'A little throatcutting in the meantime, so that there may still be something going on!'
(Seneca, *Epistles* 7.2–5)

Herod builds an arena in Jerusalem.

524. There was also a supply of wild beasts, a great many lions and other animals having been brought together for him, such as were of extraordinary strength or of very rare kinds. When the practice began of involving them in combat with one another or setting condemned men to fight against them, foreigners were astonished at the expense and at the same time entertained by the dangerous spectacle, but to the natives it meant an open break with the customs held in honour by them. For it seemed glaring impiety to throw men to wild beasts for the pleasure of

other men as spectators, and it seemed a further impiety to change their established ways for foreign practices. But more than all else it was the trophies that irked them, for in the belief that these were images surrounded by weapons, which it was against their national custom to worship, they were exceedingly angry.
(Josephus, *Antiquities* 15.273–76)[62]

Social Clubs (#525–27; cf. #86).

Pliny to Trajan.

525. The free and confederate city of Amisus enjoys, with your permission, the privilege of administering its own laws. I am sending with this letter a petition handed to me there which deals with the subject of benefit societies, so that you, Sir, may decide whether and to what extent these clubs are to be permitted or forbidden.
(Pliny the Younger, *Letters* 10.92)

Trajan to Pliny.

526. If the citizens of Amisus, whose petition you send with your letter, are allowed by their own laws, granted to them by formal treaty, to form a benefit society, there is no reason why we should interfere: especially if the contributions are not used for riotous and unlawful assemblies, but to relieve cases of hardship among the poor. In all other cities which are subject to our own law these institutions must be forbidden.
(Pliny the Younger, *Letters* 10.93)

Constitution of a burial society operating in Lanuvium in 136 CE.

The society was established in honour of Diana and Antinous (the defied lover of the emperor Hadrian).

527. (Clause from the Decree of the Senate of the Roman People)

These are permitted to assemble, convene, and maintain a society: those who desire to make monthly contributions for funerals may assemble in such a society, but they may not assemble in the name of such society except once a month for the sake of making contributions to provide burial for the dead.

It was voted further that if a slave member of this society dies, and his master or mistress unreasonably refuses to relinquish his body for burial, and he has not left written instructions, a token funeral ceremony shall be held.

It was voted further that on the festive days of his term of office each *quinquennalis* is to conduct worship with incense and wine and is to perform his other functions clothed in white, and that on the birthdays of Diana and Antinoüs he is to provide oil for the society in the public bath before they banquet.
(*CIL* volume 14, no. 2112 [Lewis and Reinhold, *Roman Civilization: Sourcebook II, The Empire*, pp. 273, 274, 275])[63]

7.12. War

Among the Greeks of the Hellenistic era, warfare was still prosecuted by citizen armies. From the first century BCE the armies of generals were almost constantly on the field. This contributed to the end of the Republic, and the diminution of the authority of the Senate. Long campaigns earlier in the first century BCE conducted by generals such as Marius, Sulla and Julius Caesar meant that troops became more loyal to their general than to the Senate, and were dependent on their generals to provide land and other benefits on discharge. Troops were used to press their general's political claims. Augustus owed his power and authority ultimately to his repute among his troops and veterans. He created a standing army out of the 25 legions personally loyal to him and which survived from the era of the civil wars.

Legionary troops were recruited from the ranks of Roman citizens, initially from among those with property. Each legion numbered roughly 5500 infantry and 120 cavalry. During early Imperial times each ordinary soldier drew an annual pay of 225 denarii (see Tacitus, *Annals* 1.17). Soldiers had to provide their own food, clothing and weapons. Auxiliary units, cohorts of about 500 men, were attached to each legion. Their numbers were drawn from non-citizens in the Imperial provinces. Citizenship was bestowed on auxiliaries on completion of 25 years' service.

With the exception of major defeats at the hands of Hannibal and the occasional disaster at the hands of the Parthians, Roman troops were invariably victorious wherever they were deployed. As Polybius noted in the mid second century BCE, Roman military power had already proven irresistible. Superior tactical ability, dependable resources, the Roman temperament, and ease of deployment all played a part in this success. Among the Romans, victory in battle was considered a major source of personal glory (see #489 above).[64]

Sources

The Roman army.

In his *Histories* 6.19–42 Polybius describes the personnel, the equipment and formation of the typical Roman army camp of his day (mid second century BCE). In sections 27–32 he describes the camp. The Roman camp appeared as a town with regular patterns of streets set at right angles.

528. (27) The manner in which they form their camp is as follows. When the site for the camp has been chosen, the position in it giving the best general view and most suitable for issuing orders is assigned to the general's tent (*praetorium*). Fixing an ensign on the spot where they are about to pitch it, they measure off round this ensign a square plot of ground each side of which is one hundred feet distant, so that the total area measures four plethra [a square plethron is about 10,000 square feet, or 930 square metres]. Along one side of this square in the direction which seems to give the greatest facilities for watering and foraging, the Roman legions are disposed as follows. As I have said, there are six tribunes in each legion; and since each consul has always two Roman legions with him, it is evident there are twelve tribunes in the army of each. They place then the tents of these all in one line parallel to the side of the square selected and fifty feet distant from it, to give room for the horses, mules, and baggage of the tribunes. These tents are pitched with their backs turned to the *praetorium* and facing the outer side of the camp, a direction of which I will always speak as 'the front.' The tents of the tribunes are at an equal distance from each other, and at such a distance that they extend along the whole breadth of the space occupied by the legions.

(28) They now measure a hundred feet from the front of all these tents, and starting from the line drawn at this distance parallel to the tents of the tribunes they begin to encamp the legions, managing matters as follows. Bisecting the above line, they start from this spot and along a line drawn at right angles to the first, they encamp the cavalry of each legion facing each other and separated by a distance of fifty feet, the last-mentioned line exactly half-way between them. The manner of encamping the cavalry and the infantry is very similar, the whole space occupied by the maniples and squadrons being a square. This square faces one of the streets or *viae* and is of a fixed length of one hundred feet, and they usually try to make the depth the same except in the case of the allies. When they employ the larger legions they add proportionately to the length and depth.

(31) The spaces behind the tents of the tribunes to right and left of the praetorium, are used in the one case for the market and in the other for the office of the quaestor and the supplies of which he is in charge…

The whole camp thus forms a square, and the way in which the streets are laid out and its general arrangement give it the appearance of a town. The agger is on all sides at a distance of 200 feet from the tents, and this empty space is of important service in several respects. To begin with it provides the proper facilities for marching the troops in and out, seeing that they all march out into this space by their own streets and thus do not come into one street in a mass and throw down or hustle each other. Again it is here that they collect the cattle brought into camp and all booty taken from the enemy, and keep them safe during the night. But the most important thing of all is that in night attacks neither fire can reach them nor missiles except a very few, which are almost

harmless owing to the distance and the space in front of the tents.
(Polybius, *Histories* 6.27–28; 31.1, 10–14)[65]

Augustus founded 28 colonies for veterans in Italy out of his personal resources (see also *Res Gestae* 3, 16). Earlier foundations had been at the cost of large-scale confiscations of land, such as Virgil's.

529. After having thus set the city and its affairs in order, he added to the population of Italy by personally establishing twenty-eight colonies; furnished many parts of it with public buildings and revenues; and even gave it, at least to some degree, equal rights and dignity with the city of Rome, by devising a kind of votes which the members of the local senate were to cast in each colony for candidates for the city offices and send under seal to Rome against the day of the elections. To keep up the supply of men of rank and induce the commons to increase and multiply, he admitted to the equestrian military career those who were recommended by any town, while to those of the commons who could lay claim to worthy sons or daughters when he made his rounds of the districts he distributed a thousand sesterces for each child.
(Suetonius, *Augustus* 46)

Lack of discipline among Roman troops in North Africa led to the punitive decimation of a cohort.

530. When the news reached Lucius Apronius [the proconsul of Africa, 18–20 CE]..., perturbed more by the disgrace of his own troops than by the success of the enemy, he resorted to a measure rare in that period and reminiscent of an older world, drawing by lot and flogging to death every tenth man in the dishonoured cohort. And so effective was the severity that, when the same forces of Tacfarinas assaulted a stronghold named Thala, they were routed by a company of veterans not more than five hundred in number.
(Tacitus, *Annals* 3.21)[66]

Dio Cassius's epitomist, Zonaras, describes the typical Roman triumph.

531. Now the celebration of the triumph was somewhat as follows. When any great success, worthy of a triumph, had been gained, the general was immediately saluted as *imperator* by the soldiers, and he would bind sprigs of laurel upon the fasces and deliver them to the messengers who announced the victory to the city. On arriving home he would assemble the senate and ask to have the triumph voted him. And if he obtained a vote from the senate and from the people, his title of *imperator* was confirmed. If he still occupied the office which he had held when he won his victory, he continued to hold it while celebrating the festival; but if his term of office had expired, he received some other title appropriate to the office, since it was forbidden a private individual to hold a triumph. Arrayed in the triumphal dress and wearing armlets, with a laurel crown upon his head, and holding a branch in his right hand, he called together the people. After praising collectively the troops who had served with him, and some of them individually, he presented them with money and honoured them also with decorations. Upon some he bestowed armlets and spears without the iron; to others he gave crowns, sometimes of gold, sometimes of silver, bearing the name of each man and the representation of his particular feat. For example, if a man had been first to mount a wall, the crown bore the figure of a wall; or if he had also captured some point by storm, both of the feats were depicted. A man might have won a battle at sea, in which case the crown was adorned with ships, or he might have won a cavalry fight and some equestrian figure was represented. He who had rescued a citizen from battle or other peril, or from a siege, had the greatest praise and would receive a crown fashioned of oak, which was esteemed as far more honourable than all the other crowns, whether of silver or of gold. And these rewards were not only given to men singly, as the result of individual deeds of prowess, but were also bestowed upon whole companies and armies. A large part of the spoils also was assigned to the soldiers who had taken part in the campaign; but some victors have distributed the spoils even among the entire populace and have devot-

ed them toward the expenses of the festival or turned them over to the treasury; if anything was left over, they would spend it for temples, porticos or some other public work.

After these ceremonies the triumphant general would mount his chariot. Now this chariot did not resemble one used in games or in war, but was fashioned in the shape of a round tower. And he would not be alone in the chariot, but if he had children or relatives, he would make the girls and the infant male children get up beside him in it and place the older ones upon the horses—outriggers as well as the yoke-pair; if there were many of them, they would accompany the procession on chargers, riding along beside the victor. None of the rest rode, but all went on foot wearing laurel wreaths. A public slave, however, rode with the victor in the chariot itself, holding over him the crown of precious stones set in gold, and kept saying to him, 'Look behind!' that is, 'Look at what comes after—at the ensuing years of life—and do not be elated or puffed up by your present fortune.' Both a bell and a whip were fastened to the chariot, signifying that it was possible for him to meet with misfortune also, to the extent even of being scourged or condemned to death. For it was customary for those who had been condemned to die for any crime to wear a bell, to the end that no one should approach them as they walked along and so be contaminated. Thus arrayed, they entered the city, having at the head of the procession the spoils and trophies and figures representing the captured forts, cities, mountains, rivers, lakes, and seas—everything, in fact, that they had taken. If one day did not suffice for the exhibition of these things in procession, the celebration was held during a second and a third day. When these adjuncts had gone on their way, the victorious general arrived at the Roman Forum, and after commanding that some of the captives be led to prison and put to death, he rode up to the Capitol. There he performed certain rites and made offerings and dined in the porticos up there, after which he departed homeward toward evening, accompanied by flutes and pipes. Such were the triumphs in olden times; but factions and powerful cliques effected many changes in them.

(Zonaras, *Epitome of Dio Cassius* 7.21)[67]

Roman citizenship was bestowed upon veterans. The following is an extract from the diptych of M. Valerius Quadratus, a veteran of the Jerusalem campaign as a member of the legion X Fretensis. It was uncovered in Philadelphia in the Fayum (in Egypt), and dates from 2 July 94 CE. The editor has provided textual emendations in square brackets [ ] and glosses in parentheses ( ). The Emperor Domitian issued the decree.

532. (column 2) 'It seemed good to me to signify by decree: The veteran soldiers among you all (?) ought to be made free and exempted from all customs, havendues and tolls; they themselves, their wives and children and their parents who are living in wedlock (?) shall be able to be Roman citizens with every and the best right and shall be free and released with all exemption; and with respect to all exemption their parents and children, who are written above, shall be of the same right and of the same estate (as they)...

(column 3) [? The Imperator has allowed the citizenship of those v]eterans (with their wives and children above written, inscribed on brass, or if they are unmarried, with those whom they afterwards shall have married, each severally) who have served at Hierosolymna in the 10th Fretensian Legion, [having been] discharged with an honourable discharge, after full time served...'

(Deissmann, *Light from the Ancient East*, p. 446 [column 2, ll. 12–18; column 3, ll. 1–4])

7.13. Atrocities

The following extracts illustrate the violence of the Graeco-Roman era, which was no worse, one supposes, than at other times in history. Many of the sources below emanate from the theatre of war. The violence inflicted on the innocent, especially those caught up in a siege, is frequently noted by writers. Massacres of provincials by Roman soldiers are a depressingly common occurrence in the sources.[68] However, violence was also endemic to social life, as the extracts from Juvenal and Seneca testify.

Sources

The end of the siege of Tyre.

533. The king [Alexander] sold the women and children into slavery and crucified all the men of military age. These were not less than two thousand [cf. Curtius, 4.4.17—2000 men]. Although most of the non-combatants had been removed to Carthage, those who remained to become captive were found to be more than thirteen thousand. (Diodorus Siculus, *Histories* 17.46.4)

In the fourth century BCE, Thebes, having resisted Alexander's hegemony, was successfully besieged by Alexander and the city's former allies. Diodorus Siculus describes what happened in the aftermath.

534. So it was that many terrible things befell the city. Greeks were mercilessly slain by Greeks, relatives were butchered by their own relatives, and even a common dialect induced no pity. In the end, when night finally intervened, the houses had been plundered and children and women and aged persons who had fled into the temples were torn from sanctuary and subjected to outrage without limit.
(Diodorus Siculus, *Histories* 17.13.6.
See also 17.14.1–4. Note, by contrast, Josephus's idealized presentation of Moses's commands for the conduct of war by the Israelites in *Against Apion* 2.111–12).

The following passage comes from Appian's account of the Third Punic War (149–146 BCE). The war resulted in the complete destruction of Carthage. Here the historian reports the carnage inside the city at the moment of its capture.

535. Then came the new scenes of horror. The fire spread and carried everything down, and the soldiers did not wait to destroy the buildings little by little, but pulled them all down together. So the crashing grew louder, and many fell with the stones into the midst dead. Others were seen still living, especially old men, women and young children who had hidden in the inmost nooks of the houses, some of them wounded, some more or less burned, and uttering horrible cries. Still others, thrust out and falling from such a height with the stones, timbers, and fire, were torn asunder into all kinds of horrible shapes, crushed and mangled. Nor was this the end of their miseries, for the street cleaners, who were removing the rubbish with axes, mattocks, and boathooks, and making the roads passable, tossed with these instruments the dead and the living together into holes in the ground, sweeping them along like sticks and stones or turning them over with their iron tools, and man was used for filling up a ditch. Some were thrown in head foremost, while their legs, sticking out of the ground, writhed a long time. Others fell with their feet downward and their heads above ground. Horses ran over them, crushing their faces and skulls, not purposely on the part of the riders, but in their headlong haste. Nor did the street cleaners either do these things on purpose; but the press of war, the glory of approaching victory, the rush of the soldiery, the confused noise of heralds and trumpeters all round, the tribunes and centurions changing guard and marching the cohorts hither and thither—all together made everybody frantic and heedless of the spectacle before their eyes.
(Appian, *History of Rome* 8.129)

The Romans used crucifixion as a weapon of terror. The following passage describes the fate of those endeavouring to escape from Jerusalem during the final stages of the siege.

536. When caught, they were driven to resist, and after a conflict it seemed too late to sue for mercy. They were accordingly scourged and subjected to torture of every description, before being killed, and then crucified opposite the walls. Titus indeed commiserated their fate, five hundred or sometimes more being captured daily; on the other hand, he recognized the risk of dismissing prisoners of war, and that the custody of such numbers would amount to the imprisonment of their custodians; but his main reason for not stopping the crucifixions was

the hope that the spectacle might perhaps induce the Jews to surrender, for fear that continued resistance would involve them in a similar fate. The soldiers out of rage and hatred amused themselves by nailing their prisoners in different postures; and so great was their number, that space could not be found for the crosses nor crosses for the bodies.
(Josephus, *Jewish War* 5.449–51)[69]

The mistreatment of prisoners of war is also encountered in Appian's account of the capture of Carthage in 146 BCE. See also #535.

537. When daylight came, Hasdrubal, enraged at the attack upon Megara, took the Roman prisoners whom he held, brought them upon the walls, in full sight of their comrades, and tore out their eyes, tongues, tendons, or private parts with iron hooks; of some he lacerated the soles of the feet, of others he cut off the fingers, and some he flayed alive, hurling them all, still living, from the top of the walls. He intended to make reconciliation between the Carthaginians and Romans impossible, and sought to fire them with the conviction that their only safety was in fighting: but the result was contrary to his intention. For the Carthaginians, conscience-stricken by these nefarious deeds, became timid instead of courageous, and hated Hasdrubal for depriving them even of all hope of pardon. Their senate especially denounced him for committing these savage and outrageous cruelties in the midst of such great domestic calamities. But he actually arrested some of the complaining senators and put them to death. Making himself feared in every way he came to be more like a tyrant than a general, for he considered himself secure only if he were an object of terror to them, and for this reason difficult to attack.
(Appian, *History of Rome* 8.118)[70]

Troops going beserk on the German frontier, 68 CE.

538. The army approached the Treviri with a sense of security which they naturally felt among allies. But at Divodurum, a town of the Mediomatrici, though received with all courtesy, the army was struck with sudden panic; the soldiers hurriedly seized their arms to massacre the innocent citizens, not for booty or from a desire to loot, but prompted by wild fury, the cause of which was uncertain and the remedies therefore more difficult. Finally, however, they were quieted by their general's appeals and refrained from completely destroying the community; still about 4,000 had been massacred, and such terror spread over the Gallic provinces that later on, as the army advanced, entire communities headed by their magistrates came out to meet it with appeals, women and children prostrating themselves along the roads, while everything else that can appease an enemy's wrath was offered to secure peace, although there was no war.
(Tacitus, *Histories* 1.63)

The toll of warfare on the land and people.

539. After the spectacles [Caesar's triumphs celebrated on his return from his African campaign of 46 BCE], a census of the people [according to Suetonius, *Caesar* 41, the census was of those entitled to receive the food dole in Rome] was taken, and instead of the three hundred and twenty thousand of the preceding lists there were enrolled only one hundred and fifty thousand. So great was the calamity which the civil wars had wrought, and so large a portion of the people of Rome had they consumed away, to say nothing of the misfortunes that possessed the rest of Italy and the provinces.
(Plutarch, *Julius Caesar* 55.3)

The execution of Sejanus's son and daughter.

540. It was determined that the surviving children of Sejanus should pay the penalty, though the anger of the populace was nearly spent and the majority of men had been placated by the earlier executions. They were therefore carried to the dungeon, the boy conscious of the fate in store for him, the girl so completely ignorant that she asked repeatedly what her offence had been and to what place they were dragging her: she would do wrong no more, and she could be cautioned with the usual childish beating. It is recorded by authors of the period that, as it was considered an unheard-of thing for capital punishment to be inflicted on a virgin, she was violated by the executioner with the hal-

ter beside her: they were then strangled, and their young bodies thrown on to the Gemonian Stairs.
(Tacitus, *Annals* 5.9)[71]

Philo reflects on the human propensity for cruelty; this in the context of failure to pay taxes.

541. An example of this was given a little while ago in our own district by a person who was appointed to serve as a collector of taxes. When some of his debtors whose default was clearly due to poverty took flight in fear of the fatal consequences of his vengeance, he carried off by force their womenfolk and children and parents and their other relatives and beat and subjected them to every kind of outrage and contumely in order to make them either tell him the whereabouts of the fugitive or discharge his debt themselves. As they could do neither the first for want of knowledge, nor the second because they were as penniless as the fugitive, he continued this treatment until while wringing their bodies with racks and instruments of torture he finally dispatched them by newly-invented methods of execution. He filled a large basket with sand and having hung this enormous weight by ropes round their necks set them in the middle of the market-place in the open air, in order that while they themselves sank under the cruel stress of the accumulated punishments, the wind, the sun, the shame of being seen by the passers-by and the weights suspended on them, the spectators of their punishments might suffer by anticipation. Some of these, whose souls saw facts more vividly than did their eyes, feeling themselves maltreated in the bodies of others, hastened to take leave of their lives with the aid of the sword or poison or halter, thinking that in their evil plight it was a great piece of luck to die without suffering torture. The others who had seized the opportunity to dispatch themselves were brought out in a row, as is done in the awarding of inheritances, first those who stood in the first degrees of kinship, after them the second, then the third and so on till the last. And when there were no kinsmen left, the maltreatment was passed on to their neighbours and sometimes even to villages and cities which quickly became desolate and stripped of their inhabitants who left their homes and dispersed to places where they expected to remain unobserved.
(Philo, *Special Laws* 3.159–62.
See also *Special Laws* 2.92–94)

Juvenal reflects on the violence men perpetrate against each other.

542. But in these days there is more amity among serpents than among men; wild beasts are merciful to beasts spotted like themselves. When did the stronger lion ever take the life of the weaker? In what wood did a boar ever breathe his last under the tusks of a boar bigger than himself? The fierce tigress of India dwells in perpetual peace with her fellow; grim bears live in harmony with bears. But man finds it all too little to have forged the deadly blade on an impious anvil; for whereas the first artificers only wearied themselves with forging rakes and hoes, spades and ploughshares, not knowing how to beat out swords, we now behold a people whose wrath is not assuaged by slaying someone, but who deem that a man's breast, arms, and face afford a kind of food. What would Pythagoras say, or to what place would he not flee, if he beheld these horrors of to-day,—he who refrained from every living creature as if it were human, and would not indulge his belly with every kind of pulse?
(Juvenal, *Satires* 15.159–74)

Seneca's advice on avoiding violent people.

543. Reflect on the things which goad man into destroying man: you will find that they are hope, envy, hatred, fear, and contempt. Now, of all these, contempt is the least harmful, so much so that many have skulked behind it as a sort of cure. When a man despises you, he works you injury, to be sure, but he passes on; and no one persistently or of set purpose does hurt to a person whom he despises. Even in battle, prostrate soldiers are neglected: men fight with those who stand their ground. And you can avoid the envious hopes of the wicked so long as you have nothing which can stir the evil desires of others, and so long as you possess nothing remarkable. For people crave even

little things, if these catch the attention or are of rare occurrence.

You will escape envy if you do not force yourself upon the public view, if you do not boast your possessions, if you understand how to enjoy things privately. Hatred comes either from running foul of others: and this can be avoided by never provoking anyone; or else it is uncalled for: and common-sense will keep you safe from it. Yet it has been dangerous to many; some people have been hated without having had an enemy. As to not being feared, a moderate fortune and an easy disposition will guarantee you that; men should know that you are the sort of person who can be offended without danger; and your reconciliation should be easy and sure. Moreover, it is as troublesome to be feared at home as abroad; it is as bad to be feared by a slave as by a gentleman. For every one has strength enough to do you some harm. Besides, he who is feared, fears also; no one has been able to arouse terror and live in peace of mind.
(Seneca, *Epistles* 105.1–4)

7.14. Government

The historian Polybius, a keen and astute observer of Rome, sought to account for its imperial success. It seemed to him that the seeds of Roman ascendancy were located in Rome's constitution, a uniquely balanced mix, he argued, of monarchy, oligarchy and democracy (see #544 below). It was, he claimed, the best of all constitutions. The proof of this lay in the fact that it had shown itself capable of delivering Rome (as Polybius had recorded) in all emergencies and had secured the state from the extremes of any one of the forms of government.

In time, however, Rome found itself at the mercy of successful generals, whose soldiers were prepared to do their bidding. The civil wars and strife of the first two generations of the first century BCE were resolved in the principate of Augustus. Rome essentially reverted to a monarchy, as perceptively noted by Appian (see #70). No one doubted that supreme power resided in the emperor, at least as long as he could rely on the loyalty and backing of the army. The Senate and councils of the plebs continued to transact their business. The consuls continued to be elected, and were sent as governors to the provinces. However, all affairs of government were transacted under the watchful, and occasionally intrusive, eye of the emperor and his bureaucracy.

A feature both of Republican and early Imperial times was the role played by Roman citizenship in the dissemination of Roman power. In no small part Roman rule had been effectively established through the discriminating extension of citizenship to Roman allies in Italy and later to provincials.[72] In the first century CE Roman citizenship was still counted a privilege. Citizens were not subject, for instance, to summary punishment such as being beaten, and could appeal to Rome when accused (see Acts 25:10, 12).[73] Paul was a Roman citizen, and had been born as such (Acts 22:28).

Sources

Polybius asserted the superiority of the Roman constitution. He argues that the constitution features the main components of monarchy, oligarchy and democracy, and that these existed in balance and creative tension.

544. (11) The three kinds of government that I spoke of above all shared in the control of the Roman state. And such fairness and propriety in all respects was shown in the use of these three elements for drawing up the constitution and in its subsequent administration that it was impossible even for a native to pronounce with certainty whether the whole system was aristocratic, democratic, or monarchical. This was indeed only natural. For if one fixed one's eyes on the power of the consuls, the constitution seemed completely monarchical and royal; if on that of the senate it seemed again to be aristocratic; and when one looked at the power of the masses, it seemed clearly to be a democracy. The parts of the state falling under the control of each element were and with a few modifications still are as follows.

(12) The consuls, previous to leading out their legions, exercise authority in Rome over all public affairs, since all the other magistrates except the tribunes are under them and bound to obey them, and it is they who introduce embassies to the senate. Besides this it is they who consult the senate on matters of urgency, they who carry out in detail the provisions of its decrees. Again as concerns all affairs of state administered by the people it is their duty to take these under their charge, to summon assemblies, to introduce measures, and to preside over the execution of the popular decrees. As for preparation for war and the general conduct of operations in the field, here their power is almost uncontrolled; for they are empowered to make what demands they choose on the allies, to appoint military tribunes, to levy soldiers and select those who are fittest for service. They also have the right of inflicting, when on active service, punishment on anyone under their command; and they are authorized to spend any sum they decide upon from the public funds, being accompanied by a quaestor who faithfully executes their instructions. So that if one looks at this part of the administration alone, one may reasonably pronounce the constitution to be a pure monarchy or kingship...

(13) To pass to the senate. In the first place it has the control of the treasury, all revenue and expenditure being regulated by it. For with the exception of payments made to the consuls, the quaestors are not allowed to disburse for any particular object without a decree of the senate. And even the item of expenditure which is far heavier and more important than any other—the outlay every five years by the censors on public works, whether construction or repairs—is under the control of the senate, which makes a grant to the censors for the purpose. Similarly crimes committed in Italy which require a public investigation, such as treason, conspiracy, poisoning, and assassination, are under the jurisdiction of the senate. Also if any private person or community in Italy is in need of arbitration or indeed claims damages or requires succour or protection, the senate attends to all such matters. It also occupies itself with the dispatch of all embassies sent to countries outside of Italy for the purpose either of settling differences, or of offering friendly advice, or indeed of imposing demands, or of receiving submission, or of declaring war; and in like manner with respect to embassies arriving in Rome it decides what reception and what answer should be given to them. All these matters are in the hands of the senate, nor have the people anything whatever to do with them. So that again to one residing in Rome during the absence of the consuls the constitution appears to be entirely aristocratic; and this is the conviction of many Greek states and many of the kings, as the senate manages all business connected with them.

(Polybius, *Histories* 6.11.11–13; 12.1–9; 13)

After discussing the three arms of government in Rome (consuls, Senate, councils of the plebs), Polybius draws the following conclusions.

545. Such being the power that each part has of hampering the others or co-operating with them, their union is adequate to all emergencies, so that it is impossible to find a better political system than this. For whenever the menace of some common danger from abroad compels them to act in concord and support each other, so great does the strength of the state become, that nothing which is requisite can be neglected, as all are zealously competing in devising means of meeting the need of the hour, nor can any decision arrived at fail to be executed promptly, as all are co-operating both in public and in private to the accomplishment of the task they have set themselves; and consequently this peculiar form of constitution possesses an irresistible power of attaining every object upon which it is resolved. When again they are freed from external menace, and reap the harvest of good fortune and affluence which is the result of their success, and in the enjoyment of this property are corrupted by flattery and idleness and wax insolent and overbearing, as indeed happens often enough, it is then especially that we see the state providing

itself a remedy for the evil from which it suffers. For when one part having grown out of proportion to the others aims at supremacy and tends to become too predominant, it is evident that, as for the reasons above given none of the three is absolute, but the purpose of the one can be counterworked and thwarted by the others, none of them will excessively outgrow the others or treat them with contempt. All in fact remains *in statu quo*, on the one hand, because any aggressive impulse is sure to be checked and from the outset each estate stands in dread of being interfered with by the others...
(Polybius, *Histories* 6.18)[74]

Increasingly during the Imperial period the Senate became essential for the Greek east, which became dependent on it for settling disputes.

The overuse of the rights of sanctuary in the east, the submission of all constitutions to Rome.

546. Tiberius, however, while tightening his grasp on the solid power of the principate, vouchsafed to the senate, a shadow of the past by submitting the claims of the provinces to the discussion of its members. For throughout the Greek cities there was a growing laxity, and impunity, in the creation of rights of asylum. The temples were filled with the dregs of the slave population; the same shelter was extended to the debtor against his creditor and to the man suspected of a capital offence; nor was any authority powerful enough to quell the factions of a race which protected human felony equally with divine worship. It was resolved, therefore, that the communities in question should send their charters and deputies to Rome. A few abandoned without a struggle the claims they had asserted without a title: many relied on hoary superstitions or on their services to the Roman nation. It was an impressive spectacle which that day afforded, when the senate scrutinized the benefactions of its predecessors, the constitutions of the provinces, even the decrees of kings whose power antedated the arms of Rome, and the rites of the deities themselves, with full liberty as of old to confirm or change.
(Tacitus, *Annals* 3.60)[75]

The quest for glory and fame through the holding of public office is the subject of Sallust's observations below. The lure and danger of politics is clearly evoked. Sallust himself held a succession of offices in the late 50s and 40s BCE.

547. But among these pursuits, in my opinion, magistracies and military commands, in short all public offices, are least desirable in these times, since honour is not bestowed upon merit, while those who have gained it wrongfully are neither safe nor the more honourable because of it. For to rule one's country or subjects by force, although you both have the power to correct abuses, and do correct them, is nevertheless tyrannical; especially since all attempts at change foreshadow bloodshed, exile, and other horrors of war. Moreover, to struggle in vain and after wearisome exertion to gain nothing but hatred, is the height of folly, unless haply one is possessed by a dishonourable and pernicious passion for sacrificing one's personal honour and liberty to the power of a few men.

But among intellectual pursuits, the recording of the events of the past is especially serviceable; but of that it becomes me to say nothing, both because many men have already spoken of its value, and in order that no one may suppose that I am led by vanity to eulogize my own favourite occupation. I suppose, too, that since I have resolved to pass my time aloof from public affairs, some will apply to this arduous and useful employment of mine the name of idleness, certainly those who regard courting the people and currying favour by banquets as the height of industriousness. But if such men will only bear in mind in what times I was elected to office, what men of merit were unable to attain the same honour and what sort of men have since come into the senate, they will surely be convinced that it is rather from justifiable motives than from indolence that I have changed my opinion, and that greater profit will accrue to our country from my inactivity than from others' activity.

I have often heard that Quintus Maximus, Publius Scipio, and other eminent men of our country, were in the habit of declaring that their hearts were set mightily aflame for the pursuit of virtue whenever they gazed upon the masks of their ancestors. Of course they did not mean to imply that the wax or the effigy had any such power over them, but rather that it is the memory of great deeds that kindles in the breasts of noble men this flame that cannot be quelled until they by their own prowess have equalled the fame and glory [*fama atque gloria*] of their forefathers.

But in these degenerate days, on the contrary, who is there that does not vie with his ancestors in riches and extravagance rather than in uprightness and diligence? Even the 'new men', who in former times always relied upon worth to outdo the nobles, now make their way to power and distinction by intrigue and open fraud rather than by noble practices; just as if a praetorship, a consulship, or anything else of the kind were distinguished and illustrious in and of itself and were not valued according to the merit of those who live up to it. But in giving expression to my sorrow and indignation at the morals of our country I have spoken too freely and wandered too far away from my subject. To this I now return.
(Sallust, *War with Jugurtha* 3–4)

Electioneering.

Quintus Cicero, the brother of the famous orator, wrote an exhortatory treatise on electioneering to help Cicero prepare his campaign for the consulship of 63 BCE. Cicero was elected.

548. (35) You should know how each man is disposed towards you, so that you can decide, accordingly, how much confidence to place in each. Now as to the escorts, inasmuch as their services are more important than those of the callers, indicate clearly that they are more gratifying to you, and so far as possible, go down to the Forum at regular hours; a large company of daily escorts makes a great impression and adds great prestige. The third item under this heading is the supply of full-time attendants. To those who are volunteers, make it clear that you are forever in their debt for a very great kindness. To those who owe you this service, insist absolutely that any who are not too old or too busy should regularly attend on you themselves, and that those who cannot themselves do so should appoint their relatives to this duty. I am very anxious that you should always have a crowd about you; I think it important to the occasion. Further, it will bring you great credit and high prestige if you have around you those whom you have defended, who have been preserved and saved from condemnation by you. Demand of them plainly that since it is due to your unpaid efforts that they have retained their property, or their reputation, or their life and all their fortunes, and since there will never be another chance for them to thank you, they should repay you by this service.

(41) Now that enough has been said of instituting friendships, I must now speak of the other part of the canvass, which concerns method in dealing with the People. This requires a memory for names, an ingratiating manner, constant attendance, generosity, publicity, a fine political image. First, show off your habit of *knowing people* so that it is obvious, and increase and improve it daily; nothing, to my mind, is so popular and gratifying. Then, be determined that what you lack by nature should be so well simulated that it seems a natural act. You are not wanting in the pleasant manners proper to a kind and agreeable man, but what you urgently need is *ingratiation*, which may be a base fault in the rest of life, but in a canvass it is indispensable. For it is vile when flattery is used to corrupt a man, but less execrable when used to conciliate friendship, and indispensable for a candidate, whose facial expression and conversation must be modified and adapted to the humour and the inclination of all whom he meets.

(52) Lastly, see that your whole canvass is a *fine show*, brilliant, resplendent, and popular, with the utmost display and prestige; and also, if it can be managed at all, that there should be scandalous talk, in character, about the crimes, lusts, and briberies of your competitors. Above all, it must be shown in this canvass that high hopes and good opinions are entertained for your political future. Yet, during your canvass, you must not deal

with politics either in the Senate or in political meetings of the People. Instead, you must keep in mind that the Senate should deem you, on your life's record, to be in future an upholder of its authority; the Roman Knights and men of worth and substance, from your past life, to be devoted to peace and quiet times; the masses, to be favourably inclined to their interests, since you have been 'Popular' at least in your speeches in political meetings and lawcourts. (Quintus Cicero, *Handbook of Electioneering* 35–38, 41–42, 52–53)

Roman Law: The Twelve Tables *(#549, #551–53).*

The Twelve Tables preserve fifth-century BCE Roman law codes on various matters, dealing, for instance, with the rights of fathers, the family, the place of women, and property rights. The early history of the development of Roman law can be traced in *The Twelve Tables.*

The rights of the pater familias *regarding the destruction of deformed infants.*

549. Quickly killed, as the Twelve Tables ordain that a dreadfully deformed child shall be killed [by the father].
(*Twelve Tables* 4.1)

The power of the *pater familias* is well illustrated in Sallust's account of the Catiline conspiracy.

550. [T]here were many outside the ranks of the conspiracy who, when hostilities began, went to join Catiline. Among them was Fulvius, a senator's son, who was brought back and put to death by order of his father. (Sallust, *War with Catiline* 39.5)

The status of women with regard to guardianship.

551. Our ancestors have seen fit that females, by reason of levity in disposition, should remain in guardianship even when they have attained their majority.
(*Twelve Tables* 5.1)[76]

Freedmen and patrons.

552. The inheritance of a Roman citizen-freedman is, by the Law of the Twelve Tables, made over to his patron, if the freedman has died intestate and having no self-successor.
(*Twelve Tables* 5.8)

No burial or cremation was allowed within the Roman pomerium, i.e. the city boundaries.

553. A dead man says a law in the Twelve—shall not be buried or burned within the city...
(*Twelve Tables* 10.1)

Capital punishment.

The following extract is from the early third-century CE jurist Iulius Paulus. Glosses are included within parentheses ( ).

554. Concerning Seditious Persons.

Instigators of sedition and riot or rousers of the people are, according to the nature of their rank, either crucified, thrown to wild beasts, or deported to an island. As for those who dig up or plow up boundary stones or destroy boundary trees, if slaves do it of their own volition, they are condemned to the mines; if humble persons, to (labor on) public works; if of superior rank, they are deprived of one third of their property and relegated to an island or driven into exile. Roman citizens who permit themselves or their slaves to be circumcised under the Jewish rite are deprived of their property and relegated to an island for life; the physicians (who perform the operation) suffer capital punishment...

On the Cornelian Law Concerning Assassins and Poisoners (a law of Sulla passed in 81 BCE).

Persons who perform, or cause to be performed, impious or nocturnal rites in order to enchant, bewitch, or bind, are crucified or thrown to wild beasts... It has been decreed that persons who are privy to the art of magic shall be visited with the supreme penalty, that is, be thrown to wild beasts or crucified. The magicians themselves are burned alive. No one is permitted to have books on the art of magic in his possession; those in whose possession they are found (the books are burned in public) are deprived of their property and deported to an island if of superior rank, and suffer capital punishment if humble. Not only the

profession but even the knowledge of this art is prohibited...
(Iulius Paulus, *Opinions* 5.22–24)

7.15. Natural Disasters

Earthquakes, famines, fires, building collapses, and storms are frequently narrated in the Graeco-Roman sources. Disasters of any sort are often the subject of poignant and rhetorically effective narrative. The following extracts have been included to underscore the contribution of natural disasters to the already tenuous existence of the people of the period. I have cited in full Pliny the Younger's letter describing the famous eruption of Mount Vesuvius in 79 CE.

Sources

Destruction of corn fleet at the mouth of the Tiber during the reign of Nero.

555. [A]t Rome trophies over the Parthians and arches were being erected in the middle of the Capitoline Hill: they had been voted by the senate while the issue of the war was still open, and now they were not abandoned—appearances being consulted, though known truth had to be ignored. Moreover, to cloak his uneasiness as to the situation abroad, Nero had the grain for the populace—which had been spoilt by age—thrown into the Tiber, as proof that the corn-supply was not a matter for anxiety. The price was not raised, though some two hundred vessels actually in port had been destroyed by a raging tempest, and a hundred more, which had made their way up the Tiber, by a chance outbreak of fire. (Tacitus, *Annals* 15.18)

In 79 CE Mount Vesuvius erupted. Pliny the Younger, later Governor of Bithynia during the time of Trajan, was an eye-witness. In the following letter to the historian Tacitus he describes what happened. His uncle, the natural historian Pliny the Elder, perished in the disaster. Note also Pliny's flattery of the recipient. Tacitus's record of the event (assuming he recorded it) is lost.

556. To Cornelius Tacitus

Thank you for asking me to send you a description of my uncle's death so that you can leave an accurate account of it for posterity; I know that immortal fame awaits him if his death is recorded by you. It is true that he perished in a catastrophe which destroyed the loveliest regions of the earth, a fate shared by whole cities and their people, and one so memorable that it is likely to make his name live for ever: and he himself wrote a number of books of lasting value: but you write for all time and can still do much to perpetuate his memory. The fortunate man, in my opinion, is he to whom the gods have granted the power either to do something which is worth recording or to write what is worth reading, and most fortunate of all is the man who can do both. Such a man was my uncle, as his own books and yours will prove. So you set me a task I would choose for myself, and I am more than willing to start on it.

My uncle was stationed at Misenum, in active command of the fleet. On 24 August, in the early afternoon, my mother drew his attention to a cloud of unusual size and appearance. He had been out in the sun, had taken a cold bath, and lunched while lying down, and was working at his books. He called for his shoes and climbed up to a place which would give him the best view of the phenomenon. It was not clear at that distance from which mountain the cloud was rising (it was afterwards known to be Vesuvius); its general appearance can best be expressed as being like a pine rather than any other tree, for it rose to a great height on a sort of trunk and then split off into branches, I imagine because it was thrust upwards by the first blast and then left unsupported as the pressure subsided, or else it was borne down by its own weight so that it spread out and gradually dispersed. Sometimes it looked white, sometimes blotched and dirty, according to the amount of soil and ashes it carried with it. My uncle's scholarly acumen saw at once that it was important enough for a closer inspection, and he ordered a fast boat to be made ready, telling me I could come with him if I wished. I replied that I preferred to go on with my studies, and as it happened he had himself given me some writing to do.

As he was leaving the house he was handed a message from Rectina, wife of Tascius, whose house was at the foot of the mountain, so that escape was impossible except by boat. She was terrified by the danger threatening her and implored him to rescue her from her fate. He changed his plans, and what he had begun in a spirit of inquiry he completed as a hero. He gave orders for the warships to be launched and went on board himself with the intention of bringing help to many more people besides Rectina, for this lovely stretch of coast was thickly populated. He hurried to the place which everyone was hastily leaving, steering his course straight for the danger zone. He was entirely fearless, describing each new movement and phase of the portent to be noted down exactly as he observed them. Ashes were already falling, hotter and thicker as the ships drew near, followed by bits of pumice and blackened stones, charred and cracked by the flames: then suddenly they were in shallow water, and the shore was blocked by debris from the mountain. For a moment my uncle wondered whether to turn back, but when the helmsman advised this he refused, telling him that Fortune stood by the courageous and they must make for Pomponianus at Stabiae. He was cut off there by the breadth of the bay (for the shore gradually curves round a basin filled by the sea) so that he was not as yet in danger, though it was clear that this would come nearer as it spread. Pomponianus had therefore already put his belongings on board ship, intending to escape if the contrary wind fell. This wind was of course full in my uncle's favour, and he was able to bring his ship in. He embraced his terrified friend, cheered and encouraged him, and thinking he could calm his fears by showing his own composure, gave orders that he was to be carried to the bathroom. After his bath he lay down and dined; he was quite cheerful, or at any rate he pretended he was, which was no less courageous.

Meanwhile on Mount Vesuvius broad sheets of fire and leaping flames blazed at several points, their bright glare emphasized by the darkness of night. My uncle tried to allay the fears of his companions by repeatedly declaring that these were nothing but bonfires left by the peasants in their terror, or else empty houses on fire in the districts they had abandoned. Then he went to rest and certainly slept, for as he was a stout man his breathing was rather loud and heavy and could be heard by people coming and going outside his door. By this time the courtyard giving access to his room was full of ashes mixed with pumice-stones, so that its level had risen, and if he had stayed in the room any longer he would never have got out. He was wakened, came out and joined Pomponianus and the rest of the household who had sat up all night. They debated whether to stay indoors or take their chance in the open, for the buildings were now shaking with violent shocks, and seemed to be swaying to and fro as if they were torn from their foundations. Outside on the other hand, there was the danger of falling pumice-stones, even though these were light and porous; however, after comparing the risks they chose the latter. In my uncle's case one reason outweighed the other, but for the others it was a choice of fears. As a protection against falling objects they put pillows on their heads tied down with cloths.

Elsewhere there was daylight by this time, but they were still in darkness, blacker and denser than any night that ever was, which they relieved by lighting torches and various kinds of lamp. My uncle decided to go down to the shore and investigate on the spot the possibility of any escape by sea, but he found the waves still wild and dangerous. A sheet was spread on the ground for him to lie down, and he repeatedly asked for cold water to drink. Then the flames and smell of sulphur which gave warning of the approaching fire drove the others to take flight and roused him to stand up. He stood leaning on two slaves and then suddenly collapsed, I imagine because the dense fumes choked his breathing by blocking his windpipe which was constitutionally weak and narrow and often inflamed. When daylight returned on the 26th—two days after the last day he had seen—his body was found intact and uninjured, still fully clothed and looking more like sleep than death.

Meanwhile my mother and I were at Misenum, but this is not of any historic interest, and you only wanted to hear about my uncle's death. I will say no more, except to add that I have described in detail every incident which I either witnessed myself or heard about immediately after the event, when reports were most likely to be accurate. It is for you to select what best suits your purpose, for there is a great difference between a letter to a friend and history written for all to read.
(Pliny the Younger, *Letters* 6.16)

Dio Cassius describes the earthquake in Antioch that occurred while Trajan was visiting the city.

557. While the emperor was tarrying in Antioch a terrible earthquake occurred; many cities suffered injury, but Antioch was the most unfortunate of all. Since Trajan was passing the winter there and many soldiers and many civilians had flocked thither from all sides in connexion with law-suits, embassies, business or sightseeing, there was no nation or people that went unscathed; and thus in Antioch the whole world under Roman sway suffered disaster. There had been many thunderstorms and portentous winds, but no one would ever have expected so many evils to result from them. First there came, on a sudden, a great bellowing roar, and this was followed by a tremendous quaking. The whole earth was upheaved, and buildings leaped into the air; some were carried aloft only to collapse and be broken in pieces, while others were tossed this way and that as if by the surge of the sea, and overturned, and the wreckage spread out over a great extent even of the open country. The crash of grinding and breaking timbers together with tiles and stones was most frightful; and an inconceivable amount of dust arose, so that it was impossible for one to see anything or to speak or hear a word. As for the people, many even who were outside the houses were hurt, being snatched up and tossed violently about and then dashed to the earth as if falling from a cliff; some were maimed and others were killed. Even trees in some cases leaped into the air, roots and all. The number of those who were trapped in the houses and perished was past finding out; for multitudes were killed by the very force of falling débris, and great numbers were suffocated in the ruins. Those who lay with a part of their body buried under the stones or timbers suffered terribly, being able neither to live any longer nor to find an immediate death.

Nevertheless, many even of these were saved, as was to be expected in such a countless multitude; yet not all such escaped unscathed. Many lost legs or arms, some had their heads broken, and still others vomited blood; Pedo the consul was one of these, and he died at once. In a word, there was no kind of violent experience that those people did not undergo at that time. And as Heaven continued the earthquake for several days and nights, the people were in dire straits and helpless, some of them crushed and perishing under the weight of the buildings pressing upon them, and others dying of hunger, whenever it so chanced that they were left alive either in a clear space, the timbers being so inclined as to leave such a space, or in a vaulted colonnade. When at last the evil had subsided, someone who ventured to mount the ruins caught sight of a woman still alive. She was not alone, but had also an infant; and she had survived by feeding both herself and her child with her milk. They dug her out and resuscitated her together with her babe, and after that they searched the other heaps, but were not able to find in them anyone still living save a child sucking at the breast of its mother, who was dead. As they drew forth the corpses they could no longer feel any pleasure even at their own escape.

So great were the calamities that had overwhelmed Antioch at this time. Trajan made his way out through a window of the room in which he was staying. Some being, of greater than human stature, had come to him and led him forth, so that he escaped with only a few slight injuries; and as the shocks extended over several days, he lived out of doors in the hippodrome. Even Mt. Casius itself was so shaken that its peaks seemed to lean over and break off and to be

falling upon the very city. Other hills also settled, and much water not previously in existence came to light, while many streams disappeared.
(Dio Cassius, *Roman History* 68.24.1–25.6)

7.16. Sickness and Death

The extracts cited below illustrate the Graeco-Roman encounter with physical frailty, and death and dying. Attempts to account for the meaning of life when faced by death are also included here (see also #243). In contrast to the literature of condolence, Christian and Jewish writers of the period had much more to offer by way of hope in a life after death. The epitaphs are eloquent, often simple and humble, witnesses of the worth of the dead to those who set up their funerary monuments.

Sources

Remedies.

Books 28–30 of Pliny the Elder's *Natural History* are given over to remedies for various complaints and illnesses.

558. Sexual intercourse was disapproved of by Democritus, as being merely the act whereby one human being springs from another. Heaven knows, the less indulgence in this respect the better. Athletes, however, when sluggish regain by it their activity, and the voice, when it has lost its clearness and become husky, is restored. It cures pain in the loins, dulness of vision, unsoundness of mind and melancholia.
(Pliny the Elder, *Natural History* 28.58)

Many of the remedies involve exotic animals.

559. The blood of an elephant, particularly that of the male, checks all the fluxes that are called *rheumatismi*. Ivory shavings with Attic honey are said to remove dark spots on the face, and ivory dust whitlows [inflammation of the deeper tissues of a toe or finger]. By the touch of the trunk headache is relieved, more successfully if the animal also sneezes. The right side of the trunk used as an amulet with the red earth of Lemnos is aphrodisiac. The blood too is good for consumption, and the liver for epilepsy.

Lion fat with rose oil preserves fairness of complexion and keeps the face free from spots; it also cures frost-bite and swollen joints.
(Pliny the Elder, *Natural History* 28.88–89)

Exposure of deformed infants and abortion (#560–63).

560. As to exposing or rearing the children born, let there be a law that no deformed child shall be reared; but on the ground of number of children, if the regular customs hinder any of those born being exposed, there must be a limit fixed to the procreation of offspring, and if any people have a child as a result of intercourse in contravention of these regulations, abortion must be practised on it before it has developed sensation and life; for the line between lawful and unlawful abortion will be marked by the fact of having sensation and being alive.
(Aristotle, *Politics* 7.14.10)[77]

561. These poor women, however, endure the perils of child-birth, and all the troubles of nursing to which their lot condemns them; but how often does a gilded bed contain a woman that is lying in? So great is the skill, so powerful the drugs, of the abortionist, paid to murder mankind within the womb. Rejoice, poor wretch; give her the stuff to drink whatever it be, with your own hand: for were she willing to get big and trouble her womb with bouncing babies, you might perhaps find yourself the father of an Ethiopian; and some day a coloured heir, whom you would rather not meet by daylight, would fill all the places in your will.
(Juvenal, *Satires* 6.592–601)[78]

Ilarion to Alis.

562. 'Ilarion to Alis his sister, many greetings, and to my dear Berous and Apollonarion. Know that I am still even now at Alexandria; and do not worry if they come back altogether (?), but I remain at Alexandria. I urge and entreat you to be careful of the child, and if I receive a present soon I will send it up to you. If (Apollonarion?) bears offspring, if it

is a male let it be, if a female expose it. You told Aphrodisias "Don't forget me." How can I forget you? I urge you therefore not to worry…'
(P.Oxy 744 [1 BCE])

Abortion and infanticide are condemned in Jewish and Christian writings.

563. But the second commandment of the teaching is this; 'Thou shalt do no murder; thou shalt not commit adultery'; thou shalt not commit sodomy; thou shalt not commit fornication; thou shalt not steal; thou shalt not use magic; thou shalt not use philtres; thou shalt not procure abortion, nor commit infanticide…
(*Didache* 2.1–2)

Seneca and Epictetus on sickness and death (#564–66).

564. (5) [M]y counsel to you is this,—and it is a cure, not merely of this disease of yours, but of your whole life,—'Despise death.' There is no sorrow in the world, when we have escaped from the fear of death. There are these three serious elements in every disease: fear of death, bodily pain, and interruption of pleasures. Concerning death enough has been said, and I shall add only one word: this fear is not a fear of disease, but a fear of nature. Disease has often postponed death, and a vision of dying has been many a man's salvation. You will die, not because you are ill, but because you are alive; even when you have been cured, the same end awaits you; when you have recovered, it will be not death, but ill-health, that you have escaped.

(20) 'But,' you object, 'my illness does not allow me to be doing anything; it has withdrawn me from all my duties.' It is your body that is hampered by ill-health, and not your soul as well. It is for this reason that it clogs the feet of the runner and will hinder the handiwork of the cobbler or the artisan; but if your soul be habitually in practice, you will plead and teach, listen and learn, investigate and meditate. What more is necessary? Do you think that you are doing nothing if you possess self-control in your illness? You will be showing that a disease can be overcome, or at any rate endured. There is, I assure you, a place for virtue even upon a bed of sickness. It is not only the sword and the battle-line that prove the soul alert and unconquered by fear; a man can display bravery even when wrapped in his bedclothes. You have something to do: wrestle bravely with disease. If it shall compel you to nothing, beguile you to nothing, it is a notable example that you display. O what ample matter were there for renown, if we could have spectators of our sickness! Be your own spectator; seek your own applause.

(25) All these things, however, can be easily endured—gruel, warm water, and anything else that seems insupportable to a fastidious man, to one who is wallowing in luxury, sick in soul rather than in body—if only we cease to shudder at death. And we shall cease, if once we have gained a knowledge of the limits of good and evil; then, and then only, life will not weary us, neither will death make us afraid. For surfeit of self can never seize upon a life that surveys all the things which are manifold, great, divine; only idle leisure is wont to make men hate their lives. To one who roams through the universe, the truth can never pall; it will be the untruths that will cloy. And, on the other hand, if death comes near with its summons, even though it be untimely in its arrival, though it cut one off in one's prime, a man has had a taste of all that the longest life can give. Such a man has in great measure come to understand the universe. He knows that honourable things do not depend on time for their growth; but any life must seem short to those who measure its length by pleasures which are empty and for that reason unbounded.
(Seneca, *Epistles* 78.5–7, 20–21, 25–27)[79]

565. There is no need, therefore, for you to hurry to the tomb of your son; what lies there is his basest part and a part that in life was the source of much trouble—bones and ashes are no more parts of him than were his clothes and the other protections of the body. He is complete—leaving nothing of himself behind, he has fled away and wholly departed from earth; for a little while he tarried above us while he was being purified and was ridding himself of all the blemishes and stain that still clung to him from his mortal existence, then soared

aloft and sped away to join the souls of the blessed.
(Seneca, *To Marcia, On Consolation* 25)

566. Never say about anything, 'I have lost it,' but only 'I have given it back.' Is your child dead? It has been given back. Is your wife dead? She has been given back. 'I have had my farm taken away.' Very well, this too has been given back. 'Yet it was a rascal who took it away.' But what concern is it of yours by whose instrumentality the Giver called for its return? So long as He gives it you, take care of it as of a thing that is not your own, as travellers treat their inn.
(Epictetus, *Encheiridion* 11)

A second-century CE *letter of condolence.*

567. Irene to Taonnophris and Philo good cheer!

'I was as much grieved and shed as many tears over Eumoerus as I shed for Didymas, and I did everything that was fitting, and so did all my friends, Epaphroditus and Thermouthion and Philion and Apollonius and Plantas. But still there is nothing one can do in the face of such trouble. So I leave you to comfort yourselves. Goodbye. Athyr 1.'
(P.Oxy 115 [second century CE]).

The following extract is a Jewish epitaph written in Latin at the beginning of the second century CE. It was found in Rome in the catacomb on the Monteverde.

The Epitaph of Regina.

568. Here Regina is buried, in sepulchre so fair, which her husband, requiting her love, hath erected. She, after twice ten years with him, had ended a year and a fourth month, eight days remaining; again she will live, she will return to the light again. For she is able to hope that she rise again for evermore as hath been promised—and this faith is true—to the worthy and the godly, she who hath deserved to have a throne in that blessed country. This will thy godliness have gotten thee, this thy grave life, this also thy love of thy stock, this thy observation of the law, thy deserts in respect of marriage, the glory whereof was thy care. For these things done thou mayest hope things to come, whence also thy sorrowful husband seeketh consolation.
(Deissmann, *Light from the Ancient East*, p. 448)

Paul on death.

The passage below is evidence not only of Paul's conviction in the resurrection but also that the parousia is imminent. Note that he believes that at the appearance of Christ some of his readers will not have died.

569. But we do not want you to be uninformed, brothers and sisters, about those who have died, so that you may not grieve as others do who have no hope. For since we believe that Jesus died and rose again, even so, through Jesus, God will bring with him those who have died. For this we declare to you by the word of the Lord, that we who are alive, who are left until the coming of the Lord, will by no means precede those who have died. For the Lord himself, with a cry of command, with the archangel's call and with the sound of God's trumpet, will descend from heaven, and the dead in Christ will rise first. Then we who are alive, who are left, will be caught up in the clouds together with them to meet the Lord in the air; and so we will be with the Lord forever. Therefore encourage one another with these words.
(1 Thessalonians 4:13–18)

Juvenal on old age.

570. 'Give me length of days, give me many years, O Jupiter!' Such is your one and only prayer, in days of strength or of sickness; yet how great, how unceasing, are the miseries of old age! Look first at the misshapen and ungainly face, so unlike its former self; see the unsightly hide that serves for skin; see the pendulous cheeks and the wrinkles like those which a matron baboon carves upon her aged jaws where Thabraca spreads her shaded glades. The young men differ in various ways: this man is handsomer than that, and he than another; one is far stronger than another: but old men all look alike. Their voices are as shaky as their limbs, their heads without hair, their noses drivelling as in childhood. Their bread, poor wretches, has to be munched by toothless gums; so offen-

sive do they become to their wives, their children and themselves, that even the legacy-hunter, Cossus, turns from them in disgust. Their sluggish palate takes joy in wine or food no longer, and all the pleasures of the flesh have been long ago forgotten…
(Juvenal, *Satires* 10.188–204)

Epitaphs (#571–77).

Epitaph of a Roman soldier from Sidon buried on the German frontier (dating from the beginning of the Imperial period).

571. Tiberius Julius Abdes Pantera, of Sidon, aged 62, a soldier of 40 years' service, of the 1st cohort of archers, lies here.
(Deissmann, *Light from the Ancient East*, p. 74)

Epitaph of a child.

572. To you, father Fronto and mother Flaccilla, I commend this girl, my pet and darling. Little Erotion must not be frightened by the dark shades and the monstrous mouths of Tartarus' hound. She was due to complete the chills of a sixth midwinter, no more, if she had not lived that many days too few. Let her now play and frolic with her old patrons and lispingly chatter my name. Not hard be the turf that covers her soft bones, be not heavy upon her, earth; she was not heavy upon you.
(Martial, *Epigrams* 5.34.
Cf. 5.37; 10.61; 11.91)

The following epitaph is from a Greek stele dating from the second half of the first century CE. It was found in Bithynia.

573. In this place Chrestos buried aged Italos; he wept for his faithful slave when he died. In return for (Italos') good life and industrious servitude (Chrestos) fulfilled these sacred rites for him as a favour.
(*New Docs* III, p. 39)

This Greek stone epitaph dates from the Imperial period and was found in Rome.

574. When I had just tasted life fate snatched me, an infant, and I did not see my father's pattern; but I died after enjoying the light of eleven months, then I returned it. I lie in the tomb forever, no longer seeing the light; but you, stranger, read this and weep as you come upon the tomb of Eunoe.
(*New Docs* IV, p. 40)

Latin funerary mensa (table) dating from the first half of the second century CE, found in Caesarea in Mauretania.

575. Marcia Rogata… Cytisis, aged 15 years, …months. She was pious and wise beyond her age, as though mind was competing with the swift onset of death.
(*New Docs* III, p. 47)

Late first-century/early second-century CE epitaph of a virtuous woman. The inscription is written on two sides of a coffin cartonnage.

576. Here lies Valeria, daughter of Marcus, of free-born status from Caesarea in Mauritania. She was kind, affectionate, dignified, blameless; (side 2) she loved her husband and her children, and was faithful to her marriage. Out of respect and love for what is good her husband, Lucius Dexios from Herculaneum, buried her.
(*New Docs* III, p. 40)

Epitaph of a gladiator (Imperial period).[80]

577. I who was brimful of confidence in the stadium, now you see me a corpse, wayfarer, a retiarius from Tarsos, a member of the second squad, Melanippos (by name). No longer do I hear the sound of the beaten-bronze trumpet, nor do I rouse the din of flutes during one-sided contests. They say that Herakles completed 12 labours; but I, having completed the same (number), met my end at the thirteenth. Thallos and Zoe made this for Melanippos as a memorial at their own expense.
(*New Docs* IV, p. 19)

Notes

1. Edwin A. Judge, *The Social Pattern of Christian Groups in the First Century* (London: Tyndale, 1960), p. 34; Scullard, *From the Gracchi to Nero*, pp. 302–303. Note also Philippians 4:22.
2. See Horace, *Odes* 4.5 ll. 25–28; *Carmen Saeculare* ll. 17–20; Augustus, *Res Gestae* 6.

See Tacitus, *Annals* 2.85 for immorality on the part of women as a contributing reason for Augustus's initiatives.

3. See Rodney Stark, *The Rise of Christianity* (San Francisco: HarperCollins, 1997), pp. 95–128. See also Sarah B. Pomeroy, *Goddesses, Whores, Wives, and Slaves* (New York: Schocken, 1995), pp. 164–70.
4. Note Augustus's treatment of his free-spirited and adulterous daughter, Julia. Suetonius, *Augustus* 65.
5. During the principate of Tiberius the Senate had to amend the *lex Papia Poppaea*, passed in 9 CE (see Tacitus, *Annals* 3.25). Dio Cassius provides a summary of the legislation, which can be accessed at #479 (see also Suetonius, *Augustus* 24).
6. The Younger Pliny discusses a divorce case in *Letters* 6.31.4–6. For Messalina's divorce of the emperor Claudius, see Tacitus, *Annals* 11.26–27.
7. I have not included the attestations and the signatures, which follow the cited text and are written in Aramaic.
8. Commentators note that Jesus' teaching as recorded in Mark's Gospel reflects the Roman context which did allow women to divorce their husbands, and that such permission was not available to Jewish women under Jewish law. Matthew 5:31–32 represents the situation under Jewish law, namely that a woman was not permitted to divorce her husband. However, see #413 cited from the Babatha archive which seems to allow for the possibility. For discussion of the role of women in Roman marriage, see Pomeroy, *Goddesses, Whores, Wives, and Slaves*, pp. 150–63.
9. Note the remarks of Apuleius on the magnetic attractiveness of women's hair in *Golden Ass* 2.8–9. Note also the necessity for women to cover their hair in meetings of the church in 1 Corinthians 11:5–15—a decorous social convention that was required (in Paul's words) 'because of the angels' (see J.A. Fitzmyer, 'A Feature of Qumran Angelology and the Angels of 1 Cor 11:10', *NTS* 4 [1957–58], pp. 48–58). Angels were perceived to be present in the congregation in a manner similarly imagined in the Qumran texts (see #649–50). In the early church and in Tertullian's time there were women who chose to remain virgins. Much to Tertullian's outrage, they were encouraged to appear unveiled in church. See Peter R.L. Brown, *The Body and Society: Men, Women, and Sexual Renunciation in Early Christianity* (New York: Columbia University, 1988), pp. 80–82.
10. See also, e.g., Tacitus, *Annals* 3.34 for the 'natural frailty' of women with respect to susceptibility to sexual desire.
11. Juvenal (*Satires* 13.187–91) argues that the desire for vengeance, the 'delight of a little, weak, and petty mind', is removed by philosophy. That is why, he continues, 'no one so rejoices in vengeance as a woman'.
12. The word used for 'deception' can refer to seduction. The seduction of Eve by the serpent is alluded to by Paul in 2 Corinthians 11:3. Cf. *Apocalypse of Abraham* 23:1–5 (c. 100 CE); *2 Enoch* 31:6 (c. 100 CE); *Protevangelium of James* 13:1 (second century CE).
13. The later emperor Vitellius, so Suetonius reports, had been one of Tiberius's *spintria* (*Vitellius* 3).
14. The penalty about which Paul speaks in this passage may be the loss of maleness as the passive and subordinated (i.e. the penetrated) partner in such sexual activity. Such men have, in effect, become women. They have succumbed, like women, to sexual desire and are unable to exercise the self-mastery that characterized men as penetrators. See Stanley Stowers, *A Rereading of Romans* (New Haven: Yale University Press, 1994), p. 95. Mark Antony's relationship with Cleopatra was cast in terms of his having become enslaved to passion thereby surrendering his manhood under the spell of a woman. Instead of dominating the woman he was dominated by her.
15. For a document of manumission, see P.Oxy 722 (91 or 107 CE).
16. Although it was acknowledged that former slaves could rise to positions of great eminence, their social superiors could be quite unforgiving in assessing their worth. See, e.g., Tacitus's comment on Felix (*Histories* 5.9; #580). The wealthy Trimalchio, whose banquet is the great set piece of the extant portion of Petronius's *Satyricon*, as satirized as the vulgar freedman *par excellence*.
17. Stambaugh and Balch, *The New Testament in its Social Environment*, p. 113. See also #404–405.
18. See Plato, *Republic* 6.495D–E; Aristotle, *Politics* 3.3.
19. Sphragis, the young slave, is a 'Sidonian', a

name often given to those from Palestine. Note that the guarantor is a Jew: he has a Jewish father (Ananias). He is a member of the military unit, called the 'Persians', serving under Toubias the kleruch. Toubias is also a Jew, the father of Joseph, whose story is told by Josephus in *Antiquities* 12.154–236 (see #111).

20. Julius Caesar distributed slaves to his soldiers (Suetonius, *Julius Caesar* 26).
21. Note Cicero's letter to this man at #61. The mistreatment of slaves is underscored in a story related in Dio Cassius, *Roman History* 54.23.1–4 about Vedius Pollio, who kept huge man-eating lampreys in reservoirs to which he threw those of his slaves he desired to put to death. For mistreatment of slaves see also Martial, *Epigrams* 2.66; 3.13; Herodas, *Mime* V (*The Jealous Woman*). Tacitus, *Annals* 14.42–44 relates the execution of 400 slaves, the total number in the household of the murdered Prefect of Rome, Pedanius Secundus, one of whom had murdered him. The punishment was required by convention. Hadrian legislated for an amelioration of this practice (see #453).
22. For slavery among Jews, see also the ostracon no. 1 discovered in 1996 in the cemetery wall at Qumran. The text refers to the gift of a slave called Hisday to a man named 'El'azar by a certain Honi, who had joined the community (for text, see Vermes, *Complete Dead Sea Scrolls in English*, p. 596). For a fuller discussion, see F.M. Cross and E. Eshel, 'Ostraca from Khirbet Qumran', *IEJ* 47 (1997), pp. 17–28.
23. Julius Caesar took a course in rhetoric from Apollonius Milo in Rhodes (Suetonius, *Julius Caesar* 4). Augustus also studied rhetoric (Suetonius, *Augustus* 84). Tiberius was taught by Theodorus of Gadara. Nero was the first emperor who needed assistance in his speeches. For Caesar, Seneca, and Claudius as orators, see Tacitus, *Annals* 13.3.
24. Quintilian, *Institutio Oratoria* 2.15.38.
25. This is not to say that there were no critics of the rhetorical emphasis in the educational curriculum. Note Petronius's criticisms of rhetorical education (*Satyricon* 1–2); Seneca, *Letters* 108.23.
26. Stambaugh and Balch, *The New Testament in its Social Environment*, p. 122.
27. See Quintilian, *Institutio Oratoria* 1.3.13–14 for his disapproval of the flogging of school children. Note Paul's use of the word *paidagōgos* of the law of Moses in Galatians 3:24.
28. Comparisons were often made between Demosthenes and Cicero. See, e.g., Quintilian, *Institutio Oratoria* 10.1.105–110; Longinus, *On the Sublime* 12.3–5.
29. According to Seneca, liberal studies do not teach virtue but prepare the soul for the reception of virtue (see *Epistles* 88.20). Cf. #368.
30. On Paul's education, see E.A. Judge, 'St Paul and Classical Society', *JAC* 15 (1972), pp. 19-36 (29–31).
31. At the conclusion of his 'speech' (cited above) Paul parodies the award of the mural crown, bestowed upon the first soldier to scale the wall of a besieged town. See Livy, *History of Rome* 23.18.7; Aulus Gellius, *Attic Nights* 5.6.16.
32. Herod the Great underwrote the Olympic Games in 9 BCE (see Josephus, *Jewish War* 1.426–27) and was a conspicuous bestower of benefactions throughout the eastern Mediterranean. On the culture of benefaction, see Frederick W. Danker, *Benefactor: Epigraphic Study of a Graeco-Roman and New Testament Semantic Field* (St Louis: Clayton, 1982); James R. Harrison, *Paul's Language of Grace (Charis) in its Graeco-Roman Context* (Tübingen: J.C.B. Mohr [Paul Siebeck], forthcoming).
33. See L. William Countryman, *The Rich Christian in the Age of the Early Empire: Contradictions and Accommodations* (New York/ Toronto: Edwin Mellen, 1980) and Reggie M. Kidd, *Wealth and Beneficence in the Pastoral Epistles* (Atlanta: Scholars Press, 1990).
34. See Judge, *Social Pattern*, pp. 60, 76.
35. Note also the ethical value placed on 'lowliness' and 'meekness' in Judaism and early Christian exhortation. See, e.g., Matthew 5:5; Romans 12:16; James 4:6; Philippians 2:8; Galatians 5:22–26 (#670). The Romans, by contrast, relished the competition for glory and fame.
36. There were developments towards the agglomeration of estates in Judaea as well, which were farmed by tenants (see Matthew 21:33–41). Herod the Great, like his Roman contemporaries, also confiscated the lands of his opponents.

37. See also Appian, *Civil Wars* 1.54.
38. See also R. Kearsley's study of a late first-century BCE/early first-century CE honorary inscription from Kyme in *New Docs* VII, pp. 233–41.
39. See also Cicero, *Letters to Atticus* 5.16; Appian, *Civil Wars* 2.92. For the burden of taxation in Gaul see Tacitus, *Annals* 4.72.
40. Bruce J. Malina, *The New Testament World: Insights from Cultural Anthropology* (London: SCM Press, 1981), p. 27. 'Honor', he continues, 'is a claim to worth along with the social acknowledgement of worth'. Note Sirach 44–50 for an early Jewish affirmation of the righteous deeds of the godly who have died.
41. See, e.g., Mark 8:34–38 (parr.); Philippians 2:5–13; Hebrew 12:2; 13:13. See also the following socially sensitive studies: Jerome H. Neyrey, *Honor and Shame in the Gospel of Matthew* (Louisville, KY: Westminster/John Knox Press, 1998); David H. Desilva, *Despising the Shame: Honor Discourse and Community Maintenance in the Epistle to the Hebrews* (Atlanta: Scholars Press, 1996); Barth L. Campbell, *Honor, Shame, and the Rhetoric of 1 Peter* (Atlanta: Scholars Press, 1998).
42. Cf. Sallust's comments in his *War with Jugurtha* 1–3, 41–42.
43. Sallust traces the historical background of the particular expression of the Roman love of glory in his *War with Catiline* 7.1–7. For the masks of ancestors, see also #325.
44. The ephebate was an institution originally designed to impart military training to the youth of a Greek *polis*. In the Roman period, the ephebate was much more an institution supplementing the secondary educational curriculum as a preparation for active involvement in civic affairs. Gymnasia were established all over the Greek world. One was built in Jerusalem immediately preceding the Maccabaean emergency (see #117). See also 2 Maccabees 4:7–17, 18–20; Josephus, *Antiquities* 12.240–41.
45. Paul sees Rome as a strategic base for his future western missionary enterprise in Spain (Romans 1:13; 15:23–24).
46. See Josephus, *Antiquities* 17.300–301; *Jewish War* 2.80–81 which mention a crowd of 8000 Roman Jews (men?) who gathered in Rome with 50 Jewish deputies from Judaea to argue the case for Jewish autonomy after the death of Herod in 4 BCE.
47. See A. Scobie, 'Slums, Sanitation and Mortality in the Roman World', *Klio* 68 (1986), pp. 399–433.
48. Philippi was a colony founded in 42 BCE when Octavian and Antony settled their veterans there (after they had defeated Brutus and Cassius). As a colony it was a miniature Rome. Paul visited the city (see Acts 16) and wrote a letter to the church there.
49. See Goodman, 'The First Jewish Revolt', pp. 417–27.
50. One iugerum is equal to 0.625 of an acre.
51. There is a fine example in the Herodian palace complex at Masada.
52. J. Carcopino observes that Attica resisted the demand for spectacles on the Roman model. See his *Daily Life in Ancient Rome* (Harmondsworth: Penguin Books, 1956), p. 246.
53. See Richard C. Beacham, *Spectacle Entertainments of Early Imperial Rome* (New Haven: Yale University Press, 1999).
54. See Pliny, *Letters* 4.22 for the abolishing of the Greek-style athletics games in Vienne because 'they had long been a corrupting influence of the town'. See also his *Panegyricus* 33, which celebrates the consulship of Trajan in 100 CE, an occasion marked by numerous events bestowed by the Emperor: 'Next came a public entertainment—nothing lax or dissolute to weaken and destroy the manly spirit of his subjects, but one to inspire them to face honourable wounds and look scorn on death, by exhibiting love of glory and desire for victory even in the persons of criminals and slaves. What generosity went to provide this spectacle!' See also Cicero, *Tusculan Disputations* 2.41: 'A gladiatorial show is apt to seem cruel and brutal to some eyes, and I incline to think that it is so, as now conducted. But in the days when it was criminals who crossed swords in the death struggle, there could be no better schooling against pain and death at any rate for the eyes, though for the ear perhaps there might be many'. Nero, on the other hand, represented all that was effeminate with respect to manly virtue. Tacitus, *Annals* 14.15 describes the debilitating moral effects of Nero's love of the theatre.

55. See Carcopino (in ironic mood), *Daily Life in Ancient Rome*, p. 239. When Cicero was proconsul of the province of Asia he wrote to M. Caelius Rufus, a curule aedile with responsibilities for providing beast shows for the populace, that he was unlikely to find a ready supply of the panthers he wanted since it had been reported to him that their numbers (not surprisingly) had become fewer. See *Letters to his Friends* 2.11 (51 BCE).
56. Stambaugh and Balch, *The New Testament in its Social Environment*, pp. 124–27; Robert L. Wilken, *The Christians as the Romans Saw Them* (New Haven: Yale University Press, 1984), pp. 31–47.
57. For the New Testament and the Graeco-Roman background, see Stephen C. Barton and G.H.R. Horsley, 'A Hellenistic Cult Group and the New Testament Churches', *JAC* 24 (1981), pp. 7–41; John S. Kloppenborg and Stephen G. Wilson (eds.), *Voluntary Associations in the Graeco-Roman World* (London/New York: Routledge, 1996).
58. The Secular Games, supposedly held every 100 years, were staged in 17 BCE. Horace's *Carmen Saeculare* was composed for the celebration.
59. Dio Cassius also records Claudius's love of the theatrical brutality of the arena in his *Roman History* 60.13.
60. See also Dio Cassius, *History of Rome* 66.25; Suetonius, *Titus* 7.3.
61. Laureolus was a famous bandit, the central character in the famous mime of the same name. After a tumultuous career, Laureolus was captured and crucified. In the epigram cited above, a condemned criminal is substituted for the actor and crucified in the arena. See also Carcopino, *Daily Life in Ancient Rome*, pp. 231–32. Prisoners also fought in *en masse* in staged naval battles (see Tacitus, *Annals* 12.56).
62. See also Josephus, *Antiquities* 16.137 for Herod's elaborate celebrations marking the completion of Caesarea. These included music contents, athletic exercises, as well as gladiatorial contests, wild beast fights, and horse races.
63. The *quinquennalis* was the chief officer of the society, and held office for five years.
64. See Gibbon's perceptive comment on human character: 'Trajan was ambitious of fame; and as long as mankind shall continue to bestow more liberal applause on their destroyers than on their benefactors, the thirst for military glory will ever be the vice of most exalted characters' (*The History of the Decline and Fall of the Roman Empire* [London: Folio Society, 1983], I, p. 34).
65. Note also Josephus, *Jewish War* 3.79–84. The Roman legionary formation and the phalanx are compared in Polybius, *Histories* 18.31–32. As envisaged by the Qumran community, the battle formation of soldiers in the war against the Sons of Darkness (that is, the 'Kittim', and Jewish renegades) owes much to the formation of the Roman legion. See 1QM5; Vermes (following Yadin and others), *Complete Dead Sea Scrolls in English*, pp. 162–63.
66. See also Suetonius, *Augustus* 24.
67. See also Appian, *History of Rome* 8.66.
68. Note, for instance, the massacre of 30,000 Lusitanians by Servius Galba, a second-century BCE ancestor of the emperor Galba (see Suetonius, *Galba* 3.2). For the massacre of 80,000 Romans and Italians in one day on the orders of Mithridates, see #50.
69. The Romans were not the only people to use crucifixion. See the actions of Alexander (#533) and Alexander Jannaeus (#128).
70. The rape of Boudicca's captive daughters and the flogging of Boudicca, Queen of the Britons, are reported in Tacitus, *Annals* 14.31.
71. The incident was well known. See the reports in Suetonius, *Tiberius* 61 and Dio Cassius, *Roman History* 58.11.5.
72. Note the remarks of Claudius, reported by Tacitus, on the benefits of selectively extending citizenship (*Annals* 11.24).
73. See Appian, *Civil Wars* 2.26; Acts 16:37; 22:24–25.
74. Contrast Polybius's disparaging comments on the constitution of the Athenians (*Histories* 6.44.3–4).
75. See Wallbank, *The Hellenistic World*, p. 249: The whole empire coalesced into 'a single cultural continuum in which many aspects of the hellenistic world lived on, adapted to the provincial organisations imposed from Rome'.
76. The translator, Warmington, notes that this statute had lost much of its force by imperial times.

77. Augustus refused to acknowledge or allow to be reared the daughter of his disgraced daughter Julia (see Suetonius, *Augustus* 65).
78. See also Ovid, *Amores* 2.13, 14.
79. See also *Epistles* 63.12–13; 91; 107.
80. A *retiarius* fought with a net, a dagger and a trident. Note the comments about this and another gladiator inscription in *New Docs* IV, pp. 18–20.

8. Early Judaism and Christianity

Introduction

It has been estimated that the number of Jews at the time of Augustus was about 4.5 million, 500,000–750,000 of these living in Palestine.[1] The scattering of Jews from their homeland due to enforced exile, enslavement and through serving as mercenaries occurred from the sixth century BCE. As a result Jews were to be found all around the Mediterranean, concentrated in the towns and cities, but also working subsistence farms in the Jewish homeland. Thus Judaism of the Hellenistic and Graeco-Roman eras assumed the characteristics of a world religious system.

Yet Jews possessed a distinctive culture. Their beliefs and practices attracted mostly negative comment from their contemporaries. Although not untouched by the influence of Hellenistic culture, even in Palestine, Jerusalem included, Jews maintained an uncompromising belief in one God—the creator and Lord of heaven and earth—who had expressly forbade the making of idols and who had revealed his moral will, and had entered into an exclusive covenant relationship with his people. In Persian times Judaean Jews began to consolidate their epic tradition, legal deposit, and prophetic oracles into what would become settled scriptures. The Torah, comprising the five books of Moses, probably reached definitive form by the late fifth century BCE (see topic 2.1). The setting aside of the weekly Sabbath as a day of rest and the keeping of strictly delineated food and purity laws were mandated. Significantly, Jews believed that moral integrity and moral performance were integral to their religious commitment. In this they were clearly distinguishable from the worshippers of the gods in so far as the ground of the Jewish moral code was conceived primarily in theological, not philosophical, terms. The Jewish life-commitment was the subject of the revelation of the divine will. Moreover, the Jewish commitment was exclusive of other religious loyalties. It was thus well-nigh impossible for Jews to escape the attention of their neighbours. They were not participants in civic cults or in the mystery religions. They were not citizens of Greek cities. Their food laws meant that social contact with their non-Jewish neighbours was severely limited. Not surprisingly Jews earned a reputation for misanthropy. There are a number of Roman and Greek writers who repeated and embellished this charge. Jewish beliefs and practices were the subject of much misinformation and prejudice.[2] The same was true of Roman responses to the early Christians.

8.1. Descriptions of Judaea

Josephus is the best witness to Jewish culture in the Graeco-Roman era. His knowledge of the Jewish homeland is unparalleled among extant sources. He also preserved fragments of non-Jewish writers on the Jews.

Several Graeco-Roman observers wrote about the geography of Judaea and Jewish customs. To them the Jewish homeland was an exotic place, made even more so by the presence of the Jews. The somewhat incidental remarks of Pliny the Elder on the Essenes in his description of the land have assumed a significant place in scholarly discussion of the Qumran community. Tacitus's observations, though seriously compromised by anti-Jewish sentiment, are an important witness to the geography, history and customs of the Jews as seen through the eyes of a sophisticated Roman.

Sources

Josephus reports the observations of Hecataeus of Abdera.

Hecataeus flourished about 300 BCE, and was active under Ptolemy I.[3]

578. [T]hough many myriads of our race had already been deported to Babylon by the Persians [*sic*], yet after Alexander's death myriads more migrated to Egypt and Phoenicia in consequence of the disturbed condition of Syria. The same writer [Hecataeus of Abdera] has referred to the extent and beauty of the country which we inhabit in the following words: 'They occupy almost three million *arourae* of the most excellent and fertile soil, productive of every variety of fruits. Such is the extent of Judaea.' (Josephus, *Against Apion* 1.194–95)[4]

Pliny the Elder's description of the land of Judaea and the Decapolis.

He is writing soon after the destruction of Jerusalem in 70 CE.

579. Beyond Idumaea and Samaria stretches the wide expanse of Judaea. The part of Judaea adjoining Syria is called Galilee, and that next to Arabia and Egypt Peraea. Peraea is covered with rugged mountains, and is separated from the other parts of Judaea by the river Jordan. The rest of Judaea is divided into ten Local Government Areas in the following order: the district of Jericho, which has numerous palm-groves and springs of water, and those of Emmaus, Lydda, Joppa, Accrabim, Jufna, Timnath-Serah, Bethlebaoth, the Hills, the district that formerly contained Jerusalem, by far the most famous city of the East and not of Judaea only, and Herodium with the celebrated town of the same name.

The source of the river Jordan is the spring of Panias from which Caesarea described later takes its second name. It is a delightful stream, winding about so far as the conformation of the locality allows, and putting itself at the service of the people who dwell on its banks, as though moving with reluctance towards that gloomy lake, the Dead Sea, which ultimately swallows it up, its much-praised waters mingling with the pestilential waters of the lake and being lost. For this reason at the first opportunity afforded by the formation of the valleys it widens out into a lake usually called the Sea of Gennesareth. This is 16 miles long and 5 broad, and is skirted by the pleasant towns of Bethsaida and Hippo on the east, El Kereh on the south (the name of which place some people also give to the lake), and Tabaraiah with its salubrious hot springs on the west. The only product of the Dead Sea is bitumen, the Greek word for which gives it its Greek name, Asphaltites. The bodies of animals do not sink in its waters, even bulls and camels floating; this has given rise to the report that nothing at all can sink in it. It is more than 100 miles long, and fully 75 miles broad at the broadest part but only 6 miles at the narrowest. On the east it is faced by Arabia of the Nomads, and on the south by Machaerus, at one time next to Jerusalem the most important fortress in Judaea. On the same side there is a hot spring possessing medicinal value, the name of which, Callirrhoë, itself proclaims the celebrity of its waters.

On the west side of the Dead Sea, but out of range of the noxious exhalations of the coast, is the solitary tribe of the Essenes, which is remarkable beyond all the other tribes in the whole world, as it has no women and has renounced all sexual desire, has no money, and has only palm-trees for company. Day by day the throng of refugees is recruited to an equal number by numerous accessions of persons tired of life and driven thither by the waves of fortune to adopt their manners. Thus through thousands of ages (incredible to relate) a race in which no one is born lives on for ever: so prolific for their advantage is other men's weariness of life!

Lying below the Essenes was formerly the town of Engedi, second only to Jerusalem in the fertility of its land and in its groves of palm-trees, but now like Jerusalem a heap of ashes. Next comes Masada, a fortress on a rock, itself also not far from the Dead Sea. This is the limit of Judaea. (Pliny the Elder, *Natural History* 5.70–73)[5]

Tacitus's survey of Jewish origins, national character and history.

At the beginning of the fifth book of the *Histories*, Tacitus spends no little time in describing the Jews and the country of Judaea. He is, he points out, about to embark on the narrative of the last days of Jerusalem (see 5.2). He has been describing Titus's return to Judaea to take charge of the war effort now that his father, Vespasian, had left Judaea to press his claim as emperor.

580. A great part of Judea is covered with scattered villages, but there are some towns also; Jerusalem is the capital of the Jews. In it was a temple possessing enormous riches. The first line of fortifications protected the city, the next the palace, and the innermost wall the temple. Only a Jew might approach its doors, and all save the priests were forbidden to cross the threshold. While the East was under the dominion of the Assyrians, Medes, and Persians, the Jews were regarded as the meanest of their subjects; but after the Macedonians gained supremacy, King Antiochus endeavoured to abolish Jewish superstition and to introduce Greek civilization; the war with the Parthians, however, prevented his improving this basest of peoples; for it was exactly at that time that Arsaces had revolted. Later on, since the power of Macedon had waned, the Parthians were not yet come to their strength, and the Romans were far away, the Jews selected their own kings. These in turn were expelled by the fickle mob; but recovering their throne by force of arms, they banished citizens, destroyed towns, killed brothers, wives, and parents, and dared essay every other kind of royal crime without hesitation; but they fostered the national superstition, for they had assumed the priesthood to support their civil authority.

The first Roman to subdue the Jews and set foot in their temple by right of conquest was Gnaeus Pompey: thereafter it was a matter of common knowledge that there were no representations of the gods within, but that the place was empty and the secret shrine contained nothing. The walls of Jerusalem were razed, but the temple remained standing. Later, in the time of our civil wars, when these eastern provinces had fallen into the hands of Mark Anthony, the Parthian prince, Pacorus, seized Judea, but he was slain by Publius Ventidius, and the Parthians were thrown back across the Euphrates: the Jews were subdued by Gaius Sosius. Antony gave the throne to Herod, and Augustus, after his victory, increased his power. After Herod's death, a certain Simon assumed the name of king without waiting for Caesar's decision. He, however, was put to death by Quintilius Varus, governor of Syria; the Jews were repressed; and the kingdom was divided into three parts and given to Herod's sons. Under Tiberius all was quiet. Then, when Caligula ordered the Jews to set up his statue in their temple, they chose rather to resort to arms, but the emperor's death put an end to their uprising. The princes now being dead or reduced to insignificance, Claudius made Judea a province and entrusted it to Roman knights or to freedmen; and of the latter, Antonius Felix, practised every kind of cruelty and lust, wielding the power of king with all the instincts of a slave; he had married Drusilla, the granddaughter of Cleopatra and Antony, and so was Antony's grandson-in-law, while Claudius was Antony's grandson.

Still the Jews' patience lasted until Gessius Florus became procurator: in his time war began. When Cestius Gallus, governor of Syria, tried to stop it, he suffered varied fortunes and met defeat more often than he gained victory. On his death, whether in the course of nature or from vexation, Nero sent out Vespasian, who, aided by his good fortune and reputation as well as by his excellent subordinates, within two summers occupied with his victorious army the whole of the level country and all the cities except Jerusalem. The next year was taken up with civil war, and thus was passed in inactivity so far as the Jews were concerned. When peace had been secured throughout Italy, foreign troubles began again; and the fact that the Jews alone had failed to surrender increased our resentment; at the same time, having regard to all the possibilities and hazards of a new reign, it seemed expedient for Titus to remain with the army.

(Tacitus, *Histories* 5.8–10)

8.2. The Elephantine Community

The collection of Elephantine papyri and ostraca was discovered in 1890. The collection and the community which produced them warrant separate treatment. Elephantine is an island in the Nile on which a Jewish garrison was stationed during Persian times. The papyri date from 419 (5th year of Darius II) to 400 BCE, and are written in Aramaic. The community had a temple dedicated not only to Yahu (cf. Yahweh) but also to Bethel and Anat. Celebration of Passover is attested in this corpus.

Scholars speculate that these Jews were descendants of exiles from the northern kingdom of Israel, which had finally succumbed to Assyria in 722 BCE. Bethel was a cult centre of Jeroboam I. Anat was the sister/consort of Baal. The Elephantine temple dates from before the coming of the Persians. The Persian Cambyses found the temple in the 520s when he occupied Egypt, and left it intact (see #582). Other gods are testified to in the oaths preserved. During the time of Darius II (423–405 BCE) the temple was destroyed by Egyptians, perhaps during a nationalistic uprising. Political, rather than religious, motives for this destruction may have been predominant.

The Jews sought permission to rebuild the temple, though they made it clear to the local governor that only meal offerings and incense would be offered on the altar out of respect for the governor's abhorrence of animal sacrifices. He was a Zoroastrian, a follower of the god Ahuramazda. In their petition the Jews refer to the high priest Johanan (see Nehemiah 12:22). It also mentions the sons of Sanballat (governor of Samaria in the book of Nehemiah).

Sources

The Judaism of the Elephantine community allows for considerable latitude in religious expression. Note the syncretistic attitude expressed in the following letter.

Letter of one Jew to another of superior station (an ostracon).

581. To my lord Micaiah, your servant Giddel. I send you welfare and life. I bless you by Yaho and Khn(ub). Now, send me the garment that is on you and they will mend it. I send the note for your welfare.
(*ANET* p. 491)[6]

The Jewish temple in Elephantine was dedicated not only to Yahu (cf. Yahweh) but also to Bethel and Anat. In the following document the Jews of Elephantine petition the governor of Judah for permission to rebuild the temple ruined by Egyptians. In the second, the governor's positive response is recorded. Arsames was the satrap of Egypt.

Papyrus copy of a petition for the authorization to rebuild the temple (407 BCE).

582. To our lord Bagoas, governor of Judah, your servants Yedoniah and his colleagues, the priests who are in the fortress of Elephantine… In the month of Tammuz in the 14th year of King Darius, when Arsames departed and went to the king, the priests of the god Khnub, who is in the fortress of Elephantine, conspired with Vidaranag, who was commander-in-chief here, to wipe out the temple of the god Yaho from the fortress of Elephantine. So that wretch Vidaranag sent to his son Nefayan, who was in command of the garrison of the fortress of Syene, this order, 'The temple of the god Yaho in the fortress of Yeb is to be destroyed'. Nefayan thereupon led the Egyptians with the other troops. Coming with their weapons to the fortress of Elephantine, they entered that temple and razed it to the ground… Now, our forefathers built this temple in the fortress of Elephantine back in the days of the kingdom of Egypt, and when Cambyses [king of Persia, 529–522] came to Egypt he found it built. They knocked down all the temples of the gods of Egypt, but no one did any damage to this temple.
(*ANET* p. 492)

Advice of the Governors of Judah and Samaria to the Jews of Elephantine.

583. Memorandum of what Bagoas and Delaiah said to me: Let this be an instruction to you in Egypt to say before Arsames about the house of offering of the God of Heaven which had been in existence in the fortress of Elephantine since ancient times, before Cambyses, and was destroyed by that wretch Vidaranag in the year 14 of King Darius: to rebuild it on its site as it was before, and the meal-offering and incense to be made on that altar as it used to be.
(*ANET* p. 492)[7]

8.3. The Jewish Diaspora

The spread of the Jews to the towns and cities of the Mediterranean is attested by Graeco-Roman writers and confirmed by archaeological evidence. This diaspora was occasioned primarily by the effects of enforced deportations and by enslavement of Jews after war. The migration of Jews to Egypt can be traced to the period of turmoil following the death of Alexander and the subsequent wars of Alexander's successors.[8] The presence of a sizable, but apparently non-citizen, Jewish population in Alexandria led to civic volatility in the New Testament era (see the topic 8.5 on Jewish civic rights).

It is frequently noted by New Testament scholars that the missionary enterprise of Paul the Apostle throughout the eastern Mediterranean was only possible because of the existence of urban concentrations of Jews throughout the east, replete with synagogues and other aspects of Jewish community life. During the reign of Augustus, it is estimated that 40,000 (or 5%) of the Roman population was Jewish.

Sources

Strabo on the ubiquity of the Jews.

584. There were four classes in the state of Cyrene; the first consisted of citizens, the second of farmers, the third of resident aliens (metics), and the fourth of Jews. This people has already made its way into every city, and it is not easy to find any place in the habitable world which has not received this nation and in which it has not made its power felt.
(Strabo as preserved in Josephus, *Antiquities* 14.115. See also Philo, *Flaccus* 45–46)

The Jewish presence in Egypt.

Josephus paraphrases Hecataeus of Abdera to the effect that many Jews migrated to Egypt after the death of Alexander the Great because of turmoil in Syria (see also #578).

585. [H]e goes on to speak of our vast population, stating that, though many myriads of our race had already been deported to Babylon by the Persians [*sic*], yet after Alexander's death myriads more migrated to Egypt and Phoenicia in consequence of the disturbed condition of Syria.
(Josephus, *Against Apion* 1.194)

Onias IV, son of the deposed high priest Onias III, built a temple in Leontopolis. After the destruction of the Temple in Jerusalem in 70 CE, the Romans also destroyed this one.

586. Ptolemy [V Philometor] gave him a tract, a hundred and eighty furlongs distant from Memphis, in the so-called nome of Heliopolis. Here Onias erected a fortress and built his temple (which was not like that in Jerusalem, but resembled a tower) of huge stones and sixty cubits in altitude. The altar, however, he designed on the model of that in the home country, and adorned the building with similar offerings, the fashion of the lampstand excepted; for, instead of making a stand, he had a lamp wrought of gold which shed a brilliant light and was suspended by a golden chain. The sacred precincts were wholly surrounded by a wall of baked brick, the doorways being of stone. The king, moreover, assigned him an extensive territory as a source of revenue, to yield both abundance for the priests and large provision for the service of God. In all this, however, Onias was not actuated by honest motives; his aim was rather to rival the Jews at Jerusalem, against whom he harboured resentment for his exile, and he hoped by erecting this temple to attract the multitude away from them to it. There had, moreover, been an ancient prediction made some six hundred years before by one named Esaias, who had foretold the erection of this temple in Egypt by a man of Jewish birth [see Isaiah 19:18–23]. Such, then, was the origin of this temple.
(Josephus, *Jewish War* 7.426–32)

A mid second-/first-century BCE Jewish inscription praising God for deliverance found near the Temple of Pan near Redesieh in the Thebaid.

587. Praise be to God. Theodotos the son of Dorion, a Jew, saved from the sea (made this).
(*New Docs* IV, p. 113)

Philo and the pogrom during the reign of Caligula.

Note Philo's remarks concerning the character of Pontius Pilate in the following extract.

588. What of your other grandfather Tiberius Caesar? Did he not evidently adopt the same policy? At any rate in the twenty-three years during which he was emperor he maintained the tradition observed in the temple from distant ages and destroyed or disturbed no part of it. I can quote in addition one act showing a fine spirit. For though I experienced many ills when he was alive, truth is dear, and is held in honour by you. One of his lieutenants was Pilate, who was appointed to govern Judaea. He, not so much to honour Tiberius as to annoy the multitude, dedicated in Herod's palace in the holy city some shields coated with gold. They had no image work traced on them nor anything else forbidden by the law apart from the barest inscription stating two facts, the name of the person who made the dedication and of him in whose honour it was made. But when the multitude understood the matter which had by now become a subject of common talk, having put at their head the king's four sons, who in dignity and good fortune were not inferior to a king, and his other descendants and the persons of authority in their own body, they appealed to Pilate to redress the infringement of their traditions caused by the shields and not to disturb the customs which throughout all the preceding ages had been safeguarded without disturbance by kings and by emperors. When he, naturally inflexible, a blend of self-will and relentlessness, stubbornly refused they clamoured, 'Do not arouse sedition, do not make war, do not destroy the peace; you do not honour the emperor by dishonouring ancient laws. Do not take Tiberius as your pretext for outraging the nation; he does not wish any of our customs to be overthrown. If you say that he does, produce yourself an order or a letter or something of the kind so that we may cease to pester you and having chosen our envoys may petition our lord.' It was the final point which particularly exasperated him, for he feared that if they actually sent an embassy they would also expose the rest of his conduct as governor by stating in full the briberies, the insults, the robberies, the outrages and wanton injuries, the executions without trial constantly repeated, the ceaseless and supremely grievous cruelty. So with all his vindictiveness and furious temper, he was in a difficult position. He had not the courage to take down what had been dedicated nor did he wish to do anything which would please his subjects. At the same time he knew full well the constant policy of Tiberius in these matters. The magnates saw this and understanding that he had repented of his action but did not wish to appear penitent sent letters of very earnest supplication to Tiberius. When he had read them through what language he used about Pilate, what threats he made! The violence of his anger, though he was not easily roused to anger, it is needless to describe since the facts speak for themselves. For at once without even postponing it to the morrow he wrote to Pilate with a host of reproaches and rebukes for his audacious violation of precedent and bade him at once take down the shields and have them transferred from the capital to Caesarea on the coast surnamed Augusta after your great-grandfather, to be set up in the temple of Augustus, and so they were. So both objects were safeguarded, the honour paid to the emperor and the policy observed from of old in dealing with the city.
(Philo, *On the Embassy to Gaius* 298–305)[9]

The Jews of the Eastern Mediterranean.

According to Josephus in *Antiquities* 12.119, Seleucus I granted equal citizenship to the Jews in Antioch, and in other cities he founded, with the Macedonians and Greeks. This decision was upheld, Josephus notes, at least with respect to Jews who had not taken part in the Jewish War, by Vespasian and Titus (see *Antiquities* 12.121–24) even when the Alexandrians and Antiochenes requested the rescinding of these privileges.[10] Josephus also relates the conversion of Izates, the prince of Adiabene, by a Jewish merchant (*Antiquities* 20.17–48).

In 210 BCE Antiochus III ordered 2000 Jewish families to settle in Phrygia and Lydia from Mesopotamia. There were unfortunate civic consequences.

589. But, as these quarrelled and fought jealously with one another, each for his own kingdom, the result was that continual and prolonged wars arose, and the cities suffered through their struggles and lost many of their inhabitants, so that all of Syria at the hands of Ptolemy, the son of Lagus, who was then called *Soter* (Saviour), suffered the reverse of that which was indicated by his surname. And this king seized Jerusalem by resorting to cunning and deceit. For he entered the city on the Sabbath as if to sacrifice, and, as the Jews did not oppose him—for they did not suspect any hostile act—and, because of their lack of suspicion and the nature of the day, were enjoying idleness and ease, he became master of the city without difficulty and ruled it harshly. (Josephus, *Antiquities* 12.3–4)

The Jewish presence in Rome.

590. He [Augustus] was aware that the great section of Rome on the other side of the Tiber is occupied and inhabited by Jews, most of whom were Roman citizens emancipated. For having been brought as captives to Italy they were liberated by their owners and were not forced to violate any of their native institutions. He knew therefore that they have houses of prayer and meet together in them, particularly on the sacred sabbaths when they receive as a body a training in their ancestral philosophy. He knew too that they collect money for sacred purposes from their firstfruits and send them to Jerusalem by persons who would offer the sacrifices. (Philo, *On the Embassy to Gaius* 155–56)

Sejanus and the Jews.

Sejanus was Praetorian Prefect under Tiberius until his fall from grace in 31 CE. Philo attests the protection of Jewish rights everywhere under Tiberius as legacy of Augustus's earlier reverence for those rights.

591. Therefore everyone everywhere, even if he was not naturally well disposed to the Jews, was afraid to engage in destroying any of our institutions, and indeed it was the same under Tiberius though matters in Italy became troublesome when Sejanus was organizing his onslaughts. For Tiberius knew the truth, he knew at once after Sejanus's death that the accusations made against the Jewish inhabitants of Rome were false slanders, invented by him because he wished to make away with the nation, knowing that it would take the sole or the principal part in opposing his unholy plots and actions, and would defend the emperor when in danger of becoming the victim of treachery. (Philo, *On the Embassy to Gaius* 159–60. For Sejanus, see also *Flaccus* 1)

8.4. Reactions to Judaism

The extracts below are from Graeco-Roman authors on Judaism. They provide an insight into the manner in which the Jews were regarded in the era. There is ample evidence of misrepresentation of Jewish beliefs and customs, as well as resentment at attempts by Jews to 'infect' Roman customs and thus weaken Roman identity. That some Romans were converted to Judaism seems likely. Jewish practices, such as circumcision and the keeping of the Sabbath—un-Roman practices to say the least—seemed highly tainted with the overwrought religious sensibility the Romans called 'superstition' (*superstitio*; see, e.g., #603). There was also the matter of civil unrest. Roman anxiety on the matter of law and order was fuelled by the unruliness of alien ethnic (and religious) minorities. While ordinarily tolerant of the religious customs of others, Romans were extraordinarily vigilant with respect to the threat to public order which other religions sometimes occasioned (see the suppression of the Bacchanalia, #349). On at least three instances the conduct of Jews in Rome gave the civic authorities sufficient cause to order the expulsion of the Jews from the city.

Sources

In his speech in defence of Lucius Valerius Flaccus (59 BCE), who was accused of maladministration as governor of the province of

Asia, Cicero appeals to anti-Jewish sentiment. The Jews who might witness against Flaccus would make poor witnesses, he argues. Flaccus, to his credit, actually forbade the remitting of the Temple tax to Judaea from his province. That money, Cicero asserts, remains in the provincial treasury such was the steadfastness of Flaccus.

592. There follows the odium that is attached to Jewish gold. This is no doubt the reason why this case is being tried not far from the Aurelian Steps. You procured this place and that crowd, Laelius, for this trial. You know what a big crowd it is, how they stick together, how influential they are in informal assemblies. So I will speak in a low voice so that only the jurors may hear; for those are not wanting who would incite them against me and against every respectable man. I shall not help them to do this more easily. When every year it was customary to send gold to Jerusalem on the order of the Jews from Italy and from all our provinces, Flaccus forbade by an edict its exportation from Asia. Who is there, gentlemen, who could not honestly praise this action? The senate often earlier and also in my consulship most urgently forbade the export of gold. But to resist this barbaric superstition was an act of firmness, to defy the crowd of Jews when sometimes in our assemblies they were hot with passion, for the welfare of the state was an act of the greatest seriousness. 'But Gnaeus Pompey when Jerusalem was captured laid his victorious hands on nothing in that shrine.' In that he was especially wise—as in many other matters. In a state so given to suspicion and calumny he left his critics no opportunity for gossip. But I do not think that illustrious general was hindered by the religious feelings of the Jews and his enemies, but by his sense of honour. (Cicero, *Pro Flacco* 66–68)

Julius Gaius's letter to the people of Parium, c. 43 BCE.

593. 'Julius Gaius, Praetor, Consul of the Romans, to the magistrates, council and people of Parium, greeting. The Jews in Delos and some of the neighbouring Jews, some of your envoys also being present, have appealed to me and declared that you are preventing them by statute from observing their national customs and sacred rites. Now it displeases me that such statutes should be made against our friends and allies and that they should be forbidden to live in accordance with their customs and to contribute money to common meals and sacred rites, for this they are not forbidden to do even in Rome. For example, Gaius Caesar, our consular praetor, by edict forbade religious societies to assemble in the city, but these people alone he did not forbid to do so or to collect contributions of money or to hold common meals. Similarly do I forbid other religious societies but permit these people alone to assemble and feast in accordance with their native customs and ordinances. And if you have made any statutes against our friends and allies, you will do well to revoke them because of their worthy deeds on our behalf and their goodwill toward us.' (Josephus, *Antiquities* 14.213–16)[11]

In both 19 and 49 CE the Jews were expelled from Rome. An earlier expulsion of Jews took place in 139 BCE. This event is attested in a fourth-century epitome of the early first-century CE writer Valerius Maximus.

594. Cn. Cornelius Hispalus, *praetor peregrinus* in the year of the consulate of M. Popilius Leanas and L. Calpurnius, ordered the astrologers by an edict to leave Rome and Italy within 10 days, since by a fallacious interpretation of the stars they perturbed fickle and silly minds, thereby making profit out of their lies. The same praetor compelled the Jews, who attempted to infect the Roman customs with the cult of Jupiter Sabazius, to return to their homes. (Paris, from the *Epitome of Valerius Maximus*)[12]

The following three extracts relate to the expulsion that occurred in 19 BCE.

Josephus relates the reasons for the expulsion of the Jews under Tiberius.

595. There was a certain Jew, a complete scoundrel, who had fled his own country because he was accused of transgressing certain laws and feared punishment on this

account. Just at this time he was resident in Rome and played the part of an interpreter of the Mosaic law and its wisdom. He enlisted three confederates not a whit better in character than himself; and when Fulvia, a woman of high rank who had become a Jewish proselyte, began to meet with them regularly, they urged her to send purple and gold to the temple in Jerusalem. They, however, took the gifts and used them for their own personal expenses, for it was this that had been their intention in asking for gifts from the start. Saturninus, the husband of Fulvia, at the instigation of his wife, duly reported this to Tiberius, whose friend he was, whereupon the latter ordered the whole Jewish community to leave Rome. The consuls drafted four thousand of these Jews for military service and sent them to the island of Sardinia; but they penalized a good many of them, who refused to serve for fear of breaking the Jewish law. And so because of the wickedness of four men the Jews were banished from the city.
(Josephus, *Antiquities* 18.81–84)[13]

596. As the Jews had flocked to Rome in great numbers and were converting many of the natives to their ways, he [Tiberius] banished most of them.
(Dio Cassius, *Roman History* 57.18.5a)

In the following, Seneca is recounting his early attraction to the philosophy of Pythagoras. He alludes incidentally to the expulsion of the Jews.

597. I was imbued with his teaching, and began to abstain from animal food; at the end of a year the habit was as pleasant as it was easy. I was beginning to feel that my mind was more active; though I would not to-day positively state whether it really was or not. Do you ask how I came to abandon this practice? It was this way: The days of my youth coincided with the early part of the reign of Tiberius Caesar. Some foreign rites were at that time being inaugurated [the translator reads *vovebantur*; the text reads *movebantur*, 'were being expelled'], and abstinence from certain kinds of animal food was set down as a proof of interest in the strange cult. So at the request of my father, who did not fear prosecution, but detested philosophy, I returned to my previous habits; and it was no very hard matter to induce me to dine more comfortably.
(Seneca, *Epistles* 108.22)[14]

The banishing of the Jews from Rome in 49 CE.

598. Since the Jews constantly made disturbances at the instigation of Chrestus [*impulsore Chresto*], he expelled them from Rome.
(Suetonius, *Claudius* 25.4)[15]

Petronius on the Jews.

599. The Jew may worship his pig-god and clamour in the ears of high heaven, but unless he also cuts back with a knife the region of his groin, and unless he unlooses by art the knotted head, he shall go forth from the holy city cast forth from the people, and transgress the sabbath by breaking the law of fasting.
(Petronius, *Satyricon* Poems 24)

Juvenal on the Jews.

600. For while all his goods and chattels were being packed upon a single wagon, my friend halted at the dripping archway of the old Porta Capena. Here Numa held his nightly assignations with his mistress; but now the holy fount and grove and shrine are let out to Jews, who possess a basket and a truss of hay for all their furnishings.
(Juvenal, *Satires* 3.10–14)

In the following extract Juvenal laments the fact that many of the children of Jewish sympathizers become Jewish proselytes (cf. #596). Note the perception of Jews as inveterately lazy.

601. Some who have had a father who reveres the Sabbath, worship nothing but the clouds, and the divinity of the heavens [*caeli numen adorant*], and see no difference between eating swine's flesh, from which their father abstained, and that of man; and in time they take to circumcision. Having been wont to flout the laws of Rome, they learn and practise and revere the Jewish law, and all that Moses handed down in his secret tome, forbidding to point out the way to any not worshipping the same rites, and conducting none but the circumcised

to the desired fountain. For all which the father was to blame, who gave up every seventh day to idleness, keeping it apart from all the concerns of life.
(Juvenal, *Satires* 14.96–106)[16]

Epictetus mentions the Jews several times. It is possible that the following passage refers to Christians rather than Jews.

602. [W]henever we see a man halting between two faiths, we are in the habit of saying, 'He is not a Jew, he is only acting the part.' But when he adopts the attitude of mind of the man who has been baptized and has made his choice, then he both is a Jew in fact and is also called one. So we also are counterfeit 'baptists,' ostensibly Jews, but in reality something else, not in sympathy with our own reason, far from applying the principles which we profess, yet priding ourselves upon them as being men who know them.
(Epictetus, *Discourses* 2.9.20–21)[17]

Plutarch on the superstition of the Jews.

Plutarch defines superstition as 'ignorance and blindness in regard to the gods' (see his *Superstition* 164E).

603. Hesiod advises that the farmer before ploughing and sowing should

Pray to Zeus of the world below and holy Demeter

with his hand on the plough-handle; and Homer says that Ajax, as he was about to engage in single combat with Hector, bade the Greeks pray to the gods for him, and then, while they were praying, donned his armour; and when Agamemnon enjoined on the fighting men,

See that each spear is well sharpened, and each man's shield in good order,

at the same time he asked in prayer from Zeus,

Grant that I raze to the level of earth the palace of Priam;

for God is brave hope, not cowardly excuse. But the Jews, because it was the Sabbath day, sat in their places immovable, while the enemy were planting ladders against the walls and capturing the defences, and they did not get up, but remained there, fast bound in the toils of superstition as in one great net.
(Plutarch, *Superstition* 169B–C)[18]

8.5. The Civic Rights of the Jews

From the earliest phases of the Roman expansion eastward, Romans had encountered communities of Jews within larger urban settings. In Books 14 and 16 of his *Antiquities* Josephus preserves a selection of first-century BCE Roman and civic decrees affecting Jewish privileges and rights of assembly in Asia Minor and Greece. The decrees cited in Josephus testify to a consistent pattern of the upholding the rights of Jews as 'resident aliens' (metics) in the empire by Rome. In every instance the decrees are either initiated by Roman officials directing various cities and localities to protect and uphold Jewish privileges or are decrees of cities acting on Roman directives. In this way Josephus is seeking to demonstrate that the Jews have been long treated with respect, and have not been prevented by their rulers from practising their ancestral laws, but, on the contrary, even had their rulers' cooperation in preserving the Jewish religion and way of life.

In his *Antiquities* 12.8, Josephus records Ptolemy I's grant of equal citizenship to Jews in Alexandria.[19] This is at odds with *3 Maccabees* 2:25–30, 31–33 in which the promise of citizenship is held out to Alexandrian Jews if they renounce Judaism. However, it seems more likely that while there may have been some (apostate) Jews who were citizens, and who participated in the worship of the civic gods and other civic responsibilities, the majority of Jews enjoyed the status of a venerable ethnic community as Claudius himself attests (see #608 below).

Josephus is not the only writer who is exercised by the issue of Jewish civic rights. Towards the end of his life, the Jewish philosopher Philo of Alexandria had cause to represent the Jewish case for civic equality before Caligula in Rome following serious civic unrest in Alexandria (see #588). Claudius, however, dashed Alexandrian Jewish hopes.

Sources

A decree of Julius Caesar, 'passed by the Senate', for the people of Sidon concerning the Jews.

604. 'Gaius Julius Caesar, Imperator and Pontifex Maximus, Dictator for the second time, to the magistrates, council and people of Sidon, greeting. If you are in good health, it is well; I also and the army are in good health. I am sending you a copy of the decree, inscribed on a tablet, concerning Hyrcanus, son of Alexander [Jannaeus], the high priest and ethnarch of the Jews, in order that it may be deposited among your public records. It is my wish that this be set up on a tablet of bronze in both Greek and Latin. It reads as follows. "I, Julius Caesar, Imperator and Pontifex Maximus, Dictator for the second time, have decided as follows with the advice of the council. Whereas the Jew Hyrcanus, son of Alexander, both now and in the past, in time of peace as well as in war, has shown loyalty and zeal toward our state, as many commanders have testified on his behalf, and in the recent Alexandrian war came to our aid with fifteen hundred soldiers, and being sent by me to Mithridates, surpassed in bravery all those in the ranks, for these reasons it is my wish that Hyrcanus, son of Alexander, and his children shall be ethnarchs of the Jews and shall hold the office of high priest of the Jews for all time in accordance with their national customs, and that he and his sons shall be our allies and also be numbered among our particular friends; and whatever high-priestly rights or other privileges exist in accordance with their laws, these he and his children shall possess by my command. And if, during this period, any question shall arise concerning the Jews' manner of life, it is my pleasure that the decision shall rest with them. Nor do I approve of troops being given winter-quarters among them or of money being demanded of them." '
(Josephus, *Antiquities* 14.190–95)[20]

The decree affecting the Jews of Halicarnassus was passed on the motion of the (Roman) official Marcus Alexander. It states that Jewish 'sacred services to God and customary festivals and gatherings should be maintained', and, proceeds to allow the following:

605. '[T]hose Jewish men and women who so wish may observe their Sabbaths and perform their sacred rites in accordance with the Jewish laws, and may build places of prayer [*proseuchai*] near the sea in accordance with their native custom.'
(Josephus, *Antiquities* 14.258)

Jewish civic rights were upheld by Marcus Agrippa on his tour of the east (16–13 BCE).

606. Thereupon Agrippa, who perceived that they had been subjected to violence, replied that because of Herod's goodwill and friendship for him he was ready to grant the Jews all they might ask for, and, he said, their requests seemed just in themselves, so that even if they were to ask for still more, he would not hesitate to give them this, provided, of course, that it did not cause the Roman government any trouble. And since they asked that the rights which they had formerly received should not be annulled, he would confirm their right to continue to observe their own customs without suffering mistreatment.
(Josephus, *Antiquities* 16.60)

In 70 CE Titus was petitioned twice by the Senate and people of Antioch to expel the Jews from the city. His reply to the second of these entreaties and the response of the Antiochenes were as follows:

607. 'But their own country to which, as Jews, they ought in that case to be banished, has been destroyed, and no other place would now receive them'. So relinquishing their first request the Antiochenes turned to a second, petitioning him to remove the brazen tablets on which were inscribed the privileges of the Jews. But this, too, Titus refused, and, leaving the status of the Jews of Antioch exactly as it was before, he set out for Egypt.
(Josephus, *Jewish War* 7.109–111)

Claudius's repudiation of Jewish hopes for citizenship in Alexandria.

The following extract from a papyrus (P.London 1912, ll. 73–104) refers to serious ethnic rioting that took place in Alexandria in 38 CE, which was described by Philo in his apologetic work *Flaccus*. Flaccus, the Prefect of Egypt at the time, had acted in league with anti-Jewish elements in Alexandria by proposing to erect statues of Caligula in the synagogues. Jewish refusal resulted in a pogrom—a 'war', according to Claudius—in which Jews were killed, some by crucifixion, and Jewish property destroyed. Josephus's edict of Claudius (reproduced in *Antiquities* 19.280–85) which upholds Jewish access to the citizenship roles in Alexandria is, in part, a forgery.[21]

608. With regard to the responsibility for the disturbances and rioting, or rather, to speak the truth, the war, against the Jews, although your ambassadors, particularly Dionysios the son of Theon, argued vigorously and at length in the disputation, I have not wished to make an exact inquiry, but I harbour within me a store of immutable indignation against those who renewed the conflict. I merely say that, unless you stop this destructive and obstinate mutual enmity, I shall be forced to show what a benevolent ruler can be when he is turned to righteous indignation. Even now, therefore, I conjure the Alexandrians to behave gently and kindly towards the Jews who have inhabited the same city for many years, and not to dishonour any of their customs in their worship of their god, but to allow them to keep their own ways, as they did in the time of the god Augustus and as I too, having heard both sides, have confirmed. The Jews, on the other hand, I order not to aim at more than they have previously had and not in future to send two embassies as if they lived in two cities, a thing which has never been done before, and not to intrude themselves into the games presided over by the *gymnasiarchoi* and the *kosmetai*, since they enjoy what is their own, and in a city which is not their own they possess an abundance of all good things. Nor are they to bring in or invite Jews coming from Syria or Egypt, or I shall be forced to conceive graver suspicions. If they disobey, I shall proceed against them in every way as fomenting a common plague for the whole world. If you both give up your present ways and are willing to live in gentleness and kindness with one another, I for my part will care for the city as much as I can, as one which has long been closely connected with us.
(*CPJ* no. 153)

In 41 CE two high-ranking Alexandrians, Isidorus and Lampon sought to indict the Jewish king Agrippa I before Claudius for fomenting a Jewish rebellion in the city. The charge failed, and both were executed. The affair is the subject of one of a related set of early third-century anti-Roman papyri known collectively as the *Acts of the Alexandrian Martyrs*.[22]

8.6. The Sabbath

Along with monotheism, aniconic worship, the keeping of food laws, and circumcision, the observing of the Sabbath was one of chief distinguishing boundary markers of Jewish identity. The practice is well known to the Greek and Roman writers of the era, who invariably interpreted the practice as evidence of Jewish indolence.[23] Sabbath-keeping contributed to the particularity and separateness of the Jews in mixed ethnic settings. It was one of the reasons why Jews were unable to serve in the Roman army. Indeed, the issue of whether Jews should fight on the Sabbath or not had been keenly debated (see 1 Maccabees 2:29–41 cited at #132). The Dead Sea sect took a resolutely stringent position on this issue, refusing, one suspects, to bow to the kind of compromise devised at the time of the Maccabaean Revolt.

The Gospels reveal just how anxious were Jesus' contemporaries among the Pharisees about his apparent disregard for the Sabbath. Tensions on this score undoubtedly contributed to his alienation from those who wielded power in Judaean society. Jewish-Christians continued to observe the Sabbath, while Gentile Christianity soon lost any sense of obligation to keep the day separate. The Dead Sea sect was more strict in the observance of the Sabbath than their contemporaries, as the extract from the Damascus Document cited below at #645 demonstrates.

Sources

The book of *Jubilees* is particularly focused on Sabbath observance.

609. And he gave us a great sign, the sabbath day, so that we might work six days and observe a sabbath from all work on the seventh day. And he told us—all of the angels of the presence and all of the angels of sanctification, these two great kinds—that we might keep the sabbath with him in heaven and on earth. And he said to us, 'Behold I shall separate for myself a people from among all the nations. And they will also keep the sabbath. And I will sanctify them for myself, and I will bless them. Just as I have sanctified and shall sanctify the sabbath day for myself thus shall I bless them. And they will be my people and I will be their God. And I have chosen the seed of Jacob from among all that I have seen. And I have recorded him as my firstborn son, and have sanctified him for myself forever and ever. And I will make known to them the sabbath day so that they might observe therein a sabbath from all work.'

    And thus he created therein a sign by which they might keep the sabbath with us on the seventh day, to eat and drink and bless the one who created all things just as he blessed and sanctified for himself a people who appeared from all the nations so that they might keep the sabbath together with us. And he caused their desires to go up as pleasing fragrance, which is acceptable before him always.
    (*Jubilees* 2:17–22)

Agatharchides was a second-century BCE historian and geographer from Alexandria. Josephus records his observations on the Sabbath.

610. 'The people known as Jews, who inhabit the most strongly fortified of cities, called by the natives Jerusalem, have a custom of abstaining from work every seventh day; on these occasions they neither bear arms nor take any agricultural operations in hand, nor engage in any other form of public service [*leitourgia*], but pray with outstretched hands in the temples [*hieroi*] until the evening. Consequently, because the inhabitants, instead of protecting their city, persevered in their folly, Ptolemy, son of Lagus, was allowed to enter with his army; the country was thus given over to a cruel master, and the defect of a practice enjoined by law was exposed. That experience has taught the whole world, except that nation, the lesson not to resort to dreams and traditional fancies about the law, until its difficulties are such as to baffle human reason.'
    (Josephus, *Against Apion* 1.209–211)[24]

Ovid on the Sabbath.

Just as sailors and farmers observe seasons for their respective activities, Ovid contends, so the lover should be aware that there are better times than others for courting.

611. You may begin on the day on which woeful Allia flows stained with the blood of Latian wounds, or on that day, less fit for business, whereon returns the seventh-day feast that the Syrian of Palestine observes. But hold in awful dread your lady's birthday; let that be a black day whereon a present must be given.
    (Ovid, *Art of Love* 1.413–18)

Jesus and the Sabbath.

612. Again he [Jesus] entered the synagogue, and a man was there who had a withered hand. They [the Pharisees] watched him to see whether he would cure him on the sabbath, so that they might accuse him. And he said to the man who had the withered hand, 'Come forward.' Then he said to them, 'Is it lawful to do good or to do harm on the sabbath, to save life or to kill?' But they were silent. He looked around at them with anger; he was grieved at their hardness of heart and said to the man, 'Stretch out your hand.' He stretched it out, and his hand was restored. The Pharisees went out and immediately conspired with the Herodians against him, how to destroy him.
    (Mark 3:1–6)

The rabbis on the Sabbath.

613. He who makes the Sabbath a delight shall have the wishes of his heart fulfilled.
    (*Babylonian Talmud, Sabbath* 118b)

614. 'Therefore the Lord blessed the Sabbath day and sanctified it.' It has no partner. All the other days of the week go in pairs, but the seventh day has no partner. The Sabbath said to God, 'All the other days have partners; I have no partner.' God said, 'Israel shall be thy partner.'
(*Pesiḳta Rabbati* 117b)

8.7. The Temple

There had been a temple in Jerusalem from the days of Solomon. That temple had been destroyed by the Babylonians in 586 BCE. After 539 BCE it was rebuilt in stages by exiles returning from Babylonia. Though defiled by Antiochus Epiphanes, it was re-dedicated by Judas Maccabaeus and stood until the last decades of the first century BCE. The building programme of Herod the Great saw the transformation of the existing sanctuary by the erection of a splendid edifice overflowing the whole site. Began in 20 BCE, the building was not completed until the outbreak of the Revolt in 66 CE. Its destruction in 70 deprived the world of a monument of unparalleled artistic achievement, its fame and beauty reported by Jewish and non-Jewish writers.

In common with the religious practices of non-Jews, the offering of sacrifice was a central act within the Jewish cult. Sacrifices were offered to God accompanied by prayers beseeching his favour or expressing thanks and praise for his care of individuals and the nation. The daily liturgical round began and ended with sacrifice. However, after the closure of all other shrines during reforms undertaken in the reign of Josiah (640–609 BCE), a reform which was subsequently mandated after the event in scripture, sacrifice could only be offered at 'the place the Lord your God will choose out of all your tribes as his habitation to put his name there' (see Deuteronomy 12:5), namely, the Jerusalem Temple. This meant that very few Jews living in the diaspora were present on sacrificial occasions. Nevertheless pilgrims did travel to Jerusalem (see Luke 2:41–44; Acts 2:5–11).[25] The annual Temple tax of two drachmas was also levied on all Jewish males throughout the homeland and the diaspora.

Sacrifices were offered by priests in accordance with the stipulations recorded in the books of Leviticus and Numbers and ascribed to Moses. According to Numbers 8 the tribe of Levi stood between God and the people of Israel to guarantee his continued presence among the nation. Levi bridged the chasm between a holy God, who consented to dwell in the midst of his people, and the people. The people participated in ritual uncleanness of all kinds, namely, bodily emissions and contact with corpses, as well as certain sins of commission and omission. The Levites functioned, therefore, as 'bridge-builders' (*pontifices*) between God and the people. The high priest was analogous to the *pontifex maximus* in Rome. Sacrifice cleansed the people, the sanctuary and the 'camp' of pollution. The Levites' devotion to priestly duty thus enabled the ongoing fellowship of God with the people of Israel.

There is a powerful connection between the pre-70 CE priestly caste and the rabbis operating after the destruction of the Temple and its priesthood in 70 CE. The priestly regulations were self-applied by the rabbis, and were promoted by them to all Jews. This was also the case with their spiritual predecessors, the Pharisees, even before 70. The concern for priestly purity had the effect of turning the Pharisees and the rabbis into lay-priests. They did not sacrifice, but represented to the people a living bond with the ritual purity of the Temple and the priestly establishment. Their performance of these regulations was most visible in their table etiquette. They exercised strict control of what they ate (in strict accordance with the food laws of scripture), how they ate it (with washed hands), and with whom they ate (no Gentile and non-observant Jewish contacts). By contrast Jesus' inclusive table fellowship represented a challenge to ascendant notions of purity.

The Temple's sanctity was jealously guarded by the Jews. No Gentile could go beyond the outer court; no woman could go beyond the court of women; no Jewish layman could proceed beyond the court of Israel; only priests could enter the Holy Place; and only the high priest into the Most Holy Place (Holy of Holies).

The Fourth Gospel depicts Jesus discoursing with the Jews a number of times in the Temple (John 7:14; 10:23). However, he is never reported to have offered sacrifice himself, except directing the slaughtering of the Passover lamb (see Mark 14:12 parr.). He is also portrayed directing one of those he had healed of leprosy to offer the required sacrifice, and to show himself to the priests for a clean bill of health (Mark 1:44).

Herod doubled the size of the Temple area to 35 acres. He had the platform raised to 450 feet ('300 cubits'), using blocks of stone measuring 60 feet long in the southwest corner. Some of the huge foundation blocks weighing some 400 tons can still be seen.[26] The present 'Wailing Wall' was part of the western outer wall. This is all that remains of the Temple above ground. The Temple was by no means abandoned by the early Christians. They met in the spacious colonnades offered by the precincts and are present at cultically significant times, namely at the 'hour of prayer' at the time of the evening sacrifice (see Acts 3:1).

Sources

A decree (in the form of a letter) of Antiochus III proclaiming the sanctity of the Temple.

615. 'It is unlawful for any foreigner to enter the enclosure of the temple which is forbidden to the Jews, except to those of them who are accustomed to enter after purifying themselves in accordance with the law of the country. Nor shall anyone bring into the city the flesh of horses or of mules or of wild or tame asses, or of leopards, foxes or hares or, in general, of any animals forbidden to the Jews. Nor is it lawful to bring in their skins or even to breed any of these animals in the city. But only the sacrificial animals known to their ancestors and necessary for the propitiation of God shall they be permitted to use. And the person who violates any of these statutes shall pay to the priests a fine of three thousand drachmas of silver.'
(Josephus, *Antiquities* 12.145–46)

Temple inscription.

Compare the tenor of this (Greek) inscription with the account of Paul's arrest in the Temple precincts in Acts 21:26–30.

616. Let no foreigner enter within the screen and enclosure surrounding the sanctuary. Whosoever is taken so doing will be the cause that death overtaketh him.
(Deissmann, *Light from the Ancient East*, p. 80)

Hecataeus's description of Jerusalem and the Temple.

617. Again, here is his [Hecataeus's] description of Jerusalem itself, the city which we have inhabited from remote ages, of its great beauty and extent, its numerous population, and the temple buildings: 'The Jews have many fortresses and villages in different parts of the country, but only one fortified city, which has a circumference of about fifty *stades* and some hundred and twenty thousand inhabitants; they call it Jerusalem. Nearly in the centre of the city stands a stone wall, enclosing an area about five *plethra* long and a hundred cubits broad, approached by a pair of gates. Within this enclosure is a square altar, built of heaped up stones, unhewn and unwrought; each side is twenty cubits long and the height ten cubits. Beside it stands a great edifice, containing an altar and a lampstand, both made of gold, and weighing two talents; upon these is a light which is never extinguished by night or day. There is not a single statue or votive offering, no trace of a plant, in the form of a sacred grove or the like. Here priests pass their nights and days performing certain rites of purification, and abstaining altogether from wine while in the temple.'
(Josephus, *Against Apion* 1.196–99)[27]

Herod and the Temple.

618. Though the temple, as I said, was seated on a strong hill, the level area on its summit originally barely sufficed for shrine and altar, the ground around it being precipitous and

steep. But king Solomon, the actual founder of the temple, having walled up the eastern side, a single portico was reared on this made ground; on its other sides the sanctuary remained exposed. In course of ages, however, through the constant additions of the people to the embankment, the hill-top by this process of levelling up was widened. They further broke down the north wall and thus took in an area as large as the whole temple enclosure subsequently occupied. Then, after having enclosed the hill from its base with a wall on three sides, and accomplished a task greater than they could ever have hoped to achieve—a task upon which long ages were spent by them as well as all their sacred treasures, though replenished by the tributes offered to God from every quarter of the world—they built around the original block the upper courts and the lower temple enclosure. The latter, where its foundations were lowest, they built up from a depth of three hundred cubits; at some spots this figure was exceeded. The whole depth of the foundations was, however, not apparent; for they filled up a considerable part of the ravines, wishing to level the narrow alleys of the town. Blocks of stone were used in the building measuring forty cubits; for lavish funds and popular enthusiasm led to incredible enterprises, and a task seemingly interminable was through perseverance and in time actually achieved.
(Josephus, *Jewish War* 5.184–89.[28]
See also Philo's description in *Special Laws* 1.71–78)

Pilgrimage.

There was a flourishing trade centred on the Temple. In addition, Jews from all over the world conducted pilgrimages to Jerusalem to coincide with the major festivals.

619. Countless multitudes from countless cities come, some over land, others over sea, from east and west and north and south at every feast. They take the [Jerusalem] temple for their port as a general haven and safe refuge from the bustle and great turmoil of life, and there they seek to find calm weather, and, released from the cares whose yoke has been heavy upon them from their earliest years, to enjoy a brief breathing-space in scenes of genial cheerfulness. Thus filled with comfortable hopes they devote the leisure, as is their bounden duty, to holiness and the honouring of God. Friendships are formed between those who hitherto knew not each other, and the sacrifices and libations are the occasion of reciprocity of feeling and constitute the surest pledge that all are of one mind.
(Philo, *Special Laws* 1.69–70)[29]

Despite the destruction of the Temple in 70 CE, Jews still thought of the cult as operative in daily life. Josephus writes the following towards the end of the first century, a generation after the destruction.

620. We have but one temple for the one God (for like ever loveth like), common to all as God is common to all. The priests are continually engaged in His worship, under the leadership of him who for the time is head of the line. With his colleagues he will sacrifice to God, safeguard the laws, adjudicate in cases of dispute, punish those convicted of crime. Any who disobey him will pay the penalty as for impiety towards God Himself. Our sacrifices are not occasions for drunken self-indulgence—such practices are abhorrent to God—but for sobriety. At these sacrifices prayers for the welfare of the community must take precedence of those for ourselves; for we are born for fellowship, and he who sets its claims above his private interests is specially acceptable to God. We should beseech God not to give us blessings, for He has given them spontaneously and put them at the disposal of all, but for capacity to receive, and, having received, to keep them. In view of the sacrifices the Law has prescribed purifications for various occasions: after a funeral, after child-birth, after conjugal union, and many others.
(Josephus, *Against Apion* 2.193–98)[30]

621. God foresaw that the Temple would be destroyed, and He said, 'While the Temple exists, and you bring sacrifices, the Temple atones for you; when the Temple is not there, what shall atone for you? Busy yourselves with the words of the Law, for they are equivalent to sacrifices, and they will atone for you.'
(*Tanḥuma (Buber)*, Aḥare Mot 35a)

8.8. The Synagogue

The synagogue was the most significant and distinctive Jewish institution of the Hellenistic and Graeco-Roman eras in Palestine and the diaspora. It was the public locus of the expression of Jewish piety and communal identity. It was the place in which the salvation history and traditions of the Jews were publicly rehearsed. It was the theatre for the dissemination of Jewish learning and religious culture. It was a house of prayer (*beth ha-Tefillah*), a school house (*beth ha-Sefer, beth ha-Midrash*), a house of meeting (*beth ha-Kenesseth*), a court (*beth Din*), and a centre for social services. Since Jews and Gentiles lived throughout the Graeco-Roman era as neighbours, even in Palestine, synagogue buildings were accessible to non-Jews. A number of Graeco-Roman writers, Josephus, Acts and the inscriptions bear witness to this. This accessibility promoted understanding between Jews and their Gentile neighbours, but also provoked tension.

In contrast to the Jerusalem Temple, which was a priestly preserve, the synagogue functioned as the assembly of the laity. The rabbi was not a priest.[31] Whereas in the Temple the Jewish laity kept their distance, in the synagogue any Jewish adult male could participate in the significant acts and rites, namely, the reading of the scriptures, the benedictions and prayers, and could deliver the homily (see Luke 4:16–30; Acts 13:15). The earliest synagogue that has been excavated is on the Aegean island of Delos.[32]

Many scholars contend that the origins of the synagogue are to be traced to the exile of the Jews in the sixth century BCE. Cut off from the cultic institutions of their Palestinian homeland, exiled Jews began to meet for mutual encouragement and edification. Passages such as Ezekiel 8:1; 14:1 and 20:1, in which the elders of Israel are pictured gathered in the presence of the prophet, are claimed as evidence of the beginnings of the synagogue.[33]

Nehemiah 8 speaks of an assembly of Jews in the postexilic era, during Ezra's ministry, at which the Law of Moses was read to the gathering (see #106). Because the people no longer understood Hebrew, learned priests explained in Aramaic (the *lingua franca*) the meaning of what was read. We know from much later times that in eastern synagogues not only did the Torah continue to be read in Hebrew, but that Aramaic paraphrases of what was read accompanied the readings. The substantial Aramaic targumic deposit is the result of the lack of facility in Hebrew.

The New Testament book of Acts represents one of the main contemporary literary sources for the Jewish institution of the synagogue in Hellenistic and Graeco-Roman times, reporting a multiplicity of synagogues in Palestine, Asia Minor and Greece in which Moses is read 'in every city', Sabbath by Sabbath.[34] The decrees of the Romans recorded in Books 14 and 16 of Josephus's *Antiquities* guaranteed that Jews would be able to continue practising their laws, to keep the Sabbath, to remit the Temple tax unhindered to Jerusalem, to be exempt from military service, and to meet in their synagogues.[35] These privileges were upheld in the first century by Claudius and Vespasian. Even after the revolt of 66–70, Jews were allowed to continue meeting in their synagogues and to continue practising the customs of their religion. To this extent it is right to conclude that, both before and after the Revolt, Judaism was regarded as a 'licensed religion', and that the Romans were satisfied that Judaism was not a political threat and its ethical stance was in accord with accepted convention and notions of public order.

Paul attended the synagogue as a matter of custom (see Acts 17:2). This was where he preached the message of Jesus Christ as the fulfilment of the promises of the Hebrew Bible. He drew his converts from the synagogue—from the ranks of Jews, proselytes to Judaism, and Godfearing Gentiles. Luke portrays him repeatedly worsting the unbelieving Jews in debate, which leads to outbreaks of violence, sometimes murderous in intent, as at Lystra in Acts 14:19–20.

There is no reason to doubt the attraction Judaism held for those, especially among the upper classes, who identified with the high ethics and monotheism of Judaism. It seems that more women than men were attracted to Judaism on these scores. Josephus (and the author of Acts) informs his readers of a class of Gentile adherents to Judaism called 'God-worshippers' (*sebomenoi ton theon*).[36] He informs his readers that Jews and 'God-worshippers' from all over the world contributed to the wealth of the Temple. These were Paul's links between the world of Jewish privilege and custom and the Gentile world, as Acts eloquently attests.

The synagogue service comprised three parts, namely, prayer, reading of scripture, and homily. The most famous prayer is the 'Eighteen Benedictions', sometimes called the Amidah because it was prayed standing. According to rabbinic tradition, the 'Eighteen Benedictions' were standardized at the end of the first century CE after the destruction of the Temple as part of the process of normalizing and restoring Judaism. The themes of the Benedictions amount to a compendium of early Jewish theological insights and eschatological expectations. Salvation history (Benediction 1), the need for repentance and confidence in God's mercy and will to forgive (6), the recognition of affliction (7), and a prayer for good harvests (9) are some of the themes articulated. An eschatological note is struck in Benedictions 2 (resurrection hope), 10 (the expectation of re-gathering of the dispersed people [cf. Isaiah 11:10]) and 14 (a prayer for the re-establishment of the throne of David). It is quite clear from the Benedictions that apocalyptic fervour was not extinguished even in the wake of the calamity of the First Revolt.[37]

But not all the Benedictions comprise praise and blessings. Benediction 12 is a malediction (a curse) on those Jews who are apostates (*minim* in Hebrew), which may have been expanded to include the *Nozrim* (Nazarenes, i.e. Christians). According to Jerome (c. 340–420 CE) Jews cursed Christians in the synagogue prayers of the fourth century. Note too the desire for vengeance on Rome ('the arrogant kingdom').

In addition to the prayers there was a lectionary for the regular reading of scripture. Moses, so Luke notes, is read and preached every Sabbath in every city (Acts 15:21; cf. Philo, *Moses* 2.215). The reading of the prophets is attested in Luke 4 and in Acts 13:15. The homily was based on the scripture readings. The preacher was not necessarily a rabbi. A visiting Jew could give the sermon if the synagogue rulers invited him to do so (e.g. Acts 13:15b). It has been suggested that *4 Maccabees* and Hebrews reflect the style of synagogue sermons. Hebrews is especially rhetorically effective, and bears all the marks of sophisticated moral exhortation. The letter mounts a sophisticated argument for the supersession of the Levitical priesthood and underscores the importance of perseverance in the faith in the light of the surpassing revelation of God in the person of Jesus Christ.

Sources

The mid first-century CE *'Theodotus' inscription from Jerusalem.*

622. Theodotus the son of Vettenus, priest and ruler of the synagogue, son of a ruler of the synagogue, son's son of a ruler of the synagogue, built the synagogue for reading of the law and for teaching of the commandments, also the strangers' lodging and the chambers and the conveniencies of waters for an inn for them that need it from abroad, of which (synagogue) his fathers and the elders and Simonides did lay the foundation.
(Deissmann, *Light from the Ancient East*, p. 440)

Evidence of synagogues in the diaspora.

The earliest two references to synagogues emanate from Egypt in Ptolemy III's reign (246–221 BCE). The following inscription was found at Schedia.[38]

623. For King Ptolemy and Queen Berenike, his sister and wife, and for their children, the Jews built the synagogue.
(*New Docs* III, p. 121)

'God-fearers'.

624. But no one need wonder that there was so much wealth in our temple, for all the Jews throughout the habitable world, and those who worshipped God [*sebomenoi ton theon*], even those from Asia and Europe, had been contributing to it for a very long time. (Josephus, *Antiquities* 14.110)

Extracts from the 'Eighteen Benedictions' (the Amidah*).*

625. (1) Blessed art thou, O Lord our God and God of our fathers, God of Abraham, God of Isaac, and God of Jacob, the great, mighty and revered God, the most high God, who bestowest lovingkindnesses, and possessest all things; who rememberest the pious deeds of the patriarchs, and in love wilt bring a redeemer to their children's children for thy name's sake. O King, Helper, Saviour and Shield. Blessed art thou, O Lord, the Shield of Abraham.

(2) Thou, O Lord, art mighty for ever, thou quickenest the dead, thou art mighty to save. Thou sustainest the living with lovingkindness, quickenest the dead with great mercy, supportest the falling, healest the sick, loosest the bound, and keepest thy faith to them that sleep in the dust. Who is like thee, lord of mighty acts, and who resembleth thee, O King, who killest and quickenest, and causest salvation to spring forth? Yea, faithful art thou to quicken the dead. Blessed art thou, O Lord, who quickenest the dead.

(10) Sound the great horn for our freedom; lift up the ensign to gather our exiles, and gather us from the four corners of the earth. Blessed art thou, O Lord, who gatherest the banished ones of thy people Israel.

(11) Restore our judges as at first, and our counsellors as at the beginning; remove from us grief and suffering; reign over us, O Lord, thou alone, in lovingkindness and tender mercy, and justify us in judgment. Blessed art thou, the King who lovest righteousness and judgment.

(12) And for slanderers let there be no hope, and let all wickedness perish as in a moment; let all thine enemies be speedily cut off, and the dominion of arrogance do thou uproot and crush, cast down and humble speedily in our days. Blessed art thou, O Lord, who breakest our enemies and humblest the arrogant.

(14) And to Jerusalem, thy city, return in mercy, and dwell therein as thou hast spoken; rebuild it soon in our days as an everlasting building, and speedily set up therein the throne of David. Blessed art thou, O Lord, who rebuildest Jerusalem.

(15) Speedily cause the offspring of David, thy servant, to flourish, and let his horn be exalted by thy salvation, because we wait for thy salvation all the day. Blessed art thou, O Lord, who causest the horn of salvation to flourish.

(18) Accept, O Lord our God, thy people Israel and their prayer; restore the service to the oracle of thy house; receive in love and favour both the fire-offerings of Israel and their prayer; and may the service of thy people Israel be ever acceptable unto thee. (*The Amidah*, Benedictions 1, 2, 10–12, 14–15, 18)

8.9. Pharisees

The 'party' of the Pharisees is likely to have originated in the struggle for Jewishness at the time of Greek cultural and political dominance which reached a climax with the Maccabaean Revolt. The Hasidim were their likely forbears.[39] 1 Maccabees speaks of the Hasidim (see 1 Maccabees 2:42), a term meaning 'pious ones', who expressed outrage at Syrian interference in Jewish religious and political affairs. The Pharisees are first mentioned by name during the high priesthood of John Hyrcanus 1 (134–104 BCE) (see *Antiquities* 13.171–72).[40] They are depicted by Josephus as antagonistic to Hyrcanus and the Hasmonaean assumption of the 'throne of David'. They were cruelly punished under Alexander Jannaeus (103–76 BCE) during his war with the Seleucid king Demetrius III Eukairos (see #145).[41]

Under Queen Salome, Jannaeus's widow, the Pharisees were restored to favour (Josephus, *Jewish War* 1.111). They became increasingly intolerant of the Herodian dynasty. The hacking down of the Eagle which Herod had erected over the gates of the Temple was provoked and carried out by Pharisees in extreme zeal for the Law.[42] Another Pharisee, Saddok, was responsible for the ideology behind the movement presented by Josephus as the 'Fourth Philosophy', which advocated direct action against the Romans.[43]

In the New Testament they are scrupulous laymen concerned about ritual purity, tithing, Sabbath-keeping and the application of oral tradition throughout Judaea and Galilee. They formed themselves into local associations. They were found within the Sanhedrin.[44] Josephus estimates their numbers at 6000 at the time of Herod's death. They held themselves rigorously separate from the ordinary bulk of the people, the 'people of the land' (*'am ha-'arets*; see John 7:49), who were regarded as 'accursed'. Yet they were highly regarded by the people. They insisted that the priestly purity rules were to be followed by all. Table fellowship was a potent strategy for delineating identity. By Jesus' day Pharisaism was not as politically active as it had been in the previous century.

According to Josephus, the Pharisees believed in divine providence and predestination, the resurrection of the body, angels and demons (cf. Acts 23:8), and the linkage of scripture and tradition (cf. Mark 7:3). The Sadducees denied these doctrines preferring, one assumes, to adhere to the old ways as encapsulated in the Pentateuch.

After the fall of Jerusalem in 70 CE, it is Pharisaic Judaism alone of the Jewish groups which was able to regroup and maintain and propagate a distinctive Jewish witness. They were amenable to tradition and prepared to adapt to new social and political realities. Josephus reports that they were more friendly to strangers than the Sadducees (*Jewish War* 2.166), they were followed by the masses (*Antiquities* 13.298) and interpreted the law more freely than the Sadducees (*Antiquities* 18.12).

Another Jewish group, the scribes, were closely connected to the Pharisees. Scribes were a professional scholarly body drawn from Judaea and Galilee (see Luke 5:17). Their task was to commit to writing the oral traditions of the earlier generations, and to teach authoritatively what was in accordance with Jewish practice and doctrine. All social classes provided scribes. Their role as teachers and lawyers can be seen in Mark 1:22 where it is acknowledged that Jesus taught with authority 'not as the scribes'.[45]

Whereas Pharisees were non-professional expounders and teachers of the traditions and the scriptures, scribes spent their time in undistracted study. In effect they were the professional legal body. Many scribes belonged to the Pharisees, and the two are often mentioned together in the New Testament.[46] Gamaliel was a scribe, a Pharisee and a member of the Sanhedrin (Acts 5:34). The work of scribes provided the authority behind the movement of the Pharisees.

Sources

Josephus and the Pharisees.

626. (162) Of the two first-named schools, the Pharisees, who are considered the most accurate interpreters of the laws, and hold the position of the leading sect, attribute everything to Fate and to God; they hold that to act rightly or otherwise rests, indeed, for the most part with men, but that in each action Fate co-operates. Every soul, they maintain, is imperishable, but the soul of the good alone passes into another body, while the souls of the wicked suffer eternal punishment.

(166) The Pharisees are affectionate to each other and cultivate harmonious relations with the community. The Sadducees, on the contrary, are, even among themselves, rather boorish in their behaviour, and in their intercourse with their peers are as rude as to aliens.

(Josephus, *Jewish War* 2.162–63, 166)

Pharisees in the New Testament.

627. Now when the Pharisees and some of the scribes who had come from Jerusalem gathered around him, they noticed that some of

his disciples were eating with defiled hands, that is, without washing them. (For the Pharisees, and all the Jews, do not eat unless they thoroughly wash their hands, thus observing the tradition of the elders; and they do not eat anything from the market unless they wash it; and there are also many other traditions that they observe, the washing of cups, pots, and bronze kettles.)
(Mark 7:1–4.
Cf. Matthew 15:1–2)

628. Now all the tax collectors and sinners were coming near to listen to him. And the Pharisees and the scribes were grumbling and saying, 'This fellow welcomes sinners and eats with them.'
(Luke 15:1–2.
Cf. Matthew 9:10–13)

After the apostles performed many healings, the Sadducees arrested them, intending to do away with them. Peter and the Apostles are brought before the Sanhedrin. Gamaliel counsels caution in dealing with the Christians in the face of many who want to have them killed.

629. [A] Pharisee in the council named Gamaliel, a teacher of the law, respected by all the people, stood up and ordered the men [Peter and the other apostles] outside for a short time. Then he said to them, 'Fellow Israelites, consider carefully what you propose to do to these men. For some time ago Theudas rose up, claiming to be somebody, and a number of men, about four hundred, joined him; but he was killed, and all who followed him were dispersed and disappeared. After him Judas the Galilean rose up at the time of the census and got people to follow him; he also perished, and all who followed him were scattered. So in the present case, I tell you, keep away from these men and let them alone; because if this plan or this undertaking is of human origin, it will fail; but if it is of God, you will not be able to overthrow them—in that case you may even be found fighting against God!'
(Acts 5:34–39)[47]

Paul before the Sanhedrin.

630. When Paul noticed that some were Sadducees and others were Pharisees, he called out in the council, 'Brothers, I am a Pharisee, a son of Pharisees. I am on trial concerning the hope of the resurrection of the dead.' When he had said this, a dissension began between the Pharisees and the Sadducees, and the assembly was divided. (The Sadducees say that there is no resurrection, or angel, or spirit; but the Pharisees acknowledge all three.)
(Acts 23:6–8)

8.10. Sadducees

The Sadducees are first mentioned during the high priesthood of Hyrcanus I.[48] Whereas the Pharisees belonged to what was largely a lay movement taking its inspiration from the Law and the deposit of tradition, the Sadducees had come to terms with the Hasmonaeans. They served as magistrates and priests, as well as lay nobility. Taxes to support the priesthood were levied in the form of sacrificial portions and tithes.[49] In the New Testament the Sadducees appear as supporters of the religious status quo, eager to secure the best deal for the people and for themselves.[50] Their numbers were small, confined to a few patrician families.

Josephus outlines the beliefs of the Sadducees as negations of the doctrines of the Pharisees and Essenes. The Sadducees did not find the doctrine of the resurrection in their authoritative scripture, the Pentateuch (cf. Mark 12:18–27). Josephus also draws attention to their haughty manner, and their harshness in dealing with others, even with one another (see #631 below). They were swept away in the Jewish War. Having provided leadership of the revolt at the outset, their leaders were soon replaced by the radicals and the mob. It had been Eleazar (son of Ananias, the Sadducaean high priest who appears in Acts 23:1), who, as Captain of the Temple, had persuaded the Temple priests not to offer sacrifices for the emperor, thus precipitating the revolt. Josephus was born into a high priestly family with, one suspects, an impeccable Sadducaean pedigree (*Life* 1–6).

The 'high priests' were the families of the leading priests. The New Testament calls them 'Chief Priests'. There were 28 high priests from 4 BCE to 70 CE. Two were contemporaries of Jesus: Annas (Luke 3:2), appointed by the Syrian legate Quirinius in 6 CE, and his son-in-law Caiaphas (18–36). The Gospels depict Annas still wielding considerable power (see Luke 3:2; John 18:3). Annas founded a dynasty. Five of his sons and a grandson, Annas II, became high priests.[51]

High priests, Pharisees, Sadducees and scribes were represented in the Sanhedrin, a term derived from the Greek *sunedrion*. The Sanhedrin functioned as the Jewish senate. It was also called the Council of the Elders (*presbyterion*; Luke 22:66). It had 70 mostly aristocratic members (Numbers 11:16). The high priest was the convener (see Matthew 26:57; Mark 14:53). The Sanhedrin did not survive the War. Leadership within Palestinian Judaism passed to the scholars, namely the Pharisees and scribes who met at Jamnia with Roman approval (see #192).

Sources

Josephus on the Sadducees.

631. The Sadducees, the second of the orders, do away with Fate altogether, and remove God beyond, not merely the commission, but the very sight, of evil. They maintain that man has the free choice of good or evil, and that it rests with each man's will whether he follows the one or the other. As for the persistence of the soul after death, penalties in the underworld, and rewards, they will have none of them. The Pharisees are affectionate to each other and cultivate harmonious relations with the community. The Sadducees, on the contrary, are, even among themselves, rather boorish in their behaviour, and in their intercourse with their peers are as rude as to aliens.
(Josephus, *Jewish War* 2.164–66)

A major difference between the Pharisees and the Sadducees.

632. [T]he Pharisees had passed on to the people certain regulations handed down by former generations and not recorded in the Laws of Moses, for which reason they are rejected by the Sadducaean group, who hold that only those regulations should be considered valid which were written down (in Scripture), and that those which had been handed down by former generations need not be observed.
(Josephus, *Antiquities* 13.297.
Cf. the mishnaic tractate *Aboth* 1 for the succession of rabbis)

8.11. Essenes

The Essenes are mentioned by Josephus, Philo, and Pliny the Elder. Both Josephus and Philo agree that they numbered c. 4000 throughout Palestine. Philo also speaks of a group of Jewish ascetics in Egypt whom he calls *therapeutae*. They bear considerable affinity with the Essenes of Palestine. According to Josephus, the Essenes, together with the Pharisees and Sadducees, had been in existence since 'ancient times'.[52] It is frequently argued that the Essenes, like the Pharisees, originated in the movement of the Hasidim, who opposed the measures taken by Antiochus Epiphanes (see 1 Maccabees 2:42).[53]

The Essenes were similar to the Pharisees in their concern for ritual purity and carefully defined social boundaries. Josephus describes Essenes who were celibate. Celibacy was unusual in early Judaism, and may indicate an acute anxiety by those who practised it about the ritual defilement occasioned by sexual intimacy (Leviticus 15:16–18; 18:19). They lived in communities in which possessions were shared (cf. Acts 2:44–45), observed ascetic discipline, and avoided unnecessary contact even with other Jews. Josephus also describes in detail the lifestyle in which Essenes engaged wherever they settled, which included strict rules for admission and probation.

Herod the Great favoured the Essenes out of respect for the ability of one of them to foretell the future (see *Antiquities* 15:373–79).[54] Josephus reports that at the commencement of the Jewish Revolt, the Jewish leadership assigned John the Essene the defence of the district of Thamna in Judaea. Josephus was impressed by the rigour of their discipline and their endurance under suffering during the Revolt (see *Jewish War* 2.152–53).

Sources

Josephus provides a detailed description of the beliefs of the Essenes in Book 2 of his *Jewish War*.

633. (119) The Jewish philosophy, in fact, takes three forms. The followers of the first school are called Pharisees, of the second Sadducees, of the third Essenes.

The Essenes have a reputation for cultivating peculiar sanctity. Of Jewish birth, they show a greater attachment to each other than do the other sects. They shun pleasures as a vice and regard temperance and the control of the passions as a special virtue. Marriage they disdain, but they adopt other men's children, while yet pliable and docile, and regard them as their kin and mould them in accordance with their own principles. They do not, indeed, on principle, condemn wedlock and the propagation thereby of the human race, but they wish to protect themselves against women's wantonness, being persuaded that none of the sex keeps her plighted troth to one man.

Riches they despise, and their community of goods is truly admirable; you will not find one among them distinguished by greater opulence than another. They have a law that new members on admission to the sect shall confiscate their property to the order, with the result that you will nowhere see either abject poverty or inordinate wealth; the individual's possessions join the common stock and all, like brothers, enjoy a single patrimony. Oil they consider defiling, and anyone who accidentally comes in contact with it scours his person; for they make a point of keeping a dry skin and of always being dressed in white. They elect officers to attend to the interests of the community, the special services of each officer being determined by the whole body.

They occupy no one city, but settle in large numbers in every town. On the arrival of any of the sect from elsewhere, all the resources of the community are put at their disposal, just as if they were their own; and they enter the houses of men whom they have never seen before as though they were their most intimate friends. Consequently, they carry nothing whatever with them on their journeys, except arms as a protection against brigands. In every city there is one of the order expressly appointed to attend to strangers, who provides them with raiment and other necessaries. In their dress and deportment they resemble children under rigorous discipline. They do not change their garments or shoes until they are torn to shreds or worn threadbare with age. There is no buying or selling among themselves, but each gives what he has to any in need and receives from him in exchange something useful to himself; they are, moreover, freely permitted to take anything from any of their brothers without making any return.

(137) A candidate anxious to join their sect is not immediately admitted. For one year, during which he remains outside the fraternity, they prescribe for him their own rule of life, presenting him with a small hatchet, the loin-cloth already mentioned [see §128], and white raiment. Having given proof of his temperance during this probationary period, he is brought into closer touch with the rule and is allowed to share the purer kind of holy water, but is not yet received into the meetings of the community. For after this exhibition of endurance, his character is tested for two years more, and only then, if found worthy, is he enrolled in the society. But, before he may touch the common food, he is made to swear tremendous oaths: first that he will practise piety towards the Deity, next that he will observe justice towards men: that he will wrong none whether of his own mind or under another's orders; that he will for ever hate the unjust and fight the battle of the just; that he will for ever keep faith with all men, especially with the powers that be, since no ruler attains his office save by the will of God; that, should he himself bear rule, he will never abuse his authority nor, either in dress or by other outward marks of superiority, outshine his subjects; to be for ever a lover of truth and to expose liars; to keep his hands

from stealing and his soul pure from unholy grain; to conceal nothing from the members of the sect and to report none of their secrets to others, even though tortured to death. He swears, moreover, to transmit their rules exactly as he himself received them; to abstain from robbery; and in like manner carefully to preserve the books of the sect and the names of the angels. Such are the oaths by which they secure their proselytes.

Those who are convicted of serious crimes they expel from the order; and the ejected individual often comes to a most miserable end. For, being bound by their oaths and usages, he is not at liberty to partake of other men's food, and so falls to eating grass and wastes away and dies of starvation. This has led them in compassion to receive many back in the last stage of exhaustion, deeming that torments which have brought them to the verge of death are a sufficient penalty for their misdoings.

(160) There is yet another order of Essenes, which, while at one with the rest in its mode of life, customs, and regulations, differs from them in its views on marriage. They think that those who decline to marry cut off the chief function of life, the propagation of the race, and, what is more, that, were all to adopt the same view, the whole race would very quickly die out. They give their wives, however, a three years' probation, and only marry them after they have by three periods of purification given proof of fecundity. They have no intercourse with them during pregnancy, thus showing that their motive in marrying is not self-indulgence but the procreation of children. In the bath the women wear a dress, the men a loin-cloth. Such are the usages of this order. (Josephus, *Jewish War* 2.119–27, 137–44, 160–61)

Philo's description of the Essenes.

634. Palestinian Syria, too, has not failed to produce high moral excellence. In this country live a considerable part of the very populous nation of the Jews, including as it is said, certain persons, more than four thousand in number, called Essenes. Their name which is, I think, a variation, though the form of the Greek is inexact, of ὁσιότης [*hosiotēs*] (holiness), is given them, because they have shown themselves especially devout in the service of God, not by offering sacrifices of animals, but by resolving to sanctify their minds. The first thing about these people is that they live in villages and avoid the cities because of the iniquities which have become inveterate among city dwellers, for they know that their company would have a deadly effect upon their own souls, like a disease brought by a pestilential atmosphere. Some of them labour on the land and others pursue such crafts as co-operate with peace and so benefit themselves and their neighbours. They do not hoard gold and silver or acquire great slices of land because they desire the revenues therefrom, but provide what is needed for the necessary requirements of life. For while they stand almost alone in the whole of mankind in that they have become moneyless and landless by deliberate action rather than by lack of good fortune, they are esteemed exceedingly rich, because they judge frugality with contentment to be, as indeed it is, an abundance of wealth. As for darts, javelins, daggers, or the helmet, breastplate or shield, you could not find a single manufacturer of them, nor, in general, any person making weapons or engines or plying any industry concerned with war, nor, indeed, any of the peaceful kind, which easily lapse into vice, for they have not the vaguest idea of commerce either wholesale or retail or marine, but pack the inducements to covetousness off in disgrace. Not a single slave is to be found among them, but all are free, exchanging services with each other, and they denounce the owners of slaves, not merely for their injustice in outraging the law of equality, but also for their impiety in annulling the statute of Nature, who mother-like has born and reared all men alike, and created them genuine brothers, not in mere name, but in very reality, though this kinship has been put to confusion by the triumph of malignant covetousness, which has wrought estrangement instead of affinity and enmity instead of friendship. As for philosophy they abandon the logical part to quibbling verbalists as unnecessary for the acquisition of virtue, and the physical to visionary praters as

beyond the grasp of human nature, only retaining that part which treats philosophically of the existence of God and the creation of the universe. But the ethical part they study very industriously, taking for their trainers the laws of their fathers, which could not possibly have been conceived by the human soul without divine inspiration.

In these they are instructed at all times, but particularly on the seventh days. For that day has been set apart to be kept holy and on it they abstain from all other work and proceed to sacred spots which they call synagogues. There, arranged in rows according to their ages, the younger below the elder, they sit decorously as befits the occasion with attentive ears. Then one takes the books and reads aloud and another of especial proficiency comes forward and expounds what is not understood. For most of their philosophical study takes the form of allegory, and in this they emulate the tradition of the past. They are trained in piety, holiness, justice, domestic and civic conduct, knowledge of what is truly good, or evil, or indifferent, and how to choose what they should and avoid the opposite, taking for their defining standards these three, love of God, love of virtue, love of men. Their love of God they show by a multitude of proofs, by religious purity constant and unbroken throughout their lives, by abstinence from oaths, by veracity, by their belief that the Godhead is the cause of all good things and nothing bad; their love of virtue, by their freedom from the love of either money or reputation or pleasure, by self-mastery and endurance, again by frugality, simple living, contentment, humility, respect for law, steadiness and all similar qualities; their love of men by benevolence and sense of equality, and their spirit of fellowship, which defies description, though a few words on it will not be out of place. First of all then no one's house is his own in the sense that it is not shared by all, for besides the fact that they dwell together in communities, the door is open to visitors from elsewhere who share their convictions.

Again they all have a single treasury and common disbursements; their clothes are held in common and also their food through their institution of public meals. In no other community can we find the custom of sharing roof, life and board more firmly established in actual practice. And that is no more than one would expect. For all the wages which they earn in the day's work they do not keep as their private property, but throw them into the common stock and allow the benefit thus accruing to be shared by those who wish to use it. The sick are not neglected because they cannot provide anything, but have the cost of their treatment lying ready in the common stock, so that they can meet expenses out of the greater wealth in full security. To the elder men too is given the respect and care which real children give to their parents, and they receive from countless hands and minds a full and generous maintenance for their latter years.

Such are the athletes of virtue produced by a philosophy free from the pedantry of Greek wordiness, a philosophy which sets its pupils to practise themselves in laudable actions, by which the liberty which can never be enslaved is firmly established. Here we have a proof.

(Philo, *Every Good Man is Free* 75–89)[55]

Philo dedicated his work *On the Contemplative Life* to the Therapeutae, an ascetic Jewish group based in Egypt but especially near Alexandria, who renounced a life within cities to pursue a life of fellowship with God in community. The Therapeutae bore many similarities to the Palestinian Essenes, and anticipate later Christian monastic communities in Egypt.

635. This kind exists in many places in the inhabited world, for perfect goodness must needs be shared both by Greeks and the world outside Greece, but it abounds in Egypt in each of the nomes as they are called and especially round Alexandria. But the best of these votaries journey from every side to settle in a certain very suitable place which they regard as their fatherland. This place is situated above the Mareotic Lake on a somewhat low-lying hill very happily placed both because of its security and the pleasantly tempered air. The safety is secured by the farm buildings and villages round about and

the pleasantness of the air by the continuous breezes which arise both from the lake which debouches into the sea and from the open sea hard by. For the sea breezes are light, the lake breezes close and the two combining together produce a most healthy condition of climate.

The houses of the society thus collected are exceedingly simple, providing protection against two of the most pressing dangers, the fiery heat of the sun and the icy cold of the air. They are neither near together as in towns, since living at close quarters is troublesome and displeasing to people who are seeking to satisfy their desire for solitude, nor yet at a great distance because of the sense of fellowship which they cherish, and to render help to each other if robbers attack them. In each house there is a consecrated room which is called a sanctuary or closet and closeted in this they are initiated into the mysteries of the sanctified life. They take nothing into it, either drink or food or any other of the things necessary for the needs of the body, but laws and oracles delivered through the mouth of prophets, and psalms and anything else which fosters and perfects knowledge and piety. They keep the memory of God alive and never forget it, so that even in their dreams the picture is nothing else but the liveliness of divine excellences and powers. Indeed many when asleep and dreaming give utterance to the glorious verities of their holy philosophy. Twice every day they pray, at dawn and at eventide; at sunrise they pray for a fine bright day, fine and bright in the true sense of the heavenly daylight which they pray may fill their minds. At sunset they ask that the soul may be wholly relieved from the press of the senses and the objects of sense and sitting where she is consistory and council chamber to herself pursue the quest of truth. The interval between early morning and evening is spent entirely in spiritual exercise. They read the Holy Scriptures and seek wisdom from their ancestral philosophy by taking it as an allegory, since they think that the words of the literal text are symbols of something whose hidden nature is revealed by studying the underlying meaning.

They have also writings of men of old, the founders of their way of thinking, who left many memorials of the form used in allegorical interpretation and these they take as a kind of archetype and imitate the method in which this principle is carried out. And so they do not confine themselves to contemplation but also compose hymns and psalms to God in all sorts of metres and melodies which they write down with the rhythms necessarily made more solemn.

For six days they seek wisdom by themselves in solitude in the closets mentioned above, never passing the outside door of the house or even getting a distant view of it. But every seventh day they meet together as for a general assembly and sit in order according to their age in the proper attitude, with their hands inside the robe, the right hand between the breast and the chin and the left withdrawn along the flank. Then the senior among them who also has the fullest knowledge of the doctrines which they profess comes forward and with visage and voice alike quiet and composed gives a well-reasoned and wise discourse. He does not make an exhibition of clever rhetoric like the orators or sophists of to-day but follows careful examination by careful expression of the exact meaning of the thoughts, and this does not lodge just outside the ears of the audience but passes through the hearing into the soul and there stays securely. All the others sit still and listen showing their approval merely by their looks or nods.

This common sanctuary in which they meet every seventh day is a double enclosure, one portion set apart for the use of the men, the other for the women. For women too regularly make part of the audience with the same ardour and the same sense of their calling. The wall between the two chambers rises up from the ground to three or four cubits built in the form of a breast work, while the space above up to the roof is left open. This arrangement serves two purposes; the modesty becoming to the female sex is preserved, while the women sitting within ear-shot can easily follow what is said since there is nothing to obstruct the voice of the speaker.

(Philo, *On the Contemplative Life* 21–33. See also sections 66–68)

Pliny the Elder's description of the Essenes.

It is probable that Pliny is describing the Qumran community.

636. On the west side of the Dead Sea, but out of range of the noxious exhalations of the coast, is the solitary tribe of the Essenes, which is remarkable beyond all the other tribes in the whole world, as it has no women and has renounced all sexual desire, has no money, and has only palm-trees for company. Day by day the throng of refugees is recruited to an equal number by numerous accessions of persons tired of life and driven thither by the waves of fortune to adopt their manners. Thus through thousands of ages (incredible to relate) a race in which no one is born lives on for ever: so prolific for their advantage is other men's weariness of life!
(Pliny the Elder, *Natural History* 5.72)

8.12. The Qumran Community

From the time of their discovery the Dead Sea Scrolls have been associated with the Essenes. The accidental discovery of the scrolls in 1947 (followed by similar manuscript discoveries over the next 10 years in 10 more caves) alerted scholars to the possible connection between the caves, the documents and the ruins of Qumran nearby. Excavation of the ruins in the 1950s by Roland de Vaux seems to bear out the hypothesis that there was indeed a monastic-like community at Qumran whose library and literary output had been secreted in the caves nearby before the destruction of the settlement in 68 CE.[56]

The ruins suggest that the community could have supported no more than c. 300 people at any one time. Some graves in the main cemetery have been excavated, revealing male remains in every case, the bodies buried on a north–south axis. Graves in an extension nearby have brought to light the remains of some women and children. It is reported that burials in the extension postdate those in the main cemetery, and have been buried in Moslem fashion on an east–west axis.[57]

Three types of documents have been discovered in the caves near the ruins of Qumran: (1) copies of books of the Hebrew Bible, notably two scrolls of Isaiah, one complete;[58] (2) copies of certain books of the Pseudepigrapha, namely, fragments of *1 Enoch* (though not chapters 37–71), *Jubilees*, and the deutero-canonical book of Tobit; (3) documents presumably composed by Qumran Essenes such as the Thanksgiving Scroll (1QH), the Rule of the Community (1QS), the War Scroll (1QM), and the Pesharim. The sectarian documents can be divided into the categories of regulations, prayers and hymns, biblical exposition, and apocalyptic scenarios.

Documents in the third group express the distinctive theology of the Qumran Essenes. With the exception of the so-called Damascus Document (CD) found in the Cairo Synagogue Genizah (store-room) at the end of the nineteenth century, fragmentary copies of which turned up in the Qumran caves, none of these documents was known before 1947. Fragments of the Songs of the Sabbath Sacrifice (4QShirShab) were found at Masada.

There is keen debate about the origins of the Qumran community. The consensus, if one can call it that, argues that the Qumran community came into existence in the middle of the second century BCE. It arose out of a bitter dispute within priestly circles in Jerusalem concerning the integrity of the priestly establishment. According to CD the community had experienced a 20-year period of 'wandering' during a time of 'wrath' when God delivered up his people to the sword and forsook his sanctuary (#640). This period could well correspond to the years c. 175–164 BCE, the years of the hellenization programme of Jason and Menelaus and the emergency occasioned by the desecration of the Temple by Antiochus IV Epiphanes. During this time God kept his faithful ones safe, though leaderless. After 20 years, God raised up for this 'remnant' a 'Righteous Teacher'. However, he was opposed by a 'Wicked Priest' (1QpHab 8; #643), perhaps the same person also referred to as the

'Scoffer' (CD 1). After the confrontation the Righteous Teacher led his people to 'Damascus' (CD 7) where they entered into a 'new covenant' (CD 8). The cause of the exile seems to have been centred on the issues of the alleged flouting of the Levitical Holiness Code by the priests not associated with the Teacher and the maintenance of the lunar calendar by the priestly establishment. The Qumran sect adopted a solar calendar. The members replaced animal sacrifice with the sacrifice of praise and thanksgiving, and saw themselves as having been joined to the congregation of the angels (see, e.g., #649, #650, 1QH 11.19–22; 19.10–13). 1QS describes in detail the procedure by which one became a member of the community.

Sources[59]

The Damascus Document (CD) describes the origins of the sect during a period of apostasy in Israel. In the Scrolls 'Belial' denotes Satan.

637. During all these years Belial shall be unleashed against Israel, as He spoke by the hand of Isaiah, son of Amoz, saying, *Terror and the pit and the snare are upon you, O inhabitant of the land* (Isaiah 24:17). Interpreted, these are the three nets of Belial with which Levi son of Jacob said that he catches Israel by setting them up as three kinds of righteousness. The first is fornication, the second is riches, and the third is profanation of the Temple. Whoever escapes the first is caught in the second, and whoever saves himself from the second is caught in the third (Isaiah 24:18).

The 'builders of the wall' (Ezekiel 13:10) who have followed after 'Precept'—'Precept' was a spouter of whom it is written, *They shall surely spout* (Micah 2:6)—shall be caught in fornication twice by taking a second wife while the first is alive, whereas the principle of creation is, *Male and female created He them* (Genesis 1:27). **V** Also, those who entered the Ark went in two by two. And concerning the prince it is written, *He shall not multiply wives to himself* (Deuteronomy 17:17); but David had not read the sealed book of the Law which was in the ark (of the Covenant), for it was not opened in Israel from the death of Eleazar and Joshua, and the elders who worshipped Ashtoreth. It was hidden and (was not) revealed until the coming of Zadok. And the deeds of David rose up, except for the murder of Uriah, and God left them to him.

Moreover, they profane the Temple because they do not observe the distinction (between clean and unclean) in accordance with the Law, but lie with a woman who sees her bloody discharge.

And each man marries the daughter of his brother or sister, whereas Moses said, *You shall not approach your mother's sister; she is your mother's near kin* (Leviticus 18:13). But although the laws against incest are written for men, they also apply to women. When, therefore, a brother's daughter uncovers the nakedness of her father's brother, she is (also his) near kin.

Furthermore, they defile their holy spirit and open their mouth with a blaspheming tongue against the laws of the Covenant of God saying, 'They are not sure.' They speak abominations concerning them; *they are all kindlers of fire and lighters of brands* (Isaiah 50:11), *their webs are spiders' webs and their eggs are vipers' eggs* (Isaiah 59:5). No man that approaches them shall be free from guilt; the more he does so, the guiltier shall he be, unless he is pressed. For (already) in ancient times God visited their deeds and His anger was kindled against their works; *for it is a people of no discernment* (Isaiah 27:11), *it is a nation void of counsel inasmuch as there is no discernment in them* (Deuteronomy 32:28). For in ancient times, Moses and Aaron arose by the hand of the Prince of Lights and Belial in his cunning raised up Jannes and his brother when Israel was first delivered.

And at the time of the desolation of the land there arose removers of the bound who led Israel astray. And the land was ravaged because they preached rebellion against the commandments of God given by the hand of Moses and **VI** of His holy anointed ones, and because they prophesied lies to turn Israel away from following God. But God remembered the Covenant with the forefathers, and he raised from Aaron men of dis-

cernment and from Israel men of wisdom, and He caused them to hear.
(Damascus Document 4.12–6.3)

The document known as 4QMMT ('Some Observances of the Law') refers to the separation by the community from the establishment over a range of differences concerning the correct interpretation of the law for daily living (*halakoth*).

638. [And you know that] we have separated from the mass of the peo[ple]...and from mingling with them in these matters and from being in contact with them in these (matters). And you k[now that no] treachery or lie or evil is found in our hands for we give for [these] th[e...
(4Q397 fragments 7, 8.7–9)

639. We have also written to you (sing.) concerning some of the observances of the Law (*miqsat ma'ase ha-Torah*[60]), which we think are beneficial to you and your people. For [we have noticed] that prudence and knowledge of the Law are with you.

Understand all these (matters) and ask Him to straighten your counsel and put you far away from thoughts of evil and the counsel of Belial. Consequently, you will rejoice at the end of time when you discover that some of our sayings are true. And it will be reckoned for you as righteousness when you perform what is right and good before Him, for your own good and for that of Israel.
(4Q398 fragment 2 conflated with 4Q399)[61]

According to the Damascus Document, the forerunners of the community had experienced a 20-year period of 'wandering' during a time of national apostasy when God delivered up his people to the sword and forsook his sanctuary.

640. Listen now all you who know righteousness, and consider the works of God; for He has a dispute with all flesh and will condemn all those who despise him.

For when they were unfaithful and forsook Him, He hid His face from Israel and His Sanctuary and delivered them up to the sword. But remembering the Covenant of the forefathers, He left a remnant to Israel and did not deliver it up to be destroyed. And in the age of wrath, three hundred and ninety years after He had given them into the hand of King Nebuchadnezzar of Babylon, He visited them, and He caused a plant root to spring from Israel and Aaron to inherit His land and to prosper on the good things of His earth. And they perceived their iniquity and recognized that they were guilty men, yet for twenty years they were like blind men groping for the way.

And God observed their deeds, that they sought Him with a whole heart, and He raised for them a Teacher of Righteousness to guide them in the way of His heart. And he made known to the latter generations that which God had done to the latter generation, the congregation of traitors, to those who departed from the way. This was the time of which it is written, *Like a stubborn heifer thus was Israel stubborn* (Hosea 4:16), when the Scoffer arose who shed over Israel the water of lies. He caused them to wander in a pathless wilderness, laying low the everlasting heights, abolishing the ways of righteousness and removing the boundary with which the forefathers had marked out their inheritance, that he might call down on them the curses of His Covenant and deliver them up to the avenging sword of the Covenant. For they sought smooth things and preferred illusions (Isaiah 30:10) and they watched for breaks (Isaiah 30:13) and chose the fair neck; and they justified the wicked and condemned the just, and they transgressed the Covenant and violated the Precept. They banded together against the life of the righteous (Psalm 94:21) and loathed all who walked in perfection; they pursued them with the sword and exulted in the strife of the people. And the anger of God was kindled against **II** their congregation so that He ravaged all their multitude; and their deeds were defilement before Him.
(Damascus Document 1.1–2.1)

The Habbakuk *pesher* (1QpHab) is an interpretation of the book of Habbakuk. It discloses important insights into the history of the community and the crucial role of the Teacher of Righteousness for the spiritual guidance and health of the community, as well as his unique insights into the meaning of the prophetic text. The scroll proceeds by citing the biblical text (in italics), followed by an interpretation (*pesher*).

641. *I will take my stand to watch and will station myself upon the fortress. I will watch to see what He will say to me and how [He will answer] my complaint. And the Lord answered [and said to me, 'Write down the vision and make it plain] upon the tablets, that [he who reads] may read it speedily'* (2:1–2).

...**VII** and God told Habbakuk to write down that which would happen to the final generation, but He did not make known to him when time would come to an end. And as for that which He said, *That he who reads may read it speedily*: interpreted this concerns the Teacher of Righteousness, to whom God made known all the mysteries of the words of His servants the Prophets.
(1QpHab 6.12–7.5)

In the following section of the Habbakuk *pesher* the writer attests the rapacity of the Romans. The term 'Kittim' is a code word in the scrolls for the Romans (see Part 2 n. 22).

642. *Thou dealest with men like the fish of the sea, like creeping things, to rule over them. They draw [them all up with a fish-hook], and drag them out with their net, and gather them in [their seine. Therefore they sacrifice] to their net. Therefore they rejoice [and exult and burn incense to their seine; for by them] their portion is fat [and their sustenance rich]* (1:14–16).

...**VI** the Kittim. And they shall gather in their riches together with all their booty, like the *fish of the sea*. And as for that which He said, *Therefore they sacrifice to their net and burn incense to their seine*: interpreted, this means that they sacrifice to their standards and worship their weapons of war. *For through them their portion is fat and their sustenance rich*: interpreted, this means that they divide their yoke and their tribute—*their sustenance*—over all the peoples year by year, ravaging many lands.

Therefore their sword is ever drawn to massacre nations mercilessly (1:17).

Interpreted, this concerns the Kittim who cause many to perish by the sword—youths, grown men, the aged, women and children—and who even take no pity on the fruit of the womb.
(1QpHab 5.12–6.12)

The following passage reveals the crucial role of the Teacher for the eschatological felicity of the members of the community. The passage also introduces the Wicked Priest, the great opponent and persecutor of the Teacher.

643. [*But the righteous shall live by his faith*] (2:4b).

VIII Interpreted, this concerns all those who observe the Law in the House of Judah, whom God will deliver from the House of Judgement because of their suffering and because of their faith in the Teacher of Righteousness.

Moreover, the arrogant man seizes wealth without halting. He widens his gullet like Hell and like Death he has never enough. All the nations are gathered to him and all the peoples are assembled to him. Will they not all of them taunt him and jeer at him saying, 'Woe to him who amasses that which is not his! How long will he load himself up with pledges?' (2:5–6).

Interpreted, this concerns the Wicked Priest who was called by the name of truth when he first arose. But when he ruled over Israel his heart became proud, and he forsook God and betrayed the precepts for the sake of riches. He robbed and amassed the riches of the men of violence who rebelled against God, and he took the wealth of the peoples, heaping sinful iniquity upon himself. And he lived in the ways of abomination amidst every unclean defilement
(1QpHab 8.1–13)[62]

The Wicked Priest persecuted the Righteous Teacher. In the following passage there is an incidental acknowledgment that the Qumran community followed a different calendar than that followed by the priestly establishment.

644. *Woe to him who causes his neighbours to drink; who pours out his venom to make them drunk that he may gaze on their feasts* (2:15).

Interpreted, this concerns the Wicked Priest who pursued the Teacher of Righteousness to the house of his exile that he might confuse him with his venomous fury. And at the time appointed for rest, for the Day of Atonement, he appeared before them to confuse them, and to cause them to stumble on the Day of Fasting, their Sabbath of repose. (1QpHab 11.2–8)

The observance of the Sabbath.

645. No man shall work on the sixth day from the moment when the sun's orb is distant by its own fulness from the gate (wherein it sinks); for this is what He said, *Observe the Sabbath day to keep it holy* (Deuteronomy 5:12). No man shall speak any vain or idle word on the Sabbath day. He shall make no loan to his companion. He shall make no decision in matters of money and gain. He shall say nothing about work or labour to be done on the morrow.

No man shall walk in the field to do business on the Sabbath. He shall not walk more than one thousand cubits beyond the town.

No man shall eat on the Sabbath day except that which is already prepared. He shall eat nothing lying in the fields. He shall not drink except in the camp. **XI** If he is on a journey and goes down to bathe, he shall drink where he stands, but shall not draw water into a vessel. He shall send out no stranger on his business on the Sabbath day. No man shall wear soiled garments, or garments brought to the store, unless they have been washed with water and rubbed with incense. No man shall willingly mingle (with others) on the Sabbath.

No man shall walk more than two thousand cubits after a beast to pasture it outside his town. He shall not raise his hand to strike it with his fist. If it is stubborn he shall not take it out of his house.

No man shall take anything out of the house or bring anything in. And if he is in a booth, let him neither take anything out nor bring anything in. He shall not open a sealed vessel on the Sabbath.

No man shall carry perfumes on himself whilst going and coming on the Sabbath. He shall lift neither stone nor dust in his dwelling.

No man minding a child shall carry it whilst going and coming on the Sabbath.

No man shall chide his manservant or maidservant or labourer on the Sabbath. No man shall assist a beast to give birth on the Sabbath day. And if it should fall into a cistern or pit, he shall not lift it out on the Sabbath.

No man shall spend the Sabbath in a place near to Gentiles on the Sabbath.

No man shall profane the Sabbath for the sake of riches or gain on the Sabbath day. But should any man fall into water or (fire), let him not be pulled out with the aid of a ladder or rope or (some such) utensil.

No man on the Sabbath shall offer anything on the altar except the Sabbath burnt-offering; for it is written thus: *Except your Sabbath offerings* (Leviticus 23:38).

No man shall send to the altar any burnt-offering, or cereal offering, or incense, or wood, by the hand of one smitten with any uncleanness, permitting him thus to defile the altar. For it is written, *The sacrifice of the wicked is an abomination, but the prayer of the just is an agreeable offering* (Proverbs 15:8).

No man entering the house of worship shall come away unclean and in need of washing. And at the sounding of the trumpets for assembly, he shall go there before or after (the meeting), and shall not cause the whole service to stop, **XII** for it is a holy service.

No man shall lie with a woman in the city of the Sanctuary, to defile the city of the Sanctuary with their uncleanness. (Damascus Document 10.14–12.2)[63]

The following passage from the Community Rule (1QS) has invited comparison with the Fourth Gospel and other early Jewish and Christian literature. Note especially the concept of the 'two ways' and strong predestinarian tenor of this passage.

646. The Master shall instruct all the sons of light and shall teach them the nature of all the children of men according to the kind of spirit which they possess, the signs identifying their works during their lifetime, their visitation for chastisement, and the time for their reward.

From the God of Knowledge comes all that is and shall be. Before ever they existed He established their whole design, and when, as ordained for them, they come into being, it is in accord with His glorious design that they accomplish their task without change. The laws of all things are in His hand and He provides them with all their needs.

He has created man to govern the world, and has appointed for him two spirits in which to walk until the time of His visitation: the spirits of truth and injustice. Those born of truth spring from a fountain of light, but those born of injustice spring from a source of Darkness. All the children of righteousness are ruled by the Prince of Light and walk in the ways of light, but all the children of injustice are ruled by the Angel of Darkness and walk in the ways of darkness. The Angel of Darkness leads all the children of righteousness astray, and until his end, all their sin, iniquities, wickedness, and all their unlawful deeds are caused by his dominion in accordance with the mysteries of God. Every one of their chastisements, and every one of the seasons of their distress, shall be brought about by the rule of his persecution; for all his allotted spirits seek the overthrow of the sons of light.

But the God of Israel and His Angel of Truth will succour all the sons of light. For it is He who created the spirits of Light and Darkness and founded every action upon them and established every deed [upon] their [ways]. And He loves the one **IV** everlastingly and delights in its works for ever; but the counsel of the other He loathes and for ever hates its ways.

These are their ways in the world for the enlightenment of the heart of man, and so that all the paths of true righteousness may be made straight before him, and so that the fear of the laws of God may be instilled in his heart: a spirit of humility, patience, abundant charity, unending goodness, understanding, and intelligence; (a spirit of) mighty wisdom which trusts in all the deeds of God and leans on His great loving-kindness; a spirit of discernment in every purpose, of zeal for just laws, of holy intent with steadfastness of heart, of great charity towards all the sons of truth, of admirable purity which detests all unclean idols, of humble conduct sprung from an understanding of all things, and of faithful concealment of the mysteries of truth. These are the counsels of the spirit to the sons of truth in this world.

And as for the visitation of all who walk in this spirit, it shall be healing, great peace in a long life, and fruitfulness, together with every everlasting blessing and eternal joy in life without end, a crown of glory and a garment of majesty in unending light.

But the ways of the spirit of falsehood are these: greed, and slackness in the search for righteousness, wickedness and lies, haughtiness and pride, falseness and deceit, cruelty and abundant evil, ill-temper and much folly and brazen insolence, abominable deeds (committed) in a spirit of lust, and ways of lewdness in the service of uncleanness, a blaspheming tongue, blindness of eye and dullness of ear, stiffness of neck and heaviness of heart, so that man walks in all the ways of darkness and guile.

And the visitation of all who walk in this spirit shall be a multitude of plagues by the hand of all the destroying angels, everlasting damnation by the avenging wrath of the fury of God, eternal torment and endless disgrace together with shameful extinction in the fire of the dark regions. The times of all their generations shall be spent in sorrowful mourning and in bitter misery and in calamities of darkness until they are destroyed without remnant or survivor.

The nature of all the children of men is ruled by these (two spirits), and during their life all the hosts of men have a portion of their divisions and walk in (both) their ways. And the whole reward for their deeds shall be, for everlasting ages, according to whether each man's portion in their two divisions is great or small. For God has established the spirits in equal measure until the final age, and has set everlasting hatred between their divisions. Truth abhors the works of injustice, and injustice hates all the ways of truth. And their struggle is fierce in all their arguments for they do not walk together. But in the mysteries of His understanding, and in His glorious wisdom, God has ordained an end for injustice, and at the time of the visitation He will destroy it for ever. Then truth, which has wallowed in the ways of wickedness during the dominion of injustice until the appointed time of judgement, shall rise in the world for ever. God will then purify every deed of man with His truth; He will refine for Himself the human frame by rooting out all spirit of injustice from the bounds of his flesh. He will cleanse him of all wicked deeds with the spirit of holiness; like purifying waters He will shed upon him the spirit of truth (to cleanse him) of all abomination and injustice. And he shall be plunged into the spirit of purification, that he may instruct the upright in the knowledge of the Most High and teach the wisdom of the sons of heaven to the perfect way. For God has chosen them for an everlasting Covenant and all the glory of Adam shall be theirs. There shall be no more lies and all the works of injustice shall be out to shame.

Until now the spirits of truth and injustice struggle in the hearts of men and they walk in both wisdom and folly. According to his portion of truth so does a man hate injustice, and according to his inheritance in the realm of injustice so is he wicked and so hates truth. For God has established the two spirits in equal measure until the determined end, and until the Renewal, and He knows the reward of their deeds from all eternity. He has allotted them to the children of men that they may know good [and evil, and] that the destiny of all the living may be according to the spirit within [them at the time] of the visitation.
(1QS 3.13–4.26)

The scroll of Thanksgiving Hymns (1QH) was one of the original seven scrolls discovered in cave 1 in 1947. Some of these hymns are in the first person while others are communal. Scholars have debated whether the former were composed by the Righteous Teacher. The depth of feeling, especially in the laments, is striking. The indebtedness of the Thanksgiving Hymns to the canonical book of Psalms is evident.

The following two extracts recall the indispensable ministry of the Righteous Teacher in the community. See also #293.

647. Through me Thou hast illumined
the face of the Congregation
and hast shown Thine infinite power.
For Thou hast given me knowledge
through Thy marvellous mysteries,
and hast shown Thyself mighty within me
in the midst of Thy marvellous Council.
Thou hast done wonders before the Congregation
for the sake of Thy glory,
that they may make known Thy mighty deeds to all the living.
(1QH 12.27–29)

648. I [thank Thee, O Lord,
for] Thou hast placed me beside a fountain of streams
in an arid land,
and close to a spring of waters
in a dry land,
and beside a watered garden
[in a wilderness].
[For Thou didst set] a plantation
of cypress, pine, and cedar for Thy glory,
trees of life beside a mysterious fountain
hidden among the trees by the water,
and they put out a shoot
of the everlasting Plant.
But before they did so, they took root
and sent out their roots to the watercourse
that its stem might be open to the living waters
and be one with the everlasting spring.
(1QH 16.4–8)[64]

The perception that the community believed that it worshipped God with the angels and shared their lot is encountered in the scrolls. In the first of the following extracts (from 1QS 11) the psalmist praises God for granting the community unique access to the 'marvellous mysteries' and for providing access to the worship of God with the angels in heaven. In the second (from 1QH) the immediacy of the fellowship of the men of the community with the angels is stressed. In the third (from the Songs of the Sabbath Sacrifice) the community sees itself united with the angels in heaven worshipping God.[65] This immediacy can be paralleled in the New Testament.[66] The presence of angels is a sign both of the dawning eschatological era and the sanctified status of the community to which the privilege is granted.

649. God has given them to His chosen ones
as an everlasting possession,
and has caused them to inherit
the lot of the Holy Ones.
He has joined their assembly
to the Sons of Heaven
to be a Council of the Community,
a foundation of the Building of Holiness,
and eternal Plantation throughout all ages
to come.
(1QS 11.7–8)

650. For Thou wilt bring Thy glorious [salvation]
to all the men of Thy Council,
to those who share a common lot
with the Angels of the Face.
And among them shall be no mediator to
[invoke Thee],
And no messenger [to make] reply...
(1QH 14.12–13)

651. For the Mas[ter. Song of the holocaust of] the twelfth [S]abbath [on the twenty-first of the third month.]

[Praise the God of...w]onder, and exalt Him...of glory in the te[nt of the God of] knowledge. The [cheru]bim prostrate themselves before Him and bless. As they rise, a whispered divine voice [is heard], and there is a roar of praise. When they drop their wings, there is a [whispere]d divine voice. The cherubim bless the image of the throne-chariot above the firmament, [and] they praise [the majes]ty of the luminous firmament beneath His seat of glory. When the wheels advance, angels of holiness come and go. From between His glorious wheels, there is as it were a fiery vision of most holy spirits. About them, the appearance of rivulets of fire in the likeness of gleaming brass, and a work of...radiance in many-coloured glory, marvellous pigments, clearly mingled. The spirits of the living 'gods' move perpetually with the glory of the marvellous chariot(s). The whispered voice of blessing accompanies the roar of their advance, and they praise the Holy One on their way of return. When they ascend, they ascend marvellously and when they settle, they stand still. The sound of joyful praise is silenced and there is a whispered blessing of the 'gods' in all the camps of God. And the sound of praise...from among all their divisions...and all their numbered ones praise, each in his turn.
(4Q405 fragments 20, 21, 22)[67]

The War Rule (#652–53).

This scroll is a manual for the community's climactic, eschatological engagement with the enemies of God, including the Kittim and those Jews not affiliated with the Community.

652. For the M[aster. The Rule of]War on the unleashing of the attack of the sons of light against the company of the sons of darkness, the army of Belial: against the band of Edom, Moab, and the sons of Ammon, and [against the army of the sons of the East and] the Philistines, and against the bands of the Kittim of Assyria and their allies the ungodly of the Covenant.

The sons of Levi, Judah, and Benjamin, the exiles in the desert, shall battle against them in...all their bands when the exiled sons of light return from the Desert of the Peoples to camp in the Desert of Jerusalem; and after the battle they shall go up from there (to Jerusalem?).

[The king] of the Kittim [shall enter] into Egypt, and in his time he shall set out in great wrath to wage war against the kings of the north, that his fury may destroy and cut the horn of [Israel]. This shall be a time of salvation for the people of God, an age of dominion for all the members of His company, and of everlasting destruction for all the company of Belial. The confusion of the sons of Japheth shall be [great] and Assyria shall fall unsuccoured. The dominion of the Kittim shall come to an end and iniquity shall be vanquished, leaving no remnant; [for the sons] of darkness there shall be no escape. [The sons of righteous]ness shall shine over all the ends of the earth; they shall go on shining until all the seasons of darkness are consumed and, at the season appointed by God, His exalted greatness shall shine eternally to the peace, blessing, glory, joy, and long life of all the sons of light.

On the day when the Kittim fall, there shall be battle and terrible carnage before the God of Israel, for that shall be the day appointed from ancient times for the battle of destruction of the sons of darkness. At that time, the assembly of gods and the hosts of men shall battle, causing great carnage; on the day of calamity, the sons of light shall battle with the company of darkness amid the shouts of a mighty multitude and the clamour of gods and men to (make manifest) the might of God. And it shall be a time of [great] tribulation for the people which God shall redeem; of all its afflictions none shall be as this, from its sudden beginning until its end in eternal redemption.

On the day of their battle against the Kittim [they shall set out for] carnage. In three lots shall the sons of light brace themselves in battle to strike down iniquity, and in three lots shall Belial's host gird itself to thrust back the company [of God. And when the hearts of the detach]ments of foot-soldiers faint, then shall the might of God fortify [the hearts of the sons of light]. And with the seventh lot, the mighty hand of God shall bring down [the army of Belial, and all] the angels of his kingdom, and all the members [of his company in everlasting destruction]...
(1QM 1.1–16)

In the following excerpt from the War Scroll the writer describes the camp. Note the strict enforcement of the priestly codes relating to nakedness and bodily emissions (see Exodus 20:24–26; Leviticus 15).

653. **VII** The men of the army shall be from forty to fifty years old. The inspectors of the camps shall be from fifty to sixty years old. The officers shall be from forty to fifty years old. The despoilers of the slain, the plunderers of booty, the cleansers of the land, the keepers of the baggage, and those who furnish the provisions shall be from twenty-five to thirty years old.

No boy or woman shall enter their camps, from the time they leave Jerusalem and march out to war until they return. No man who is lame, or blind, or crippled, or afflicted with a lasting bodily blemish, or smitten with a bodily impurity, none of these shall march out to war with them. They shall all be freely enlisted for war, perfect in spirit and body and prepared for the Day of Vengeance. And no man shall go down with them on the day of battle who is impure because of his 'fount,' for the holy angels shall be with their hosts. And there shall be a space of about two thousand cubits between all their camps for the place serving as a latrine, so that no indecent nakedness may be seen in the surroundings of their camps.

When the battle formations are marshalled facing the enemy, formation facing formation, seven Priests of the sons of Aaron shall advance from the middle gates to the place between the formations. They shall be clothed in vestments of white cloth of flax, in a fine linen tunic and fine linen breeches; and they shall be girdled with a fine cloth of flax embroidered with blue, purple, and scarlet thread, a many-coloured design worked by a craftsman. And on their heads they shall wear mitred turbans. These shall be battle raiment; they shall not take them into the Sanctuary.
(1QM 7.1–12)

The Temple Scroll is the longest of those discovered in the caves. It presents an idealized picture of a new temple in Jerusalem in which God's will is perfectly realized on earth.

654. **XXX**... You shall make...for stairs, a stair[case]...in the house which you shall build...You [shall make] a staircase north of the Temple, a square house, twenty cubits from one corner to the other alongside its four corners. Its distance from the wall of the Temple shall be seven cubits on the north-west. You shall make the width of its wall four cubits...like the Temple and its inside from corner to corner twelv[e cubits.] (There shall be) a square column in its middle, in the centre; its width four cubits on each side around which the stairs wind... **XXXI** In the upper chamber of [this] ho[use you shall make a ga]te opening to the roof of the Temple and a way (shall be) made

through this gate towards the entrance...of the Temple by which one can reach the upper chamber of the Temple. Overlay with gold [a]ll this stairhouse, its walls, its gates and its roof, from inside [and from] outside, its column and its stairs. [You] shall do everything as I tell you. You shall make a square house for the laver in the south-east, on all its sides, (each) twenty-one cubits; fifty cubits distant from the altar. The width of the wall shall be four cubits, and the height [t]wenty cubits...Make gates for it on the east, on the north and on the west. The width of the gates shall be four cubits and the height seven **XXXII** ... You shall make in the wall of this house, on the inside, recesses, and in them...one cubit (in) width and their height four cubits above the ground. They shall be overlaid with gold on which they shall place their clothes which they have worn on arrival. Above the house of the...when they come to minister in the sanctuary. You shall make a trench around the laver beside its house and the trench shall go [from the house of] the laver to a cavity. It shall descend [rapid]ly to the ground where the water shall flow and disappear. It shall not be touched by any man for it is mingled with the blood of the holocaust.
(11QT 30–32)

The following passages from the scrolls parallel ideas in the New Testament. In the first the son of God/son of the Most High terminology strikingly parallels titles ascribed to Jesus in Luke 1:32. The second, a collection of beatitudes, mirrors the beatitudes of Matthew 5:3–11. The third, 4Q521 (Messianic Apocalypse), evokes the days of the Messiah in terms of the programme of Isaiah 61:1, and anticipates the raising of the dead. Jesus, as recorded in Luke 4:18–19 and Matthew 11:2–6, perceived himself as Israel's Messiah in line with early Jewish expectations as exemplified in this text.

655. The son of God he will be proclaimed (or: proclaim himself) and the son of the Most High they will call him.
(4Q246 column 2.1)

656. [Blessed is]...with a pure heart
and does not slander with his tongue.
Blessed are those who hold to her (Wisdom's) precepts
and do not hold to the ways of iniquity.
Blessed are those who rejoice in her,
and do not burst forth in ways of folly.
Blessed are those who seek her with pure hands,
and do not pursue her with a treacherous heart.
Blessed is the man who has attained Wisdom,
and walks in the Law of the Most High.
He directs his heart towards her ways,
and restrains himself by her corrections,
and always takes delight in her chastisements.
He does not forsake her when he sees distress,
nor abandon her in time of strain.
(4Q525 fragment 2.1–5)

657. ...[the hea]vens and the earth will listen to His Messiah, and none therein will stray from the commandments of the holy ones.
Seekers of the Lord, strengthen yourselves in His service!
All you hopeful in (your) heart, will you not find the Lord in this?
For the Lord will consider the pious (*hasidim*) and call the righteous by name.
Over the poor His spirit will hover and will renew the faithful with His power.
And He will glorify the pious on the throne of the eternal Kingdom.
He who liberates the captives, restores sight to the blind, straightens the b[ent] (Psalm 146:7–8).
And f[or] ever I will clea[ve to the h]opeful and in His mercy...
And the fr[uit...] will not be delayed for anyone
And the Lord will accomplish glorious things which have never been as [He...]
For He will heal the wounded, and revive the dead and bring good news to the poor (Isaiah 61:1).
... He will lead the uprooted and knowledge...and smoke (?)[68]
(4Q521 fragment 2, column 2.1–13)

8.13. The 'Fourth Philosophy', Bandits and *Sicarii*

Josephus marks the rise of the 'Fourth Philosophy' (the Pharisees, Sadducees and Essenes are the first three) with the removal of Archelaus and the imposition of direct Roman rule in Judaea in 6 CE. Followers of this 'philosophy' adhered to the teaching of Judas the Galilaean. This Judas had enlisted the support of the Pharisee Saddok (see *Antiquities* 18.4–10). Josephus ascribes the teaching of the 'Fourth Philosophy' to both Judas and Saddok. It was not lawful, they taught, to pay tribute to Rome and to tolerate 'mortal masters' after having God as their lord (*Jewish War* 2.118; *Antiquities* 18.23). According to Josephus, the 'Fourth Philosophy' adopted policies of direct action against the Roman overlords and their Jewish collaborators, and were to be sharply distinguished from the other Jewish groups.

Any discussion of the 'Fourth Philosophy' must also take account of the problem posed to Roman rule by bandits, also prepared to take direct action. Josephus draws family links between earlier bandit leaders and Judas the Galilaean, who, in turn, is the forebear of leaders of bandits and *sicarii* later in the first century CE. Herod had put them down efficiently and ruthlessly, but the causes of the problem, were, of course, not remedied by violence. There were outbreaks of banditry in 4 BCE led by Judas, the son of the Hezekiah executed by Herod in the 40s BCE.[69] Disturbances were in evidence again in 6 CE.[70] Bandit uprisings continued to feed on harsh economic conditions. There was a severe famine in 46–48 (see Acts 11:27).

Outbreaks of banditry infested the country during the procuratorship of Felix (52–59) (Josephus, *Jewish War* 2.238). The situation has rightly been described as a wholesale peasant rebellion against the Romans, the bandits able to find support, sympathy and protection at will.[71] After the outbreak of the War, the bandits, easily defeated by the well-armed Romans troops, streamed into well-fortified Jerusalem. They wrested the leadership from the aristocratic establishment. Under their leaders they began to direct the war effort.

The *sicarii* originated during Felix's procuratorship. The name is derived from the Latin *sica*, a dagger. Their practice was to mingle with the crowd and assassinate Jewish collaborators. Their first victim was a former high priest, Jonathan, who had arranged for Felix to become procurator. Jonathan was a son of the former high priest Annas, active still at the time of the trial of Jesus. The deeds of the *sicarii* provoked great terror, as Josephus reports. Under their leader Menahem they made a bid for leadership of the Revolt in Jerusalem in the early days of the War. However, Menahem was killed and his followers ousted from the city. They retreated to Masada, which they had captured at the beginning of the revolt. They held out until the successful Roman siege of 73/74 CE (see #227–28). According to Josephus, Menahem was a son of Judas the Galilaean (*Jewish War* 2.433).

Sources

The revolt of Judas the Galilaean, the instigator of the 'Fourth Philosophy'.

658. The territory of Archelaus was now reduced to a province, and Coponius, a Roman of the equestrian order, was sent out as procurator, entrusted by Augustus with full powers, including the infliction of capital punishment. Under his administration, a Galilaean, named Judas, incited his countrymen to revolt, upbraiding them as cowards for consenting to pay tribute to the Romans and tolerating mortal masters, after having God for their lord. This man was a sophist who founded a sect of his own, having nothing in common with the others.
(Josephus, *Jewish War* 2.117–18.
See also Acts 5:37)

The advent of the sicarii.

659. But while the country was thus cleared of these pests, a new species of banditti was springing up in Jerusalem, the so-called *sicarii*, who committed murders in broad daylight in the heart of the city. The festivals were their special seasons, when they would

mingle with the crowd, carrying short daggers concealed under their clothing, with which they stabbed their enemies. Then, when they fell, the murderers joined in the cries of indignation and, through this plausible behaviour, were never discovered. The first to be assassinated by them was Jonathan the high-priest; after his death there were numerous daily murders. The panic created was more alarming than the calamity itself; every one, as on the battlefield, hourly expecting death. Men kept watch at a distance on their enemies and would not trust even their friends when they approached. Yet, even while their suspicions were aroused and they were on their guard, they fell; so swift were the conspirators and so crafty in eluding detection.
(Josephus, *Jewish War* 2.254–57)

8.14. Herodians, Hellenists and Samaritans

A group called the Herodians is mentioned infrequently in the Gospels. Josephus does not mention them at all. In Mark 3:6 they are recorded taking council with the Pharisees to plot Jesus' destruction. They also appear in Mark 12:13 (and Matthew 22:16) questioning Jesus about the propriety of paying the tribute money. Presumably they were first-century CE supporters of the Herodian family and wanted Judaea and later Galilee to be ruled once more by members of Herod's family rather than by Roman governors. Their best hopes lay in Agrippa I—hopes that were dashed with his sudden death in 44 CE.[72]

The Hellenists appear in Acts 6:1 and 9:29. They were Palestinian Jews who spoke Greek without speaking a Semitic language. The Septuagint (as it was in the first century) was their version of the Bible. Originally the Hellenists were proselytes to Judaism, perhaps forcibly converted in the days of John Hyrcanus I (134–104 BCE). Hellenists who had not converted to Christianity strongly opposed Paul and sought to kill him. It is possible that the opposition to Stephen (see Acts 6:9) was inspired by Jewish Hellenists.

The Samaritans of the Graeco-Roman era were descendants of local Israelites and Assyrian colonists, who took possession of Samaria, the capital of the northern kingdom of Israel, in 722 BCE. Alexander the Great permitted them to build their own temple on Mount Gerizim.[73] Their request indicates that there is keen competition between Samaritan and Judaean Jews for the ownership of the heritage of ancient Israel.[74] Josephus reports that some apostate priests from Jerusalem joined the Samaritans in building this temple (*Antiquities* 11.347). According to 2 Maccabees 6:2 (see #171), it was re-dedicated to Zeus Xenios ('Zeus of the Foreigner') during the depredations of Antiochus IV Epiphanes. It was destroyed by Hyrcanus I in 128 BCE (*Antiquities* 13.275–83), rebuilt after the Bar Kokhba revolt, and destroyed by Christians in 484 CE. The Samaritans are encountered only infrequently in the sources. It is evident that their relationships with Jews were strained. Herod rebuilt Samaria, renaming it Sebaste (*Antiquities* 13.275; 15.296–98). The Samaritans withdrew to Shechem where their descendants still live. The community possesses its own version of the Pentateuch.

In his *Praeparatio Evangelica* 9.17, 18 Eusebius preserves two fragments of a Samaritan author known as Pseudo-Eupolemos. In the first, the writer refers to Abraham's battle with the 'Armenians' (cf. Genesis 14) and of his being treated as a guest by Melchizedek in the temple Argarizin (i.e. Gerizim).[75]

Sources

Christian Hellenists.

660. Now during those days, when the disciples were increasing in number, the Hellenists complained against the Hebrews because their widows were being neglected in the daily distribution of food.
(Acts 6:1)

Non-Christian Hellenists.

661. He [Paul] spoke and argued with the Hellenists; but they were attempting to kill him.
(Acts 9:29)

The Samaritans.

662. Two nations my soul detests,
 and the third is not even a people:
 Those who live in Seir [Samaria], and the Philistines,
 and the foolish people that live in Shechem.
 (Sirach 50:25–26)

An association of Samaritans on Delos.

The following inscription dates from 150–50 BCE, and was found just north of the second-century BCE synagogue.[76]

663. The Israelites of Delos who contribute to sacred Mount Gerizim crown with a golden crown Sarapion, son of Jason, from Knossos because of his benefaction towards them. (*New Docs* VIII, p. 148)

8.15. Early Christianity

Christianity began as a reform movement within Judaism. Sean Freyne terms the Jesus movement a 'Galilaean protest movement'. It was conducted within society, not outside of it as in the case of the Essenes.[77] It took root in agrarian and small-town Galilee. From the beginning the movement found itself in tension with the urban reform movement sponsored by the Pharisees.[78] Jesus does not frequent sophisticated urban centres such as Tiberias, Sepphoris and the cities of the Decapolis. He is the champion of the non-observant 'people of the land', the *'am ha-'aretz*, so despised by the Pharisees.

In its Palestinian and Syrian forms especially, the movement was marked by wandering charismatic teachers and healers, such as Jesus himself (see, e.g., Mark 6:7–13). The community that gathered around him attests a levelling of the hierarchical distinctions operating in the Graeco-Roman world and among the Pharisees. Women are numbered among his followers (see Luke 8:2–3). The Kingdom (or rule) of God, the nearness of which is the central focus of the message of Jesus, is to be entered as a child (slave) (see Mark 10:15).[79] According to the most trustworthy traditions about Jesus, he had preached open community and inclusivism in the face of the closing of ethnic and factional ranks among other Jews. Moreover, Jesus also practised open commensality (note, e.g., Luke 15:1–2): he did not draw the precise distinctions at the table the Pharisees drew in their keeping of food and purity laws. Thus the ministry of Jesus posed a challenge to religious authority and prevailing social convention in its way of creating community. The Pharisees, alternatively, promoted a social ideal based on sustaining and sharpening the differences between observant and non-observant Jews. Quite intentionally Jesus subverted the function of the Law as understood by the Pharisees, which was to create and maintain the social divide between the observant and non-observant, whether they be Gentiles or Jews. In this manner the Pharisees sought to protect Jewish ethnic integrity. Jesus also appointed 12 as his inner circle, symbolically foundational of a new Israel. In speaking of himself as 'temple' (see Mark 14:58; John 2:19, 21), he further challenged traditional perceptions of the place of the Jerusalem Temple in the life of the people. Not surprisingly, therefore, confrontations between Jesus and the Pharisees did occur in his ministry. The ministry of Paul, though in many respects more accepting than was Jesus of the hierarchical status quo, also challenged the relentlessly discriminating social ideal of the Pharisees in whose fellowship Paul had spent the first half of his life. By contrast, the later New Testament, the post-Pauline literature especially, shows early Christianity coming to terms with and assimilating itself to conventional social (including hierarchical) structures.[80]

Paul took the radical message of Jesus and translated it into the urban context of the Graeco-Roman culture of the Mediterranean basin. Like Jesus he sought to build up communities that reflected the radical egalitarianism of the dawning Kingdom of God. In the Pauline communities, as in the community gathered around Jesus, the prevailing social values and hierarchies were necessarily undermined (see Galatians 3:28; #668). Although he continued to regard himself as a faithful

Jew he effectively subverted conventional Jewish ethnic integrity. He rejected the necessity of maintaining a specific Jewish identity, as initiated and sustained by observing the covenantal requirements of the Law, as still acceptable to God in the face of the Christ-event. Paul proclaimed an exclusive *faith* response to the redemptive initiative of God in Christ. He decisively rejected the Law with its demand of ethnic separateness. Paul insisted that its distinctive social framework, which underscored ethnic divisions, was incompatible with the dawning of eschatological realities in the Christ-event. He termed these now unacceptable, at best optional, demands 'works of the Law'. Paul's stress on freedom from such restraint undoubtedly appealed to Gentiles, though his appeal to the fulfilment of divine promises in Christ would have appealed to his Jewish listeners.[81] Luke–Acts takes this a step further by insisting that the Christians, not the Jews, are the true heirs of the promises made to Israel through Moses and the prophets. According to Luke, Judaism has been superseded; a view also expressed in the letter to the Hebrews. This was not a view shared by other early Christian traditions articulated in the New Testament, including the undisputed Pauline letters.[82]

Neither Jesus nor Paul were motivated by the desire to create a new religion. However, as we have seen, there are seeds of disjunction with Judaism in the activity and words recorded of Jesus and in the undisputed letters of Paul. Yet some early Christians saw themselves comprising but one of several Jewish groups co-existing in the eastern Mediterranean. However, by the end of the first century some believers were finding that maintaining their membership of the synagogue was becoming increasingly untenable.[83] Other Christian communities had already tested the social boundaries that distinguished Jews from other Jews and from non-Jews. It was Hellenist Jewish Christians who first took the gospel to Antioch and beyond the Jewish boundaries in which the message had hitherto been articulated.[84] They were in a better position than the Twelve to take the message outside Jerusalem. Persecution under Nero would have undoubtedly helped to consolidate a growing sense of a distinctive, though vulnerable, Christian identity over against Roman power and imperial ideology.[85] The stories of the trial, death and resurrection of Jesus—repeated at each celebration of the eucharist—would have also served as a protest against Roman imperial claims and prevailing strategies for the acquisition of fame and glory.[86]

It would be a mistake to characterize early Christianity as monolithic in any sense. Like early Judaism, it is best to speak of early Christian traditions and ways of interpreting the significance of the Christ-event being upheld by different Christian communities located throughout the eastern Mediterranean. In Syria and Palestine especially, as noted above, some communities of early Christians perceived that they were living in continuity with Judaism. These kept the Law and upheld Jewish culture. The community centred on the leadership of James the brother of Jesus was one such.[87] Existing traditions about Jesus, such as those articulated in Mark's Gospel which seemed to subvert this Jewish-orientated identity, were re-worked in other documents of early Christianity to give credence to a greater sense of continuity with Judaism. Nevertheless, the early Christians were united in the belief that Jesus was the Messiah of Jewish expectation and that though he had been crucified in weakness and shame he had been vindicated by God and raised to life. These two themes, resurrection and messianism, so significant for understanding the significance of Jesus in early Christian traditions in the context of early Judaism, are treated below (see topics 8.16 and 8.17 below).

Early Christianity was based on the household, especially in the ministries of Paul and his colleagues. The household provided a sense of belonging for the poor and dispossessed who were otherwise ground down by the rigid hierarchies and authority structures of the wider society.[88] Jewish households were a precedent (see #678). From the beginning Christians practised participation in two symbolic acts as a way of initiating and incorporating believers into Christ. These acts were baptism, a rite of entry into the community through identification with the death of Christ, and the eucharist, in which believers shared in the benefits of the ongoing presence of Jesus the God-human. In common with Judaism, Christianity saw the believer's life-commitment in religious terms. The new faith avoided the technical terms of the Graeco-Roman cults, even applying cultic terms to the everyday life of believers.[89] Even the term *sōtēr* ('saviour') prominently used in ruler cults, came into prominence in Christianity later rather than earlier.[90]

Sources

The presence of eschatological newness in the Christ event (#664–67).

664. Now after John was arrested, Jesus came to Galilee, proclaiming the good news of God, and saying, 'The time is fulfilled, and the kingdom of God has come near; repent, and believe in the good news.'
(Mark 1:14–15)

665. When John heard in prison what the Messiah was doing, he sent word by his disciples and said to him, 'Are you the one who is to come, or are we to wait for another?' Jesus answered them, 'Go and tell John what you hear and see: the blind receive their sight, the lame walk, the lepers are cleansed, the deaf hear, the dead are raised, and the poor have good news brought to them. And blessed is anyone who takes no offense at me.'
(Matthew 11:2–6)

666. [I]f anyone is in Christ, there is a new creation: everything old has passed away; see, everything has become new!
(2 Corinthians 5:17)

667. And the virginity of Mary, and her giving birth were hidden from the Prince of this world, as was also the death of the Lord. Three mysteries of a cry which were wrought in the stillness of God. How then was he manifested to the world? A star shone in heaven beyond all the stars, and its light was unspeakable, and its newness caused astonishment, and all the other stars, with the sun and moon, gathered in chorus round this star, and it far exceeded them all in its light; and there was perplexity, whence came this new thing, so unlike them. By this all magic was dissolved and every bond of wickedness vanished away, ignorance was removed, and the old kingdom was destroyed, for God was manifest as man for the 'newness' of eternal life, and that which had been prepared by God received its beginning. Hence all things were disturbed, because the abolition of death was being planned.
(Ignatius, *Letter to the Ephesians* 19)

The breaking down of social hierarchies (#668–70).

668. There is no longer Jew or Greek, there is no longer slave or free, there is no longer male and female; for all of you are one in Christ Jesus.
(Galatians 3:28)[91]

The following two passages repudiate the competitiveness that marked Graeco-Roman society in favour of a community based on humility and the setting aside of claims to status.

669. Bless those who persecute you; bless and do not curse them. Rejoice with those who rejoice, weep with those who weep. Live in harmony with one another; do not be haughty, but associate with the lowly; do not claim to be wiser than you are. Do not repay anyone evil for evil, but take thought for what is noble in the sight of all. If it is possible, so far as it depends on you, live peaceably with all. Beloved, never avenge yourselves, but leave room for the wrath of God; for it is written, 'Vengeance is mine, I will repay, says the Lord.'
(Romans 12:14–19)

670. For you were called to freedom, brothers and sisters; only do not use your freedom as an opportunity for self-indulgence, but through love become slaves to one another. For the whole law is summed up in a single commandment, 'You shall love your neighbor as yourself.' If, however, you bite and devour one another, take care that you are not consumed by one another.

Live by the Spirit, I say, and do not gratify the desires of the flesh. For what the flesh desires is opposed to the Spirit, and what the Spirit desires is opposed to the flesh; for these are opposed to each other, to prevent you from doing what you want. But if you are led by the Spirit, you are not subject to the law. Now the works of the flesh are obvious: fornication, impurity, licentiousness, idolatry, sorcery, enmities, strife, jealousy, anger, quarrels, dissensions, factions, envy, drunkenness, carousing, and things like these. I am warning you, as I warned you before: those who do such things will not inherit the kingdom of God.

By contrast, the fruit of the Spirit is love, joy, peace, patience, kindness, generosity, faithfulness, gentleness, and self-control. There is no law against such things. And those who belong to Christ Jesus have crucified the flesh with its passions and desires. If we live by the Spirit, let us also be guided by the Spirit. Let us not become conceited, competing against one another, envying one another.
(Galatians 5:13–26)

The setting aside of food laws.

671. 'Do you not see that whatever goes into a person from outside cannot defile, since it enters, not the heart but the stomach, and goes out into the sewer?'
(Thus he declared all foods clean.)
(Mark 7:18b–19)[92]

Early Christian wandering charismatic teachers and healers.

672. Let every Apostle who comes to you be received as the Lord, but let him not stay more than one day, or if need be a second as well; but if he stay three days, he is a false prophet. And when an Apostle goes forth let him accept nothing but bread till he reach his night's lodging; but if he ask for money, he is a false prophet.
(*Didache* 11:4–6.
Cf. Mark 10:28; 2 John 10; 3 John 5–8)

Charismatically endowed ministries were operative in the first generation Pauline churches.

673. (4) Now there are varieties of gifts, but the same Spirit; and there are varieties of services, but the same Lord; and there are varieties of activities, but it is the same God who activates all of them in everyone.
(27) Now you are the body of Christ and individually members of it. And God has appointed in the church first apostles, second prophets, third teachers; then deeds of power, then gifts of healing, forms of assistance, forms of leadership, various kinds of tongues.
(1 Corinthians 12:4–6, 27–28)

The earliest churches also developed more settled, institutionalized, forms of ministry which, in the case of the community for which the *Didache* was written (c. 100 CE), existed alongside the ministry of wandering charismatics.

674. Appoint therefore for yourselves bishops and deacons worthy of the Lord, meek men, and not lovers of money, and truthful and approved, for they also minister to you the ministry of the prophets and teachers. Therefore do not despise them, for they are your honourable men together with the prophets and teachers.
(*Didache* 15:1–2)

In the post-Pauline context charismatically endowed ministries were superseded by more institutionalized forms of ministry. Leadership in the post-Pauline churches became much more closely linked to the ideal of the virtuous (male) householder.

675. The saying is sure: whoever aspires to the office of bishop desires a noble task. Now a bishop must be above reproach, married only once, temperate, sensible, respectable, hospitable, an apt teacher, not a drunkard, not violent but gentle, not quarrelsome, and not a lover of money. He must manage his own household well, keeping his children submissive and respectful in every way—for if someone does not know how to manage his own household, how can he take care of God's church?
(1 Timothy 3:1–5.
Cf. Titus 1:5–9)

Paul's mission was particularly focused on the household. The faith was, in Edwin Judge's apt phrase, 'sponsored' by householders to their dependents.[93] In the following extract from the Letter to the Romans, Paul commends Phoebe to the Roman church. She is described as a benefactor (*prostatis*) of many in the church.

676. I commend to you our sister Phoebe, a deacon of the church at Cenchreae, so that you may welcome her in the Lord as is fitting for the saints, and help her in whatever she may require from you, for she has been a benefactor [*prostatis*] of many and of myself as well.

Greet Prisca and Aquila, who work with me in Christ Jesus, and who risked their necks for my life, to whom not only I give thanks, but also all the churches of the Gentiles. Greet also the church in their house. (Romans 16:1–5a)

Early Christians adapted the Hellenistic household code, which articulated the duties of three basic household pairs, namely, wives and husbands, slaves and masters, and children and fathers. The codes take their inspiration from philosophical discourse on the *topos* (topic) of household management.[94] They are encountered in the post-Pauline literature of the New Testament.[95] In the hands of these writers, the codes represent a community-protection strategy designed to relate the newly founded churches to the hierarchical social conventions operating in the Graeco-Roman environment.[96] While it is true that the Christian codes mandate certain responsibilities of the superior party in each pair—husbands, masters, fathers—they underscore the submission of the naturally inferior to the naturally superior in the interests of maintaining social cohesion. They ensure, certainly with respect to the churches for whom the Pastoral Epistles were written, that leaders in the church will be male householders. The appearance of the codes in the Pauline churches marks the eclipse of earlier emancipist and fraternal tendencies that had existed in tension with Paul's deference to social convention.[97]

677. Wives, be subject to your husbands as you are to the Lord. For the husband is the head of the wife just as Christ is the head of the church, the body of which he is the Savior. Just as the church is subject to Christ, so also wives ought to be, in everything, to their husbands.

Husbands, love your wives, just as Christ loved the church and gave himself up for her, in order to make her holy by cleansing her with the washing of water by the word, so as to present the church to himself in splendor, without a spot or wrinkle or anything of the kind—yes, so that she may be holy and without blemish. In the same way, husbands should love their wives as they do their own bodies. He who loves his wife loves himself. For no one ever hates his own body, but he nourishes and tenderly cares for it, just as Christ does for the church, because we are members of his body. 'For this reason a man will leave his father and mother and be joined to his wife, and the two will become one flesh.' This is a great mystery, and I am applying it to Christ and the church. Each of you, however, should love his wife as himself, and a wife should respect her husband.

Children, obey your parents in the Lord, for this is right. 'Honor your father and mother'—this is the first commandment with a promise: 'so that it may be well with you and you may live long on the earth.'

And, fathers, do not provoke your children to anger, but bring them up in the discipline and instruction of the Lord.

Slaves, obey your earthly masters with fear and trembling, in singleness of heart, as you obey Christ; not only while being watched, and in order to please them, but as slaves of Christ, doing the will of God from the heart. Render service with enthusiasm, as to the Lord and not to men and women, knowing that whatever good we do, we will receive the same again from the Lord, whether we are slaves or free.

And, masters, do the same to them. Stop threatening them, for you know that both of you have the same Master in heaven, and with him there is no partiality.
(Ephesians 5:22–6:9)

The celebration of Passover in the Jewish household.

678. On this day every dwelling-house is invested with the outward semblance and dignity of a temple. The victim is then slaughtered and dressed for the festal meal which befits the occasion. The guests assembled for the banquet have been cleansed by purificatory lustrations, and are there not as in other festive gatherings, to indulge the belly with wine and viands, but to fulfil with prayers and hymns the custom handed down by their fathers.
(Philo, *Special Laws* 2.148)

Early Christian corporate 'worship' in the Corinthian church.

679. What should be done then, my friends? When you come together, each one has a hymn, a lesson, a revelation, a tongue, or an interpretation. Let all things be done for building up. If anyone speaks in a tongue, let there be only two or at most three, and each in turn; and let one interpret. But if there is no one to interpret, let them be silent in church and speak to themselves and to God. Let two or three prophets speak, and let the others weigh what is said. If a revelation is made to someone else sitting nearby, let the first person be silent. For you can all prophesy one by one, so that all may learn and all be encouraged. And the spirits of prophets are subject to the prophets, for God is a God not of disorder but of peace.

(As in all the churches of the saints, women should be silent in the churches. For they are not permitted to speak, but should be subordinate, as the law also says. If there is anything they desire to know, let them ask their husbands at home. For it is shameful for a woman to speak in church. Or did the word of God originate with you? Or are you the only ones it has reached?)

Anyone who claims to be a prophet, or to have spiritual powers, must acknowledge that what I am writing to you is a command of the Lord. Anyone who does not recognize this is not to be recognized. So, my friends, be eager to prophesy, and do not forbid speaking in tongues; but all things should be done decently and in order.
(1 Corinthians 14:26–40.
The section in brackets may be an interpolation)

The following passage reflects a pattern of corporate worship in a post-Pauline church.

680. Let the word of Christ dwell in you richly; teach and admonish one another in all wisdom; and with gratitude in your hearts sing psalms, hymns, and spiritual songs to God. And whatever you do, in word or deed, do everything in the name of the Lord Jesus, giving thanks to God the Father through him.
(Colossians 3:16–17)

The book of Acts recalls the worship and community focus of the Jerusalem church in the immediate post-Easter period

681. All who believed were together and had all things in common; they would sell their possessions and goods and distribute the proceeds to all, as any had need. Day by day, as they spent much time together in the temple, they broke bread at home and ate their food with glad and generous hearts, praising God and having the goodwill of all the people. And day by day the Lord added to their number those who were being saved.
(Acts 2:44–47)

The eucharist (#682–83).

The term is derived from the Greek verb meaning to give thanks. The words spoken at the eucharistic meal grew out of Jewish blessings before a meal. From earliest times the eucharist was closely associated with sacrifice (see #683). The church offered its praise and thanksgiving, and participated in a meal of bread and wine in the context of the liturgical re-presentation of Jesus' death (the breaking of his body and the shedding of his blood) and its benefits understood in sacrificial terms.[98]

682. And concerning the Eucharist, hold Eucharist thus: First concerning the Cup, 'We give thanks to thee, our Father, for the Holy Vine of David thy child, which, thou didst make known to us through Jesus thy child; to thee be glory for ever.' And concerning the broken Bread; 'We give thee

thanks, our Father, for the life and knowledge which thou didst make known to us through Jesus thy child. To thee be glory for ever. As this broken bread was scattered upon the mountains, but was brought together and became one, so let thy Church be gathered together from the ends of the earth into thy kingdom, for thine is the glory and the power through Jesus Christ for ever.' But let none eat or drink of your Eucharist except those who have been baptised in the Lord's Name. For concerning this also did the Lord say, 'Give not that which is holy to the dogs.'
(*Didache* 9)

683. On the Lord's Day of the Lord come together, break bread and hold Eucharist, after confessing your transgressions that your offering [*thusia*, sacrifice] may be pure; but let none who has a quarrel with his fellow join in your meeting until they be reconciled, that your sacrifice [*thusia*] be not defiled. For this is that which was spoken by the Lord, 'In every place and time offer me a pure sacrifice, for I am a great king,' saith the Lord, 'and my name is wonderful among the heathen' [see Malachi 1:11, 14].
(*Didache* 14.
See also *Didache* 10)

Josephus on Jesus.

Josephus has been describing events that took place in Judaea during Pilate's governorship, when he turns his attention briefly to Jesus. In all probability, the following excerpt from the *Antiquities* is in its entirety not originally what Josephus wrote. There are strong grounds for believing that there is a Christian overlay of the historian's acknowledgment of the career and death of Jesus.

684. About this time there lived Jesus, a wise man, if indeed one ought to call him a man. For he was one who wrought surprising feats and was a teacher of such people as accept the truth gladly. He won over many Jews and many of the Greeks. He was the Messiah. When Pilate, upon hearing him accused by men of the highest standing amongst us, had condemned him to be crucified, those who had in the first place come to love him did not give up their affection for him. On the third day he appeared to them restored to life, for the prophets of God had prophesied these and countless other marvellous things about him. And the tribe of Christians, so called after him, has still to this day not disappeared.
(Josephus, *Antiquities* 18.63–64)[99]

Agrippa I orders the murder of James the Apostle.

685. About that time King Herod [Agrippa I] laid violent hands upon some who belonged to the church. He had James, the brother of John, killed with the sword. After he saw that it pleased the Jews, he proceeded to arrest Peter also.
(Acts 12:1–3)

The death of James the Just, the brother of Jesus.

Josephus is narrating events that happened in Jerusalem between the death of the procurator Festus and the arrival of his successor Albinus in 62 CE. Without Roman consent, the high priest, Ananus (Annas II), took the opportunity to mastermind the execution of James, known as the brother of the Lord. Ananus is described as daring and hot tempered, a member of the Sadducees, 'who are indeed more heartless than any of the other Jews' (20.199; cf. §207). Eusebius asserts that the martyrdom of James was the immediate cause for the destruction of the city (*Ecclesiastical History* 2.23). The Christians fled to Pella (see #711 below).

686. Possessed of such a character, Ananus thought that he had a favourable opportunity because Festus was dead and Albinus was still on the way. And so he convened the judges of the Sanhedrin and brought before them a man named James, the brother of Jesus who was called the Christ, and certain others. He accused them of having transgressed the law and delivered them up to be stoned. Those of the inhabitants of the city who were considered the most fair-minded and who were strict in observance of the law were offended at this. They therefore secretly sent to King Agrippa urging him, for Ananus had not even been correct in his first

step, to order him to desist from any further such actions.
(Josephus, *Antiquities* 20.200–201)[100]

A saying of Jesus about James not found in the canonical Gospels.

687. The disciples said to Jesus, 'We are aware that you will depart from us. Who will be our leader?' Jesus said to them, 'No matter where you come it is to James the Just that you shall go, for whose sake heaven and earth have come to exist.'
(*Coptic Gospel of Thomas* 12)

Paul (#688–90).

Paul recalls his pedigree as Jew and Pharisee.

688. If anyone else has reason to be confident in the flesh, I have more: circumcised on the eighth day, a member of the people of Israel, of the tribe of Benjamin, a Hebrew born of Hebrews; as to the law, a Pharisee; as to zeal, a persecutor of the church; as to righteousness under the law, blameless.
(Philippians 3:4b–6)

The following two extracts reveal something of the content of Paul's apocalyptic hope. Paul affirms the imminent triumph of God including the re-appearing (parousia) of Jesus as God's appointed eschatological agent (#690), the renewal of creation (#689) and the resurrection of believers (#690).

The renewal of creation.

689. We know that the whole creation has been groaning in labor pains until now; and not only the creation, but we ourselves, who have the first fruits of the Spirit, groan inwardly while we wait for adoption, the redemption of our bodies.
(Romans 8:22–23)

The nearness of the parousia and the certainty of the resurrection of believers.

690. But we do not want you to be uninformed, brothers and sisters, about those who have died, so that you may not grieve as others do who have no hope. For since we believe that Jesus died and rose again, even so, through Jesus, God will bring with him those who have died. For this we declare to you by the word of the Lord, that we who are alive, who are left until the coming of the Lord, will by no means precede those who have died. For the Lord himself, with a cry of command, with the archangel's call and with the sound of God's trumpet, will descend from heaven, and the dead in Christ will rise first. Then we who are alive, who are left, will be caught up in the clouds together with them to meet the Lord in the air; and so we will be with the Lord forever. Therefore encourage one another with these words.

Now concerning the times and the seasons, brothers and sisters, you do not need to have anything written to you. For you yourselves know very well that the day of the Lord will come like a thief in the night. When they say, 'There is peace and security,' then suddenly destruction will come upon them, as labor pains come upon a pregnant woman, and there will be no escape!
(1 Thessalonians 4:13–5:3)[101]

8.16. Resurrection

The doctrines of the eternal felicity of the soul and the resurrection of the dead are not encountered in the Bible until a select number of texts of the postexilic era.[102] It is commonly acknowledged that Jews first encountered ideas of the survival of the soul after death during the exile under the Persians after the mid sixth century BCE. Cyrus the Persian was influenced by the teachings of Zoroaster, who was an early sixth-century religious teacher. From a later Jewish point of view, his teaching anticipates the worldview of the apocalyptic literature of early Judaism. He taught a doctrine of the ascent of the soul to heaven as a just reward for righteous suffering in this life (see #12). His teaching also underscored the exclusion of the wicked from the blessed life of the faithful.

The resurrection of the body became a part of a number of speculative scenarios which are grouped under the category of Jewish eschatological apocalypticism, a worldview that emerged out of prophetic eschatology, which anticipated the fulfillment of divine promises in the historical arena.

R.B. Wright argues that the best explanation for the apocalyptic worldview is that Jews, experiencing oppression from a succession of empires, no longer saw history 'as a viable vehicle for covenantal promises'.[103] The hallmarks of apocalyptic thinking are dualism—often expressed in terms of a clear demarcation between this world and the world to come—and a confidence in God's imminent, catastrophic interruption of history in order to establish his rule, to vindicate his elect and to punish those who harass them.[104]

The doctrine of rewards and punishments in the afterlife is axiomatic for the Jewish eschatological apocalypses, though it is not confined to that genre (see, e.g., *Jubilees* 23:31). The more particular doctrine of the resurrection of the body is present in Daniel 12 (#694; see also the *Testament of Judah* 25:1) and *1 Enoch* 51 (#695; though less certainly in *1 Enoch* 10:17; 103:4), but is not a particularly widespread doctrine in early Jewish literature. In *Jewish War* 2.154–58, Josephus claims that the Essenes believed in the doctrine of the immortality of the soul. This may be Josephus's euphemism for the resurrection of the dead for his sophisticated Roman audience, though it must also be admitted that life after death in any form is rarely encountered in the Dead Sea Scrolls (however, see #657).[105]

Early Christians affirmed that Jesus had died but had also been raised from death. More than other assertion about Jesus, the resurrection marks early Christianity as an apocalyptic movement. Paul, the mediator of the message of the resurrected Messiah of Israel, subscribes to an apocalyptic worldview. In fact, in Galatians 1:12 he states that the message he preached did not come through human mediation, but through revelation—an apocalypse (*apokalupsis*).

Sources

The following three extracts from the corpus of Zoroastrian texts disclose beliefs that can be paralleled in the literature of early Judaism and Christianity. It is quite possible that the eschatological dualism encountered in early Judaism, the belief in the resurrection of the body, and the doctrine of rewards and punishments after death passed into Judaism under Persian influence. The first and third extracts, #691 and #693, are from the collection of texts known as the *Avesta*, which was collated in the Sasanid period (third–seventh centuries CE) from much earlier written traditions purporting to preserve the teaching of Zoroaster.

Resurrection (#691–92).

691. Let Angra Mainyu be hid beneath the earth. Let the Daevas likewise disappear. Let the dead arise (unhindered by these foes), and let bodily life be sustained in these now lifeless bodies.
(*Zend Avesta*, Miscellaneous Fragments 4.3)[106]

The following extract is from a ninth-century CE Zoroastrian cosmological work. It bears comparison with Paul's discourse on the resurrection in 1 Corinthians 15 (#698) (see also 2 Corinthians 5:1–5) on which it does not seem to be dependent.

692. (4) After Soshyans comes they prepare the raising of the dead, as it says, that Zaratust asked of Auharmazd thus: 'Whence does a body form again, which the wind has carried and the water conveyed? and how does the resurrection occur?' Auharmazd answered thus:... (6) 'Observe that when that which was not was then produced, why is it not possible to produce again that which was? for at that time one will demand the bone from the spirit of the earth, the blood from the water, the hair from the plants, and the life from fire, since they were delivered to them in the original creation.' (7) First the bones of Gayomard are roused up, then those of Mashya and Mashyoi, then those of the rest of mankind; in the fifty-seven years of the Soshyans they prepare all the dead, and all men stand up; whoever is righteous and whoever is wicked, every human creature, they rouse up from the spot where its life departs... (10) Then is the assembly of the Sadvastaran, where all mankind will stand at this time; in that assembly every one sees his own good deeds and his own evil deeds; and then, in that assembly, a wicked man

becomes as conspicuous as a white sheep among those that are black… (12) Afterwards, they set the righteous man apart from the wicked; and then the righteous is for heaven, and they cast the wicked back to hell. (13) Three days and nights they inflict punishment bodily in hell, and then he beholds bodily those three days' happiness in heaven… (19) Afterwards, the fire and halo melt the metal of Shatvairo, in the hills and mountains, and it remains on this earth like a river. (20) Then all men will pass into that melted metal and will become pure; when one is righteous, then it seems to him just as though he walks continually in warm milk; but when wicked, then it seems to him in such manner as though, in the world, he walks continually in melted metal… (26) This, too, it says, that whoever has been the size of a man, they restore him then with an age of forty years; they who have been little when not dead, they restore then with an age of fifteen years; and they give every one his wife, and show him his children with the wife; so they act as now in the world, but there is no begetting of children. (27) Afterwards, Soshyans and his assistants, by order of the creator Auharmazd, give every man the reward and recompense suitable to his deeds; this is even the righteous existence where it is said that they convey him to paradise, and the heaven of Auharmazd takes up the body as itself requires; with that assistance he continually advances for ever and everlasting. (28) This too, it says, that whoever has performed no worship, and has ordered no Geti-kharid, and has bestowed no clothes as a righteous gift, is naked there; and he performs the worship of Auharmazd, and the heavenly angels provide him the use of his clothing. (29) Afterwards, Auharmazd seizes on the evil spirit… (30) Then two fiends remain at large, Aharman and Az; Auharmazd comes to the world, himself the Zota and Srosh the Raspi, and holds the Kusti in his hand; defeated by the Kusti formula the resources of the evil spirit and Az act most impotently, and by the passage through which he rushed into the sky he runs back to gloom and darkness. (31) Gokihar burns the serpent in the melted metal, and the stench and pollution which were in hell are burned in that metal, and it [hell] becomes quite pure. (32) He [Auharmazd] sets the vault into which the evil spirit fled, in that metal; he brings the land of hell back for the enlargement of the world; the renovation arises in the universe by his will, and the world is immortal for ever and everlasting.
(*Bundahis* 30.4–32)

Dualism. The words in parentheses are ancient glosses.

693. (Yea) when the two spirits came together at the first to make life, and life's absence, and to determine how the world at the last shall be (ordered), for the wicked (Hell) the worst life, for the holy (Heaven) the Best Mental State. (Then when they had finished each his part in the deeds of creation, they chose distinctly each his separate realm.) He who was the evil of them both (chose the evil), thereby working the worst of possible results, but the more bounteous spirit chose the (Divine) Righteousness…
(*Yasna* 30.4–5)

Resurrection in early Jewish and Christian texts (#694–98).

694. 'At that time Michael, the great prince, the protector of your people, shall arise. There shall be a time of anguish, such as has never occurred since nations first came into existence. But at that time your people shall be delivered, everyone who is found written in the book. Many of those who sleep in the dust of the earth shall awake, some to everlasting life, and some to shame and everlasting contempt. Those who are wise shall shine like the brightness of the sky, and those who lead many to righteousness, like the stars forever and ever.'
(Daniel 12:1–3)

695. In those days, Sheol will return all the deposits which she had received and hell will give back all that which it owes. And he shall choose the righteous and the holy ones from among (the risen dead), for the day when they shall be selected and saved has arrived. In those days, (the Elect One) shall sit on my throne, and from the conscience of his mouth shall come out all the secrets of wisdom, for the Lord of the Spirits has given them to him and glorified him. In those days, mountains shall dance like rams; and the hills

shall leap like kids satiated with milk. And the faces of all the angels in heaven shall glow with joy, because on that day the Elect One has arisen. And the earth shall rejoice; and the righteous ones shall dwell upon her and the elect ones shall walk upon her.
(*1 Enoch* 51)

The torture of the seven brothers in 2 Maccabees 7 provides grim theatre indeed. The affirmation of the resurrection is clearly articulated. In the extract below the first two brothers defiantly go to their deaths at the hands of Antiochus Epiphanes.

696. 'The Lord God is watching over us and in truth has compassion on us, as Moses declared in his song that bore witness against the people to their faces, when he said, "And he will have compassion on his servants." '

After the first brother had died in this way, they brought forward the second for their sport. They tore off the skin of his head with the hair, and asked him, 'Will you eat rather than have your body punished limb by limb?' He replied in the language of his ancestors and said to them, 'No.' Therefore he in turn underwent tortures as the first brother had done. And when he was at his last breath, he said, 'You accursed wretch, you dismiss us from this present life, but the King of the universe will raise us up to an everlasting renewal of life, because we have died for his laws.'
(2 Maccabees 7:6–9)

Pseudo-Phocylides on resurrection.

697. It is not good to dissolve the human frame;
for we hope that the remains of the departed will soon come to light (again)
out of the earth; and afterward they will become gods.
For the souls remain unharmed among the deceased.
For the spirit is a loan of God to mortals, and (his) image.
For we have a body out of earth, and when afterward we are resolved again into earth
we are but dust; and then the air has received our spirit.
When you are rich, do not be sparing; remember that you are mortal.
It is impossible to take riches and money (with you) into Hades.
All alike are corpses, but God rules over the souls.
Hades is (our) common eternal home and fatherland,
a common place for all, poor and kings.
We humans live not a long time but for a season.
But (our) soul is immortal and lives ageless forever.
(*Sentences of Pseudo-Phocylides*, ll. 102–115)

Paul affirms the resurrection hope.

698. But someone will ask, 'How are the dead raised? With what kind of body do they come?' Fool! What you sow does not come to life unless it dies. And as for what you sow, you do not sow the body that is to be, but a bare seed, perhaps of wheat or of some other grain. But God gives it a body as he has chosen, and to each kind of seed its own body. Not all flesh is alike, but there is one flesh for human beings, another for animals, another for birds, and another for fish. There are both heavenly bodies and earthly bodies, but the glory of the heavenly is one thing, and that of the earthly is another. There is one glory of the sun, and another glory of the moon, and another glory of the stars; indeed, star differs from star in glory.

So it is with the resurrection of the dead. What is sown is perishable, what is raised is imperishable. It is sown in dishonor, it is raised in glory. It is sown in weakness, it is raised in power. It is sown a physical body, it is raised a spiritual body. If there is a physical body, there is also a spiritual body. Thus it is written, 'The first man, Adam, became a living being'; the last Adam became a life-giving spirit. But it is not the spiritual that is first, but the physical, and then the spiritual. The first man was from the earth, a man of dust; the second man is from heaven. As was the man of dust, so are those who are of the dust; and as is the man of heaven, so are those who are of heaven. Just as we have borne the image of the man of dust, we will also bear the image of the man of heaven.

What I am saying, brothers and sisters, is this: flesh and blood cannot inherit the kingdom of God, nor does the perishable inherit the imperishable. Listen, I will tell you a mystery! We will not all die, but we will all be changed, in a moment, in the twinkling of an eye, at the last trumpet. For the trumpet will sound, and the dead will be raised imperishable, and we will be changed. For this perishable body must put on imperishability, and this mortal body must put on immortality. When this perishable body puts on imperishability, and this mortal body puts on immortality, then the saying that is written will be fulfilled:

'Death has been swallowed up in victory.'
'Where, O death, is your victory?
Where, O death, is your sting?'

The sting of death is sin, and the power of sin is the law. But thanks be to God who gives us the victory through our Lord Jesus Christ.

Therefore, my beloved, be steadfast, immovable, always excelling in the work of the Lord, because you know that in the Lord your labor is not in vain.
(1 Corinthians 15:35–58)

8.17. Messianism

There is ambiguity in the writings of the early Judaism concerning Messianic expectation. There is no agreed Messianic agenda, and no universal expectation of a Messiah. The *Testaments of the Twelve Patriarchs* (*T12P*) testify to an expectation of two Messiahs, one of Aaron who takes precedence, and one of David. This expectation is in line with certain Qumran scrolls. In *4 Ezra* 7:26–29 the Messiah dies without performing any function. The great apocalyptic vision in *Testament of Moses* 10 sees God alone as the one who executes vengeance on his enemies and establishes his rule. On the other hand, *Psalms of Solomon* 17 is one of the clearest statements concerning the coming Davidic Messiah before the advent of Jesus.

Although there is a diversity of expectations, there is a confident expectation in the early Jewish literature and the New Testament that God will intervene on behalf of his beleaguered people and translate them to his place under his rule having destroyed their enemies. In the *Psalms of Solomon*, the Messiah will restore the ancient tribal divisions, usher in the everlasting rule of God, bring the diaspora Jews home, and punish the wicked and the Gentiles. He is titled 'Son of David' and '*Lord* Messiah'. This linkage anticipates Luke 1–2 (especially 2:11).

The synoptic evangelists are agreed that Jesus deflected any expectation that he would take direct action as Messiah against the oppressors of Israel. Rather he spoke of himself as the suffering Son of Man (see #702). Nevertheless, the evangelists are agreed that Jesus was indeed the Messiah, the anointed agent of God, who was rightfully the unique and vindicated Son of God, and who had truly exercised his kingship in a life of service and humiliation, and, pre-eminently, in his death.[107]

Sources

The *Psalms of Solomon* were written late in the first century BCE. The following expresses the psalmist's expectation of a royal Davidic Messiah after the model of David. This psalm is unprecedented in scope and detail. After detailing the offences of the 'arrogant' against the people of God, the psalmist expresses a confident hope in the coming of the anointed one, a king.

699. See, Lord, and raise up for them their king,
the son of David, to rule over your servant Israel
in the time known to you, O God.
Undergird him with the strength to destroy the unrighteous rulers,
to purge Jerusalem from gentiles
who trample her to destruction;
in wisdom and in righteousness to drive out
the sinners from the inheritance;
to smash the arrogance of sinners
like a potter's jar;
To shatter all their substance with an iron rod;
to destroy the unlawful nations with the word of his mouth;
At his warning the nations will flee from his presence;
and he will condemn sinners by the thoughts of their hearts.

He will gather a holy people
whom he will lead in righteousness;
and he will judge the tribes of the people
that have been made holy by the Lord their God.
He will not tolerate unrighteousness (even) to pause among them,
and any person who knows wickedness shall not live with them.
For he shall know them
that they are all children of their God.
He will distribute them upon the land
according to their tribes;
the alien and the foreigner will no longer live near them.
He will judge peoples and nations in the wisdom of his righteousness.
Pause.
And he will have gentile nations serving him under his yoke,
and he will glorify the Lord in (a place) prominent (above) the whole earth.
And he will purge Jerusalem
(and make it) holy as it was even from the beginning,
(for) nations to come from the ends of the earth to see his glory,
to bring as gifts her children who had been driven out,
and to see the glory of the Lord
with which God has glorified her.
And he will be a righteous king over them, taught by God.
There will be no unrighteousness among them in his days,
for all shall be holy,
and their king shall be the Lord Messiah.
(For) he will not rely on horse and rider and bow,
nor will he collect gold and silver for war.
Nor will he build up hope in a multitude for a day of war.
The Lord himself is his king,
the hope of the one who has a strong hope in God.
He shall be compassionate to all the nations
(who) reverently (stand) before him.
He will strike the earth with the word of his mouth forever;
he will bless the Lord's people with wisdom and happiness.
And he himself (will be) free from sin, (in order) to rule a great people.
He will expose officials and drive out sinners
by the strength of his word.
And he will not weaken in his days, (relying) upon his God,
for God made him
powerful in the holy spirit
and wise in his counsel of understanding,
with strength and righteousness.
And the blessing of the Lord will be with him in strength,
and he will not weaken;
His hope (will be) in the Lord.
Then who will succeed against him,
mighty in his actions
and strong in the fear of God?
Faithfully and righteously shepherding the Lord's flock,
he will not let any of them stumble in their pasture.
He will lead them all in holiness
and there will be no arrogance among them,
that any should be oppressed.
This is the beauty of the king of Israel
which God knew,
to raise him over the house of Israel
to discipline it.
His words will be purer than the finest gold, the best.
He will judge the peoples in the assemblies,
the tribes of the sanctified.
His words will be as the words of the holy ones,
among sanctified peoples.
Blessed are those born in those days
to see the good fortune of Israel
which God will bring to pass in the assembly of the tribes.
May God dispatch his mercy to Israel;
may he deliver us from the pollution of profane enemies;
The Lord Himself is our king forevermore.
(*Psalms of Solomon* 17:21–46)[108]

Dual messianic expectation (#700–701).

700. 'And Levi and Judah were glorified by the Lord among the sons of Jacob. The Lord made choice among them: To the one he gave the priesthood and to the other, the kingship. Subject yourselves to them, and live in integrity as did your father…' (*Testament of Issachar* 5.7–8)[109]

Dual expectation in the Qumran Scrolls.

701. [This shall be the ass]embly of the men of renown [called] to the meeting of the Council of the Community

When God engenders (the Priest-) Messiah, he shall come with them [at] the head of the whole congregation of Israel with all [his brethren, the sons] of Aaron the Priests, [those called] to the assembly, the men of renown; and they shall sit [before him, each man] in the order of his dignity. And then [the Mess]iah of Israel shall [come], and the chiefs of the [clans of Israel] shall sit before him, [each] in the order of his dignity, according to [his place] in their camps and marches. And before them shall sit all the heads of [family of the congreg] ation, and the wise men of [the holy congregation,] each in the order of his dignity.
(1QSa 2.11–15)

Messianism in the New Testament is imbued with the affirmation that Jesus, the Messiah, has already come. As one who was prepared to suffer, Jesus was a surprising and unexpected messianic figure indeed. The early Christians preached that the suffering of Jesus was essential for understanding his Messiahship.

702. Jesus went on with his disciples to the villages of Caesarea Philippi; and on the way he asked his disciples, 'Who do people say that I am?' And they answered him, 'John the Baptist; and others, Elijah; and still others, one of the prophets.' He asked them, 'But who do you say that I am?' Peter answered him, 'You are the Messiah.' And he sternly ordered them not to tell anyone about him.

Then he began to teach them that the Son of Man must undergo great suffering, and be rejected by the elders, the chief priests, and the scribes, and be killed, and after three days rise again.
(Mark 8:27–31)

703. Jesus said to her, 'Woman, believe me, the hour is coming when you will worship the Father neither on this mountain nor in Jerusalem. You worship what you do not know; we worship what we know, for salvation is from the Jews. But the hour is coming, and is now here, when the true worshipers will worship the Father in spirit and truth, for the Father seeks such as these to worship him. God is spirit, and those who worship him must worship in spirit and truth.' The woman said to him, 'I know that Messiah is coming' (who is called Christ). 'When he comes, he will proclaim all things to us.' Jesus said to her, 'I am he, the one who is speaking to you.'
(John 4:21–26)

704. Paul, a servant of Jesus Christ, called to be an apostle, set apart for the gospel of God, which he promised beforehand through his prophets in the holy scriptures, the gospel concerning his Son, who was descended from David according to the flesh and was declared to be Son of God with power according to the spirit of holiness by resurrection from the dead, Jesus Christ our Lord…
(Romans 1:1–4)

705. And I began to weep bitterly because no one was found worthy to open the scroll or to look into it. Then one of the elders said to me, 'Do not weep. See, the Lion of the tribe of Judah, the Root of David, has conquered, so that he can open the scroll and its seven seals.'

Then I saw between the throne and the four living creatures and among the elders a Lamb standing as if it had been slaughtered, having seven horns and seven eyes, which are the seven spirits of God sent out into all the earth.
(Revelation 5:4–6)

706. Let all the Lord's babes praise him,
and let us receive the truth of his faith.
And his children shall be acknowledged by him,
therefore let us sing by his love.
We live in the Lord by his grace,
and life we receive by his Messiah.
For a great day has shined upon us,
and wonderful is he who has given to us of his glory.
(*Odes of Solomon* 41:1–4.
Cf. #295)

8.18. Christians under the Empire

Unlike Judaism, with which the Romans had had a long history of dealings, the early Christians appeared to be a particularly offensive 'superstition' lacking all the hallmarks of venerability to which the Jews could appeal. Tacitus's account of the tortures inflicted on the Christians by Nero after the fire of Rome in 64 CE reveals both the historian's deep sense of loathing of the Christians and his revulsion at the actions of Nero.

The correspondence of Pliny the Younger reveals the risks Christians faced when accused before magistrates charged with the responsibility of rooting out sedition and social deviance as a threat to the state. It is significant that bearing and not renouncing the name of 'Christian' seems to be sufficient cause for execution. This practice may stem from the execution of Christians by Nero in 64.[110] The letter reveals an extraordinary penetration of Christians in the province to the detriment of the cults. Trajan's reply commends the governor for his resolute judicial action, but urges Pliny not to accept anonymous accusations.

Sources

The book of Acts defends the new movement as law-abiding. The Romans need not fear outbreaks of anti-social behaviour.

Jews and Christians before Gallio.

707. [W]hen Gallio was proconsul of Achaia, the Jews made a united attack on Paul and brought him before the tribunal. They said, 'This man is persuading people to worship God in ways that are contrary to the law.' Just as Paul was about to speak, Gallio said to the Jews, 'If it were a matter of crime or serious villainy, I would be justified in accepting the complaint of you Jews; but since it is a matter of questions about words and names and your own law, see to it yourselves; I do not wish to be a judge of these matters.' And he dismissed them from the tribunal. Then all of them seized Sosthenes, the official of the synagogue, and beat him in front of the tribunal. But Gallio paid no attention to any of these things.
(Acts 18:12–17)[111]

Paul expresses the following sentiments regarding the responsibility of believers to the state.

708. Let every person be subject to the governing authorities; for there is no authority except from God, and those authorities that exist have been instituted by God. Therefore whoever resists authority resists what God has appointed, and those who resist will incur judgment. For rulers are not a terror to good conduct, but to bad. Do you wish to have no fear of the authority? Then do what is good, and you will receive its approval; for it is God's servant for your good. But if you do what is wrong, you should be afraid, for the authority does not bear the sword in vain! It is the servant of God to execute wrath on the wrongdoer. Therefore one must be subject, not only because of wrath but also because of conscience. For the same reason you also pay taxes, for the authorities are God's servants, busy with this very thing. Pay to all what is due them—taxes to whom taxes are due, revenue to whom revenue is due, respect to whom respect is due, honor to whom honor is due.
(Romans 13:1–7.
Contrast the cries for vengeance against Rome in Revelation)[112]

The persecution of Christians (#709–716).

Tacitus wrote a famous account of Nero's persecution of the Christians, whom he blamed for the fire of Rome in 64. Eusebius is the chief witness of a persecution against Christians that was sponsored by Domitian. The extracts from the corpus of the correspondence of Pliny show something of the political pressure that was brought to bear on believers on occasion. Finally I have included an extract from Ignatius's letter to the Romans.

709. But neither human help, nor imperial munificence, nor all the modes of placating Heaven, could stifle scandal or dispel the belief that the fire had taken place by order. Therefore, to scotch the rumour, Nero sub-

stituted as culprits, and punished with the utmost refinements of cruelty, a class of men, loathed for their vices, whom the crowd styled Christians. Christus, the founder of the name, had undergone the death penalty in the reign of Tiberius, by sentence of the procurator Pontius Pilatus, and the pernicious superstition was checked for a moment, only to break out once more, not merely in Judaea, the home of the disease, but in the capital itself, where all things horrible or shameful in the world collect and find a vogue. First, then, the confessed members of the sect were arrested; next, on their disclosures, vast numbers were convicted, not so much on the count of arson as for hatred of the human race. And derision accompanied their end: they were covered with wild beasts' skins and torn to death by dogs; or they were fastened on crosses, and, when daylight failed were burned to serve as lamps by night. Nero had offered his Gardens for the spectacle, and gave an exhibition in his Circus, mixing with the crowd in the habit of a charioteer, or mounted on his car. Hence, in spite of a guilt which had earned the most exemplary punishment, there arose a sentiment of pity, due to the impression that they were being sacrificed not for the welfare of the state but to the ferocity of a single man.
(Tacitus, *Annals* 15.44)[113]

710. During his [Nero's] reign many abuses were severely punished and put down, and no fewer new laws were made: a limit was set to expenditures; the public banquets were confined to a distribution of food; the sale of any kind of cooked viands in the taverns was forbidden, with the exception of pulse and vegetables, whereas before every sort of dainty was exposed for sale. Punishment was inflicted on the Christians, a class of men given to a new and mischievous superstition.
(Suetonius, *Nero* 16.2)

In 66 CE, as the Jewish revolt was being set in train, the Christians escaped from Jerusalem and fled to Pella. The following extract from Eusebius testifies to the persistent charge that the Jews had been responsible for the deaths of Jesus and the apostles. The view is noticeably present in Luke–Acts.[114]

711. [T]he people of the church in Jerusalem were commanded by an oracle given by revelation before the war to those in the city who were worthy of it to depart and dwell in one of the cities of Perea which they called Pella. To it those who believed in Christ migrated from Jerusalem, that when holy men had altogether deserted the royal capital of the Jews and the whole land of Judaea, the judgement of God might at last overtake them for all their crimes against the Christ and his Apostles, and all that generation of the wicked be utterly blotted out from among men.
(Eusebius, *Ecclesiastical History* 3.5.3)

Some high born Christians suffered for their faith in the time of Domitian.

1 Clement *and the persecutions in Rome in the mid 60s and 90s* CE.

712. But, to cease from the examples of old time, let us come to those who contended in the days nearest to us; let us take the noble examples of our own generation. Through jealousy and envy the greatest and most righteous pillars of the Church were persecuted and contended unto death. Let us set before our eyes the good apostles: Peter, who because of unrighteous jealousy suffered not one or two but many trials, and having thus given his testimony went to the glorious place which was his due. Through jealousy and strife Paul showed the way to the prize of endurance; seven times he was in bonds, he was exiled, he was stoned, he was a herald both in the East and in the West, he gained the noble fame of his faith, he taught righteousness to all the world, and when he had reached the limits of the West he gave his testimony before the rulers, and thus passed from the world and was taken up into the Holy Place,—the greatest example of endurance.

To these men with their holy lives was gathered a great multitude of the chosen, who were the victims of jealousy and offered among us the fairest example in their endurance under many indignities and tortures. Through jealousy women were persecuted as Danaids and Dircae, suffering terrible and unholy indignities; they steadfastly finished the course of faith, and received a

noble reward, weak in the body though they were. Jealousy has estranged wives from husbands, and made of no effect the saying of our father Adam, 'This is now bone of my bone and flesh of my flesh.' Jealousy and strife have overthrown great cities, and rooted up mighty nations.
(*1 Clement* 5–6)

Eusebius reports the persecution under Domitian.

713. When Domitian had given many proofs of his great cruelty and had put to death without any reasonable trial no small number of men distinguished at Rome by family and career, and had punished without a cause myriads of other notable men by banishment and confiscation of their property, he finally showed himself the successor of Nero's campaign of hostility to God. He was the second to promote persecution against us, though his father, Vespasian, had planned no evil against us.

At this time, the story goes, the Apostle and Evangelist John was still alive, and was condemned to live in the island of Patmos for his witness to the divine word [Revelation 1:9]. At any rate Irenaeus, writing about the number of the name ascribed to the anti-Christ in the so-called Apocalypse of John, states this about John in so many words in the fifth book against Heresies. 'But if it had been necessary to announce his name plainly at the present time, it would have been spoken by him who saw the apocalypse. For it was not seen long ago but almost in our own time, at the end of the reign of Domitian.'

The teaching of our faith shone so brilliantly in the days described that even writers foreign to our belief did not hesitate to commit to their narratives the persecutions and the martyrdoms in it, and they even indicated the time accurately, relating that in the fifteenth year of Domitian, Flavia Domitilla, who was the niece of Flavius Clemens, one of the consuls at Rome at that time, was banished with many others to the island of Pontia as testimony to Christ.

The same Domitian gave orders for the execution of those of the family of David and an ancient story goes that some heretics accused the grandsons of Judas (who is said to have been the brother, according to the flesh, of the Saviour) saying that they were of the family of David and related to the Christ himself. Hegesippus relates this exactly as follows. 'Now there still survived of the family of the Lord grandsons of Judas, who was said to have been his brother according to the flesh, and they were delated as being of the family of David. These the officer brought to Domitian Caesar, for, like Herod, he was afraid of the coming of the Christ. He asked them if they were of the house of David and they admitted it. Then he asked them how much property they had, or how much money they controlled, and they said that all they possessed was nine thousand denarii between them, the half belonging to each, and they stated that they did not possess this in money but that it was the valuation of only thirty-nine plethra of ground on which they paid taxes and lived on it by their own work'. They then showed him their hands, adducing as testimony of their labour the hardness of their bodies, and the tough skin which had been embossed on their hands from their incessant work. They were asked concerning the Christ and his kingdom, its nature, origin, and time of appearance, and explained that it was neither of the world nor earthly, but heavenly and angelic, and it would be at the end of the world, when he would come in glory to judge the living and the dead and to reward every man according to his deeds. At this Domitian did not condemn them at all, but despised them as simple folk, released them, and decreed an end to the persecution against the church. But when they were released they were the leaders of the churches, both for their testimony and for their relation to the Lord, and remained alive in the peace which ensued until Trajan. Hegesippus tells this; moreover, Tertullian also has made similar mention of Domitian. 'Domitian also once tried to do the same as he, for he was a Nero in cruelty, but, I believe, inasmuch as he had some sense, he stopped at once and recalled those whom he had banished.'
(Eusebius, *Ecclesiastical History* 3.17–20)[115]

Pliny encountered Christians while Governor of Bithynia. His famous letter to Trajan, dated about 110 CE, reveals rare detail concerning the structure and content of early Christian meetings as well as the Roman judicial process in cases in which charges were brought against Christians.

714. Pliny to the Emperor Trajan

> It is my custom to refer all my difficulties to you, Sir, for no one is better able to resolve my doubts and to inform my ignorance.
>
> I have never been present at an examination of Christians. Consequently, I do not know the nature or the extent of the punishments usually meted out to them, nor the grounds for starting an investigation and how far it should be pressed. Nor am I at all sure whether any distinction should be made between them on the grounds of age, or if young people and adults should be treated alike; whether a pardon ought to be granted to anyone retracting his beliefs, or if he has once professed Christianity, he shall gain nothing by renouncing it; and whether it is the mere name of Christian which is punishable, even if innocent of crime, or rather the crimes associated with the name.
>
> For the moment this is the line I have taken with all persons brought before me on the charge of being Christians. I have asked them in person if they are Christians, and if they admit it, I repeat the question a second and third time, with a warning of the punishment awaiting them. If they persist, I order them to be led away for execution; for, whatever the nature of their admission, I am convinced that their stubbornness and unshakeable obstinacy ought not to go unpunished. There have been others similarly fanatical who are Roman citizens. I have entered them on the list of persons to be sent to Rome for trial.
>
> Now that I have begun to deal with this problem, as so often happens, the charges are becoming more widespread and increasing in variety. An anonymous pamphlet has been circulated which contains the names of a number of accused persons. Among these I considered that I should dismiss any who denied that they were or ever had been Christians when they had repeated after me a formula of invocation to the gods and had made offerings of wine and incense to your statue (which I had ordered to be brought into court for this purpose along with the images of the gods), and furthermore had reviled the name of Christ: none of which things, I understand, any genuine Christian can be induced to do.
>
> Others, whose names were given to me by an informer, first admitted the charge and then denied it; they said that they had ceased to be Christians two or more years previously, and some of them even twenty years ago. They all did reverence to your statue and the images of the gods in the same way as the others, and reviled the name of Christ. They also declared that the sum total of their guilt or error amounted to no more than this: they had met regularly before dawn on a fixed day to chant verses alternately among themselves in honour of Christ as if to a god, and also to bind themselves by oath, not for any criminal purpose, but to abstain from theft, robbery and adultery, to commit no breach of trust and not to deny a deposit when called upon to restore it. After this ceremony it had been their custom to disperse and reassemble later to take food of an ordinary, harmless kind; but they had in fact given up this practice since my edict, issued on your instructions, which banned all political societies. This made me decide it was all the more necessary to extract the truth by torture from two slave-women, whom they call deaconesses. I found nothing but a degenerate sort of cult carried to extravagant lengths.
>
> I have therefore postponed any further examination and hastened to consult you. The question seems to me to be worthy of your consideration, especially in view of the number of persons endangered; for a great many individuals of every age and class, both men and women, are being brought to trial, and this is likely to continue. It is not only the towns, but villages and rural districts too which are infected through contact with this wretched cult. I think though that it is still possible for it to be checked and directed to better ends, for there is no doubt that people have begun to throng the temples which had been almost entirely deserted for a long time; the sacred rites which had been allowed to lapse are being performed again, and flesh of sacrificial vic-

tims is on sale everywhere, though up till recently scarcely anyone could be found to buy it. It is easy to infer from this that a great many people could be reformed if they were given an opportunity to repent.
(Pliny the Younger, *Letters* 10.96)

Trajan's measured reply to Pliny's letter has been preserved.

715. Trajan to Pliny

You have followed the right course of procedure, my dear Pliny, in your examination of the cases of persons charged with being Christians, for it is impossible to lay down a general rule to a fixed formula. These people must not be hunted out; if they are brought before you and the charge against them is proved, they must be punished, but in the case of anyone who denies that he is a Christian, and makes it clear that he is not by offering prayers to our gods, he is to be pardoned as a result of his repentance however suspect his past conduct may be. But pamphlets circulated anonymously must play no part in any accusation. They create the worst sort of precedent and are quite out of keeping with the spirit of our age.
(Pliny the Younger, *Letters* 10.97)

Ignatius was Bishop of Antioch. In about the year 110 he was brought to trial and sentenced *ad bestiam*, the punishment to be carried out in Rome. As he made the journey through Asia Minor and Greece, he wrote six letters to Christian communities he encountered along the way. He also wrote a letter to Polycarp Bishop of Smyrna. Polycarp would himself be martyred 40 years later.

Ignatius prepares for martyrdom.

716. I am writing to all the Churches, and I give injunctions to all men, that I am dying willingly for God's sake, if you do not hinder it. I beseech you, be not 'an unseasonable kindness' to me. Suffer me to be eaten by the beasts, through whom I can attain to God. I am God's wheat, and I am ground by the teeth of wild beasts that I may be found pure bread of Christ. Rather entice the wild beasts that they may become my tomb, and leave no trace of my body, that when I fall asleep I be not burdensome to any. Then shall I be truly a disciple of Jesus Christ, when the world shall not even see my body. Beseech Christ on my behalf, that I may be found a sacrifice through these instruments. I do not order you as did Peter and Paul; they were Apostles, I am a convict; they were free, I am even until now a slave. But if I suffer I shall be Jesus Christ's freedman, and in him I shall rise free. Now I am learning in my bonds to give up all desires.

From Syria to Rome I am fighting with wild beasts, by land and sea, by night and day, bound to ten 'leopards' (that is, a company of soldiers), and they become worse for kind treatment. Now I become the more a disciple for their ill deeds, 'but not by this am I justified.' I long for the beasts that are prepared for me; and I pray that they may be found prompt for me; I will even entice them to devour me promptly; not as has happened to some whom they have not touched from fear; even if they be unwilling of themselves, I will force them to it. Grant me this favour. I know what is expedient for me; now I am beginning to be a disciple. May nothing of things seen or unseen envy me my attaining to Jesus Christ. Let there come on me fire, and cross, and struggles with wild beasts, cutting, and tearing asunder, rackings of bones, mangling of limbs, crushing of my whole body, cruel tortures of the devil, may I but attain to Jesus Christ!
(Ignatius, *Letter to the Romans* 4–5)

Not all early references to Christians are found in contexts of persecution and judicial process. In his *Golden Ass*, Apuleius depicts a woman who appears to be a Christian rather than a Jew, since none of the usual prejudices against Jews surfaces here, and there may be a reference to participation in an early morning eucharist. She is the wife of a baker who had bought Lucius. Her faith is the source of her vices.

717. [S]he was crabbed, cruel, cursed, drunken, obstinate, niggish, covetous in base robberies, riotous in filthy expenses, an enemy to faith and chastity, a despiser of all the gods whom others did honour, one that affirmed that she had instead of our religion an only god by herself, whereby, inventing

empty rites and ceremonies, she deceived all men, but especially her poor husband, delighting in drinking wine, yea, early in the morning, and abandoning her body to continual whoredom.
(Apuleius, *Golden Ass* 9.14)

Notes

1. E. Lohse, *The New Testament Environment* (London: SCM Press, 1976), p. 122.
2. It is for this reason that Jewish writers such as Josephus and Philo are concerned to mount an apology for Judaism. See, e.g., #280 and Josephus, *Antiquities* 8.111–18. The novella *3 Maccabees* is particularly devoted to this theme (see esp. 3:4–5).
3. Given the pro-Jewish sentiment of this and other fragments purporting to have been written by Hecataeus, it is possible that Josephus is actually citing a Jewish writer posing as Hecataeus of Abdera. Hecataeus is cited not only by Josephus (*Antiquities* 1.159; *Against Apion* 2.43) but also by the writer of the *Letter of Aristeas* (§31), and by Diodorus Siculus (*Histories* 40.3.1–8), Clement of Alexandria (*Stromateis* 5.113), and Origen (*Against Celsus* 1.15b). See R. Doran's discussion in *OTP* II, pp. 905–908, and the fragments collected in *OTP* II, pp. 909–919. Doran believes that, apart from the fragments of Hecataeus cited in *Antiquities* 1 and Clement of Alexandria, the remainder, including this one cited by Josephus in *Against Apion* 1.183–205, are genuine.
4. An aroura was an Egyptian measure of land equal to about half an acre. See H.St.J. Thackeray (trans.), *The Life, Against Apion* (Loeb Classical Library; Cambridge, MA: Harvard University Press, 1926), p. 197 (n. c). Three million arourae would be approximately 4500 square miles or 11,500 square kilometres. The modern state of Israel encompasses 7992 square miles or 20,400 square kilometres and supports a population of just over five million (1996).
5. See also the descriptions in Strabo, *Geography* 16.34–46; *Letter of Aristeas* 83–120; Diodorus Siculus, *Histories* 40.3.1–8.
6. Yaho is the rendition of the name for the God of the Jews. Khnub, if that is the correct emendation, is another god besides Yaho.
7. In another papyrus the Jews of Elephantine promise to pay tribute to Arsames, satrap of Egypt, if he allows the rebuilding of their temple.
8. See Josephus, *Antiquities* 12.7–10, which refers to Samaritans and Jews being deported to Egypt, though some Jews did migrate there of their own accord. See also Philo, *On the Embassy to Gaius* 281 for a list of Jewish colonies.
9. See Josephus, *Jewish War* 2.169–71 and his description of Pilate's introduction of iconic standards into Jerusalem.
10. See #607 with respect to Antioch.
11. See Suetonius, *Julius Caesar* 42.3 for Caesar's dissolving of the guilds (*collegia*) 'except those of ancient origin'. M. Pucci ben Zeev identifies the writer of the letter cited above with Octavian, who had taken the name Julius Gaius during his consulship of 43 BCE. See his 'Who Wrote a Letter Concerning the Delian Jews?', *RB* 103 (1996), pp. 237–43.
12. The God of the Jews is here identified as Jupiter Sabazius. Sabazius is an epithet of a god of Anatolian (especially Phrygian) provenance. A connection between Dionysus and the god of the Jews is noted by Tacitus, *Histories* 5.5. The *praetor peregrinus* had authority over foreigners in Rome. For discussion of the expulsion, see Smallwood, *The Jews under Roman Rule*, pp. 128–30.
13. Tacitus also knows of this expulsion. See *Annals* 2.85.
14. Cf. Suetonius, *Augustus* 76 which cites Augustus's letter to Tiberius referring in disparaging terms to fasting like the Jews. Jewish food laws are also mentioned in Epictetus, *Discourses* 1.11.12–13.
15. This expulsion, Suetonius records, was also contemporaneous with the expulsion of the druids. Some scholars have argued that the civil unrest was occasioned by fierce debate between Jews and Jewish-Christians about Christus (Christ), not that the discord was fomented by an agitator called Chestus. See John P. Meier, *A Marginal Jew: Rethinking the Historical Jesus* (New York: Doubleday, 1991), I, pp. 91–92.
16. For a similar view that the keeping of the Sabbath is evidence of the laziness of the Jews, see Tacitus, *Histories* 5.4 (#580). The earliest mention in Greek writers of the practice of

circumcision among the 'Syrians of Palestine' occurs in Herodotus, *Histories* 2.104.

17. Epictetus refers to the 'madness' (i.e. irrationality) of the 'Galilaeans' in *Discourses* 4.7.6.
18. See also #610.
19. According to Josephus, *Antiquities* 14.188, Julius Caesar confirmed these rights in Alexandria.
20. See also #593 concerning Julius Caesar's protection of Jewish civic rights in Parium.
21. So Tcherikover (*CPJ* I, p. 70). Note Tcherikover's excellent review of scholarship on the question up to 1957 (*CPJ* I, pp. 70–74). See also Smallwood, *The Jews under Roman Rule*, pp. 220–56.
22. For discussion see *CPJ* II, pp. 55–107.
23. See #580, #601, and Tacitus, *Histories* 5.4.
24. Cf. #589. For fighting on the Sabbath, see 1 Maccabees 2:29–38, 39–41.
25. Deuteronomy 16:16 obliges all Jewish males to present themselves three times per annum for the feasts of Passover, Weeks (Pentecost) and Tabernacles.
26. Note Jesus' disciples' great wonder at the immensity of Herod's temple (Mark 13:1). With justification Tacitus calls the Jerusalem Temple a citadel (*Histories* 5.12).
27. A stade is roughly equivalent to 1/4 of a mile. A plethron is roughly equivalent to 100 feet.
28. Josephus is a mine of information about the Temple. He reports, e.g., that the gold for the gates had been donated by Philo's brother, Alexander the Alabarch (Josephus, *Jewish War* 5.205–206; Alexander's nephew was Tiberius Alexander, the Prefect). For its layout and splendour, see Josephus, *Jewish War* 5.184–227 (222–24 for the blinding splendour of the edifice); with information regarding the priests and the high priestly vestments in *Jewish War* 5.228–37. There were golden grape vines in the sanctuary with clusters of grapes the size of an adult (*Jewish War* 5.210). Note also Josephus's further remarks on the Temple in *Against Apion* 2.103–109. According to Josephus the edifice was 'doomed' (see *Jewish War* 6.250–53; #186).
29. Philo visited Jerusalem once (see *On Providence* 64). For pilgrimage, see also Acts 2:5, 9–11. Gentiles would also go on pilgrimage to Jerusalem (see *Antiquities* 3.318; John 12:20; Acts 20:4, 16).
30. See also Josephus, *Against Apion* 2.193–98; *Antiquities* 3.224–57; *1 Clement* 41:2–3; Hebrews 10:1–3; *The Epistle to Diognetus* 3; and frequently in the Mishnah.
31. This point is well made by J.J. Petuchowski in 'The Liturgy of the Synagogue: History, Structure, and Contents', in W.S. Green (ed.), *Approaches to Ancient Judaism*, IV (Chico, CA: Scholars Press, 1983), pp. 1-64 (2).
32. Synagogues have also been excavated at Herodium, Masada, Chorazin(?), Gamala and Tarichaea (Magdala). See Stambaugh and Balch, *The New Testament in its Social Environment*, p. 85.
33. See George Foot Moore, *Judaism in the First Centuries of the Christian Era*, I (New York: Schocken, 1971), p. 283. Note also Lee I. Levine, *The Ancient Synagogue* (New Haven: Yale University Press, 2000). Levine argues that the synagogue arose as a focus of Jewish communal identity as a substitute for meetings at the city gate in the towns of Judaea. In alien environments such meetings could not be held in a public thoroughfare.
34. See Acts 6:9; 13:5, 14; 14:1; 15:21. Note also Philo, *Moses* 2.216; Josephus, *Against Apion* 2.175.
35. See, e.g., *Antiquities* 14.213–16 (cited at #593) for Julius Gaius's (Augustus?) letter to the people of Parium upholding the right of Jews to meet unhindered in their synagogue and to conduct themselves as they do even in Rome.
36. Among these high-born 'sympathizers' were the Roman matrons Fulvia, wife of Saturninus (see *Antiquities* 18.81–84; cited at #595), and Flavia Domitilla, wife of the heir appointed by Emperor Domitian (see Dio Cassius, *History of Rome* 67.14.1–3; cited at #103). See also the presence of 'Godfearers' in the third-century CE inscription at Aphrodisias discussed in J. Reynolds and R. Tannenbaum, *Jews and Godfearers at Aphrodisias* (Cambridge: Cambridge Philological Society, 1987).
37. J.A. Fitzmyer advises caution linking eschatology and messianism. See his 'Qumran Messianism', in *idem*, *The Dead Sea Scrolls and Christian Origins* (Grand Rapids: Eerdmans, 2000), pp. 73–110.
38. Note the wealth of Jewish inscriptional material, much of it associated with synagogues, in *CIJ* I, and David Noy, *Jewish Inscriptions of Western Europe* (2 vols.; Cambridge: Cambridge University Press, 1993, 1995).

39. This hypothesis has its complexities. See John Kampen, *The Hasideans and Origins of Pharisaism: A Study in 1 and 2 Maccabees* (Atlanta: Scholars Press, 1988). Kampen argues that the Hasidim were originally scribes, and that the Pharisees derived from them. Freyne, *World of the New Testament*, pp. 110–11, agrees that the Pharisees derived from the Hasidaean movement, and that it was originally priestly but in time became lay in its membership.
40. The term 'pharisee' seems to derive from the Hebrew *paras* (פרשׁ), a root meaning (a) to separate or (b) to expound. The following three theories have been offered: (1) The Pharisees were given this name because they were separatists, eager to maintain the laws of Levitical purity. (2) The Pharisees were named thus because they were expounders of the Law, had a great interest in Scripture and the tradition of its interpretation, and were interested in the codifying of tradition and in the task of applying the Law to contemporary life. To the ordinary people they represented an authoritative voice. (3) 'Pharisee' means a 'Persianizer', the name levelled at them by Sadducees, who perceived that distinctive Pharisaic doctrines such as belief in resurrection and the existence of angels and demons were postexilic borrowings from Persia and were deviations from the scriptural deposit. For the first two suggestions, see Moore, *Judaism*, I, pp. 60–62 (cf. #12, #691–93). T.W. Manson discusses all three suggestions, opting for the third in his *The Servant-Messiah* (Cambridge: Cambridge University Press, 1953), pp. 16–23.
41. Though Josephus does not name the victims, 4QpNah 1 speaks of the Jewish king, the 'young lion', who exacts revenge on the 'seekers after smooth things', a Qumran phrase likely to be a reference to the Pharisees, and hangs men alive. Demetrius had sought an alliance with the 'seekers after smooth things' in order to gain access to Jerusalem.
42. Judas and Matthias were the instigators of the hacking down of the golden eagle on the grounds that the representation compromised the ban on the making of idols (Josephus, *Antiquities* 17.149–67; cf. *Life* 65; Exodus 20:4; Deuteronomy 5:8–9). Both men are described as scholars who were 'unrivalled interpreters of the ancestral laws', and educators of the youth (*Antiquities* 17.149). They appealed to the cause of upholding the ancestral laws of the people.
43. See *Antiquities* 18.4–10. Saddok aided Judas the Gaulanite in his rebellion against the Romans in 6 CE. Judas was the instigator of the Fourth Philosophy, and is referred to by Josephus as Judas the Galilaean in *Antiquities* 18.23 and *Jewish War* 2.118 (see also Acts 5:37).
44. See John 3:1; Acts 5:34, 23:6.
45. In Matthew 22:25 Jesus is questioned regarding a point of Law (the identity of the greatest commandment) by a *nomikos* (i.e. lawyer/scribe). See too Luke 10:25 where a lawyer asks Jesus, 'Who is my neighbour?' after 'testing' Jesus with the question 'How shall I inherit eternal life?' See Luke 5:17 and Acts 5:34 for the phrase 'teacher of the law'.
46. Matthew 23:13; Mark 2:16; Luke 5:17; 15:2. Josephus reports that there were Scribes of the Pharisees and Scribes of the Sadducees (*Jewish War* 6.291).
47. For the rebellion of Theudas, see Josephus, *Antiquities* 20.97–98. The author of Acts errs in placing this rebellion, which was put down by the procurator Fadus (44–46 CE), before that of Judas the Galilaean at the time of the census conducted by Quirinius in 6 CE (note also Luke 2:2, which places the census in the time of the Herod).
48. The derivation of the term is obscure. The term 'Sadducee', it has been argued, may be traced to Zadok, high priest under Solomon (according to 1 Kings 2:35; and in the idealized Temple, Ezekiel 40:46; 43:19; 44:15; 48:11), and whose family provided the high priests down to the advent of Antiochus Epiphanes. See Moore, *Judaism*, I, pp. 68–69. Others have suggested that 'Sadducee' is derived from *tsaddiq* ('righteous') or from *sundikos*, a member of the Council. See Manson, *Servant-Messiah*, pp. 11–20.
49. See Stambaugh and Balch, *The New Testament in its Social Environment*, p. 98.
50. The religion of Jesus was an attack on Temple religion, so Freyne, *World of the New Testament*, p. 102.
51. Annas II was responsible for the judicial murder of James the 'Lord's brother' in 62 CE.
52. Josephus, *Antiquities* 18.11. Cf. Pliny the Elder (*Natural History* 5.72 [#636]). He writes that the Essenes have been conducting their ascetic and celibate lifestyle yet perpetuating their numbers 'through thousands of ages'.

53. Some scholars have identified the prominent Maccabaean era warriors, the Hasidaeans of 1 Maccabees, with the Essenes. The etymology of the terms 'Essene' and 'Hasidaean' are similar. See Hartmut Stegemann, *The Library of Qumran* (Grand Rapids: Eerdmans, 1998), pp. 150–51; Vermes, *Complete Dead Sea Scrolls in English*, p. 18. However, for a critique of this position, see García Martínez, 'Origins', in Martínez and Barrera, *The People of the Dead Sea Scrolls*, pp. 77–96 (especially 86–91). García Martínez argues that the sect had its origins in apocalypticism, and that the writer of the Enochic Book of Dreams (*1 Enoch* 83–90) recounts the origins of the group (to which he belongs) in chapter 90 (cited at #252). See also Part 4 n. 3.
54. See also the prophetic gifts of Judas the Essene reported by Josephus in *Antiquities* 13.311 during the time of Aristobulus I.
55. Philo provides another description of the Essenes in *Hypothetica* (11.1–18), an apologetic work.
56. The Romans seem to have used Qumran as a camp. Roman coins of the period have been found above the destruction layer of ash. De Vaux's hypothesis linking the scrolls in the caves with the ruins at Qumran has been criticized recently and alternatives suggested, e.g. that the ruins are those of a villa. However, these have failed so far to persuade the majority of scholars. The recent discovery of first-century inscribed ostraca in the cemetery wall establishes an even more probable connection between the community of the scrolls and the ruins (see Frank Moore Cross, Jr, and E. Eshel, 'Ostraca from Khirbet Qumran', *IEJ* 47 (1997), pp. 17–28; Vermes, *Complete Dead Sea Scrolls in English*, pp. 21, 596–97). According to Josephus (*Jewish War* 4.451) Vespasian campaigned in Jericho and visited the shores of the Dead Sea in 68 (*Jewish War* 4.477). For a proposed four-stage history of the community, see James H. Charlesworth, 'The Origin and Subsequent History of the Authors of the Dead Sea Scrolls: Four Transitional Phases among the Qumran Essenes', *RevQ* 10 (1981), pp. 213–33. For a critique of the view that Qumran was a villa, see Jodi Magness, 'A Villa at Qumran?', *RevQ* 16 (1994), pp. 397–419, and *idem*, 'Archaeology', in Peter W. Flint and James C. VanderKam (eds.), *The Dead Sea Scrolls after Fifty Years: A Comprehensive Assessment*, I (Leiden: E.J. Brill, 1998), pp. 46–75.
57. Joseph Zias, 'The Cemeteries of Qumran and Celibacy: The Confusion Laid to Rest?', *Dead Sea Discoveries* 7 (2000), pp. 220–53.
58. These Hebrew manuscripts extend knowledge of the biblical text 1000 years earlier than previously existing Hebrew manuscripts. Fragments of all the books of the Hebrew Bible except Esther have been brought to light.
59. The texts that follow are taken from Vermes, *Complete Dead Sea Scrolls in English*. Vermes places references to biblical quotations, italicized Hebrew words and phrases, and glosses in parentheses ( ). Vermes's textual reconstructions are enclosed in square brackets [ ]. Roman numerals in bold type indicate scroll columns. A line of dots indicate lacunae in the text which are incapable of textual reconstruction.
60. The Greek equivalent of the Hebrew phrase translated as 'works of the law' is used by Paul in Romans and Galatians (*erga tou nomou*; see Rom. 3:20, 28; Gal. 2:16; 3:2, 5, 10). For discussion see, e.g., J.G.D. Dunn's two-volume commentary on the letter to the Romans (Waco, TX: Word Books, 1988). Dunn outlines the position he will take in his Commentary in I, p. lxxii. The 'works of the law' are those requirements of the law which initiate and sustain a Jewish identity.
61. In this extract, note that doing what the law demands will 'be reckoned as righteousness' (cf. Genesis 15:6). In other words, doing the works of the law is counted by God as satisfying the condition for bestowing on the doer the status of being a sound covenant partner. Contrast Paul's point of view in Romans 4:1–12. For Paul faith in Christ, not living a life orientated to the law, will be reckoned as righteousness. Paul claims that doing the required works of the law would be tantamount to earning the righteousness that Paul asserts can come only by gift (v. 4). Such people might boast of their accomplishment (v. 2). Moreover, if righteousness only came through doing Jewish works, that would imply that those 'without works', i.e. Gentiles whose lives are not orientated to doing the law, would be excluded from receiving righteousness. Yet, Paul argues, scripture supports the view that righteousness can be bestowed on those with-

out works, even on the uncircumcised (such as Abraham) (vv. 5–12).

62. Note the assertion of 'faith in the Teacher of Righteousness' as essential for eschatological felicity. Contrast Paul in Romans 1:17, citing Genesis 15:6, in which the righteous one will live by confidence (or faith) in the divine promise.
63. Contrast the teaching of Jesus on the Sabbath in Matthew 12:9–14 with the teaching here.
64. The Hebrew preposition translated by Vermes 'beside' and 'close to' in ll. 2, 4 and 6 could be translated 'as'.
65. In addition to the texts cited here, note 1QSa 2.8–9 and 1QSb 4.26. Note Colossians 2:18 in which the 'worship of angels' is likely to mean participating in the worship offered by the angels to God rather than the worship offered to angels as is often supposed. The Qumran Songs of the Sabbath Sacrifice record the hymns of praise offered by the angels in the heavenly cult, access to which the men of the community believed they shared.
66. See, e.g., 1 Corinthians 11:10 (see discussion in Part 7 n. 9) and Hebrews 12:22–23.
67. This scroll is much indebted to the vision of God's throne chariot (*merkavah*) in Ezekiel 1; 3:12–15, 22–24; 8:1–4; 10:1–22; and 43:1–7. This vision gave rise to an extensive literature in which a mystic ascended to heaven to see the dwellings (palaces; *hekaloth*) of God culminating with a vision of the *merkavah*. See, e.g., *3 Enoch*. Cf. 2 Corinthians 12:3–4.
68. Rather than the Messiah raising the dead in this scroll, it is more likely that it is God who will do this.
69. See #152; Josephus, *Antiquities* 14.420–30.
70. Bandits were crucified with Jesus. The Fourth Gospel terms Barabbas a bandit (John 18:40). He had committed murder in an insurrection (Mark 15:7; Luke 23:19), and was clearly popular with the mob, as each of the Gospels attests.
71. See R.A. Horsley with John S. Hanson, *Bandits, Prophets, and Messiahs: Popular Movements at the Time of Jesus* (San Francisco: Harper & Row, 1988), pp. 48–87.
72. See further Smallwood, *The Jews under Roman Rule*, pp. 163–64, 184.
73. See Deuteronomy 11:29; 27:12–13; Josephus, *Antiquities* 11.321.
74. See Josephus, *Antiquities* 12.257–64. In a letter sent to Antiochus Epiphanes, Josephus reports the Samaritans repudiating any claim to Jewish ethnicity. They argue that in fact they are 'Sidonians' and colonists of the Medes and Persians not Jews.
75. In Genesis 14:18, Melchizedek was, of course, king of Salem (Jerusalem). The fragments of Pseudo-Eupolemos are conveniently included in *OTP* II, pp. 880–82.
76. For the Jewish community on Delos, see 1 Maccabees 15:23; Josephus, *Antiquities* 14.213–16 (cited at #593), 231–32.
77. Freyne, *World of the New Testament*, p. 162. While Jesus visited the cosmopolitan towns of Galilee, there is no record of him visiting Sepphoris or Tiberias, civic foundations after the Greek style.
78. See Josephus, *Antiquities* 18.15 for the urban base of the Pharisees.
79. The word for child (*pais*) was also used of servants and slaves. There is no mention of converts to the movement acquiring 'fathers' in Mark 3:31–35 and 10:28–30, though they will gain brothers, sisters and mothers (see also Matthew 23:9). See Stambaugh and Balch, *The New Testament in its Social Environment*, p. 106.
80. In this regard, note David C. Verner, *The Household of God: The Social World of the Pastoral Epistles* (SBLDS, 71; Chico, CA: Scholars Press, 1983).
81. See Freyne, *The World of the New Testament*, pp. 185–87.
82. See J. Christiaan Beker, *Paul the Apostle* (Philadelphia: Fortress Press, 1980), pp. 328–47.
83. Here I have in mind the experience of the members of the Johannine community in relation to the synagogue. The Fourth Gospel reveals something of the tension issuing in excommunication and violence that was beginning to surface by virtue of the fact that believers acknowledged Christ as Lord and Messiah (see, e.g., John 9; 16:1–4). The Gospel is written on two levels—it is the story of the ministry of Jesus as well as a reflection on the part of the evangelist of events and issues in the community's life. See J. Louis Martyn, *History and Theology in the Fourth Gospel* (Nashville: Abingdon Press, 1968).
84. See Acts 11:19–21; Freyne, *World of the New Testament*, p. 171. It would appear that those who preached the gospel in Antioch were

Greek-speaking Jews 'from Cyprus and Cyrene'. It was they who, on arriving in Antioch, preached to the 'Hellenists' (NRSV). Elsewhere the term is usually taken to mean Jews who spoke Greek and not a semitic language, though the implication of the passage is that these 'Hellenists' were not Jews in fact (see v. 19). Not surprisingly the Greek manuscript tradition also strongly attests 'Greeks' at this juncture. For an extensive discussion, see Bruce M. Metzger, *A Textual Commentary on the Greek New Testament* (Stuttgart: United Bible Societies, 1975), pp. 386–89. There is no doubt that, according to Luke, the action of the preachers in Antioch marked a new strategy in the early Christian mission.

85. Freyne, *World of the New Testament*, p. 172.
86. The issue of protest is highlighted in Mark Taylor's provocative article, 'The Executed God: The Way of the Cross in Lockdown America', *Princeton Seminary Bulletin* 21 (2000), pp. 301–323.
87. See Richard Bauckham, *James: Wisdom of James, Disciple of Jesus the Sage* (London/New York: Routledge, 1999).
88. Freyne, *World of the New Testament*, p. 172.
89. See R. Bultmann, *Theology of the New Testament*, I (New York: Charles Scribner's Sons, 1951), p. 121.
90. Stambaugh and Balch, *The New Testament in its Social Environment*, p. 138. Although 'Saviour' is used of Jesus by Paul in Philippians 3:20 (c. 60 CE), it is more common in writings usually dated late in the first-century CE. See, e.g., Titus 1:3, 4; 2:10, 13; 3:4, 6; and five times in 2 Peter.
91. However, note 1 Corinthians 11:2–16. See also the discussion of the limits beyond which Paul was not prepared to countenance feminine freedom and independence in Brown, *The Body and Society*, pp. 44–57.
92. Matthew, writing for a community that saw itself more in continuity with Judaism, omits the crucial statement in parentheses in his presentation of what defiles a person in Matthew 15:1–20. The issue of food was a complex one for New Testament communities. See #332–35.
93. See Judge, *Social Pattern*, pp. 60, 76. See also L. Michael White, 'Finding the Ties that Bind: Issues from Social Description', *Semeia* 56 (1992), pp. 3–22 and *idem*, 'Social Networks: Theoretical Orientation and Historical Applications', *Semeia* 56 (1992), pp. 23–36.
94. See, e.g., Aristotle, *Politics* book 1, extracts from which are to be found at #403–405. For modern scholarly comment, see David L. Balch, *Let Wives be Submissive: The Household Code in 1 Peter* (SBLMS, 26; Chico, CA: Scholars Press, 1981); David L. Balch and Carolyn Osiek, *Families in the New Testament World: Households and House Churches* (Louisville: John Knox, 1997).
95. See Ephesians 5:22–6:9 (cited at #677); Colossians 3:18–4:1; 1 Timothy 2:8–15; 5:1–2; 6:1–2; Titus 2:1–10; 3:1–2; 1 Peter 2:18–3:7.
96. See Margaret Y. MacDonald, *The Pauline Churches: A Socio-historical Study of Institutionalization in the Pauline and Deutero-Pauline Writings* (SNTSMS, 60; Cambridge: Cambridge University Press, 1988).
97. Cf. Galatians 3:28 (#668) and Paul's concerns about the need for women to conform in their dress to social convention in 1 Corinthians 11:2–16.
98. See 1 Corinthians 11:23–26; Ignatius, *Epistle to the Smyrnaeans* 7.1.
99. For a cogent attempt to distinguish the original text from Christian redaction see Meier, *A Marginal Jew*, I, pp. 59–69.
100. Ananus was promptly deposed by Agrippa II. Josephus's note that James was the brother of Jesus 'who was called the Christ' appears to be exactly what he wrote.
101. Note also Paul's affirming of the nearness of the parousia in 1 Corinthians 7:29–31; 15:51; Romans 13:11.
102. Immortality/resurrection is absent in the second-century BCE work Sirach, which affirms the older view that there is no life after death. Note 14:12–19; 38:16–23. In 30:4, the father lives on in his son; in 44:13–15 the godly live on in their continuing progeny.
103. See *OTP* II, p. 646.
104. See also topic 4.1 and the survey of apocalypses.
105. For a brief discussion, see John J. Collins, *Apocalypticism in the Dead Sea Scrolls* (London/New York: Routledge, 1997), pp. 87–89.
106. 'Angra Mainyu' denotes the evil principle opposed to the supreme deity Ahuramazda. The Daevas were tribespeople who opposed

the Zoroastrians and worshipped Daeva. For the concept of blessedness after death in an early text (sixth century BCE) see also #12.

107. See O. Cullmann, *New Testament Christology* (London: SCM Press, 1959), pp. 111–36.
108. See also *Psalms of Solomon* 18 (*OTP* II, pp. 669–70) cited at #294.
109. See also, *inter alia*, *Testament of Reuben* 6.8; *Testament of Naphtali* 5.1–5.
110. See P. Keresztes, 'The Imperial Government and the Christian Church, I: From Nero to the Severi', *ANRW* 2.23.1 (1979), pp. 247–315.
111. Gallio, the pro-consul of Achaea in 50/51 CE, was the brother of Seneca, the philosopher.
112. See Klaus Wengst, *Pax Romana and the Peace of Jesus Christ* (Philadelphia: Fortress Press, 1987), pp. 72–89 (Paul), 118–35 (book of Revelation).
113. See also Eusebius, *Ecclesiastical History* 2.25.5–8.
114. Compare the accounts of the trial of Jesus in the Gospels. Luke 23:26 has the Jewish accusers of Jesus, not the soldiers under Pilate, lead him away to execution. See further discussion of Luke–Acts and the Jews in Jack T. Sanders, *The Jews in Luke–Acts* (Philadelphia: Fortress Press, 1987); Harding, 'On the Historicity of Acts', pp. 518–38; and more generally with respect to the Gospels and early Christian literature, John Dominic Crossan, *Who Killed Jesus?* (San Francisco: HarperSanFrancisco, 1995).
115. Dio Cassius also records this persecution (see #103). However, he does not specify that Flavius Clemens and Domitilla (who, Dio reports, was Clemen's wife) were Christians but that they were charged with 'atheism' because, like others, they had drifted into 'Jewish ways'. According to Suetonius, *Domitian* 15, Flavius Clemens was a man of 'contemptible laziness' (because he kept the Sabbath?).

Bibliography

Primary Sources

Apostolic Fathers, I (LCL, 24; trans. Kirsopp Lake; Cambridge, MA: Harvard University Press, 1912).
Appian, *History of Rome*, I–IV (LCL, 2, 3, 4, 5; trans. Harold White; Cambridge, MA: Harvard University Press, 1912, 1912, 1913, 1913).
Apuleius, *The Golden Ass* (trans. W. Adlington; rev. S. Gaselee; Cambridge, MA: Harvard University Press, 1915).
Aristotle, *Works*, XVI (LCL, 317; trans. H. Rackham; Cambridge, MA: Harvard University Press, 1937).
—*Works*, XXI (LCL, 264; trans. H. Rackham; Cambridge, MA: Harvard University Press, 1944).
—*Works*, XXII (LCL, 193; trans. J.H. Freese; Cambridge, MA: Harvard University Press, 1926).
—*Works*, XXIII (LCL, 199; trans. W. Rhys Roberts; Cambridge, MA: Harvard University Press, 1932).
Arrian, *Anabasis of Alexander*, I (LCL, 236; trans. P.A. Brunt; Cambridge, MA: Harvard University Press, 1976).
—*Anabasis of Alexander*, II (LCL, 269; trans. E. Iliff Robson; Cambridge, MA: Harvard University Press, 1933).
Athenaeus, *Deipnosophistae*, III (LCL, 224; trans. Charles Burton Gulick; Cambridge, MA: Harvard University Press, 1929).
Augustus, *Res Gestae Divi Augusti* (introduction and commentary P.A. Brunt and J.M. Moore; Oxford: Oxford University Press, 1967).
Austin, M.M., *The Hellenistic World from Alexander to the Roman Conquest: A Selection of Ancient Sources in Translation* (Cambridge: Cambridge University Press, 1981).
Bailey, C., *Epicurus: The Extant Remains* (Oxford: Oxford University Press, 1926).
Barrett, C.K., *The New Testament Background: Selected Documents* (New York: Harper & Row, 2nd edn, 1987; rev. edn, 1989).
Betz, H.D., *Greek Magical Papyri in Translation* (Chicago: Chicago University Press, 2nd edn, 1992).
Bevan, E., *Later Greek Religion* (London: Dent, 1927).
Boring, M.E., K. Berger and C. Colpe (eds.), *Hellenistic Commentary to the New Testament* (Nashville: Abingdon Press, 1995).
Caesar, Julius, *Civil Wars* (LCL, 39; trans. A.G. Peskett; Cambridge, MA: Harvard University Press, 1914).
Cartlidge, D.R., and David L. Dungan (eds.), *Documents for the Study of the Gospels* (Minneapolis: Fortress Press, 1994).
Cato and Varro, *On Agriculture* (LCL, 283; trans. Harrison Boyd Ash and William Davis Hooper; Cambridge, MA: Harvard University Press, 1935).
Catullus, *Poems* (LCL, 6; trans. Francis Warre Cornish; Cambridge, MA: Harvard University Press, 1913).
Charlesworth, J.H. (ed.), *Old Testament Pseudepigrapha* (Garden City, NY: Doubleday, 1983, 1985).
Cicero, *Works*, VII (LCL, 221; trans. L.H.G. Greenwood; Cambridge, MA: Harvard University Press, 1928).
—*Works*, X (LCL, 324; trans. Louis E. Ford; Cambridge, MA: Harvard University Press, 1937).
—*Works*, XI (LCL, 158; trans. N.H. Watts; Cambridge, MA: Harvard University Press, 1923).
—*Works*, XVI (LCL, 213; trans. Clinton Walker Keyes; Cambridge, MA: Harvard University Press, 1928).
—*Works*, XIX (LCL, 268; trans. H. Rackham; Cambridge, MA: Harvard University Press, 1933).
—Works, XXII (LCL, 7; trans. E.O. Winstedt; Cambridge, MA: Harvard University Press, 1912).
—*Works*, XXIV (LCL, 97; trans. E.O. Winstedt; Cambridge, MA: Harvard University Press, 1918).

—*Works*, XXV (LCL, 205; trans. W. Glynn Williams; Cambridge, MA: Harvard University Press, 1927).
—*Works*, XXVII (LCL, 230; trans. W. Glynn Williams; Cambridge, MA: Harvard University Press, 1926).
—*Works*, XXVIII (LCL, 462; trans. W. Glynn Williams, M. Cary and Mary Isobel Henderson; Cambridge, MA: Harvard University Press, 1972).
Cross, F.M., and E. Eshel, 'Ostraca from Khirbet Qumran', *IEJ* 47 (1997), pp. 17–28.
Curtius, *History of Alexander*, II (LCL, 369; trans. John C. Rolfe; Cambridge, MA: Harvard University Press, 1946).
Deissmann, A., *Light from the Ancient East* (London: Hodder & Stoughton, 4th edn, 1927).
Demosthenes, *Works*, VI (LCL, 351; trans. A.T. Murray; Cambridge, MA: Harvard University Press, 1939).
Dio Cassius, *Roman History*, I (LCL, 32; trans. Earnest Cary; Cambridge, MA: Harvard University Press, 1914).
—*Roman History*, V (LCL, 82; trans. Earnest Cary; Cambridge, MA: Harvard University Press, 1917).
—*Roman History*, VI (LCL, 83; trans. Earnest Cary; Cambridge, MA: Harvard University Press, 1917).
—*Roman History*, VII (LCL, 175; trans. Earnest Cary; Cambridge, MA: Harvard University Press, 1924).
—*Roman History*, VIII (LCL, 176; trans. Earnest Cary; Cambridge, MA: Harvard University Press, 1925).
Diodorus Siculus, *Histories*, VIII (LCL, 422; trans. C. Bradford Welles; Cambridge, MA: Harvard University Press, 1963).
Diogenes Laertius, *Lives of Eminent Philosophers*, II (LCL, 185; trans. R.D. Hicks; Cambridge, MA: Harvard University Press, 1925).
Epictetus, *Discourses*, I (LCL, 131; trans. W.A. Oldfather; Cambridge, MA: Harvard University Press, 1925).
—*Discourses*, II (LCL, 218; trans. W.A. Oldfather; Cambridge, MA: Harvard University Press, 1928).
Eusebius, *Ecclesiastical History*, I (LCL, 153; trans. Kirsopp Lake; Cambridge, MA: Harvard University Press, 1926).
Feldman, L.H., and M. Reinhold, *Jewish Life and Thought among Greeks and Romans: Primary Readings* (Minneapolis: Fortress Press, 1996).
Freedman, H., and M. Simon (eds.), *Midrash Rabbah, Lamentations* (London/New York: Soncino, 1983).
Gellius Aulus, *Attic Nights*, II (LCL, 200; trans. John C. Rolfe; Cambridge, MA: Harvard University Press, 1927).
—*Attic Nights*, III (LCL, 212; trans. John C. Rolfe; Cambridge, MA: Harvard University Press, 1927).
Grenfell, B.P., and A.S. Hunt, *The Oxyrhynchus Papyri, Part I* (London: Egypt Exploration Society, 1898).
—*Oxyrhynchus Papyri, Part II* (London: Egypt Exploration Fund, 1899).
Grenfell, B.P., A.S. Hunt and C.C. Edgar, *Oxyrhynchus Papyri, Part IV* (London: Egypt Exploration Society, 1904).
Grenfell, B.P., A.S. Hunt and J.G. Smyly, *Tebtunis Papyri* (London: Egypt Exploration Fund, 1902).
Gropp, D.M. *et al.*, *Wadi Daliyeh II and Qumran Cave 4* (DJD, 28; Oxford: Clarendon Press, 2001)
Heisserer, A.J., *Alexander the Great and the Greeks: The Epigraphic Evidence* (Norman, OK: University of Oklahoma, 1980).
Herodotus, *Histories*, I (LCL, 117; trans. A.D. Godley; Cambridge, MA: Harvard University Press, 1926).
—*Histories*, II (LCL, 118; trans. A.D. Godley; Cambridge, MA: Harvard University Press, 1938).
Horace, *Odes and Epodes* (LCL, 33; trans. C.E. Bennett; Cambridge, MA: Harvard University Press, 1927).
Horsley, G.H.R., *New Documents Illustrating Early Christianity* (Macquarie University: Ancient History Documentary Research Centre, 1981).
—*New Documents Illustrating Early Christianity*, II (Macquarie University: Ancient History Documentary Research Centre, 1982).

—*New Documents Illustrating Early Christianity*, III (Macquarie University: Ancient History Documentary Research Centre, 1983).

—*New Documents Illustrating Early Christianity*, IV (Macquarie University: Ancient History Documentary Research Centre, 1987).

Hunt, A.S., *The Oxyrhynchus Papyri, Part VIII* (London: Egypt Exploration Society, 1911).

Isocrates, *Works*, I (LCL, 209; trans. George Norlin; Cambridge, MA: Harvard University Press, 1928).

—*Works*, III (LCL, 373; trans. LaRue Van Hook; Cambridge, MA: Harvard University Press, 1945).

Josephus, *Works*, I (LCL, 186; trans. H.St.J. Thackeray; Cambridge, MA: Harvard University Press, 1926).

—*Works*, II (LCL, 203; trans. H.St.J. Thackeray; Cambridge, MA: Harvard University Press, 1927).

—*Works*, III (LCL, 210; trans. H.St.J. Thackeray; Cambridge, MA: Harvard University Press, 1928).

—*Works*, IV (LCL, 242; trans. H.St.J. Thackeray; Cambridge, MA: Harvard University Press, 1930).

—*Works*, V (LCL, 281; trans. H.St.J. Thackeray; Cambridge, MA: Harvard University Press, 1934).

—*Works*, VI (LCL, 326; trans. Ralph Marcus; Cambridge, MA: Harvard University Press, 1937).

—*Works*, VII (LCL, 365; trans. Ralph Marcus; Cambridge, MA: Harvard University Press, 1937).

—*Works*, VIII (LCL, 410; trans. Ralph Marcus and Allen Wikgren; Cambridge, MA: Harvard University Press, 1963).

—*Works*, IX (LCL, 433; trans. L.H. Feldman; Cambridge, MA: Harvard University Press, 1965).

—*Works*, X (LCL, 456; trans. L.H. Feldman; Cambridge, MA: Harvard University Press, 1965).

Juvenal, *Satires* (LCL, 91; trans. G.G. Ramsay; Cambridge, MA: Harvard University Press, 1940).

Knox, A.D. (ed.), *Herodas: Mimes and Fragments* (Cambridge: Cambridge University Press, 1922).

Layton, B., *The Gnostic Scriptures* (Garden City, NY: Doubleday, 1987).

Lewis, N. (ed.), *Judean Desert Studies: The Documents from the Bar Kokhba Period in the Cave of Letters* (Jerusalem: Israel Exploration Society, 1989).

Lewis, N., and M. Reinhold, *Roman Civilization: Sourcebook I, The Republic* (New York: Harper & Row, 1966).

—*Roman Civilization: Sourcebook II, The Empire* (New York: Harper & Row, 1966).

Livy, *History of Rome*, I (LCL, 114; trans. B.O. Foster; Cambridge, MA: Harvard University Press, 1936).

—*History of Rome*, XI (LCL, 313; trans. Evan T. Sage; Cambridge, MA: Harvard University Press, 1936).

Llewelyn, S.R., with R.A. Kearsley, *New Documents Illustrating Early Christianity*, VII (Macquarie University: Ancient History Documentary Research Centre, 1994).

Llewelyn, S.R., *New Documents Illustrating Early Christianity*, VIII (Macquarie University: Ancient History Documentary Research Centre, 1998).

Lucian, *Works*, I (LCL, 14; trans. A.M. Harmon; Cambridge, MA: Harvard. University Press, 1913).

Lucian, *Works*, III (LCL, 130; trans. A.M. Harmon; Cambridge, MA: Harvard University Press, 1921).

Lucretius, *On the Nature of the Universe* (LCL, 181; trans. W.H.D. Rouse; Cambridge, MA: Harvard University Press, 1937).

Maher, M., *Targum Pseudo-Jonathan: Genesis* (Edinburgh: T. & T. Clark, 1992).

Martial, *Epigrams*, I (LCL, 94; trans. D.R. Shackleton Bailey; Cambridge, MA: Harvard University Press, 1993).

—*Epigrams*, II (LCL, 95; trans. D.R. Shackleton Bailey; Cambridge, MA: Harvard University Press, 1993).

—*Epigrams*, II (LCL; trans. Walter C.A Ker; Cambridge, MA: Harvard University Press, 1920).

Mills, L.H. (trans.), *The Zend Avesta*, in F. Max Müller (ed.), *The Sacred Books of the East*, XXXI (Oxford: Oxford University Press, 1887).

Montefiore, C.G., and H. Loewe, *A Rabbinic Anthology* (New York: Schocken Books, 1974).

Neusner, J., *The Mishnah: A New Translation* (New Haven: Yale University Press, 1988).

New Revised Standard Edition Bible, copyright 1989, Division of Christian Education of the National Council of the Churches of Christ in the United States of America. Used by permission. All rights reserved.

Nock, A.D., *Early Gentile Christianity and its Hellenistic Background* (New York: Harper & Row, 1964).
Noy, D., *Jewish Inscriptions of Western Europe* (2 vols.; Cambridge: Cambridge University Press, 1993, 1995).
Ovid, *Works*, I (LCL, 41; trans. Grant Showerman; Cambridge, MA: Harvard University Press, 1977).
—*Works*, II (LCL, 232; trans. J.R. Mozely; Cambridge, MA: Harvard University Press, 1979).
Petronius, *The Satyricon* (LCL, 15; trans. Michael Heseltine and E.H. Warmington; Cambridge, MA: Harvard University Press, 1969).
Philo, *Works*, I (LCL, 226; trans. F.H. Colson and G.H. Whitaker; Cambridge, MA: Harvard University Press, 1929).
—*Works*, IV (LCL, 261; trans. F.H. Colson and G.H. Whitaker; Cambridge, MA: Harvard University Press, 1932).
—*Works*, VI (LCL, 289; trans. F.H. Colson and G.H. Whitaker; Cambridge, MA: Harvard University Press, 1935).
—*Works*, VII (LCL, 320; trans. F.H. Colson and G.H. Whitaker; Cambridge, MA: Harvard University Press, 1935).
—*Works*, IX (LCL, 363; trans. F.H. Colson; Cambridge, MA: Harvard University Press, 1941).
—*Works*, X (LCL, 379; trans. F.H. Colson; Cambridge, MA: Harvard University Press, 1962).
Pliny the Elder, *Natural History*, II (LCL, 352; trans. R. Rackham; Cambridge, MA: Harvard University Press, 1942).
—*Natural History*, VIII (LCL, 418; trans. H. Rackham; Cambridge, MA: Harvard University Press, 1963).
—*Natural History*, IX (LCL, 394; trans. H. Rackham; Cambridge, MA: Harvard University Press, 1952).
Pliny, *Letters and Panegyricus*, I (LCL, 55; trans. Betty Radice; Cambridge, MA: Harvard University Press, 1969).
—*Letters and Panegyricus*, II (LCL, 59; trans. Betty Radice; Cambridge, MA: Harvard University Press, 1969).
Plutarch, *Lives*, II (LCL, 47; trans. Bernadotte Perrin; Cambridge, MA: Harvard University Press, 1914).
—*Lives*, IV (LCL, 80; trans. Bernadotte Perrin; Cambridge, MA: Harvard University Press, 1916).
—*Lives*, VII (LCL, 99; trans. Bernadotte Perrin; Cambridge, MA: Harvard University Press, 1919).
—*Moralia*, II (LCL, 222; trans. F.C. Babbitt; Cambridge, MA: Harvard University Press, 1928).
Polybius, *Histories*, I (LCL, 128; trans. W.R. Paton; Cambridge, MA: Harvard University Press, 1922).
—*Histories*, II (LCL, 137; trans. W.R. Paton; Cambridge, MA: Harvard University Press, 1922).
—*Histories*, III (LCL, 138 [?]; trans. W.R. Paton; Cambridge, MA: Harvard University Press, 1923).
—*Histories*, IV (LCL, 159 [?]; trans. W.R. Paton; Cambridge, MA: Harvard. University Press, 1925).
—*Histories*, V (LCL, 160; trans. W.R. Paton; Cambridge, MA: Harvard University Press, 1926).
—*Histories*, VI (LCL, 161; trans. W.R. Paton; Cambridge, MA: Harvard University Press, 1927).
Pritchard, J.B., *Ancient Near Eastern Texts Relating to the Old Testament* (Princeton: Princeton University Press, 1950, 1955).
Propertius, *Elegies* (LCL, 18; trans. H.E. Butler; Cambridge, MA: Harvard University Press, 1933).
Quintilian, *Institutio Oratoria*, I (LCL, 124; trans. H.E. Butler, Cambridge, MA: Harvard University Press, 1920).
Remains of Old Latin, III, IV (LCL, 329, 357; trans. E.H. Warmington; Cambridge, MA: Harvard University Press, 1938, 1940).
Reynolds, J., and R. Tannenbaum, *Jews and Godfearers at Aphrodisias* (Cambridge: Cambridge Philological Society, 1987).
Roberts, A., and J. Donaldson (eds.), *Ante-Nicene Fathers*, I (Grand Rapids: Eerdmans, 1987 repr. of the 1885–96 edn published by T. & T. Clark).
Sallust, *Works* (LCL, 116; trans. J.C. Rolfe; Cambridge, MA: Harvard University Press, 1931).
Scriptores Historiae Augustae, I (LCL, 139; trans. David Magie; Cambridge, MA: Harvard University Press, 1921).

Seneca the Elder, *Controversiae and Suasoriae*, I (LCL, 463; trans. M. Winterbottom; Cambridge, MA: Harvard University Press, 1974).
—*Controversiae and Suasoriae*, II (LCL, 464; trans. M. Winterbottom; Cambridge, MA: Harvard University Press, 1974).
Seneca, *Works*, I (LCL, 214; trans. J.W. Basore; Cambridge, MA: Harvard University Press, 1928).
—*Works*, II (LCL, 254; trans. J.W. Basore; Cambridge, MA: Harvard University Press, 1932).
—*Works*, IV (LCL, 75; trans. Richard M. Gummere; Cambridge, MA: Harvard University Press, 1917).
—*Works*, V (LCL, 76; trans. Richard M. Gummere; Cambridge, MA: Harvard University Press, 1920).
—*Works*, VI (LCL, 77; trans. Richard M Gummere; Cambridge, MA: Harvard University Press, 1925).
Singer, S. (trans.), *The Authorised Daily Prayer Book* (London: Eyre & Spottiswoode, 10th edn, 1916).
Smith, S. (ed.), *Babylonian Historical Texts* (Hildesheim: Georg Olms, 1975).
Stern, M., *Greek and Latin Authors on Jews and Judaism*, I (Jerusalem: Israel Academy of Sciences and Humanities, 1976).
Strabo, *Geography*, VII (LCL, 241; trans. Horace Leonard Jones; Cambridge, MA: Harvard University Press, 1983).
Suetonius, *The Twelve Caesars*, I (LCL, 31; trans. John C. Rolfe; Cambridge, MA: Harvard University Press, 1951).
—*The Twelve Caesars*, II (LCL, 38; trans. John C. Rolfe; Cambridge, MA: Harvard University Press, 1914).
Tacitus, *Works*, I (LCL, 35; trans. M. Hutton; Cambridge, MA: Harvard University Press, 1914).
—*Works*, II (LCL, 111; trans. Clifford H. Moore; Cambridge, MA: Harvard University Press, 1925).
—*Works*, III (LCL, 249; trans. Clifford H. Moore and John Jackson; Cambridge, MA: Harvard University Press, 1931).
—*Works*, IV (LCL, 249; trans. John Jackson; Cambridge, MA: Harvard University Press, 1937).
—*Works*, V (LCL, 322; trans. John Jackson; Cambridge, MA: Harvard University Press, 1937).
Tcherikover, Viktor A., and A. Fuks (eds.), *Corpus Papyrorum Judaicarum* (vols. 1, 2; Cambridge, MA: Harvard University Press, 1957, 1960).
Thucydides, *Peloponnesian War*, I (LCL, 108; trans. Charles Forster Smith; Cambridge, MA: Harvard University Press, 1928).
Vermes, G., *The Complete Dead Sea Scrolls in English* (Harmondsworth: Penguin Books, 1998).
Virgil, *Works*, I (LCL, 63; trans. H. Rushton Fairclough; Cambridge, MA: Harvard University Press, 1935).
West, E.W. (trans.), *The Pahlavi Texts*, in F. Max Müller (ed.), *The Sacred Books of the East*, V (Oxford: Oxford University Press, 1880).
Whitaker, M., *Jews and Christians: Graeco-Roman Views* (Cambridge: Cambridge University Press, 1984).
Xenophon, *Works*, II (LCL, 89; trans. Carleton L. Bownson; Cambridge, MA: Harvard University Press, 1921).
Yadin, Y., *Bar-Kokhba* (London: Weidenfeld & Nicolson, 1971).

Secondary Sources

Aune, D.E., *The New Testament in its Literary Environment* (Philadelphia: Westminster Press, 1986).
Balch, D.L., *Let Wives be Submissive: The Household Code in 1 Peter* (SBLMS, 26; Chico, CA: Scholars Press, 1981).
Balch, D.L., and C. Osiek, *Families in the New Testament World: Households and House Churches* (Louisville: John Knox, 1997).
Barton, S.C., and G.H.R. Horsley, 'A Hellenistic Cult Group and the New Testament Churches', *JAC* 24 (1981), pp. 7–41.
Bauckham, R., *James: Wisdom of James, Disciple of Jesus the Sage* (London/New York: Routledge, 1999).
Beacham, R.C., *Spectacle Entertainments of Early Imperial Rome* (New Haven/London: Yale University Press, 1999).
Beker, J.C., *Paul the Apostle* (Philadelphia: Fortress Press, 1980).

Brown, P.R.L., *The Body and Society: Men, Women, and Sexual Renunciation in Early Christianity* (New York: Columbia University, 1988).
Bultmann, R., *Theology of the New Testament*, I (New York: Charles Scribner's Sons, 1951).
Campbell, B.L., *Honor, Shame, and the Rhetoric of 1 Peter* (Atlanta: Scholars Press, 1998).
Carcopino, J., *Daily Life in Ancient Rome* (ICC; Harmondsworth: Penguin Books, 1956).
Charles, R.H., *Revelation* (2 vols.; Edinburgh: T. & T. Clark, 1920).
Charlesworth, J.H., 'The Origin and Subsequent History of the Authors of the Dead Sea Scrolls: Four Transitional Phases among the Qumran Essenes', *RevQ* 10 (1981), pp. 213–33.
—'Jewish Interest in Astrology during the Hellenistic and Roman Period', *ANRW* 2.20.2 (1987), pp. 926–50.
Charlesworth, J.H. (ed.), *The Lord's Prayer and Other Prayer Texts from the Greco-Roman Era* (Valley Forge, PA: Trinity Press International, 1994).
Collins, J.J., *Apocalypticism in the Dead Sea Scrolls* (London/New York: Routledge, 1997).
Countryman, L.W., *The Rich Christian in the Age of the Early Empire: Contradictions and Accommodations* (New York/Toronto: Edwin Mellen, 1980).
Crossan, J.D., *The Historical Jesus: The Life of a Mediterranean Jewish Peasant* (San Francisco: HarperCollins, 1991).
—*Who Killed Jesus?* (San Francisco: HarperSanFrancisco, 1995).
Cullmann, O., *New Testament Christology* (London: SCM Press, 1959).
Danker, F.W., *Benefactor: Epigraphic Study of a Graeco-Roman and New Testament Semantic Field* (St Louis: Clayton, 1982).
Desilva, D.H., *Despising the Shame: Honor Discourse and Community Maintenance in the Epistle to the Hebrews* (Atlanta: Scholars Press, 1996).
Dodd, C.H., *The Apostolic Preaching and its Developments* (London: Hodder & Stoughton, 1936).
Downing, F.G., *Christ and the Cynics: Jesus and Other Radical Preachers in First-Century Tradition* (JSOT Manuals, 4; Sheffield: Sheffield Academic Press, 1988).
Dunn, J.G.D., *Romans* (2 vols.;Waco, TX: Word Books, 1988).
Ferguson, E., *Backgrounds of Early Christianity* (Grand Rapids: Eerdmans, 1987).
Fitzmyer, J.A., 'A Feature of Qumran Angelology and the Angels of 1 Cor 11:10', *NTS* 4 (1957–58), pp. 48–58.
—'The Languages of Palestine in the First Century A.D.', in *idem, A Wandering Aramean: Collected Aramaic Essays* (SBLMS, 25; Chico, CA: Scholars Press, 1979), pp. 29–56.
—'Qumran Messianism', in *idem, The Dead Sea Scrolls and Christian Origins* (Grand Rapids: Eerdmans, 2000), pp. 73–110.
Flusser, D., 'The Magnificat, the Benedictus and the War Scroll', in *idem, Judaism and the Origins of Christianity* (Jerusalem: Magnes Press, 1988), pp. 126–49.
Freyne, S., *The World of the New Testament* (Wilmington, DE: Michael Glazier, 1980).
García Martínez, F., 'The Origins of the Essene Movement and of the Qumran Sect', in Florentino García Martínez and Julio Trebolle Barrera, *The People of the Dead Sea Scrolls: Their Writings, Beliefs and Practices* (Leiden: E.J. Brill, 1995), pp. 77–96.
Gibbon, E., *The History of the Decline and Fall of the Roman Empire* (London: Folio Society, 1983).
Goodman, M., 'The First Jewish Revolt: Social Conflict and the Problem of Debt', *JJS* 33 (1982), pp. 417–27.
—*The Ruling Classes of Judaea: The Origins of the Jewish Revolt Against Rome A.D. 66–70* (Cambridge: Cambridge University Press, 1987).
Goulder, M.D., *Midrash and Lection in Matthew* (London: SPCK, 1974).
Gowing, A.M., *The Triumphal Narratives of Appian and Cassius Dio* (Ann Arbor: University of Michigan Press, 1992).
Grant, M., *Roman Literature* (Harmondsworth: Penguin Books, 1958).
Hanson, P.D., *The Dawn of Apocalyptic* (Philadelphia: Fortress Press, 1979).
Harding, M., 'On the Historicity of Acts: Comparing Acts 9:23–5 with 2 Cor 11:32–3', *NTS* 39 (1993), pp. 518–38.

Harrison, J.R., *Paul's Language of Grace (Charis) in its Graeco-Roman Context* (Tübingen: J.C.B. Mohr [Paul Siebeck], forthcoming).

Horsley, R.A., with J.S. Hanson, *Bandits, Prophets, and Messiahs: Popular Movements at the Time of Jesus* (San Francisco: Harper & Row, 1988).

Judge, E.A., *The Social Pattern of Christian Groups in the First Century* (London: Tyndale, 1960).

—'St Paul and Classical Society', *JAC* 15 (1972), pp. 19–36.

Kampen, J., *The Hasideans and Origins of Pharisaism: A Study in 1 and 2 Maccabees* (Atlanta: Scholars Press, 1988).

Keresztes, P., 'The Imperial Government and the Christian Church, I: From Nero to the Severi', *ANRW* 2.23.1 (1979), pp. 247–315.

Kidd, R.M., *Wealth and Beneficence in the Pastoral Epistles* (Atlanta: Scholars Press, 1990).

Kearsley, R., 'A Civic Benefactor of the First Century in Asia Minor', in Stephen R. Llewelyn, *New Documents Illustrating Early Christianity*, VII (Macquarie University: Ancient History Documentary Research Centre, 1994), pp. 233–41.

Kloppenborg, J.S., and S.G. Wilson (eds.), *Voluntary Associations in the Graeco-Roman World* (London/New York: Routledge, 1996).

Levine, L.I., 'The Jewish–Greek Conflict in First Century Caesarea', *JJS* 25 (1974), pp. 281–97.

—*The Ancient Synagogue* (New Haven: Yale University Press, 2000).

Lintott, A.W., *Violence in Republican Rome* (Oxford: Clarendon Press, 1968).

Lohse, E., *The New Testament Environment* (London: SCM Press, 1976).

MacDonald, M.Y., *The Pauline Churches: A Socio-historical Study of Institutionalization in the Pauline and Deutero-Pauline Writings* (SNTSMS, 60; Cambridge: Cambridge University Press, 1988).

Magness, J., 'A Villa at Qumran?', *RevQ* 16 (1994), pp. 397–419.

—'Archaeology', in Peter W. Flint and James C. VanderKam (eds.), *The Dead Sea Scrolls after Fifty Years: A Comprehensive Assessment*, I (Leiden: E.J. Brill, 1998), pp. 46–75.

Malherbe, A.J., ' "Gentle as a Nurse": The Cynic Background to 1 Thessalonians 2', *NovT* 12 (1970), pp. 203–217.

—*Ancient Epistolary Theorists* (Atlanta: Scholars Press, 1988).

Malina, B.J., *The New Testament World: Insights from Cultural Anthropology* (London: SCM Press, 1981).

Manson, T.W., *The Servant-Messiah* (Cambridge: Cambridge University Press, 1953).

Martyn, J.L., *History and Theology in the Fourth Gospel* (Nashville: Abingdon Press, 1968).

Mason, S., *Josephus and the New Testament* (Peabody, MA: Hendrikson, 1992).

—*Flavius Josephus on the Pharisees: A Composition-Critical Study* (Leiden: E.J. Brill, 1991).

May, H.G. (ed.), *The Oxford Bible Atlas* (London: Oxford University, 2nd edn, 1974).

Meier, J.P., *A Marginal Jew: Rethinking the Historical Jesus*, I (New York: Doubleday, 1991).

Metzger, B.M., *A Textual Commentary on the Greek New Testament* (Stuttgart: United Bible Societies, 1975).

Moore, G.F., *Judaism in the First Centuries of the Christian Era*, I (New York: Schocken Books, 1971).

Neyrey, J.H., *Honor and Shame in the Gospel of Matthew* (Louisville, KY: Westminster/John Knox Press, 1998).

Petuchowski, J.J., 'The Liturgy of the Synagogue: History, Structure, and Contents', in W.S. Green (ed.), *Approaches to Ancient Judaism*, IV (Chico, CA: Scholars Press, 1983), pp. 1–64.

Pomeroy, S.B., *Goddesses, Whores, Wives, and Slaves* (New York: Schocken Books, 1995).

Rappaport, U., 'Jewish-Pagan Relations and the Revolt against Rome in 66–70 C.E.', in Lee I. Levine, *The Jerusalem Cathedra: Studies in the History, Archaeology, Geography and Ethnography of the Land of Israel* (Jerusalem: Wayne State University Press, 1981), pp. 81–95.

Sanders, J.T., *The Jews in Luke–Acts* (Philadelphia: Fortress Press, 1987).

Schürer, E., *The History of the Jewish People in the Age of Jesus Christ (175 B.C.–A.D. 135)*, I (rev. and ed. Geza Vermes and Fergus Millar; Edinburgh: T. & T. Clark, 1973).

Scobie, A., 'Slums, Sanitation and Mortality in the Roman World', *Klio* 68 (1986), pp. 399–433.

Scullard, H.H., *From the Gracchi to Nero* (London: Methuen, 1963).

Seow, C.-L., 'The Socioeconomic Context of "The Preacher's Hermeneutic" ', *Princeton Seminary Bulletin* 17 (1996), pp. 168–95.

Sherwin-White, A.N., *Roman Society and Roman Law in the New Testament* (Oxford: Oxford University Press, 1963).
Smallwood, E.M., *The Jews under Roman Rule* (Leiden: E.J. Brill, 1981).
Spong, J.S., *Liberating the Gospels: Reading the Gospels with Jewish Eyes* (San Francisco: HarperSanFrancisco, 1996).
Stambaugh, J.E., and D.L. Balch, *The New Testament in its Social Environment* (Philadelphia: Westminster Press, 1986).
Stark, R., *The Rise of Christianity* (San Francisco: HarperCollins, 1997).
Stegemann, H., *The Library of Qumran* (Grand Rapids: Eerdmans, 1998).
Stowers, S., *A Rereading of Romans* (New Haven: Yale University Press, 1994).
Syme, R., *Roman Revolution* (Cambridge: Cambridge University Press, 1939).
Taylor, M., 'The Executed God: The Way of the Cross in Lockdown America', *Princeton Seminary Bulletin* 21 (2000), pp. 301–23.
Vermes, G., *Jesus the Jew* (London: Collins, 1973).
Verner, D.C., *The Household of God: The Social World of the Pastoral Epistles* (SBLDS, 71; Chico, CA: Scholars Press, 1983).
Wallbank, F.W., *The Hellenistic World* (Glasgow: Fontana, 1981).
Wengst, K., *Pax Romana and the Peace of Jesus Christ* (Philadelphia: Fortress Press, 1987).
White, L.M., 'Finding the Ties that Bind: Issues from Social Description', *Semeia* 56 (1992), pp. 3–22.
—'Social Networks: Theoretical Orientation and Historical Applications', *Semeia* 56 (1992), pp. 23–36.
Wilken, R.L., *The Christians as the Romans Saw Them* (New Haven: Yale University Press, 1984).
Winter, P., 'Magnificat and Benedictus—Maccabaean Psalms?', *BJRL* 37 (1954–55), pp. 328-47.
Zeev, M.P. ben, 'Who Wrote a Letter Concerning the Delian Jews?', *RB* 103 (1996), pp. 237–43.
Zias, J., 'The Cemeteries of Qumran and Celibacy: The Confusion Laid to Rest?', *Dead Sea Discoveries* 7 (2000), pp. 220–53.

Numerical List of Sources

1. From the Nabonidus Chronicle.
   ANET p. 305.
2. From Nabonidus and the Clergy of Babylon.
   ANET p. 315.
3. From the Cyrus Cylinder.
   ANET pp. 315–16.
4. Isaiah 41:2–3 (NRSV).
5. Isaiah 44:24–45:4 (NRSV).
6. Daniel 5:30–6:1 (NRSV).
7. Josephus, *Antiquities* 10.248 (trans. Ralph Marcus).
8. From the Cyrus Cylinder.
   ANET p. 316.
9. Herodotus, *Histories* 3.89 (trans. A.D. Godley).
10. Herodotus, *Histories* 1.192 (trans. A.D. Godley).
11. Nehemiah 5:14–18 (NRSV).
12. Foundation Tablet from Persepolis.
    ANET pp. 316–17.
13. Xenophon, *Hellenica* 5.1.31 (trans. Carleton L. Bownson).
14. Isocrates, *Panegyricus* 150–51 (trans. George Norlin).
15. Isocrates, *To Philip* 113–15 (trans. George Norlin).
16. Arrian, *Anabasis of Alexander* 2.6.4–7 (trans. P.A. Brunt).
17. Arrian, *Anabasis of Alexander* 2.7.4–5 (trans. P.A. Brunt).
18. Arrian, *Anabasis of Alexander* 3.3.1–2; 4.1–5 (trans. P.A. Brunt).
19. Curtius, *History of Alexander* 10.3.11–14 (trans. John C. Rolfe).
20. Plutarch, *Alexander* 45.1–3 (trans. Bernadotte Perrin).
21. Plutarch, *Alexander* 47.3 (trans. Bernadotte Perrin).
22. Arrian, *Anabasis of Alexander* 7.29–30 (trans. E. Iliff Robson).
23. Diodorus Siculus, *Histories* 17.1.5 (trans. C. Bradford Welles).
24. Plutarch, *Alexander* 2.4 (trans. Bernadotte Perrin).
25. Curtius, *History of Alexander* 7.3.23 (trans. John C. Rolfe).
26. *Sibylline Oracles* 3.381–87 (trans. J.J. Collins).
27. Josephus, *Antiquities* 12.1–3 (trans. Ralph Marcus).
28. Appian, *History of Rome* 11.55 (trans. Horace White).
29. Daniel 11:5–9 (NRSV).
30. Polybius, *Histories* 9.28–29 (trans. W.R. Paton).
31. Appian, *History of Rome* 11.1 (trans. Horace White).
32. Polybius, *Histories* 5.86.7–11 (trans. W.R. Paton).
33. Polybius *Histories* 21.42 (trans. W.R. Paton).
34. Appian, *History of Rome* 11.45 (trans. Horace White).
35. Polybius, *Histories* 26.1a (trans. W.R. Paton).
36. Polybius, *Histories* 29.27 (trans. W.R. Paton).
37. Daniel 11:29–30a (NRSV).
38. Appian, *History of Rome* 11.48–50 (trans. Horace White).
39. Livy, *History of Rome* 1.16.6–7 (trans. B.O. Foster).
40. Polybius, *Histories* 1.3.6 (trans. W.R. Paton).
41. Polybius, *Histories* 1.6.3–8 (trans. W.R. Paton).
42. Polybius, *Histories* 8.1 (trans. W.R. Paton).
43. Polybius, *Histories* 3.90.7–14 (trans. W.R. Paton).
44. Polybius, *Histories* 3.115 (trans. W.R. Paton).
45. Polybius, *Histories* 3.118.1–9 (trans. W.R. Paton).
46. Polybius, *Histories* 5.101.9–102.1 (trans. W.R. Paton).
47. Polybius, *Histories* 9.11a (trans. W.R. Paton).
48. Polybius, *Histories* 15.13–14 (trans. W.R. Paton).
49. Polybius, *Histories* 38.22 (trans. W.R. Paton).
50. Appian, *History of Rome* 12.22–23 (trans. Horace White).
51. Appian, *History of Rome* 12.117 (trans. Horace White).
52. Sallust, *War with Jugurtha* 41–42 (trans. J.C. Rolfe).
53. Sallust, *War with Jugurtha* 85.13–16 (trans. J. C. Rolfe).
54. Appian, *Civil Wars* 1.95–96 (trans. Horace White).
55. Suetonius, *Julius Caesar* 19 (trans. John C. Rolfe).

56. Suetonius, *Julius Caesar* 6.1 (trans. John C. Rolfe).
57. Suetonius, *Julius Caesar* 25 (trans. John C. Rolfe).
58. Caesar, *Civil Wars* 1.4 (trans. A.G. Peskett).
59. Suetonius, *Julius Caesar* 74–75 (trans. John C. Rolfe).
60. Suetonius, *Julius Caesar* 76–80 (trans. John C. Rolfe).
61. Cicero, *Letters to his Friends* 6.15 (trans. W. Glynn Williams).
62. Plutarch, *Julius Caesar* 69.1–2 (trans. Bernadotte Perrin).
63. Horace, *Odes* 2.7 ll. 1–16 (trans. C.E. Bennett).
64. Appian, *Civil Wars* 4.5 (trans. Horace White).
65. Lucretius, *On the Nature of the Universe* 1.29–49 (trans. W.H.D. Rouse).
66. Augustus, *Res Gestae Divi Augusti* 1 (trans. P.A. Brunt and J.M. Moore).
67. Augustus, *Res Gestae Divi Augusti* 3 (trans. P.A. Brunt and J.M. Moore).
68. Augustus, *Res Gestae Divi Augusti* 34 (trans. P.A. Brunt and J.M. Moore).
69. Dio Cassius, *Roman History* 53.2.3–4 (trans. Earnest Cary).
70. Appian, *History of Rome* Preface 6 (trans. Horace White).
71. Suetonius, *Augustus* 22 (trans. J.C. Rolfe).
72. Tacitus, *Annals* 1.2 (trans. John Jackson).
73. Tacitus, *Annals* 1.3–4 (trans. Clifford H. Moore).
74. Tacitus, *Annals* 1.9 (trans. Clifford H. Moore).
75. Tacitus, *Annals* 1.10 (trans. Clifford H. Moore).
76. Dio Cassius, *Roman History* 53.16.6–8 (trans. Earnest Cary).
77. Dio Cassius, *Roman History* 53.12 (trans. Earnest Cary).
78. Suetonius, *Augustus* 48, 60 (trans. J.C. Rolfe).
79. Augustus, *Res Gestae Divi Augusti* 27 (trans. P.A. Brunt and J.M. Moore).
80. Tacitus, *Annals* 2.59 (trans. John Jackson).
81. Tacitus, *Annals* 12.27 (trans. John Jackson).
82. Tacitus, *Histories* 4.14 (trans. Clifford H. Moore).
83. Tacitus, *Annals* 4.6–7 (trans. John Jackson).
84. Suetonius, *Tiberius* 36 (trans. J.C. Rolfe).
85. Suetonius, *Gaius* 11, 32.1 (trans. J.C. Rolfe).
86. Dio Cassius, *Roman History* 60.6.6 (trans. Earnest Cary).
87. Dio Cassius, *Roman History* 60.8.1–3 (trans. Earnest Cary).
88. Suetonius, *Claudius* 25.4, 5 (trans. J.C. Rolfe).
89. Josephus, *Antiquities* 20.195 (trans. L.H. Feldman).
90. Josephus, *Life* 15–16 (trans. H.St.J. Thackeray).
91. Suetonius, *Nero* 35.3 (trans. J.C. Rolfe).
92. Suetonius, *Nero* 38.1–2 (trans. J.C. Rolfe).
93. Suetonius, *Nero* 40.2 (trans. J.C. Rolfe).
94. Tacitus, *Histories* 1.10 (trans. Clifford H. Moore).
95. Suetonius, *Nero* 57 (trans. J.C. Rolfe).
96. Tacitus, *Histories* 1.2–3 (trans. Clifford H. Moore).
97. Martial, *On the Spectacles* 2 (trans. D.R. Shackleton Bailey).
98. Suetonius, *Vespasian* 4.5–6, 5.6 (trans. J.C. Rolfe).
99. Josephus, *Jewish War* 3.399–404 (trans. H.St.J. Thackeray).
100. Martial, *Epigrams* 2.2 (trans. D.R. Shackleton Bailey).
101. Dio Cassius, *Roman History* 67.13.3–4 (trans. Earnest Cary).
102. Suetonius, *Domitian* 13.1–2 (trans. J.C. Rolfe).
103. Dio Cassius, *Roman History* 67.14 (trans. Earnest Cary).
104. Dio Cassius, *Roman History* 68.14 (trans. Earnest Cary).
105. 2 Chronicles 36:22–23 (NRSV).
106. Nehemiah 8:1–3, 7–8 (NRSV).
107. Nehemiah 13:1, 3, 15, 23–25 (NRSV).
108. Zechariah 9:9–13 (NRSV).
109. Josephus, *Antiquities* 12.4 (trans. Ralph Marcus).
110. Josephus, *Antiquities* 12.129–33 (trans. Ralph Marcus).
111. Josephus, *Antiquities* 12.154–55, 175–76 (trans. Ralph Marcus).
112. 2 Maccabees 3:1–3 (NRSV).
113. Josephus, *Antiquities* 12.226–27 (trans. Ralph Marcus).
114. Letter of Aristeas 301–303, 307–311 (trans. R.J.H. Shutt).
115. Sirach 2:12–14 (NRSV).
116. *Jubilees* 3:30–31 (trans. O.S. Wintemute).
117. 1 Maccabees 1:11–15 (NRSV).
118. Daniel 11:21 (NRSV).
119. 1 Maccabees 1:10 (NRSV).
120. Daniel 11:22 (NRSV).
121. 2 Maccabees 4:7–17 (NRSV).
122. Daniel 9:24–27 (NRSV).
123. 2 Maccabees 4:23–26 (NRSV).

124. Josephus, *Antiquities* 12.242–45 (trans. Ralph Marcus).
125. 1 Maccabees 1:20–24 (NRSV).
126. Josephus, *Antiquities* 12.248–52 (trans. Ralph Marcus).
127. Daniel 11:29–35 (NRSV).
128. Josephus, *Antiquities* 12.253–56 (trans. Ralph Marcus).
129. 1 Maccabees 1:54–64 (NRSV).
130. 2 Maccabees 6:1–2 (NRSV).
131. 1 Maccabees 2:19–28 (NRSV).
132. 1 Maccabees 2:29–41 (NRSV).
133. 1 Maccabees 2:42–48 (NRSV).
134. 1 Maccabees 4:41–46 (NRSV).
135. 1 Maccabees 4:52–59 (NRSV).
136. 1 Maccabees 6:43–46 (NRSV).
137. 1 Maccabees 8:1–4a, 5–6, 12b–16 (NRSV).
138. 1 Maccabees 8:20 (NRSV).
139. 1 Maccabees 8:23–29, 31–32 (NRSV).
140. 1 Maccabees 7:12–16a (NRSV).
141. 1 Maccabees 13:3–11 (NRSV).
142. 1 Maccabees 14:4–15 (NRSV).
143. 1 Maccabees 14:41–43 (NRSV).
144 Josephus, *Antiquities* 13.288–92 (trans. Ralph Marcus).
145. Josephus, *Antiquities* 13.379–81 (trans. Ralph Marcus).
146. *Psalms of Solomon* 1:4–8 (trans. R.B. Wright).
147. Josephus, *Antiquities* 14.69–75, 77–79 (trans. Ralph Marcus).
148. *Psalms of Solomon* 2:1–10 (trans. R.B. Wright).
149. Josephus, *Jewish War* 1.193–94 (trans. H.St.J. Thackeray).
150. Josephus, *Jewish War* 1.199–200 (trans. H.St.J. Thackeray).
151. Suetonius, *Julius Caesar* 84.5 (trans. J.C. Rolfe).
152. Josephus, *Jewish War* 1.204–207 (trans. H.St.J. Thackeray).
153. Dio Cassius, *Roman History* 48.24.4–7 (trans. Earnest Cary).
154. Dio Cassius, *Roman History* 49.22.3–6 (trans. Earnest Cary).
155. Josephus, *Jewish War* 1.282–85 (trans. H.St.J. Thackeray).
156. Josephus, *Jewish War* 1.435–37 (trans. H.St.J. Thackeray).
157. Josephus, *Antiquities* 15.292–98 (trans. Ralph Marcus and Allen Wikgren).
158. Matthew 2:1–4, 12–15a, 16 (NRSV).
159. Josephus, *Jewish War* 2.10–13 (trans. H.St.J. Thackeray).
160. Josephus, *Jewish War* 2.55–57, 60, 65 (trans. H.St.J. Thackeray).
161. Strabo, *Geography* 16.46 (trans. Horace Leonard Jones).
162. Luke 2:1–2 (NRSV).
163. Josephus, *Antiquities* 18.29–31, 176–77 (trans. L.H. Feldman).
164. Josephus, *Jewish War* 2.169–74 (trans. H.St.J. Thackeray).
165. Josephus, *Jewish War* 2.175–77 (trans. H.St.J. Thackeray).
166. Josephus, *Antiquities* 18.116–19 (trans. L.H. Feldman).
167. Mark 6:17–29 (NRSV).
168. Luke 23:6–12 (NRSV).
169. Josephus, *Jewish War* 2.181–83 (trans. H.St.J. Thackeray).
170. Josephus, *Antiquities* 18.257–62 (trans. L.H. Feldman).
171. Josephus, *Antiquities* 19.287–91 (trans. L.H. Feldman).
172. Josephus, *Antiquities* 19.343–50 (trans. L.H. Feldman).
173. Acts 12:20–23 (NRSV).
174. Josephus, *Jewish War* 2.361–64 (trans. H.St.J. Thackeray).
175. Josephus, *Jewish War* 2.390–94 (trans. H.St.J. Thackeray).
176. Suetonius, *Claudius* 28 (trans. J.C. Rolfe).
177. Josephus, *Jewish War* 2.258–65 (trans. H.St.J. Thackeray).
178. Josephus, *Jewish War* 2.305–308 (trans. H.St.J. Thackeray).
179. Josephus, *Jewish War* 2.456–58 (trans. H.St.J. Thackeray).
180. Josephus, *Life* 67 (trans. H.St.J. Thackeray).
181. Josephus, *Jewish War* 2.562–71 (trans. H.St.J. Thackeray).
182. Josephus, *Life* 417–21 (trans. H.St.J. Thackeray).
183. Josephus, *Jewish War* 6.420–21 (trans. H.St.J. Thackeray).
184. Dio Cassius, *Roman History* 65.4.1–7.2 (trans. Earnest Cary).
185. Tacitus, *Histories* Fragment 2 (trans. Clifford H. Moore).
186. Josephus, *Jewish War* 6.249–53 (trans. H.St.J. Thackeray).
187. Josephus, *Jewish War* 7.1–4 (trans. H.St.J. Thackeray).
188. Josephus, *Jewish War* 7.23–24 (trans. H.St.J. Thackeray).

189. Josephus, *Jewish War* 7.148–50 (trans. H.St.J. Thackeray).
190. *Aboth de Rabbi Nathan* IV, 11a.
C.G. Montefiore and H. Loewe, *A Rabbinic Anthology* (New York: Schocken Books, 1974), pp. 430–31 (no. 1200).
191. *2 Baruch* 35 (trans. A.F.J. Klijn).
192. *Aboth de Rabbi Nathan* IV, 11b–12a.
Montefiore and Loewe, *Rabbinic Anthology*, p. 266 (no. 680).
193. Josephus, *Jewish War* 7.304–319 (trans. H.St.J. Thackeray).
194. Josephus, *Jewish War* 7.323–36 (trans. H.St.J. Thackeray).
195. A Governor of Judaea under Vespasian.
New Docs III, p. 122.
196. Suetonius, *Domitian* 12.2 (trans. J.C. Rolfe).
197. Martial, *Epigrams* 7.55 (trans. D.R. Shackleton Bailey).
198. Ostracon from Apollinopolis Magna in the Nile Delta.
CPJ no. 171 (II, p. 122).
199. Eusebius, *Ecclesiastical History* 4.2 (trans. Kirsopp Lake).
200. Dio Cassius, *Roman History* 68.32.1–3 (trans. Earnest Cary).
201. Appian, *Civil Wars* 2.90 (trans. Horace White).
202. Jewish victories in the Hermopoulite District (June 116–January 117 CE).
CPJ no. 438 (II, p. 238).
203. Confiscation of Jewish property (117/118 [?] CE).
CPJ no. 445 (II, p. 252).
204. Dio Cassius, *Roman History* 69.12.1–14.3 (trans. Earnest Cary).
205. Justin, *Apology* 1.31 (ANF I, p. 173).
206. Appian, *History of Rome* 11.50 (trans. Horace White).
207. Letter of Shimeon bar Kosiba to the men of En-gedi.
Y. Yadin, *Bar-Kokba* (London: Weidenfeld & Nicolson, 1971), p. 133.
208. *m. Taanit* 4.6.
J. Neusner, *The Mishnah: A New Translation* (New Haven: Yale University Press, 1988), p. 315.
209. *Jerusalem Talmud, Ta'anit* IV, section 8, f. 68d, l. 43.
Montefiore and Loewe, *Rabbinic Anthology*, pp. 261–64 (no. 675).
210. Herodotus, *Histories* 1.1 (trans. A.D. Godley).
211. Thucydides, *Peloponnesian War* 1.22 (trans. Charles Forster Smith).
212. Polybius, *Histories* 2.56.10–12 (trans. W.R. Paton).
213. Polybius, *Histories* 12.25b (trans. W.R. Paton).
214. Livy, *History of Rome* Preface 1–12 (trans. B.O. Foster).
215. Tacitus, *Agricola* 1 (trans. M. Hutton).
216. Tacitus, *Agricola* 46 (trans. M. Hutton).
217. Demetrius, *On Style* 223–25, 227–28, 231–32 (trans. W. Rhys Roberts).
218. Cicero, *Letters to his Friends* 2.4.1 (trans. W. Glynn Williams).
219. Cicero, *Letters to his Friends* 16.16 (trans. W. Glynn Williams).
220. Cicero, *Letters to Atticus* 1.18 (trans. E.O. Winstedt).
221. Cicero, *Letters to Atticus* 15.15 (trans. E.O. Winstedt).
222. Pliny the Younger, *Letters* 8.24 (trans. Betty Radice).
223. 1 Thessalonians 2:1–12; 4:9–12 (NRSV).
224. Horace, *Odes* 4.5 (trans. C.E. Bennett).
225. Catullus, *Poems* 5 (trans. Francis Warre Cornish).
226. Catullus, *Poems* 13 (trans. Francis Warre Cornish).
227. Catullus, *Poems* 31 (trans. Francis Warre Cornish).
228. Virgil, *Eclogue* 1.64–78 (trans. H. Rushton Fairclough).
229. Virgil, *Eclogue* 4 (trans. H. Rushton Fairclough).
230. Virgil, *Aeneid* 1.257–96 (trans. H. Rushton Fairclough).
231. Virgil, *Aeneid* 6.548–627 (trans. H. Rushton Fairclough).
232. Virgil, *Aeneid* 6.637–71 (trans. H. Rushton Fairclough).
233. Virgil, *Aeneid* 6.724–51 (trans. H. Rushton Fairclough).
234. Propertius, *Elegies* 2.13A, ll. 1–36 (trans. H.E. Butler).
235. Propertius, *Elegies* 2.27 (trans. H.E. Butler).
236. Propertius, *Elegies* 3.4 (trans. H.E. Butler).
237. Ovid, *Amores* 1.5 (trans. Grant Showerman).
238. Ovid, *Art of Love* 1.163–76 (trans. J.H. Mozley).
239. Ovid, *Art of Love* 1.269–78 (trans. J.H. Mozley).
240. Isocrates, *To Demonicus* 9–10 (trans. George Norlin).
241. Isocrates, *To Demonicus* 13–17 (trans. George Norlin).

242. Isocrates, *Busiris* 1–3 (trans. Larue van Hook).
243. Seneca, *To Marcia, On Consolation* 19.4–5 (trans. John W. Basore)
244. Apuleius, *Golden Ass* 11.15 (trans. W. Adlington, rev. S. Gaselee).
245. Apuleius, *Golden Ass* 11.25 (trans. W. Adlington, rev. S. Gaselee).
246. Isaiah 27:1 (NRSV).
247. Isaiah 51:9–10 (NRSV).
248. Psalms 74:12–13 (NRSV).
249. *1 Enoch* 7, 10 (trans. E. Isaac).
250. *1 Enoch* 21 (trans. E. Isaac).
251. *1 Enoch* 72:1–5 (trans. E. Isaac).
252. *1 Enoch* 90:6–27 (trans. E. Isaac).
253. Daniel 7:1–18 (NRSV).
254. *4 Ezra* 11:1–12:3 (trans. B.M. Metzger).
255. *2 Baruch* 6–8 (trans. A.F.J. Klijn).
256. *2 Baruch* 25 (trans. A.F.J. Klijn).
257. *2 Baruch* 26–29 (trans. A.F.J. Klijn).
258. *Sibylline Oracles* 3.46–62 (trans. J.J. Collins).
259. *Sibylline Oracles* 5.162–78 (trans. J.J. Collins).
260. 4Q554 fragment 1, column 2.8–13 (trans. G. Vermes). G. Vermes, *Complete Dead Sea Scrolls in English* (Harmondsworth: Penguin Books, 1998), p. 569.
261. 5Q15 fragment 1, column 1.1–7 (trans. Vermes [*Complete Dead Sea Scrolls in English*, p. 569]).
262. 4Q246 column 2.1–8 (Aramaic Apocalypse) (trans. G. Vermes [*Complete Dead Sea Scrolls in English*, p. 577]).
263. Revelation 13:1–18 (NRSV).
264. Revelation 17:1–6 (NRSV).
265. Revelation 20:1–6 (NRSV).
266. Revelation 21:1–4 (NRSV)
267. Mark 13:1–37 (NRSV).
268. *Testament of Levi* 13; 18:1–5; 19 (trans. H.C. Kee).
269. 4Q548 (from Testament of Amram [4Q543–48; trans. G. Vermes (*Complete Dead Sea Scrolls in English*, pp. 535–36)]).
270. *Testament of Moses* 5–6 (trans. J. Priest).
271. Tobit 13 (NRSV).
272. 2 Timothy 3:1–9 (NRSV).
273. 2 Timothy 4:1–22 (NRSV).
274 *Jubilees* 2:1–3 (trans. O.S. Wintermute).
275. *Jubilees* 23:16–32 (trans. O.S. Wintermute).
276. *Joseph and Aseneth* 8:1–7 (trans. C. Burchard).
277. *Life of Adam and Eve* 18 (trans. M.D. Johnson).
278. *Life of Adam and Eve*, Appendix 51:3–9 (trans. M.D. Johnson).
279. 1QapGen 2.1–23 (trans. G. Vermes [*Complete Dead Sea Scrolls in English*, p. 449]).
280. Josephus, *Antiquities* 1.154–57, 166–68 (trans. H.St.J.Thackeray).
281. *Targum Pseudo-Jonathan*, Genesis 3:1–20 (trans. M. Maher). M. Maher, *Targum Pseudo-Jonathan: Genesis* (Edinburgh: T. & T. Clark, 1992), pp. 25–29.
282. Sirach 24 (NRSV).
283. Wisdom of Solomon 13:1–14:14 (NRSV).
284. Sentences of Pseudo-Phocylides ll. 3–8, 59–69b, 175–76, 213–16 (trans. P.W. van der Horst).
285. *4 Maccabees* 1:1–4, 30b–35 (NRSV).
286. *4 Maccabees* 8:27–9:9 (NRSV).
287. Matthew 8:18–22 (NRSV).
288. Matthew 6:24–34 (NRSV).
289. *Coptic Gospel of Thomas* 21 (trans. Bentley Layton).
290. *Coptic Gospel of Thomas* 45 (trans. Bentley Layton).
291. James 3:1–18 (NRSV).
292. *Didache* 1 (trans. Kirsopp Lake).
293. 1QH 10.20–30 (trans. G. Vermes [*Complete Dead Sea Scrolls in English*, pp. 257–58]).
294. *Psalms of Solomon* 18 (trans. R.B. Wright).
295. *Odes of Solomon* 24 (trans. James H. Charlesworth).
296. *Prayer of Manasseh* 1–8 (NRSV).
297. Luke 1:46–55 (NRSV).
298. *Joseph and Aseneth* 8:10–11 (trans. C. Burchard).
299 Matthew 6:7–13 (NRSV).
300. *1 Clement* 59:3–61:3 (trans. Kirsopp Lake).
301. *Didache* 10 (trans. Kirsopp Lake).
302. 1 Maccabees 3:1–9 (NRSV).
303. 2 Maccabees 15:11–16 (NRSV).
304. Josephus, *Life* 9–12 (trans. H.St.J. Thackeray).
305. Josephus, *Life* 422–23, 428–29 (trans. H.St.J. Thackeray).
306. Josephus, *Jewish War* 1.1–3 (trans. H.St.J. Thackeray).
307. Luke 1:1–4 (NRSV).
308. Acts 10:36–43 (NRSV).
309. Matthew 4:13–17 (NRSV).
310. Matthew 12:15–21 (NRSV).
311. Matthew 13:44–50 (NRSV).
312. *Coptic Gospel of Thomas* 8 (trans. Bentley Layton).
313. Justin, *Apology* 1.21–22 (*ANF* 1.170).
314. Mark 1:32–34 (NRSV).
315. Acts 19:11–12 (NRSV).

316. Marble tablet of 138 CE, probably from the Temple of Asclepius in Rome.
A. Deissmann, *Light from the Ancient East* (London: Hodder & Stoughton, 4th edn, 1927), p. 135.
317. *Odes of Solomon* 19:4–8 (trans. James H. Charlesworth).
318. Luke 24:36–43 (NRSV).
319. Livy, *History of Rome* 1.16.1 (trans. B.O. Foster).
320. Philo, *Moses* 2.291 (trans. F.H. Colson).
321. Luke 24:50–53 (NRSV).
322. Livy, *History of Rome* 1.20 (trans. B.O. Foster).
323. Cicero, *On the Nature of the Gods* 3.5 (trans. H. Rackham).
324. Polybius, *Histories* 6.56.6–12 (trans. W.R. Paton).
325. Pliny the Elder, *Natural History* 35.6–7 (trans. H. Rackham).
326. Herodas, *Mime IV: Dedications and Sacrifices to Asklepios* ll. 1–20.
A.D. Knox (ed.), *Herodas: Mimes and Fragments* (Cambridge: Cambridge University Press, 1922), p. 167. Notes by A.C. Headlam.
327. Invitation to a temple banquet.
New Docs I, p. 5.
328. Invitation to a temple banquet.
New Docs I, p. 5.
329. 1 Corinthians 8:10 (NRSV).
330. 1 Corinthians 9:13 (NRSV).
331. 1 Corinthians 10:20–21 (NRSV).
332. 1 Corinthians 10:25 (NRSV).
333. *Didache* 6:3 (trans. Kirsopp Lake).
334. Revelation 2:20 (NRSV).
335. Acts 15:28–29 (NRSV).
336. Isocrates, *To Philip* 116–17 (trans. George Norlin).
337. Lucian, *On Sacrifices* 9, 12–13 (trans. A.M. Harmon).
338. Dio Cassius, *Roman History* 52.36.1–3 (trans. Earnest Carey).
339. Pliny the Elder, *Natural History* 28.10–11 (trans. W.H.S. Jones).
340. Seneca, *Epistles* 16.4–6 (trans. Richard M. Gummere).
341. Plutarch, *Lysander* 18.3 (trans. Bernadotte Perrin).
342. Diodorus Siculus, *Histories* 16.95.1 (trans. C. Bradford Welles).
343. Athenaeus, *Deipnosophistae* 6.253e (trans. Charles Burton Gulick).
344. Dio Cassius, *Roman History* 56.46.1–2 (trans. Earnest Carey).
345. Dio Cassius, *Roman History* 59.4.4 (trans. Earnest Carey).
346. Seneca, *Apocolocyntosis divi Claudii* 5 (trans. W.H.D. Rouse).
347. Seneca, *Apocolocyntosis divi Claudii* 10, 11 (trans. W.H.D. Rouse).
348. Epictetus, *Discourses* 3.21.10–16 (trans. W. A. Oldfather).
349. Livy, *History of Rome* 39.8 (trans. Evan T. Sage).
350. Apuleius, *Golden Ass* 11.23 (trans. W. Adlington, rev. S. Gaselee).
351. Aretalogy of Isis, ll. 14–33.
New Docs I, p. 11.
352. Martial, *Epigrams* 5.41 (trans. D.R. Shackleton Bailey).
353. Catullus, *Poems* 63.50–73 (trans. Francis Warre Cornish).
354. Cicero, *Laws* 2.14.36 (trans. Clinton Walker Keyes).
355. 1 Timothy 3:16 (NRSV).
356. Appian, *Civil Wars* 1.83 (trans. Horace White).
357. Matthew 27:45–53 (NRSV).
358. P.Oxy 1148.
A.S. Hunt, *The Oxyrhynchus Papyri, Part VIII* (London: Egypt Exploration Society, 1911), p. 249.
359. Answer from an Oracle.
New Docs II, p. 37.
360. *Paris Magical Papyrus*, ll. 3007–3027.
Deissmann, *Light from the Ancient East*, pp. 259–60.
361. Love charm.
New Docs II, p. 45.
362. Pliny the Elder, *Natural History* 30.11 (trans. W.H.S. Jones).
363. Josephus, *Antiquities* 8.45–48 (trans. H.St.J. Thackeray and Ralph Marcus).
364. Acts 13:4–12 (NRSV).
365. Acts 19:13–20 (NRSV).
366. Romans 8:38–39 (NRSV).
367. Galatians 4:8–11 (NRSV).
368. Seneca, *Epistles* 5.4–5 (trans. Richard M. Gummere).
369. Epicurus, *To Herodotus* 81–82 (trans. Cyril Bailey). Cyril Bailey, *Epicurus: The Extant Remains* (Oxford: Oxford University Press, 1926), p. 53.
370. Epicurus, *Principal Doctrines* 12, 21, 28, 40 (trans. Cyril Bailey [*Epicurus*, pp. 97, 99, 101, 105]).
371. Epicurus, *To Menoeceus* 123–32 (trans. Cyril Bailey [*Epicurus*, pp. 83–85, 87]).

372. Lucretius, *On the Nature of the Universe* 2.37–61 (trans. W.H.D. Rouse).
373. Lucretius, *On the Nature of the Universe* 3.59–93 (trans. W.H.D. Rouse).
374. P.Oxy 215.
B.P. Grenfell and A.S. Hunt, *Oxyrhynchus Papyri, Part II* (London: Egypt Exploration Fund, 1899), p. 32.
375. Cleanthes, 'Hymn to Zeus'.
E. Bevan, *Later Greek Religion* (London: Dent, 1927), pp. 14–15.
376. Epictetus, *Discourses* 2.8.9–14 (trans. W.A. Oldfather).
377. Epictetus, *Discourses* 1.9.1–9 (trans. W.A. Oldfather).
378. Fragment from the works of Musonius Rufus.
Bevan, *Later Greek Religion*, pp. 102–103.
379. Seneca, *Epistles* 28.4 (trans. Richard M. Gummere).
380. Seneca, *Epistles* 90.26–29 (trans. Richard M. Gummere).
381. Seneca, *Epistles* 41.8–9 (trans. Richard M. Gummere).
382. Epictetus, *Discourses* 1.26.1 (trans. W.A. Oldfather).
383. Cicero, *On the Nature of the Gods* 2.4–5 (trans. H. Rackham).
384. Cicero, *On the Nature of the Gods* 2.117–18 (trans. H. Rackham).
385. Aulus Gellius, *Attic Nights* 7.1.1–6 (trans. John C. Rolfe).
386. Seneca, *On Providence* 2.1–4 (trans. J.W. Basore).
387. Epictetus, *Discourses* 1.16.15–21 (trans. W.A. Oldfather).
388. Epictetus, *Discourses* 3.26.28–30 (trans. W.A. Oldfather).
389. Epictetus, *Encheiridion* 31.1, 5 (trans. W.A. Oldfather).
390. Epictetus, *Discourses* 2.14.11–13 (trans. W.A. Oldfather).
391. Cicero, *On the Nature of the Gods* 1.11 (trans. H. Rackham).
392. Cicero, *On the Nature of the Gods* 1.1 (trans. H. Rackham).
393. Diogenes Laertius, *Lives of Eminent Philosophers* 6.22–23 (trans. R.D. Hicks).
394. Diogenes Laertius, *Lives of Eminent Philosophers* 6.38 (trans. R.D. Hicks).
395. Diogenes Laertius, *Lives of Eminent Philosophers* 6.60 (trans. R.D. Hicks).
396. Epictetus, *Discourses* 1.24.6–10 (trans. W.A. Oldfather).
397. Epictetus, *Discourses* 3.22.45–49 (trans. W.A. Oldfather).
398. Martial, *Epigrams* 4.53 (trans. D.R. Shackleton Bailey).
399. Philo, *On the Creation* 17–20 (trans. F.H. Colson and G.H. Whitaker)
400. Philo, *On the Creation* 165–66 (trans. F.H. Colson and G.H. Whitaker).
401. Philo, *Who is the Heir?* 205–206 (trans. F.H. Colson and G.H. Whitaker).
402. John 1:1–5, 14 (NRSV).
403. Aristotle, *Politics* 1.2.1–3 (trans. H. Rackham).
404. Aristotle, *Politics* 1.2.11–15 (trans. H. Rackham).
405. Aristotle, *Politics* 1.5.6 (trans. H. Rackham).
406. Juvenal, *Satires* 5.12–56 (trans. G.G. Ramsay).
407. Papyrus letter (first/second century CE).
New Docs I, p. 57.
408. Aulus Gellius, *Attic Nights* 10.23 (trans. John C. Rolfe).
409. Dio Cassius, *Roman History* 54.16 (trans. Earnest Cary).
410. Marriage Contract from Egypt (P.Tebt 104 [92 BCE]).
B.P. Grenfell, A.S. Hunt and J.G. Smyly, *Tebtunis Papyri* (London: Egypt Exploration Fund, 1902), p. 452.
411. Juvenal, *Satires* 6.142–60 (trans. G.G. Ramsay).
412. Josephus, *Against Apion* 2.199–203 (trans. H.St.J. Thackeray).
413. Marriage Contract (trans. Y. Yadin).
N. Lewis (ed.), *Judean Desert Studies: The Documents from the Bar Kokhba Period in the Cave of Letters* (Jerusalem: Israel Exploration Society, 1989), p. 80 (no. 18).
414. 1 Corinthians 7:1–4 (NRSV).
415. A Jewish bill of divorce (Mur 19) (c. 111 CE) (trans. M. Eugene Boring).
Boring, Berger and Colpe (eds.), *Hellenistic Commentary to the New Testament*, pp. 58–59 (no. 35).
416. Deed of divorce.
CPJ no. 144 (II, p. 12).
417. Damascus Document 4.19–21 (trans. G. Vermes [*Complete Dead Sea Scrolls in English*, p. 130]).
418. Josephus, *Life* 426 (H.St.J. Thackeray).

419. *Babylonian Talmud, Giṭṭin* 90b.
Montefiore and Loewe, *Rabbinic Anthology*, p. 509 (no. 1436).
420. Mark 10:2–12 (NRSV).
421. 1 Corinthians 7:10–13, 15 (NRSV).
422. Demosthenes, *Against Neaera* 122 (trans. A.T. Murray).
423. Martial, *Epigrams* 8.12 (trans. D.R. Shackleton Bailey).
424. Plutarch, *Advice to Bride and Groom* 16 (trans. F.C. Babbitt).
425. Plutarch, *Advice to Bride and Groom* 32 (trans. F.C. Babbitt).
426. Plutarch, *Advice to Bride and Groom* 33 (trans. F.C. Babbitt).
427. Juvenal, *Satires* 6.133–35 (trans. G.G. Ramsay).
428. Juvenal, *Satires* 6.542–47 (trans. G.G. Ramsay).
429. Juvenal, *Satires* 6.45–51 (trans. G.G. Ramsay).
430. Juvenal, *Satires* 6.200–30 (trans. G.G. Ramsay).
431. Juvenal, *Satires* 6.231–41 (trans. G.G. Ramsay).
432. Diogenes Laertius, *Lives of Eminent Philosophers* 6.52 (trans. R.D. Hicks).
433. *Testament of Reuben* 5 (trans. H.C. Kee).
434. *4 Maccabees* 18:6–8 (NRSV).
435. 1 Timothy 2:8–15 (NRSV).
436. Tacitus, *Annals* 6.1 (trans. J. Jackson).
437. Martial, *Epigrams* 7.67 (trans. D.R. Shackleton Bailey).
438. Diogenes Laertius, *Lives of Eminent Philosophers* 6.65 (trans. R.D. Hicks).
439. 1 Thessalonians 4:2–7 (NRSV).
440. 1 Corinthians 6:18 (NRSV).
441. Philo, *Special Laws* 3.37 (trans. F.H. Colson).
442. Wisdom of Solomon 14:22–27 (NRSV).
443. Romans 1:24–27 (NRSV).
444. *Epistle of Barnabas* 19:4 (trans. Kirsopp Lake).
445. Sale of a slave girl.
CPJ no. 1 (I, p. 120).
446. Polybius, *Histories* 3.17.9–10 (trans. W.R. Paton).
447. Plutarch, *Marcus Cato* 5.1–2, 5 (trans. Bernadotte Perrin).
448. Appian, *Civil Wars* 3.98 (trans. Horace White).
449. Suetonius, *Claudius* 25.2 (trans. J.C. Rolfe).
450. Epictetus, *Discourses* 4.1.34–37 (trans. W.A. Oldfather).
451. Tacitus, *Histories* 2.72 (trans. Clifford H. Moore).
452. Seneca, *Epistles* 47.1, 5–8, 10–14 (trans. Richard M. Gummere).
453. *Scriptores Historiae Augustae, Life of Hadrian* 18.7–11 (trans. David Magie).
454. Epictetus, *Discourses* 1.13 (trans. W.A. Oldfather).
455. Martial, *Epigrams* 10.31 (trans. D.R. Shackleton Bailey).
456. *Exodus Rabbah*, Beshallaḥ 21.4.
Montefiore and Loewe, *Rabbinic Anthology*, p. 346 (no. 910).
457. 1 Timothy 6:1–2 (NRSV).
458. Quintilian, *Institutio Oratoria* 1.1.8–9 (trans. H.E. Butler).
459. Seneca the Elder, *Controversiae* 2.7 (trans. M. Winterbottom).
460. Seneca the Elder, *Controversiae* 1.3 (trans. M. Winterbottom).
461. Seneca the Elder, *Suasoriae* 2.1 (trans. M. Winterbottom).
462. Seneca the Elder, *Suasoriae* 7.1 (trans. M. Winterbottom).
463. Josephus, *Against Apion* 2.204 (trans. H.St.J. Thackeray).
464. Aristotle, *Art of Rhetoric* 1.2.1–6 (trans. J.H. Freese).
465. Quintilian, *Institutio Oratoria* Preface 9–14, 18–20 (trans. H.E. Butler).
466. Aristotle, *Art of Rhetoric* 1.3.1–5 (trans. J.H. Freese).
467. Quintilian, *Institutio Oratoria* 3.7.6–12 (trans. H.E. Butler).
468. *Rhetoric to Alexander* 1425b36–40 (trans. H. Rackham).
469. Sallust, *War with Jugurtha* 85.26–37 (trans. John C. Rolfe).
470. Cicero, *Against Verres* 1.12–15 (trans. L.H.G. Greenwood).
471. *Rhetoric to Alexander* 1440b29–1441a8 (trans. H. Rackham).
472. Seneca, *Epistles* 88.1–2 (trans. Richard M. Gummere).
473. Epicetus, *Discourses* 2.16.5–8 (trans. W.A. Oldfather).
474. 2 Corinthians 11:21b–33 (NRSV).
475. 1 Corinthians 2:1–5 (NRSV).
476. Appian, *Civil Wars* 1.7 (trans. Horace White).
477. Aristotle, *Politics* 1.3.23 (trans. H. Rackham).
478. An inscription from Aletrium, 135–90 BCE.
CIL volume 1, no. 1529.
N. Lewis and M. Reinhold, *Roman Civilization: Sourcebook I, The Republic* (New York: Harper & Row, 1966), pp. 428–29.

479. Inscription in a bathing room at Interamna.
CIL volume 1 part 2, 1903.
Warmington, *Remains of Old Latin*, IV, p. 149.
480. Marble inscription from Pergamum.
Deissmann, *Light from the Ancient East*, p. 312.
481. The Priene Inscription (9 BCE).
A.D. Nock, *Early Gentile Christianity and its Hellenistic Background* (New York: Harper & Row, 1964), p. 37.
482. Luke 22:24–27 (NRSV).
483. Matthew 6:2–4 (NRSV).
484. Titus 2:11–13 (NRSV).
485. Appian, *Civil Wars* 5.4 (trans. Horace White).
486. Tacitus, *Annals* 2.42 (trans. John Jackson).
487. Petronius, *Satyricon* 76 (trans. Michael Heseltine).
488. Josephus, *Antiquities* 16.153–54, 156–59 (trans. Ralph Marcus and Allen Wikgren).
489. Plutarch, *Sulla* 7.1 (trans. Bernadotte Perrin).
490. Sallust, *War with Jugurtha* 95.3–4 (trans. J.C. Rolfe).
491. Sallust, *War with Catiline* 10–12, 14 (trans. J.C. Rolfe).
492. Sallust, *War with Jugurtha* 4.5–6 (trans. J.C. Rolfe).
493. Cicero, *Pro Archia Poeta* 11.28–29 (trans. N.H. Watts).
494. Ovid, *Art of Love* 3.113–28 (trans. J.H. Mozley).
495. Juvenal, *Satires* 3.58–65 (trans. G.G. Ramsay).
496. Aulus Gellius, *Attic Nights* 16.13.6–9 (trans. John C. Rolfe).
497. Dio Cassius, *Roman History* 55.10.1 (trans. Earnest Cary).
498. Martial, *Epigrams* 7.61 (trans. D.R. Shackleton Bailey).
499. Juvenal, *Satires* 3.1–9 (trans. G.G. Ramsay).
500. Juvenal, *Satires* 3.190–202 (trans. G.G. Ramsay).
501. Juvenal, *Satires* 3.232–77 (trans. G.G. Ramsay).
502. Cato, *On Agriculture* 5.1–5 (trans. William Davis Hooper and Harrison Boyd Ash).
503. Cato, *On Agriculture* 143.1–2 (trans. William Davis Hooper and Harrison Boyd Ash).
504. Cato, *On Agriculture* 159 (trans. William Davis Hooper and Harrison Boyd Ash).
505. Marcus Terentius Varro, *On Agriculture* 1.18.1 (trans. William Davis Hooper and Harrison Boyd Ash).
506. Marcus Terentius Varro, *On Agriculture* 1.17.4–5 (trans. William Davis Hooper and Harrison Boyd Ash).
507. Virgil, *Georgics* 2.136–76 (trans. H. Rushton Fairclough).
508. Epigram 1 ascribed to Martial (trans. Walter C.A. Ker).
509. Lucian, *Hippias* 5–8 (trans. A.M. Harmon).
510. Petronius, *Satyricon* 31 (trans. Michael Heseltine).
511. Juvenal, *Satires* 11.1–23 (trans. G.G. Ramsay).
512. Martial, *Epigrams* 10.48 (trans. D.R. Shackleton Bailey).
513. Juvenal, *Satires* 11.162–82 (trans. G.G. Ramsay).
514. Dio Cassius, *Roman History* 51.22.4–6 (trans. Earnest Cary).
515. Augustus, *Res Gestae Divi Augusti* 22–23 (trans. P.A. Brunt and J.M. Moore).
516. Dio Cassius, *Roman History* 55.10.6–8 (trans. Earnest Cary).
517. Juvenal, *Satires* 10.72–81 (trans. G.G. Ramsay).
518. Suetonius, *Claudius* 34 (trans. J.C. Rolfe).
519. Martial, *On the Spectacles* 9 (trans. D.R. Shackleton Bailey).
520. Martial, *On the Spectacles* 14 (trans. D.R. Shackleton Bailey).
521. Martial, *On the Spectacles* 21 (trans. D.R. Shackleton Bailey).
522. Inscription from Pompeii.
'From the Walls of Pompeii (i)'.
N. Lewis and M. Reinhold, *Roman Civilization: Sourcebook II, The Empire* (New York: Harper & Row, 1966), p. 359 (*CIL* volume 4, no. 3884).
523. Seneca, *Epistles* 7.2–5 (trans. Richard M. Gummere).
524. Josephus, *Antiquities* 15.273–76 (trans. Ralph Marcus and Allen Wikgren).
525. Pliny the Younger, *Letters* 10.92 (trans. Betty Radice).
526. Pliny the Younger, *Letters* 10.93 (trans. Betty Radice).
527. By-laws of a society.
Lewis and Reinhold, *Roman Civilization: Sourcebook II, The Empire*, pp. 273, 274, 275 (*CIL* volume 14, no. 2112).
528. Polybius, *Histories* 6.27–28; 31.1, 10–14 (trans. W.R. Paton).
529. Suetonius, *Augustus* 46 (trans. John C. Rolfe).
530. Tacitus, *Annals* 3.21 (trans. John Jackson).

531. Zonaras, *Epitome of Dio Cassius* 7.21 (trans. Earnest Cary).
532. Extract from the diptych of M. Valerius Quadratus.
Deissmann, *Light from the Ancient East*, p. 446 (column 2, ll. 12–18; column 3, ll. 1–4).
533. Diodorus Siculus, *Histories* 17.46.4 (trans. C. Bradford Welles).
534. Diodorus Siculus, *Histories* 17.13.6 (trans. C. Bradford Welles).
535. Appian, *History of Rome* 8.129 (trans. Horace White).
536. Josephus, *Jewish War* 5.449–51 (trans. H.St.J. Thackeray).
537. Appian, *History of Rome* 8.118 (trans. Horace White).
538. Tacitus, *Histories* 1.63 (trans. Clifford H. Moore).
539. Plutarch, *Julius Caesar* 55.3 (trans. Bernadotte Perrin).
540. Tacitus, *Annals* 5.9 (trans. John Jackson).
541. Philo, *Special Laws* 3.159–62 (trans. F.H. Colson).
542. Juvenal, *Satires* 15.159–74 (trans. G.G. Ramsay).
543. Seneca, *Epistles* 105.1–4 (trans. Richard M. Gummere).
544. Polybius, *Histories* 6.11.11–13; 12.1–9; 13 (trans. W.R. Paton).
545. Polybius, *Histories* 6.18 (trans. W.R. Paton).
546. Tacitus, *Annals* 3.60 (trans. John Jackson).
547. Sallust, *War with Jugurtha* 3–4 (trans. J.C. Rolfe).
548. Quintus Cicero, *Handbook of Electioneering* 35–38, 41–42, 52–53 (trans. Mary Isobel Henderson).
549. *Twelve Tables* 4.1 (trans. E.H. Warmington).
550. Sallust, *War with Catiline* 39.5 (trans. J.C. Rolfe).
551. *Twelve Tables* 5.1 (trans. E.H. Warmington).
552. *Twelve Tables* 5.8 (trans. E.H. Warmington).
553. *Twelve Tables* 10.1 (trans. E.H. Warmington).
554. Iulius Paulus, *Opinions* 5.22–24.
Lewis and Reinhold, *Roman Civilization: Sourcebook II, The Empire*, pp. 548, 549.
555. Tacitus, *Annals* 15.18 (trans. John Jackson).
556. Pliny the Younger, *Letters* 6.16 (trans. Betty Radice).
557. Dio Cassius, *Roman History* 68.24.1–25.6 (trans. Earnest Cary).
558. Pliny the Elder, *Natural History* 28.58 (trans. W.H.S. Jones).
559. Pliny the Elder, *Natural History* 28.88–89 (trans. W.H.S. Jones).
560. Aristotle, *Politics* 7.14.10 (trans. H. Rackham).
561. Juvenal, *Satires* 6.592–601 (trans. G.G. Ramsay).
562. Ilarion to Alis (P.Oxy 744 [1 BCE]).
B.P Grenfell, A.S. Hunt and C.C. Edgar, *Oxyrhynchus Papyri, Part IV* (London: Egypt Exploration Society, 1904), p. 244.
563. *Didache* 2.1–2 (trans. Kirsopp Lake).
564. Seneca, *Epistles* 78.5–7, 20–21, 25–27 (trans. Richard M. Gummere).
565. Seneca, *To Marcia, On Consolation* 25 (trans. John W. Basore).
566. Epictetus, *Encheiridion* 11 (trans. W.A. Oldfather).
567. A letter of condolence (P.Oxy 115) (second century CE).
B.P. Grenfell and A.S. Hunt, *The Oxyrhynchus Papyri, Part I* (London: Egypt Exploration Society, 1898), pp. 181–82.
568. The Epitaph of Regina.
Deissmann, *Light from the Ancient East*, p. 448.
569. 1 Thessalonians 4:13–18 (NRSV).
570. Juvenal, *Satires* 10.188–204 (trans. G.G. Ramsay).
571. Epitaph of a Roman soldier.
Deissmann, *Light from the Ancient East*, p. 74.
572. Epitaph of a child.
Martial, *Epigrams* 5.34 (trans. D.R. Shackleton Bailey).
573. Funerary stele.
New Docs III, p. 39.
574. Funerary epitaph.
New Docs IV, p. 40.
575. Funerary mensa.
New Docs III, p. 47.
576. Epitaph of a virtuous woman.
New Docs III, p. 40.
577. Epitaph of a gladiator.
New Docs IV, p. 19.
578. Josephus, *Against Apion* 1.194–95 (trans. H.St.J. Thackeray).
579. Pliny the Elder, *Natural History* 5.70–73 (trans. H. Rackham).
580. Tacitus, *Histories* 5.8–10 (trans. Clifford H. Moore).
581. Letter of one Jew to another of superior station.
ANET p. 491.

582. Petition for the authorization to rebuild the temple (11.1–14).
ANET p. 492.
583. Advice of the Governors of Judah and Samaria to the Jews of Elephantine.
ANET p. 492.
584. Strabo as preserved in Josephus, *Antiquities* 14.115 (trans. Ralph Marcus).
585. Josephus, *Against Apion* 1.194 (trans. H.St.J. Thackeray).
586. Josephus, *Jewish War* 7.426–32 (trans. H.St.J. Thackeray).
587. Jewish inscription.
New Docs IV, p. 113.
588. Philo, *On the Embassy to Gaius* 298–305 (trans. F.H. Colson).
589. Josephus, *Antiquities* 12.3–4 (trans. Ralph Marcus).
590. Philo, *On the Embassy to Gaius* 155–56 (trans. F.H. Colson).
591. Philo, *On the Embassy to Gaius* 159–60 (trans. F.H. Colson).
592. Cicero, *Pro Flacco* 66–68 (trans. Louis E. Ford).
593. Josephus, *Antiquities* 14.213–16 (trans. Ralph Marcus).
594. Paris, *Epitome of Valerius Maximus* (*Facta et Dicta Memorabilia* I.3:3).
M. Stern, *Greek and Latin Authors on Jews and Judaism*, I (Jerusalem: Israel Academy of Sciences and Humanities, 1976), p. 358 (no. 147b).
595. Josephus, *Antiquities* 18.81–84 (trans. L.H. Feldman).
596. Dio Cassius, *Roman History* 57.18.5a (trans. Herbert Baldwin Foster).
597. Seneca, *Epistles* 108.22 (trans. Richard M. Gummere).
598. Suetonius, *Claudius* 25.4 (trans. J.C. Rolfe).
599. Petronius, *Satyricon* Poems 24 (trans. M. Heseltine and E.H. Warmington).
600. Juvenal, *Satires* 3.10–14 (trans. G.G. Ramsay).
601. Juvenal, *Satires* 14.96–106 (trans. G.G. Ramsay).
602. Epictetus, *Discourses* 2.9.20–21 (trans. W.A. Oldfather).
603. Plutarch, *Superstition* 169B–C (trans. F.C. Babbitt).
604. Josephus, *Antiquities* 14.190–95 (trans. Ralph Marcus).
605. Josephus, *Antiquities* 14.258 (trans. Ralph Marcus)
606. Josephus, *Antiquities* 16.60 (trans. Ralph Marcus and Allen Wikgren).
607. Josephus, *Jewish War* 7.109–111 (trans. H.St.J. Thackeray).
608. The Letter of Claudius to the Alexandrians (P.London 1912, ll. 73–104).
CPJ no. 153 (II, p. 43).
609. *Jubilees* 2:17–22 (trans. O.S. Wintermute).
610. Josephus, *Against Apion* 1.209–211 (trans. H.St.J. Thackeray).
611. Ovid, *Art of Love* 1.413–18 (trans. J.H. Mozley).
612. Mark 3:1–6 (NRSV).
613. *Babylonian Talmud, Sabbath* 118b.
Montefiore and Loewe, *Rabbinic Anthology*, p. 194 (no. 517).
614. *Pesikta Rabbati* 117b.
Montefiore and Loewe, *Rabbinic Anthology*, p. 195 (no. 523).
615. Josephus, *Antiquities* 12.145–46 (trans. Ralph Marcus).
616. Jerusalem Temple inscription (in Greek).
Deissmann, *Light from the Ancient East*, p. 80.
617. Josephus, *Against Apion* 1.196–99 (trans. H.St.J. Thackeray).
618. Josephus, *Jewish War* 5.184–89 (trans. H.St.J. Thackeray).
619. Philo, *Special Laws* 1.69–70 (trans. F.H. Colson).
620. Josephus, *Against Apion* 2.193–98 (trans. H.St.J. Thackeray).
621. *Tanḥuma (Buber)*, Aḥare Mot 35a.
Montefiore and Loewe, *Rabbinic Anthology*, p. 119 (no. 313).
622. Theodotus Inscription.
Deissmann, *Light from the Ancient East*, p. 440.
623. Synagogue Inscription.
New Docs III, p. 121.
624. Josephus, *Antiquities* 14.110 (trans. Ralph Marcus).
625. *The Amidah*, Benedictions 1, 2, 10–12, 14–15, 18.
S. Singer (trans.), *The Authorised Daily Prayer Book* (London: Eyre & Spottiswoode, 10th edn, 1916), pp. 44, 45, 48, 49, 50.
626. Josephus, *Jewish War* 2.162–63, 166 (trans. H.St.J. Thackeray).
627. Mark 7:1–4 (NRSV).
628. Luke 15:1–2 (NRSV).
629. Acts 5:34–39 (NRSV).
630. Acts 23:6–8 (NRSV).

631. Josephus, *Jewish War* 2.164–66 (trans. H.St.J. Thackeray).
632. Josephus, *Antiquities* 13.297 (trans. Ralph Marcus).
633. Josephus, *Jewish War* 2.119–27, 137–44, 160–61 (trans. H.St.J. Thackeray).
634. Philo, *Every Good Man is Free* 75–89 (trans. F.H. Colson).
635. Philo, *On the Contemplative Life* 21–33 (trans. F.H. Colson).
636. Pliny the Elder, *Natural History* 5.72 (trans. H. Rackham).
637. Damascus Document 4.12–6.3 (trans. G. Vermes [*Complete Dead Sea Scrolls in English*, pp. 130–31]).
638. 4Q397 fragments 7, 8.7–9 (trans. G. Vermes [*Complete Dead Sea Scrolls in English*, p. 227]).
639. 4Q398 fragment 2 conflated with 4Q399 (trans. G. Vermes [*Complete Dead Sea Scrolls in English*, p. 228]).
640. Damascus Document 1.1–2.1 (trans. G. Vermes [*Complete Dead Sea Scrolls in English*, pp. 127–28]).
641. 1QpHab 6.12–7.5 (trans. G. Vermes [*Complete Dead Sea Scrolls in English*, p. 481]).
642. 1QpHab 5.12–6.12 (trans. G. Vermes [*Complete Dead Sea Scrolls in English*, p. 481]).
643. 1QpHab 8.1–13 (trans. G. Vermes [*Complete Dead Sea Scrolls in English*, p. 482]).
644. 1QpHab 11.2–8 (trans. G. Vermes [*Complete Dead Sea Scrolls in English*, p. 484]).
645. Damascus Document 10.14–12.2 (trans. G. Vermes [*Complete Dead Sea Scrolls in English*, pp. 139–40]).
646. 1QS 3.13–4.26 (trans. G. Vermes [*Complete Dead Sea Scrolls in English*, pp. 101–103]).
647. 1QH 12.27–29 (trans. G. Vermes [*Complete Dead Sea Scrolls in English*, p. 265]).
648. 1QH 16.4–8 (trans. G. Vermes [*Complete Dead Sea Scrolls in English*, pp. 178–79]).
649. 1QS 11.7–8 (trans. G. Vermes [*Complete Dead Sea Scrolls in English*, p. 115]).
650. 1QH 14.12–13 (trans. G. Vermes [*Complete Dead Sea Scrolls in English*, p. 272]).
651. 4Q405 fragments 20, 21, 22 (trans. G. Vermes [*Complete Dead Sea Scrolls in English*, p. 328]).
652. 1QM 1.1–16 (trans. G. Vermes [*Complete Dead Sea Scrolls in English*, pp. 163–64]).
653. 1QM 7.1–12 (trans. G. Vermes [*Complete Dead Sea Scrolls in English*, p. 170]).
654. 11QT 30–32 (trans. G. Vermes [*Complete Dead Sea Scrolls in English*, pp. 200–201]).
655. 4Q246 column 2.1 (Aramaic Apocalypse) (trans. G. Vermes [*Complete Dead Sea Scrolls in English*, p. 577]).
656. 4Q525 fragment 2.1–5 (Beatitudes) (trans. G. Vermes [*Complete Dead Sea Scrolls in English*, p. 424]).
657. 4Q521 fragment 2, column 2.1–13 (trans. G. Vermes [*Complete Dead Sea Scrolls in English*, pp. 391-92]).
658. Josephus, *Jewish War* 2.117–18 (trans. H.St.J. Thackeray).
659. Josephus, *Jewish War* 2.254–57 (trans. H.St.J. Thackeray).
660. Acts 6:1 (NRSV).
661. Acts 9:29 (NRSV).
662. Sirach 50:25–26 (NRSV).
663. An association of Samaritans in Delos (second century BCE).
New Docs VIII, p. 148.
664. Mark 1:14–15 (NRSV).
665. Matthew 11:2–6 (NRSV).
666. 2 Corinthians 5:17 (NRSV).
667. Ignatius, *Letter to the Ephesians* 19 (trans. Kirsopp Lake).
668. Galatians 3:28 (NRSV).
669. Romans 12:14–19 (NRSV).
670. Galatians 5:13–26 NRSV).
671. Mark 7:18b–19 (NRSV).
672. *Didache* 11:4–6 (trans. Kirsopp Lake).
673. 1 Corinthians 12:4–6, 27–28 (NRSV).
674. *Didache* 15:1–2 (trans. Kirsopp Lake).
675. 1 Timothy 3:1–5 (NRSV).
676. Romans 16:1–5a (NRSV).
677. Ephesians 5:22–6:9 (NRSV).
678. Philo, *Special Laws* 2.148 (trans. F.H. Colson).
679. 1 Corinthians 14:26–40 (NRSV).
680. Colossians 3:16–17 (NRSV).
681. Acts 2:44–47 (NRSV).
682. *Didache* 9 (trans. Kirsopp Lake).
683. *Didache* 14 (trans. Kirsopp Lake). See also *Didache* 10.
684. Josephus, *Antiquities* 18.63–64 (trans. L.H. Feldman).
685. Acts 12:1–3 (NRSV).
686. Josephus, *Antiquities* 20.200–201 (trans. L.H. Feldman).
687. *Coptic Gospel of Thomas* 12 (trans. Bentley Layton).
688. Philippians 3:4b–6 (NRSV).
689. Romans 8:22–23 (NRSV).
690. 1 Thessalonians 4:13–5:3 (NRSV).
691. *The Zend Avesta*, Miscellaneous Fragments 4.3.

L.H. Mills (trans.), *The Zend Avesta*, in F. Max Müller (ed.), *The Sacred Books of the East*, XXXI (Oxford: Oxford University Press, 1887), pp. 390–91.

692. *Bundahis* 30.4–32.
E.W. West (trans.), *The Pahlavi Texts*, in F. Max Müller (ed.), *The Sacred Books of the East*, V (Oxford: Oxford University Press, 1880), pp. 121–29.
693. *Yasna* 30.4–5.
L.H. Mills (trans.), *The Zend Avesta*, in F. Max Müller (ed.), *The Sacred Books of the East*, XXXI (Oxford: Oxford University Press, 1887), pp. 30–31.
694. Daniel 12:1–3 (NRSV).
695. *1 Enoch* 51 (trans. E. Isaac).
696. 2 Maccabees 7:6–9 (NRSV).
697. *Sentences of Pseudo-Phocylides*, ll. 102–115 (trans. P.W. van der Horst).
698. 1 Corinthians 15:35–58 (NRSV).
699. *Psalms of Solomon* 17:21–46 (trans. R.B. Wright).
700. *Testament of Issachar* 5.7–8 (trans. H.C. Kee).
701. 1QSa 2.11–15 ('the Messianic Rule') (trans. G. Vermes, *Complete Dead Sea Scrolls in English*, p. 159).
702. Mark 8:27–31 (NRSV).
703. John 4:21–26 (NRSV).
704. Romans 1:1–4 (NRSV).
705. Revelation 5:4–6 (NRSV).
706. *Odes of Solomon* 41:1–4 (trans. J.H. Charlesworth).
707. Acts 18:12–17 (NRSV).
708. Romans 13:1–7 (NRSV).
709. Tacitus, *Annals* 15.44 (trans. John Jackson).
710. Suetonius, *Nero* 16.2 (trans. J.C. Rolfe).
711. Eusebius, *Ecclesiastical History* 3.5.3 (trans. Kirsopp Lake).
712. *1 Clement* 5–6 (trans. Kirsopp Lake).
713. Eusebius, *Ecclesiastical History* 3.17–20 (trans. Kirsopp Lake).
714. Pliny the Younger, *Letters* 10.96 (trans. Betty Radice).
715. Pliny the Younger, *Letters* 10.97 (trans. Betty Radice).
716. Ignatius, *Letter to the Romans* 4–5 (trans. Kirsopp Lake).
717. Apuleius, *Golden Ass* 9.14 (trans. W. Adlington; rev. S. Gaselee).

Index of Sources

Numbers of sources in the text have been placed in the second column.

III. Biblical Texts

III.1 Old Testament

III.2 Apocrypha

Subject Index

Index of Names